Essentials of Understanding Psychology

fifth edition

Essentials of Understanding Psychology

Robert S. Feldman

University of Massachusetts—Amherst

Boston   Burr Ridge, IL   Dubuque, IA   Madison, WI   New York   San Francisco   St. Louis
Bangkok   Bogotá   Caracas   Kuala Lumpur   Lisbon   London   Madrid   Mexico City
Milan   Montreal   New Delhi   Santiago   Seoul   Singapore   Sydney   Taipei   Toronto

McGraw-Hill Higher Education

A Division of The McGraw-Hill Companies

ESSENTIALS OF UNDERSTANDING PSYCHOLOGY
FIFTH EDITION

Published by McGraw-Hill, a business unit of The McGraw-Hill Companies, Inc., 1221 Avenue of the Americas, New York, NY 10020. Copyright © 2003, 2000, 1997, 1994, 1989 by The McGraw-Hill Companies, Inc. All rights reserved. No part of this publication may be reproduced or distributed in any form or by any means, or stored in a database or retrieval system, without the prior written consent of The McGraw-Hill Companies, Inc., including, but not limited to, in any network or other electronic storage or transmission, or broadcast for distance learning.

Some ancillaries, including electronic and print components, may not be available to customers outside the United States.

This book is printed on acid-free paper.

1 2 3 4 5 6 7 8 9 0 QPD/QPD 0 9 8 7 6 5 4 3 2

ISBN 0–07–249426–3

Vice president and editor-in-chief: *Thalia Dorwick*
Publisher: *Stephen D. Rutter*
Senior sponsoring editor: *Melissa Mashburn*
Developmental editor: *Cheri Dellelo*
Senior marketing manager: *Chris Hall*
Project manager: *Vicki Krug*
Production supervisor: *Enboge Chong*
Coordinator of freelance design: *Michelle D. Whitaker*
Cover/interior designer: *Christopher Reese*
Cover images: *ibid.*
Lead photo research coordinator: *Carrie K. Burger*
Photo research: *Toni Michaels/PhotoFind, LLC*
Supplement producer: *David A. Welsh*
Media technology senior producer: *Sean Crowley*
Compositor: *GTS Graphics, Inc.*
Typeface: *10/12 Times Roman*
Printer: *Quebecor World Dubuque, IA*

The credits section for this book begins on page AK.1 and is considered an extension of the copyright page.

Library of Congress Control Number: 2002100215

www.mhhe.com

About the Author

Robert S. Feldman first became seriously interested in psychology when he took an introductory psychology course as an undergraduate at Wesleyan University. "After I carried out a small observational study (on hitchhiking!) for a class project," he said, "I was hooked."

After graduating with high honors from Wesleyan, where he wrote a senior psychology thesis titled "The Determinants of Dissent" (it was the Vietnam War era), his interests in the field led him to graduate school at the University of Wisconsin in Madison, where he received his M.S. and Ph.D.

Today, Feldman is Professor in the Department of Psychology at the University of Massachusetts at Amherst, where he is Director of Undergraduate Studies. Professor Feldman is also a Hewlett Teaching Fellow and a Senior Online Instruction Fellow. His proudest accomplishment is winning the College Distinguished Teacher Award at UMass.

Professor Feldman has also taught courses at Mount Holyoke College, Wesleyan University, and Virginia Commonwealth University. As Director of Undergraduate Studies, he initiated the Minority Mentoring Program and participates in the Talent Advancement Program. His introductory psychology classes range in size from 20 to 475 students, and he also teaches an online distance-learning introductory psychology course.

A Fellow of both the American Psychological Association and the American Psychological Society, Professor Feldman is a winner of a Fulbright Senior Research Scholar and Lecturer award, and he has written more than 100 books, book chapters, and scientific articles. His books, which have been translated into many languages, including Spanish, French, Chinese, and Albanian, include *Fundamentals of Nonverbal Behavior, Development of Nonverbal Behavior in Children, Social Psychology, Development Across the Life Span,* and *P.O.W.E.R. Learning: Strategies for Success in College and Life.* His research interests encompass the development of nonverbal behavior in children and the social psychology of education and have been supported by grants from the National Institute of Mental Health and the National Institute on Disabilities and Rehabilitation Research.

Professor Feldman's spare time is most often devoted to gourmet cooking and earnest, but unpolished, piano playing. He has three children and lives with his wife, also a psychologist, overlooking the Holyoke mountain range in Amherst, Massachusetts.

To

Ethel Radler,

with love

Contents in Brief

Contents

Chapter Three

Sensation and Perception   74

Chapter Four

States of Consciousness 114

Chapter Five

Learning   148

Chapter Six

Memory   180

Chapter Seven

Thinking, Language, and Intelligence 210

Chapter Eight

Motivation and Emotion   248

Chapter Eleven

Health Psychology: Stress, Coping, and Well-Being 356

Chapter Twelve

Psychological Disorders 380

Chapter Thirteen

Treatment of Psychological Disorders   414

Chapter Fourteen

Social Psychology
440

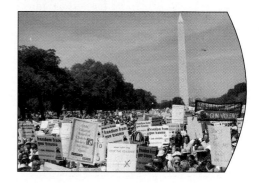

Preface

Estella Ramirez gained a better understanding of her mother's lifelong battle with major depression after learning about its possible causes in her introductory psychology course. She also developed a new appreciation for the struggles her mother faced in coping with this disorder.

* * *

As a new father, Phil Westport realized that he didn't know very much about infants, including his own daughter. He decided to take introductory psychology in part to learn more about child development. Applying what he learned in the course, Phil gained new insights into his daughter's behavior and more confidence in his ability to be a good parent.

* * *

Although he enrolled in introductory psychology because it was the only class that fit conveniently into his schedule, Jacob Rakovitch found himself increasingly interested in the subject matter. He became fascinated by the relationship between the brain and behavior, and by the end of the term he was seriously thinking about majoring in psychology.

* * *

Joanne Chu is planning to become a special education teacher after graduating from college. Her aspirations have been fueled by studying how people learn and how psychologists explain variations in intelligence in her introductory psychology course.

Psychology speaks with many voices to the diversity of students that we teach, offering a personal message to each one. To some, the discipline is a vehicle that can provide a better understanding of others' behavior; for others it is a pathway to self-understanding. To some, psychology offers the potential of a future career; others are drawn to psychology because it gives them an opportunity for intellectual discovery.

Essentials of Understanding Psychology, fifth edition, is designed to present the discipline of psychology in a way that engages and excites students about the field of psychology—no matter what led them to take the introductory course or what level of motivation they initially bring to the course. It is designed to draw them into its way of looking at the world and to inform their understanding of psychological issues. The book provides a broad introduction to the essentials of the field of psychology, covering basic theories and research findings, as well as highlighting current applications outside the laboratory.

In revising *Essentials of Understanding Psychology,* I had four major goals:

1. To provide broad coverage of the field of psychology, introducing the theories, research, and applications that constitute the discipline.
2. To impel readers to think critically about psychological phenomena, particularly those that have an impact on their everyday lives.
3. To illustrate the substantial diversity both within the field of psychology and in society as a whole by presenting material that reflects the discipline's increasing concern with cultural, gender, racial, and ethnic issues.
4. To arouse intellectual curiosity and build an appreciation of how psychology can increase students' understanding of the world around them.

In short, *Essentials of Understanding Psychology* is meant not only to expose readers to the content—and promise—of psychology, but also to do so in a way that will bring to life basic concepts and research findings, and sustain interest in the discipline long after they have completed their first encounter with the field.

The Scope and Structure of *Essentials of Understanding Psychology*

Essentials of Understanding Psychology is based on the sixth edition of *Understanding Psychology*, a broad and comprehensive introduction to the field of psychology. Like the book from which it is derived, *Essentials of Understanding Psychology* includes coverage of the traditional topical areas of psychology—such as the biological foundations of behavior, sensation and perception, learning, cognition, development, personality, abnormal behavior, and the social psychological foundations of behavior.

Unlike its predecessor, however, *Essentials of Understanding Psychology* is a briefer, 14-chapter volume. It focuses on the essence of psychology, providing a broad introduction to the field. The book also shows how the field's theories and research have an impact on readers' everyday lives by emphasizing the applications of psychology.

The flexibility of the book's organizational structure, a hallmark of this text, is considerable. Each chapter is divided into three or four manageable, self-contained units, allowing instructors to choose and omit sections in accordance with their syllabus.

Building on its strong tradition of facilitating student learning, the fifth edition of *Essentials of Understanding Psychology* contains several new and improved features:

- **The option of using a systematic study strategy built into the book—the P.O.W.E.R. Learning system.** The new edition of *Essentials of Understanding Psychology* provides students with the option of using *P.O.W.E.R. Learning*, a systematic approach to learning and studying based on five key steps (**P**repare, **O**rganize, **W**ork, **E**valuate, and **R**ethink). Based on empirical research, *P.O.W.E.R. Learning* systematizes the acquisition of new material by providing a learning framework. The system stresses the importance of learning objectives, self-evaluation, and critical thinking. The elements of the *P.O.W.E.R. Learning* can also be used in conjunction with other learning systems, such as *SQ3R*. (A more detailed description of the use of the *P.O.W.E.R. Learning* system follows in the Student Guide section of the Preface.)
- **Fine-tuning of definitions.** Definitions of key terms and concepts introduced in the text, which appear in the margins and in the end-of-book glossary, have been revised and made more precise.
- **Inclusion of additional thought-provoking examples.** Great care has been taken to select relevant and high-interest examples that motivate students to read as well as to explain key concepts.
- **Addition of Web-based exercises.** New to this edition, every chapter includes several exercises that require students to use the World Wide Web to identify and research information related to psychology.
- **Addressing diverse student learning styles.** Our prepublication research revealed that an increasing number of instructors find that the presentation of material in multiple modalities facilitates student mastery of material. Consequently, this edition includes several features that speak to the diverse learning styles of students. For example, there are more, and improved, figures. Each figure has been drawn to maximize clarity and pedagogical value, and many include annotations that draw attention to major points in the illustrations. Furthermore, there are additional photos, with captions that directly support learning. Photos have been carefully chosen to support the learning of key concepts, as well as for their visual impact. Captions have been improved and expanded, and many now include questions designed to promote critical thinking.

This edition incorporates a significant amount of new and updated information, reflecting the advances in the field and the suggestions of reviewers. *Overall, more than a thousand new citations have been added, with most of those from articles and books published within the last three years.*

For instance, advances in such areas as evolutionary perspectives, brain and behavior, mapping the human genome, cognition, emotions, and cultural approaches to psychological phenomena receive expanded and new coverage. In addition to the extensive updating, a broad range of new topics have been incorporated. The following sample of new and revised topics featured in this edition provides a good indication of the currency of the revision:

- Evolutionary perspectives (Chapter 1)
- The Human Genome Project and behavioral genetics (Chapter 2)
- Cochlear implants (Chapter 3)
- PET scan data and psychoanalytic explanations of dreaming (Chapter 4)
- "Date rape" drugs (Chapter 4)
- Effects of violent video games (Chapter 5)
- Spreading activation and associative memory models (Chapter 6)
- Being too smart for a job (Chapter 7)
- Intrinsic motivation (Chapter 8)
- Gene therapy (Chapter 9)
- Teratogens (Chapter 9)
- Estrogen replacement therapy (Chapter 9)
- Self-efficacy (Chapter 10)
- Well-being and happiness (Chapter 11)
- Depression and ADHD (Chapter 12)
- Virtual therapy and St. John's wort (Chapter 13)
- Industrial/organizational psychology (Chapter 14)
- Psychographics (Chapter 14)

Despite the extensive changes in this edition of *Essentials of Understanding Psychology,* one constant remains: the basic student-friendliness of the text. *Essentials of Understanding Psychology,* fifth edition, remains a textbook devoted to student success. In aiding students' efforts to master the body of material that the field of psychology encompasses, the book is designed to nurture students' excitement about psychology and keep that excitement alive throughout their lives.

The Learning Features of *Essentials of Understanding Psychology*

Essentials of Understanding Psychology, fifth edition, contains many features designed to help students learn, study, and master the text's content. These include the following:

- **Prologue.** Each chapter starts with an account of a real-life situation that demonstrates the relevance of basic principles and concepts of psychology to pertinent issues and problems. These prologues depict well-known people and events, such as the terrorist attack on the World Trade Center in New York, Michael J. Fox's fight against Parkinson's disease, and Lance Armstrong's motivation to win in the Tour de France.
- **Looking Ahead.** These sections follow each *Prologue,* expressing the key themes and issues discussed within the chapter.
- **Prepare and Organize.** Each major section of the chapter incorporates the first two steps of the optional *P.O.W.E.R. Learning* system: *Prepare* and *Organize.* The *Prepare* section includes several broad questions designed to orient students to the major topics of the chapter. The *Organize* section provides an outline of the material. Together, they offer a framework for conceptualizing and organizing the material that follows.
- **Applying Psychology in the 21st Century.** These boxes—which highlight the relevance of psychology—illustrate applications of current psychological theory and research findings to real-world problems, focusing on current advances and future

possibilities. For example, these discussions explore such topics as the use of brain waves to command computers, the consequences of playing violent video games on actual aggressive behavior, cloning and gene therapy, and Internet addiction.

- **Psychology at Work.** These interviews provide biographical sketches of people working in professions that make use of the findings of psychology. Some of the individuals profiled are psychologists, some work in other fields; all of them draw on psychological principles on a daily basis. For example, there are interviews with a preschool teacher, a psychologist who works for the Secret Service evaluating threats against the president of the United States, and an advertising executive.

- **Exploring Diversity.** In addition to a substantial amount of material relevant to diversity integrated throughout the text, every chapter also includes a special section devoted to an aspect of racial, ethnic, gender, or cultural diversity. These sections highlight how psychology informs (and is informed by) issues relating to the increasing multiculturalism of our global society. The *Exploring Diversity* topics include cross-cultural differences in memory, cultural perspectives on female circumcision, and the use of race to establish test norms.

- **PsychLinks.** *PsychLinks* are marginal icons providing brief descriptions and Web addresses of relevant websites. Each *PsychLink* has a corresponding hot-link on the *Essentials of Understanding Psychology* website at http://www.mhhe.com/feldmaness5.

- **Becoming an Informed Consumer of Psychology.** Each chapter includes material designed to make readers more informed consumers of psychological information by giving them the ability to evaluate critically what the field of psychology offers. These discussions also provide sound, useful guidance concerning common problems. For example, these unique sections discuss such topics as how to assess research claims, identify drug and alcohol problems, lose weight successfully, assess personality assessments, and choose a therapist.

- **Evaluate and Rethink.** Every major chapter section concludes with an *Evaluate* and *Rethink* section as part of the *P.O.W.E.R. Learning* system. The *Evaluate* sections test recall of the material, assessing the degree of initial learning. The *Rethink* sections provide thought-provoking questions designed to provoke critical thinking about the material.

- **Running Glossary.** Key terms are highlighted in boldface type within the text where they are introduced and are defined in the margin of the page, with pronunciation guides for difficult words. There is also an end-of-book glossary.

- **Looking Back.** To facilitate both review and synthesis of the information covered, a number of end-of-chapter features reinforce student learning. First, a chapter summary emphasizes the key points of the chapter and is organized according to the *Prepare* questions posed at the beginning of every major section. Second, a list of *Key Terms and Concepts,* including the page numbers where they are introduced, encourages student review. Third, *Psychology on the Web* takes students online to analyze psychological issues relevant to the chapter content. Fourth, the *OLC Preview* suggests that students visit the book website for self quizzes, activities, and additional information.

- **Epilogue.** Each chapter ends with an *Epilogue* that incorporates critical thinking questions relating to the *Prologue* at the opening of the chapter. These thought-provoking questions provide a way to tie the chapter together and illustrate how the concepts addressed in the chapter apply to the real-world situation described in the *Prologue.*

Supplements Package

A complete, integrated multimedia package supports the fifth edition of *Essentials of Understanding Psychology.*

FOR THE INSTRUCTOR

Instructor's Manual (ISBN 0-07-249427-1)

By Saundra K. Ciccarelli, Gulf Coast Community College, Florida

This thoroughly revised manual provides instructors of introductory psychology with all the tools and resources they need to present and enhance their course. The Instructor's Manual includes detailed chapter outlines, learning objectives, ideas for lectures, activities, and student projects, ready-to-use handouts, overhead masters, and multimedia references. Fully integrated with the *P.O.W.E.R. Learning* system, this manual has tips and activities that have a usefulness beyond any particular teaching approach.

Test Bank (ISBN 0-07-249430-1)

By Shirley Cassarà, Bunker Hill Community College, Massachusetts

The Test Bank has been thoroughly upgraded to reflect the new content in *Essentials of Understanding Psychology,* fifth edition. The Test Bank contains more than 2,000 testing items, classified by cognitive type and level of difficulty, and keyed to the appropriate learning objective and section in the textbook. Items that test knowledge of material in the textbook's boxes are indicated for easy reference. Grading suggestions make the Test Bank easy to use.

Computerized Test Bank (ISBN 0-07-249432-8)

Available in a cross-platform format, this CD-ROM makes all the items from the Test Bank easily available to instructors to create their own tests. The test-generating program facilitates the selection of questions from the Test Bank and the printing of tests and answer keys, and also allows instructors to import questions from other sources.

Online Learning Center (ISBN 0-07-249435-2)

The Online Learning Center for Instructors houses downloadable versions of the Instructor's Manual and PowerPoint slides, a variety of other text-specific instructor resources, including a bank of 145 images and a newsletter written by Robert Feldman, and access to our acclaimed customized website creation tool, PageOut! Instructors in need of assistance can contact their McGraw-Hill sales representative via e-mail from the Online Learning Center. Visit us at http://www.mhhe.com/feldmaness5.

Instructor's Resource CD-ROM (ISBN 0-07-253103-7)

The CD-ROM contains every key instructor's resource in one flexible format. The Instructor's Manual, the Test Bank, PowerPoint presentations, and 145-item Image Bank are included along with an easy-to-use interface for the design and delivery of multimedia classroom presentations.

Image Bank

Over 145 illustrations can be downloaded from the Image Bank on the Online Learning Center and used on your course website or in PowerPoint presentations.

In-Class Activities Manual for Instructors of Introductory Psychology (ISBN 0-07-238431-X)

By Patricia A. Jarvis, Cynthia R. Nordstrom, and Karen B. Williams, Illinois State University

Geared to instructors of large introductory psychology courses, this activities manual covers every major topic in introductory psychology. Nineteen chapters include 58 separate activities, all of which have been used successfully in the authors' classes in introductory psychology. Each activity includes a short description of the demonstration, the approximate time needed to complete the activity, the materials needed, step-by-step procedures, practical tips, and suggested readings related to the activity. The manual also includes advice and syllabus, what to consider when structuring your large section, how to select and manage a teaching assistant, and other key topics.

Annual Editions Online: Psychology (ISBN 0-07-234602-7)
By Karen G. Duffy, SUNY at Geneseo, New York
With Annual Editions Online: Psychology, you'll have online access to current, carefully selected articles from the public press. The abridged version contains 20 online readings that are supported with well-researched links of interest and built-in assessment in the form of online quizzes and article reviews. An online search engine to connect with additional articles and an online Instructor's Resource Guide are also included. If you are interested in packaging Annual Editions Online with a McGraw-Hill textbook, contact your sales representative for details.

Annual Editions: Psychology 01/02, 31/e (ISBN 0-07-243377-9)
By Karen G. Duffy, SUNY at Geneseo, New York
This reader of public press articles explores the science of psychology; biological bases of behavior; perceptual processes; learning and remembering; cognitive processes; emotion and motivation; development; personality processes; social processes; psychological disorders; and psychological treatments. Annual Editions is supported by Dushkin Online (www.dushkin.com/online/), a student website that provides study support tools and links to related websites.

Taking Sides: Clashing Views on Controversial Psychological Issues, 11/e (ISBN 0-07-237142-0)
By Brent Slife, Brigham Young University, Utah
This debate reader is designed to introduce students to controversies in psychology. The readings, which represent the arguments of leading psychologists and commentators, reflect a variety of viewpoints and have been selected for their liveliness and substance and because of their value in a debate framework. By requiring students to analyze opposing viewpoints and reach considered judgments, Taking Sides actively develops critical thinking skills.

Sources: Notable Sections in Psychology, 3/e (ISBN 0-07-303187-9)
By Terry F. Pettijohn, Ohio State University–Marion
This volume contains approximately 40 selections of enduring intellectual value—classic articles, book excerpts, and research studies—that have shaped the study of psychology and our contemporary understanding of it.

FOR THE STUDENT

Study Guide (ISBN 0-07-2494298)
By Barbara L. Radigan, Community College of Allegheny County, Pennsylvania
The Study Guide integrates the *P.O.W.E.R. Learning* system into a comprehensive review of the text material. Multiple-choice practice tests and essay questions allow students to gauge their understanding of the material. An answer key provides answers to all of the chapter's exercises, including feedback for all multiple-choice items. A list of activities and projects that encourage students to apply psychology to their daily lives is also included. New to this edition is additional information that is designed to help non-native speakers of English understand and retain key course information.

Online Learning Center (ISBN 0-07-2494352)
The Student Online Learning Center houses an array of chapter-by-chapter study tools, including detailed chapter outlines, concepts and learning objectives, key words, self-quizzes, essay questions, activities and projects, explanations of American idiomatic expressions for ESL students, answers to *Epilogue* questions in the textbook, crossword puzzles, interesting Web links, and interactive exercises. Visit us at http://www.mhhe.com/feldmaness5.

Making the Grade CD-ROM (ISBN 0-07-249434-4)

Packaged free with each copy of the text, this CD-ROM is designed to help students perform at their best. It contains practice quizzes for each text chapter, a learning styles assessment, study skills primer, guide to electronic research, and link to the text website.

New! In-Psych Student CD-ROM (ISBN 0-07-249428-X)

In-Psych sets a new standard for introductory psychology multimedia. The CD-ROM is organized according to the textbook chapter outlines and features over 60 interactive exercises chosen to illustrate especially difficult core introductory psychology concepts. Each exercise showcases one of three types of media assets—an audio clip, a video clip, or a simulation—and includes a pretest, follow-up assignments, and Web resources. In-Psych also includes chapter quizzes, a student research guide, and an interactive timeline that puts events, key figures, and research in psychology in historical perspective. A learning styles assessment tool helps students identify what kind of learners they are—kinesthetic, auditory, or visual—and then provides them with study tips tailored to their own particular learning style.

WebQuester: Psychology (ISBN 0-07-240850-2)

By Terry F. Pettijohn, Ohio State University–Marion

WebQuester is a series of online interactive exercises covering approximately 20 core topics in psychology. Each website includes 1 to 3 multiple-choice questions, short-answer questions, and essay questions. A 150-page Guidebook to the Web provides practical information and tips; topic areas include Searching the Web, Evaluating Information, Thinking Critically in the World of Information, and Computer Ethics.

Acknowledgments

One of the most important features of *Essentials of Understanding Psychology* is the involvement of both professionals and students in the review process. The fifth edition of *Essentials of Understanding Psychology* has relied heavily on—and profited substantially from—the advice of instructors and students from a wide range of backgrounds.

First, the manuscript was evaluated by traditional academic reviewers, who served in their capacity as content experts and teachers of psychology. These reviewers helped ensure that the coverage and presentation was accurate, incorporated state-of-the-art research findings, and remained focused on the diverse needs of introductory psychology courses. They include the following:

Richard Baiardo
Evergreen Valley College, California

Manolya Bayar
Harford Community College, Maryland

Kathleen Bey
Palm Beach Community College, Central Campus, Florida

Theresa Botts
Eastern Kentucky University

Dominic Brucato
Miami-Dade Community College–North Campus, Florida

Linda Chaparro
Oxnard College, California

Carolyn Cohen
Massachusetts Bay Community College

Bob Conkright
Austin Community College, Cypress Campus, Texas

Natividad DeAnda
Los Medanos College, Pittsburg, California

Giselle Diaz
Palm Beach Community College, Florida

Karen Douglas
San Antonio College, Texas

Todd Farrar
Virginia College, Alabama

Aaron Fielder
Virginia College, Alabama

Stanley Fitch
El Camino College, California

Classie Foat
Skyline College, California

Tracy Forte
Potomac College, District of Columbia

Christopher Frost
Southwest Texas State University

Rod Gillis
University of Miami, Florida

Anthony Gordon
Contra Costa College, California

Joseph Hanak
Corning Community College, New York

Sarah Harrison
Evergreen Valley College, California

Milton Hatcher
Arkansas State University

Toni Haynes
Palm Beach Community College, South Campus, Florida

Alylene Hegar
Eastfield College, Texas

Kerry Hinkel
Valdosta State University, Georgia

Wayne Hren
Los Angeles Pierce College, California

Robert Hutchinson
Modesto Junior College, California

Shirin Khosropour
Austin Community College, Pinnacle Campus, Texas

Barbara Lusk
Collin County Community College, Texas

Leslie Martin
La Sierra University, California

Michael T. Miles
Palm Beach Community College, Central Campus, Florida

Gwen Murdock
Missouri Southern State College

Glen Musgrove
Broward Community College, Central Campus, Florida

Glenda Nichols
Tarrant County Junior College, South Campus, Texas

Sonya Nieves
Broward Community College, South Campus, Florida

Carol Ponday
Los Angeles Pierce College, California

Ben Price
San Jose City College, California

Kimberly Rector
Academy of Business College, Arizona

George Riday
Citrus College, California

MaryLou Robbins
San Jacinto College South Campus, Texas

Harry Saterfield
Foothill College, California

Bishop Scott
College of Alameda, California

Sharon Scott
South Plains College, Texas

Elizabeth Shaw
Texarkana College, Texas

Charlotte Simon
Montgomery College–Rockville, Maryland

Jean Spaulding
Northwest College HCC, Texas

Mary Helen Spear
Prince George's Community College, Maryland

Brian Spillane
Antelope Valley College, California

Patricia Stephenson
Miami-Dade Community College–Kendall Campus, Florida

Janet Stubbs
Salem State College, Massachusetts

Robert Templeton
Palm Beach Community College, Central Campus, Florida

Donald Thompson
Troy State University–Montgomery, Alabama

Joe Tinnin
Richland College, Texas

Richard Townsend
Miami-Dade Community College, South Campus, Florida

Barbara Turner
Pasadena City College, California

Robin Vallacher
Florida Atlantic University, Florida

Jean Volckmann
Pasadena City College, California

Gwen Walker
Los Angeles Mission College, California

Sandra Wilcox
California State University–Dominguez Hills, California

Stephen Wurst
State University of New York at Oswego

Andrea Zabel
Midland College, Texas

Several people also gave us their input in reviews and interviews about the ancillary package. I am grateful to the following teachers of psychology:

Marilyn Andrews
Hartnell College, California

Richard Baiardo
Evergreen Valley College, California

Louis Banderet
Northeastern University, Massachusetts

Carol Batt
Sacred Heart University, Connecticut

Steven L. Berman
Florida International University, Florida

Kathleen Bey
Palm Beach Atlantic University, Florida

David Bjorklund
Florida Atlantic University, Florida

Don Borden
Corning Community College, New York

Deb Brihl
Valdosta State University, Georgia

Richard Cavasina
California University of Pennsylvania

Natividad DeAnda
Los Mendosa College, California

Karen T. Douglas
San Antonion College, Texas

Stanley K. Fitch
El Camino College, California

Linda Flickinger
St. Clair County Community College, Michigan

Dave Harrison
Virginia Polytechnic Institute and State University, Virginia

Sara Hart Harrison
Evergreen Valley College, California

Lisa M. Henry
Loyola Marymount University, California

Judith M. Horowitz
Medaille College, New York

Loreen Huffman
Missouri Southern State College

Robert Hynes
Limestone College, South Carolina

Robert Jensen
California State University–Sacramento

Norman E. Kinney
Southeast Missouri State University

W. Richard Krall
Gateway Community College, Arizona

Len Larsen
Eastfield College, Texas

Joe Manganello
Gloucester County College, New Jersey

Michael R. Markham
Florida International University, Florida

Leslie R. Martin
La Sierra University, California

John Mastenbrook
Del Mar College, Texas

Dorothy L. Mercer
Eastern Kentucky University

Michael Miles
Palm Beach Community College, Florida

Richard Miller
Navarro College, Texas

Mindy Miserendino
Sacred Heart University, Connecticut

Glenn J. Musgrove
Broward Community College, Central Campus, Florida

Jerry Newell
Citrus Community College, California

Geri Olson
Sonoma State University, California

Dan Quinn
Northeastern University, Massachusetts

Barbara Radigan
*Community College of Allegheny County,
   Pennsylvania*

Christopher K. Randall
Troy State University–Montgomery, Alabama

Karen Pitts Saenz
Houston Community College–Southeast, Texas

Nicole Schnopp-Wyatt
Pikeville College, Kentucky

Norman Schorr
Montgomery College–Rockville, Maryland

Sharon Scott
South Plains College, Texas

Ann Shaver
Fairmont State College, West Virginia

Debjani Sinha
University of Cincinnati, Ohio

Nathan Slaughter
Merritt College, California

Jeanne Spaulding
Houston Community College, Texas

William Vasquez
Palo Alto College, California

Charles Verschoor
Miami-Dade Community College, Florida

Sandra G. Wilcox
California State University–Dominguez Hills

Matthew P. Winslow
Eastern Kentucky University

Andrea Zabel
Midland College, Texas

Another group of reviewers consisted of a panel of students who had used *Understanding Psychology* in their introductory psychology class. Over the course of a subsequent semester, they reviewed the entire book, literally line-by-line. Their insights, suggestions, and sometimes all-too-enthusiastic criticism were invaluable to me as I prepared this revision. The student review panel consisted of Cherilyn Johnson, Louis Meunier, Stacey Whitbourne, and Phil Zeyte.

Finally, dozens of students read parts of the manuscript to ensure that the material was clear and engaging. Their suggestions are incorporated throughout the text. I am grateful to all of these reviewers who provided their time and expertise to help ensure that *Essentials of Understanding Psychology* reflects the best that psychology has to offer.

I also owe a great deal to numerous others. My thinking has been shaped by many teachers along my educational path. I was introduced to psychology at Wesleyan University, where several committed and inspiring teachers—in particular Karl Scheibe—conveyed their sense of excitement about the field and made its relevance clear to me. Karl epitomizes the teacher-scholar combination to which I aspire, and I continue to marvel at my fortune in having such a role model.

By the time I left Wesleyan I could envision no other career for myself but that of psychologist. Although the University of Wisconsin, where I did my graduate work, could not have been more different from the much smaller Wesleyan, the excitement and inspiration were similar. Once again, a cadre of excellent teachers—led, especially, by the late Vernon Allen—molded my thinking and taught me to appreciate the beauty and science of the discipline of psychology.

My colleagues and students at the University of Massachusetts at Amherst provide ongoing intellectual stimulation, and I thank them for making the University a fine place to work. Several people also provided extraordinary research and editorial help. In particular, I am grateful to my superb students, past and present, including Erik Coats, Sara Levine, Jim Forrest, Darren Spielman, Dan Hrubes, Jim Tyler, Brent Weiss, and Christopher Poirier. Chris, in particular, provided a good deal of help and advice on this edition of the book. Edward Murphy helped in a variety of important ways, providing highly useful and intelligent editorial input and advice. Finally, I am extremely grateful to John Graiff, whose hard work and dedication helped immeasurably on just about everything involving this book.

I also offer thanks to the McGraw-Hill editorial team. I especially thank President Steve Debow, Vice President and Editor-in-Chief Thalia Dorwick, and Publisher Steve Rutter, whose hands-on interest in the project helped it along at critical junctures. Melissa Mashburn, sponsoring editor, brought a thoughtful, creative energy and strong commitment to the book, and I am very grateful for her support. Cheri Dellelo also provided editorial support, and I thank her. Finally, every reader of this book owes a debt to Rhona Robbin, developmental editor on prior editions of *Essentials of Understanding Psychology*. Her relentless pursuit of excellence helped form this book, and she taught me a great deal about the craft and art of writing.

Other people at McGraw-Hill were central to the design, production, and marketing process, especially Project Manager Vicki Krug and Designer Michelle Whitaker. Thanks, also, to Merrily Mazza, who directs this superb team. I am also appreciative of marketing manager Chris Hall, whose expertise and savvy I count on. I am proud to be a part of this world-class team.

Finally, I remain completely indebted to my family. My parents, Leah Brochstein and the late Saul D. Feldman, provided a lifetime foundation of love and support, and I continue to see their influence in every corner of my life. My extended family also plays a central role in my life. They include, more or less in order of age, my nieces and nephews, my brother, assorted brothers- and sisters-in-law, Ethel Radler, and Harry Brochstein. Finally, my mother-in-law, the late Mary Evans Vorwerk, had an important influence on this book, and I remain ever grateful to her.

Ultimately, my children, Jonathan, Joshua, and Sarah, and my wife, Katherine, remain the focal point of my life. I thank them, with immense love.

Robert S. Feldman
Amherst, Massachusetts

The student review panel, who reviewed the material in this book in depth, consisted of Phil Zeyte, Cherilyn Johnson, Louis Meunier, and Stacey Whitbourne.

Using *Essentials of Understanding Psychology:* A Guide for Students

If you're reading this passage, you're probably taking an introductory psychology course. Maybe you're studying psychology because you've always been interested in what makes people tick. Or perhaps you've had a friend or family member who has sought assistance for a psychological disorder. Or maybe you have no idea of what psychology is all about, but you know that taking an introductory psychology course would fulfill a degree requirement.

Whatever your motivation for taking the course and reading this book, here's my commitment to you: by the time you finish this text, you will have a better understanding of why people—including you—behave the way they do. You will know how, and why, psychologists conduct research, and you'll have an understanding of the theories that guide their research. You will become acquainted with the breadth of the field, and you'll obtain practical, useful information. In short, you'll gain a wealth of knowledge that hopefully will excite your curiosity and increase your understanding of people's behavior.

To meet this commitment, *Essentials of Understanding Psychology* has been written with you, the reader, in mind. At every step in the development of the book, students and instructors have been consulted extensively in an effort to identify the combination of learning tools that would maximize readers' ability to learn and retain the subject matter of psychology. The result is a book that contains features that will not only help you to understand psychology, but also make it the discipline that is a part of your life.

Now it's your turn; you'll need to take several steps to maximize the effectiveness of the learning tools in this book. These steps include familiarizing yourself with the scope and structure of the book, using the built-in learning aids, and employing a systematic study strategy.

Prologue

Looking Ahead

3–4 Major Topical Sections

Looking Back

Epilogue

Familiarize Yourself with the Scope and Organization of *Essentials of Understanding Psychology*

Begin by reading the list of chapters and skimming the detailed Contents pages. From this you will get a sense of the topics covered and the logic of the sequence of chapters. Then take some time to flip through the book. Choose a chapter that sounds particularly interesting to you, skim it, and see for yourself how it is laid out. Note that every chapter follows the same diamond-shaped pattern.

The heart of each chapter consists of several self-contained units that provide logical starting and stopping points for reading and studying. You can plan your studying around the three or four major sections of each chapter. For instance, if your instructor assigns a chapter to read over the course of a week, you might plan to read and study one major section each day, using later days in the week to review the material.

Use the Built-in Learning Aids

Once you have acquired a broad overview of *Essentials of Understanding Psychology,* you are ready to begin reading and learning about psychology. Each chapter contains learning aids that will help you master the material. In addition, the book incorporates the *P.O.W.E.R. Learning* system. As we'll discuss in further detail later, the *P.O.W.E.R. Learning* system is based on a series of five steps: **P**repare, **O**rganize, **W**ork, **E**valuate, and **R**ethink. Each major section of a chapter starts with a **P**repare and **O**rganize segment, and—after you do the **W**ork of reading the section—ends with an **E**valuate and **R**ethink segment. Making use of the *P.O.W.E.R. Learning* system and the other built-in features will help you study more easily and effectively.

- **Prologue and Epilogue**
  Each chapter begins with a *Prologue* and ends with an *Epilogue.* The *Prologue* sets the stage for the chapter, providing a brief account of a real-life event that is relevant to the chapter content, and demonstrating why the material in the chapter is important. The *Epilogue* refers back to the *Prologue,* seeking to place it in the context of the chapter subject matter and asking questions designed to encourage you to think critically about what you've read.

- **Looking Ahead**

  The *Looking Ahead* section, which follows the *Prologue*, identifies the key themes and issues addressed in the chapter. It alerts you to what you'll have learned after reading and studying the chapter.

- **PsychLinks**

  These marginal icons provide a brief description and Web address of a web site relevant to the material being discussed in the text. For your convenience, each *PsychLink* has a corresponding link on the *Essentials of Understanding Psychology* website (http://www.mhhe.com/feldmaness5) that takes you directly to the site.

- **Prepare and Organize segments**

  The *Prepare* section consists of learning objectives to help focus your thinking about the chapter content. (The same questions are used to organize the chapter summary at the end of the chapter.) The *Organize* section provides an outline of the material to orient you to the topics that will be covered.

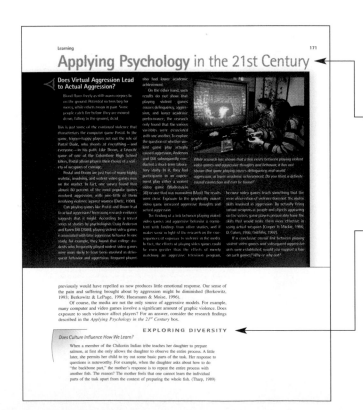

- **Applying Psychology in the 21st Century**

  These boxes describe psychological research that is being applied to everyday problems. Read them to understand how psychology promises to improve the human condition, in ways ranging from new approaches to treating psychological disorders to using brain waves to overcome physical disabilities.

- **Exploring Diversity**

  Each chapter includes a section devoted to an aspect of racial, ethnic, gender, or cultural diversity. These features illustrate the contributions of psychology to a better understanding of multicultural issues that are so central a part of our global society.

- **Psychology at Work**
  These boxes present brief interviews with psychologists and other professionals who draw on psychological principles and findings in their work. These biographical sketches provide a glimpse of the broad range of professions that use psychology. They can help answer your questions on how to use your knowledge of psychology as you follow your own career path.

- **Running Glossary**
  When a key term or concept appears in the text, it appears either in boldface or italics. Boldfaced words are of primary importance; italicized words are of secondary importance. Terms and concepts in bold are defined in the text where they are introduced and in the text margins, and in the end-of-book glossary. In addition, boldfaced terms are included in the page-referenced list of *Key Terms and Concepts* at the end of every chapter. You might want to highlight these terms with a marker.

- **Becoming an Informed Consumer of Psychology**
  One of the major goals of *Essentials of Understanding Psychology* is to make readers more informed, critical consumers of information relating to psychological issues. These discussions, found in every chapter, give you the tools to evaluate information concerning human behavior that you might hear or read about in the media or on the Web.

- **Evaluate and Rethink segments**
  Every major section ends with an *Evaluate* and *Rethink* segment. *Evaluate* sections provide a series of questions on the chapter content that ask for concrete information, in a multiple-choice, fill-in, or true-false format. The questions that appear in the *Rethink* sections are designed to encourage you to think critically about a topic or issue, and they often have more than one correct answer.

  Answer *Evaluate* and *Rethink* questions! Your responses will indicate both your degree of mastery of the material and the depth of your knowledge. If you have no trouble with the questions, you can be confident that you are studying effectively. Use questions with which you have difficulty as a basis for further study.

- **Looking Back**
  These end-of-chapter sections include four parts: a chapter summary, a list of *Key Terms and Concepts, Psychology on the Web,* and *OLC Preview.* The summary is organized around the *Prepare* questions from each major section. The *Key Terms and Concepts* list includes a page number where the term is first introduced in the chapter. To find its definition, you have two choices: turn to the margin of the page where the term is introduced, or consult the end-of-book glossary, which contains every *Key Term and Concept. Psychology on the Web* exercises take you online to help you learn more about topics covered in the chapter. The *OLC Preview* points you to the book website, where you can test your knowledge, do additional activities, and find interesting resources.

You'll find the same set of features in every chapter. Consequently, the book provides a set of familiar landmarks to help you chart your way through new material. This structure will help you organize each chapter's content, as well as learn and remember the material.

One final note: This text uses a reference citation style endorsed by the American Psychological Association (APA). According to APA style, citations include a name and date, typically set off in parentheses at the end of a sentence specifying the author of the work being cited and the year of publication—e.g., "(Anderson & Dill, 2000)." Each of these author-date citations refers to a book or article in the Reference List at the end of this book.

Using *P.O.W.E.R. Learning,* a Proven Strategy for Effective Study and Critical Thinking

Now that you are acquainted with the special features of *Essentials of Understanding Psychology* that are designed to help you understand and master this book's content, you should consider consistently applying the *P.O.W.E.R. Learning* system incorporated in the book. By using *P.O.W.E.R. Learning,* you can increase your ability to learn and retain information and to think critically, not only in your psychology course but in all academic subjects.

As noted earlier, the *P.O.W.E.R. Learning* strategy includes five key steps: *P*repare, *O*rganize, *W*ork, *E*valuate, and *R*ethink. *P.O.W.E.R. Learning* systematizes the acquisition of new material by providing a learning framework. It stresses the importance of learning objectives and appropriate preparation prior to beginning to study, as well as the significance of self-evaluation and the incorporation of critical thinking into the learning process. Specifically, use of the *P.O.W.E.R. Learning* system entails the following steps:

- **Prepare.** Before starting any journey, we need to know where we are headed. Academic journeys are no different; we need to know what our goals are. The *Prepare* stage consists of thinking about what we hope to attain from reading a particular section of the text by identifying specific goals that we seek to accomplish. In *Essentials of Understanding Psychology,* these goals are presented in the form of broad questions that start each major section.
- **Organize.** Once we know what our goals are, we need to develop a route to accomplish those goals. The *Organize* stage involves developing a mental roadmap of where we are headed. *Essentials of Understanding Psychology* highlights the organization of each upcoming section. Read the outline to get an idea of what topics are covered and how they are organized.
- **Work.** The heart of the *P.O.W.E.R. Learning* system entails actually reading and studying the material presented in the book. In some ways *Work* is the easy part, because if you have carried out the steps in the preparation and organization stage, you'll know where you're headed and how you'll get there. Of course it's not so simple—you'll need the motivation to conscientiously read and think about the material presented in the chapter. And remember, the main text isn't the only material that you need to read and think about. It's also important to read the boxes, the marginal glossary terms, and the special sections in order to gain a full understanding of the material, so be sure to include them as part of the *Work* of reading the chapter.
- **Evaluate.** The fourth step, *Evaluate,* provides you with the opportunity to determine how effectively you have mastered the material. *Essentials of Understanding Psychology* has a series of questions at the end of each section

that permit a rapid check of your understanding of the material. Evaluating your progress is essential to assessing your degree of mastery of the material.

- **Rethink.**   The final step in *P.O.W.E.R. Learning* involves critical thinking, which entails reanalyzing, reviewing, questioning, and challenging assumptions. It provides the opportunity to look at the big picture by thinking about how material fits with other information that you have already learned. Every major section of *Essentials of Understanding Psychology,* fifth edition, ends with a *Rethink* section that contains thought-provoking questions. Answering them will help you understand the material more fully and at a deeper level.

If you want to maximize your potential to master the material in *Essentials of Understanding Psychology,* fifth edition, use *P.O.W.E.R. Learning!* Taking the time and effort to work through the steps of the system is a proven technique for understanding and learning the material.

Supplementing *P.O.W.E.R. Learning* with *SQ3R*

Although *P.O.W.E.R. Learning* is the learning strategy that is built into the book and consequently is the easiest to use, it is not the only system compatible with the book. For example, some readers may wish to supplement the *P.O.W.E.R. Learning* system with the *SQ3R* method, which includes a series of five steps, designated by the initials *S-Q-R-R-R.* The first step is to *survey* the material by reading the chapter outlines, chapter headings, figure captions, recaps, and *Looking Ahead* and *Looking Back* sections, providing yourself with an overview of the major points of the chapter. The next step—the *Q* in *SQ3R*—is to *question.* Formulate questions about the material—either aloud or in writing—prior to actually reading a section of the material. The queries posed in the *Prepare* sections and the *Evaluate* and *Rethink* questions that end each part of the chapter are also a good source of questions.

The next three steps in *SQ3R* ask you to *read, recite,* and *review* the material. *Read* carefully and, even more importantly, read actively and critically. While you are reading, answer the questions you have asked yourself. Critically evaluate material by considering the implications of what you are reading, thinking about possible exceptions and contradictions, and examining underlying assumptions. The *recite* step involves describing and explaining to yourself (or to a friend) the material you have just read and answering the questions you have posed earlier. Recite aloud; the recitation process helps to identify your degree of understanding of the material you have just read. Finally, *review* the material, looking it over, reading the *Looking Back* summaries, and answering the in-text review questions.

Some Final Comments

The *P.O.W.E.R. Learning* system (as well as *SQ3R*) provides a proven means of increasing your study effectiveness. Yet you need not feel tied to a particular strategy. You might want to combine other elements into your own study system. For example, learning tips and strategies for critical thinking will be presented throughout *Essentials of Understanding Psychology,* such as in Chapter 6 when the use of mnemonics (memory techniques for organizing material to help its recall) are discussed. If these tactics help you to successfully master new material, stick with them.

By using the *P.O.W.E.R. Learning* system, you will maximize your understanding of the material in this book and will master techniques that will help you learn and think critically in all of your academic endeavors. More importantly, you will optimize your understanding of the field of psychology. It is worth the effort: the excitement, challenges, and promise that psychology holds for you are significant.

Essentials of Understanding Psychology

Chapter One

Introduction to Psychology

Prologue

From Terrorism to Heroism

The attacks on the World Trade Towers and Pentagon raised a variety of psychological issues, ranging from efforts to explain the motivation of the attackers to the extraordinary bravery of the rescue workers.

It began as a bright morning on the East Coast of the United States, filled with promise, but it soon turned into a day that would be remembered for the most deadly acts of terrorism the world had ever experienced.

Groups of terrorists hijacked four planes, leveled the World Trade Center towers, severely damaged the Pentagon, and caused the crash of another jetliner in Pennsylvania, killing just under 3,000 people. For Americans it was a catastrophe of unprecedented scale. The scope of the carnage was so vast that people had difficulty comprehending it, let alone dealing with it.

In the midst of the tragedy, however, the best of humanity was also evident. Firefighters, paramedics, and other brave rescuers sifted through the rubble, putting themselves at risk as they sought to help. Thousands of people gave blood, seeking to aid those who were injured. And millions of citizens, far removed from the sites of the terrorist acts, made generous donations to help those whose lives had been shattered by the attacks.

Looking Ahead

The behaviors that were seen in the September 11 terrorist attacks and their aftermath—ranging from the deadly aggression of the terrorists to the selfless actions of those who came to the aid of the victims—raise many issues of a psychological nature. Consider, for example, how different kinds of psychologists would look at the incident:

- Psychologists studying the biology underlying behavior would consider changes in internal bodily activity as individuals dealt with the situation.
- Those psychologists who study learning and memory would examine what people remember afterward of the incident.
- Psychologists who study thinking processes would consider how people calculated what action to take during the crisis.
- Psychologists who focus on motivation would seek to explain the reasons behind the terrorists' actions.
- Developmental psychologists, who study growth and change throughout the life span, would ask how witnessing the incident would affect students' lives in the future.
- Health psychologists would examine the kinds of stress reactions and illnesses that might later occur as a result of the incident.
- Clinical and counseling psychologists would try to identify the most effective ways to help people cope with the loss of life.
- Social psychologists would attempt to explain the causes of aggression in society, as well as examine the humane and compassionate efforts of those who provided assistance during the incident.

Although the approaches taken by different types of psychologists in studying the impact of the attack are diverse, there is a common link: each represents a specialty area within the general field of study of **psychology**, the scientific study of behavior and mental processes.

Since the first stirrings of the discipline, psychologists have debated what the scope of the field should be. Should psychologists limit themselves to the study of outward, observable behavior? Is it possible to study thinking scientifically? Should the field encompass the study of such diverse topics as physical and mental health, perception, dreaming, and motivation? Is it appropriate to focus solely on human behavior, or should the behavior of non-humans be included?

This definition seems straightforward, but its simplicity is deceptive. Most psychologists have answered these questions with the argument that the field should be receptive to a variety of viewpoints and approaches. Consequently, the phrase *behavior and mental processes* in the definition of psychology must be understood to mean many things: It encompasses not just what people do, but also their thoughts, feelings, perceptions, reasoning processes, memories, and even the biological activities that maintain bodily functioning.

When we speak of the "study" of behavior and mental processes, psychology's perspective is equally broad. Psychologists try to describe, predict, and explain human behavior and mental processes, as well as help change and improve the lives of people and the world in which they live. The use of scientific methods allows psychologists to find answers that are far more valid and legitimate than those resulting from mere intuition and speculation. And what a variety and range of questions psychologists seek to answer! Consider these examples: How long can we live without sleep? What is the best way to study? What is intelligence? What is normal sexual behavior? Can people change their dysfunctional behavior? Can aging be delayed? How does stress affect our lives? How can we reduce violence?

These questions provide just a hint of the various topics that we will encounter as we explore the field of psychology. Our discussions will take us through the range of what is known about behavior and mental processes. At times, we will explore animal behavior because it provides important clues about human behavior. Many psychologists study non-human species in order to determine general laws of behavior that pertain to *all* organisms. But we will always return to the everyday problems that confront human beings.

This book incorporates several features that illustrate how psychology can affect each of our lives. You will see how psychologists are applying what they have learned to resolve practical problems of daily life (*Applying Psychology in the 21st Century* boxes). You will

psychology: The scientific study of behavior and mental processes.

 PsychLink

Psychology organization home pages
www.mhhe.com/
feldmaness5-01links

meet people who have experienced firsthand how valuable a background in psychology can be in their professional lives (*Psychology at Work* boxes). You will learn how psychology contributes to our understanding of the multicultural world in which we live (*Exploring Diversity* sections). And you will find material in each chapter that is intended to help you incorporate psychology into your everyday life (*Becoming an Informed Consumer of Psychology*).

This introductory chapter presents several topics central to an understanding of psychology. We begin our journey through the field of psychology by describing the different types of psychologists and the various roles they play. Next, we examine the major perspectives that guide the work psychologists do, and identify the major issues that underlie psychologists' views of the world and human behavior. Finally, we examine how psychologists conduct research and what challenges they face.

Psychologists at Work

A month after losing his arm in an industrial accident, Henry Washington sits with his eyes closed as Hector Valdez, a research psychologist who studies the perception of touch, dribbles warm water on his cheek. Washington is startled as he reports feeling the water not only on his cheek, but running down his missing arm. The sensation is so strong that he checks to be sure that the arm is still missing.

***

Evelyn Poirier welcomes to her lab the Chow brothers, a pair of identical twins who were adopted by different families just after they were born. They have come to participate in her study examining similarities in the behavioral and personality traits of twins. By comparing twins who have lived together virtually all their lives to those who have been separated from birth, Poirier is seeking to determine the relative influence of heredity and experience on human behavior.

***

Methodically—and painfully—recounting events that occurred in his youth, the college student discloses a childhood secret that he has revealed previously to no one. The listener, psychologist Jonnetta Pennybaker, responds with support, suggesting to him that his concern is in fact shared by many people.

Each of these episodes describes work carried out by contemporary psychologists. Psychologists address extraordinarily different types of behavior, ranging from the most basic biological processes to how people are affected by their culture.

The Subfields of Psychology: Psychology's Family Tree

The diversity of topical areas within psychology has resulted in the development of a number of subfields (described in Table 1-1). The subfields of psychology can be likened to an extended family, with assorted nieces and nephews, aunts and uncles, and cousins who, although they might not interact on a day-to-day basis, are related to one another because they share a common goal: understanding behavior. Several basic questions about behavior that are addressed by key subfields include the following:

What Are the Biological Foundations of Behavior?

In the most fundamental sense, people are biological organisms. *Biopsychology* is the subfield of psychology that specializes in the biological bases of behavior. While they study a broad range of topics, biopsychologists focus on the operation of the brain and nervous system, considering how our body influences our behavior. For example, they might examine the link between specific sites in the brain and the muscular tremors of

Prepare

What is the science of psychology?
What are the major specialties in the field of psychology?
Where do psychologists work?

Organize

Psychologists at Work
The Subfields of Psychology
Working at Psychology

Table 1-1 The Major Subfields of Psychology

Subfield	Description
Biopsychology	*Biopsychology* examines how biological structures and functions of the body affect behavior.
Clinical psychology	*Clinical psychology* deals with the study, diagnosis, and treatment of psychological disorders.
Clinical neuropsychology	*Clinical neuropsychology* unites the areas of biopsychology and clinical psychology, focusing on the relationship between biological factors and psychological disorders.
Cognitive psychology	*Cognitive psychology* focuses on the study of higher mental processes.
Counseling psychology	*Counseling psychology* focuses primarily on educational, social, and career adjustment problems.
Cross-cultural psychology	*Cross-cultural psychology* investigates the similarities and differences in psychological functioning in and across various cultures and ethnic groups.
Developmental psychology	*Developmental psychology* examines how people grow and change from the moment of conception through death.
Educational psychology	*Educational psychology* is concerned with teaching and learning processes, such as the relationship between intelligence and school performance and the development of better teaching techniques.
Environmental psychology	*Environmental psychology* considers the relationship between people and their physical environment, including how our physical environment affects our emotions and the amount of stress we experience in a particular setting.
Evolutionary psychology	*Evolutionary psychology* considers how behavior is influenced by our genetic inheritance from our ancestors.
Experimental psychology	*Experimental psychology* studies the processes of sensing, perceiving, learning, and thinking about the world.
Forensic psychology	*Forensic psychology* focuses on legal issues, such as deciding on criteria for determining whether a defendant was legally sane at the time a crime was committed.
Health psychology	*Health psychology* explores the relationship between psychological factors and physical ailments or disease.
Industrial/organizational psychology	*Industrial/organizational psychology* is concerned with the psychology of the workplace.
Personality psychology	*Personality psychology* focuses on the consistency in people's behavior over time and the traits that differentiate one person from another.
Program evaluation	*Program evaluation* focuses on assessing large-scale programs, such as the Head Start preschool program, to determine whether they are effective in meeting their goals.
Psychology of women	*Psychology of women* focuses on issues such as discrimination against women, structural differences in women's and men's brains, and the causes of violence against women.
School psychology	*School psychology* is devoted to counseling children in elementary and secondary schools who have academic or emotional problems.
Social psychology	*Social psychology* is the study of how people's thoughts, feelings, and actions are affected by others.
Sport psychology	*Sport psychology* applies psychology to athletic activity and exercise.

people affected by Parkinson's disease (discussed in Chapter 2) or attempt to determine how our emotions are related to physical sensations (Chapter 8).

How Do People Sense, Perceive, Learn, and Think About the World?

PsychLink

Journey through biopsychology
www.mhhe.com/
feldmaness5-01links

If you have ever wondered why you are susceptible to optical illusions, how your body registers pain, or how you can study with the greatest effectiveness, an experimental psychologist can answer your questions. *Experimental psychology* is the branch of psychology that studies the processes of sensing, perceiving, learning, and thinking about the world. (The term *experimental psychologist* is somewhat misleading. Psychologists in every specialty area use experimental techniques, and experimental psychologists do not use only experimental methods.)

Several subspecialties of experimental psychology have become specialties in their own right. One example is *cognitive psychology,* which focuses on higher mental processes, including thinking, memory, reasoning, problem solving, judging, decision making, and language (as we will discuss in Chapter 7).

What Are the Sources of Change and Stability in Behavior Across the Life Span?

A baby producing her first smile . . . taking her first step . . . saying her first word. These universal milestones in development are also singularly special and unique for each person. *Developmental psychology* studies how people grow and change from the moment of conception through death (Chapter 9). *Personality psychology* focuses on the consistency in people's behavior over time and the traits that differentiate one person from another (Chapter 10).

How Do Psychological Factors Affect Physical and Mental Health?

If you are frequently depressed, feel constant stress, or seek to overcome a fear that prevents you from carrying out your normal activities, your problems would interest a health psychologist. *Health psychology* explores the relationship between psychological factors and physical ailments or disease. For example, health psychologists are interested in how long-term stress (a psychological factor) can affect physical health and in identifying ways to promote behavior that brings about good health (Chapter 11).

    Clinical psychology deals with the study, diagnosis, and treatment of psychological disorders. Clinical psychologists are trained to diagnose and treat problems ranging from the everyday crises of life, such as unhappiness over the breakup of a relationship, to more extreme conditions, such as profound, lingering depression. Some clinical psychologists also research and investigate issues that range from identifying the early signs of psychological disturbance to studying the relationship between family communication patterns and psychological disorders (Chapters 12 and 13).

How Do Our Social Networks Affect Behavior?

The complex networks of social interrelationships that are part of our world are the focus of study for a number of subfields of psychology. For example, *social psychology* is the study of how people's thoughts, feelings, and actions are affected by others. Social psychologists focus on such diverse topics as human aggression, liking and loving, persuasion, and conformity.

    Cross-cultural psychology investigates the similarities and differences in psychological functioning in and across the various cultures and ethnic groups of the world. For example, cross-cultural psychologists examine how cultures differ in their use of punishment during child rearing, or why certain cultures view academic success as being determined mostly by hard work while others see it as being determined mostly by innate ability (J. G. Miller, 1999; Rosenzweig, 1999; Aycan, 2000).

Expanding Psychology's Frontiers

As a science, psychology's boundaries are constantly growing. Two newer members of the field's family tree—clinical neuropsychology and evolutionary psychology—have sparked particular excitement, and debate, within psychology.

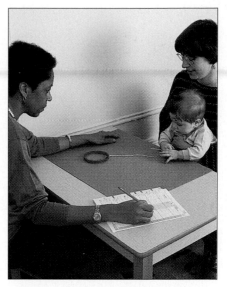

Experimental psychologists study how people sense the world. How do you think researchers adapt their experimental techniques when working with children?

PsychLink

Health psychology
www.mhhe.com/
feldmaness5-01links

Counseling psychologists who staff college centers advise students on career choices, methods of study, as well as strategies for coping with everyday adjustment problems.

Clinical neuropsychology unites the areas of biopsychology and clinical psychology: It focuses on the relationship between biological factors and psychological disorders. Building on advances in our understanding of the structure and chemistry of the brain, the specialty is leading to promising new treatments for psychological disorders, as well as debates over the use of medication to control behavior.

Evolutionary psychology considers how behavior is influenced by our genetic inheritance from our ancestors. The evolutionary approach suggests that the chemical coding of information in our cells not only determines such traits as hair color and race, but also holds the key to understanding a broad variety of behaviors that helped our ancestors survive and reproduce (Geary & Bjorklund, 2000).

Evolutionary concepts have been used to explain similarities in behavior across cultures, such as the qualities desired in potential mates. However, such explanations have stirred up controversy by suggesting that many significant behaviors are wired into the human species as a result of evolution and occur automatically.

Working at Psychology

Help Wanted: Assistant professor at a small liberal arts college. Teach undergraduate courses in introductory psychology and courses in specialty areas of cognitive psychology, perception, and learning. Strong commitment to quality teaching and student advising necessary. The candidate must also provide evidence of scholarship and research productivity.

Help Wanted: Industrial-organizational consulting psychologist. International firm is seeking psychologists for full-time career positions as consultants to management. Candidates must have the ability to establish a rapport with senior business executives and to help them find innovative, practical, and psychologically sound solutions to problems concerning people and organizations.

Help Wanted: Clinical psychologist. Ph.D., internship experience, and license required. Comprehensive clinic seeks psychologist to work with children and adults providing individual and group therapy, psychological evaluations, crisis intervention, and development of behavior treatment plans on multidisciplinary team. Broad experience with substance-abuse problems is desirable.

PsychLink

Industrial/organizational psychology
www.mhhe.com/
feldmaness5-01links

As these advertisements suggest, psychologists are employed in a variety of settings. Most doctoral-level psychologists are employed by institutions of higher learning (universities and colleges) or are self-employed, usually working as private practitioners treating clients. Other work sites include hospitals, clinics, mental health centers, counseling centers, government human-services organizations, and schools (American Psychological Association [APA], 2000).

Why do so many psychologists work in academic settings? Because these are effective settings for the three major roles played by psychologists in society—teacher, scientist, and clinical practitioner. Many psychology professors are also actively involved in research or in serving clients. Whatever their particular job site, however, psychologists share a commitment to improving individual lives as well as society in general.

Psychologists: A Statistical Portrait

Is there an "average" psychologist in terms of personal characteristics? Probably not. About half of U.S. psychologists are men and about half are women. It is predicted that by the year 2010 the number of women in the field will exceed the number of men (Pion et al., 1996).

Although most psychologists today are found in the United States, about one-third of the world's 500,000 psychologists are found in other parts of the world. Psychologists outside the United States are increasingly influential in adding to the knowledge base and practices of psychology (Mays et al., 1996; Pawlik & d'Ydewalle, 1996).

One issue of great concern is the relative lack of racial and ethnic diversity among psychologists in the United States. According to figures compiled by the American Psychological Association (APA), of those psychologists who identify themselves in surveys by race and ethnic origin—four-fifths of respondents—the vast majority are white. Past educational and occupational discrimination and a lack of encouragement for minorities to enter the field have resulted in only 6 percent of psychologists being members of minority groups. Although the numbers of minority psychologists and graduate students of psychology have increased, they have not kept up with the growth of the minority population at large (Tomes, 1998; Waters, 2000).

The underrepresentation of racial and ethnic minorities among psychologists is significant for several reasons. First, the field of psychology is diminished by a lack of the diverse perspectives and talents provided by minority group members. Furthermore, minority-group psychologists serve as role models for members of minority communities; their lack of representation within the profession might deter other minority group members from seeking to enter the field. Finally, because members of minority groups frequently prefer to receive psychological therapy from treatment providers of their own race or ethnic group, the rarity of minority psychologists can discourage some members of minority groups from seeking treatment (King, 1993; Chamberlin, 1998).

The Education of a Psychologist

How do people become psychologists? The most common route is a long one. Most psychologists have a doctorate, either a *Ph.D.* or (less frequently) a *Psy.D.* The Ph.D. is a research degree, requiring a dissertation based on an original investigation. The Psy.D. is obtained by psychologists who wish to focus on the treatment of psychological disorders. Both the Ph.D. and the Psy.D. typically take four or five years of work past the bachelor's level. Some fields of psychology involve education beyond the doctorate. For instance, doctoral-level clinical psychologists, who deal with people with psychological disorders, typically spend an additional year on an internship.

About a third of people working in the field of psychology have a master's degree as their highest degree, which is earned following two or three years of graduate work. Master's-level psychologists teach, conduct research under the supervision of a doctoral-level psychologist, or work in specialized programs dealing with drug abuse or crisis intervention. Some work in universities, government, and business, collecting and analyzing data.

An undergraduate major in psychology provides good preparation for a variety of occupations, although it does not allow professional work in psychology per se. For instance, many people in business, nursing, law, social work, and other professions report that an undergraduate background in psychology has proven invaluable in their careers. Some 20 percent of recipients of bachelor's degrees in psychology work in the social services or in some other form of public affairs. Furthermore, undergraduates who specialize in psychology typically have good analytical skills, are trained to think critically, and are able to synthesize and evaluate information well—skills that are held in high regard by employers in business, industry, and the government (APA, 2000).

Evaluate

1. Match each subfield of psychology with an issue or question posed below.

a. Biopsychology

b. Experimental psychology

c. Cognitive psychology

d. Developmental psychology

e. Personality psychology

f. Health psychology

g. Clinical psychology

h. Counseling psychology

i. Educational psychology

j. School psychology

k. Social psychology

l. Industrial/organizational psychology

1. Joan, a college freshman, is panicking. She needs to learn better organizational skills and study habits to cope with the demands of college.

2. At what age do children generally begin to acquire an emotional attachment to their fathers?

3. It is thought that pornographic films that depict violence against women can prompt aggressive behavior in some men.

4. What chemicals are released in the human body as a result of a stressful event? What are their effects on behavior?

5. Luis is unique in his manner of responding to crisis situations, with an even temperament and a positive outlook.

6. The teachers of 8-year-old Jack are concerned that he has recently begun to withdraw socially and show little interest in schoolwork.

7. Janetta's job is demanding and stressful. She wonders if her lifestyle is making her more prone to certain illnesses, such as cancer and heart disease.

8. A psychologist is intrigued by the fact that some people are much more sensitive to painful stimuli than others are.

9. A strong fear of crowds leads a young woman to seek treatment for her problem.

10. What mental strategies are involved in solving complex word problems?

11. What teaching methods most effectively motivate elementary school students to successfully accomplish academic tasks?

12. Jessica is asked to develop a management strategy that will encourage safer work practices in an assembly plant.

Rethink

1. Why might the study of twins who were raised together and twins who were not be helpful in distinguishing the effects of heredity and environment?

2. Suppose you know a 7-year-old child who is having problems learning to read and you want to help. Imagine that you can consult as many psychologists as you want to. How might each type of psychologist approach the problem?

Answers to Evaluate Questions

1. a-4, b-8, c-10, d-2, e-5, f-7, g-9, h-1, i-11, j-6, k-3, l-12

Prepare

What are the historical roots of the field of psychology?

What are the major approaches used by contemporary psychologists?

Organize

A Science Evolves

The Roots of Psychology

Today's Perspectives

A Science Evolves: The Past, the Present, and the Future

Some half-million years ago, people assumed that psychological problems were caused by evil spirits. To allow these spirits to escape the person's body, ancient healers performed an operation called trephining. Trephining consisted of chipping away at a patient's skull with crude stone instruments until a hole was cut through the bone.

***

According to the seventeenth-century philosopher Descartes, nerves were hollow tubes through which "animal spirits" conducted impulses in the same way that water is transmitted through a pipe. When a person put a finger too close to a fire, heat was transmitted into the brain through the tubes.

***

Franz Josef Gall, an eighteenth-century physician, argued that a trained observer could discern intelligence, moral character, and other basic personality characteristics from the shape and number of bumps on a person's skull. His theory gave rise to the "science" of phrenology, employed by hundreds of devoted practitioners in the nineteenth century.

Though these explanations might sound far-fetched, in their own times they represented the most advanced thinking regarding what might be called the psychology of the era. Our understanding of behavior has advanced tremendously since these earlier views were formulated, yet most of the advances have been recent—for, as sciences go, psychology is one of the "new kids on the block."

Psychology's roots can be traced back to the ancient Greeks and Romans, and philosophers argued for hundreds of years about some of the questions psychologists grapple with today. However, the formal beginning of psychology as a science is generally set at 1879, when Wilhelm Wundt established in Leipzig, Germany, the first experimental laboratory devoted to psychological phenomena. At about the same time, William James was setting up his laboratory in Cambridge, Massachusetts.

The Roots of Psychology

When Wilhelm Wundt set up the first psychology laboratory in 1879, his aim was to study the building blocks of the mind. He considered psychology to be the study of conscious experience, and he developed a perspective that came to be known as structuralism. **Structuralism** focused on the basic elements that constitute the foundation of perception, consciousness, thinking, emotions, and other kinds of mental states and activities.

To come to an understanding of how basic sensations combined to produce our perception of the world, Wundt and other structuralists used a procedure called **introspection** to study the mind. In introspection, people were presented with a stimulus—such as a bright green object or a sentence printed on a card—and were asked to describe, in their own words and in as much detail as they could manage, what they were experiencing. Wundt argued that, by analyzing the reports people offered of their reactions, psychologists could come to better understand the structure of the mind.

Over time, psychologists challenged Wundt's structuralism. They became increasingly dissatisfied with the assumption that introspection could unlock the fundamental elements of the mind. Introspection was not a truly scientific technique. There were few ways an outside observer could confirm the accuracy of others' introspections. Moreover, people had difficulty describing some kinds of inner experiences, such as emotional responses. Such drawbacks led to the evolution of new approaches, which largely supplanted structuralism.

However, the heritage of structuralism still exists. As we will see in Chapter 7, there has been a renewed interest in people's descriptions of their inner experience. Cognitive psychologists, who focus on higher mental processes such as thinking, memory, and problem solving, have developed innovative techniques that help us understand people's conscious experience and that overcome many of the difficulties inherent in introspection.

The main perspective that came to replace structuralism as psychology evolved is known as functionalism. Rather than focusing on the mind's components, **functionalism** concentrated on what the mind *does* and how behavior *functions*. Functionalists, whose perspective became prominent in the early 1900s, asked what roles behavior plays in allowing people to better adapt to their environments. Led by the American psychologist William James, the functionalists examined how behavior allows people to satisfy their needs. The famous American educator John Dewey used functionalism to develop the field of school psychology, proposing ways to best meet students' educational needs.

Another important reaction to structuralism was the development of gestalt psychology in the early 1900s. **Gestalt psychology** is a perspective focusing on how perception is organized. Instead of considering the individual parts that make up thinking, gestalt psychologists took the opposite tack, concentrating on how people consider individual elements together as units or wholes. Their credo was "The whole is different from the sum of its parts," meaning that, when considered together, the basic elements that compose our perception of objects produce something greater and more

Wilhelm Wundt

 PsychLink

History of psychology
www.mhhe.com/
feldmaness5-01links

structuralism: Wundt's approach, which focuses on the basic elements that form the foundation of thinking, consciousness, emotions, and other kinds of mental states and activities.

introspection: A procedure used to study the structure of the mind, in which subjects are asked to describe in detail what they are experiencing when they are exposed to a stimulus.

functionalism: An early approach to psychology that concentrated on what the mind does—the functions of mental activity—and the role of behavior in allowing people to adapt to their environments.

William James

meaningful than those individual elements alone. As we will see in Chapter 3, gestalt psychologists have made substantial contributions to our understanding of perception.

Women in Psychology: Founding Mothers

As in many scientific fields, societal constraints hindered women's participation during the early development of psychology. Despite the hurdles they faced, several women made major contributions to psychology, although until recently their contributions were largely overlooked. For example, Leta Stetter Hollingworth was one of the first psychologists to focus on child development and on women's issues. She collected data to refute the view, popular in the early 1900s, that women's abilities regularly declined during parts of the menstrual cycle (Benjamin & Shields, 1990; Hollingworth, 1943/1990; Denmark & Fernandez, 1993).

Mary Whiton Calkins, who studied memory in the early part of the twentieth century, became the first female president of the American Psychological Association. Karen Horney (pronounced "HORN-eye") focused on the social and cultural factors behind personality, and June Etta Downey spearheaded the study of personality traits and became the first woman to head a psychology department at a state university. Anna Freud (daughter of Sigmund Freud) also made notable contributions to the treatment of abnormal behavior (Horney, 1937; Stevens & Gardner, 1982).

Today's Perspectives

The women and the men who worked to build the foundations of psychology shared a common goal: to explain and understand behavior, using scientific methods. Seeking to achieve this same goal, the tens of thousands of psychologists who followed these early pioneers embraced—and often rejected—a variety of broad perspectives (Benjamin, 1997; Robins, Gosling, & Craik, 1999).

The various perspectives offer distinct outlooks and emphasize different factors. Just as we can use more than one map to find our way around a particular region—for instance, a map that shows roads and highways and another map that shows major landmarks—psychologists developed a variety of approaches to understanding behavior. When considered jointly, the different perspectives provide the means to explain behavior in its amazing variety.

Mary Whiton Calkins

gestalt (geh SHTALLT) psychology: An approach to psychology that focuses on the organization of perception and thinking in a "whole" sense, rather than on the individual elements of perception.

The Major Perspectives of Psychology

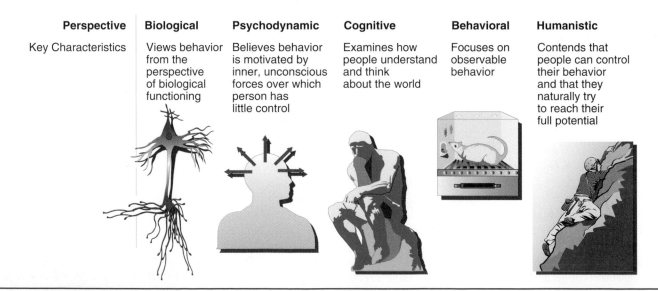

Perspective	Biological	Psychodynamic	Cognitive	Behavioral	Humanistic
Key Characteristics	Views behavior from the perspective of biological functioning	Believes behavior is motivated by inner, unconscious forces over which person has little control	Examines how people understand and think about the world	Focuses on observable behavior	Contends that people can control their behavior and that they naturally try to reach their full potential

Figure 1–1 The major perspectives used by psychologists.

Today, the field of psychology involves five major perspectives (summarized in Figure 1-1). Each of these broad perspectives emphasizes different aspects of behavior and mental processes, and each takes our understanding of behavior in somewhat different directions.

The Biological Perspective: Blood, Sweat, and Fears

When we get down to the basics, human beings are animals made of skin and bones. The **biological perspective** considers how people and nonhumans function biologically: how individual nerve cells are joined together, how the inheritance of certain characteristics from parents and other ancestors influences behavior, how the functioning of the body affects hopes and fears, which behaviors are instinctual, and so forth. Even more complex kinds of behaviors, such as a baby's response to strangers, are viewed as having critical biological components by psychologists using the biological perspective. This perspective includes the study of heredity and evolution, and how heredity might influence behavior.

Because every behavior can at some level be broken down into its biological components, the biological perspective has broad appeal. Psychologists who subscribe to this perspective have made major contributions to the understanding and betterment of human life, ranging from developing cures for certain types of deafness to identifying medications to treat people with severe mental disorders.

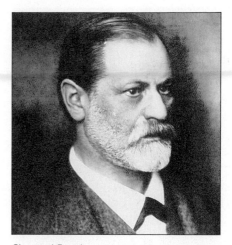

Sigmund Freud

biological perspective: The approach that views behavior from the perspective of biological functioning.

The Psychodynamic Perspective: Understanding the Inner Person

To many people who have never taken a psychology course, psychology begins and ends with the psychodynamic perspective. Proponents of the **psychodynamic perspective** believe that behavior is motivated by inner forces and conflicts about which we have little awareness or control. Dreams and slips of the tongue are viewed as indications of what a person is truly feeling within a seething cauldron of unconscious psychic activity.

The psychodynamic view is intimately linked with one individual: Sigmund Freud. Freud was a Viennese physician in the early 1900s whose ideas about unconscious determinants of behavior had a revolutionary effect on twentieth-century thinking, not just in psychology but in related fields as well. Although some of the original principles of psychodynamic thinking have been roundly criticized, contemporary use of the perspective has provided a means not only to understand and treat some kinds of psychological disorders, but also to understand everyday phenomena such as prejudice and aggression.

psychodynamic perspective: The approach based on the belief that behavior is motivated by unconscious inner forces over which the individual has little control.

The Cognitive Perspective: Identifying the Roots of Understanding

The route to understanding behavior leads some psychologists straight into the mind. Evolving in part from structuralism, the **cognitive perspective** focuses on how people think, understand, and know about the world. The emphasis is on learning how people comprehend and represent the outside world within themselves, and how our ways of thinking about the world influence our behavior.

Psychologists using the cognitive perspective often compare human thinking to the workings of a computer, considering how information is input, transformed, stored, and retrieved. In this view, thinking is *information processing*.

Psychologists relying on the cognitive perspective ask questions ranging from how people make decisions to whether a person can watch television and study at the same time. The common elements that link cognitive approaches are an emphasis on how people understand and think about the world and a concern to describe the patterns and irregularities in the operation of our minds.

cognitive perspective: The approach that focuses on how people think, understand, and know about the world.

The Behavioral Perspective: Observing the Outer Person

Whereas the biological, psychodynamic, and cognitive approaches look inside the organism to determine the causes of its behavior, the behavioral perspective takes a very different approach. The **behavioral perspective** grew out of a rejection of

behavioral perspective: The approach that suggests that observable behavior that can be measured objectively should be the focus of study.

John B. Watson

psychology's early emphasis on the inner workings of the mind, suggesting instead that the field should focus on observable behavior that can be measured objectively.

John B. Watson was the first major American psychologist to advocate a behavioral approach. Working in the 1920s, Watson was adamant in his view that one could gain a complete understanding of behavior by studying and modifying the environment in which people operated. In fact, he believed rather optimistically that it was possible to elicit any desired sort of behavior by controlling a person's environment. This philosophy is clear in his own words: "Give me a dozen healthy infants, well-formed, and my own specified world to bring them up in and I'll guarantee to take any one at random and train him to become any type of specialist I might select—doctor, lawyer, artist, merchant-chief, and yes, even beggar-man and thief, regardless of his talents, penchants, tendencies, abilities, vocations and race of his ancestors" (Watson, 1924). The behavioral perspective was later championed by B.F. Skinner, who until his death in 1990 was probably the best-known psychologist. Much of our understanding of how people learn new behaviors is based on the behavioral perspective.

As we will see, the behavioral perspective crops up along every byway of psychology. Along with its influence in the area of learning processes, this perspective has also made contributions in such diverse areas as treating mental disorders, curbing aggression, resolving sexual problems, and ending drug addiction.

The Humanistic Perspective: The Unique Qualities of Homo Sapiens

Rejecting the views that behavior is determined largely by automatic biological forces, by unconscious processes, or by the environment, the **humanistic perspective** instead suggests that all individuals naturally strive to grow, develop, and be in control of their lives and behavior. Humanistic psychologists maintain that each of us has the capacity to seek and reach fulfillment.

According to Carl Rogers and Abraham Maslow, who were central figures in the development of the humanistic perspective, people will strive to reach their full potential if given the opportunity. The emphasis of the humanistic perspective is on *free will,* the ability to freely make decisions about one's own behavior and life. The notion of free will stands in contrast to *determinism,* which sees behavior as caused, or determined, by things beyond a person's control.

The humanistic perspective assumes that people have the ability to make their own choices about their behavior rather than rely on societal standards. More than any other approach, it stresses the role of psychology in enriching people's lives and helping them to achieve self-fulfillment. The humanistic perspective has had an important influence on psychologists, reminding them of their commitment to the individual person in society.

It is important not to let the abstract qualities of the broad approaches we have discussed lull you into thinking that they are purely theoretical: These perspectives underlie ongoing work of a practical nature, as we will discuss throughout this book. As a start in seeing this, read the *Applying Psychology in the 21st Century* box.

Applying Psychology in the 21st Century

Psychology and the Reduction of Violence

A 6-year-old boy brings a gun to school and shoots a classmate with whom he had a playground dispute the previous day.

An elderly woman is killed by two teenage muggers during a robbery; she had less than $2 for them to steal.

Three white men tie a black man to a truck and drag him at high speed down a country road; he dies a gruesome death.

Violence in the United States has reached epidemic levels, and there are few signs that it will let up. Surveys consistently reveal that violence and crime rank near the top of the list of social problems that concern Americans most (Stone & Kelner, 2000; Taylor, 2000).

Yet violence has not gone unchallenged, and the field of psychology is playing a key role in efforts to reduce this social ill. Psychologists specializing in diverse areas and employing the major perspectives of the field are making a concerted effort to answer key questions relating to violence. These are some examples:

- *Does watching violence on television and in movies lead viewers to be violent?* Most social and developmental psychologists agree that observation of aggression in the media enhances the likelihood that viewers will act aggressively. Furthermore, it desensitizes viewers to displays of aggression, leading them to react with passivity to actual incidents of aggression, and it makes the world seem to be a more dangerous place (Seppa, 1997; American Academy of Pediatrics, 1999b).
- *What is the effect of extremely violent video games on the people who play them?* Playing violent video games has consequences similar to watching violence in the media: an increase in subsequent aggression, desensitization to actual

violence, and a view of the world as being more hostile (Anderson & Dill, 1999).
- *How can youth violence be reduced?* Cultural, societal, and individual psychological factors—including parental neglect, frequent observation of violence, poverty, prejudice, and discrimination—are associated with higher rates of violence. Successful training programs have been designed to teach inner-city students with a history of aggression to respond to provocative

The role of guns in American culture is a widely discussed and controversial topic. What can psychologists add to the discussion?

situations without violence (Staub, 1996; Spielman & Staub, 2000; Enserink, 2000b).
- *How can rape be prevented?* According to some estimates, one in four women in the United States stands a chance of being raped at some point during her lifetime (Koss, 1993). Psychologists from different subfields of the field—including clinical psychology, developmental psychology, and the psychology of women—have been

working to reduce sexually aggressive behavior by teaching values that make aggression, of any kind, less likely (Hall & Barongan, 1997).
- *Is there a "cycle of violence" that extends violence from one generation to another?* Many child abusers were victims of abuse in their own childhood. According to the "cycle of violence" explanation, abuse and neglect during their childhood make people more likely to abuse and neglect their own children. On the other hand, developmental psychologists who study growth and change throughout the life span have found that being abused does not inevitably lead to abusing one's own children. Why some people are able to break the cycle of violence, while others succumb to it, remains a key question for psychologists (Wileman & Wileman, 1995; Peled, Jaffe, & Edleson, 1995).
- *What role do biological factors play in aggression?* Some psychologists have considered whether aggression is linked to biological factors. For instance, biopsychologists and social psychologists have found a link between aggressive behavior and the presence of certain hormones in the body. These findings suggest the possibility that medical treatments might reduce violence in perpetrators (Dabbs, Hargrove, & Heusel, 1996; Davidson, Putnam, & Larson, 2000).

Clearly, psychologists are taking a variety of approaches to combating violence. And violence is not the only societal problem to which psychologists are contributing their expertise in an effort to alleviate human suffering. As we will explore in the *Applying Psychology in the 21st Century* boxes in every chapter, psychology's basic principles help address and solve a wide range of social problems.

Assuming that the research on video games is confirmed, should violent video games be restricted to certain age groups? Should they be banned entirely? Why or why not?

Evaluate

1. Wundt described psychology as the study of conscious experience, a perspective he called _____.

2. Early psychologists studied the mind by asking people to describe what they were experiencing when exposed to various stimuli. This procedure was known as _____.

3. The statement, "In order to study human behavior, we must consider the whole of perception rather than its component parts" might be made by a person subscribing to the _____ perspective.

4. Jeanne's therapist asks her to recount a violent dream she recently experienced in order to gain insight into the unconscious forces affecting her behavior. Jeanne's therapist is working from a _____ perspective.

5. "We should study observable behavior, not the suspected inner workings of the mind." This statement was most likely made by someone with which perspective:

   a. cognitive perspective

   b. biological perspective

   c. humanistic perspective

   d. behavioral perspective

6. "My therapist is wonderful! She always points out my positive traits. She dwells on my uniqueness and strength as an individual. I feel much more confident about myself—as if I'm really growing and reaching my potential." The therapist being described most likely practices from a _____ perspective.

Answers to Evaluate Questions

1. structuralism 2. introspection 3. gestalt 4. psychodynamic 5. d 6. humanistic

Rethink

1. How might today's major perspectives of psychology be related to the earliest perspectives, such as structuralism, functionalism, and gestalt psychology?

2. Select one of the five major perspectives in use today (biological, psychodynamic, cognitive, behavioral, or humanistic), and describe the sorts of research questions and studies that researchers using that perspective might pursue.

Prepare

What are psychology's key issues and controversies?

What is the future of psychology likely to hold?

Organize

Psychology's Key Issues
Psychology's Future

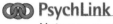 **PsychLink**

Nature vs. nurture
www.mhhe.com/
feldmaness5-01links

Psychology's Key Issues

As you consider the many topics and perspectives that make up psychology, which range from a narrow focus on minute biochemical influences on behavior to a broad focus on social behaviors, you might find yourself thinking that the discipline lacks cohesion. Yet the field is actually more unified than a first glimpse might suggest. For one thing, no matter what topical area a psychologist specializes in, he or she will rely on one of the five major perspectives. For example, a developmental psychologist who specializes in the study of children could make use of the cognitive perspective *or* the psychodynamic perspective *or* any of the other major perspectives.

Psychologists also agree on what the key issues of the field are. Although major arguments exist regarding how to best address and resolve these, psychology is a unified science because of this collective acknowledgment that these issues must be addressed in order for the field to advance.

As you contemplate these key issues (described below and summarized in Table 1-2), try not to think of them in "either/or" terms. Instead, consider the opposing viewpoints on each issue as opposite ends of a continuum, with the positions of individual psychologists typically falling somewhere between the two ends.

- *Nature (heredity) versus nurture (environment).* How much of our behavior is due to heredity (or "nature") and how much is due to environment ("nurture"), and what is the interplay between the two forces? This question has deep philosophical and historical roots and it is a factor in many topics of psychology.

   A psychologist's take on this issue depends partly on which major perspective she or he subscribes to. For example, developmental psychologists, whose focus is on how people grow and change throughout the course of their lives, might be most interested in learning more about hereditary influences if

Table 1-2 Positions Taken by Psychologists Using the Major Perspectives of Psychology

	PERSPECTIVE				
Issue	Biological	Psychodynamic	Cognitive	Behavioral	Humanistic
Nature (heredity) vs. nurture (environment)	Nature (heredity)	Nature (heredity)	Both	Nurture (environment)	Nurture (environment)
Conscious vs. unconscious determinants of behavior	Unconscious	Unconscious	Both	Conscious	Conscious
Observable behavior vs. internal mental processes	Internal emphasis	Internal emphasis	Internal emphasis	Observable emphasis	Internal emphasis
Free will vs. determinism	Determinism	Determinism	Free will	Determinism	Free will
Individual differences vs. universal principles	Universal emphasis	Universal emphasis	Individual emphasis	Both	Individual emphasis

they were employing a biological perspective. On the other hand, developmental psychologists who are proponents of the behavioral perspective would be more likely to focus on environment.

- *Conscious versus unconscious causes of behavior.* How much of our behavior is produced by forces of which we are fully aware, and how much is due to unconscious activity—mental processes that are not accessible to the conscious mind? This question represents one of the great controversies in the field of psychology. For example, clinical psychologists adopting a psychodynamic perspective argue that much of abnormal behavior is motivated by unconscious factors, whereas others employing the cognitive perspective suggest that abnormal behavior is largely the result of faulty thinking processes. The specific approach taken has a clear impact on how abnormal behavior is diagnosed and treated.

- *Observable behavior versus internal mental processes.* Should psychology concentrate solely on behavior that can be seen by outside observers? Or should it focus on unseen thinking processes? Some psychologists, particularly those relying on the behavioral perspective, contend that the only legitimate source of information for psychologists is behavior that can be observed directly. Other psychologists, building on the cognitive perspective, argue that what goes on inside a person's mind is critical and that we cannot understand behavior without concerning ourselves with mental processes.

- *Free will versus determinism.* How much of behavior is a matter of *free will* (choices made freely by an individual), and how much is subject to *determinism,* the notion that behavior is largely produced by factors beyond people's willful control? An issue long debated by philosophers, the free-will/determinism argument is also central to the field of psychology (Kimble, 1989; Hoeller, 1990). For example, some psychologists specializing in psychological disorders argue that people make intentional choices and that those who display so-called "abnormal behavior" should be considered responsible for their actions. Other psychologists disagree and contend that such individuals are the victims of forces beyond their control. The position psychologists take on this issue has important implications for how they will treat abnormal behavior, especially in deciding whether treatment should be forced on individuals who reject it.

- *Individual differences versus universal principles.* How much of our behavior is a consequence of our unique and special qualities and how much reflects the culture and society in which we live? How much of our behavior is universally human? Psychologists relying on the biological perspective tend to look for universal

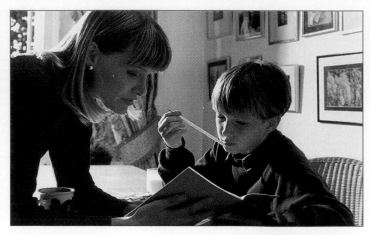

Members of different cultures attribute academic success to different factors. How might different cultural perspectives affect the performance of Asian versus North American students?

principles of behavior, such as how our nervous system operates or the way certain hormones automatically prime us for sexual activity. Such psychologists concentrate on the similarities in our behavioral destinies despite vast differences in our upbringing. In contrast, psychologists employing the humanistic perspective focus more on the uniqueness of every individual. They consider how every person's behavior is a reflection of distinct and special qualities.

The question of the degree to which psychologists can identify universal principles that apply to all people has taken on new significance in light of the tremendous demographic changes now occurring in the United States. For instance, the proportion of people of Hispanic descent in the United States by 2050 is projected to be more than twice what it is today. Soon after that, non-Hispanic whites will be a numerical minority in the United States. Similar demographic changes are slated to occur across the world. As we discuss next, these and other changes raise new and critical issues for the discipline of psychology in the twenty-first century.

 PsychLink

Cross-cultural psychology
www.mhhe.com/
feldmaness5-01links

Psychology's Future

We've examined psychology's foundations. But what does the future hold for the discipline? Although the course of scientific development is difficult to predict, several trends do seem likely to emerge in the near future:

- As its knowledge base grows, psychology will become increasingly specialized and new perspectives will evolve (Robins, Gosling, & Craik, 1999).
- More psychologists will focus on the prevention of psychological disorders rather than just on their treatment. Psychological treatment will become more available and socially acceptable as the number of psychologists increases (APA, 1999).
- Psychology's influence on issues of public interest will grow. The major problems of our time—such as violence, racial and ethnic prejudice, poverty, and environmental and technological disasters—have important psychological aspects, and it is likely that psychologists will make important practical contributions toward their resolution (Cialdini, 1997; Lerner, Fisher, & Weinberg, 2000).
- As the population of the United States becomes more diverse, issues of diversity—embodied in the study of racial, ethnic, linguistic, and cultural factors—will become more critical to psychologists providing services and doing research. The result will be a field that can provide an understanding of human behavior in its broadest sense (J. G. Miller, 1999; Rosenzweig, 1999; Leong & Blustein, 2000).

Evaluate

1. What perspective suggests that abnormal behavior is largely the result of unconscious forces?
2. "Psychologists should worry only about behavior that is directly observable." This statement would most likely be made by a person using which psychological perspective?
3. Psychology is currently moving toward increased specialization. True or false?

Answers to Evaluate Questions

1. psychodynamic 2. behavioral 3. True

Rethink

1. "The fact that some businesses now promote their ability to help people 'expand their mind beyond virtual reality' shows the great progress psychology has made lately." Criticize this statement in light of what you know about professional psychology and pseudo-psychology.
2. How do some of the key issues identified in this chapter relate to law enforcement and criminal justice?

Research in Psychology

A 30-year-old male Haitian immigrant named Abner Louima was hustled into a New York City police station lobby. Stripped naked from the waist down, he was taken, in handcuffs, to the station bathroom. There a police officer, who borrowed a pair of protective gloves from a colleague, raped Louima with a toilet plunger. He then thrust the plunger into Louima's mouth, breaking several teeth. The immigrant was then put in a holding cell. An ambulance was called an hour later, only because other occupants of the cell noted that he was bleeding. Louima was eventually transported to a hospital, where he lay near death for several days.

The bathroom where the assault took place was in the center of the police station, and it is difficult to imagine that no one heard Louima's screams of pain while he was being attacked. In fact, several days later some officers admitted that they had witnessed the incident. Yet no one offered any help, and for several days other officers refused to admit that they had any knowledge of the attack.

The question remains: Why did no one come to Louima's aid?

Were this an isolated incident, we might be able to attribute the bystanders' inaction to something specific about the situation. However, events such as this one are all too common.

For example, in another infamous case, a woman named Kitty Genovese was attacked by a man near an apartment building in New York City in the mid 1960s. At one point during the assault, which lasted thirty minutes, she managed to free herself and screamed, "Oh, my God, he stabbed me. Please help me!" In the stillness of the night, no fewer than thirty-eight neighbors heard her screams. Windows opened and lights went on. One couple pulled chairs up to the window and turned off the lights so they could see better. Someone called out, "Let that girl alone." But shouts were not enough to scare off the killer. He chased her, stabbing her eight more times, and sexually molested her before leaving her to die. And how many of those thirty-eight witnesses came to her aid? As with Abner Louima, not one person helped (Rogers & Eftimiades, 1995).

The cases of Abner Louima and Kitty Genovese remain dismaying—and puzzling— examples of "bad Samaritanism." The general public, as well as psychologists, found it difficult to explain how so many people could stand by without coming to the aid of the victims.

One easy explanation, supplied by many editorial writers, was that the incidents could be attributed to the basic shortcomings of "human nature." But such an assumption is woefully inadequate. For one thing, there are numerous examples of people who have placed their own lives at risk to help others in dangerous situations.

Prepare

What is the scientific method, and how do psychologists use theory and research to answer questions of interest?
What are the different research methods employed by psychologists?
How do psychologists establish cause-and-effect relationships in research studies?

Organize

Research in Psychology
  The Scientific Method
  Psychological Research

Abner Louima received no help when he was attacked. Why did no one come to his aid?

Clearly, then, "human nature" encompasses a wide range of both negative and positive responses. Consequently, "it was human nature" is not a very satisfying explanation for the bystanders' unhelpful behavior. The mystery of the lack of bystander intervention in both incidents remains unsolved.

Psychologists in particular puzzled over the problem for many years. After much research they finally reached an unexpected conclusion: Both Abner Louima and Kitty Genovese might well have been better off had there been just a few people who heard their cries for help rather than many. In fact, had there been just one bystander present in each instance, the chances of that person intervening might have been fairly high. For it turns out that the *fewer* witnesses present in situations like the two in question, the better the victim's chances of getting help.

How did psychologists come to such a curious conclusion? After all, logic and common sense clearly suggest that the presence of more bystanders would produce a greater likelihood that someone would help a person in need. This seeming contradiction—and the way psychologists resolved it—illustrates a central task for the field of psychology: the challenge of asking and answering questions of interest.

The Scientific Method

The challenge of posing appropriate questions and properly answering them has been met through reliance on the scientific method. The **scientific method** is the approach used by psychologists to systematically acquire knowledge and understanding about behavior and other phenomena of interest. As illustrated in Figure 1-2, it consists of three main steps: (1) identifying questions of interest, (2) formulating an explanation, and (3) carrying out research designed to lend support to or refute the explanation.

Theories: Specifying Broad Explanations

In using the scientific method, psychologists start with the kinds of observations about behavior we are all familiar with. If you have ever asked yourself why a particular teacher is so easily annoyed, why a friend is always late for appointments, or how your dog understands your commands, you have been formulating questions about behavior. Psychologists, too, ask questions about the nature and causes of behavior, and this questioning is the first step in the scientific method: identifying questions of interest.

Once a question has been identified, the next step in the scientific method involves developing theories to explain the phenomenon that has been observed. **Theories** are broad explanations and predictions concerning phenomena of interest. They provide a framework for understanding the relationships among a set of otherwise unorganized facts or principles.

PsychLink

Guide for beginning researchers
www.mhhe.com/
feldmaness5-01links

scientific method: The approach used by psychologists to systematically acquire knowledge and understanding about behavior and other phenomena of interest.

theories: Broad explanations and predictions concerning phenomena of interest.

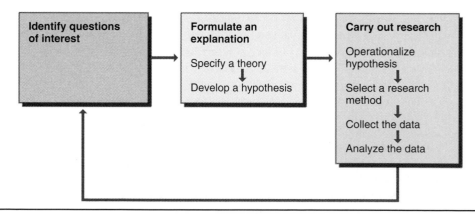

Figure 1–2 The scientific method, which encompasses the process of identifying, asking, and answering questions, is used by psychologists, and by researchers from every other scientific discipline, to come to an understanding about the world. What do you think are the advantages of this method?

All of us have developed our own informal theories of human behavior, such as "People are basically good" or "People's behavior is usually motivated by self-interest." However, psychologists' theories are more formal and focused. They are established on the basis of a careful study of the psychological literature to identify relevant research conducted and theories formulated previously, as well as psychologists' general knowledge of the field (Sternberg, 1990; Sternberg & Beall, 1991; McGuire, 1997).

Growing out of the diverse models of psychology, theories vary both in their breadth and in the level of detail they employ. For example, one theory might seek to explain and predict as broad a phenomenon as emotional experience in general. A narrower theory might purport to predict how people display the emotion of fear nonverbally after receiving a threat. An even more specific theory might attempt to explain how the muscles of the face work together to produce expressions of fear.

Psychologists Bibb Latané and John Darley, responding specifically to the Kitty Genovese case, developed a theory based on a phenomenon they called *diffusion of responsibility* (Latané & Darley, 1970). According to their theory, the greater the number of bystanders or witnesses to an event that calls for helping behavior, the more the responsibility for helping is perceived to be shared by all the bystanders. Because of this sense of shared responsibility, then, the more people present in an emergency situation, the less personal responsibility each person feels—and the less likely it is that any single person will come forward to help.

Hypotheses: Crafting Testable Predictions

Although such a theory makes sense, it represented only the beginning phase of Latané and Darley's investigative process. Their next step was to devise a way of testing their theory. To do this, they needed to create a hypothesis. A **hypothesis** is a prediction stated in a way that allows it to be tested. Hypotheses stem from theories; they help to test the underlying validity of theories.

In the same way as we develop our own broad theories about the world, we also construct hypotheses about events and behavior. They can range from trivialities (such as why our English instructor wears those weird shirts) to more meaningful matters (such as what is the best way to study for a test). Although we rarely test these hypotheses systematically, we do try to determine whether they are right. Perhaps we try comparing two strategies: cramming the night before an exam versus spreading out our study over several nights. By assessing which approach yields better test performance, we have created a way to compare the two strategies.

Latané and Darley's hypothesis was a straightforward prediction from their more general theory of diffusion of responsibility: The more people who witness an emergency situation, the less likely it is that help will be given to a victim. They could, of course, have chosen another hypothesis (for instance, that people with greater skills related to emergency situations will not be affected by the presence of others), but their initial formulation seemed to offer the most direct test of the theory.

Psychologists rely on formal theories and hypotheses for many reasons. For one thing, theories and hypotheses allow psychologists to make sense of unorganized, separate observations and bits of information by permitting them to place the pieces within a structured and coherent framework. In addition, theories and hypotheses offer psychologists the opportunity to move beyond already known facts and principles and make deductions about as yet unexplained phenomena. In this way, theories and hypotheses provide a reasoned guide to the direction that future investigation ought to take.

In sum, then, theories and hypotheses help psychologists pose appropriate questions. But how are such questions answered? As we shall see, the answers come from research.

hypothesis: A prediction, stemming from a theory, stated in a way that allows it to be tested.

Psychological Research

Research, systematic inquiry aimed at the discovery of new knowledge, is a central ingredient of the scientific method in psychology. It provides the key to understanding the degree to which theories and hypotheses are accurate.

Just as we can apply different theories and hypotheses to explain the same phenomena, we can use a number of alternative methods to conduct research on the same problem (Ray, 2000). First, though, the hypothesis must be restated in a way that will allow it to be tested, a procedure known as operationalization. **Operationalization** is the process of translating a hypothesis into specific, testable procedures that can be measured and observed.

There is no single way to go about operationalizing a hypothesis; it depends on logic, the equipment and facilities available, the psychological model being employed, and ultimately the creativity of the researcher. For example, one researcher might develop a hypothesis in which she operationalizes "fear" as an increase in heart rate. In contrast, another psychologist might operationalize "fear" as a written response to the question, "How much fear are you experiencing at this moment?"

We will consider several of the major tools in the psychologist's research kit. As we discuss these research methods, keep in mind that their relevance extends beyond testing and evaluating theories and hypotheses in psychology. Even people who do not have degrees in psychology, for instance, often carry out elementary forms of research on their own. For example, a supervisor might need to evaluate an employee's performance; a physician might systematically test the effects of different dosages of a drug on a patient; a salesperson might compare different persuasive strategies. Each of these situations calls for the use of the research practices we are about to discuss.

Furthermore, a knowledge of the research methods used by psychologists permits us to better evaluate the research that others conduct. The media constantly bombard us with claims about research studies and findings. Knowledge of research methods allows us to sort out what is credible from what should be ignored. Finally, there is evidence that by studying some kinds of research methods in depth, people learn to reason more critically and effectively. Understanding the methods by which psychologists conduct research can enhance our ability to analyze and evaluate the situations we encounter in our everyday lives (Lehman, Lempert, & Nisbett, 1988; Shaughnessy, Zechmeister, & Zechmeister, 2000; Shadish, Cook, & Campbell, 2002).

Archival Research

Suppose that, like psychologists Latané and Darley, you were interested in finding out more about emergency situations in which bystanders did not provide help. One of the first places you might turn to would be historical accounts. By using newspaper records, for example, you might find support for the notion that a decrease in helping behavior historically has accompanied an increase in the number of bystanders.

Using newspaper articles is an example of archival research. In **archival research,** existing data, such as census documents, college records, or newspaper clippings, are examined to test a hypothesis. For example, college records might be used to determine if there are gender differences in academic performance.

Archival research is a relatively inexpensive means of testing a hypothesis because someone else has already collected the basic data. Of course, the use of existing data has several drawbacks. For one thing, the data might not be in a form that allows the researcher to test a hypothesis fully. The information could be incomplete, or it could have been collected haphazardly (Stewart & Kamins, 1993).

Most archival research is hampered by the simple fact that records with the necessary information do not exist. In these instances, researchers often turn to another research method: naturalistic observation.

---

operationalization: The process of translating a hypothesis into specific, testable procedures that can be measured and observed.

PsychLink

Research methods
www.mhhe.com/
feldmaness5-01links

archival research: Research in which existing data, such as census documents, college records, or newspaper clippings, are examined to test a hypothesis.

Naturalistic Observation

In **naturalistic observation,** the investigator simply observes some naturally occurring behavior and does not make a change in the situation. For example, a researcher investigating helping behavior might observe the kind of help given to victims in a high-crime area of a city. The important point to remember about naturalistic observation is that the researcher is passive and simply records what occurs (Erlandson et al., 1993; Adler & Adler, 1994; Schmidt, 1999).

Although the advantage of naturalistic observation is obvious—we get a sample of what people do in their "natural habitat"—there is also an important drawback: the inability to control any of the factors of interest. For example, we might find so few naturally occurring instances of helping behavior that we would be unable to draw any conclusions. Because naturalistic observation prevents researchers from making changes in a situation, they must wait until appropriate conditions occur. Furthermore, if people know that they are being watched, they might alter their reactions, producing behavior that is not truly representative of the group in question.

Survey Research

There is no more straightforward way of finding out what people think, feel, and do than asking them directly. For this reason, surveys are an important research method. In **survey research,** a *sample* of people chosen to represent some larger group of interest (a *population*) are asked a series of questions about their behavior, thoughts, or attitudes. Survey methods have become so sophisticated that even with a very small sample researchers are able to infer with great accuracy how a larger group would respond. For instance, a sample of just a few thousand voters is sufficient to predict within one or two percentage points who will win a presidential election—if the representative sample is chosen with care (Weisberg, Krosnick, & Bowen, 1996; Fink & Kosecoff, 1998).

Researchers investigating helping behavior might conduct a survey by asking people to complete a questionnaire in which they indicate their reasons for not wanting to come forward to help another individual. Similarly, researchers interested in learning about sexual practices have carried out surveys to learn which practices are common and which are not, and to chart changing notions of sexual morality over the past several decades.

Asking people directly about their behavior seems in some ways the most straightforward approach to understanding what people do, but survey research has several potential drawbacks. For one thing, people might give inaccurate responses because of memory lapses or because they don't want the researcher to know what they really believe about a particular issue. Moreover, people sometimes offer responses they think the researcher wants to hear—or, in just the opposite instance, responses they assume the researcher *doesn't* want to hear. Finally, if the sample of people who are surveyed are not representative of the broader population of interest, the results of the survey have little meaning.

The Case Study

When the police officers who participated in Abner Louima's assault were arrested, many people wondered what it was about the officers' personalities or backgrounds that might have led to their behavior. To answer this question, psychologists might conduct a case study. In contrast to a survey, in which many people are studied, a **case study** is an in-depth, intensive investigation of an individual or a small group of people. Case studies often include *psychological testing,* a procedure in which a carefully designed set of questions is used to gain some insight into the personality of the individual or group being studied (Kvale, 1996; Sommer & Sommer, 1997; Gass et al., 2000).

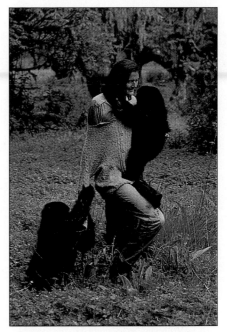

Dian Fossey, a pioneer in the study of gorillas in their native habitat, relied on naturalistic observation for her research. What are the advantages of this approach?

naturalistic observation: Research in which an investigator simply observes some naturally occurring behavior and does not make a change in the situation.

survey research: Research in which people chosen to represent some larger population are asked a series of questions about their behavior, thoughts, or attitudes.

case study: An in-depth, intensive investigation of an individual or small group of people.

"This is the New York 'Times' Business Poll again, Mr. Landau. Do you feel better or worse about the economy than you did twenty minutes ago?"

When case studies are used as a research technique, the goal is often not only to learn about the few individuals being examined, but to use the insights gained from the study to improve our understanding of people in general. Sigmund Freud built his theories through case studies of individual patients. Similarly, case studies of suicide bombers might help identify those who are prone to violence.

Correlational Research

In using the research methods that we have described, researchers often wish to determine the relationship between two variables. **Variables** are behaviors, events, or other characteristics that can change, or vary, in some way. For example, we might want to find out if there is a relationship between the variable of religious service attendance and the variable of helpfulness in emergency situations. If we did find such a relationship, we could say that there was an association—or correlation—between attendance at religious services and helpfulness in emergencies.

In **correlational research,** the relationship between two sets of variables is examined to determine whether they are associated, or "correlated." The strength and direction of the relationship between the two variables is represented by a mathematical score, known as a *correlation* (or, more formally, a *correlation coefficient*), that can range from +1.0 to −1.0.

A *positive correlation* indicates that as the value of one variable increases, we can predict that the value of the other variable will also increase. For example, if we predict that the more that students study for a test, the higher their subsequent grades on the test will be, and that the less they study, the lower their test scores will be, we are expecting to find a positive correlation. (Higher values of the variable "amount of study time" would be associated with higher values of the variable "test score," and lower values of "amount of study time" would be associated with lower values of "test score.") The correlation, then, would be indicated by a positive number, and the stronger the association between studying and test scores, the closer the number would be to +1.0. For example, we might find a correlation of +.85 between test scores and amount of studying time, indicating a strong positive association.

On the other hand, a *negative correlation* tells us that as the value of one variable increases, the value of the other decreases. For instance, we might predict that as the number of hours spent studying increases, the number of hours spent in partying decreases. Here, we are expecting a negative correlation, ranging between 0 and −1.0. More studying is associated with less partying, and less studying is associated with more partying. The stronger the association between study and partying, the closer the correlation would be to −1.0. For instance, a correlation of −.85 would indicate a strong negative association between partying and studying.

Of course, it's quite possible that little or no relationship exists between two variables. For instance, we would probably not expect to find a relationship between number of study hours and height. Lack of a relationship would be indicated by a correlation close to 0. For example, if we found a correlation of −.02 or +.03, it would indicate that there is virtually no association between the two variables; knowing how much someone studies does not tell us anything about how tall he or she is.

When we find that two variables are strongly correlated with one another, it is tempting to presume that one variable causes the other. For example, if we find that more study time is associated with higher grades, we might guess that more studying *causes* higher grades. Although this is not a bad guess, it remains just a guess—because finding that two variables are correlated does not mean that there is a causal relationship between them. Although the strong correlation suggests that knowing how much a person studies can help us predict how she or he will do on a test, it does not mean that the studying caused the test performance. It might be, for instance, that people who are interested in the subject matter tend to study more than those who are less interested, and that the

---

variables: Behaviors, events, or other characteristics that can change, or vary, in some way.

 PsychLink

Correlational research designs
www.mhhe.com/
feldmaness5-01links

correlational research: Research that examines the relationship between two sets of variables to determine whether they are associated, or "correlated."

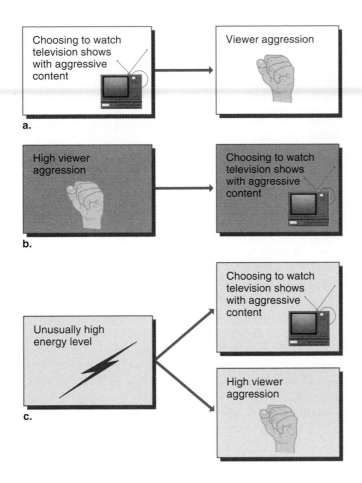

a.

b.

c.

Figure 1-3 If we find that frequent viewing of television programs having aggressive content is associated with high levels of aggressive behavior, we might cite several plausible causes, as suggested in this figure. For example, choosing to watch shows with aggressive content could produce aggression *(a);* or being a highly aggressive person might cause one to choose to watch televised aggression *(b);* or having a high energy level might cause a person to *both* choose to watch aggressive shows and act aggressively *(c).* Correlational findings, then, do not permit us to determine causality. Can you think of a way to study the effects of televised aggression on aggressive behavior that is not correlational?

experiment: The investigation of the relationship between two (or more) variables by deliberately producing a change in one variable in a situation and observing the effects of that change on other aspects of the situation.

Many studies show that the observation of violence in the media is associated with aggression in viewers. Can we conclude that the observation of violence causes aggression?

amount of interest, not the number of hours spent studying, predicts test performance. The mere fact that two variables occur together does not mean that one causes the other.

Another example illustrates the critical point that correlations tell us nothing about cause and effect but only provide a measure of the strength of a relationship between two variables. We might find that children who watch a lot of television programs featuring high levels of aggression are likely to demonstrate a relatively high degree of aggressive behavior, and that those who watch few television shows that portray aggression are apt to exhibit a relatively low degree of such behavior (see Figure 1-3). But we cannot say that the aggression is *caused* by the TV viewing, because several other explanations are possible.

For instance, it could be that children who have an unusually high level of energy seek out programs with aggressive content *and* are more aggressive. The children's energy level, then, could be the true cause of the children's higher incidence of aggression. Finally, it is also possible that people who are already highly aggressive choose to watch shows with high aggressive content *because* they are aggressive. Clearly, then, any number of causal sequences are possible—none of which can be ruled out by correlational research.

The inability of correlational research to demonstrate cause-and-effect relationships is a crucial drawback to its use. There is, however, an alternative technique that does establish causality: the experiment.

Experimental Research

The *only* way psychologists can establish cause-and-effect relationships through research is by carrying out an experiment. In a formal **experiment,** the relationship between two (or more) variables is investigated by deliberately producing a change

In this experiment, preschoolers' reactions to the puppet are monitored. Can you think of a hypothesis that might be tested in this way?

experimental manipulation: The change that an experimenter deliberately produces in a situation.

treatment: In an experiment, the manipulation implemented by the experimenter.

experimental group: Any group receiving a treatment in an experiment.

control group: A group that receives no treatment in an experiment.

 PsychLink

Two-group randomized experiment
www.mhhe.com/
feldmaness5-01links

in one variable in a situation and observing the effects of that change on other aspects of the situation. In an experiment, then, the conditions required to study a question of interest are created by an experimenter, who deliberately makes a change in those conditions in order to observe the effects of that change.

The change that an experimenter deliberately produces in a situation is called the **experimental manipulation.** Experimental manipulations are used to detect relationships between different variables.

Several steps are involved in carrying out an experiment, but the process typically begins with the development of one or more hypotheses for the experiment to test. Recall, for example, the hypothesis derived by Latané and Darley to test their theory of helping behavior: The more people who witness an emergency situation, the less likely it is that any of them will help the victim. We can trace the way these researchers designed an experiment to test this hypothesis.

Their first step was to operationalize the hypothesis by conceptualizing it in a way that could be tested. Doing so required that Latané and Darley take into account the fundamental principle of experimental research mentioned earlier. Experimenters must manipulate at least one variable in order to observe the effects of the manipulation on another variable. But the manipulation cannot be viewed by itself, in isolation; if a cause-and-effect relationship is to be established, the effects of the manipulation must be compared with the effects of no manipulation or a different kind of manipulation.

Experimental research requires, then, that the responses of at least two groups be compared with each other. One group will receive some special **treatment**—the manipulation implemented by the experimenter—and another group will receive either no treatment or a different treatment. Any group receiving a treatment is called an **experimental group;** a group that receives no treatment is called a **control group.** (In some experiments there are multiple experimental and control groups, each of which is compared with another.)

By employing both experimental and control groups in an experiment, researchers are able to rule out the possibility that something other than the experimental manipulation produced the results observed in the experiment. With no control group, we couldn't be sure that some other variable, such as the temperature at the time we were running the experiment, the color of the experimenter's hair, or even the mere passage of time, wasn't causing the changes observed.

For example, consider a medical researcher who thinks she has invented a medicine that cures the common cold. To test her claim, she gives the medicine one day to a group of twenty people who have colds, and finds that ten days later all of them are cured. Eureka? Not so fast. An observer viewing this flawed study might reasonably argue that the people would have gotten better even without the medicine. What the researcher obviously needed was a control group consisting of people with colds who *don't* get the medicine, and whose health is also checked ten days later. Only if there is a difference between experimental and control groups can the effectiveness of the medicine be assessed. Through the use of control groups, then, researchers can isolate specific causes for their findings—and draw cause-and-effect inferences.

Returning to Latané and Darley's experiment, we note that the researchers needed a means of operationalizing their hypothesis in order to proceed. They decided they would create a false emergency situation that would appear to require the aid of a bystander. As their experimental manipulation, they decided to vary the number of bystanders present. They could have had just one experimental group with, say, 2 people present, and a control group for comparison purposes with just 1 person present. Instead, they settled on a more complex procedure involving three groups—consisting of 2, 3, and 6 people—that could be compared with one another.

Latané and Darley had now identified what is called the experimenter's independent variable. The **independent variable** is the variable that is manipulated by an experimenter. (You can think of the independent variable as being independent of the actions of those taking part in an experiment; it is controlled by the experimenter.) In the case of the Latané and Darley experiment, the independent variable was the number of people present, manipulated by the experimenters.

The next step was to decide how they were going to determine the effect that varying the number of bystanders had on behavior of those in the experiment. Crucial to every experiment is the **dependent variable,** the variable that is measured and is expected to change as a result of changes caused by the experimenter's manipulation of the independent variable. The dependent variable is dependent on the actions of the *participants* or *subjects,* the people taking part in the experiment.

Latané and Darley had several possible choices for their dependent measure. One might have been a simple yes/no measure of the participants' helping behavior. But the investigators also wanted a more precise analysis of helping behavior. Consequently, they also measured the amount of time it took for a participant to provide help.

Latané and Darley now had all the necessary components of an experiment. The independent variable, manipulated by them, was the number of bystanders present in an emergency situation. The dependent variable was the measure of whether bystanders in each of the groups provided help and the amount of time it took them to do so. Consequently, like all experiments, this one had both an independent and a dependent variable. (To remember the difference, recall that a hypothesis predicts how a dependent variable *depends* on the manipulation of the independent variable.) *All* true experiments in psychology fit this straightforward model.

The Final Step: Random Assignment of Participants   To make the experiment a valid test of the hypothesis, the researchers needed to add a final step to the design: properly assigning participants to receive a particular treatment.

The significance of this step becomes clear when we examine various alternative procedures. For example, the experimenters might have assigned just males to the group with 2 bystanders, just females to the group with 3 bystanders, and both males and females to the group with 6 bystanders. Had they done so, however, any differences they found in helping behavior could not be attributed with any certainty solely to group size, because the differences might just as well be due to the composition of the group. A more reasonable procedure would be to ensure that each group had the same composition in terms of gender; then the researchers would be able to make comparisons across groups with considerably more accuracy.

Participants in each of the experimental groups ought to be comparable, and it is easy enough to create groups that are similar in terms of gender. The problem becomes a bit more tricky, though, when we consider other participant characteristics. How can we ensure that participants in each experimental group will be equally intelligent, extroverted, cooperative, and so forth, when the list of characteristics—any one of which could be important—is potentially endless?

The solution is a simple but elegant procedure called **random assignment to condition:** Participants are assigned to different experimental groups or "conditions" on the basis of chance and chance alone. The experimenter might, for instance, put the names of all potential participants into a hat and draw names to make assignments to specific groups. The advantage of this technique is that participant characteristics have an equal chance of being distributed across the various groups. By using random assignment, chances are that each of the groups will have approximately the same proportion of intelligent people, cooperative people, extroverted people, males and females, and so on.

Bibb Latané and John Darley

 PsychLink

Random assignment explained
www.mhhe.com/
feldmaness5-01links

independent variable: The variable that is manipulated by an experimenter.
dependent variable: The variable that is measured and is expected to change as a result of changes caused by the experimenter's manipulation.
random assignment to condition: A procedure in which participants are assigned to different experimental groups or "conditions" on the basis of chance and chance alone.

The following set of key elements is important to keep in mind as you consider whether a research study is truly an experiment:

- An independent variable, the variable that is manipulated by the experimenter
- A dependent variable, the variable that is measured by the experimenter and expected to change as a result of the manipulation of the independent variable
- A procedure that randomly assigns participants to different experimental groups or "conditions" of the independent variable
- A hypothesis that predicts what effect the independent variable will have on the dependent variable.

Only if each of these elements is present can a research study be considered a true experiment in which cause-and-effect relationships can be determined. (For a summary of the different types of research we've discussed, see Table 1-3.)

Were Latané and Darley Right?   By now, you must be wondering whether Latané and Darley were right when they hypothesized that increasing the number of bystanders in an emergency situation would lower the degree of helping behavior.

According to the results of the experiment they carried out, their hypothesis was right on target. To test the hypothesis, they used a laboratory setting in which participants were told that the purpose of the experiment was to hold a discussion about personal problems associated with college. The discussion was to be held over an intercom, supposedly to avoid the potential embarrassment of face-to-face contact. Chatting about personal problems was not, of course, the true purpose of the experiment, but participants were told that it was as a way of keeping their expectations about the experiment from biasing their behavior. (Consider how they would have been affected if they had been told that their helping behavior in emergencies was being tested. The experimenters could never have gotten an accurate assessment of what the participants would actually do in an emergency. By definition, emergencies are rarely announced in advance.)

Table 1-3 Research Strategies		
	Correlational Research	**Experimental Research**
General Process	Researcher observes a previously existing situation but does not make a change in the situation	Researcher manipulates a situation in order to observe the outcome of the manipulation
Intended Result	Identifies associations between factors	Learns how changes in one variable cause changes in another variable
Type	Archival research (examines records to confirm hypothesis)	Experiment (investigator produces a change in one variable to observe the effects of that change on other variables)
	Naturalistic observation (observation of naturally occurring behavior, without making a change in the situation)	
	Case study (intensive investigation of an individual or small group)	

The sizes of the discussion groups were 2, 3, and 6 people, which constituted the manipulation of the independent variable of group size. Participants were randomly assigned to these groups upon their arrival at the laboratory.

As the participants in each group were holding their discussion, they suddenly heard through the intercom one of the other participants (in reality a trained *confeder-ate,* or employee, of the experimenters) having what sounded like an epileptic seizure and calling for help.

The participants' behavior was now what counted. The dependent variable was the time that elapsed from the start of the "seizure" to the time a participant began trying to help the "victim." If six minutes went by without a participant's offering help, the experiment was ended.

As predicted by the hypothesis, the size of the group had a significant effect on whether a participant provided help (Latané & Darley, 1970). In the 2-person group (in which participants thought they were alone with the victim), the average elapsed time was 52 seconds; in the 3-person group (the participant, the victim, and one other person), the average elapsed time was 93 seconds; and in the 6-person group (the participant, the victim, and four others), the average time was 166 seconds. Considering a simple yes/no measure of whether help was given confirms the elapsed-time pattern. Eighty-five percent of the participants in the 2-person-group condition helped, 62 percent in the 3-person-group condition helped, and only 31 percent in the 6-person-group condition helped.

Because these results are so straightforward, it seems clear that the original hypothesis was confirmed. However, Latané and Darley could not be sure that the results were truly meaningful until they determined whether the results represented a **significant outcome.** Through various statistical analyses, researchers can determine whether a numeric difference is meaningful or trivial. Only when differences between groups are large enough that statistical tests show them to be significant is it possible for researchers to confirm a hypothesis (Estes, 1997; Cwikel, Behar, & Rabson-Hare, 2000).

significant outcome: Meaningful results that make it possible for researchers to feel confident that they have confirmed their hypotheses.

Moving Beyond the Study   The Latané and Darley study contains all the elements of an experiment: an independent variable, a dependent variable, random assignment to conditions, and multiple experimental groups. Consequently, we can say with some confidence that group size *caused* changes in the degree of helping behavior.

Of course, one experiment alone does not forever resolve the question of bystander intervention in emergencies. Psychologists require that findings be **replicated,** or repeated, sometimes using other procedures, in other settings, with other groups of participants, before full confidence can be placed in the validity of any single experiment. A procedure called *meta-analysis* permits psychologists to combine the results of many separate studies into one overall conclusion (Hunt, 1999).

replication: The repetition of research, sometimes using other procedures, settings, and other groups of participants, in order to increase confidence in prior findings.

In addition to replicating experimental results, psychologists need to test the limitations of their theories and hypotheses in order to determine under which specific circumstances they do and do not apply. It seems unlikely, for instance, that increasing the number of bystanders *always* results in less helping. Therefore it is critical to understand the conditions in which exceptions to this general rule occur. For example, we might speculate that in cases in which onlookers believe that a victim's difficulties could later affect them in some way, they will be more willing to help (Aronson, 1988). Testing this hypothesis (for which, in fact, there is some support) requires additional experimentation.

Like any science, then, psychology increases our understanding in small, incremental steps, with each step building upon previous work. The work is carried out on many fronts and involves many people—individuals such as Mary Garrett, who is doing research on AIDS as she studies to become a psychologist (see the *Psychology at Work* box on page 30).

Psychology at Work

Mary Garrett

**San Francisco State College,
San Francisco, California**

Education: A.A., City College of San Francisco;
B.A., San Francisco State College; enrolled in M.A.
program, San Francisco State College

Home: San Francisco, California

Mary Garrett

Most high school students have only a vague idea of what they will do with their lives, but for Mary Garrett there was absolutely no question what she wanted: She yearned to be a psychologist.

In her forties, Garrett finally began to make her dream come true. After a gap of many years in her education, she enrolled in a graduate program in research psychology at San Francisco State College.

> "I've always been interested in people, in people's behavior, and why they do what they do."

"I've always been interested in people, in people, in people's behavior, and why they do what they do," she says. "Even when I was in high school I wanted to be a psychologist, and now I plan to teach and do research in psychology at the college level."

As part of her graduate studies, Garrett is working on an innovative and potentially significant study of African American women with the AIDS virus. "The study is intended to increase our knowledge about the nature of the effects of stress on the mental and physical health of African American women with HIV and AIDS, and the coping processes that mediate these effects, in order to design effective psychosocial intervention," she says.

The impetus for the study was a similar project conducted by one of her professors. He had done an initial study on coping with AIDS, using only men in his sample. Garrett became interested in comparing how women and men deal with the disease.

"I want to find out if the coping strategies and processes are different for women. Women do have different stressors than men, such as being single mothers or being a black female in this society," she says.

The research, according to Garrett, will involve three phases: an initial exploratory study, in-depth interviews, and a written questionnaire. She attributes much of her ability to design the study to her undergraduate training as a psychology major. "It was in my methods class

> "All of my undergraduate work in psychology was instrumental in preparing for this current study."

that I learned how to develop and give surveys. I'll also be using material I've learned from classes in statistics, methods, and aging and adult development," Garrett adds. "All of my undergraduate work in psychology was instrumental in preparing for this current study."

Evaluate

1. An explanation about a phenomenon of interest is known as a _____.
2. An experimenter is interested in studying the relationship between hunger and aggression. He defines aggression as the number of times a participant will hit a punching bag. What is the process of defining this variable called?
3. Match the following forms of research to their definition:

   1. Archival research
   2. Naturalistic observation
   3. Survey research
   4. Case study

   a. Directly asking a sample of people questions about their behavior
   b. Examining existing records to test a hypothesis
   c. Looking at behavior in its true setting without intervening in the setting
   d. In-depth investigation of a person or small group

3. Match each of the following research methods with a problem basic to it:

   1. Archival research
   2. Naturalistic observation
   3. Survey research
   4. Case study

   a. Might not be able to generalize to the population at large.
   b. People's behavior could change if they know they are being watched.
   c. The data might not exist or might be unusable.
   d. People might lie in order to present a good image.

5. A psychologist wants to study the effect of attractiveness on willingness to help a person with a math problem. Attractiveness would be the _____ variable, while amount of helping would be the _____ variable.

Rethink

1. Starting with the theory that diffusion of responsibility causes responsibility for helping to be shared among bystanders, Latané and Darley derived the hypothesis that the more people who witness an emergency situation, the less likely it is that help will be given to a victim. How many other hypotheses can you think of based on the same theory of diffusion of responsibility?

2. Can you describe how a researcher might use naturalistic observation, case study methods, and survey research to investigate gender differences in aggressive behavior at the workplace? First state a hypothesis, then describe your research approaches. What positive and negative features does each method have?

Answers to Evaluate Questions

1. theory 2. Operationalization 3. 1. b; 2. c; 3. a 4. 1. c; 2. b; 3. d; 4. a 5. independent; dependent

Research Challenges: Exploring the Process

Prepare
What major issues underlie the process of conducting research?

Organize
Research Challenges
The Ethics of Research
Should Animals Be Used in Research?
Threats to Experiments

It is probably apparent by now that there are few simple formulas psychologists can follow as they carry out research. They must make choices about the type of study to conduct, the measures to take, and the most effective way to analyze the results. Even after they make these essential decisions, they must still consider several critical issues. We turn first to the most fundamental of these issues: ethics.

The Ethics of Research

Put yourself in the place of one of the participants in the Latané and Darley experiment. How would you feel when you learned that the person you thought was having a seizure was, in reality, a paid accomplice of the experimenter?

Although you might at first experience relief that there had been no real emergency, you might also feel some resentment that you had been deceived by the experimenter. And you might also experience concern that you had been placed in an unusual situation—one that might have dealt a blow to your self-esteem, depending on how you had behaved.

Most psychologists argue that the use of deception is sometimes necessary to prevent participants from being influenced by what they think the study's true purpose is. (If you knew that Latané and Darley were actually studying your helping behavior, wouldn't you automatically have been tempted to intervene in the emergency?) To avoid such outcomes, researchers must occasionally use deception.

Nonetheless, because research has the potential to violate the rights of participants, psychologists are expected to adhere to a strict set of ethical guidelines aimed at protecting participants (APA, 1992). These guidelines advocate the following:

PsychLink
Ethics in research
www.mhhe.com/
feldmaness5-01links

- Protection of participants from physical and mental harm
- The right of participants to privacy regarding their behavior
- The assurance that participation in research is completely voluntary
- The necessity of informing participants about the nature of procedures prior to their participation in the experiment

Although the guidelines do allow the use of deception, all experiments involving deception must be reviewed by an independent panel before their use—as must all research that uses human beings as participants (Rosnow et al., 1993; Rosenthal, 1994; Fisher & Fyrberg, 1994; Gurman, 1994; Bersoff, 1995; Kimmel, 1996).

One of the key ethical principles followed by psychologists is **informed consent.** Before participating in an experiment, participants must sign a document affirming that they have been told the basic outlines of the study and are aware of what their participation will involve, what risks the experiment may hold, and the fact that their participation is purely voluntary and may be terminated at any time. Furthermore, following participation in a study, participants must be given a *debriefing* in which they receive an explanation for the study and the procedures involved. The only time informed consent and a debriefing can be eliminated is in experiments in which the risks are minimal, as in a purely observational study on a street corner or in another public location (Koocher & Keith-Spiegel, 1998; Chastain & Landrum, 1999).

informed consent: A document signed by participants affirming that they have been told the basic outlines of a research study and are aware of what their participation will involve.

While readily available and widely used as research subjects, college students may not represent the population at large. What are some advantages and drawbacks of using college students as subjects?

EXPLORING DIVERSITY

Choosing Participants Who Represent the Scope of Human Behavior

When Latané and Darley, both college professors, decided who should be used as participants in their experiment, they turned to the people who were most readily accessible to them: college students. In fact, college students are used so frequently in experiments that psychology has been called—somewhat contemptuously—the "science of the behavior of the college sophomore" (Rubenstein, 1982).

The use of college students as participants has both advantages and drawbacks. The big benefit is their availability. Because most research occurs in university settings, college students are readily available. Typically, they participate for either extra course credit or a relatively small monetary payment, making the cost to the researcher minimal.

The problem with relying on college students for participants is that they might not adequately represent the general population. College students tend to be younger and better educated than a significant percentage of the rest of the population of the United States. Moreover, their attitudes are likely to be less well formed, and they are apt to be more susceptible than older adults to social pressures from authority figures and peers (Sears, 1986).

Furthermore, college students are disproportionately white and middle class. In fact, even research that does not employ college students tends to use white, middle-class participants. In particular, the use of African Americans, Latinos, Asians, and other minorities as participants is low (Graham, 1992; Guthrie, 1998).

Researchers are increasingly sensitive to the importance of using participants in experiments who represent the general population.

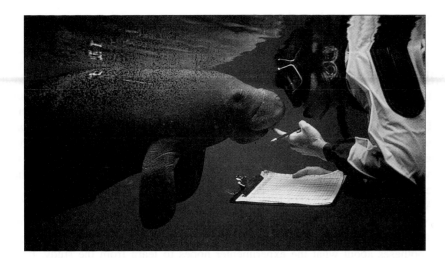

Research involving animals is controversial, but, when conducted within ethical guidelines, yields significant benefits for humans.

When a science that purports to explain human behavior in general disregards a significant proportion of the population in drawing conclusions, something is amiss. Consequently, psychological researchers have become increasingly sensitive to the importance of using participants who are fully representative of the general population (Rogler, 1999).

Should Animals Be Used in Research?

Like those who work with humans, researchers who use animals in experiments have their own set of exacting guidelines to ensure that the animals do not suffer. Specifically, researchers must make every effort to minimize discomfort, illness, and pain, and procedures subjecting animals to distress may be used only when an alternative procedure is unavailable and when the research is justified by its prospective value. Moreover, there are federal regulations specifying how animals are to be housed, fed, and maintained. Not only must researchers strive to avoid physical discomfort in the animals, they are also required to promote the *psychological* well-being of some species of animals—such as primates—that are used in research (Novak & Petto, 1991; APA, 1993).

Why should animals be used for research in the first place? Is it really possible to learn about human behavior from the results of research employing rats, gerbils, and pigeons? The answer is that psychological research that does employ animals has a different focus and is designed to answer different questions than research that uses humans. For example, the shorter life span of animals (rats live an average of two years) allows researchers to learn about the effects of aging in a much more rapid time frame than if they studied aging using human participants. Finally, some studies require large numbers of participants who share similar backgrounds or who have been exposed to particular environments—conditions that could not practically be met with human beings (Gallagher & Rapp, 1997; Mukerjee, 1997).

Research using animals has provided psychologists with information that has profoundly benefited humans. For instance, animal research furnished the keys to detecting eye disorders in children early enough to prevent permanent damage, communicating more effectively with severely retarded children, and reducing chronic pain in people, to name just a few results (APA, 1988; Botting & Morrison, 1997).

Despite the value of research that uses animals as participants, their use in psychological research is highly controversial. For example, some critics believe that animals have rights no less significant than those of humans, and that because animals are unable to consent to participation in studies, their use is unethical. Others say it is impossible to generalize from findings on nonhuman species to humans.

Because the issues involve complex moral and philosophical concerns, they are not easily resolved. As a consequence, review panels, which must approve all research before

 PsychLink

Ethical research using animals
www.mhhe.com/
feldmaness5-01links

Looking Back

What is the science of psychology?

- Psychology is the scientific study of behavior and mental processes, encompassing not just what people do, but their biological activities, feelings, perceptions, memory, reasoning, and thoughts. (p. 4)

What are the major specialties in the field of psychology?

- Biopsychologists focus on the biological basis of behavior, whereas experimental psychologists study the processes of sensing, perceiving, learning, and thinking about the world. (p. 5)
- Cognitive psychology, an outgrowth of experimental psychology, studies higher mental processes, including memory, knowing, thinking, reasoning, problem solving, judging, decision making, and language. (p. 6)
- Developmental psychologists study how people grow and change throughout the life span. (p. 7)
- Personality psychologists consider the consistency and change in an individual's behavior as he or she moves through different situations, as well as the individual differences that distinguish one person's behavior from another's when each is placed in the same situation. (p. 7)
- Health psychologists study psychological factors that affect physical disease; clinical psychologists consider the study, diagnosis, and treatment of psychological disorders. (p. 7)
- Social psychology is the study of how people's thoughts, feelings, and actions are affected by others. (p. 7)
- Cross-cultural psychology examines the similarities and differences in psychological functioning across various cultures. The psychology of women concentrates on psychological factors relating to women's behavior and development. (p. 7)

Where do psychologists work?

- Psychologists are employed in a variety of settings. Although the primary sites of employment are universities and colleges, many psychologists are found in hospitals, clinics, community mental health centers, and counseling centers. (p. 8)

What are the historical roots of the field of psychology?

- The foundations of psychology were established by Wilhelm Wundt in Germany in 1879. (p. 11)
- Early perspectives that guided the work of psychologists were structuralism, functionalism, and gestalt theory. (p. 11)

What are the major approaches used by contemporary psychologists?

- The biological approach focuses on the biological functioning of people and animals, considering the most basic components of behavior. (p. 13)
- The psychodynamic perspective suggests that there are powerful, unconscious inner forces and conflicts that people have little or no awareness of and that are primary determinants of behavior. (p. 13)
- Cognitive approaches to behavior consider how people know, understand, and think about the world. (p. 13)
- The behavioral perspective deemphasizes internal processes and concentrates instead on observable behavior, suggesting that an understanding and control of a person's environment is sufficient to fully explain and modify behavior. (p. 13)

- The humanistic perspective emphasizes that people are uniquely inclined toward psychological growth and higher levels of functioning and that they will strive to reach their full potential. (p. 14)

What are psychology's key issues and controversies?

- Among the key issues are the questions of nature versus nurture, conscious versus unconscious determinants of behavior, observable behavior versus internal mental processes, free will versus determinism, and individual differences versus universal principles. (p. 16)

What is the future of psychology likely to hold?

- Psychology will become increasingly specialized, will pay increasing attention to prevention instead of just treatment, will become increasingly concerned with the public interest, and will take the growing diversity of the nation's population into account more fully. (p. 18)

What is the scientific method, and how do psychologists use theory and research to answer questions of interest?

- The scientific method is an approach psychologists use to understand the unknown. It consists of three steps: identifying questions of interest, formulating an explanation, and carrying out research that is designed to support the explanation. (p. 20)
- Research in psychology is guided by theories (broad explanations and predictions of phenomena of interest) and hypotheses (derivations of theories that are predictions stated in a way that allows them to be tested). (p. 22)

What are the different research methods employed by psychologists?

- Archival research uses existing records, such as old newspapers or other documents, to test a hypothesis. In naturalistic observation, the investigator acts mainly as an observer, making no change in a naturally occurring situation. In survey research, people are asked a series of questions about their behavior, thoughts, or attitudes. The case study is an in-depth interview and examination of one person. (p. 22)
- These methods rely on correlational techniques, which describe associations between various variables but cannot determine cause-and-effect relationships. (p. 24)

How do psychologists establish cause-and-effect relationships in research studies?

- In a formal experiment, the relationship between variables is investigated by deliberately producing a change—called the experimental manipulation—in one of them and observing changes in the other. (p. 25)
- For a hypothesis to be tested, it must be operationalized: A researcher must translate the abstract concepts of the hypothesis into the actual procedures used in the study. (p. 26)
- In an experiment, at least two groups must be compared with each other to assess cause-and-effect relationships. The group receiving the treatment (the special procedure devised by the experimenter) is the experimental group; the second group (which receives no treatment) is the control group. There also may be multiple experimental groups; each of which is subjected to a different procedure and then compared with the others. (p. 26)

- The variable that experimenters manipulate is the independent variable. The variable that they measure and expect to change as a result of manipulation of the independent variable is called the dependent variable. (p. 27)
- In a formal experiment, participants must be assigned to treatment conditions randomly so that participant characteristics are evenly distributed across the different conditions. (p. 27)

What major issues underlie the process of conducting research?

- One of the key ethical principles followed by psychologists is that of informed consent. Participants must be informed, prior to participation, about the basic outline of the experiment and the risks and potential benefits of their participation. (p. 31)
- Although the use of college students as participants has the advantage of easy availability, there are drawbacks too. For instance, students do not necessarily represent the population as a whole. The use of animals as participants also has costs in terms of generalizability, although the benefits of using animals in research have been profound. (p. 32)
- Experiments are subject to a number of threats, or biases. Experimenter expectations can produce bias when an experimenter unintentionally transmits cues to participants about her or his expectations regarding their behavior in a given experimental condition. Participant expectations can also bias an experiment. To help eliminate bias, researchers use placebos and double-blind procedures. (p. 34)

Key Terms and Concepts

psychology (p. 4)
structuralism (p. 11)
introspection (p. 11)
functionalism (p. 11)
gestalt psychology (p. 12)
biological perspective (p. 13)
psychodynamic perspective (p. 13)
cognitive perspective (p. 13)
behavioral perspective (p. 13)
humanistic perspective (p. 14)
scientific method (p. 20)
theories (p. 20)
hypothesis (p. 21)
operationalization (p. 22)
archival research (p. 22)
naturalistic observation (p. 23)
survey research (p. 23)

case study (p. 23)
variables (p. 24)
correlational research (p. 24)
experiment (p. 25)
experimental manipulation (p. 26)
treatment (p. 26)
experimental group (p. 26)
control group (p. 26)
independent variable (p. 27)
dependent variable (p. 27)
random assignment to condition (p. 27)
significant outcome (p. 29)
replication (p. 29)
informed consent (p. 31)
experimental bias (p. 34)
placebo (p. 34)

Psychology on the Web

1. Practice using several search strategies to find out more information on the Internet about one of the key issues in psychology (e.g., free will versus determinism, nature versus nurture, or conscious versus unconscious determinants of behavior):
   a. Go to a "general purpose" search engine (such as Alta Vista at www.altavista.com).
   b. Go to a more specialized search engine (such as Yahoo's Psychology section, under the "Social Science" heading, at www.yahoo.com).

c. Go to one of the more specialized psychology websites listed in PsychLinks on the *Essentials of Understanding Psychology* website (www.mhhe/feldmaness5). Summarize and then compare the kind of information you have found through each strategy. List any useful websites you encounter in your searches.

2. Find a website that focuses on an important social issue (e.g., urban violence, gender differences in hiring or promotion, poverty) and locate descriptions of a research study about the issue. Evaluate the study by identifying the hypotheses that were tested, the methods used to test them, and the validity of the results reported.

Epilogue

The field of psychology, as we have seen, is broad and diverse. It encompasses many subfields and specialties practiced in a variety of settings, with new subfields arising and coming to prominence all the time. Furthermore, we have seen that even within the various subfields of the field, it is possible to adopt several different approaches, including the biological, psychodynamic, cognitive, behavioral, and humanistic perspectives.

We have also seen that, for all its diversity, psychology is united in its use of the scientific method and its reliance on creating productive theories and crafting testable hypotheses. We've considered the basic methods psychologists use to conduct research studies, and we've explored some of the major challenges that psychologists have to deal with when conducting research, including ethical considerations, potential bias, and the question of significance.

Before we turn to a discussion of the biology that underlies behavior, return for a moment to the opening prologue of this chapter, which discusses the terrorist attacks on New York and the Pentagon. In light of what you've learned about the branches, perspectives, and methods of psychology, consider the following questions:

1. How might a psychodynamic perspective explain why the terrorists decided to carry out suicide attacks? How would this explanation differ from the approach taken by a psychologist using the behavioral perspective?
2. Assume that two developmental psychologists are considering the effects of a child's observation of the attack on the World Trade Center towers on the child's later development. How would the questions and studies of interest to the psychologists differ if one employed the biological perspective and the other employed the behavioral perspective?
3. How might social psychologists explore the effects of watching news reports of the terrorist incident on viewers' later aggression?
4. How might researchers conduct an experiment to test a drug that they believe reduces aggression? What would the independent variable and dependent variable be in such an experiment?

OLC Preview

For additional quizzing and a variety of interactive resources, visit the *Essentials of Understanding Psychology* Online Learning Center at

www.mhhe.com/feldmaness5

Chapter Two

The Biology Underlying Behavior

Michael J. Fox was freed of the worst symptoms of Parkinson's following an operation called a thalamotomy.

Prologue

The Fight of His Life

Michael J. Fox simply could not get out of the limousine. He and actress wife Tracy Pollan had just pulled up to the Beverly Hilton for the Golden Globe Awards last January, and the actor realized he was in serious trouble. Outside, reporters and photographers stood poised to greet the star of ABC's hit sitcom *Spin City*, but Fox, 37, was in no shape to greet them. Like so many times before, his left arm and leg were shaking uncontrollably. Behind the limo's darkened windows, Pollan began squeezing Fox's hand and massaging his foot. But she could provide only temporary relief. For the tremors to fully subside, the couple would have to wait for his medication to kick in. Fox asked the driver to circle the block once. Then a second time. And a third. "He probably thought I was nuts," says Fox with a faint smile. "But I just couldn't get out of the car and let my arm go, or mumble, or shuttle." (Schneider & Gold, 1998, p. 136)

Looking Ahead

Fox's symptoms were produced by Parkinson's disease, a disorder marked by varying degrees of muscular rigidity and shaking. Parkinson's afflicts about a million people in the United States alone (including former Attorney General Janet Reno and Muhammad Ali), strikes for no known reason, and typically progresses with age.

Happily, though, Fox was freed of the worst symptoms of the disease, following a painstaking four-hour operation called a thalamotomy. In this procedure, surgeons bored a hole into Fox's brain and located and destroyed misfiring brain cells.

The ability of surgeons to identify damaged portions of the brain and carry out repairs is little short of miraculous. But the greater miracle is the brain itself. As we shall see in this chapter, the brain, an organ roughly half the size of a loaf of bread, controls our behavior through every waking and sleeping moment. The brain and the nerves that extend throughout the body constitute the human nervous system. Our movements, thoughts, hopes, aspirations, dreams—our very awareness that we are human—are all intimately related to this system.

Because of the importance of the nervous system in controlling behavior, and because humans at their most basic level are biological beings, psychologists and researchers from other fields as diverse as computer science, zoology, and medicine have paid special attention to the biological underpinnings of behavior. These experts are collectively called *neuroscientists* (Beatty, 2000).

Psychologists who specialize in considering the ways in which biological structures and functions of the body affect behavior are known as **biopsychologists** (or **behavioral neuroscientists**). These specialists seek to answer questions such as these: What are the bases for voluntary and involuntary functioning of the body? How are messages communicated to and from the brain to other parts of the body? What is the physical structure of the brain, and how does this structure affect behavior? Can the causes of psychological disorders be traced to biological factors, and how can such disorders be treated?

This chapter addresses such questions, focusing on the biological structures of the body that are of interest to biopsychologists. Initially, we discuss nerve cells, called neurons, which allow messages to travel through the brain and body; we learn that through their growing knowledge of neurons and the nervous system, psychologists are increasing their understanding of human behavior and are uncovering important clues in their efforts to cure certain kinds of diseases. Then we turn to the structure and main divisions of the nervous system, explaining how they work to control voluntary and involuntary behaviors. In the process we also examine how the various parts of the nervous system operate together in emergency situations to produce lifesaving responses to danger.

Next, we consider the brain itself, examining its major structures and how these affect behavior. We see how the brain controls movement, our senses, and our thought processes. We also consider the fascinating notion that the two halves of the brain might have different specialties and strengths. Finally, we examine the chemical messenger system of the body, the endocrine system.

As we discuss these biological processes, it is important to keep in mind the rationale for doing so: Our understanding of human behavior cannot be complete without knowledge of the fundamentals of the brain and the rest of the nervous system. As we'll see in future chapters, biological factors have an important impact on our sensory experiences, states of consciousness, motivation and emotion, development throughout the life span, and physical and psychological health. Advances in biopsychology have paved the way for the creation of drugs and other treatments for psychological and physical disorders. In short, we cannot understand behavior—the moods, motivations, goals, and desires that are central to the human condition—without an understanding of our biological makeup.

---

biopsychologists (or behavioral neuroscientists): Psychologists who specialize in considering the ways in which biological structures and functions of the body affect behavior

---

PsychLink

Description of neuropsychology
www.mhhe.com/
feldmaness5-02links

Neurons: The Elements of Behavior

If you have ever watched the precision with which a well-trained athlete or dancer executes a performance, you may have marveled at the complexity—and wondrous abilities—of the human body. But even the most everyday tasks, such as picking up a pencil, writing, and speaking, require a sophisticated sequence of events that is itself truly impressive. For instance, the difference between saying the words *dime* and *time* rests primarily on whether the vocal cords are relaxed or tense during a period lasting no more than one one-hundredth of a second. Yet it is a distinction that almost everyone can make with ease.

The nervous system provides the pathways that permit us to carry out such precise activities. To understand how it is able to exert such exacting control over our bodies, we must begin by examining neurons, the most basic parts of the nervous system, and considering how nerve impulses are transmitted throughout the brain and body.

Prepare

Why do psychologists study the brain and nervous system?

What are the basic elements of the nervous system?

How does the nervous system communicate electrical and chemical messages from one part to another?

Organize

Neurons
  The Structure of the Neuron
  Firing the Neuron
  Where Neurons Meet
  Neurotransmitters

The Structure of the Neuron

The ability to play the piano, drive a car, or hit a tennis ball depends, at one level, merely on muscle coordination. But if we consider *how* the muscles involved in such activities are activated, we see that there are more fundamental processes involved. It is necessary for the body to provide messages to the muscles and to coordinate those messages, for the muscles to be able to produce the complex movements that characterize successful physical activity.

Such messages—as well as those that enable us to think, remember, and experience emotion—are passed through specialized cells called neurons. **Neurons,** or nerve cells, are the basic elements of the nervous system. Their quantity is staggering—perhaps as many as one *trillion* neurons throughout the body are involved in the control of behavior. Although there are several types of neurons, they all have a similar basic structure, as illustrated in Figure 2-1. Like all cells in the body, neurons have a cell body, containing a nucleus. The nucleus incorporates the inherited material that establishes how the cell will function. Neurons are physically held in place by *glial cells,* which provide nourishment and insulate them (Bear, Connors, & Paradiso, 2000).

In contrast to most other cells, however, neurons have a distinctive feature: the ability to communicate with other cells and transmit information, sometimes across relatively long distances. As you can see in Figure 2-1, neurons have clusters of fibers called **dendrites** at one end. These fibers, which look like the twisted branches of a tree, receive messages from other neurons. At the opposite end, neurons have a long, slim, tubelike extension called an **axon,** the part of the neuron that carries messages destined for other neurons. The axon is considerably longer than the rest of the neuron. Although most axons are several millimeters in length, some can be as long as three feet. Axons end in small bulges called **terminal buttons** that send messages to other neurons.

The messages that travel through the neuron are purely electrical in nature. Although there are exceptions, these electrical messages generally move across neurons as if they were traveling on a one-way street. They follow a route that begins with the dendrites, continues into the cell body, and leads ultimately down the tubelike extension, the axon. *D*endrites, then, *d*etect messages from other neurons; *a*xons carry signals *a*way from the cell body.

To prevent messages from short-circuiting one another, axons must be insulated in some fashion (just as electrical wires must be insulated). In most axons, this is done with a **myelin sheath,** a protective coating of specialized fat and protein cells that wrap themselves around the axon.

The myelin sheath also serves to increase the velocity with which the electrical impulses travel through the axons. Those axons that carry the most important and most urgently required information have the greatest concentrations of myelin. If your hand

neurons: Nerve cells, the basic elements of the nervous system

dendrites: A cluster of fibers at one end of a neuron that receive messages from other neurons

axon: The part of the neuron that carries messages destined for other neurons

terminal buttons: Small bulges at the end of axons that send messages to other neurons

myelin sheath: Specialized cells of fat and protein that wrap themselves around the axon, providing a protective coating

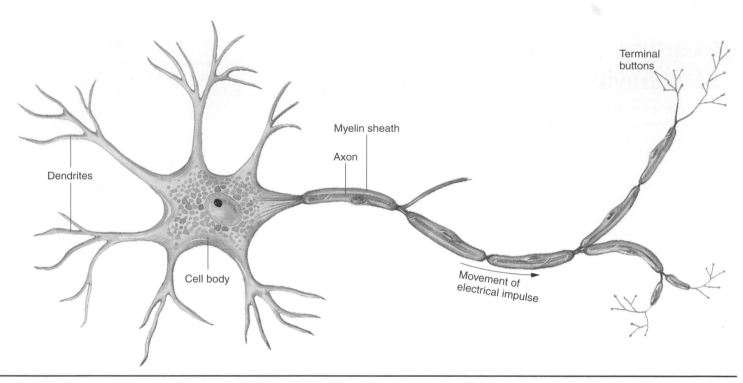

Figure 2-1 The primary components of the specialized cell called the neuron, the basic element of the nervous system (Van de Graaff, 2000). What advantages does the treelike structure of the neuron provide?

After K. Van De Graaff. Copyright © The McGraw-Hill Companies.

all-or-none law: The rule that neurons are either on or off

resting state: The state in which there is a negative electrical charge of about −70 millivolts within the neuron

Taken with the aid of an electron microscope, this photograph shows cell bodies, dendrites, and axons in a cluster of neurons.

touches a painfully hot stove, for example, the information regarding the pain is passed through axons in the hand and arm that have a relatively thick coating of myelin, speeding the message of pain to the brain. In certain diseases, such as multiple sclerosis, the myelin sheath surrounding the axon deteriorates, exposing parts of the axon that are normally covered. This short-circuits messages between the brain and muscles and results in symptoms such as the inability to walk, vision difficulties, and general muscle impairment.

Firing the Neuron

Like a gun, neurons either fire or don't fire; there is no in-between stage, just as pulling harder on a gun trigger doesn't make the bullet travel faster or move more surely. Similarly, neurons follow an **all-or-none law:** they are either on or off, with nothing in between the on or off state. Once triggered beyond a certain point, a neuron fires.

Before a neuron is triggered—that is, when it is in a **resting state**—it has a negative electrical charge of about −70 millivolts (a millivolt is one one-thousandth of a volt). This charge is caused by the presence of more negatively charged ions (a type of molecule) within the neuron than outside it. You might think of the neuron in terms of a miniature car battery, with the inside of the neuron representing the negative pole and the outside of the neuron the positive pole.

However, when a message arrives, the cell walls in the neuron allow positively charged ions to rush in, at rates as high as 100 million ions per second. The sudden arrival of these positive ions causes the charge within that part of the cell to change momentarily from negative to positive. When the charge reaches a critical level, the "trigger" is pulled, and an electrical nerve impulse, known as an **action potential,** travels down the axon of the neuron (see Figures 2-2 and 2-3).

The action potential moves from one end of the axon to the other like a flame moving across a fuse toward an explosive. As the impulse travels along the axon, the movement of ions causes a sequential change in charge from negative to positive (see Figure 2-2). After the passage of the impulse, positive ions are pumped out of the axon, and the neuron charge returns to negative.

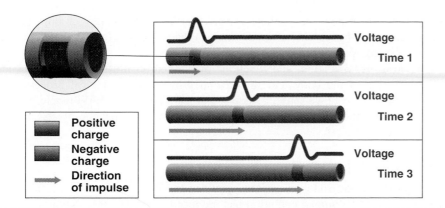

Positive charge
Negative charge
Direction of impulse

Voltage
Time 1

Voltage
Time 2

Voltage
Time 3

Figure 2–2 Movement of an action potential across an axon. Just prior to time 1, positively charged ions enter the cell walls, changing the charge within that part of the cell from negative to positive. The action potential is thus triggered, traveling down the axon, as illustrated in the changes occurring from Time 1 to Time 3 (from top to bottom in this drawing). Following the passage of the action potential, positive ions are pumped out of the axon, restoring its charge to negative. The change in voltage illustrated at the top of the axon can be seen in greater detail in Figure 2-3.

Just after an action potential has passed, the neuron cannot fire again immediately, no matter how much stimulation it receives. It is as if the gun has to be painstakingly reloaded after each shot. There then follows a period in which, though it is possible for the neuron to fire, a stronger stimulus is needed than would be needed if the neuron had reached its normal resting state. Eventually, though, the neuron is ready to be fired once again.

These complex events can occur at dizzying speeds, although there is great variation among different neurons. The particular speed at which an action potential travels along an axon is determined by the axon's size and the thickness of its myelin sheath. Axons with small diameters carry impulses at about 2 miles per hour; longer and thicker ones can average speeds of more than 225 miles per hour.

Neurons differ not only in terms of how quickly an impulse moves across the axon, but in their potential rate of firing. Some neurons have the potential to fire as many as a thousand times per second; others have a maximum potential rate that is much lower. The intensity of a stimulus that provokes a neuron determines how much of this potential rate is reached. A strong stimulus, such as a bright light or a loud sound, leads to a higher rate of firing than a less intense stimulus does. Thus, even though all impulses move at the same strength or speed across a particular axon—

action potential: An electric nerve impulse that travels through a neuron when it is set off by a "trigger," changing the neuron's charge from negative to positive

PsychLink
The Myelin Project
www.mhhe.com/
feldmaness5-02inks

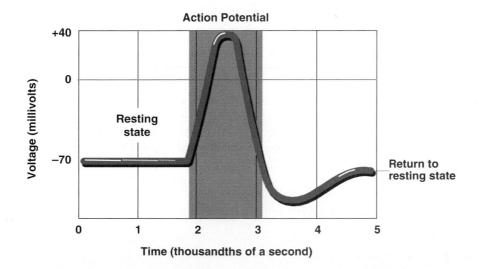

Action Potential

+40

0

−70

Voltage (millivolts)

Resting state

Return to resting state

0   1   2   3   4   5

Time (thousandths of a second)

Figure 2–3 Changes in the electrical charge of a neuron during the passage of an action potential. In its normal resting state, a neuron has a negative charge of around −70 millivolts. When an action potential is triggered, however, the cell charge becomes positive, increasing to about +40 millivolts. Following the passage of the action potential, the charge becomes even more negative than it is in its typical state. It is not until the charge returns to its resting state that the neuron will be fully ready to be triggered once again.

because of the all-or-none law—there is variation in the frequency of impulses, providing a mechanism by which we can distinguish the tickle of a feather from the weight of someone standing on our toe.

The structure, operation, and functions of the neuron illustrate how fundamental biological aspects of the body underlie several primary psychological processes. Our understanding of the way we sense, perceive, and learn about the world would be greatly restricted without the information about the neuron that biopsychologists and other researchers have acquired.

Where Neurons Meet: Bridging the Gap

If you've ever looked inside a computer, you've seen that each part is physically connected to another. In contrast, evolution has produced a neural transmission system that at some points has no need for a structural connection between its components. Instead, a chemical connection bridges the gap, known as a synapse, between two neurons (see Figure 2-4). The **synapse** is the space between two neurons where the axon of a sending neuron communicates with the dendrites of a receiving neuron using chemical messages.

When a nerve impulse comes to the end of the axon and reaches a terminal button, the terminal button releases a chemical courier called a neurotransmitter. **Neurotransmitters** are chemicals that carry messages across the synapse to the dendrite (and sometimes the cell body) of a receiver neuron. Like a boat that ferries passengers across a river, these chemical messengers move toward the shorelines of other neurons. The chemical mode of message transmission that occurs between neurons is strikingly different from the means by which communication occurs inside neurons. It is important to remember, then, that although messages travel in electrical form *within* a neuron, they move *between* neurons through a chemical transmission system.

There are several types of neurotransmitters, and not all receiver neurons are capable of making use of the chemical message carried by a particular neurotransmitter. In the same way as a jigsaw puzzle piece can fit in only one specific location in a puzzle, so each kind of neurotransmitter has a distinctive configuration that allows it to fit into a specific type of receptor site on the receiving neuron (see Figure 2-4b). It is only when a neurotransmitter fits precisely into a receptor site that successful chemical communication is possible.

If a neurotransmitter does fit into a site on the receiving neuron, the chemical message it delivers is basically one of two types: excitatory or inhibitory. **Excitatory messages** make it more likely that a receiving neuron will fire and an action potential will travel down its axon. **Inhibitory messages,** in contrast, do just the opposite; they provide chemical information that prevents or decreases the likelihood that the receiving neuron will fire.

Because the dendrites of a neuron receive both excitatory and inhibitory messages simultaneously, the neuron must integrate the messages by using a kind of chemical calculator. If the concentration of excitatory messages is greater than the concentration of inhibitory ones, the neuron fires. On the other hand, if the inhibitory messages outweigh the excitatory ones, nothing happens, and the neuron remains in its resting state (Thomson, 1997; Miles, 2000).

If neurotransmitters remained at the site of the synapse, receptor neurons would be awash in a continual chemical bath, producing constant stimulation of the receptor neurons—and effective communication across the synapse would no longer be possible. To solve this problem, neurotransmitters are either deactivated by enzymes or—more frequently—reabsorbed by the terminal button in an example of chemical recycling called **reuptake.** Like a vacuum cleaner sucking up dust, neurons reabsorb the neurotransmitters that are now clogging the synapse. All this activity occurs at lightning speed, with the process taking just several milliseconds (Helmuth, 2000).

---

synapse: The space between two neurons where the axon of a sending neuron communicates with the dendrites of a receiving neuron using chemical messages

PsychLink

All about synapses
www.mhhe.com/
feldmaness5-02links

neurotransmitters: Chemicals that carry messages across the synapse to the dendrite (and sometimes the cell body) of a receiver neuron

excitatory message: A chemical message that makes it more likely that a receiving neuron will fire and an action potential will travel down its axons

inhibitory message: A chemical message that prevents a receiving neuron from firing

reuptake: The reabsorption of neurotransmitters by a terminal button a.

STEP 1: Neurotransmitters are produced and stored in the axon

Neurotransmitters

Axon

STEP 2: If an action potential arrives, the axon releases neurotransmitters

Dendrite

Synapse

Neurotransmitter

STEP 3: Neurotransmitters travel across the synapse to receptor sites on another neuron's dendrite

Synapse

Receptor site

Neurotransmitter

STEP 4: When a neurotransmitter fits into a receptor site, it delivers an excitatory or inhibitory message. If enough excitatory messages are delivered, the neuron will fire

Figure 2-4 *(a)* A synapse is the junction between an axon and a dendrite. The gap between the axon and the dendrite is bridged by chemicals called neurotransmitters (Mader, 2000). *(b)* Just as the pieces of a jigsaw puzzle can fit in only one specific location in a puzzle, each kind of neurotransmitter has a distinctive configuration that allows it to fit into a specific type of receptor cell (Johnson, 2000). Why is it advantageous for axons and dendrites to be linked by temporary chemical bridges rather than by the hard wiring typical of a radio connection or telephone hookup?

(a) After S. S. Mader. Copyright © The McGraw-Hill Companies.

(b) After G. B. Johnson. Copyright © The McGraw-Hill Companies.

b.

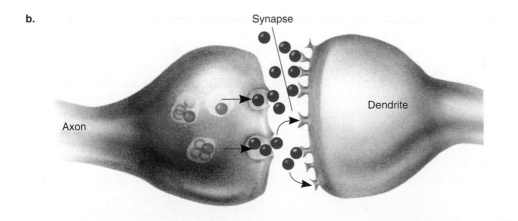

Synapse

Dendrite

Axon

Neurotransmitters: Multitalented Chemical Couriers

Neurotransmitters are a particularly important link between the nervous system and behavior. Not only are they important for maintaining vital brain and body functions, but a deficiency or an excess of a neurotransmitter can produce severe behavior disorders. More than a hundred chemicals have been found to act as neurotransmitters, and biopsychologists believe that more may ultimately be identified (Purves et al., 1997; Penney, 2000).

Neurotransmitters vary significantly in terms of how strong their concentration must be to trigger a neuron to fire. Furthermore, the effects of a given neurotransmitter vary, depending on the area of the nervous system in which it is produced. The same neurotransmitter, then, can cause a neuron to fire when it is secreted in one part of the brain and can inhibit the firing of neurons when it is produced in another part. (The major neurotransmitters are described in Table 2-1.)

One of the most common neurotransmitters is *acetylcholine* (or *ACh,* its chemical symbol), which is found throughout the nervous system. ACh is involved in our every move, because—among other things—it transmits messages relating to our skeletal muscles. ACh is also involved in memory capabilities, and a diminished production of ACh might be related to Alzheimer's disease (Selkoe, 1997).

Another common excitatory neurotransmitter, *glutamate,* plays a role in memory. As we'll discuss in Chapter 6, memories appear to be produced by specific biochemical changes at particular synapses, and glutamate, along with other neurotransmitters, plays an important role in this process (Gibbs et al., 1996; Li et al., 1999; Bennett, 2000).

Gamma-amino butyric acid (GABA), found in both the brain and the spinal cord, appears to be the nervous system's primary inhibitory neurotransmitter. It moderates a variety of behaviors, ranging from eating to aggression. Several common substances, such as the tranquilizer Valium and alcohol, are effective because they permit GABA to operate more efficiently (Tabakoff & Hoffman, 1996).

Another major neurotransmitter is *dopamine (DA).* The discovery that certain drugs can have a marked effect on dopamine release has led to the development of effective treatments for a wide variety of physical and mental ailments. For instance, Parkinson's disease, from which actor Michael J. Fox suffers, is caused by a deficiency of dopamine in the brain. Techniques for increasing the production of dopamine in Parkinson's patients are proving effective (Schapira, 1999; LeWitt, 2000).

Table 2-1 Some Major Neurotransmitters

Name	Location	Effect	Function
Acetylcholine (ACh)	Brain, spinal cord, peripheral nervous system, especially some organs of the parasympathetic nervous system	Excitatory in brain and autonomic nervous system; inhibitory elsewhere	Muscle movement; cognitive functioning
Glutamate	Brain, spinal cord	Excitatory	Memory
Gamma-amino butyric acid (GABA)	Brain, spinal cord	Main inhibitory neurotransmitter	Eating, aggression, sleeping
Dopamine (DA)	Brain	Inhibitory or excitatory	Muscle disorders, mental disorders, Parkinson's disease
Serotonin	Brain, spinal cord	Inhibitory	Sleeping, eating, mood, pain, depression
Endorphins	Brain, spinal cord	Primarily inhibitory, except in hippocampus	Pain suppression, pleasurable feelings, appetites, placebos

In other instances, *over*production of dopamine produces negative consequences. For example, researchers have hypothesized that schizophrenia and some other severe mental disturbances are affected or perhaps even caused by the presence of unusually high levels of dopamine. Drugs that block the reception of dopamine reduce the symptoms displayed by some people diagnosed with schizophrenia, as we will examine further in Chapters 12 and 13 (Kahn, Davidson, & Davis, 1996).

Another neurotransmitter, *serotonin,* is associated with the regulation of sleep, eating, mood, and pain. A growing body of research points toward a broader role for serotonin, suggesting its involvement in such diverse behaviors as coping with stress, alcoholism, depression, suicide, impulsivity, and aggression (Smith, Williams, & Cowen, 2000).

Endorphins, another class of neurotransmitters, are a family of chemicals produced by the brain that are similar in structure to painkilling drugs such as morphine. The production of endorphins seems to reflect the brain's effort to deal with pain. For instance, people who are afflicted with diseases that produce long-term, severe pain often develop large concentrations of endorphins in their brains—suggesting an effort by the brain to control the pain. Endorphins can also produce the euphoric feelings that runners sometimes experience after long runs. The exertion and perhaps even the pain involved in a long run stimulate the production of endorphins—ultimately resulting in what has been called "runner's high" (Kremer & Scully, 1994; Dishman, 1997).

Endorphin release might also explain other phenomena that have long puzzled psychologists. For example, acupuncture and placebos (pills or other substances that contain no actual drugs but that patients *believe* will make them better) might induce the release of endorphins, leading to the reduction of pain (Mikamo et al., 1994; Murray, 1995).

Evaluate

1. The _____ is the fundamental element of the nervous system.
2. Neurons receive information through their _____ and they send messages through their _____.
3. Just as electrical wires have an outer coating, so axons are insulated by a coating called the _____ _____.
4. The gap between two neurons is bridged by a chemical connection called a _____.
5. Endorphins are one kind of _____, the chemical "messengers" between neurons.

Answers to Evaluate Questions

1. neuron 2. dendrites; axons 3. myelin sheath 4. synapse 5. neurotransmitter

Rethink

1. Can you use your knowledge of psychological research methods to suggest how researchers can study the effects of neurotransmitters on human behavior?
2. In what ways might endorphins help produce the placebo effect? Is there a difference between believing that one's pain is reduced and actually experiencing reduced pain? Why or why not?

The Nervous System

Given the complexity of individual neurons and the neurotransmission process, it should come as no surprise that the connections and structures formed by the neurons are complicated. Because just one neuron can be connected to 80,000 other neurons, the total number of possible connections is astonishing. For instance, estimates of the number of neural connections within the brain fall in the neighborhood of 1 quadrillion—a 1 followed by 15 zeros; some experts put the number even higher (McGaugh, Weinberger, & Lynch, 1990; Estes, 1991; Eichenbaum, 1993).

Whatever the actual number of neural connections, the human nervous system has both a logic and an elegance. We turn now to its basic structures.

Prepare

In what way are the structures of the nervous system tied together?

Organize

The Nervous System
  The Central and Peripheral Nervous Systems
  The Evolutionary Foundations of the Nervous System
  Behavioral Genetics

Figure 2-5 A schematic diagram of the relationship of the parts of the nervous system.

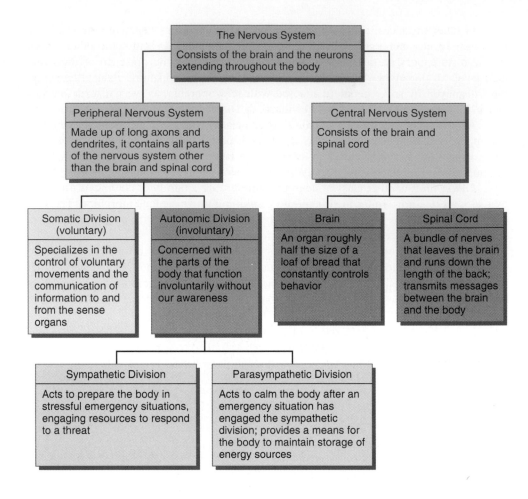

The Central and Peripheral Nervous Systems

central nervous system (CNS): The system that includes the brain and spinal cord

spinal cord: A bundle of nerves that leaves the brain and runs down the length of the back and is the main means for transmitting messages between the brain and the body

reflexes: Automatic, involuntary responses to incoming stimuli

sensory (afferent) neurons: Neurons that transmit information from the perimeter of the body to the central nervous system

motor (efferent) neurons: Neurons that communicate information from the nervous system to muscles and glands of the body

interneurons: Neurons that connect sensory and motor neurons, carrying messages between the two

peripheral nervous system: The part of the nervous system that includes the autonomic and somatic subdivisions; made up of long axons and dendrites, it branches out from the spinal cord and brain and reaches the extremities of the body

As you can see from the schematic representation in Figure 2-5, the nervous system is divided into two main parts: the central nervous system and the peripheral nervous system. The **central nervous system (CNS)** is composed of the brain and spinal cord. The **spinal cord,** about the thickness of a pencil, contains a bundle of nerves that leaves the brain and runs down the length of the back (see Figure 2-6, p. 51). It is the primary means for transmitting messages between the brain and the body.

However, the spinal cord is not just a communications conduit. It also controls some simple kinds of behaviors on its own, without any involvement of the brain. One example is the way your knee jerks forward when it is tapped with a rubber hammer. Such behaviors, called **reflexes,** are automatic, involuntary responses to incoming stimuli. Similarly, when you touch a hot stove and immediately withdraw your hand, a reflex is at work. Although the brain eventually analyzes and reacts to the situation ("Ouch—hot stove—pull away!"), the initial withdrawal is directed only by neurons in the spinal cord.

Three sorts of neurons are involved in reflexes. **Sensory (afferent) neurons** transmit information from the perimeter of the body to the central nervous system. **Motor (efferent) neurons** communicate information from the nervous system to muscles and glands of the body. **Interneurons** connect sensory and motor neurons, carrying messages between the two.

The importance of the spinal cord and reflexes is illustrated by the outcome of accidents in which the cord is injured or severed. Actor Christopher Reeve, who was injured in a horse-riding accident, suffers from *quadriplegia,* a condition in which voluntary muscle movement below the neck is lost. In a less severe but still debilitating condition, *paraplegia,* people are unable to voluntarily move any muscles in the lower half of their body.

As suggested by its name, the **peripheral nervous system** branches out from the spinal cord and brain and reaches the extremities of the body. Made up of long axons and dendrites, the peripheral nervous system encompasses all parts of the nervous system other than the brain and spinal cord. There are two major divisions, the somatic division and the autonomic division, both of which connect the central nervous system with the sense organs, muscles, glands, and other organs. The **somatic division** specializes in the control of voluntary movements—such as the motion of the eyes to read this sentence or of the hand to turn this page—and the communication of information to and from the sense organs. On the other hand, the **autonomic division** is concerned with the parts of the body that keep us alive—the heart, blood vessels, glands, lungs, and other organs that function involuntarily without our awareness. As you are reading at this moment, the autonomic division of the peripheral nervous system is pumping blood through your body, pushing your lungs in and out, overseeing the digestion of the meal you had a few hours ago, and so on—all without a thought or care on your part.

Activating the Divisions of the Autonomic Nervous System

The autonomic division plays a particularly crucial role during emergency situations. Suppose as you are reading you suddenly sense that a stranger is watching you through the window. As you look up, you see the glint of something that just might be a knife. As confusion races through your mind and fear overcomes your attempts to think rationally, what happens to your body? If you are like most people, you react immediately on a physiological level. Your heart rate increases, you begin to sweat, and you develop goose bumps all over your body.

The physiological changes that occur result from the activation of one of the two parts that make up the autonomic division: the **sympathetic division.** The sympathetic division acts to prepare the body in stressful emergency situations, engaging all of the organism's resources to respond to a threat. This response often takes the form of "fight or flight." In contrast, the **parasympathetic division** acts to calm the body after the emergency situation is resolved. When you find, for instance, that the stranger at the window is actually your roommate who has lost his keys and is climbing in the window to avoid waking you, your parasympathetic division begins to predominate, lowering your heart rate, stopping your sweating, and returning your body to the state it was in prior to your fright. The parasympathetic division also provides a means for the body to maintain storage of energy sources such as nutrients and oxygen. The sympathetic and parasympathetic divisions work together to regulate many functions of the body (see Figure 2-7). For instance, sexual arousal is controlled by the parasympathetic division but sexual orgasm is a function of the sympathetic division.

The Evolutionary Foundations of the Nervous System

The complexities of the nervous system can be understood only by taking the course of evolution into consideration. The forerunner of the human nervous system is found in the earliest simple organisms to have a spinal cord. Basically, these organisms were simple input-output devices: When the upper side of their spinal cord was stimulated by for instance, being touched, they reacted with a simple response, such as jerking away. Such responses were completely a consequence of the organism's genetic makeup.

Over millions of years, the front end of the spinal cord became more specialized, and organisms became capable of distinguishing between different kinds of stimuli and responding appropriately to them. Ultimately, the front end of the spinal cord evolved into what we would consider a primitive brain. At first, it had just three parts, devoted to close stimuli (such as smell), more distant stimuli (such as sights and sounds), and the ability to maintain balance and bodily coordination. In fact, many animals, such as fish, still have a nervous system that is structured in roughly similar fashion today. In contrast, the human brain evolved from this three-part configuration into an organ that is far more complex and differentiated (Merlin, 1993).

Furthermore, the nervous system is *hierarchically organized,* meaning that relatively newer (from an evolutionary point of view) and more sophisticated regions of the brain regulate the older, and more primitive, parts of the nervous system. As we move up along

Brain

Spinal cord

- Central nervous system
- Autonomic division of the peripheral nervous system
- Somatic division of the peripheral nervous system

Figure 2-6 The central nervous system—consisting of the brain and spinal cord—and the peripheral nervous system.

After E. Loftus and C. Wortmann. Copyright © The McGraw-Hill Companies.

somatic division: The part of the nervous system that specializes in the control of voluntary movements and the communication of information to and from the sense organs

autonomic division: The part of the nervous system that controls involuntary movement (the actions of the heart, glands, lungs, and other organs)

Figure 2-7 The major functions of the autonomic nervous system. The sympathetic division acts to prepare certain organs of the body for stressful emergency situations, and the parasympathetic division acts to calm the body after the emergency situation is resolved. Can you explain why each response of the sympathetic division might be useful in an emergency?

Sympathetic | | Parasympathetic

Pupil widens	Eyes	Pupil constricts
Dry	Mouth	Salivation increases
Accelerates	Heart	Slows
Swell	Lungs	Constrict
Slows	Digestion	Increases
Climax	Sex organs	Arousal
Sweating increases	Sweat glands	No sweating

sympathetic division: The part of the autonomic division of the nervous system that acts to prepare the body in stressful emergency situations, engaging all the organism's resources to respond to a threat

parasympathetic division: The part of the autonomic division of the nervous system that acts to calm the body after the emergency situation is resolved

evolutionary psychology: The branch of psychology that seeks to identify behavior patterns that result from our genetic inheritance from our ancestors

 PsychLink

Human behavioral genetic data
www.mhhe.com/
feldmaness5-02links

behavioral genetics: The study of the effects of heredity on behavior

PsychLink

The Human Genome Project
www.mhhe.com/
feldmaness5-02links

the spinal cord and continue upward into the brain, then, the functions controlled by various regions become progressively more advanced.

Why should we care about the evolutionary background of the human nervous system? The answer comes from researchers working in the area of **evolutionary psychology,** the branch of psychology that seeks to identify how behavior is influenced and produced by our genetic inheritance from our ancestors. They argue that the course of evolution is reflected in the structure and functioning of the nervous system, and that evolutionary factors consequently have a significant influence on our everyday behavior. Their work, and that of other scientists, has led to the development of a new field: behavioral genetics.

Behavioral Genetics

Our evolutionary heritage manifests itself not only through the structure and functioning of the nervous system, but through our behavior as well. In the view of a blossoming new area of study, people's personality and behavioral habits are affected in part by their genetic heritage. **Behavioral genetics** studies the effects of heredity on behavior. Behavioral genetics researchers are finding increasing evidence that cognitive abilities, personality traits, sexual orientation, and psychological disorders are determined to some extent by genetic factors (Funder, 1997; Craig et al., 2000).

Behavioral genetics gets to the heart of the nature-nurture issue that we first discussed in Chapter 1. Although no one would argue that our behavior is *solely* determined by inherited factors, evidence collected by behavioral geneticists does suggest that our genetic inheritance predisposes us to respond in particular ways to our environment, and even to seek out particular kinds of environments. For instance, research indicates that genetic factors might be related to such diverse behavior as level of family conflict, schizophrenia, learning disabilities, and general sociability (Elkins, McGue, & Iacono, 1997; Berrettini, 2000).

Furthermore, important human characteristics and behaviors are related to the presence (or absence) of particular *genes,* the genetic material that controls the transmission of traits. For example, researchers have found evidence that novelty-seeking behavior is determined, at least in part, by a certain gene.

Researchers have identified some 30,000 individual genes, each of which appears in a specific sequence on particular chromosomes. Scientists only recently succeeded in mapping these genes as part of a massive, multibillion-dollar project known as the Human Genome Project, which, after a decade of effort, identified the sequence of the 3 billion chemical pairs that make up the DNA in genes. By understanding the basic structure of the human *genome,* the "map" of humans' total genetic makeup, scientists are a giant step closer to understanding the biochemical recipes that direct human functioning (Human Genome Project, 2000; Pennisi, 2000).

Despite its relative infancy, the field of behavioral genetics has already made substantial contributions. By understanding the relationship between our genetic heritage and the structures of the nervous system, we are gaining new knowledge about the development of various behavioral difficulties, such as the psychological disorders we'll discuss in Chapter 12. Perhaps more importantly, behavioral genetics holds the promise of developing new treatment techniques to remedy genetic deficiencies that can lead to physical and psychological difficulties. For example, analysis of a drop of blood might tell a woman whether she has a form of breast cancer that is likely to be deadly or is treatable, and scientists might be able to analyze our children's genes to determine if they are susceptible to heart disease, as we'll discuss in detail in Chapter 9 (Risch & Merikangas, 1996; Haseltine, 1997; Begley, 2000).

We turn now to a consideration of the particular structures of the brain and the primary functions to which they are related. However, a caution is in order. Although we'll be discussing how specific brain areas are tied to specific behaviors, this approach is an oversimplification. No simple one-to-one correspondence between a distinct part of the brain and a particular behavior exists. Instead, behavior is produced by complex interconnections among sets of neurons located in many areas of the brain: Our behavior, emotions, thoughts, hopes, and dreams are produced by a variety of neurons throughout the nervous system, working in concert (Grillner, 1996; Joseph, 1996; Sharma, Angelucci, & Sur, 2000).

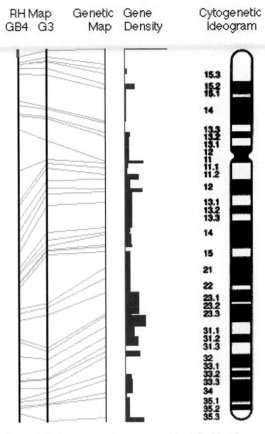

Chromosome 5: pTEL-D5S678

Part of the human DNA sequence, identified by the Human Genome Project, which has mapped the specific location and sequence of every gene.

Evaluate

1. If you should put your hand on a red-hot piece of metal, the immediate response of pulling it away would be an example of a(n) _____.
2. The central nervous system is composed of the _____ and _____ .
3. In the peripheral nervous system, the _____ division controls voluntary movements, whereas the _____ division controls organs that keep us alive and function without our awareness.
4. Maria saw a young boy run into the street and get hit by a car. When she got to the fallen child, she was in a state of panic. She was sweating and her heart was racing. Her biological state resulted from the activation of what division of the nervous system?

   a. Parasympathetic

   b. Central

   c. Sympathetic

5. The increasing complexity and hierarchy of the nervous system over millions of years is the subject of study for researchers working in the field of _____ _____.
6. The emerging field of _____ _____ studies how our genetic inheritance predisposes us to behave in certain ways.

Rethink

1. How might communication within the nervous system result in human consciousness?
2. How is the "fight or flight" response helpful to organisms in emergency situations?

Answers to Evaluate Questions

1. reflex 2. brain; spinal cord 3. somatic; autonomic 4. c 5. evolutionary psychology 6. behavioral genetics

The Brain

It is not much to look at. Soft, spongy, mottled, and pinkish-gray in color, it can hardly be said to possess much in the way of physical beauty. Despite its physical appearance, however, it ranks as the greatest natural marvel we know of and possesses a beauty and sophistication all its own.

The object to which this description applies? The human brain. Our brain is responsible for our loftiest thoughts—and our most primitive urges. It is the overseer of the intricate workings of the human body. If one were to attempt to design a computer to mimic the range of capabilities of the brain, the task would be nearly impossible; in fact, it has proved difficult even to come close. The sheer quantity of nerve cells in the brain is enough to daunt even the most ambitious computer engineer. Many billions of nerve cells make up a structure weighing just three pounds in the average adult. However, the most astounding thing about the brain is not its number of cells but its ability to allow human intellect to flourish as it guides our behavior and thoughts.

Studying the Brain's Structure and Functions: Spying on the Brain

The brain has posed a continual challenge to those wishing to study it. For most of history, its examination was possible only after an individual was dead. Only then could the skull be opened and the brain cut into without serious injury.

Although this was informative, such a limited procedure could hardly tell us much about the functioning of the healthy brain.

Today, however, important advances have been made in the study of the brain through the use of brain-scanning techniques. Using brain scanning, investigators can take a snapshot of the internal workings of the brain without having to cut surgically into a person's skull. The major scanning techniques, described below, are illustrated in Figure 2-8.

a.

b.

c.

d.

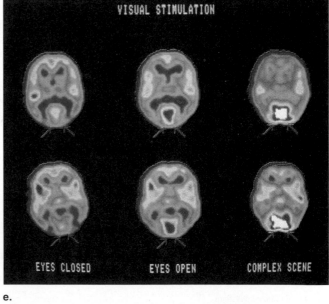

e.

Figure 2-8 Brain scans produced by different techniques. *(a)* A computer-produced EEG image. *(b)* This CAT scan shows the structures of the brain. *(c)* The MRI scan uses a magnetic field to detail the parts of the brain. *(d)* The SQUID scan shows the neural activity of the brain *(e)* The PET scan displays the functioning of the brain at a given moment and is sensitive to the person's activities.

- The *electroencephalogram (EEG)* records electrical activity in the brain through electrodes placed on the outside of the skull. Although traditionally the EEG could produce only a graph of electrical wave patterns, new techniques are now able to transform the brain's electrical activity into a pictorial representation of the brain that allows the diagnosis of such problems as epilepsy and learning disabilities.
- The *computerized axial tomography (CAT) scan* uses a computer to construct an image of the structures of the brain by combining thousands of separate X rays taken at slightly different angles. It is very useful for showing abnormalities in the structure of the brain, such as swelling and enlargement of certain parts, but does not provide information about brain activity.
- The *magnetic resonance imaging (MRI) scan* provides a detailed, three-dimensional computer-generated image of brain structures and activity by aiming a powerful magnetic field at the body. For example, it is capable of producing vivid images of individual bundles of nerves, opening the way for improved diagnosis of such ailments as chronic back pain.
- The *superconducting quantum interference device (SQUID)* is sensitive to tiny changes in magnetic fields that occur when neurons fire. Using SQUID, researchers can pinpoint the location of neural activity.
- The *positron emission tomography (PET) scan* shows biochemical activity within the brain at a given moment in time. PET scans begin by injecting into the bloodstream a radioactive (but safe) liquid that makes its way to the brain. By locating radiation within the brain, a computer can determine which are the more active regions, providing a striking picture of the brain at work.

The brain may not be much to look at, but it represents one of the great marvels of human development. Why do most scientists believe that it will be difficult, if not impossible, to duplicate the brain's abilities?

 PsychLink

Numerous brain scans
www.mhhe.com/
feldmaness5–02links

 PsychLink

Information about NMR
www.mhhe.com/
feldmaness5–02links

Each of these techniques offers exciting possibilities not only for the diagnosis and treatment of brain disease and injuries, but also for an increased understanding of the normal functioning of the brain. In addition, researchers are developing ways to combine separate scanning techniques (such as integrated, simultaneous PET and MRI scans) to produce even more effective portraits of the brain, such as three-dimensional reconstructions of the brain that can be used during surgery (Grimson et al., 1999).

Advances in brain scanning are also aiding the development of new methods for harnessing the brain's neural signals. We consider some of these intriguing findings in the *Applying Psychology in the 21st Century* box on page 57.

The Central Core: Our "Old Brain"

Even though the capabilities of the human brain far exceed those of the brain of any other species we know of, it is not surprising that the basic functions that we share with more primitive animals, such as breathing, eating, and sleeping, are directed by a relatively primitive part of the brain. The portion of the brain known as the **central core** (see Figure 2-9) is quite similar to that found in all vertebrates (species with backbones). The central core is sometimes referred to as the "old brain" because its evolutionary underpinnings can be traced back some 500 million years to primitive structures found in nonhuman species.

To get a better view of the brain, researchers are experimenting with various scanning techniques; this photo combines PET and MRI scans.

Figure 2–9 The major divisions of the brain: the cerebral cortex and the central core.

After R. Seeley, et al. Copyright © The McGraw-Hill Companies.

Cerebral cortex (the "new brain")

Central core (the "old brain")

central core: The "old brain," which controls such basic functions as eating and sleeping and is common to all vertebrates

cerebellum (ser uh BELL um): The part of the brain that controls bodily balance

If we were to move up the spinal cord from the base of the skull to locate the structures of the central core of the brain, the first part we would come to would be the *hindbrain,* which contains the medulla, pons, and cerebellum (see Figure 2-10). The *medulla* controls a number of critical body functions, the most important of which are breathing and heartbeat. The *pons* comes next, joining the two halves of the cerebellum, which lies adjacent to it. Containing large bundles of nerves, the pons acts as a transmitter of motor information, coordinating muscles and integrating movement between the right and left halves of the body. It is also involved in the control of sleep.

The **cerebellum** is found just above the medulla and behind the pons. Without the help of the cerebellum we would be unable to walk in a straight line without staggering and lurching forward, for it is the job of the cerebellum to control bodily balance. It constantly monitors feedback from the muscles to coordinate their placement, movement, and tension. In fact, drinking too much alcohol seems to depress the activity of the cerebellum, leading to the unsteady gait and movement characteristic of drunkenness. The cerebellum is also involved in several intellectual functions, ranging from analysis of sensory information to problem solving (Gao et al., 1996; Wickelgren, 1998a).

Figure 2–10 The major structures in the brain.

After G. B. Johnson. Copyright © The McGraw-Hill Companies.

Cerebral cortex

Corpus callosum
Bridge of fibers passing information between the two cerebral hemispheres

Thalamus
Relay center for cortex; handles incoming and outgoing signals

Cerebellum
Controls bodily balance

Pons
Involved in sleep and arousal

Reticular formation
A network of neurons related to sleep, arousal, and attention

Medulla
Responsible for regulating largely unconscious functions such as breathing and circulation

Hypothalamus
Responsible for regulating basic biological needs: hunger, thirst, temperature control

Pituitary gland
"Master" gland that regulates other endocrine glands

Spinal cord
Responsible for communication between brain and rest of body; involved with simple reflexes

Applying Psychology in the 21st Century

Mind over Cursor: Using Brain Waves to Overcome Physical Limitations

For four years, Hans-Peter Balzmann, a lawyer suffering from Lou Gehrig's disease, was locked within his own body. Paralyzed by the disease and unable to eat, speak, or even breathe on his own, he had relied on a respirator and feeding tube to survive. Although his mind functioned normally, he was unable to communicate with the outside world.

All that changed, however, after Balzmann obtained an experimental device that allows brain waves to be translated into written communication. Using EEG scanning techniques that react to the pattern of brain waves originating in the brain, Balzmann learned to boost and curtail certain types of brain waves. After hundreds of hours of practice, he was able to select letters that appear on a video screen. By stringing letters

together, he could spell out messages. The process, which makes use of brain waves called "slow cortical potentials," permitted Balzmann to communicate effectively for the first time in years. Although the method is slow and tedious—Balzmann can produce only about two characters per minute—it holds great promise (Birbaumer et al., 1999).

Other increasingly sophisticated procedures may permit faster communication with brain waves in the future. For example, neurosurgeon Philip Kennedy of Emory University is experimenting with a procedure in which he implants electrodes into a paralyzed patient's motor cortex. When the patient thinks about moving her hands, tongues, or eyes, the brain produces electrical signals that are amplified by the implant and translated into the movement of a cursor. Using this system, the patient can spell out words and hit icons (such as "I'm cold") on the computer screen ("Mind over Matter," 1999).

Technological advances offer the possibility of treating other brain disorders. For example, an experimental system is being tested to treat seizures due to epilepsy. The system consists of a pacemaker-like device, implanted into the chest, that sends signals to the brain to block seizures. When patients feel that a seizure is about to occur, they can activate the system, short-circuiting the seizure (Forest, 1997).

Ultimately, systems such as these might be useful not just for people with illnesses and disabilities, but for anyone. For instance, it is conceivable that one day you will be able to control your computer's cursor by simply thinking about moving it. Mind-over-cursor could be in everyone's future.

Can you think of a mechanism that would permit brain-wave communication between two people? What implications would there be if people gained the ability to communicate with each other in this way?

The **reticular formation** extends from the medulla through the pons, passing through the middle section of the brain—or *midbrain*—and into the front-most part of the brain, called the *forebrain*. Like an ever-vigilant guard, the reticular formation is made up of groups of nerve cells that can immediately activate other parts of the brain to produce general bodily arousal. If you are startled by a loud noise, for example, your reticular formation can put you into a heightened state of awareness so you can determine whether a response is necessary. In addition, the reticular formation serves a different function when we are sleeping, seeming to filter out background stimuli to allow us to sleep undisturbed.

Hidden within the forebrain, the **thalamus** acts primarily as a busy relay station, mostly for information concerning the senses. Messages from the eyes, ears, and skin travel to the thalamus to be communicated upward to higher parts of the brain. The thalamus also integrates information from higher parts of the brain, sorting it out so that it can be sent to the cerebellum and medulla.

reticular formation: The part of the brain from the medulla through the pons made up of groups of nerve cells that can immediately activate other parts of the brain to produce general bodily arousal

thalamus: The part of the brain located in the middle of the central core that acts primarily as a busy relay station, mostly for information concerning the senses

While the cerebellum is involved in several intellectual functions, its main duty is to control balance, constantly monitoring feedback from the muscles to coordinate their placement, movement, and tension. Do you think the cerebellum is under conscious or automatic control as people negotiate difficult balancing tasks?

The **hypothalamus** is located just below the thalamus. Although tiny—about the size of a fingertip—the hypothalamus plays an inordinately important role. One of its major functions is to maintain *homeostasis*, a steady internal environment for the body. The hypothalamus helps maintain a constant body temperature and monitors the amount of nutrients stored in the cells. It also produces and regulates behavior that is critical to the basic survival of the species, such as eating, self-protection, and sex.

The Limbic System: Beyond the Central Core

In an eerie view of the future, some science fiction writers have suggested that people will someday routinely have electrodes implanted in their brains. These electrodes will permit them to receive tiny shocks that produce the sensation of pleasure by stimulating certain centers of the brain. When they feel upset, people will simply activate their electrodes to achieve an immediate high.

Although farfetched, and ultimately improbable, such a futuristic fantasy is based on fact. The brain does have pleasure centers in several areas, including some in the **limbic system.** Consisting of a series of doughnut-shaped structures including the *amygdala, hippocampus,* and *fornix,* the limbic system borders the top of the central core and has connections with the cerebral cortex (see Figure 2-11).

The structures of the limbic system jointly control a variety of basic functions relating to emotions and self-preservation, such as eating, aggression, and reproduction. Injury to the limbic system can produce striking changes in behavior. It can turn animals that are usually docile and tame into belligerent savages. Conversely, those that are usually wild and uncontrollable might become meek and obedient (Bedard & Parsinger, 1995).

Research examining the effects of mild electric shocks to parts of the limbic system and other parts of the brain have produced some thought-provoking findings (Olds & Milner, 1954; Olds & Fobes, 1981). In one experiment, rats who pressed a bar received mild electric stimulation through an electrode implanted in their brain, which produced pleasurable feelings. Even starving rats on their way to food would stop to press the bar as many times as they could. Some rats would actually stimulate themselves literally thousands of times an hour—until they collapsed with fatigue (Routtenberg & Lindy, 1965).

Figure 2-11 *(a)* The limbic system consists of a series of doughnut-shaped structures that are involved in self-preservation, learning, memory, and the experience of pleasure (After A. Schneider and B. Tarshih. Copyright © The McGraw-Hill Companies). *(b)* This computer-generated image provides another view of the limbic system (Courtesy of Dr. Robert B. Livingston, University of California-San Diego, and Philip J. Mercurio, Neurosciences Institute).

The extraordinarily pleasurable quality of certain kinds of stimulation has also been experienced by humans, who, as part of treatment for certain kinds of brain disorders, have received electrical stimulation to certain areas of the limbic system. Although at a loss to describe just what it feels like, these people report the experience to be intensely pleasurable, similar in some respects to sexual orgasm.

The limbic system also plays an important role in learning and memory, a finding demonstrated in patients with epilepsy. In an attempt to stop their seizures, such patients have had portions of the limbic system removed. One unintended consequence of the surgery is that these individuals sometimes have difficulty learning and remembering new information.

The limbic system, then, is involved in several important functions, including self-preservation, learning, memory, and the experience of pleasure. These functions are hardly unique to humans; in fact, the limbic system is sometimes referred to as the "animal brain" because its structures and functions are so similar to those of other mammals. To identify the part of the brain that provides the complex and subtle capabilities that are uniquely human, we need to turn to another structure—the cerebral cortex.

Evaluate

1. _____ _____ is a procedure whereby a picture of the brain can be taken without opening the skull.
2. Match the name of each brain scan with the appropriate description:

   a. EEG
   b. CAT
   c. PET

   1. By locating radiation within the brain, a computer can provide a striking picture of brain activity.
   2. Electrodes placed around the skull record the electrical signals transmitted through the brain.
   3. A computer image combines thousands of X-ray pictures into one.

3. Control of such functions as breathing and sleep is located in the _____ _____.
4. Match the portion of the brain with its function:

   a. medulla
   b. pons
   c. cerebellum
   d. reticular formation

   1. Maintains breathing and heartbeat
   2. Controls bodily balance
   3. Coordinates and integrates muscle movements
   4. Activates other parts of the brain to produce general bodily arousal

5. The _____, a fingertip-sized portion of the brain, is responsible for the regulation of the body's internal environment.

Answers to Evaluate Questions

1. Brain scanning 2. a-2; b-3; c-1 3. central core or "old brain" 4. a-1; b-3; c-2; d-4 5. hypothalamus

Rethink

1. How would you answer the argument that "psychologists should leave the study of neurons and synapses and the nervous system to biologists"?
2. Before sophisticated brain-scanning techniques were developed, biopsychologists' understanding of the brain was largely based on the brains of people who had died. What limitations would this pose, and in what areas would you expect the most significant advances once brain-scanning techniques were possible?

The Cerebral Cortex: Our "New Brain"

As we have proceeded up the spinal cord and into the brain, our discussion has centered on areas of the brain that control functions similar to those found in less sophisticated organisms. But where, you may be asking, are the portions of the brain that enable humans to do what they do best, and that distinguish humans from all other animals? Those unique features of the human brain—indeed, the very capabilities that allow you to come up with such a question in the first place—are embodied in the ability to think, evaluate, and make complex judgments. The principal location of these abilities, along with many others, is the **cerebral cortex.**

The cerebral cortex is referred to as the "new brain" because of its relatively recent evolution. It consists of a mass of deeply folded, rippled, convoluted tissue that amounts to some 80 percent of the brain's total mass. Although only about one-twelfth of an inch thick, it would, if flattened out, cover an area of more than two feet square. This

cerebral cortex: The "new brain," responsible for the most sophisticated information processing in the brain; contains the lobes

Figure 2-12 The cerebral cortex of the brain. The major physical *structures* of the cerebral cortex are called lobes. This figure also illustrates the *functions* associated with particular areas of the cerebral cortex. Are any areas of the cerebral cortex present in nonhuman animals?

· **lobes:** The four major sections of the cerebral cortex: frontal, parietal, temporal, and occipital

configuration allows the surface area of the cortex to be considerably greater than if it were smoother and more uniformly packed into the skull. The uneven shape also permits a high level of integration of neurons, allowing sophisticated processing of information.

The cortex has four major sections, called **lobes.** If we take a side view of the brain, the *frontal lobes* lie at the front center of the cortex, and the *parietal lobes* lie behind them. The *temporal lobes* are found in the lower center of the cortex, with the *occipital lobes* lying behind them. These four sets of lobes are physically separated by deep grooves called sulci. Figure 2-12 shows the four areas.

Another way of describing the brain is by considering the functions associated with a given area. Figure 2-12 also shows the specialized regions within the lobes related to specific functions and areas of the body. Three major areas have been discovered: the motor areas, the sensory areas, and the association areas. Although we will discuss these areas as though they were separate and independent, keep in mind that this is an over-simplification. In most instances, behavior is influenced simultaneously by several structures and areas within the brain, operating interdependently. Furthermore, even within a given area, additional subdivisions exist. Finally, when people suffer certain kinds of brain injury, uninjured portions of the brain can sometimes take over the functions that were previously handled by the damaged area. In short, the brain is extraordinarily adaptable (Gibbons, 1990; Sharma, Angelucci, & Sur, 2000).

The Motor Area of the Cortex

PsychLink
Information about lobes
www.mhhe.com/
feldmaness5-02links

motor area: The part of the cortex that is largely responsible for the voluntary movement of particular parts of the body

If you look at the frontal lobe in Figure 2-12, you will see a shaded portion labeled the **motor area.** This part of the cortex is largely responsible for the voluntary movement of particular parts of the body. Every portion of the motor area corresponds to a specific locale within the body. If we were to insert an electrode into a particular part of the motor area of the cortex and apply mild electrical stimulation, there would be involuntary movement in the corresponding part of the body. If we moved to another part of the motor area and stimulated it, a different part of the body would move.

The motor area is so well mapped that researchers have identified the amount and relative location of cortical tissue used to produce movement in specific parts of the human body. For example, the control of body movements that are relatively large scale and require little precision, such as movement of a knee or a hip, is centered in a very small space in the motor area. In contrast, movements that must be precise and delicate, such as facial expressions and finger movements, are controlled by a considerably larger portion of the motor area.

In short, the motor area of the cortex provides a guide to the degree of complexity and the importance of the motor capabilities of specific parts of the body. Keep in mind, however, that behavior is produced by multiple sets of neurons in the nervous system, linked in elaborate ways. Like other behavior, movement is produced through the coordinated firing of a complex variety of neurons, working together but not necessarily lined up neatly in the motor area of the cortex (Sanes et al., 1995; Batista et al., 1999; Kakei, Hoffman, & Strick, 1999).

The Sensory Area of the Cortex

Given the one-to-one correspondence between motor area and body location, it is not surprising to find a similar relationship between specific portions of the cortex and the senses. The **sensory area** of the cortex includes three regions: one that corresponds primarily to body sensations (including touch and pressure), one relating to sight, and a third relating to sound. For instance, the *somatosensory area* encompasses specific locations associated with the ability to perceive touch and pressure in a particular area of the body. As with the motor area, the amount of brain tissue related to a particular location on the body determines the degree of sensitivity of that location. The greater the space within the cortex, the more sensitive that area of the body. As you can see from the weird-looking individual in Figure 2-13, parts such as the fingers are related to proportionally more space in the somatosensory area and are the most sensitive.

The senses of sound and sight are also represented in specific areas of the cerebral cortex. An *auditory area* located in the temporal lobe is responsible for the sense of hearing. If the auditory area is stimulated electrically, a person will hear sounds such as clicks or hums. It also appears that particular locations within the auditory area respond to specific pitches (deCharms, Blake, & Merzenich, 1998; Klinke et al., 1999).

The *visual area* in the cortex, located in the occipital lobe, operates analogously to the other sensory areas. Stimulation by electrodes produces the experience of flashes of light or colors, suggesting that the raw sensory input of images from the eyes is received in this area of the brain and transformed into meaningful stimuli. The visual area also provides another example of how areas of the brain are intimately related to specific areas of the body: Particular areas of the eye's retina are related to a particular part of the cortex—with, as you might guess, more space in the brain given to the most sensitive portions of the retina (Martin et al., 1995; Miyashita, 1995).

sensory area: The site in the brain of the tissue that corresponds to each of the senses, with the degree of sensitivity relating to the amount of tissue

Figure 2-13 The greater the amount of tissue in the somatosensory area of the brain that is related to a specific body part, the more sensitive is that body part. If the size of our body parts reflected the corresponding amount of brain tissue, we would look like this strange creature.

*A model of the injury
sustained by Phineas Gage.*

association areas: One of the major areas
of the brain; the site of the higher mental
processes such as thought, language,
memory, and speech

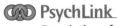 **PsychLink**

Description of aphasia
www.mhhe.com/
feldmaness5-02links

The Association Areas of the Cortex

Consider the following case:

> Twenty-five-year-old Phineas Gage, a railroad employee, was blasting rock one day
> in 1848 when an accidental explosion punched a 3-foot-long spike, about an inch in
> diameter, completely through his skull. The spike entered just under his left cheek,
> came out the top of his head, and flew into the air. Gage immediately suffered a
> series of convulsions, yet a few minutes later was talking with rescuers. In fact, he
> was able to walk up a long flight of stairs before receiving any medical attention.
> Amazingly, after a few weeks his wound healed, and he was physically close to his
> old self again. Mentally, however, there was a difference: Once a careful and hard-
> working person, Phineas now became enamored with wild schemes and was . . .
> irresponsible. As one of his physicians put it, ". . . His friends and acquaintances
> said he was 'no longer Gage'" (Harlow, 1869, p. 14).

What had happened to the old Gage? Although there is no way of knowing for
sure—science being what it was in the 1800s—we can speculate that the accident injured
the association areas of Gage's cerebral cortex. The **association areas** are generally considered to be the site of higher mental processes such as thinking, language, memory,
and speech (Rowe et al., 2000).

The association areas take up a large proportion of the cerebral cortex. Most of our
understanding of the association areas comes from patients who have suffered some type
of brain injury. In some cases the injury stemmed from natural causes such as a tumor or
a stroke, either of which would block certain blood vessels within the cerebral cortex. In
other cases, accidents were the culprits, as was true with Phineas Gage. In any event, damage to these areas can result in unusual behavioral changes, indicating the importance of
the association area to normal functioning (Herholz, 1995; Gannon et al., 1998).

Gage's case provides evidence that there are specialized areas for making rational
decisions. When this area is damaged, people undergo personality changes that affect
their ability to make moral judgments and process emotions. At the same time, people
with damage in this area can still be capable of reasoning logically, performing
calculations, and recalling information (Damasio et al., 1994).

Injuries to other parts of the association areas can produce a condition known as
apraxia. *Apraxia* occurs when an individual is unable to integrate activities in a rational
or logical manner. The disorder is most evident when people are asked to carry out a
sequence of behaviors requiring a degree of planning and foresight, suggesting that the
association areas act as "master planners," or organizers of actions.

Injuries to the association areas of the brain can also produce *aphasia,* problems
with language. In *Broca's aphasia* (caused by damage to the part of the brain first
identified by a French physician, Paul Broca, in 1861), speech becomes halting, labo-
rious, and often ungrammatical. The speaker is unable to find the right words, in a
kind of tip-of-the-tongue phenomenon that we all experience from time to time. People with aphasia, though, grope for words almost constantly, eventually blurting out
a kind of "verbal telegram." A phrase like "I put the book on the table" comes out as
"I . . . put . . . book . . . table" (Cornell, Fromkin, & Mauner, 1993; Goodglass, 1993;
Kirshner, 1995).

Wernicke's aphasia is a disorder named for Carl Wernicke, who identified it in
the 1870s. Wernicke's aphasia produces difficulties both in understanding others'
speech and in the production of language. The disorder is characterized by speech that
sounds fluent but makes no sense. For instance, one patient, asked what brought him
to a hospital, gave this rambling reply: "Boy, I'm sweating, I'm awful nervous, you
know, once in a while I get caught up, I can't mention the tarripoi, a month ago, quite
a little, I've done a lot well, I impose a lot, while, on the other hand, you know what
I mean, I have to run around, look it over, trebbin and all that sort of stuff" (Gardner,
1975, p. 68).

Mending the Brain

> Shortly after he was born, Jacob Stark's arms and legs started jerking every
> 20 minutes. Weeks later he could not focus his eyes on his mother's face. The
> diagnosis: uncontrollable epileptic seizures involving his entire brain.
>
> His mother, Sally Stark, recalled: "When Jacob was two and a half months
> old, they said he would never learn to sit up, would never be able to feed himself.
> Nothing could be done to prevent profound retardation. They told us to take him
> home, love him and find an institution." (Blakeslee, 1992, C3).

Instead, the Starks brought Jacob to the University of California at Los Angeles for brain surgery when he was five months old. Surgeons removed 20 percent of his brain. The operation was a complete success. Three years later, Jacob seems normal in every way, with no sign of seizures.

Jacob's surgery is representative of increasingly daring approaches in the treatment of brain disorders. It also illustrates how our growing understanding of the processes that underlie brain functioning can be translated into solutions to difficult problems.

The surgery that helped Jacob was based on the premise that the diseased part of his brain was producing seizures throughout the entire brain. Surgeons reasoned that if they removed the misfiring portion, the remaining parts of the brain, which appeared intact in PET scans, would take over. They bet that Jacob could still lead a normal life following surgery, particularly because the surgery was being done at so young an age. Clearly, the gamble paid off.

The success of such surgery is in part related to new findings about the regenerative powers of the brain and nervous system. Although it has been known that the brain has the ability to shift functions to different locations following injury to a specific area or in cases of surgery, it had been assumed for decades that the neurons of the spinal cord and brain could never be replaced.

However, new evidence is beginning to suggest otherwise. For instance, researchers have found that the cells from the brains of adult mice can produce new neurons, at least in a test tube environment. Similarly, researchers have reported partial restoration of movement in rats who had a 1/5-inch-long gap in their spinal cords and, as a result, were unable to move their hind limbs. The researchers transplanted neurons from the peripheral nervous system into the gap, and subsequently the rats were able to flex their legs. One year after the operation, they were able to support themselves and move their legs, and examination of the neurons in the spinal cord showed significant regeneration around the area of the transplantation (Cheng, Cao, & Olson, 1996; McDonald, 1999; Blakeslee, 2000).

The future also holds promise for people who, like Michael J. Fox, suffer from the tremors and loss of motor control produced by Parkinson's disease. Because Parkinson's is caused by a gradual loss of cells that stimulate the production of dopamine in the brain, investigators reasoned that a procedure that increases the supply of dopamine might be effective. They seem to be on the right track. When certain cells from human fetuses are injected directly into the brains of Parkinson's sufferers, they seem to take root, stimulating dopamine production. For most of those who have undergone this procedure, the preliminary results are promising, with some patients showing great improvement. On the other hand, the technique remains experimental, and it also raises some thorny ethical issues, given that the source of the implanted fetal tissue is aborted fetuses (Harvard Mental Health Letter, 2000; Pollack, 2000).

The Specialization of the Hemispheres: Two Brains or One?

The most recent development, at least in evolutionary terms, in the organization and operation of our brain probably occurred in the last million years: a specialization of the functions controlled by the two sides of the brain, which has symmetrical left and right halves.

hemispheres: The two symmetrical left and right halves of the brain; each controls the side of the body opposite to it

Specifically, the brain can be divided into two roughly similar mirror-image halves—just as we have two arms, two legs, and two lungs. Because of the way nerves are connected from the brain to the rest of the body, these two symmetrical left and right halves, called **hemispheres,** control the side of the body opposite to their location. The left hemisphere of the brain, then, generally controls the right side of the body, and the right hemisphere controls the left side of the body. Thus damage to the right side of the brain is typically indicated by functional difficulties in the left side of the body.

Despite the appearance of similarity between the two hemispheres of the brain, they are involved in somewhat different functions. It appears that certain activities are more likely to occur in one hemisphere than in the other. Early evidence for the functional differences between halves of the brain came from studies of people with aphasia. Researchers found that people with the speech difficulties characteristic of aphasia tended to have physical damage to the left hemisphere of the brain. In contrast, physical abnormalities in the right hemisphere of the brain tended to produce far fewer problems with language. This finding led researchers to conclude that for most people, language is **lateralized,** or located more in one hemisphere than in the other—in this case, in the left side of the brain (Grossi et al., 1996).

lateralization: The dominance of one hemisphere of the brain in specific functions

It now seems clear that the two hemispheres of the brain are somewhat specialized in terms of the functions they carry out. The left hemisphere concentrates more on tasks that require verbal competence, such as speaking, reading, thinking, and reasoning. The right hemisphere has its own strengths, particularly in nonverbal areas such as the understanding of spatial relationships, recognition of patterns and drawings, music, and emotional expression (Ornstein, 1998; Robertson & Ivry, 2000).

In addition, information is processed somewhat differently in the two hemispheres. The left hemisphere tends to consider information sequentially, one bit at a time; the right hemisphere tends to process information globally, considering it as a whole (Turkewitz, 1993; Banich & Heller, 1998).

On the other hand, it is important to keep in mind that the differences in specialization between the hemispheres are not great, and the degree and nature of lateralization vary from one person to another. If you are right-handed, control of language is probably concentrated more in your left hemisphere. If you are among the 10 percent of people who are left-handed or are ambidextrous (you use both hands interchangeably), it is much more likely that the language centers of your brain are located more in the right hemisphere or are divided equally between left and right hemispheres.

Researchers have also unearthed evidence that there may be subtle differences in brain lateralization patterns between males and females. In fact, some scientists have suggested that there are slight differences in the structure of the brain according to gender and culture. As we see next, such findings have led to a lively debate in the scientific community.

EXPLORING DIVERSITY

Human Diversity and the Brain

The interplay of biology and environment is particularly clear when we consider evidence suggesting that there are both sex and cultural differences in brain structure and function. Let's consider sex first. According to accumulating evidence, females and males show some intriguing differences in brain lateralization and weight, although the nature of those differences—and even their very existence—is a matter of considerable controversy (Kimura, 1992; Dorion et al., 2000).

We can be reasonably confident about some differences. For instance, most males tend to show greater lateralization of language in the left hemisphere. For them, language is clearly relegated largely to the left side of the brain. In contrast, women display less

Figure 2-14 These composite MRI brain scans show the distribution of active areas in the brains of males *(left)* and females *(right)* during a verbal task involving rhyming. In males, activation is more lateralized, or confined, to the left hemisphere, while in females, activation is bilateralized, that is, occurring in both hemispheres of the brain.

(Source: B. A. Shaywitz et al., 1995. NMR/Yale Medical School)

lateralization, with language abilities apt to be more evenly divided between the two hemispheres (Gur et al., 1982; Shaywitz et al., 1995; Kulynych et al., 1994). Such differences in brain lateralization could account, in part, for female superiority on certain measures of verbal skills, such as the onset and fluency of speech, and the fact that far more boys than girls have reading problems in elementary school (Kitterle, 1991).

Other research suggests that men's brains are somewhat bigger than women's brains, even after taking into account differences in body size. On the other hand, part of the *corpus callosum,* a bundle of fibers that connects the hemispheres of the brain, is proportionally larger in women than in men. Furthermore, some research suggests that women's brains have a higher proportion of the neurons that are actually involved in thinking than men's brains do (Witelson, 1995; Falk et al., 1999; Gur et al., 1999).

Men and women also might process information differently. For example, MRI brain scans of men sounding out words show activation of a small area of the left side of the brain, whereas women use areas on both sides of the brain (Shaywitz et al., 1995; see Figure 2-14). Similarly, PET brain scans of men and women while they are not engaged in mental activity show differences in the use of glucose (Gur et al., 1995; Gur, 1996).

The meaning of such sex differences is far from clear. Consider one possibility related to the differences that have been found in the proportional size of the corpus callosum: Its increased proportion in women might permit stronger connections to develop between those parts of the brain that control speech. In turn, this would explain why speech tends to emerge slightly earlier in girls than in boys.

Before we rush to such a conclusion, though, it is important to consider an alternative hypothesis: It is plausible that the earlier emergence of verbal abilities in girls is due to the fact that infant girls receive greater encouragement to verbalize than infant boys do. This greater early experience could foster growth of certain parts of the brain. Hence, physical brain differences might be a *reflection* of social and environmental influences, rather than a *cause* of the differences in men's and women's behavior. At this point, it is impossible to confirm which of these two alternative hypotheses is correct.

The culture in which we are raised also might give rise to differences in brain lateralization. For example, native speakers of Japanese seem to process information regarding vowel sounds primarily in the brain's left hemisphere. In contrast, North and South Americans, Europeans, and individuals of Japanese ancestry who learn Japanese later in life handle vowel sounds principally in the right hemisphere.

The reason for this cultural difference in lateralization? One explanation could be that certain characteristics of the Japanese language, such as the ability to express complex ideas using only vowel sounds, result in the development of a specific type of brain lateralization in native speakers. Differences in lateralization could account for other dissimilarities between the ways native Japanese speakers and Westerners think about the world (Tsunoda, 1985).

In general, scientists are just beginning to understand the extent, nature, and meaning of sex and cultural differences in lateralization and brain structure. Furthermore, in evaluating the research on brain lateralization, it is important to keep in mind that the two hemispheres of the brain function interdependently in deciphering, interpreting, and reacting to the world.

The Split Brain: Exploring the Two Hemispheres

The patient, V. J., had suffered severe seizures. By cutting her corpus callosum, the fibrous portion of the brain that carries messages between the hemispheres, surgeons hoped to create a firebreak to prevent the seizures from spreading. The operation did decrease the frequency and severity of V. J.'s attacks. But V. J. developed an unexpected side effect: She lost the ability to write at will, although she could read and spell words aloud. (Strauss, 1998, p. 287)

split-brain patient: A person who suffers from independent functioning of the two halves of the brain, as a result of which the sides of the body work in disharmony

People like V. J., whose corpus callosum has been surgically cut to stop seizures and who are therefore called **split-brain patients,** offer a rare opportunity for researchers investigating the independent functioning of the two hemispheres of the brain. For example, psychologist Roger Sperry—who won the Nobel Prize for his work—developed a number of ingenious techniques for studying how each hemisphere operated (Sperry, 1982; Baynes et al., 1998; Gazzaniga, 1998).

In one experimental procedure, blindfolded subjects were allowed to touch an object with their right hand and were asked to name it. Because the right side of the body is connected to the left side of the brain—the hemisphere that is most responsible for language—the split-brain patient was able to name it. But if the blindfolded subjects touched the object with their left hand, they were not able to name it aloud. However, the information had registered: When the blindfold was taken off, subjects could pick out the objects that they had touched. Information can be learned and remembered, then, using only the right side of the brain. (By the way, unless you've had a split-brain operation, this experiment won't work with you, because the bundle of fibers connecting the two hemispheres of a normal brain immediately transfer the information from one hemisphere to the other.)

It is clear from experiments like this one that the right and left hemispheres of the brain specialize in handling different sorts of information. At the same time, it is important to realize that they are both capable of understanding, knowing, and being aware of the world, albeit in somewhat different ways. The two hemispheres, then, should be regarded as different in terms of the efficiency with which they process certain kinds of information, rather than as two entirely separate brains.

The Endocrine System: Of Chemicals and Glands

endocrine system: A chemical communication network that sends messages throughout the nervous system via the bloodstream
hormones: Chemicals that circulate through the blood and affect the functioning or growth of other parts of the body

One aspect of the biopsychology of behavior that we have not yet considered is the **endocrine system,** a chemical communication network that sends messages throughout the nervous system via the bloodstream. Although not a structure of the brain itself, the endocrine system is intimately tied to the hypothalamus. The job of the endocrine system is to secrete **hormones,** chemicals that circulate through the blood and affect the functioning or growth of other parts of the body (Crapo, 1985; Kravitz, 1988).

Like neurotransmitters, hormones communicate chemical messages throughout the body, although the speed and mode of transmission are quite different. Whereas neural

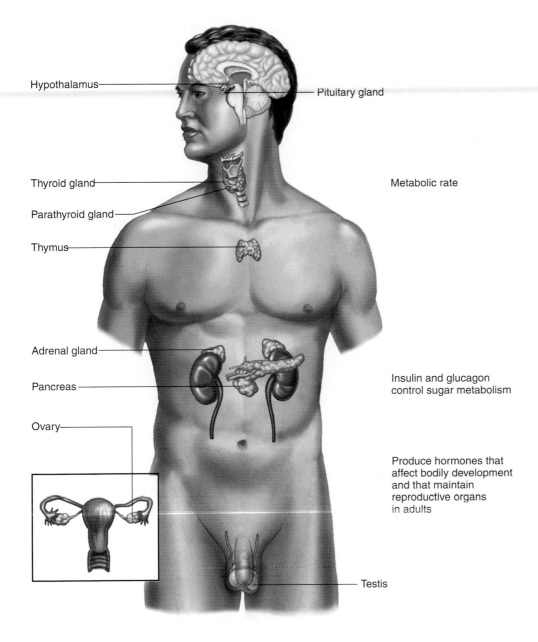

Figure 2-15 Location and function of the major endocrine glands.

After S. S. Mader. Copyright © The McGraw-Hill Companies.

Hypothalamus

Pituitary gland

Thyroid gland

Metabolic rate

Parathyroid gland

Thymus

Adrenal gland

Pancreas

Insulin and glucagon control sugar metabolism

Ovary

Produce hormones that affect bodily development and that maintain reproductive organs in adults

Testis

messages are measured in thousandths of a second, hormonal communications can take minutes to reach their destination. Furthermore, neural messages move across neurons in specific lines (as with wires strung along telephone poles), whereas hormones travel throughout the entire body, similar to the way radio waves transmit across the entire landscape. Just as radio waves evoke a response only when a radio is tuned to the correct station, so hormones flowing through the bloodstream activate only those cells that are receptive and "tuned" to the appropriate hormonal message.

A major component of the endocrine system is the **pituitary gland,** found near—and regulated by—the hypothalamus. The pituitary gland has sometimes been called the "master gland," because it controls the functioning of the rest of the endocrine system. But the pituitary gland is more than just the taskmaster of other glands; it has important functions in its own right. For instance, hormones secreted by the pituitary gland control growth. Extremely short people and unusually tall ones usually have pituitary gland abnormalities. Other endocrine glands, shown in Figure 2-15, affect emotional reactions, sexual urges, and energy levels.

Despite its designation as the "master gland," the pituitary is actually a servant of the brain, because the brain is ultimately responsible for the endocrine system's

pituitary gland: The "master gland," the major component of the endocrine system, which secretes hormones that control growth functioning. The brain regulates the internal balance of the body, ensuring that home-ostasis is maintained through the hypothalamus.

Individual hormones can wear many hats, depending on circumstances. For example, the hormone oxytocin is at the root of many of life's satisfactions and plea-sures. In new mothers, oxytocin produces an urge to nurse newborn offspring. The same hormone also seems to stimulate cuddling between species members. And, at least in rats, it encourages sexually active males to seek out females more passionately, and females to be more receptive to males' sexual advances (Angier, 1991).

BECOMING AN INFORMED CONSUMER OF PSYCHOLOGY

biofeedback: A procedure in which a person learns to control through conscious thought internal physiological processes such as blood pressure, heart and respiration rate, skin temperature, sweating, and constriction of particular muscles

Learning to Control Your Heart—and Mind—Through Biofeedback

Tammy DeMichael was cruising along the New York State Thruway with her fiancé when he fell asleep at the wheel. The car slammed into the guardrail and flipped, leaving DeMichael with what the doctors called a "splattered C-6, 7"—a broken neck and crushed spinal cord.

After a year of exhaustive medical treatment, she still had no function or feeling in her arms and legs. "The experts said I'd be a quadriplegic for the rest of my life, able to move only from the neck up," she recalls. . . . But DeMichael proved the experts wrong. Today, feeling has returned to her limbs, her arm strength is normal or better, and she no longer uses a wheelchair. "I can walk about 60 feet with just a cane, and I can go almost anywhere with crutches," she says. (Morrow & Wolf, 1991, p. 64)

The key to DeMichael's astounding recovery: biofeedback. **Biofeedback** is a proce-dure in which a person learns to control through conscious thought internal physiological processes such as blood pressure, heart and respiration rate, skin temperature, sweating, and constriction of particular muscles. Although it had traditionally been thought that the heart, respiration rate, blood pressure, and other bodily functions were under the control of parts of the brain over which we have no influence, psychologists have discovered that these responses are actually susceptible to voluntary control (Rau et al., 1996; Grimsley & Kar-riker, 1996; Bazell, 1998).

In biofeedback, a person is hooked up to electronic devices that provide con-tinuous feedback relating to particular physiological responses. For instance, a per-son interested in controlling headaches through biofeedback might have electronic sensors placed on certain muscles on her head and learn to control the constriction and relaxation of those muscles. Later, after she mastered this training, when she felt a headache starting she could relax the relevant muscles and end the pain.

In DeMichael's case, biofeedback was effective because not all of the nervous sys-tem's connections between the brain and her legs were severed. Through biofeedback, she learned how to send messages to specific muscles, "ordering" them to move. Although it took more than a year, DeMichael was successful in restoring a large degree of her mobility.

Learning to control physiological processes through the use of biofeedback is not easy, but biofeedback has been employed with success in a variety of ailments, including emotional problems (such as anxiety, depression, phobias, tension headaches, insomnia, and hyperactivity); physical illnesses with a psychological component (such as asthma, high blood pressure, ulcers, muscle spasms, and migraine headaches); and physical problems (such as DeMichael's injuries, strokes, cerebral palsy, and, as we see in Figure 2-16, curvature of the spine).

Figure 2-16 The traditional treatment for curvature of the spine employs an unsightly, cumbersome brace. In contrast, biofeedback treatment employs an unobtrusive set of straps attached to a small electronic device that produces tonal feedback when the patient is not standing straight. The person learns to maintain a position that gradually decreases the curvature of the spine until the device is no longer needed (Miller, 1985). What other disorders might biofeedback devices like this one help to treat?

Evaluate

1. A surgeon places an electrode on a portion of your brain and stimulates it. Immediately, your right wrist involuntarily twitches. The doctor has most likely stimulated a portion of the _____ area of your brain.

2. The _____ its corresponding space within the cortex, the more sensitive an area of the body is.

3. Each hemisphere controls the _____ side of the body.

4. Nonverbal realms, such as emotions and music, are controlled primarily by the _____ hemisphere of the brain, whereas the _____ hemisphere is more responsible for speaking and reading.

5. The left hemisphere tends to consider information _____, whereas the right hemisphere tends to process information _____.

6. As studies with split-brain patients have shown, information can be learned and remembered using only the nonverbal side of the brain. True or False?

Answers to Evaluate Questions

1. motor 2. greater 3. opposite 4. right; left 5. sequentially; globally 5. True

Rethink

1. Suppose that abnormalities in an association area of the brain were linked through research to serious criminal behavior. Would you be in favor of mandatory testing of individuals and surgery to repair or remove those abnormalities? Why or why not?

2. Could personal differences in people's specialization of right and left hemispheres be related to occupational success? For example, might an architect who relies on spatial skills have a different pattern of hemispheric specialization than a writer?

Looking Back

Why do psychologists study the brain and nervous system?

- A full understanding of human behavior requires knowledge of the biological influences underlying that behavior. This chapter reviews what biopsychologists (psychologists who specialize in studying the effects of biological structures and functions on behavior) have learned about the human nervous system. (p. 42)

What are the basic elements of the nervous system?

- Neurons, the most basic elements of the nervous system, allow nerve impulses to pass from one part of the body to another. Information generally follows a route that begins with the dendrites, continues into the cell body, and leads ultimately down the tubelike extension, the axon. (p. 43)

How does the nervous system communicate electrical and chemical messages from one part to another?

- Most axons are protected by a coating called the myelin sheath. When an axon receives a message to fire, it releases an action potential, an electrical charge that travels through the neuron. Neurons operate according to an all-or-none law: Either they are at rest or an action potential is moving through them. There is no in-between state. (p. 44)
- Once a neuron fires, nerve impulses are carried to other neurons through the production of chemical substances, neurotransmitters, that bridge the gaps— known as synapses—between neurons. Neurotransmitters are either excitatory (telling other neurons to fire), or inhibitory (preventing or decreasing the likelihood of other neurons firing). The major neurotransmitters include acetylcholine (ACh), which produces contractions of skeletal muscles, and dopamine, which has been linked to Parkinson's disease and certain mental disorders such as schizophrenia. (p. 46)
- Endorphins, another type of neurotransmitter, are related to the reduction of pain. Endorphins aid in the production of natural painkillers and are probably responsible for creating the kind of euphoria that joggers sometimes experience after running. (p. 48)

In what way are the structures of the nervous system tied together?

- The nervous system is made up of the central nervous system (the brain and spinal cord) and the peripheral nervous system (the remainder of the nervous system). The peripheral nervous system is made up of the somatic division, which controls voluntary movements and the communication of information to and from the sense organs, and the autonomic division, which controls involuntary functions such as those of the heart, blood vessels, and lungs. (p. 49)
- The autonomic division of the peripheral nervous system is further subdivided into the sympathetic and parasympathetic divisions. The sympathetic division prepares the body in emergency situations, and the parasympathetic division helps the body return to its typical resting state. (p. 51)
- Evolutionary psychology, the branch of psychology that seeks to identify behavior patterns that are a result of our genetic inheritance, has led to increased understanding of the evolutionary basis of the structure and organization of the human nervous system. Behavioral genetics extends this study to include the evolutionary and hereditary bases of human personality traits and behavior. (p. 51)

How do researchers identify the major parts and functions of the brain?

- Brain scans take a "snapshot" of the internal workings of the brain without having to cut surgically into a person's skull. Major brain-scanning techniques include the electroencephalogram (EEG), computerized axial tomography (CAT), the functional magnetic resonance imaging (MRI) scan, the superconducting quantum interference device (SQUID), and the positron emission tomography (PET) scan. (p. 54)

What are the major parts of the brain, and for what behaviors is each part responsible?

- The central core of the brain is made up of the medulla (which controls such functions as breathing and the heartbeat), the pons (which coordinates the muscles and the two sides of the body), the cerebellum (which controls balance), the reticular formation (which acts to heighten awareness in emergencies), the thalamus (which communicates sensory messages to and from the brain), and the hypothalamus (which maintains homeostasis, or body equilibrium, and regulates basic survival behaviors). The functions of the central core structures are similar to those found in other vertebrates. This part of the brain is sometimes referred to as the "old brain." Increasing evidence also suggests that female and male brains might differ in structure in minor ways. (p. 55)
- The cerebral cortex—the "new brain"—has areas that control voluntary movement (the motor area); the senses (the sensory area); and thinking, reasoning, speech, and memory (the association area). The limbic system, found on the border of the "old" and "new" brains, is associated with eating, reproduction, and the experiences of pleasure and pain. (p. 59)

How do the two halves of the brain operate interdependently?

- The brain is divided into left and right halves, or hemispheres, each of which generally controls the opposite side of the body. Each hemisphere can be thought of as specialized in the functions it carries out: The left is best at verbal tasks, such as logical reasoning, speaking, and reading; the right is best at nonverbal tasks, such as spatial perception, pattern recognition, and emotional expression. (p. 63)
- The endocrine system secretes hormones, allowing the brain to send messages throughout the nervous system via the bloodstream. A major component is the pituitary gland, which affects growth. (p. 66)

How can an understanding of the nervous system help us find ways to relieve disease and pain?

- Biofeedback is a procedure by which a person learns to control internal physiological processes. By controlling what were previously considered involuntary responses, people are able to relieve anxiety, tension, migraine headaches, and a wide range of other psychological and physical problems. (p. 68)

Key Terms and Concepts

biopsychologists (behavioral neuroscientists) (p. 42)
neurons (p. 43)
dendrites (p. 43)

axon (p. 43)
terminal buttons (p. 43)
myelin sheath (p. 43)
all-or-none law (p. 44)

Preview

For additional quizzing and a variety of interactive resources, visit the *Essentials of Understanding Psychology* Online Learning Center at

www.mhhe.com/feldmaness5

Psychology on the Web

1. Biofeedback research is continuously changing and being applied to new areas of human functioning. Find at least two websites that discuss recent research on biofeedback and summarize the research and any findings it has produced. Include in your summary your own best estimate of future applications of this technique.
2. Find one or more websites on Parkinson's disease and learn more about this topic. Specifically, find reports of new treatments for Parkinson's that do not involve the use of fetal tissue. Write a summary of your findings.

Epilogue

This chapter has traced the ways in which biological structures and functions of the body affect behavior. Starting with neurons, we considered each of the components of the nervous system, culminating in an examination of how the brain permits us to think, reason, speak, recall, and experience emotions—the hallmarks of being human.

Before we proceed to the next chapter, where we put our knowledge of the biology of behavior to use in a look at sensation and perception, turn back for a moment to the prologue of this chapter, involving television and movie star Michael J. Fox. Consider the following questions.

1. Using what you now know about brain structures and functioning, can you explain what might have produced Fox's Parkinson's disease in the first place?
2. The operation used to treat Fox's disorder destroyed certain cells of his brain. Speculate about what part of the brain the operation might have involved.
3. Do you think biofeedback techniques could be used to control the symptoms of Parkinson's disease? Why or why not?

Chapter Three

Sensation and Perception

Prologue

Now Hear This!

Amy Ecklund

You'd almost think Amy Ecklund is a contestant on a game show called *Guess That Sound.* "That's a glass!" she proudly exclaims as she hears a clinking noise in the New Haven pub where she's having lunch. "Silverware!" she cries at the clang of a fork. When a hammer bangs, Ecklund gets really excited. "Wow!" she says, "that is loud!"

Life's everyday clatter is a symphony to Ecklund, 29, who for four years has played deaf hospital administrator Abigail Bauer on the CBS soap *Guiding Light.* Hearing-impaired since age 6 (doctors never determined the cause), Ecklund no longer has to read lips to do scenes. Last January she had a Nucleus 24 cochlear implant put in her right ear, thus becoming one of the 2,000 people in the U.S. to have benefited from the revolutionary hearing device...[which] has allowed Ecklund to hear nearly normally, dramatically changing her life. "It's like watching a child being born," says Michael O'Leary, who plays her husband, Dr. Rick Bauer, on *Guiding Light* (Ecklund, 1999, p. 68).

Looking Ahead

Amy Ecklund is the beneficiary of a new generation of technological devices that offer the promise of restored hearing to the tens of thousands of people with hearing impairments. Still, no technological substitute has reached the ultimate level of sophistication of the human ear, or, for that matter, any of our other sense organs. In fact, our ability to sense the stimuli in our environment is remarkable, enabling us to feel the gentlest of breezes, see flickering lights miles away, and hear the soft murmuring of distant songbirds.

In this chapter we focus on the field of psychology that is concerned with the nature of the information our body takes in through its senses and with the way we interpret such information. We will explore both sensation and perception. **Sensation** encompasses the processes by which our sense organs receive information from the environment. **Perception** is the sorting out, interpretation, analysis, and integration of stimuli involving our sense organs and brain.

To a psychologist interested in understanding the causes of behavior, sensation and perception are fundamental topics, because so much of our behavior is a reflection of how we react to and interpret stimuli from the world around us. Questions ranging from "What processes enable us to see and hear?" to "How do we distinguish one person from another?" fall into the realm of sensation and perception.

Although perception clearly represents a step beyond sensation, in practice it is sometimes difficult to find the precise boundary between the two. The primary difference is that sensation can be thought of as an organism's first encounter with a raw sensory stimulus, whereas perception is the process by which the stimulus is interpreted, analyzed, and integrated with other sensory information. For example, if we were considering sensation, we might ask about the loudness of a ringing fire alarm. If we were considering perception, we might ask whether someone recognizes the ringing sound as an alarm and identifies its meaning. But both sensation and perception are necessary for transforming the physical world into our psychological reality.

This chapter begins with a discussion of the relationship between the characteristics of a physical stimulus and the kinds of sensory responses it produces. We then examine several of the major senses, including vision, hearing, balance, smell, taste, and the skin senses, which include touch and the experience of pain.

Next, the chapter explains how we organize the stimuli to which our sense organs are exposed. For instance, we consider a number of issues relating to perception, such as how we are able to perceive the world in three dimensions when our eyes are capable only of sensing two-dimensional images. Finally, we examine visual illusions, which provide us with important clues for understanding general perceptual mechanisms. As we explore these issues, we'll see how the senses work together to provide us with an integrated view and understanding of the world.

PsychLink

Perception demonstrations
www.mhhe.com/
feldmaness5-03links

sensation: The processes by which our sense organs receive information from the environment
perception: The sorting out, interpretation, analysis, and integration of stimuli involving our sense organs and brain

Prepare

What is sensation, and how do psychologists study it?
What is the relationship between a physical stimulus and the kinds of sensory responses that result from it?

Organize

Sensing the World Around Us
    Absolute Thresholds
    Difference Thresholds
    Sensory Adaptation

Sensing the World Around Us

As Isabel sat down to Thanksgiving dinner, her father carried the turkey in on a tray and placed it squarely in the center of the table. The noise level, already high from the talking and laughter of family members, grew louder still. As Isabel picked up her fork, the smell of the turkey reached her and she felt her stomach growl hungrily. The sight and sound of her family around the table, along with the smells and tastes of the holiday meal, made Isabel feel more relaxed than she had since starting school in the fall.

Put yourself in this setting and consider how different it might be if any one of your senses was not functioning. What if you were blind and unable to see the faces of your family or the welcome shape of the golden-brown turkey? What if you had no sense of hearing and could not listen to the conversations of family members, or if you were unable to feel your stomach growl, smell the dinner, or taste the food? Clearly, you would experience the dinner very differently from someone whose sensory apparatus was intact.

Moreover, the sensations mentioned here barely scratch the surface of sensory experience. Although perhaps you were taught, as I was, that there are just five senses—sight, sound, taste, smell, and touch—this enumeration is too modest. Human sensory capabilities go well beyond the basic five senses. It is well established, for example, that we are sensitive not merely to touch, but to a considerably wider set of stimuli—pain, pressure, temperature, and vibration, to name a few. In addition, vision has two subsystems—relating to day and night vision—and the ear is responsive to information that allows us not only to hear but also to keep our balance. Psychologists now believe there are at least a dozen distinct senses, all of which are interrelated.

To consider how psychologists understand the senses, and, more broadly, sensation and perception, we first need a basic working vocabulary. In formal terms, if any passing source of physical energy activates a sense organ, the energy is known as a stimulus. A **stimulus,** then, is energy that produces a response in a sense organ.

Stimuli vary in both type and intensity. Different types of stimuli activate different sense organs. For instance, we can differentiate light stimuli (which activate our sense of sight and allow us to see the colors of a tree in autumn) from sound stimuli (which, through our sense of hearing, permit us to hear the sounds of an orchestra).

Each sort of stimulus that is capable of activating a sense organ can also be considered in terms of its strength, or *intensity*. How intense a light stimulus needs to be before it is capable of being detected, or how much perfume a person must wear before it is noticed by others, are questions related to stimulus intensity.

The issue of how the intensity of a stimulus influences our sensory responses is considered in a branch of psychology known as psychophysics. **Psychophysics** is the study of the relationship between the physical aspects of stimuli and our psychological experience of them. Psychophysics played a central role in the development of the field of psychology, and many of the first psychologists studied issues related to psychophysics (Baird, 1997; Gescheider, 1997).

Absolute Thresholds: Detecting What's Out There

Just when does a stimulus become strong enough to be detected by our sense organs? The answer to this question requires an understanding of the concept of absolute threshold. An **absolute threshold** is the smallest intensity of a stimulus that must be present for it to be detected. Consider the following examples of absolute thresholds for the various senses (Galanter, 1962):

- *Sight:* A candle flame can be seen from 30 miles away on a dark, clear night.
- *Hearing:* The ticking of a watch can be heard 20 feet away under quiet conditions.
- *Taste:* Sugar can be tasted when 1 teaspoon is dissolved in 2 gallons of water.
- *Smell:* Perfume can be detected when one drop is present in a three-room apartment.
- *Touch:* A bee's wing falling from a distance of 1 centimeter can be felt on the cheek.

Such thresholds permit our sensory apparatus to detect a wide range of sensory stimulation. In fact, the capabilities of our senses are so fine-tuned that we might have problems if they were any more sensitive. For instance, if our ears were just slightly more acute, we would be able to hear the sound of air molecules in our ears knocking into our eardrum—a phenomenon that would surely prove distracting and might even prevent us from hearing sounds outside our bodies.

Of course, the absolute thresholds we have been discussing are measured under ideal conditions. Normally our senses cannot detect stimulation quite as well because of

stimulus: Energy that produces a response in a sense organ

psychophysics: The study of the relationship between the physical aspects of stimuli and our psychological experience of them

absolute threshold: The smallest intensity of a stimulus that must be present for the stimulus to be detected

 PsychLink

International Society for Psychophysics
www.mhhe.com/
feldmaness5–03links

Crowded conditions, sounds, and sights can all be considered as noise that interferes with sensation. Can you think of other examples of noise that is not auditory in nature?

the presence of noise. *Noise,* as defined by psychophysicists, is background stimulation that interferes with the perception of other stimuli. Hence, *noise* refers not just to auditory stimuli, the most obvious example, but also to stimuli that affect the other senses. Picture a talkative group of people crammed into a small, crowded, smoke-filled room at a party. The din of the crowd makes it hard to hear individual voices, and the smoke makes it difficult to see, or even taste, the food. In this case, the smoke and crowded conditions would both be considered "noise" because they are both preventing sensation at more discriminating levels.

Difference Thresholds: Noticing Distinctions Between Stimuli

Suppose you wanted to choose the six best apples from a supermarket display—the biggest, reddest, and sweetest apples. One approach would be to systematically compare one apple with another until you were left with a few so similar that you could not tell the difference between them. At that point, it wouldn't matter which ones you chose.

difference threshold: The smallest level of stimulation required to sense that a *change* in stimulation has occurred

just noticeable difference: The minimum stimulation required to detect the difference between two stimuli

Psychologists have discussed this comparison problem in terms of the **difference threshold,** the smallest level of stimulation required to sense that a *change* in stimulation has occurred. Put another way, the difference threshold is the minimum stimulation required to detect the difference between two stimuli, or a **just noticeable difference.**

The stimulus value that constitutes a just noticeable difference depends on the initial intensity of the stimulus. For instance, when the moon is visible during the late afternoon, it appears relatively dim—yet against a dark night sky, it seems quite bright.

Weber's law: One of the basic laws of psychophysics, that a just noticeable difference is in constant proportion to the intensity of an initial stimulus

The relationship between changes in the original value of a stimulus and the degree to which the change will be noticed forms one of the basic laws of psychophysics: Weber's law. **Weber's law** (with *Weber* pronounced "vay-ber") states that a just noticeable difference is a constant proportion of the intensity of an initial stimulus. For example, Weber found that the just noticeable difference for weight is 1:50. Consequently, it takes a 1-ounce increase in a 50-ounce weight to produce a noticeable difference, and it would take a 10-ounce increase to produce a noticeable difference if the initial weight were 500 ounces. In both cases, the same proportional increase is necessary to produce a just noticeable difference—1:50 = 10:500.

Sensory Adaptation: Turning Down Our Responses

You enter a bar, and the odor of cigarettes assaults you. A few minutes later, though, you barely notice the smell.

PsychLink

The fading dot
www.mhhe.com/
feldmaness5-03links

adaptation: An adjustment in sensory capacity following prolonged exposure to stimuli

The reason you acclimate to the odor is sensory adaptation. **Adaptation** is an adjustment in sensory capacity following prolonged exposure to stimuli. Adaptation occurs as people become accustomed to a stimulus and change their frame of reference. In a sense, our brains mentally turn down the volume of the stimulation they're experiencing.

One example of adaptation is the decrease in sensitivity that occurs after repeated exposure to a strong stimulus. If you were to hear a loud tone over and over again, eventually it would begin to sound softer. Similarly, although jumping into a cold lake might be temporarily unpleasant, eventually we probably will get used to the temperature.

This apparent decline in sensitivity to sensory stimuli is due to the inability of the sensory nerve receptors to constantly fire off messages to the brain. Because these receptor cells are most responsive to *changes* in stimulation, constant stimulation is not effective in producing a reaction.

Judgments of sensory stimuli are also affected by the context in which the judgments are made. This is because judgments are made, not in isolation from other stimuli, but in terms of preceding sensory experience.

Evaluate

1. _____ is the stimulation of the sense organs; _____ is the sorting out, interpretation, analysis, and integration of stimuli by our sense organs.
2. The term *absolute threshold* refers to the _____ intensity of a stimulus that must be present for the stimulus to be detected.
3. Weber discovered that in order for a difference between two stimuli to be perceptible, the stimuli must differ by at least a _____ proportion.
4. After completing a very difficult rock climb in the morning, Carmella found the afternoon climb unexpectedly easy. This case illustrates the phenomenon of _____.

Answers to Evaluate Questions

1. Sensation; perception 2. smallest 3. constant 4. adaptation

Rethink

1. Do you think it is possible to have sensation without perception? Is it possible to have perception without sensation?
2. Do you think sensory adaptation is essential for everyday psychological functioning?

Vision: Shedding Light on the Eye

If, as poets say, the eyes provide a window to the soul, they also provide us with a window to the world. Our visual capabilities permit us to admire and react to scenes ranging from the beauty of a sunset to the configuration of our lover's face to the words written on the pages of a book.

Vision starts with light, the physical energy that stimulates the eye. Light is a form of electromagnetic radiation waves, which, as shown in Figure 3-1, are measured in wavelengths. The sizes of wavelengths correspond to different types of energy. The range of wavelengths that humans are sensitive to—called the *visual spectrum*—is relatively small. Many nonhuman species have different capabilities. For instance, some reptiles and fish sense energies of longer wavelengths than humans do, and certain insects sense energies of shorter wavelengths than humans do.

Prepare

What basic processes underlie the sense of vision?
How do we see colors?

Organize

Vision
  Illuminating the Structure of the Eye
  Color Vision and Color Blindness

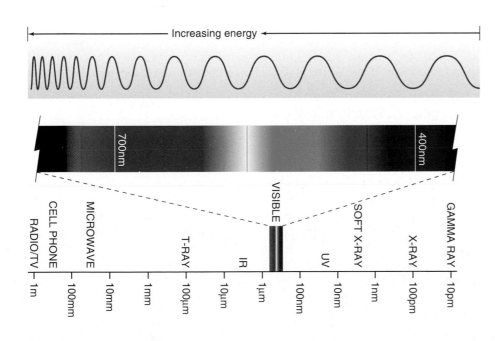

Figure 3-1 The visual spectrum—the range of wavelengths to which people are sensitive—is only a small part of the kinds of wavelengths present in our environment. Is it a benefit or disadvantage to our everyday lives that we aren't more sensitive to a broader range of visual stimuli? Why?

After R. Seeley, et al. Copyright © The McGraw-Hill Companies.

Figure 3-2 Although human vision is far more complicated than the most sophisticated camera, in some ways basic visual processes are analogous to those used in photography.

 PsychLink

Visual perception
www.mhhe.com/
feldmaness5-03links

Light waves coming from some object outside the body (imagine the light reflected off the flower in Figure 3-2) are sensed by the only organ that is capable of responding to the visual spectrum: the eye. Our eyes shape light into a form that can be used by the neurons that serve as messengers to the brain. The neurons themselves take up a relatively small percentage of the total eye. In other words, most of the eye is a mechanical device, analogous in many respects to a camera without film, as you can see in Figure 3-2.

Despite the similarities between the eye and a camera, vision involves processes that are far more complex and sophisticated than those of any camera. Furthermore, once the image reaches the neuronal receptors of the eye, the eye/camera analogy ends, for the processing of the visual image in the brain is more reflective of a computer than a camera.

Illuminating the Structure of the Eye

The ray of light we are tracing as it is reflected off the flower first travels through the *cornea,* a transparent, protective window. The cornea bends (or *refracts*) light as it passes through in order to more sharply focus it. After moving through the cornea, the light

Like the automatic lighting system on a camera, the human eye dilates to let in more light (left), and contracts to block out light (right). Can humans adjust their ears to let in more or less sound in a similar manner?

traverses the pupil. The *pupil* is a dark hole in the center of the *iris,* the colored part of the eye, which in humans ranges from a light blue to a dark brown. The size of the pupil opening depends on the amount of light in the environment. The dimmer the surroundings, the more the pupil opens in order to allow more light to enter.

Why shouldn't the pupil be opened completely all the time, thereby allowing the greatest amount of light into the eye? The answer relates to the basic physics of light. A small pupil greatly increases the range of distances at which objects are in focus. With a wide-open pupil, the range is relatively small, and details are harder to discern. The eye takes advantage of bright light by decreasing the size of the pupil and thereby becoming more discerning. In dim light the pupil expands to enable us to view the situation better—but at the expense of visual detail. (Perhaps one reason candlelight dinners are thought of as romantic is that the dim light prevents one from seeing the details of a partner's physical flaws.)

Once light passes through the pupil, it enters the *lens,* which is located directly behind the pupil. The lens acts to bend the rays of light so they are properly focused on the rear of the eye. The lens focuses light by changing its own thickness, a process called *accommodation.* The lens becomes flatter when viewing distant objects and rounder when looking at closer objects.

Reaching the Retina

Having traveled through the pupil and lens, our image of the flower finally reaches its ultimate destination in the eye—the **retina.** Here the electromagnetic energy of light is converted into the neural codes used by the brain. It is important to note that because of the physical properties of light, the image has reversed itself in traveling through the lens, and it reaches the retina upside down (relative to its original position). Although it might seem that this reversal would cause difficulties in understanding and moving about the world, this is not the case. The brain interprets the image in terms of its original position.

The retina consists of a thin layer of nerve cells at the back of the eyeball (see Figure 3-3). There are two kinds of light-sensitive receptor cells found in the retina. The names they have been given describe their shapes: rods and cones. **Rods** are thin, cylindrical receptor cells highly sensitive to light. **Cones** are cone-shaped, light-sensitive receptor cells that are responsible for sharp focus and color perception, particularly in

retina: The part of the eye that converts the electromagnetic energy of light into useful information for the brain

rods: Thin, cylindrical receptor cells in the retina that are highly sensitive to light
cones: Cone-shaped, light-sensitive receptor cells in the retina that are responsible for sharp focus and color perception, particularly in bright light

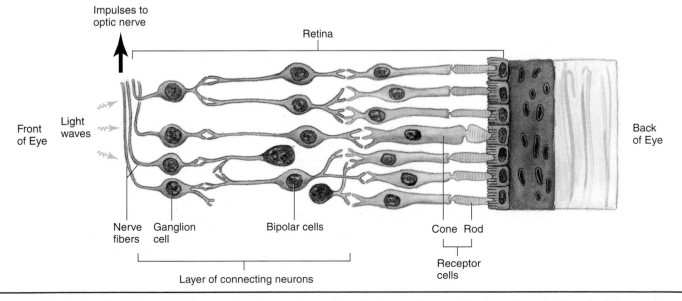

Figure 3-3 The basic cells of the eye. Light entering the eye travels through the ganglion and bipolar cells and strikes the light-sensitive rods and cones located at the back of the eye. The rods and cones then transmit nerve impulses to the brain via the bipolar and ganglion cells.
After D. Shier, et al. Copyright © The McGraw-Hill Companies.

bright light. The rods and cones are distributed unevenly throughout the retina. The greatest concentration of cones is on the part of the retina called the *fovea* (refer back to Figure 3-2). The fovea is a particularly sensitive region of the retina. If you want to focus in on something of particular interest, you will automatically try to center the image from the lens onto the area of the fovea to see it more sharply.

The density of cones declines just outside the fovea, although cones are found throughout the retina in lower concentrations. On the other hand, there are no rods in the very center of the fovea, but the density is greatest outside the fovea and then gradually declines toward the edges of the retina. Because the fovea covers only a small portion of the eye, there are fewer cones (about 7 million) than there are rods (about 125 million).

The rods and cones are not only structurally dissimilar, but they play distinctly different roles in vision. Cones are primarily responsible for the sharply focused perception of color, particularly in brightly lit situations; rods are related to vision in dimly lit situations and are largely insensitive to color and to details as sharp as those the cones are capable of recognizing. The rods play a key role in *peripheral vision*—seeing objects that are outside the main center of focus—and in night vision.

Rods and cones also are involved in *dark adaptation*, the phenomenon of adjusting to dim light after being in brighter light. (Think of the experience of walking into a dark movie theater and groping your way to a seat, but a few minutes later seeing the seats quite clearly.) The speed at which dark adaptation occurs is a result of the rate of change in the chemical composition of the rods and cones. Although the cones reach their greatest level of adaptation in just a few minutes, the rods take 15 minutes to reach the maximum level. The opposite phenomenon—*light adaptation*, or the process of adjusting to bright light after exposure to dim light—occurs much faster, taking only a minute or so.

The distinctive abilities of rods and cones make the eye analogous to a camera that is loaded with two kinds of film. One type is a highly sensitive black-and-white film (the rods). The other type is a somewhat less sensitive color film (the cones).

Sending the Message from the Eye to the Brain

When light energy strikes the rods and cones, it starts a chain of events that transforms light into neural impulses that can be communicated to the brain. Even before the neural message reaches the brain, however, some initial coding of the visual information takes place.

What happens when light energy strikes the retina depends in part on whether it encounters a rod or a cone. Rods contain *rhodopsin,* a complex, reddish-purple substance whose composition changes chemically when energized by light. The substance found in cone receptors is different, but the principles are similar. Stimulation of the nerve cells in the eye triggers a neural response that is transmitted to other nerve cells, called *bipolar cells* and *ganglion cells,* leading to the brain.

Bipolar cells receive information directly from the rods and cones. This information is then communicated to the ganglion cells. Ganglion cells collect and summarize visual information, which is gathered and moved out of the back of the eyeball through a bundle of ganglion axons called the **optic nerve.**

Because the opening for the optic nerve passes through the retina, there are no rods or cones in the area, which creates a blind spot. Normally, however, this absence of nerve cells does not interfere with vision, because you automatically compensate for the missing part of your field of vision (Ramachandran, 1995; Churchland & Ramachandran, 1995). (To find your blind spot, see Figure 3-4.)

Once beyond the eye itself, the neural signals relating to the image move through the optic nerve. As the optic nerve leaves the eyeball, its path does not take the most direct route to the part of the brain right behind the eye. Instead, the optic nerves from each eye meet at a point roughly between the two eyes—called the *optic chiasm*—where each optic nerve then splits.

optic nerve: A bundle of ganglion axons that carry visual information

PsychLink

Anatomy of the eye
www.mhhe.com/
feldmaness5-03links

Figure 3-4 To find your blind spot, close your right eye and look at the haunted house with your left eye. You will see the ghost on the periphery of your vision. Now, while staring at the house, move the page toward you. When the book is about a foot from your eye, the ghost will disappear. At this moment, the image of the ghost is falling on your blind spot.

But also notice how, when the page is at that distance, not only does the ghost seem to disappear, but the line seems to run continuously through the area where the ghost used to be. This shows how we automatically compensate for missing information by using nearby material to complete what is unseen. That's the reason you never notice the blind spot. What is missing is replaced by what is seen next to the blind spot. Can you think of any advantages that this tendency to provide missing information gives humans as a species?

When the optic nerves split, the nerve impulses coming from the right half of each retina are sent to the right side of the brain, and the impulses arriving from the left half of each retina are sent to the left side of the brain. Because the image on the retinas is reversed and upside down, however, those images coming from the right half of each retina actually originated in the field of vision to the person's left, and images coming from the left half of each retina originated in the field of vision to the person's right (see Figure 3-5). In this way, our nervous system ultimately produces the phenomenon introduced in Chapter 2, in which each half of the brain is associated with the functioning of the opposite side of the body.

Processing the Visual Message

By the time a visual message reaches the brain, it has passed through several stages of processing. One of the initial sites is the ganglion cells. Each ganglion cell gathers information from a group of rods and cones in a particular area of the eye and compares the amount of light entering the center of that area with the amount of light in the area around it. Some ganglion cells are activated by light in the center (and darkness in the surrounding area). Other ganglion cells are activated when there is darkness in the center and light in the surrounding areas. The ultimate effect of this process is to maximize the detection of variations in light and darkness. The neural image that is passed on to the brain, then, is an enhanced version of the actual visual stimulus outside the body.

The ultimate processing of visual images takes place in the visual cortex of the brain, and it is here that the most complex kinds of processing occur. Psychologists David Hubel and Torsten Wiesel won the Nobel Prize for their discovery that many neurons in the cortex are extraordinarily specialized, being activated only by visual stimuli of a particular shape or pattern—a process known as **feature detection.** They found that some cells are activated only by lines of a particular width, shape, or orientation. Other cells are activated only by moving, as opposed to stationary, stimuli (Hubel & Wiesel, 1979; Patzwahl, Zanker, & Altenmuller, 1994).

More recent work has added to our knowledge of the complex ways in which visual information coming from individual neurons is combined and processed. Different parts of the brain seem to process nerve impulses in several individual systems simultaneously. For instance, one system relates to shapes, one to colors, and others to movement, location, and depth (Moutoussis & Zeki, 1997).

If separate neural systems exist for processing information about specific aspects of the visual world, how are all these data integrated by the brain? Although the exact process is not yet well understood, it seems likely that the brain makes use of information

feature detection: The activation of neurons in the cortex by visual stimuli of specific shapes or patterns

optic tract

optic chiasm

optic nerve

primary visual area
of cerebral cortex

right visual field

left visual field

Figure 3-5 Because the optic nerve coming from each eye splits at the optic chiasm, the image to a person's right is sent to the left side of the brain, and the image to the person's left is transmitted to the right side of the brain.

After S. S. Mader. Copyright © The McGraw-Hill Companies.

regarding the frequency, rhythm, and timing of the firing of particular sets of neural cells. Furthermore, it appears that the brain's integration of visual information does not occur in any single step or location in the brain, but instead is a process that occurs on several levels simultaneously. The ultimate outcome, though, is indisputable: a vision of the world around us (Macaluso, Frith, & Driver, 2000; deGelder, 2000).

 PsychLink

Explanation of color blindness
www.mhhe.com/
feldmaness5-03links

Color Vision and Color Blindness: The Seven-Million-Color Spectrum

Although the range of wavelengths to which humans are sensitive is relatively narrow, at least in comparison with the entire electromagnetic spectrum, the portion to which we are capable of responding still allows us great flexibility in sensing the world. Nowhere is this clearer than in terms of the number of colors we can discern. A person with normal color vision is capable of distinguishing no less than seven million different colors (Bruce, Green, & Georgeson, 1997).

Although the variety of colors that people are generally able to distinguish is vast, there are certain individuals whose ability to perceive color is quite limited—the color-blind. Interestingly, the condition of these individuals has provided some of the most important clues for understanding how color vision operates (Neitz, Neitz, & Kainz, 1996).

Before continuing, though, look at the photos shown in Figure 3-6. If you have difficulty seeing the differences among the series of photos, you may well be one of the 1 in 50 men or 1 in 5,000 women who are color-blind.

a.   b.   c.

Figure 3.6 *(a)* To someone with normal vision, these hot-air balloons appear like this. *(b)* A person with red-green color blindness would see the scene like this, in hues of blue and yellow. *(c)* A person who is blue-yellow blind, conversely, would see it in hues of red and green.

For most people with color-blindness, the world looks quite dull. Red fire engines appear yellow, green grass seems yellow, and the three colors of a traffic light all look yellow. In fact, in the most common form of color blindness, all red and green objects are seen as yellow. There are other forms of color blindness as well, but they are quite rare. In yellow blue blindness, people are unable to tell the difference between yellow and blue, and in the most extreme case an individual perceives no color at all. To such a person the world looks something like the picture on a black-and-white television set.

To understand why some of us are color-blind, it is necessary to consider the basics of color vision. There appear to be two processes involved. The first process is explained by the **trichromatic theory of color vision.** This theory suggests that there are three kinds of cones in the retina, each of which responds primarily to a specific range of wavelengths. One is most responsive to blue-violet colors, one to green, and the third to yellow-red (Brown & Wald, 1964). According to trichromatic theory, perception of color is influenced by the relative strength with which each of the three kinds of cones is activated. If we see a blue sky, the blue-violet cones are primarily triggered, and the others show less activity. The trichromatic theory provides a straightforward explanation of color-blindness. It suggests that one of the three cone systems malfunctions, and colors covered by that range are perceived improperly (Nathans et al., 1989).

However, there are phenomena that the trichromatic theory is less successful at explaining. For example, the theory does not explain what happens after you stare at something like the flag shown in Figure 3-7 for about a minute. Try this yourself, and then look at a blank white page: You'll see an image of the traditional red, white, and blue U.S. flag. Where there was yellow, you'll see blue, and where there were green and black, you'll see red and white.

The phenomenon you have just experienced is called an *afterimage*. It occurs because activity in the retina continues even when you are no longer staring at the original picture. However, it also demonstrates that the trichromatic theory does not explain color vision completely. Why should the colors in the afterimage be different from those in the original?

Because trichromatic processes do not provide a full explanation of color vision, alternative explanations have been proposed. According to the **opponent-process theory of color vision,** receptor cells are linked in pairs, working in opposition to each other. Specifically, there is a blue-yellow pairing, a red-green pairing, and a black-

trichromatic theory of color vision: The theory that there are three kinds of cones in the retina, each of which responds primarily to a specific range of wavelengths

opponent-process theory of color vision: The theory that receptor cells are linked in pairs, working in opposition to each other

Figure 3-7 Stare at the dot in this flag for about a minute, and then look at a piece of plain white paper. What do you see? Most people see an afterimage that converts the colors in the figure into the traditional red, white, and blue U.S. flag. If you have trouble seeing it the first time, blink once and try again.

white pairing. If an object reflects light that contains more blue than yellow, it will stimulate the firing of the cells sensitive to blue, simultaneously discouraging or inhibiting the firing of receptor cells sensitive to yellow—and the object will appear blue. If, on the other hand, a light contains more yellow than blue, the cells that respond to yellow will be stimulated to fire while the blue ones are inhibited, and the object will appear yellow.

The opponent-process theory provides a good explanation for afterimages. When we stare at the yellow in the figure, for instance, our receptor cells for the yellow component of the yellow-blue pairing become fatigued and are less able to respond to yellow stimuli. On the other hand, the receptor cells for the blue part of the pair are not tired, because they are not being stimulated. When we look at a white surface, the light reflected off it would normally stimulate both the yellow and the blue receptors equally. But the fatigue of the yellow receptors prevents this from happening. They temporarily do not respond to the yellow, which makes the white light appear to be blue. Because the other colors in the figure do the same thing relative to their specific opponents, the afterimage produces the opponent colors—for a while. The afterimage lasts only a short time, because the fatigue of the yellow receptors is soon overcome, and the white light begins to be perceived more accurately.

Both opponent processes and trichromatic mechanisms are at work in allowing us to see color. However, they operate in different parts of the visual sensing system. Trichromatic processes work within the retina itself, whereas opponent mechanisms operate both in the retina and at later stages of neuronal processing (Leibovic, 1990; Gouras, 1991; de Valois & de Valois, 1993).

As we have gained more understanding of the processes that permit us to see, some psychologists have begun to develop new techniques to help overcome visual deficiencies in people with serious problems such as visual impairment or total blindness. One of the most promising devices is discussed in the *Applying Psychology in the 21st Century* box.

Applying Psychology in the 21st Century

Bringing Sight to People with Blindness

At first sight, it looks like an off-center ponytail flopping at the back of the head of a 62-year-old man named Jerry. But a closer look reveals that it is actually a bundle of wires entering Jerry's skull.

The purpose of the wires is to link a computer directly into Jerry's brain. The computer responds to a tiny pinhole camera mounted on one lens of a pair of sunglasses Jerry is wearing, along with an ultrasonic rangefinder mounted on the other lens. The camera and rangefinder send minute electrical charges through 68 electrodes implanted in a small area of the surface of Jerry's brain, allowing Jerry to perceive specks of light.

Admittedly, the kind of vision Jerry experiences is greatly limited. He is able to locate a mannequin in a room, find a black cap that is hanging on a wall, and place it on the head of the mannequin. He can also recognize two-inch-tall letters from five feet away.

Jerry (whose last name has not been divulged) is using an experimental device that may someday bring close to normal vision to people with blindness. Although in its current version the device permits Jerry to see only specks of flickering light, it is still sophisticated enough to permit him to perceive differences between light and dark areas (Dobelle, 2000).

Technological advances are providing other approaches to helping the blind. For instance, sensory perception psychologist Jack Loomis and colleagues are developing what they call a "personal guidance system" to help people with vision limitations move through their environment (Loomis et al., 1993; Golledge et al., 1998; Loomis, Golledge, & Klatzky, in press).

The system uses a positioning device linked to navigation satellites overhead that are able to map the ground with an accuracy of several feet. Geographic information from the satellites is

Jerry, a 62-year-old man with blindness, is able to see as the result of electrodes implanted in his brain and connected to a camera mounted on a pair of glasses. A small computer on his hip permits him to read large letters and move around large objects in a room. Do you think modern technology will ever duplicate the functions of the human eye?

transmitted to an on-ground receiver and computer strapped to a person's back. The computer translates the geographic information into acoustic stimulation that is sent to one earphone or the other. The stimulation, which for now is just a code word, becomes softer or louder, depending on the direction the person is supposed to turn.

Klatzky and Loomis predict that future versions will go beyond a single code word to provide complete verbal directions, such as "go forward ten feet, and then turn to the right." In addition, the computer will identify landmarks the person is passing by ("I'm the post office, and I'm 20 feet to your left"). Furthermore, the size of the backpack should shrink significantly, perhaps fitting into a pack around the waist.

Researchers predict that devices such as Jerry's electrodes and the personal guidance system will be commercially available within the next few years. Next on the horizon are electronic retinal implants, a kind of bionic eye, that will restore sight to people with damaged retinas. Some experts feel that such devices can be developed well before the end of the decade (Marcus, 1998; Eisenberg, 1999; Dobelle, 2000).

What psychological adjustments might be necessary when sight is restored for people who have been blind for their entire lives? Can you think of any disadvantages of the restoration of sight and why some blind individuals might decide not to have their sight restored?

How are we able to perceive the world in three dimensions when our retinas are capable of sensing only two-dimensional images?

- Depth perception is the ability to perceive distance and to view the world in three dimensions, even though the images projected on our retinas are two-dimensional. We are able to judge depth and distance as a result of binocular disparity and monocular cues, such as motion parallax, the relative size of images on the retina, and linear perspective. (p. 104)
- Motion perception depends on several cues. They include the perceived movement of an object across our retina and information about how the head and eyes are moving. (p. 105)

What clues do visual illusions give us about our understanding of general perceptual mechanisms?

- Visual illusions are physical stimuli that consistently produce errors in perception, causing judgments that do not accurately reflect the physical reality of the stimulus. One of the best-known illusions is the Müller-Lyer illusion. (p. 105)
- Visual illusions are usually the result of errors in the brain's interpretation of visual stimuli. Furthermore, culture clearly affects how we perceive the world. (p. 106)
- Subliminal perception refers to the perception of messages about which we have no awareness. The reality of the phenomenon, as well as of ESP, is open to question and debate. (p. 108)

Key Terms and Concepts

sensation (p. 76)	sound (p. 88)
perception (p. 76)	eardrum (p. 89)
stimulus (p. 77)	cochlea (p. 89)
psychophysics (p. 77)	basilar membrane (p. 89)
absolute threshold (p. 77)	hair cells (p. 89)
difference threshold (p. 78)	place theory of hearing (p. 91)
just noticeable difference (p. 78)	frequency theory of hearing (p. 92)
Weber's law (p. 78)	semicircular canals (p. 93)
adaptation (p. 78)	otoliths (p. 93)
retina (p. 81)	skin senses (p. 95)
rods (p. 81)	gate-control theory of pain (p. 96)
cones (p. 81)	gestalt laws of organization (p. 98)
optic nerve (p. 82)	feature analysis (p. 100)
feature detection (p. 83)	top-down processing (p. 102)
trichromatic theory of color vision (p. 85)	bottom-up processing (p. 103)
opponent-process theory of color vision (p. 85)	visual illusions (p. 105)

Psychology on the Web

1. Select one topic of personal interest to you that was mentioned in this chapter (e.g., psi, cochlear implants, visual/optical illusions). Find one "serious" or scientific website and one "popular" or commercial website with information about your chosen topic. Compare the type, level, and reliability of the information that you find on each site. Write a summary of your findings.
2. Are there more gestalt laws of organization than the four discussed in this chapter (i.e., closure, proximity, similarity, and simplicity)? Find the answer to this question on the Web and write a summary of any additional gestalt laws you find.

Epilogue

In this chapter we have noted the important distinction between sensation and perception, and we have examined the processes that underlie both of them. We've seen how external stimuli evoke sensory responses, and how our different senses process the information contained in those responses. We also have focused on the physical structure and internal workings of the individual senses, including vision, hearing, balance, smell, taste, and the skin senses, and we've explored how our brains organize and process sensory information to construct a consistent, integrated picture of the world around us.

Before we proceed to a discussion of consciousness in the next chapter, let's return to the opening prologue of this chapter. Consider the story of Amy Ecklund and answer the following questions, using your knowledge of sensation and perception.

1. What do you think happens when a formerly deaf person such as Amy Ecklund first hears a sound that is new to her, like the "chirping" of a modern cell telephone? What differences would there be in her *sensation* of the sound and her *perception* of it?
2. Do you think that Ecklund's cochlear implant is capable of sensory adaptation—a decrease in sensitivity after repeated exposure to a strong stimulus? If it is not, how would this affect her experience of the world?
3. Do you think Ecklund will gradually lose her ability to read lips? Will she necessarily lose her sense of belonging in the culture of the deaf? What disadvantages would this have for her?

Preview

For additional quizzing and a variety of interactive resources, visit the *Essentials of Understanding Psychology* Online Learning Center at

www.mhhe.com/feldmaness5

Chapter Four

States of Consciousness

Prologue

A Deadly Binge

Scott Krueger

The Massachusetts Institute of Technology is known as a demanding school, and Scott Krueger was ready for it. He had graduated near the top of his high-school class in upstate New York, and no one doubted that he could balance his freshman engineering classes with early-morning crew practice. But in Boston, there is another side to MIT: its 30 fraternities are a magnet for whiz kids who like to party.

Scott Krueger wasn't ready for that. During a Greek Week celebration, the Phi Gamma Delta pledge passed out after downing the equivalent of 16 shots in an hour. His frat brothers carried him back to his basement room in their stately Boston mansion, then noticed he wasn't breathing well. Rescue workers found Krueger comatose. His blood-alcohol level was a staggering .41; the state's legal driving limit is .08. Either Krueger's blood got so thick from alcohol that the oxygen wasn't able to reach his brain or he choked on his own vomit. Days later, his anguished parents took their son off life support (Rosenberg & Bai, 1997, p. 69).

Looking Ahead

 PsychLink

Information on consciousness
www.mhhe.com/
feldmaness5-04links

Binge drinking—defined as five drinks in a row for men, and four for women—is commonplace on college campuses. Although most binge drinkers are luckier than Krueger, all put themselves at serious risk. In fact, each year thousands of people die from complications of alcohol and drug overdoses, and many more are addicted to various kinds of drugs.

What leads people to use alcohol and other types of drugs to alter their normal states of consciousness? More generally, what *is* consciousness, and how does normal waking consciousness relate to states of consciousness such as sleep, hypnotic trances, or drug-induced experiences? In this chapter, we consider these questions.

Consciousness is the awareness of the sensations, thoughts, and feelings being experienced at a given moment. Consciousness is our subjective understanding of both the environment around us and our private internal world, unobservable to outsiders.

Consciousness is generally divided into two broad states: waking consciousness and altered states of consciousness, although the boundary between the two types is not always clear. In *waking consciousness,* we are awake and aware of our thoughts, emotions, and perceptions. In more active states of waking consciousness, we systematically carry out mental activity, focusing our thoughts and absorbing the world around us. In more passive states of waking consciousness, thoughts and images come to us more spontaneously; we might drift from one thought to another (Velmans, 2000).

When we enter an *altered state of consciousness,* our mental state differs significantly from waking consciousness. Some altered states of consciousness, such as sleeping and dreaming, occur naturally. Others, such as those induced by drug use or hypnosis, are triggered by deliberate attempts to alter one's state of consciousness.

Because consciousness is so personal a phenomenon, psychologists have sometimes been reluctant to study it. After all, who can say that your consciousness is similar to or, for that matter, different from anyone else's? In fact, early psychologists suggested that the study of consciousness was out of bounds for the discipline. They argued that because consciousness could be understood only by relying on the "unscientific" introspections of experimental participants about what they were experiencing at a given moment, its study was best left to disciplines such as philosophy.

However, contemporary psychologists reject the view that the study of consciousness is unsuitable for the field of psychology. Instead, they argue that several approaches permit the scientific study of consciousness. For example, biopsychologists can measure brain-wave patterns under conditions of consciousness ranging from sleep to waking to hypnotic trances. Moreover, new understanding of the chemistry of drugs such as marijuana and alcohol has provided insights into the way they produce their pleasurable—as well as adverse—effects (Shear, 1997; Damasio, 1999; Sommerhof, 2000).

Another impetus for the study of consciousness is the realization that people in many different cultures routinely seek ways to alter their states of consciousness. Across a variety of cultures, variations in states of consciousness share some basic characteristics (Ludwig, 1969; Martindale, 1981). One is an alteration in thinking, which may become shallow, illogical, or otherwise different from normal. In addition, people's sense of time can become disturbed, and their perceptions of the world and of themselves might be changed. They might experience a loss of self-control. Finally, they might feel a sense of *ineffability*—the inability to understand an experience rationally or describe it in words.

This chapter considers several states of consciousness, beginning with two that we have all experienced: sleeping and dreaming. Next, we turn to states of consciousness found under conditions of hypnosis and meditation. Finally, we examine drug-induced states of consciousness.

Sleep and Dreams

The crowd roared as running back Donald Dorff, age 67, took the pitch from his quarterback and accelerated smoothly across the artificial turf. As Dorff braked and pivoted to cut back over a tackle, a huge defensive lineman loomed in his path. One hundred twenty pounds of pluck, Dorff did not hesitate. But let the retired grocery merchandiser from Golden Valley, Minnesota, tell it:

"There was a 280-pound tackle waiting for me, so I decided to give him my shoulder. When I came to, I was on the floor in my bedroom. I had smashed into the dresser and knocked everything off it and broke the mirror and just made one heck of a mess. It was 1:30 A.M." (Long, 1987, p. 787)

Dorff, it turned out, was suffering from a rare condition (called *REM sleep behavior disorder*) where the mechanism that usually shuts down bodily movement during dreams does not function properly. People with the malady have been known to hit others, smash windows, punch holes in walls—all while fast asleep.

Luckily, Dorff's problem had a happy ending. With the help of clonazepam, a drug that suppresses movement during dreams, his malady vanished, permitting him to sleep through the night undisturbed.

Despite the success of Dorff's treatment, many unanswered questions about sleep remain, along with a considerable number of myths. (Try testing your own knowledge of sleep and dreams by answering the questions in the sleep quiz below.)

Prepare

What are the different states of consciousness?

What happens when we sleep, and what are the meaning and function of dreams?

What are the major sleep disorders and how can they be treated?

How much do we daydream?

Organize

Sleep and Dreams
  The Stages of Sleep
  REM Sleep
  Why Do We Sleep, and How Much Sleep Is Necessary?
  The Function and Meaning of Dreaming
  Sleep Disturbances
  Circadian Rhythms
  Daydreams

SLEEP QUIZ

Although sleeping is something we all do for a significant part of our lives, myths and misconceptions about the topic abound. To test your own knowledge of sleep and dreams, try answering the following questions before reading further.

_____ 1. Some people never dream. *True or false?*

_____ 2. Most dreams are caused by bodily sensations such as an upset stomach. *True or false?*

_____ 3. It has been proved that people need eight hours of sleep to maintain mental health. *True or false?*

_____ 4. When people do not recall their dreams, it is probably because they are secretly trying to forget them. *True or false?*

_____ 5. Depriving someone of sleep will invariably cause the individual to become mentally imbalanced. *True or false?*

_____ 6. If we lose some sleep, we will eventually make up all the lost sleep the next night or another night. *True or false?*

_____ 7. No one has been able to go for more than 48 hours without sleep. *True or false?*

_____ 8. Everyone is able to sleep and breathe at the same time. *True or false?*

_____ 9. Sleep enables the brain to rest, because little brain activity takes place during sleep. *True or false?*

_____ 10. Drugs have been proved to provide a long-term cure for sleeping difficulties. *True or false?*

Scoring: This is an easy set of questions to score, for every item is false. But don't lose any sleep if you missed them; they were chosen to represent the most common myths regarding sleep.

The Stages of Sleep

Most of us consider sleep a time of tranquility, as we set aside the tensions of the day and spend the night in uneventful slumber. However, a closer look at sleep shows that a good deal of activity occurs throughout the night, and that what at first appears to be a unitary state is, in fact, quite diverse.

Much of our knowledge of what happens during sleep comes from the *electro-encephalogram,* or *EEG,* a measurement of electrical activity within the brain (see Chapter 2). When probes from an EEG machine are attached to the surface of a sleeping person's scalp and face, it becomes clear that the brain is active throughout the night. It produces electrical discharges with systematic, wavelike patterns that change in height (or amplitude) and speed (or frequency) in regular sequences. Instruments that measure muscle and eye movements also reveal a good deal of physical activity.

People progress through four distinct stages of sleep during a night's rest, moving through the stages in cycles lasting about 90 minutes. Each of these four sleep stages is associated with a unique pattern of brain waves, as shown in Figure 4-1. Moreover, there are specific biological indicators of dreaming.

When people first go to sleep, they move from a waking state in which they are relaxed with their eyes closed into **stage 1 sleep,** which is characterized by relatively rapid, low-voltage brain waves. This is actually a stage of transition between wakefulness and sleep. During stage 1, images sometimes appear, as if we were viewing still photos. However, true dreaming does not occur during the initial entry into this stage, although it does happen during subsequent periods of stage 1 sleep that occur later in the night.

As sleep becomes deeper, people enter **stage 2 sleep,** which is characterized by a slower, more regular wave pattern. However, there are also momentary interruptions of sharply pointed, spiky waves that are called *sleep spindles* because of their configuration. It becomes increasingly difficult to awaken a person from stage 2 sleep, which makes up about half of the total sleep of those in their early twenties.

As people drift into **stage 3 sleep,** the next stage of sleep, the brain waves become slower, with higher peaks and lower valleys in the wave pattern. By the time sleepers arrive at **stage 4 sleep,** the pattern is even slower and more regular, and people are least responsive to outside stimulation.

stage 1 sleep: The state of transition between wakefulness and sleep, characterized by relatively rapid, low-voltage brain waves

stage 2 sleep: A sleep deeper than that of stage 1, characterized by a slower, more regular wave pattern, along with momentary interruptions of "sleep spindles"

stage 3 sleep: A sleep characterized by slow brain waves, with greater peaks and valleys in the wave pattern

stage 4 sleep: The deepest stage of sleep, during which we are least responsive to outside stimulation

Figure 4–1 Brain-wave patterns (measured by an EEG apparatus) vary significantly during the different stages of sleep (Hobson, 1989). As sleep moves from stage 1 through stage 4, brain waves become slower.

People progress through four distinct stages of sleep during a night's rest spread over cycles lasting about 90 minutes. REM sleep, which occupies only 20 percent of adults' sleeping time, occurs in stage 1 sleep. These photos, taken at different times of night, show the synchronized patterns of a couple accustomed to sleeping in the same bed.

As you can see in Figure 4-2, stage 4 sleep is most likely to occur during the early part of the night. In the first half of the night, our sleep is dominated by stages 3 and 4. The last half is characterized by lighter stages of sleep—as well as the phase of sleep during which dreams occur, as we discuss next (Dement & Wolpert, 1958). In addition to passing through regular transitions between stages of sleep, then, people tend to sleep less and less deeply over the course of the night.

REM Sleep: The Paradox of Sleep

Several times a night, while sleepers are in stage 1 sleep, something curious happens. Their heart rate increases and becomes irregular, their blood pressure rises, their breathing rate increases, and males—even male infants—have erections. Most characteristic of this period is the back-and-forth movement of their eyes, as if they were watching an action-filled movie. This period of sleep is called **rapid eye movement, or REM, sleep,** and contrasts with stages 1 through 4, which are grouped together under the label of *non-REM* (or *NREM*) sleep. REM sleep occupies a little over 20 percent of adults' total sleeping time.

rapid eye movement (REM) sleep: Sleep occupying 20 percent of an adult's sleeping time, characterized by increased heart rate, blood pressure, and breathing rate; erections; eye movements; and the experience of dreaming

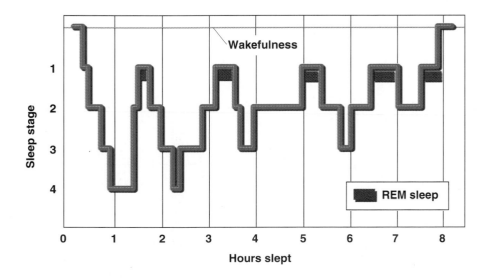

Figure 4-2 During the night, the typical sleeper passes through all four stages of sleep and several REM periods.

From E. Hartman, *The Biology of Dreaming*, 1967. Courtesy of Charles C Thomas, Publisher, Ltd., Springfield, Illinois.

Paradoxically, while all this activity is occurring, the major muscles of the body appear to be paralyzed—except in rare cases such as Donald Dorff's. In addition, REM sleep is usually accompanied by dreams, which—whether or not people remember them—are experienced by *everyone* during some part of the night.

One possible explanation for rapid eye movements is that the eyes follow the action that is occurring in the dream (Dement, 1979; Kelly, 1991). For instance, people who have reported dreaming about watching a tennis match just before they were awakened showed regular right-left-right eye movements, as if they were observing the ball flying back and forth across the net.

There is good reason to believe that REM sleep plays an important role in everyday human functioning. People deprived of REM sleep—by being awakened every time they begin to display the physiological signs of the stage—show a *rebound effect* when allowed to rest undisturbed. With this rebound effect, REM-deprived sleepers spend significantly more time in REM sleep than they normally would. It is as if the body requires a certain amount of REM sleep in order to function properly.

Why Do We Sleep, and How Much Sleep Is Necessary?

Sleep is a requirement for normal human functioning, although, surprisingly, we don't know exactly why. It is reasonable to expect that our bodies would require a tranquil "rest and relaxation" period in order to revitalize themselves, and experiments with rats show that total sleep deprivation results in death. Some researchers, using an evolutionary perspective, suggest that sleep permitted our ancestors to conserve energy at night, a time when food was relatively hard to come by. Still, this explanation is speculative, and although we know that *some* sleep is necessary, we don't fully know why we must sleep (Webb, 1992; Porkka-Heiskanen et al., 1997).

Scientists have been unable to establish just how much sleep is absolutely required. For instance, today most people sleep seven to eight hours each night, but they sleep three hours a night *less* than people did a hundred years ago. In addition, there is wide variability among individuals, with some people needing as little as three hours. Sleep requirements also vary over the course of a lifetime: As they age, people generally need less and less sleep (see Figures 4-3 and 4-4).

People who participate in sleep deprivation experiments, in which they are kept awake for stretches as long as 200 hours, show no lasting effects. It's no fun—they feel weary and irritable, can't concentrate, and show a loss of creativity, even after only minor deprivation. They also show a decline in logical reasoning ability. However, after being allowed to sleep normally, they bounce back quickly and are able to

PsychLink

Basics of sleep behavior
www.mhhe.com/
feldmaness5-04links

Figure 4-3 Although most people report sleeping between eight and nine hours per night, the amount varies a great deal (Borbely, 1996). Where would you place yourself on this graph, and why do you think you need more or less sleep than others?

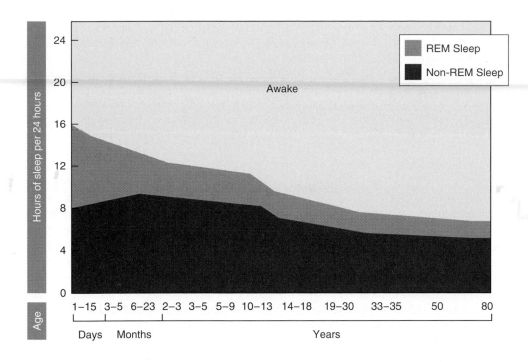

Figure 4-4 Over the course of their life span, people sleep less (Roffwarg, Muzio, & Dement, 1996). In addition, the proportion of REM sleep increases.

Reprinted with permission from H. P. Roffwarg, J. N. Munzio and W. C. Dement, "Ontogenci Development of the Human Sleep-Dream Cycle," *Science*, 152, pp. 604–619, 1966. Copyright © 1966 American Association for the Advancement of Science.

PsychLink

Comprehensive information on dreams
www.mhhe.com/feldmaness5-04links

perform at predeprivation levels after just a few days (Dement, 1976; Webb, 1992; Dinges et al., 1997).

Those of us who worry, then, that long hours of study, work, or perhaps partying are ruining our health should feel heartened. As far as anyone can tell, most people suffer no permanent consequences of such temporary sleep deprivation. At the same time, though, a lack of sleep can make us feel edgy, slow our reaction time, and lower our performance on academic tasks. In addition, we put ourselves, and others, at risk when we carry out routine activities, such as driving, when we're very sleepy.

The Function and Meaning of Dreaming

I was sitting at my desk when I remembered that this was the day of my chemistry final! I was terrified, because I hadn't studied a bit for it. In fact, I had missed every lecture all semester. In a panic, I began running across campus desperately searching for the classroom, to which I'd never been. It was hopeless; I knew I was going to fail and flunk out of college.

If you have had a similar dream—a surprisingly common dream among people involved in academic pursuits—you know how utterly convincing are the panic and fear that the events in the dream can bring about. *Nightmares,* unusually frightening dreams, occur fairly often. In one survey, almost half of a group of college students who kept records of their dreams over a two-week period reported having at least one nightmare. This works out to some twenty-four nightmares per person each year, on average (Wood & Bootzin, 1990; Berquier & Ashton, 1992; Tan & Hicks, 1995).

On the other hand, most of the 150,000 dreams the average person experiences by the age of 70 are much less dramatic (Snyder, 1970; Webb, 1992). They typically encompass such everyday events as going to the supermarket, working at the office, or preparing a meal. Students dream about going to class; professors dream about lecturing. Dental patients dream of getting their teeth

THE FAR SIDE BY GARY LARSON

"I've got it again, Larry ... an eerie feeling like there's something on top of the bed."

drilled; dentists dream of drilling the wrong tooth. The English take tea with the Queen in their dreams; in the United States, people go to a bar with the president (Solomon, 1993; Potheraju & Soper, 1995; Domhoff, 1996).

But what, if anything, do all these dreams mean? Whether dreams have a specific significance and function is a question that scientists have considered for many years, and they have developed several alternative theories.

Do Dreams Represent Unconscious Wish Fulfillment?

Sigmund Freud viewed dreams as a guide to the unconscious (Freud, 1900). In his **unconscious wish fulfillment theory,** he proposed that dreams represented unconscious wishes that dreamers desire to see fulfilled. However, because these wishes are threatening to the dreamer's conscious awareness, the actual wishes—called the **latent content of dreams**—are disguised. The true subject and meaning of a dream, then, may have little to do with its overt story line, which Freud called the **manifest content of dreams.**

To Freud, it was important to pierce the armor of a dream's manifest content to understand its true meaning. To do this, Freud tried to get people to discuss their dreams, associating symbols in the dreams to events in the past. He also suggested that certain common symbols with universal meanings appear in dreams. For example, to Freud, dreams in which the person is flying symbolize a wish for sexual intercourse. (See Table 4-1 for other common symbols.)

Today, many psychologists reject Freud's view that dreams typically represent unconscious wishes and that particular objects and events in a dream are symbolic. Instead, they believe that the direct, overt action of a dream is the focal point of its meaning. For example, a dream in which we are walking down a long hallway to take an exam for which we haven't studied does not relate to unconscious, unacceptable wishes. Instead, it simply might mean we are concerned about an impending test. Even more complex dreams can often be interpreted in terms of everyday concerns and stress (Domhoff, 1996; Nikles et al., 1998).

Moreover, we now know that some dreams reflect events occurring in the dreamer's environment as he or she is sleeping. For example, sleeping participants in one experiment were sprayed with water while they were dreaming. These unlucky volunteers reported more dreams involving water than a comparison group of participants who were left to sleep undisturbed (Dement & Wolpert, 1958).

Dreams-for-Survival Theory

According to the **dreams-for-survival theory,** dreams permit information that is critical for our daily survival to be reconsidered and reprocessed during sleep. Dreaming is seen as an inheritance from our animal ancestors, whose small brains were unable to sift sufficient information during waking hours. Consequently, dreaming provided a mechanism that permitted the processing of information twenty-four hours a day.

unconscious wish fulfillment theory: Sigmund Freud's theory that dreams represent unconscious wishes that dreamers desire to fulfill

latent content of dreams: According to Freud, the "disguised" or real meanings of dreams, hidden by more obvious subjects

manifest content of dreams: According to Freud, the overt story line of dreams

dreams-for-survival theory: The theory that dreams permit information that is critical for our daily survival to be reconsidered and reprocessed during sleep

Table 4-1 Dream Symbolism, According to Freud	
Symbol (Manifest Content of Dream)	**Interpretation (Latent Content)**
Climbing up a stairway, crossing a bridge, riding an elevator, flying in an airplane, walking down a long hallway, entering a room, train traveling through a tunnel	Sexual intercourse
Apples, peaches, grapefruits	Breasts
Bullets, fire, snakes, sticks, umbrellas, guns, hoses, knives	Male sex organs
Ovens, boxes, tunnels, closets, caves, bottles, ships	Female sex organs

Freud suggested that certain common symbols with universal meanings appear in dreams. According to his symbolism, a plane flying across the sky might represent the dreamer's wish for sexual intercourse. Can this claim be proved?

According to this theory, dreams represent concerns about our daily lives, illustrating our uncertainties, indecisions, ideas, and desires. Dreams are seen, then, as consistent with everyday living. Rather than being disguised wishes, as Freud suggested, they would represent key concerns growing out of our daily experiences (Pavlides & Winson, 1989; Winson, 1990).

Research supports the dreams-for-survival theory, suggesting that certain dreams permit people to focus on and consolidate memories, particularly dreams that pertain to "how-to-do-it" memories related to motor skills. For instance, in one experiment, participants learned a visual memory task late in the day. They were then sent to bed, but awakened at certain times during the night. When they were awakened at times that did not interrupt dreaming, their performance on the memory task typically improved the next day. But when they were awakened during rapid eye movement (REM) sleep—the stage of sleep when people dream—their performance declined. The conclusion: Dreaming can play a role in helping us remember material to which we have been previously exposed (Karni et al., 1992, 1994).

Activation-Synthesis Theory

According to psychiatrist J. Allan Hobson, who proposed **activation-synthesis theory,** the brain produces random electrical energy during REM sleep, possibly due to changes in the production of particular neurotransmitters. This electrical energy randomly stimulates memories lodged in various portions of the brain. Because we have a need to make sense of our world, even while asleep, the brain takes these chaotic memories and weaves them into a logical story line, filling in the gaps to produce a rational scenario (Hobson, 1996; Porte & Hobson, 1996).

Yet Hobson does not entirely reject the view that dreams reflect unconscious wishes. He suggests that the particular scenario a dreamer produces is not just random but instead is a clue to the dreamer's fears, emotions, and concerns. Hence, what starts out as a random process culminates in something meaningful.

activation–synthesis theory: Hobson's theory that the brain produces random electrical energy during REM sleep that stimulates memories lodged in various portions of the brain

Dream Theories in Perspective

The range of theories about dreaming (summarized in Table 4-2) clearly illustrates that dream researchers have yet to agree on the fundamental meaning of dreams. Furthermore, new research is suggesting that the different approaches might be closer together than originally thought.

For instance, according to work by Allen Braun and colleagues, the parts of the brain associated with emotions and visual imagery are strongly activated during REM sleep. Using PET scans that show brain activity, Braun's research team found that the limbic and paralimbic regions of the brain, which are associated with emotion and

Table 4-2 Three Views of Dreams

Theory	Basic Explanation	Meaning of Dreams	Is Meaning of Dream Disguised?
Unconscious wish fulfillment theory (Freud)	Dreams represent unconscious wishes the dreamer wants to fulfill	Latent content reveals unconscious wishes	Yes, by manifest content of dreams
Dreams-for-survival theory	Information relevant to daily survival is reconsidered and reprocessed	Clues to everyday concerns about survival	Not necessarily
Activation-synthesis theory (Hobson)	Dreams are the result of random activation of various memories, which are tied together in a logical story line	Dream scenario that is constructed is related to dreamer's concerns	Not necessarily

motivation, are particularly active during REM sleep. At the same time, the association areas of the prefrontal cortex, which control logical analysis and attention, are inactive during REM sleep (Braun et al., 1998; see Figure 4-5).

The results can be viewed as consistent with several aspects of Freudian theory. For example, the high activation of emotional and motivational centers of the brain during dreaming makes it more plausible that dreams might reflect unconscious wishes and instinctual needs, just as Freud suggested. Similarly, the fact that the areas of the brain responsible for emotions are highly active, while the brain regions responsible for rational thought are offline during REM sleep, suggests that the ego and superego are dormant, permitting unconscious thoughts to dominate.

On the other hand, critics of Freudian explanations for dreams disagree that the new research findings necessarily support Freud. There is still is no evidence that the meaning of dreams is hidden behind symbols found in the storyline of the dream. Furthermore, just because areas of the brain involved with motivation and emotion are activated during REM sleep does not prove that dreams relate to hidden motivations and emotions of the dreamer.

One thing is clear: Despite the advances in our understanding of the biological aspects of dreaming, the debate about the meaning of dreams is not yet resolved. But Freud would probably take satisfaction in the fact that almost a hundred years after he published his first book on the meaning of dreams, scientists are still debating his theory.

Sleep Disturbances: Slumbering Problems

At one time or another, almost all of us have difficulty sleeping—a condition known as *insomnia.* It could be due to a particular situation, such as the breakup of a relationship, concern about a test score, or the loss of a job. Some cases of insomnia, however, have no obvious cause. Some people are simply unable to fall asleep easily, or they go to sleep readily but wake up frequently during the night. Insomnia is a problem that afflicts about a quarter of the population of the United States (Hauri, 1991; Pressman & Orr, 1997).

Interestingly, some people who *think* they have sleeping problems are mistaken. For example, researchers in sleep laboratories have found that some people who report being up all night actually fall asleep in thirty minutes and stay asleep all night. Furthermore, some people with insomnia accurately recall sounds that they heard while they were asleep, which gives them the impression that they were actually awake during the night. In fact, some researchers suggest that future drugs for insomnia could function by changing people's *perceptions* of how much they have slept, rather than by making them sleep more (Engle-Friedman, Baker, & Bootzin, 1985; Klinkenborg, 1997).

Other sleep problems are less common than insomnia, although they are still widespread. For instance, some 20 million people suffer from *sleep apnea,* a condition in which a person has difficulty breathing while sleeping. The result is disturbed, fitful sleep, as the person is constantly reawakened when the lack of oxygen becomes great enough to trigger a waking response. Some people with apnea wake as many as 500

● Areas active during REM sleep

(Higher-order reasoning is inactive)

Complex visual processing

Attention

Arousal

Memory formation

Motivation

Emotion

Figure 4-5 New research has found that those parts of the brain that are associated with emotions and visual imagery are strongly activated during REM sleep. Why might this be the case?

times during the course of a night, although they might not even be aware that they have wakened. Not surprisingly, such disturbed sleep results in complaints of fatigue the next day. Sleep apnea might also account for *sudden infant death syndrome (SIDS)*, a mysterious killer of seemingly normal infants who die while sleeping (Ball et al., 1997).

Narcolepsy is uncontrollable sleeping that occurs for short periods while awake. No matter what the activity—holding a heated conversation, exercising, or driving—the narcoleptic will suddenly fall asleep. People with narcolepsy go directly from wakefulness to REM sleep, skipping the other stages. The causes of narcolepsy are not known, although there could be a genetic component because narcolepsy runs in some families (Siegel, 2000).

We know relatively little about sleeptalking and sleepwalking, two sleep disturbances that are usually harmless. Both occur during stage 4 sleep and are more frequent in children than in adults. Sleeptalkers and sleepwalkers usually have a vague consciousness of the world around them, and a sleepwalker might be able to walk with agility around obstructions in a crowded room. Unless a sleepwalker wanders into a dangerous environment, sleepwalking typically poses little risk (Hobson & Silverstri, 1999).

Circadian Rhythms: Life Cycles

The fact that we cycle back and forth between wakefulness and sleep is one example of our body's circadian rhythms. **Circadian rhythms** (from the Latin *circa diem,* or "around a day") are biological processes that occur repeatedly on approximately a 24-hour cycle. Sleep and waking, for instance, occur naturally to the beat of an internal pacemaker that works on a cycle of about 24 hours. Several other bodily functions, such as body temperature and the female menstrual cycle, also work on circadian rhythms (Oren & Terman, 1998; Czeisler et al., 1999; Young, 2000).

Circadian cycles are complex. For instance, sleepiness occurs not just in the evening, but throughout the day in regular patterns. As you can see in Figure 4-6, most of us tend to get drowsy in midafternoon—regardless of whether we have eaten a heavy lunch. By making an afternoon siesta part of their everyday habit, people in several cultures take advantage of the body's natural inclination to sleep at this time (Dement, 1989; Ogilvic & Harsh, 1994).

The brain's hypothalamus controls the beat of circadian rhythms. However, the relative amount of light and darkness, which differs with the seasons of the year, also plays a role in determining circadian rhythms. In fact, some people experience *seasonal*

PsychLink

Sleep disorders information
www.mhhe.com/
feldmaness5-04links

circadian rhythms: Biological processes that occur repeatedly on approximately a twenty-four-hour cycle

PsychLink

Circadian rhythms
www.mhhe.com/
feldmaness5-04links

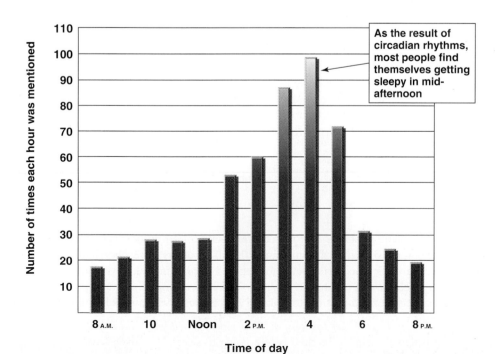

Figure 4-6 caption note: As the result of circadian rhythms, most people find themselves getting sleepy in mid-afternoon

Figure 4-6 These are the times of day that people report feeling the sleepiest (during periods when they are normally awake and trying to stay alert) (Dement, 1989). What implications does this information have for the workplace? For schools and colleges?the proportion of REM sleep increases.

From W. C. Dement, in D. F. Dinges and Broughton (eds.), Sleep and Alertness: Chronobiological, Behavioral, and Medical Aspects of Napping, 1989. Reprinted with permission of Lippincott, Wiliams and Wilkins Publishers.

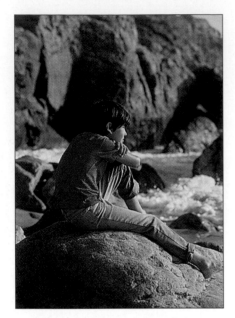

Daydreams are fantasies that people construct while they are awake. What are the similarities and differences between daydreams and night dreams?

daydreams: Fantasies that people construct while awake

affective disorder, a form of severe depression in which feelings of despair and hopelessness increase during the winter and lift during the rest of the year. The disorder appears to be a result of the brevity and gloom of winter days. Psychologists have found that several hours of daily exposure to bright lights is sometimes sufficient to improve the mood of those with the disorder (Sack et al., 1990; Roush, 1995; Oren & Terman, 1998).

Circadian rhythms explain the difficulty people have in flying through multiple time zones—the phenomenon of *jet lag*. Pilots, as well as others who must work on constantly changing time shifts (police officers and physicians), must fight their internal clocks. The result can be fatigue, irritability, and, even worse, outright error. In fact, an analysis of major disasters caused by human error finds that many, such as the Exxon *Valdez* oil spill in Alaska and the Chernobyl nuclear reactor accident, occurred late at night (Mapes, 1990; Moore-Ede, 1993).

Daydreams: Dreams Without Sleep

It is the stuff of magic: Our past mistakes can be wiped out and the future filled with noteworthy accomplishments. Fame, happiness, and wealth can be ours. In the next moment, though, the most horrible of tragedies can occur, leaving us devastated, alone, and penniless.

The source of these scenarios is **daydreams,** fantasies that people construct while awake. Unlike dreaming that occurs while sleeping, daydreams are more under people's control. Therefore their content is often more closely related to immediate events in the environment than is the content of the dreams that occur during sleep. Although they might include sexual content, daydreams also pertain to other activities or events that are relevant to a person's life.

Daydreams are a typical part of waking consciousness, even though our awareness of the environment around us declines while we are daydreaming. People vary considerably in the amount of daydreaming they do. For example, around 2 to 4 percent of the population spend at least half their free time fantasizing. Although most people daydream much less frequently, almost everyone fantasizes to some degree. Studies that ask people to identify what they are doing at random times during the day have shown that they are daydreaming about 10 percent of the time. As for the content of fantasies, most concern such mundane, ordinary events as paying the telephone bill, picking up the groceries, or solving a romantic problem (Singer, 1975; Lynn & Rhue, 1988; Lynn et al., 1996).

Frequent daydreaming might seem to suggest psychological difficulties, but there appears to be little relationship between psychological disturbance and daydreaming. Except in those rare cases in which a daydreamer is unable to distinguish a fantasy from reality (a mark of serious problems, as we discuss in Chapter 12), daydreaming seems to be a normal part of waking consciousness. Indeed, fantasy can contribute to the psychological well-being of some people by enhancing their creativity and by permitting them to use their imagination to understand what other people are experiencing (Lynn & Rhue, 1988; Pihlgren, Gidycz, & Lynn, 1993; Lynn et al., 1996).

BECOMING AN INFORMED CONSUMER OF PSYCHOLOGY

Sleeping Better

Do you have trouble sleeping? You're not alone—almost 40 million people in the United States have chronic difficulty sleeping, and 30 million others have occasional sleep problems. For those of us who spend hours tossing and turning in bed, psychologists studying sleep disturbances have a number of suggestions for overcoming insomnia (National Institutes of Health, 1996b; Kupfer & Reynolds, 1997; Scharf, 1999), including these:

* *Exercise during the day (at least six hours before bedtime) and avoid naps.* Not surprisingly, it helps to be tired before going to sleep! Moreover, learning

systematic relaxation techniques and biofeedback (see Chapter 2) can help you unwind from the day's stresses and tensions (Lehrer, 1996).

- *Choose a regular bedtime and stick to it.* Adhering to a habitual schedule helps your internal timing mechanisms regulate your body more effectively.
- *Don't use your bed as an all-purpose area.* Leave studying, reading, eating, watching TV, and other recreational activities to some other part of your living quarters. If you follow this advice, your bed will become a cue for sleeping.
- *Avoid drinks with caffeine after lunch.* The effects of beverages such as coffee, tea, and some soft drinks can linger for as long as 8 to 12 hours after they are consumed.
- *Drink a glass of warm milk at bedtime.* Your grandparents were right when they dispensed this advice: Milk contains the chemical tryptophan, which helps people fall asleep.
- *Avoid sleeping pills.* Although some prescription pills can be temporarily effective, in the long run they can cause more harm than good because they disrupt the normal sleep cycle (Haimov & Lavie, 1996; Zhdanova, Lynch, & Wurtman, 1997).
- *Try* not *to sleep.* This approach works because people often have difficulty falling asleep because they are trying so hard. A better strategy is to go to bed only when you feel tired. If you don't get to sleep within ten minutes, leave the bedroom and do something else, returning to bed only when you feel sleepy. Continue this process all night if necessary. But get up at your usual hour in the morning, and don't take any naps during the day. After three or four weeks, most people become conditioned to associate their beds with sleep—and fall asleep rapidly at night (Seltzer, 1986; Ubell, 1993; Sloan et al., 1993).

For long-term problems with sleep, you might consider visiting a sleep disorders center. For a list of accredited clinics, send a self-addressed, stamped envelope to: American Sleep Disorders Association, 6301 Bandel Road, Suite 101, Rochester, Minnesota 55901, or go to their website at http://www.asda.org.

Evaluate

1. _____ is the term used to describe our understanding of the world external to us, as well as our own internal world.
2. A great deal of neural activity goes on during sleep. True or false?
3. Dreams occur in _____ sleep.
4. _____ _____ are internal bodily processes that occur on a daily cycle.
5. Freud's theory of unconscious _____ _____ states that the actual wishes that an individual expresses in dreams are disguised because they are threatening to the person's conscious awareness.
6. Match the theory of dreaming with its definition.

   1. Activation-synthesis theory
   2. Dreams-for-survival theory
   3. Dreams as wish fulfillment

   a. Dreams permit important information to be reprocessed during sleep.
   b. The manifest content of dreams disguises the latent content of the dreams.
   c. Electrical energy stimulates random memories, which are woven together to produce dreams.

7. Match the sleep problem with its definition.

   1. Insomnia
   2. Narcolepsy
   3. Sleep apnea

   a. Condition that makes breathing while sleeping difficult
   b. Difficulty in sleeping
   c. Uncontrollable need to sleep during the day

Rethink

1. How would studying the sleep patterns of nonhuman species potentially help us figure out which of the theories of dreaming provides the best account of the functions of dreaming?

2. Suppose that a new "miracle pill" is developed that will allow a person to function with only one hour of sleep per night. However, because a night's sleep is so short, a person who takes the pill will never dream again. Knowing what you do about the functions of sleep and dreaming, what would be some advantages and drawbacks of such a pill from a personal standpoint? Would you take such a pill?

Answers to Evaluate Questions

1. Consciousness 2. True 3. REM 4. Circadian rhythms 5. wish fulfillment 6. 1-c; 2-a; 3-b 7. 1-b; 2-c; 3-a

Prepare

Are hypnotized people in a different state of consciousness?

What are the effects of meditation?

Organize

Hypnosis and Meditation
  Hypnosis
  Meditation

Hypnosis and Meditation

You are feeling relaxed and drowsy. You are getting sleepier and sleepier. Your body is becoming limp. Now you are starting to become warm, at ease, more comfortable. Your eyelids are feeling heavier and heavier. Your eyes are closing; you can't keep them open any more. You are totally relaxed.

Now, as you listen to my voice, do exactly as I say. Place your hands above your head. You will find they are getting heavier and heavier—so heavy you can barely keep them up. In fact, although you are straining as hard as you can, you will be unable to hold them up any longer.

An observer watching the above scene would notice a curious phenomenon occurring. Many of the people listening to the voice would, one by one, drop their arms to their sides, as if they were holding heavy lead weights. The reason for this strange behavior? The people have been hypnotized.

It is only recently that hypnotism has become an area considered worthy of scientific investigation. In part, the initial rejection of hypnosis relates to its bizarre eighteenth-century origins: Franz Mesmer's arguing that a form of "animal magnetism" could influence people and cure their illnesses. After a commission headed by Benjamin Franklin discredited the phenomenon, it fell into disrepute, only to rise again to respectability in the nineteenth century. But even today, as we will see, the nature of hypnosis is a matter of controversy.

Hypnosis: A Trance-Forming Experience?

hypnosis: A trancelike state of heightened susceptibility to the suggestions of others

People under **hypnosis** are in a trancelike state of heightened susceptibility to the suggestions of others. In some respects, it appears that they are asleep. Yet other aspects of their behavior contradict this notion, for these people are attentive to the hypnotist's suggestions and might carry out bizarre or silly suggestions.

Despite their compliance when hypnotized, people do not lose all will of their own. They will not suddenly become antisocial or self-destructive. They will not reveal hidden truths about themselves, and they are capable of lying when hypnotized. Moreover, people cannot be hypnotized against their will—despite popular misconceptions (Gwynn & Spanos, 1996).

There are wide variations in people's susceptibility to hypnosis. About 5 to 20 percent of the population cannot be hypnotized at all, and some 15 percent are very easily hypnotized. Most people fall somewhere in between. Moreover, the ease with which a person is hypnotized is related to a number of other characteristics. People who are readily hypnotized are also easily absorbed while reading books or listening to music, becoming unaware of what is happening around them, and they often spend

Despite common misconceptions, people such as these cannot be hypnotized against their will, nor do they lose all will of their own. In what ways is hypnosis beneficial?

an unusual amount of time daydreaming. In sum, then, they show a high ability to concentrate and to become completely absorbed in what they are doing (Rhue, Lynn, & Kirsch, 1993; Weitzenhoffer, 1999).

A Different State of Consciousness?

The question of whether hypnosis is a state of consciousness that is qualitatively different from normal waking consciousness is controversial. Psychologist Ernest Hilgard presented one side of the argument when he argued convincingly that hypnosis is a state of consciousness that differs significantly from other states. He contended that particular behaviors clearly differentiate hypnosis from other states, including higher suggestibility, increased ability to recall and construct images, and the acceptance of suggestions that clearly contradict reality. Moreover, changes in electrical activity in the brain are associated with hypnosis, supporting the position that hypnosis is a state of consciousness different from normal waking (Hilgard, 1975; Graffin, Ray, & Lundy, 1995).

On the other side of the controversy were theorists who rejected the notion that hypnosis is a significantly different state of consciousness from normal waking consciousness. They argued that altered brain-wave patterns are not sufficient to demonstrate a qualitative difference, given that no other specific physiological changes occur when a person is in a trance. Furthermore, little support exists for the contention that adults can accurately recall memories of childhood events while hypnotized. Such evidence suggests that there is nothing qualitatively special about the hypnotic trance (Spanos et al., 1993; Kirsch & Lynn, 1998).

There is increasing agreement that the controversy over the nature of hypnosis has led to extreme positions on both sides of the issue (Kirsch & Lynn, 1995). More recent approaches suggest that the hypnotic state might best be viewed as lying along a continuum, in which hypnosis is neither a totally different state of consciousness nor totally similar to normal waking consciousness.

As arguments about the true nature of hypnosis continue, though, one thing is clear: Hypnosis has been successfully used to solve practical human problems. In fact, psychologists working in many different areas have found hypnosis to be a reliable, effective tool (Rhue, Lynn, & Kirsch, 1993). Among the range of applications are the following:

- *Controlling pain.* Patients suffering from chronic pain might be given the suggestion, while hypnotized, that their pain is eliminated or reduced. Hypnosis has proved to be particularly useful during childbirth and dental procedures (Oster, 1994; Mairs, 1995; Barber, 1996).
- *Reducing smoking.* Although it hasn't been successful in stopping drug and alcohol abuse, hypnosis sometimes helps people stop smoking through hypnotic suggestions that the taste and smell of cigarettes are unpleasant (Erickson, Hershman, & Secter, 1990; Spiegel et al., 1993).
- *Treating psychological disorders.* Hypnosis sometimes is used during treatment for psychological disorders. For example, hypnosis may be employed to heighten relaxation, reduce anxiety, increase expectations of success, or modify self-defeating thoughts (Fromm & Nash, 1992).
- *Assisting in law enforcement.* Witnesses and victims are sometimes better able to recall details of a crime when hypnotized. In one case, a witness to the kidnapping of a group of California schoolchildren was placed under hypnosis and was able to recall all but one digit of the license number on the kidnapper's vehicle (Geiselman et al., 1985). On the other hand, sometimes hypnotic recollections are inaccurate, and the legal status of hypnosis is unresolved (Gibson, 1995; Lynn et al., 1997; Baker, 1998).
- *Improving athletic performance.* Athletes sometimes turn to hypnosis to improve their performance. For example, baseball player Mark McGwire used hypnotism to increase his concentration when batting, with considerable success (Udolf, 1981; Stanton, 1994; Edgette & Edgette, 1995).

PsychLink

Comprehensive hypnosis information
www.mhhe.com/
feldmaness5–04links

Figure 4-7 The body's use of oxygen declines significantly during meditation (Benson, 1993).

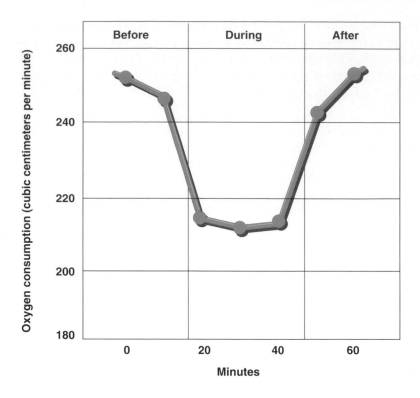

Meditation: Regulating Our Own State of Consciousness

When traditional practitioners of the ancient Eastern religion Zen Buddhism want to achieve greater spiritual insight, they turn to a technique that has been used for centuries to alter their state of consciousness: meditation.

Meditation is a learned technique for refocusing attention that brings about an altered state of consciousness. Meditation often consists of the repetition of a *mantra*—a sound, word, or syllable—over and over. In other forms of meditation, the focus is on a picture, flame, or specific part of the body. Regardless of the nature of the particular initial stimulus, the key to the procedure is concentrating on it so thoroughly that the meditator becomes unaware of any outside stimulation and reaches a different state of consciousness.

Following meditation, people report feeling thoroughly relaxed. They sometimes relate that they have gained new insights into themselves and the problems they are facing. The long-term practice of meditation can even improve health due to the biological changes it produces. For example, oxygen usage decreases, heart rate and blood pressure decline, and brain-wave patterns can change (Wallace & Benson, 1972; Holmes, 1985; Jevning et al., 1996; Zamarra et al., 1996; see Figure 4-7).

Anyone can meditate by using a few simple procedures. The fundamentals include sitting in a quiet room with eyes closed, breathing deeply and rhythmically, and repeating a word or sound—such as the word *one*—over and over. Practiced twice a day for 20 minutes, the technique is effective in bringing about relaxation (Benson & Friedman, 1985; Benson, 1993; Benson et al., 1994).

PsychLinks

Transcendental meditation research
www.mhhe.com/
feldmaness5-04links

meditation: A learned technique for refocusing attention that brings about an altered state of consciousness

EXPLORING DIVERSITY

Cross-Cultural Routes to Altered States of Consciousness

• A group of Native American Sioux sit naked in a steaming sweat lodge, as a medicine man throws water on sizzling rocks to send billows of scalding steam into the air.

- Aztec priests smear themselves with a mixture of crushed poisonous herbs, hairy black worms, scorpions, and lizards. Sometimes they drink the potion.
- During the sixteenth century, a devout Hasidic Jew lies across the tombstone of a celebrated scholar. As he murmurs the name of God repeatedly, he seeks to be possessed by the soul of the dead wise man's spirit. If successful, he will attain a mystical state, and the deceased's words will flow out of his mouth.

Each of these rituals has a common goal: suspension from the bonds of everyday awareness and access to an altered state of consciousness (Furst, 1977; Fine, 1994). Although they might seem exotic from the vantage point of many Western cultures, these rituals represent an apparently universal effort to alter consciousness.

Some scholars suggest that the quest to alter consciousness represents a basic human desire (Siegel, 1989). Whether or not one accepts such an extreme view, it is clear that different cultures have developed their own unique forms of consciousness-altering activities. Similarly, when we discuss psychological disorders in Chapter 12, we will see that what is deemed "abnormal" behavior varies considerably from one culture to another.

Of course, realizing that efforts to produce altered states of consciousness are widespread throughout the world's societies does not answer a fundamental question: Is the experience of *un*altered states of consciousness similar across different cultures?

There are two possible responses to this question. Because humans share basic biological commonalties in the ways their brains and bodies are wired, we might assume that the fundamental experience of consciousness is similar across cultures. As a result, we could suppose that consciousness shows some basic similarities across cultures.

On the other hand, cultures can differ greatly in how they interpret and view certain aspects of consciousness. For example, people in different cultures might experience the passage of time differently: One study found that Mexicans view time as passing more slowly than other North Americans do (Diaz-Guerrero, 1979).

Whatever the true nature of consciousness and why people seek to alter it, it is clear that people often seek the means to alter their everyday experience of the world. In some cases that need becomes overwhelming, as we see next when we consider the use of drugs.

Evaluate

1. _____ is a state of heightened susceptibility to the suggestions of others.
2. A friend tells you, "I once heard of a person who was murdered by being hypnotized and then told to jump from the Golden Gate Bridge!" Could such a thing have happened? Why or why not?
3. _____ is a learned technique for refocusing attention to bring about an altered state of consciousness.
4. Leslie repeats a unique sound, known as a _____, when she engages in meditation.

Answers to Evaluate Questions

1. Hypnosis 2. No: people who are hypnotized cannot be made to perform self-destructive acts. 3. Meditation 4. mantra

Rethink

1. What sorts of mental functioning does hypnosis appear to affect most strongly? Do you think it might have more effect on the left or right hemisphere of the brain, or would it affect both equally? Why?
2. Meditation produces several physical and psychological benefits. Does this suggest that we are physically and mentally burdened in our normal state of waking consciousness? Why?

Drug Use: The Highs and Lows of Consciousness

Green Bay Packers quarterback Brett Favre can tell you exactly when he changed his life, even if he doesn't remember it. It was 6 P.M. on February 27, and Favre was in his room at Bellin Hospital in Green Bay, Wisconsin, recovering from ankle surgery. A nurse was about to reinsert his IV, and the oft-injured quarterback was rolling his eyes in resignation at his longtime girlfriend, Deanna Tynes, and their 7-year-old daughter, Brittany. Then suddenly he went into convulsions. "His whole body was jerking around, his lip was folded under," says Deanna, 27, who screamed to the nurse to stop him from swallowing his tongue. Asked a terrified Brittany: "Mom, is he going to die?"

In a sense, just the opposite happened. When Favre, 26, regained consciousness minutes later, he awakened to a central fact of his life: He was an addict in need of help. For the previous five months, Favre had been taking the painkiller Vicodin—first to help him deal with a season's worth of injuries and then as a crutch for coping with fame. Doctors could not pinpoint the cause of the seizure, but it seemed clear to Favre that it was related to his dependency on the prescription drug. Three months later he checked into the Menninger Clinic in Topeka, Kansas, for six weeks of rehab. (Plummer & Pick, 1996, p. 129)

psychoactive drugs: Drugs that influence a person's emotions, perceptions, and behavior

Brett Favre was successful in his personal war on drugs: He became free of painkillers and later was able to lead his team to triumph in the Super Bowl. Others, though, are not so lucky. Each year, thousands of people die from complications of drug overdoses, and many more are addicted to various kinds of drugs.

Drugs are a part of almost everyone's life. From infancy on, most people take vitamins, aspirin, cold-relief medicine, and the like, and surveys find that 80 percent of adults in the United States have taken an over-the-counter pain reliever in the past six months. However, these drugs rarely produce an altered state of consciousness (Dortch, 1996).

On the other hand, some substances, known as psychoactive drugs, lead to an altered state of consciousness. **Psychoactive drugs** influence a person's emotions, perceptions, and behavior. Yet even these drugs are common in most of our lives. If you have ever had a cup of coffee or sipped a beer, you have taken a psychoactive drug.

A large number of individuals have used more potent—and dangerous—psychoactive drugs than coffee and beer (see Figure 4-8). For instance, surveys find that 40 percent of U.S. high school seniors have used an illegal drug within the last year, and over 60 percent report having been drunk on alcohol. The figures for the adult population are even higher (Johnston, Bachman, & O'Malley, 2000).

Of course, drugs vary widely in the effects they have on users, in part because they affect the nervous system in very different ways. Some drugs alter the limbic system, others affect the operation of specific neurotransmitters across the synapses of neurons (see Chapter 2). For example, some drugs block or enhance the release of neurotransmitters, some block the receipt or the removal of a neurotransmitter, and still others mimic the effects of particular neurotransmitters (see Figure 4-9).

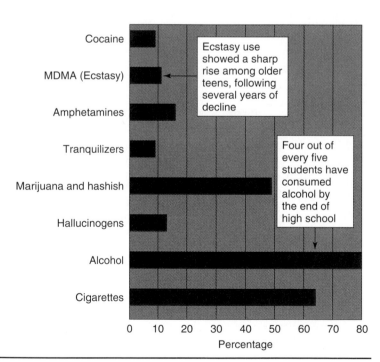

Figure 4-8 How many teenagers use drugs? Results of the most recent comprehensive survey of 14,000 high school seniors across the United States show the percentage of respondents who have used various substances for nonmedical purposes at least once (Johnston, Bachman, & O'Malley, 2000). Can you think of any reasons why teenagers—as opposed to older people—might be particularly likely to use drugs?

The most dangerous drugs are addictive. **Addictive drugs** produce a biological or psychological dependence in the user, and withdrawal from them leads to a craving for the drug that, in some cases, can be nearly irresistible. Addictions can be *biologically based,* in which case the body becomes so accustomed to functioning in the presence of a drug that it cannot function in its absence. Or addictions can be *psychologically based,* in which case people believe that they need the drug in order to respond to the stresses of daily living. Although we generally associate addiction with drugs such as heroin, everyday sorts of drugs like caffeine (found in coffee) and nicotine (found in cigarettes) have addictive aspects as well.

We know surprisingly little about the underlying causes of addiction. One of the problems in identifying the causes is that different drugs (such as alcohol and cocaine) affect the brain in very different ways—and yet can be equally addicting. Furthermore, it takes longer to become addicted to some drugs than to others, even though the ultimate consequences of addiction can be equally grave (Wickelgren, 1998b; Thombs, 1999).

Why do people take drugs in the first place? There are many reasons, ranging from the perceived pleasure of the experience itself, to the escape a drug-induced high affords from the everyday pressures of life, to an attempt to achieve a religious or spiritual state. But other factors, ones that have little to do with the nature of the experience itself, also lead people to try drugs (McDowell & Spitz, 1999).

For instance, the alleged drug use of well-known role models (such as baseball player Darryl Strawberry and film star Robert Downey, Jr.), the easy availability of some illegal drugs, and peer pressure all play a role in the decision to use drugs. In some cases, the motive is simply the thrill of trying something new. Finally, the sense of helplessness experienced by poor, unemployed individuals trapped in lives of poverty might lead them to try drugs as a way of escaping the bleakness of their lives. Regardless of the forces that lead a person to begin using drugs, drug addiction is among the most difficult of all behaviors to modify, even with extensive treatment (Dupre et al., 1995; Tucker, Donovan, & Marlatt, 1999).

Because of the difficulty in treating drug problems, there is little disagreement that the best hope for dealing with the overall societal problem of substance abuse is to prevent people from becoming involved with drugs in the first place. However, there is little accord on how to accomplish this goal. In fact, as we consider in the *Applying Psychology in the 21ˢᵗ Century* box, the effectiveness of even the most popular antidrug program is questionable.

Figure 4-9 Different drugs affect different parts of the nervous system and brain and each drug functions in one of these specific ways.

After S. S. Mader. Copyright © The McGraw-Hill Companies.

 PsychLink

Information on addiction
www.mhhe.com/
feldmaness5-04links

addictive drugs: Drugs that produce a biological or psychological dependence in the user; withdrawal from them leads to a craving for the drug that in some cases can be nearly irresistible

Stimulants: Drug Highs

It's one o'clock in the morning, and you still haven't finished reading the last chapter of the text on which you will be tested in the morning. Feeling exhausted, you turn to the one thing that might help you stay awake for the next two hours: a cup of strong, black coffee.

If you have ever found yourself in such a position, you have been relying on a major **stimulant,** caffeine, to stay awake. *Caffeine* is one of a number of stimulants that affect the central nervous system by causing a rise in heart rate, blood pressure, and muscular tension. Caffeine is present not only in coffee; it is an important ingredient in tea, soft drinks, and chocolate as well (see Figure 4-10).

Caffeine produces several reactions. The major behavioral effects of caffeine are an increase in attentiveness and a decrease in reaction time. Caffeine can also bring about an improvement in mood, most likely by mimicking the effects of a natural brain chemical, adenosine. Too much caffeine, however, can result in nervousness and insomnia. People

stimulants: Drugs that affect the central nervous system by causing a rise in heart rate, blood pressure, and muscular tension

Figure 4–10 How much caffeine are you eating and drinking? This chart shows the range of caffeine found in common foods and drinks (*New York Times*, 1991). The average person in the U.S. consumes about 200 milligrams of caffeine each day.

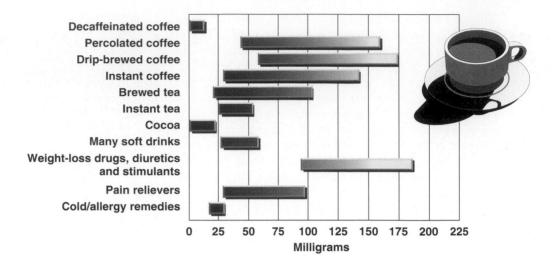

can build up a biological dependence on the drug. If they suddenly stop drinking coffee, they might experience headaches or depression. Many people who drink large amounts of coffee on weekdays have headaches on weekends because of a sudden drop in the amount of caffeine they are consuming (Silverman et al., 1992; Silverman, Mumford, & Griffiths, 1994; James, 1997).

Nicotine, found in cigarettes, is another common stimulant. The soothing effects of nicotine help explain why cigarette smoking is addictive. Smokers develop a dependence on nicotine, and those who suddenly stop smoking develop strong cravings for the drug. This is not surprising: nicotine activates neuronal mechanisms similar to those activated by cocaine, which, as we see next, is also highly addictive (Murray, 1990; Pich et al., 1997). (We will discuss smoking in greater detail in Chapter 11 when we consider health psychology.)

Cocaine

Although its use has declined over the last decade, the stimulant *cocaine* and its derivative, crack, are still a serious concern. Cocaine is inhaled or "snorted" through the nose, smoked, or injected directly into the bloodstream. It is rapidly absorbed into the body and takes effect almost immediately.

When used in relatively small quantities, cocaine produces feelings of profound psychological well-being, increased confidence, and alertness. Cocaine produces this "high"

During the late 19th century, and even into the early 20th century, cocaine was used in numerous home remedies and medicines.

Applying Psychology in the 21st Century

Just Say No—to D.A.R.E.? Finding Antidrug Programs That Work

The two eighth-graders in a classroom in New York City's Spanish Harlem can barely suppress their giggles. "You are sitting on a stalled, crowded bus," their teacher tells them. "Start up a conversation." Esther, petite and ponytailed, begins. "Well, this bus is really crowded!" "Yeah," says Luis. "I can't wait to get outta here—I'm gonna suffocate." Pause. Esther: "Nice day, isn't it? Where are you going?" Luis: "To take my girlfriend to the movies." Esther: "I have a date too." Painful pause. Luis: "The bus is certainly . . . stopped." The class cracks up, and the two scamper back to their desks. (Van Biema, 1996)

This dialogue might not sound like it has much to do with helping adolescents avoid getting hooked on drugs, but in fact it is part of a new approach to drug prevention called Life Skills Training. Unlike previous efforts, this program focuses on teaching a broad range of social skills that adolescents need to deal with the range of pressures they face.

The Life Skills program contrasts sharply with D.A.R.E. (Drug Abuse Resistance Education), currently the most popular antidrug program in the United States. Used in more than 80 percent of school districts in the United States, D.A.R.E. consists of a series of seventeen lessons on the dangers of drugs, alcohol, and gangs, taught to

fifth- and sixth-graders by a police officer. The program is highly popular with school officials, parents, and politicians.

The problem: Several well-controlled evaluations have been unable to demonstrate that the D.A.R.E. program is effective in reducing drug use over the long term. In fact, one study even showed that D.A.R.E. graduates were *more* likely to use marijuana than a comparison group of nongraduates (Clayton et al., 1996; Lynan et al., 1999).

Because of problems in identifying long-term positive effects of D.A.R.E., researchers have sought to develop alternative strategies, such as the Life Skills Training program. Instead of focusing on long-term dangers, Life Skills Training concentrates on immediate negative consequences. During 15 sessions, students are taught to be more assertive and confident, and to assess more accurately the communications they receive from their peers and popular culture. The notion is that by learning general social skills, students will be better equipped to deal with perceived peer pressure to use drugs, alcohol, and cigarettes (Botvin & Botvin, 1992; Dusenbury & Botvin, 1992).

Analysis of the Life Skills Training approach suggests that it is successful in reducing adolescent drug use. For example, an evaluation of several thousand students in Newark, New Jersey, who had participated in Life Skills Training in seventh grade and were tracked until they graduated from high school, showed that the students used drugs, tobacco, and alcohol at half the rate of their peers who had not been in the program (Botvin et al., 1994; Botvin et al., 1995; Van Biema, 1996).

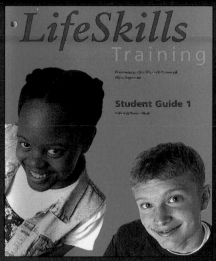

An alternative to the popular D.A.R.E. program, Life Skills Training concentrates on immediate negative consequences instead of long-term dangers. Why might this approach be more effective?

Whether the D.A.R.E. program will win continued support or be replaced by other programs, such as Life Skills Training, remains to be seen. What is clear is that teenage drug use remains a considerable social problem, and that effective approaches to stem the use of drugs are sorely needed.

Why do you think the D.A.R.E. program is so popular among the police and school boards? Do you think the students who go through the training are as supportive as the adults who sponsor its use?

through the neurotransmitter dopamine. As you'll recall from Chapter 2, dopamine is one of the chemicals that transmit between neurons messages related to ordinary feelings of pleasure. Normally when dopamine is released, excess amounts of the neurotransmitter are reabsorbed by the releasing neuron. However, when cocaine enters the brain, it blocks reabsorption of leftover dopamine. As a result, the brain is flooded with dopamine-produced pleasurable sensations (Landry, 1997; Bolla, Cadet, & London, 1998; see Table 4-3 for a summary of the effects of cocaine and other illegal drugs.)

However, there is a steep price to be paid for the pleasurable effects of cocaine. The drug is psychologically and physically addictive, and users can grow obsessed with obtaining it. Cocaine addicts indulge in binge use, administering the drug every ten to thirty minutes if it is available. During these binges, they think of nothing but cocaine; eating, sleeping, family, friends, money, and even survival have no importance. Their lives become tied to the drug. Over time, users deteriorate mentally and physically. In extreme cases, cocaine can cause hallucinations—a common one is of insects crawling over one's body (Pottieger et al., 1992; Crits-Christoph et al., 1999).

Almost 2.5 million people in the United States are occasional cocaine users, and as many as 1.5 million use the drug regularly. Given the strength of cocaine, withdrawal

Table 4-3 Drugs and Their Effects

Drug	Street Name	Effects	Withdrawal Symptoms	Adverse/Overdose Reactions
Stimulants				
Cocaine	Coke, blow, snow, lady, crack	Increased confidence, mood elevation, sense of energy and alertness, decreased appetite, anxiety, irritability, insomnia, transient drowsiness, delayed orgasm	Apathy, general fatigue, prolonged sleep, depression, disorientation, suicidal thoughts, agitated motor activity, irritability, bizarre dreams	Elevated blood pressure, increase in body temperature, face-picking, suspiciousness, bizarre and repetitious behavior, vivid hallucinations, convulsions, possible death

Amphetamines
  Benzedrine
  Dexedrine
	
	Speed
	Speed			

Depressants				
Alcohol	Booze	Anxiety reduction, impulsiveness, dramatic mood swings, bizarre thoughts, suicidal behavior, slurred speech, disorientation, slowed mental and physical functioning, limited attention span	Weakness, restlessness, nausea and vomiting, headaches, nightmares, irritability, depression, acute anxiety, hallucinations, seizures, possible death	Confusion, decreased response to pain, shallow respiration, dilated pupils, weak and rapid pulse, coma, possible death

Barbiturates
  Nembutal
  Seconal
  Phenobarbital
	
	Yellowjackets, yellows
	Reds			

Rohypnol	Roofies, rope, "date rape drug"	Muscle relaxation, amnesia, sleep	Seizures	Seizures, coma, incapacitation, inability to resist sexual assault
Narcotics				
Heroin	H, hombre, junk, smack, dope, crap, horse,	Anxiety and pain reduction, apathy, difficulty in concentration, slowed speech, decreased physical activity, drooling, itching, euphoria, nausea	Anxiety, vomiting, sneezing, diarrhea, lower back pain, watery eyes, runny nose, yawning, irritability, tremors, panic, chills and sweating, cramps	Depressed levels of consciousness, low blood pressure, rapid heart rate, shallow breathing, convulsions, coma, possible death
Morphine	Drugstore dope, cube, first line, mud			
Hallucinogens				

Cannabis
  Marijuana
  Hashish
  Hash oil
	Bhang, kif, ganja, dope, grass, pot, smoke, hemp, joint, weed, bone, Mary Jane, herb, tea	Euphoria, relaxed inhibitions, increased appetite, disoriented behavior	Hyperactivity, insomnia, decreased appetite, anxiety	Severe reactions are rare but include panic, paranoia, fatigue, bizarre and dangerous behavior, decreased testosterone over long term; immune-system effects

MDMA	Ecstasy	Heightened sense of oneself and insight, feelings of peace, empathy, energy	Not reported	Increase in body temperature, possible memory difficulties
LSD	Acid, quasey, microdot, white lightning	Heightened aesthetic responses; vision and depth distortion; heightened sensitivity to faces and gestures; magnified feelings; paranoia; panic; euphoria	Not reported	Nausea and chills; increased pulse, temperature, and blood pressure; slow, deep breathing; loss of appetite; insomnia; bizarre, dangerous behavior

 PsychLink

Factline on cocaine
www.mhhe.com/
feldmaness5-04links

from the drug is difficult. Although the use of cocaine among high school students has declined in recent years, the drug is still a major problem (Johnston, Bachman, & O'Malley, 1999).

Amphetamines

Amphetamines are strong stimulants, such as Dexedrine and Benzedrine, popularly known as "speed." When their use soared in the 1970s, the phrase "speed kills" became prevalent as the drugs caused an increasing number of deaths. Although amphetamine use has declined from its 1970s peak, many drug experts believe that speed would quickly resurface in large quantities if cocaine supplies were interrupted.

In small quantities, amphetamines—which stimulate the central nervous system—bring about a sense of energy and alertness, talkativeness, heightened confidence, and a mood "high." They increase concentration and reduce fatigue. Amphetamines also cause a loss of appetite, increased anxiety, and irritability. When taken over long periods of time, amphetamines can cause feelings of being persecuted by others, as well as a general sense of suspiciousness. People taking amphetamines can lose interest in sex. If taken in too large a quantity, amphetamines overstimulate the central nervous system to such an extent that convulsions and death can occur.

Depressants: Drug Lows

In contrast to the initial effect of stimulants, which is an increase in arousal of the central nervous system, the effect of **depressants** is to impede the nervous system by causing neurons to fire more slowly. Small doses result in at least temporary feelings of *intoxication*—drunkenness—along with a sense of euphoria and joy. When large amounts are taken, however, speech becomes slurred and muscle control becomes disjointed, making motion difficult. Ultimately, heavy users can lose consciousness entirely.

Amphetamines (shown here greatly magnified) are strong stimulants that increase alertness and energy and provide a sense of heightened confidence.

depressants: Drugs that slow down the nervous system

Alcohol

The most common depressant is *alcohol,* which is used by more people than any other drug. Based on liquor sales, the average person in the United States over the age of 14 drinks $2\frac{1}{2}$ gallons of pure alcohol over the course of a year. This works out to more than 200 drinks per person. Although alcohol consumption has declined steadily over the last decade, surveys show that more than three-fourths of college students indicate that they have had a drink within the last thirty days (Carmody, 1990; National Center on Addiction and Substance Abuse, 1994; Johnston, Bachman, & O'Malley, 2000).

One of the more disturbing trends is the high frequency of binge drinking among college students, the practice that led to the death of Scott Krueger (described in the chapter prologue). For men, *binge drinking* is defined as drinking five or more drinks in one sitting; for women, who generally weigh less than men and whose bodies absorb alcohol less efficiently, binge drinking is defined as having four or more drinks at one sitting.

As shown in Figure 4-11, some 50 percent of male college students and 40 percent of female college students responding to a nationwide survey said they had engaged in binge drinking within the prior two weeks. Some 17 percent of female students and 31 percent of male students admitted drinking on ten or more occasions during the past thirty

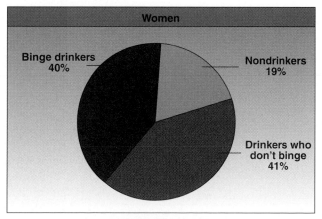

Figure 4-11 Drinking habits of college students (Wechsler et al., 2000). For men, binge drinking was defined as consuming five or more drinks in one sitting; for women, the total was four or more.

Although most alcohol consumers are casual users, there are more than 14 million alcoholics in the United States. The effects of alcohol vary significantly, depending on who is drinking it and the setting in which they are drinking. If alcohol were a newly discovered drug, do you think its sale would be legal?

 PsychLink

Alcohol and alcoholism
information
www.mhhe.com/
feldmaness5–04links

days. Furthermore, even light drinkers were affected by the high rate of alcohol use: Two-thirds of lighter drinkers said that they had had their studying or sleep disturbed by drunk students, and around one-third had been insulted or humiliated by a drunk student. A quarter of the women said they had been the target of an unwanted sexual advance by a drunk classmate (Wechsler et al., 1994; Wechsler et al., 2000).

Although alcohol consumption is widespread, there are significant gender and cultural variations in its use. For example, women are typically somewhat lighter drinkers than men—although the gap between the sexes is narrowing for older women and has closed completely for teenagers. In addition, women are usually more susceptible to the effects of alcohol, because of differences in blood volume and body fat that permit more alcohol to go directly into the bloodstream (Galanter, 1995; National Center on Addiction and Substance Abuse, 1996; Blume, 1998).

There are also ethnic differences in alcohol consumption. For example, people of East Asian backgrounds who live in the United States tend to drink significantly less than Caucasians or African Americans, and their incidence of alcohol-related problems is lower. It could be that physical reactions to drinking, which can include sweating, a quickened heartbeat, and flushing, are more unpleasant for East Asians than for other groups (Akutsu et al., 1989; Smith & Lin, 1996; Garcia-Andrade, Wall, & Ehlers, 1997).

Although alcohol is a depressant, most people claim that it increases their sense of sociability and well-being. The discrepancy between the actual and the perceived effects of alcohol lies in the initial effects it produces in the majority of individuals who use it: release of tension and stress, feelings of happiness, and loss of inhibitions (Steele & Southwick, 1985; Josephs & Steele, 1990; Steele & Josephs, 1990; Sayette, 1993). As the dose of alcohol increases, however, the depressive effects become more pronounced (see Figure 4-12). People might feel emotionally and physically unstable. They also show poor judgment and might act aggressively. Moreover, their memories are impaired, brain processing of spatial information is diminished, and speech becomes slurred and incoherent. Eventually they might fall into a stupor and pass out. If they drink enough alcohol in a short time, they can die of alcohol poisoning (Bushman, 1993; Matthews et al., 1996; Chin & Pisoni, 1997).

Although most people fall into the category of casual users, there are some 14 million alcoholics in the United States. *Alcoholics,* people with alcohol-abuse problems, come to rely on alcohol and continue to drink even though it causes serious difficulties.

Number of drinks consumed in 2 hours	Alcohol in blood, percentage	Typical effects
2	0.05	Judgment, thought, and restraint weakened; tension released, giving carefree sensation
3	0.08	Tensions and inhibitions of everyday life lessened; cheerfulness
4	0.10	Voluntary motor action affected, making hand and arm movements, walk, and speech clumsy
7	0.20	Severe impairment—staggering, loud, incoherent, emotionally unstable,100 times greater traffic risk; exuberance and aggressive inclinations magnified
9	0.30	Deeper areas of brain affected, with stimulus-response and understanding confused; stuporous; blurred vision
12	0.40	Incapable of voluntary action, sleepy, difficult to arouse; equivalent of surgical anesthesia
15	0.50	Comatose; centers controlling breathing and heartbeat anesthetized; death increasingly probable

Note: A drink refers to a typical 12-ounce bottle of beer, a 1.5-ounce shot of hard liquor, or a 5-ounce glass of wine.

Figure 4-12 The effects of alcohol. The quantities represent only rough benchmarks; the effects vary significantly depending on an individual's weight, height, recent food intake, genetic factors, and even a person's psychological state.

In addition, they become increasingly immune to the effects of alcohol. Consequently, alcoholics must drink progressively more in order to experience the initial positive feelings that alcohol produces (Galanter & Kleber, 1999).

Some alcoholics must drink constantly in order to feel well enough to function in their daily lives. Other alcoholics drink inconsistently, but occasionally go on sporadic binges in which they consume large quantities of alcohol.

It is not clear why certain people become alcoholics and develop a tolerance for alcohol, while others do not. Some evidence suggests a genetic cause, although the question of whether there is a specific inherited gene that produces alcoholism is controversial. What is clear is that the chances of becoming alcoholic are considerably higher if there are alcoholics in earlier generations of a person's family. On the other hand, not all alcoholics have close relatives who are alcoholics. In these cases, environmental stressors are suspected of playing a larger role (Pennisi, 1997a; McGue, 1999).

Even legal drugs, when used improperly, can lead to addiction.

narcotics: Drugs that increase relaxation and relieve pain and anxiety

hallucinogen: A drug that is capable of producing hallucinations, or changes in the perceptual process

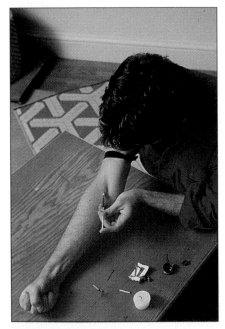

The use of heroin creates a cycle of biological and physical dependence. Combined with the strong positive feelings produced by the drug, this makes heroin addiction especially difficult to cure.

Barbiturates

Barbiturates, which include such drugs as Nembutal, Seconal, and Phenobarbital, are another form of depressant. Frequently prescribed by physicians to induce sleep or to reduce stress, barbiturates produce a sense of relaxation. Yet they also are psychologically and physically addictive, and the combination of barbiturates with alcohol can be deadly because it relaxes the muscles of the diaphragm to such an extent that the user stops breathing.

Rohypnol

Rohypnol is frequently called the "date rape drug," because when it is mixed with alcohol it can prevent victims from resisting sexual assault. Sometimes people who are unknowingly given the drug are so incapacitated that they have no memory of the assault.

Narcotics: Relieving Pain and Anxiety

Narcotics are drugs that increase relaxation and relieve pain and anxiety. Two of the most powerful narcotics, *morphine* and *heroin,* are derived from the poppy seed pod. Although morphine is used medically to control severe pain, heroin is illegal in the United States. This has not prevented its widespread use.

Heroin users usually inject the drug directly into their veins with a hypodermic needle. The immediate effect has been described as a "rush" of positive feeling, similar in some respects to a sexual orgasm—and just as difficult to describe. After the rush, a heroin user experiences a sense of well-being and peacefulness that lasts three to five hours. When the effects of the drug wear off, however, the user feels extreme anxiety and a desperate desire to repeat the experience. Moreover, larger amounts of heroin are needed each time to produce the same pleasurable effect. This leads to a cycle of biological and psychological addiction: The user is constantly either shooting up or attempting to obtain ever-increasing amounts of the drug. Eventually, the life of the addict revolves around heroin.

Because of the powerful positive feelings the drug produces, heroin addiction is particularly difficult to cure. One treatment that has shown some success is the use of methadone. *Methadone* is a synthetic chemical that satisfies a heroin user's physiological cravings for the drug without providing the "high" that accompanies heroin. When heroin users are placed on regular doses of methadone they might be able to function relatively normally. The use of methadone has one substantial drawback, however. Although it can eliminate the psychological dependence on heroin, it replaces the biological addiction to heroin with a biological addiction to methadone. Researchers are attempting to find nonaddictive chemical substitutes for heroin, as well as substitutes for other addictive drugs, that do not replace one addiction with another (Waldrop, 1989; Sinclair, 1990; Pulvirenti & Koob, 1994).

Hallucinogens: Psychedelic Drugs

What do mushrooms, jimsonweed, and morning glories have in common? Besides being fairly common plants, each can be the source of a powerful **hallucinogen,** a drug that is capable of producing hallucinations, or changes in the perceptual process.

The most common hallucinogen in widespread use today is *marijuana,* whose active ingredient—tetrahydrocannabinol (THC)—is found in a common weed, cannabis. Marijuana is typically smoked in cigarettes or pipes, although it can be cooked and eaten. More than 35 percent of high school seniors and 15 percent of eighth-graders report having used marijuana within the past year. However, these figures have shown a slight decline since 1999. (Johnston, Bachman, & O'Malley, 2000; see Figure 4-13).

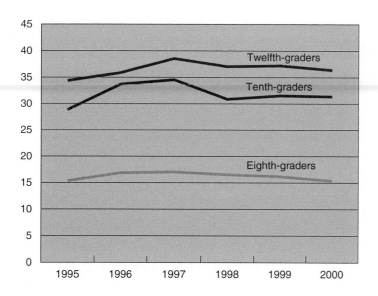

Figure 4-13 Trends in prevalence of use of marijuana for eighth-, tenth-, and twelfth-graders (Johnston, Buchman, & O'Malley, 2000).

The effects of marijuana vary from person to person, but they typically consist of feelings of euphoria and general well-being. Sensory experiences seem more vivid and intense, and a person's sense of self-importance seems to grow. Memory can be impaired, causing the user to feel pleasantly "spaced out." On the other hand, the effects are not universally positive. Individuals who use marijuana when feeling depressed can end up even more depressed, because the drug tends to magnify both good and bad feelings.

There are clear risks associated with long-term, heavy marijuana use. Although marijuana does not seem to produce addiction by itself, some evidence suggests that there are similarities in the way marijuana and drugs such as cocaine and heroin affect the brain. Furthermore, there is some evidence that heavy use at least temporarily decreases the production of the male sex hormone testosterone, potentially affecting sexual activity and sperm count (DiChiara & Reinhart, 1997; Iversen, 2000).

In addition, marijuana smoked during pregnancy has lasting effects on children who are exposed prenatally. Heavy use also diminishes the ability of the immune system to fight off germs and increases stress on the heart, although it is unclear how strong these effects are. There is one unquestionably negative consequence of smoking marijuana: The smoke damages the lungs much the way cigarette smoke does, producing an increased likelihood of developing cancer and other lung diseases (Julien, 1995; "Marijuana as Medicine," 1997).

Despite the possible dangers of marijuana use, there is little scientific evidence for the popular belief that users "graduate" from marijuana to more dangerous drugs. Furthermore, the use of marijuana is routine in certain cultures. For instance, some people in Jamaica habitually drink a marijuana-based tea for religious purposes. In addition, marijuana has several medical uses; it can prevent nausea from chemotherapy, treat some AIDS symptoms, and relieve muscle spasms for people with spinal cord injuries. In a controversial move, several states have made the use of the drug legal if it is prescribed by a physician—although it remains illegal under U.S. federal law (Brookhiser, 1997; Iverson, 2000).

PsychLink

Information on marijuana
www.mhhe.com/
feldmaness5-04links

MDMA (Ecstasy) and LSD

MDMA ("Ecstasy") and *lysergic acid diethylamide* (LSD, or "acid") fall into the category of hallucinogens. Both drugs affect the operation of the neurotransmitter serotonin in the brain, altering brain-cell activity and perception (Aghajanian, 1994; Cloud, 2000).

What are the effects of a hallucinogen on thinking? Artists have tried to depict the hallucinogenic experience, as in this yarn painting.

Ecstasy users report a sense of peacefulness and calm, increased empathy and connection with others, and feeling relaxed yet energetic. Although the data are not conclusive, some researchers have found declines in memory and performance on intellectual tasks for Ecstasy users, and such findings suggest that there can be long-term changes in serotonin receptors in the brain (McCann et al., 1999).

LSD produces vivid hallucinations. Perceptions of colors, sounds, and shapes are altered so much that even the most mundane experience—such as looking at the knots in a wooden table—can seem moving and exciting. Time perception is distorted, and objects and people might be viewed in a new way, with some users reporting that LSD increases their understanding of the world. For others, however, the experience brought on by LSD can be terrifying, particularly if users have had emotional difficulties in the past. Furthermore, people can experience flashbacks—hallucinations that start suddenly, long after they stopped using the drug.

BECOMING AN INFORMED CONSUMER OF PSYCHOLOGY

Identifying Drug and Alcohol Problems

In a society bombarded with commercials for drugs that are guaranteed to do everything from cure the common cold to give new life to "tired blood," it is no wonder that drug-related problems are a major social issue. Yet many people with drug and alcohol problems deny they have them, and even close friends and family members can fail to realize when occasional social use of drugs or alcohol has turned into abuse.

Certain signs, however, indicate when use becomes abuse (Archambault, 1992; National Institute on Drug Abuse, 2000). Among them:

- Always getting high to have a good time
- Being high more often than not
- Getting high to get oneself going
- Going to work or class while high
- Missing or being unprepared for class or work because you were high
- Feeling bad later about something you said or did while high
- Driving a car while high
- Coming in conflict with the law because of drugs
- Doing something while high that you wouldn't otherwise do
- Being high in nonsocial, solitary situations
- Being unable to stop getting high
- Feeling a need for a drink or a drug to get through the day
- Becoming physically unhealthy
- Failing at school or on the job
- Thinking about liquor or drugs all the time
- Avoiding family or friends while using liquor or drugs

Any combination of these symptoms should be sufficient to alert you to the potential of a serious drug problem. Because drug and alcohol dependence are almost impossible to cure on one's own, people who suspect that they have a problem should seek immediate attention from a psychologist, physician, or counselor.

You can also get help from national hotlines. For alcohol difficulties, call the National Council on Alcoholism at (800) 622-2255. For drug problems, call the National Institute on Drug Abuse at (800) 662-4357. You can also check your telephone book for a local listing of Alcoholics Anonymous or Narcotics Anonymous. Finally, you can write to the National Council on Alcoholism and Drug Dependence, 12 West 21st Street, New York, NY 10010, or consult their website at http://www.ncadd.org, for help with alcohol and drug problems.

Evaluate

1. Drugs that affect a person's consciousness are referred to as _____.
2. Match the type of drug to an example of that type.
   1. Narcotic—a pain reliever
   2. Amphetamine—a strong stimulant
   3. Hallucinogen—capable of producing hallucinations

   a. LSD
   b. Heroin
   c. Dexedrine or speed

3. Classify each drug listed as a stimulant (S), depressant (D), hallucinogen (H), or narcotic (N).
   1. Nicotine _____
   2. Cocaine _____
   3. Alcohol _____
   4. Morphine _____
   5. Marijuana _____
4. The effects of LSD can recur long after the drug has been taken. True or false?
5. _____ is a drug that has been used to treat people with heroin addiction.

Answers to Evaluate Questions

1. psychoactive 2. 1–b; 2–c; 3–a 3. 1–S; 2–S; 3–D; 4–N; 5–H 4. True 5. Methadone

Rethink

1. Why do you think people in almost every culture use psychoactive drugs and search for altered states of consciousness?
2. People often use the word *addiction* loosely, speaking of an addiction to candy or a television show. Can you explain the difference between this type of "addiction" and a true physiological addiction? Is there a difference between this type of "addiction" and a psychological addiction?

LookingBack

What are the different states of consciousness?

- Consciousness is a person's awareness of the sensations, thoughts, and feelings at a given moment. It can vary from more active to more passive states. (p. 116)

What happens when we sleep, and what are the meaning and function of dreams?

- Using the electroencephalogram, or EEG, to study sleep, scientists have found that the brain is active throughout the night, and that sleep proceeds through a series of stages identified by unique patterns of brain waves. (p. 118)
- REM (rapid eye movement) sleep is characterized by an increase in heart rate, a rise in blood pressure, an increase in the rate of breathing and, in males, erections. Dreams occur during this stage. (p. 119)
- According to Freud, dreams have both a manifest content (their apparent story line) and a latent content (their true meaning). He suggested that the latent content provides a guide to a dreamer's unconscious, revealing unfulfilled wishes or desires. (p. 122)
- The dreams-as-survival theory suggests that information relevant to daily survival is reconsidered and reprocessed in dreams. Finally, the activation-synthesis theory proposes that dreams are a result of random electrical energy that stimulates different memories, which are then woven into a coherent story line. (p. 122)

What are the major sleep disorders and how can they be treated?

- Insomnia is a sleep disorder characterized by difficulty sleeping. Sleep apnea is a condition in which people have difficulty sleeping and breathing at the same time. People with narcolepsy have an uncontrollable urge to sleep. Sleepwalking and sleeptalking are relatively harmless. (p. 124)
- Psychologists and sleep researchers advise people with insomnia to increase exercise during the day, avoid caffeine and sleeping pills, drink a glass of warm milk before bedtime, and try *not* to go to sleep. (p. 124)

How much do we daydream?

- Daydreaming may occur 10 percent of the time, although wide individual differences exist in the amount of time devoted to it. (p. 126)

Are hypnotized people in a different state of consciousness?

- Hypnosis produces a state of heightened susceptibility to the suggestions of the hypnotist. Under hypnosis, significant behavioral changes occur, including increased concentration and suggestibility, heightened ability to recall and construct images, lack of initiative, and acceptance of suggestions that clearly contradict reality. (p. 128)

What are the effects of meditation?

- Meditation is a learned technique for refocusing attention that brings about an altered state of consciousness. (p. 130)
- Different cultures have developed their own unique ways to alter states of consciousness. (p. 130)

What are the major classifications of drugs, and what are their effects?

- Drugs can produce an altered state of consciousness. However, they vary in how dangerous they are and in whether or not they are addictive, producing a physical or psychological dependence. Drug addiction is one of the most difficult behaviors to modify. (p. 132)
- Stimulants cause arousal in the central nervous system. Two common stimulants are caffeine (found in coffee, tea, and soft drinks) and nicotine (found in cigarettes). More dangerous are cocaine and amphetamines, or "speed." In large quantities they can overload the central nervous system, leading to convulsions and death. (p. 133)
- Depressants decrease arousal in the central nervous system, causing the neurons to fire more slowly. They can cause intoxication along with feelings of euphoria. The most common depressants are alcohol and barbiturates. (p. 137)
- Alcohol is the most frequently used depressant. Its initial effects of released tension and positive feelings yield to depressive effects as the dose of alcohol increases. Both genetic causes and environmental stressors can lead to alcoholism. (p. 137)
- Morphine and heroin are narcotics, drugs that produce relaxation and relieve pain and anxiety. Because of their addictive qualities, morphine and heroin are particularly dangerous. (p. 140)
- Hallucinogens are drugs that produce hallucinations or other changes in perception. The most frequently used hallucinogen is marijuana, which has several long-term risks. Two other hallucinogens are LSD and Ecstasy. (p. 140)
- A number of signals indicate when drug use becomes drug abuse. A person who suspects that he or she has a drug problem should get professional help. People are almost never capable of solving drug problems on their own. (p. 142)

Key Terms and Concepts

consciousness (p. 116)
stage 1 sleep (p. 118)
stage 2 sleep (p. 118)
stage 3 sleep (p. 118)
stage 4 sleep (p. 118)
rapid eye movement (REM) sleep (p. 119)
unconscious wish fulfillment theory (p. 122)
latent content of dreams (p. 122)
manifest content of dreams (p. 122)
dreams-for-survival theory (p. 122)
activation-synthesis theory (p. 123)

circadian rhythms (p. 125)
daydreams (p. 126)
hypnosis (p. 128)
meditation (p. 130)
psychoactive drugs (p. 132)
addictive drugs (p. 133)
stimulants (p. 133)
depressants (p. 137)
narcotics (p. 140)
hallucinogen (p. 140)

Psychology on the Web

1. Find a resource on the Web that interprets dreams, and another that reports the results of scientific dream research. Compare the nature and content of the two sites in terms of the topics covered, reliability of information provided, and promises made about the use of the site and its information. Write a summary of what you found.
2. There is considerable debate about the effectiveness of D.A.R.E., the Drug Abuse Resistance Education program. Find a discussion of both sides of the issue on the Web and summarize the arguments on each side. State your own preliminary conclusions about the D.A.R.E. program.

Preview

For additional
quizzing and a
variety of interactive
resources, visit the
*Essentials of
Understanding
Psychology* Online
Learning Center at

www.mhhe.com/feldmaness5

Epilogue

In this chapter we discussed consciousness in its full range from active states to passive states. We focused especially on factors that affect consciousness, from natural factors like sleep, dreaming, and daydreaming, to more intentional ways of altering consciousness, including hypnosis, meditation, and drugs. We examined some of the reasons people seek to alter their consciousness, considered both uses and abuses of consciousness-altering strategies, and attempted to address some of the most dangerous ways people alter their consciousness.

Before we turn to the subject of learning in the next chapter, return briefly to the prologue of this chapter, about Scott Krueger's death from binge drinking. Consider the following questions in light of your understanding of alcohol use and abuse.

1. What do you think might have caused Krueger's excessive drinking the evening he overdosed on alcohol?
2. Do you believe Krueger should have been considered an alcoholic? Was he addicted either physiologically or psychologically to alcohol?
3. How does alcohol affect the state of consciousness of users such as Krueger?
4. Why do you think the incidence of binge drinking is so high?

Chapter Five

Learning

Prologue

A Friend Named Ike

Elizabeth Twohy, who had polio as a child, needs to use a wheelchair most of the day, and the list of little things that are hard to do in a wheelchair is just about endless. But she has a friend, Ike, who helps out.

He picks up things she drops, turns light switches on and off, puts clothes in the dryer and takes the dishes out of the dishwasher, sorts the recyclables and brings her the telephone.

"The only thing that Ike can't do that would be really nice would be to drive the car," said Ms. Twohy, director of disability services for Brookdale Community College in Lincroft, N.J. Ike does have a license, but it's a dog license (O'Neil, 1999, p. D6).

Learning, a permanent change in behavior brought on by experience, plays a central role in practically every specialty area of psychology.

Looking Ahead

Ike's helpfulness did not just happen, of course. It is the result of painstaking training procedures—the same ones that are at work in each of our lives, illustrated by our ability to read a book, drive a car, play poker, study for a test, or perform any of the numerous activities that make up our daily routine. Like Ike, each of us must acquire and then refine our skills and abilities through learning.

Learning is a fundamental topic for psychologists and plays a central role in almost every specialty area of psychology, as we will see throughout this book. For example, a psychologist studying perception might ask, "How do we learn that people who look small from a distance are far away and not simply tiny?" A developmental psychologist might inquire, "How do babies learn to distinguish their mothers from other people?" A clinical psychologist might wonder, "Why do some people learn to be afraid when they see a spider?" A social psychologist might ask, "How do we learn to believe that we've fallen in love?" Each of these questions, although drawn from very different fields of psychology, can be answered only through an understanding of basic learning processes.

What do we mean by learning? Although psychologists have identified a number of different types of learning, a general definition encompasses them all: **Learning** is a relatively permanent change in behavior brought about by experience.

To understand learning, we need to return to the nature-nurture issue we first discussed in Chapter 1. Specifically, we must distinguish between performance changes due to *maturation* and changes brought about by experience. (Maturation is the nature part of the nature-nurture question; experience is the nurture part.) For instance, children become better tennis players as they grow older partially because their strength increases with their size—a maturational phenomenon. Maturational changes need to be differentiated from improvements due to practice, which indicate that learning has taken place.

Similarly, we must distinguish short-term changes in behavior that are due to factors other than learning, such as declines in performance resulting from fatigue or lack of effort, from performance changes that are due to actual learning. For example, if Venus Williams performs poorly in a tennis game because of tension or fatigue, this does not mean that she has not learned to play correctly or has forgotten how to play well.

In short, we begin this chapter by examining the type of learning that explains responses ranging from a dog salivating when it hears its owner opening a can of dog food to the emotions we feel when our national anthem is played. We then discuss other theories that consider how learning is a consequence of rewarding circumstances. Finally, we examine approaches that focus on the cognitive aspects of learning.

learning: A relatively permanent change in behavior brought about by experience

PsychLink

Theories on learning
www.mhhe.com/
feldmaness5-05links

Prepare

What is learning?
How do we learn to form associations between stimuli and responses?

Organize

Classical Conditioning
　The Basics of Classical Conditioning
　Applying Conditioning Principles to Human Behavior
　Extinction
　Generalization and Discrimination
　Beyond Traditional Classical Conditioning

Classical Conditioning

Does the mere sight of the golden arches in front of McDonald's make you feel pangs of hunger and think about hamburgers? If it does, then you are displaying an elementary form of learning called classical conditioning. Classical conditioning helps explain such diverse phenomena as crying at the sight of a bride walking down the aisle, fearing the dark, and falling in love.

The Basics of Classical Conditioning

Ivan Pavlov, a Russian physiologist, never intended to do psychological research. In 1904 he won the Nobel Prize for his work on digestion, testimony to his contribution to that field. Yet Pavlov is remembered not for his physiological research, but for his experiments on basic learning processes—work that he began quite accidentally (Windholz, 1997).

Pavlov had been studying the secretion of stomach acids and salivation in dogs in response to the ingestion of varying amounts and kinds of food. While doing so, he observed a curious phenomenon: Sometimes stomach secretions and salivation would begin in the dogs when they had not yet eaten any food. The mere sight of the experimenter who normally brought the food, or even the sound of the experimenter's footsteps, was enough to produce salivation in the dogs. Pavlov's genius was his ability to recognize the implications of this discovery. He saw that the dogs were responding not only on the basis of a biological need (hunger), but also as a result of learning—or, as it came to be called, classical conditioning. **Classical conditioning** is a type of learning in which a neutral stimulus (such as the experimenter's footsteps) comes to bring about a response after it is paired with a stimulus (such as food) that naturally brings about that response.

Ivan Pavlov (center) developed the principles of classical conditioning.

To demonstrate and analyze classical conditioning, Pavlov conducted a series of experiments (Pavlov, 1927). In one, he attached a tube to the salivary gland of a dog, which would allow him to measure precisely the dog's salivation. He then rang a bell and, just a few seconds later, presented the dog with meat. This pairing occurred repeatedly and was carefully planned so that each time exactly the same amount of time elapsed between the presentation of the bell and the meat. At first the dog would salivate only when the meat itself was presented, but soon it began to salivate at the sound of the bell. In fact, even when Pavlov stopped presenting the meat, the dog still salivated after hearing the sound. The dog had been classically conditioned to salivate to the bell.

As you can see in Figure 5-1, the basic processes of classical conditioning that underlie Pavlov's discovery are straightforward, although the terminology he chose is not simple. Consider first the diagram in Figure 5-1a. Before conditioning, there are two unrelated stimuli: the ringing of a bell and meat. We know that normally the ringing of a bell does not lead to salivation but to some irrelevant response, such as perking up the ears or perhaps a startle reaction. The bell is therefore called the **neutral stimulus** because it is a stimulus that, before conditioning, does not naturally bring about the response we are interested in. We also have meat, which, because of the biological makeup of the dog, naturally leads to salivation—the response that we are interested in conditioning. The meat is considered an **unconditioned stimulus,** or **UCS,** because food placed in a dog's mouth automatically causes salivation to occur. The response that the meat elicits (salivation) is called an **unconditioned response,** or **UCR**—a natural, innate response that is not associated with previous learning. Unconditioned responses are always brought about by the presence of unconditioned stimuli.

Figure 5-1b illustrates what happens during conditioning. The bell is rung just before each presentation of the meat. The goal of conditioning is for the bell to become associated with the unconditioned stimulus (meat) and therefore to bring about the same sort of response as the unconditioned stimulus. During this period, salivation gradually increases each time the bell is rung, until the bell alone causes the dog to salivate.

When conditioning is complete, the bell has evolved from a neutral stimulus to what is now called a **conditioned stimulus,** or **CS.** At this time, salivation that occurs as a response to the conditioned stimulus (bell) is considered a **conditioned response,** or **CR.** This situation is depicted in Figure 5-1c. After conditioning, then, the conditioned stimulus evokes the conditioned response.

The sequence and timing of the presentation of the unconditioned stimulus and the conditioned stimulus are particularly important (Rescorla, 1988; Wasserman & Miller, 1997). Like a malfunctioning warning light at a railroad crossing that goes on after the train has passed by, a neutral stimulus that *follows* an unconditioned stimulus has little chance of becoming a conditioned stimulus. On the other hand, just as a warning light works best if it goes on right before a train passes, a neutral stimulus that is presented *just before* the unconditioned stimulus is most apt to result in successful conditioning. Research has shown that conditioning is most effective if the neutral stimulus (which will become a conditioned stimulus) precedes the unconditioned stimulus by between a half-second and several seconds, depending on what kind of response is being conditioned.

classical conditioning: A type of learning in which a neutral stimulus comes to bring about a response after it is paired with a stimulus that naturally brings about that response

neutral stimulus: A stimulus that, before conditioning, does not naturally bring about the response of interest

unconditioned stimulus (UCS): A stimulus that brings about a response without having been learned

unconditioned response (UCR): A response that is natural and needs no training (e.g., salivation at the smell of food)

conditioned stimulus (CS): A once-neutral stimulus that has been paired with an unconditioned stimulus to bring about a response formerly caused only by the unconditioned stimulus

conditioned response (CR): A response that, after conditioning, follows a previously neutral stimulus (e.g., salivation at the ringing of a bell)

Figure 5-1 The basic process of classical conditioning. *(a)* Prior to conditioning, the ringing of a bell does not bring about salivation—making the bell a neutral stimulus. On the other hand, meat naturally brings about salivation, making the meat an unconditioned stimulus and salivation an unconditioned response. *(b)* During conditioning, the bell is rung just before the presentation of the meat. *(c)* Eventually, the ringing of the bell alone brings about salivation. We can now say that conditioning has been accomplished: The previously neutral stimulus of the bell is now considered a conditioned stimulus that brings about the conditioned response of salivation.

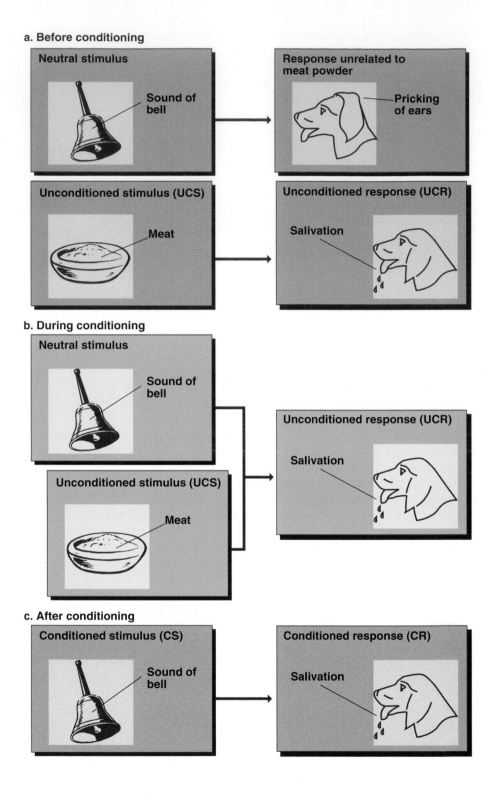

Although the terminology Pavlov used to describe classical conditioning might at first seem confusing, the following summary rules can help make the relationships between stimuli and responses easier to understand and remember:

- An *un*conditioned stimulus leads to an *un*conditioned response.
- *Un*conditioned stimulus–*un*conditioned response pairings are *un*learned and *un*trained.
- During conditioning, a previously neutral stimulus is transformed into the conditioned stimulus.

- A conditioned stimulus leads to a conditioned response, and a conditioned stimulus–conditioned response pairing is a consequence of learning and training.
- An unconditioned response and a conditioned response are similar (such as salivation in the example described earlier), but the conditioned response is learned, whereas the unconditioned response occurs naturally.

Applying Conditioning Principles to Human Behavior

Although the initial conditioning experiments were carried out with animals, classical conditioning principles were soon found to explain many aspects of everyday human behavior. Recall, for instance, the earlier illustration of how people might experience hunger pangs at the sight of McDonald's golden arches. The cause of this reaction is classical conditioning: The previously neutral arches have become associated with the food inside the restaurant (the unconditioned stimulus), causing the arches to become a conditioned stimulus that brings about the conditioned response of hunger.

Emotional responses are particularly likely to be learned through classical conditioning processes. For instance, how do some of us develop fears of mice, spiders, and other creatures that are typically harmless? In a now-famous case study designed to show that classical conditioning was at the root of such fears, an 11-month-old infant named Albert, who initially showed no fear of rats, heard a loud noise just as he was shown a rat (Watson & Rayner, 1920). The noise (the unconditioned stimulus) evoked fear (the unconditioned response). After just a few pairings of noise and rat, Albert began to show fear of the rat by itself. The rat, then, had become a CS that brought about the CR, fear. Similarly, the pairing of the appearance of certain species (such as mice or spiders) with the fearful comments of an adult may cause children to develop the same fears their parents have. (By the way, we don't know what happened to the unfortunate Albert, and Watson, the experimenter, has been condemned for using ethically questionable procedures.)

Learning via classical conditioning also occurs during adulthood. For example, you might not go to a dentist as often as you should because of prior associations of dentists and pain. Or you might have a particular fondness for the smell of a certain perfume or aftershave lotion because the feelings and thoughts of an early lover come rushing back whenever you encounter it. Classical conditioning, then, explains many of the reactions we have to stimuli in the world around us (Woodruff-Pak, 1999).

Extinction

What do you think would happen if a dog who had become classically conditioned to salivate at the ringing of a bell never again received food when the bell was rung? The answer lies in one of the basic phenomena of learning: extinction. **Extinction** occurs when a previously conditioned response decreases in frequency and eventually disappears.

To produce extinction, one needs to end the association between conditioned and unconditioned stimuli. For instance, if we had trained a dog to salivate at the ringing of a bell, we could produce extinction by ceasing to provide meat after the bell was rung. At first the dog would continue to salivate when it heard the bell, but after a few such instances, the amount of salivation would probably decline, and the dog would eventually stop responding to the bell altogether. At that point, we could say that the response had been extinguished. In sum, extinction occurs when the conditioned stimulus is repeatedly presented without the unconditioned stimulus. We should keep in mind that extinction can be a helpful phenomenon. Consider, for instance, what it would be like if the fear you experienced while watching *The Blair Witch Project* never was extinguished. You might well tremble with fright every time you entered any wooded area.

As we will describe in Chapter 13, psychologists have treated people with irrational fears, or phobias, by using a form of therapy called systematic desensitization. The goal of *systematic desensitization* is to bring about the extinction of the phobia. For example, a therapist using systematic desensitization for a client who is afraid of dogs might repeatedly expose the client to dogs, starting with a less frightening aspect (a photo

PsychLink

Classical conditioning
www.mhhe.com/
feldmaness5-05links

extinction: The decrease in frequency, and eventual disappearance, of a previously conditioned response; one of the basic phenomena of learning of a cute dog) and moving toward more feared ones (such as an actual encounter with an unfamiliar dog). As the anticipated negative consequences of exposure to the dog (e.g., being jumped on or bitten) do not occur, the fear eventually becomes extinguished.

Once a conditioned response has been extinguished, has it vanished forever? Not necessarily. Pavlov discovered this when he returned to his dog a few days after the conditioned behavior had seemingly been extinguished. If he rang a bell, the dog once again salivated—an effect known as **spontaneous recovery,** or the reemergence of an extinguished conditioned response after a period of rest.

Spontaneous recovery helps explain why it is so hard to overcome drug addictions. For example, cocaine addicts who are thought to be "cured" could experience an irresistible impulse to use the drug again if they are subsequently confronted by a stimulus with strong connections to the drug, such as a white powder (O'Brien et al., 1992; Drummond et al., 1995).

Generalization and Discrimination

Despite differences in color and shape, to most of us a rose is a rose is a rose. The pleasure we experience at the beauty, smell, and grace of the flower is similar for different types of roses. Pavlov noticed a similar phenomenon. His dogs often salivated not only at the ringing of the bell that was used during their original conditioning but at the sound of a buzzer as well.

Such behavior is the result of stimulus generalization. **Stimulus generalization** takes place when a conditioned response follows a stimulus that is similar to the original conditioned stimulus. The greater the similarity between the two stimuli, the greater the likelihood of stimulus generalization. Baby Albert, who, as we mentioned earlier, was conditioned to be fearful of rats, was later found to be afraid of other furry white things as well. He was fearful of white rabbits, white fur coats, and even a white Santa Claus mask. On the other hand, according to the principle of stimulus generalization, it is unlikely that he would have been afraid of a black dog, because its color would differentiate it sufficiently from the original fear-evoking stimulus.

The conditioned response elicited by the new stimulus is usually not as intense as the original conditioned response, although the more similar the new stimulus is to the old one, the more similar the new response will be. It is unlikely, then, that Albert's fear of the Santa Claus mask was as great as his learned fear of a rat. Still, stimulus generalization permits us to know, for example, that we ought to brake at all red lights, even if there are minor variations in size, shape, and shade.

If two stimuli are sufficiently distinct from one another so that one evokes a conditioned response but the other does not, we can say that stimulus discrimination has occurred. **Stimulus discrimination** is the ability to differentiate between stimuli. For example, the ability to discriminate between a red and a green traffic light prevents us from getting mowed down by oncoming traffic at intersections.

Beyond Traditional Classical Conditioning: Challenging Basic Assumptions

Although Pavlov hypothesized that all learning is nothing more than long strings of conditioned responses, this notion has not been supported by subsequent research. It turns out that classical conditioning provides us with only a partial explanation of how people and animals learn and that Pavlov was wrong in some of his basic assumptions (Risley & Rescorla, 1972; Hollis, 1997).

For example, according to Pavlov, the process of linking stimuli and responses occurs in a mechanistic, unthinking way. In contrast to this perspective, learning theorists influenced by cognitive psychology have argued that learners actively develop an understanding and expectancy about which particular unconditioned stimuli are matched with specific conditioned stimuli. A ringing bell, for instance, gives a dog something to

Because of a previous unpleasant experience, a person may expect a similar occurrence when faced with a comparable situation in the future, a process known as stimulus generalization. Can you think of ways this process is used in everyday life?

spontaneous recovery: The reemergence of an extinguished conditioned response after a period of rest

stimulus generalization: A response to a stimulus that is similar to but different from a conditioned stimulus; the more similar the two stimuli, the more likely generalization is to occur

stimulus discrimination: The ability to differentiate between stimuli

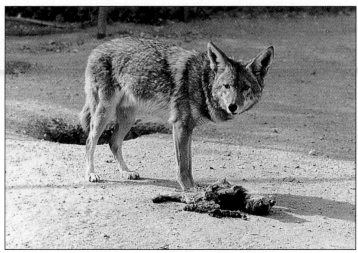

Because of prior experience with meat that had been laced with a mild poison, this coyote does not obey its natural instincts and ignores what otherwise would be a tasty meal. What principles of classical conditioning does this phenomenon contradict?

think about: the impending arrival of food (Rescorla, 1988; Clark & Squire, 1998; Woodruff-Pak, 1999).

Traditional explanations of how classical conditioning operates have also been challenged by learning psychologist John Garcia, whose research was initially concerned with the effects of exposure to nuclear radiation on laboratory animals. In the course of his experiments, he realized that rats placed in a radiation chamber drank almost no water, even though in their home cage they drank eagerly. The most obvious explanation—that it had something to do with the radiation—was soon ruled out. Garcia found that even when the radiation was not turned on, the rats still drank little or no water in the radiation chamber (Garcia, Hankins, & Rusiniak, 1974; Garcia, 1990).

Initially puzzled by the rats' behavior, Garcia eventually figured out that the drinking cups in the radiation chamber were made of plastic, thereby giving the water an unusual, plastic-like taste. In contrast, drinking cups in the home cage were made of glass and left no abnormal taste.

As a result, the plastic-tasting water had become repeatedly paired with illness brought on by exposure to radiation, and that had led the rats to form a classically conditioned association. The process began with the radiation acting as an unconditioned stimulus evoking the unconditioned response of sickness. With repeated pairings, the plastic-tasting water had become a conditioned stimulus that evoked the conditioned response of sickness.

This finding violated one of the basic rules of classical conditioning—that an unconditioned stimulus should *immediately* follow a conditioned stimulus for optimal conditioning to occur. Instead, Garcia's findings showed that conditioning could occur even when there was an interval of as long as eight hours between exposure to the conditioned stimulus and the response of sickness. Furthermore, the conditioning persisted over very long periods and sometimes occurred after just one exposure to water that was followed later on by illness.

These findings have had important practical implications. For example, to prevent coyotes from killing their sheep, some ranchers now routinely lace a sheep carcass with a drug and leave the carcass in a place where coyotes will find it. The drug temporarily makes the coyotes quite ill, but it does not permanently harm them. After just one exposure to a drug-laden sheep carcass, coyotes avoid sheep, which are normally one of their primary natural victims (Gustavson et al., 1974).

Evaluate

1. _____ involves changes brought about by experience, whereas maturation describes changes due to biological development.

2. _____ is the name of the scientist responsible for discovering the learning phenomenon known as _____ conditioning, in which an organism learns a response to a stimulus to which it would not normally respond.

Refer to the passage below to answer questions 3 through 6:

The last three times little Theresa visited Dr. Lopez for checkups, he administered a painful preventive immunization shot that left her in tears. Today, when her mother takes her for another checkup, Theresa begins to sob as soon as she comes face-to-face with Dr. Lopez, even before he has had a chance to say hello.

3. The painful shot that Theresa received during each visit was a(n)_____ _____, which elicited the _____ _____, her tears.

4. Dr. Lopez is upset because his presence has become a _____ _____ for Theresa's crying.

5. Fortunately, Dr. Lopez gave Theresa no more shots for quite some time. Over that time she gradually stopped crying and even came to like him. _____ had occurred.

6. _____ _____ occurs when a stimulus that is fairly similar to the conditioned stimulus produces the same response.

7. On the other hand, _____ _____ occurs when there is no response to a stimulus that is slightly distinct from the conditioned stimulus.

Answers to Evaluate Questions

1. Learning 2. Pavlov; classical 3. unconditioned stimulus; unconditioned response 4. conditioned stimulus 5. Extinction 6. Stimulus generalization 7. stimulus discrimination

Rethink

1. Can you think of ways that classical conditioning is used by politicians? advertisers? moviemakers? Do ethical issues arise from any of these uses?

2. Is it likely that Albert, Watson's experimental subject, went through life afraid of Santa Claus? Describe what probably happened to prevent this.

Prepare

What is the role of reward and punishment in learning?

Organize

Operant Conditioning
Thorndike's Law of Effect
The Basics of Operant Conditioning
Positive Reinforcers, Negative Reinforcers, and Punishment
The Pros and Cons of Punishment
Schedules of Reinforcement
Discrimination and Generalization in Operant Conditioning
Superstitious Behavior
Shaping
Biological Constraints on Learning

operant conditioning: Learning in which a voluntary response is strengthened or weakened, depending on its favorable or unfavorable consequences

Operant Conditioning

Very good. . . . What a clever idea. . . . Fantastic. . . . I agree. . . . Thank you. . . . Excellent. . . . Super. . . . You get an A. . . . I'm impressed. . . . Let me give you a hug. . . . You're getting a raise. . . . Have a cookie. . . . You look great. . . . I love you. . . .

Few of us mind being the recipient of any of the above comments. But what is especially noteworthy about them is that each of these simple statements can be used, through a process known as operant conditioning, to bring about powerful changes in behavior and to teach the most complex tasks. Operant conditioning is the basis for many of the most important kinds of human, and animal, learning.

Operant conditioning is learning in which a voluntary response is strengthened or weakened, depending on its favorable or unfavorable consequences. Unlike classical conditioning, in which the original behaviors are the natural, biological responses to the presence of some stimulus such as food, water, or pain, operant conditioning applies to voluntary responses, which an organism performs deliberately, to produce a desirable outcome. The term *operant* emphasizes this point: The organism *operates* on its environment to produce some desirable result. For example, operant conditioning is at work when we learn that toiling industriously can bring about a raise, or that studying hard results in good grades.

As with classical conditioning, the basis for understanding operant conditioning was laid by work with animals. We turn now to some of that early research, which began with a simple inquiry into the behavior of cats.

Figure 5–2 Edward L. Thorndike devised this puzzle box to study the process by which a cat learns to press a paddle to escape the box and receive food. Do you think Thorndike's work has relevance to the question of why humans voluntarily solve puzzles, such as crossword puzzles and jigsaw puzzles? Do they receive any rewards?

Thorndike's Law of Effect

If you placed a hungry cat in a cage and then put a small piece of food outside of it, just beyond the cat's reach, chances are the cat would eagerly search for a way out of the cage. The cat might first claw at the sides or push against an opening. Suppose, though, that you had rigged things so that the cat could escape by stepping on a small paddle that released the latch to the door of the cage (see Figure 5-2). Eventually, as it moved around the cage, the cat would happen to step on the paddle, the door would open, and the cat would eat the food.

What would happen if you then returned the cat to the box? The next time, it would probably take a little less time for the cat to step on the paddle and escape. After a few trials, the cat would deliberately step on the paddle as soon as it was placed in the cage. What would have occurred, according to Edward L. Thorndike (1932), who studied this situation extensively, was that the cat would have learned that pressing the paddle was associated with the desirable consequence of getting food. Thorndike summarized that relationship by formulating the *law of effect:* that responses that lead to satisfying consequences are more likely to be repeated, and responses followed by negative outcomes are less likely to be repeated.

Thorndike believed that the law of effect operated as automatically as leaves fall off a tree in autumn. It was not necessary for an organism to understand that there was a link between a response and a reward. Instead, Thorndike believed, over time and through experience the organism would make a direct connection between the stimulus and the response without any awareness that the connection existed.

The Basics of Operant Conditioning

Thorndike's early research served as the foundation for the work of one of the century's most influential psychologists, B. F. Skinner, who died in 1990. You may have heard of the Skinner box (shown in one form in Figure 5-3), a chamber with a highly controlled environment used to study operant conditioning processes with laboratory animals. Whereas Thorndike's goal was to get his cats to learn to obtain food by leaving the box, animals in a Skinner box learn to obtain food by operating in their environment within the box. Skinner became interested in specifying how behavior varied as a result of alterations in the environment.

Skinner, whose work went far beyond perfecting Thorndike's earlier apparatus, is considered the inspiration for a whole generation of psychologists studying operant

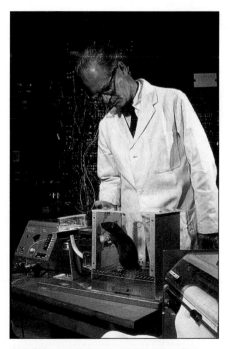

B. F. Skinner, who was the founding father of operant conditioning, developed what came to be called the "Skinner box." In what ways has Skinner's research contributed to the study of learning?

Figure 5-3 A Skinner box, used to study operant conditioning. Laboratory animals learn to press the lever in order to obtain food, which is delivered in the tray.

Lever

Food dispenser

conditioning (Delprato & Midgley, 1992; Bjork, 1993; Keehn, 1996). To illustrate Skinner's contribution, let's consider what happens to a pigeon in the typical Skinner box.

Suppose you want to teach a hungry pigeon to peck a key that is located in its box. At first the pigeon will wander around the box, exploring the environment in a relatively random fashion. At some point, however, it will probably peck the key by chance, and when it does, it will receive a food pellet. The first time this happens, the pigeon will not learn the connection between pecking and receiving food and will continue to explore the box. Sooner or later the pigeon will again peck the key and receive a pellet, and in time the frequency of the pecking response will increase. Eventually, the pigeon will peck the key continually until it satisfies its hunger, thereby demonstrating that it has learned that the receipt of food is contingent on pecking the key.

Reinforcing Desired Behavior

Skinner called the process that leads the pigeon to continue pecking the key "reinforcement." **Reinforcement** is the process by which a stimulus increases the probability that a preceding behavior will be repeated. In other words, pecking is more likely to occur again due to the stimulus of food.

reinforcement: The process by which a stimulus increases the probability that a preceding behavior will be repeated

reinforcer: Any stimulus that increases the probability that a preceding behavior will occur again

In a situation such as this one, the food is called a reinforcer. A **reinforcer** is any stimulus that increases the probability that a preceding behavior will occur again. Hence, food is a reinforcer because it increases the probability that the behavior of pecking the key (formally referred to as the *response* of pecking) will take place.

What kind of stimuli can act as reinforcers? Bonuses, toys, and good grades can serve as reinforcers—if they strengthen the probability of the response that occurred before their introduction. In each case, it is critical that the organism learn that the delivery of the reinforcer is contingent on the response occurring in the first place.

Of course, we are not born knowing that 75 cents can buy us a candy bar. Rather, through experience we learn that money is a valuable commodity because of its association with stimuli, such as food and drink, that are naturally reinforcing. This fact suggests a distinction between primary reinforcers and secondary reinforcers. A *primary reinforcer* satisfies some biological need and works naturally, regardless of a person's prior experience. Food for the hungry person, warmth for the cold person, and relief for the person in pain would all be classified as primary reinforcers. A *secondary reinforcer,* in contrast, is a stimulus that becomes reinforcing because of its association with a primary reinforcer. For instance, we

"Oh, not bad. The light comes on, I press the bar, they write me a check. How about you?"

know that money is valuable because we have learned that it allows us to obtain other desirable objects, including primary reinforcers such as food and shelter. Money thus becomes a secondary reinforcer.

What makes something a reinforcer depends on individual preferences. Though a Hershey bar could act as a reinforcer for one person, an individual who dislikes chocolate might find 75 cents more desirable. The only way we can know if a stimulus is a reinforcer for a given organism is to observe whether the frequency of a previously occurring behavior increases after the presentation of the stimulus.

Positive Reinforcers, Negative Reinforcers, and Punishment

In many respects, reinforcers can be thought of in terms of rewards; both a reinforcer and a reward increase the probability that a preceding response will occur again. But the term *reward* is limited to *positive* occurrences, and this is where it differs from a reinforcer—for it turns out that reinforcers can be positive or negative.

A **positive reinforcer** is a stimulus *added* to the environment that brings about an increase in a preceding response. If food, water, money, or praise is provided following a response, it is more likely that that response will occur again in the future. The paycheck that workers get at the end of the week, for example, increases the likelihood that they will return to their jobs the following week.

In contrast, a **negative reinforcer** refers to an unpleasant stimulus whose *removal* from the environment leads to an increase in the probability that a preceding response will occur again in the future. For example, if you have cold symptoms (an unpleasant stimulus) that are relieved when you take medicine, you are more likely to take the medicine when you experience such symptoms again. Taking medicine, then, is negatively reinforcing, because it removes the unpleasant cold symptoms. Similarly, if the radio volume is so loud that it hurts your ears, you are likely to find that turning it down relieves the problem. Lowering the volume is negatively reinforcing and you are more apt to repeat the action in the future. Negative reinforcement, then, teaches the individual that taking an action removes a negative condition that exists in the environment. Like positive reinforcers, negative reinforcers increase the likelihood that preceding behaviors will be repeated.

It is important to note that negative reinforcement is not the same as punishment. **Punishment** refers to a stimulus that *decreases* the probability that a prior behavior will occur again. Unlike negative reinforcement, which produces an *increase* in behavior, punishment reduces the likelihood of a prior response. If we receive a shock that is meant to decrease a certain behavior, then, we are receiving punishment; but if we are already receiving a shock and do something to stop that shock, the behavior that stops the shock is considered to be negatively reinforced. In the first case, the specific behavior is apt to decrease because of the punishment; in the second, it is likely to increase because of the negative reinforcement.

There are two types of punishment: positive punishment and negative punishment, just as there is positive and negative reinforcement. (In both cases, "positive" means adding something, whereas "negative" means removing something.) *Positive punishment* weakens a response through the application of an unpleasant stimulus. For instance, spanking a child for misbehaving or ten years in jail for committing a crime is positive punishment. In contrast, *negative punishment* consists of the removal of something pleasant. For instance, when a teenager is told she is "grounded" and will no longer be able to use the family car because of her poor grades, or when an employee is informed that he has been demoted with a cut in pay because of poor job evaluations, negative punishment is being administered. Both positive and negative punishment result in a decrease in the likelihood that a prior behavior will be repeated.

The distinctions between the two types of punishment, as well as positive and negative reinforcement, might seem confusing initially, but the following rules (and the summary in Table 5-1) can help you to distinguish these concepts from one another:

 PsychLink

Positive and negative reinforcers
www.mhhe.com/
feldmaness5-05links

positive reinforcer: A stimulus added to the environment that brings about an increase in a preceding response

negative reinforcer: An unpleasant stimulus whose removal leads to an increase in the probability that a preceding response will occur again in the future

punishment: A stimulus that decreases the probability that a previous behavior will occur again

Table 5-1 Types of Reinforcement and Punishment		
	EFFECT ON BEHAVIOR	
Procedure	**Increases**	**Decreases**
Presentation of Stimulus	*Positive reinforcement* *Example:* Giving a raise for good performance *Result: Increase* in frequency of response (good performance)	*Positive punishment* *Example:* Giving a spanking following misbehavior *Result: Decrease* in frequency of response (misbehavior)
Removal of Stimulus	*Negative reinforcement* *Example:* Terminating a headache by taking aspirin *Result: Increase* in frequency of response (taking aspirin)	*Negative punishment* *Example:* Removal of favorite toy after misbehavior *Result: Decrease* in frequency of response (misbehavior)

- Reinforcement *increases* the frequency of the behavior preceding it; punishment *decreases* the frequency of the behavior preceding it.
- The *application* of a *positive* stimulus brings about an increase in the frequency of behavior and is referred to as positive reinforcement; the *application* of a *negative* stimulus decreases or reduces the frequency of behavior and is called positive punishment.
- The *removal* of a *negative* stimulus that results in an increase in the frequency of behavior is termed negative reinforcement; the *removal* of a *positive* stimulus that decreases the frequency of behavior is called negative punishment.

PsychLink

Numerous articles on punishment
www.mhhe.com/
feldmaness5-05links

The Pros and Cons of Punishment: Why Reinforcement Beats Punishment

Is punishment an effective way to modify behavior? Punishment often presents the quickest route to changing behavior that, if allowed to continue, might be dangerous to an individual. For instance, a parent might not have a second chance to warn a child not to run into a busy street, so punishing the first incidence of this behavior might prove to be wise. Moreover, the use of punishment to suppress behavior, even temporarily, provides the opportunity to reinforce a person for subsequently behaving in a more desirable way.

There are some rare instances in which punishment can be the most humane approach to treating certain severe disorders. For example, some children suffer from *autism,* a psychological disorder that can lead them to abuse themselves by tearing at their skin or banging their heads against the wall, injuring themselves severely in the process. In such cases—and when all other treatments have failed—punishment in the form of a quick but intense electric shock has been used to prevent self-injurious behavior. Such punishment, however, is used only to keep the child safe and to buy time until positive reinforcement procedures can be initiated (Lovaas & Koegel, 1973; Linscheid et al., 1990; Siegel, 1996b).

Several disadvantages make the routine use of punishment questionable. For one thing, punishment is frequently ineffective, particularly if it is not delivered shortly after the undesired behavior or if the individual is able to leave the setting in which the punishment is being given. An employee who is reprimanded by the boss might quit; a teenager who loses the use of the family car might borrow a friend's instead. In such instances, the initial behavior that is being punished might be replaced by one that is even less desirable.

Even worse, physical punishment can convey to the recipient the idea that physical aggression is permissible and perhaps even desirable. A father who yells at and hits his son for misbehaving teaches the son that aggression is an appropriate, adult response. The son might soon copy his father's behavior by acting aggressively toward others. In addition, physical punishment is often administered by people who are themselves angry or enraged. It is unlikely that individuals in such an emotional state will be able to think through what they are doing or control carefully the degree of punishment they are inflicting. Ultimately, those who resort to physical punishment run the risk that they will grow to be feared. Punishment can also reduce the self-esteem of recipients unless they can understand the reasons for it.

Finally, punishment does not convey any information about what an alternative, more appropriate behavior might be. To be useful in bringing about more desirable behavior in the future, punishment must be accompanied by specific information about the behavior that is being punished, along with specific suggestions concerning a more desirable behavior. Punishing a child for staring out the window in school could merely lead her to stare at the floor instead. Unless we teach her appropriate ways to respond, we have merely managed to substitute one undesirable behavior for another. If punishment is not followed up with reinforcement for subsequent behavior that is more appropriate, little will be accomplished.

In short, reinforcing desired behavior is a more appropriate technique for modifying behavior than using punishment. Both in and out of the scientific arena, then, reinforcement usually beats punishment (Sulzer-Azaroff & Mayer, 1991; Seppa, 1996).

Schedules of Reinforcement: Timing Life's Rewards

The world would be a different place if poker players never played cards again after their first losing hand, fishermen returned to shore as soon as they missed a catch, or door-to-door salespeople turned in their samples after their first experience of being turned away. The fact that such unreinforced behaviors continue, often with great frequency and persistence, illustrates that reinforcement need not be received continually in order for behavior to be learned and maintained. In fact, behavior that is reinforced only occasionally can ultimately be learned better than behavior that is always reinforced.

When we refer to the frequency and timing of reinforcement following desired behavior, we are talking about **schedules of reinforcement.** Behavior that is reinforced every time it occurs is said to be on a **continuous reinforcement schedule;** if it is reinforced some but not all of the time, it is on a **partial reinforcement schedule.** Although learning occurs more rapidly under a continuous reinforcement schedule, behavior lasts longer after reinforcement stops when it is learned under a partial reinforcement schedule.

Why should partial reinforcement schedules result in stronger, longer-lasting learning than continuous reinforcement schedules? We can answer the question by examining how we might behave when using a candy vending machine compared with a Las Vegas slot machine. When we use a vending machine, prior experience has taught us that every time we put in the appropriate amount of money, the reinforcement, a candy bar, ought to be delivered. In other words, the schedule of reinforcement is continuous. In comparison, a slot machine offers a partial reinforcement schedule. We have learned that after putting in our cash, most of the time we will not receive anything in return. At the same time, though, we know that we will occasionally win something.

Now suppose that, unbeknownst to us, both the candy vending machine and the slot machine are broken, so that neither one is able to dispense anything. It would not be very long before we stopped depositing coins into the broken candy machine. Probably at most we would try only two or three times before leaving the machine in disgust. But the story would be quite different with the broken slot machine. Here, we would drop in money for a considerably longer time, even though there would be no payoff.

In formal terms, we can see the difference between the two reinforcement schedules: Partial reinforcement schedules (such as those provided by slot machines) maintain performance longer than continuous reinforcement schedules (such as those established in candy vending machines) before extinction—the disappearance of the conditioned response—occurs.

schedules of reinforcement: The frequency and timing of reinforcement following desired behavior

continuous reinforcement schedule: Reinforcement of behavior every time it occurs

partial reinforcement schedule: Reinforcement of behavior some but not all of the time

Figure 5–4 Typical outcomes of different reinforcement schedules. *(a)* In a fixed-ratio schedule, short pauses occur following each response. Because the more responses, the more reinforcement, fixed-ratio schedules produce a high rate of responding. *(b)* In a variable-ratio schedule, responding also occurs at a high rate. *(c)* A fixed-interval schedule produces lower rates of responding, especially just after reinforcement has been presented, since the organism learns that a specified time period must elapse between reinforcement. *(d)* A variable-interval schedule produces a fairly steady stream of responses.

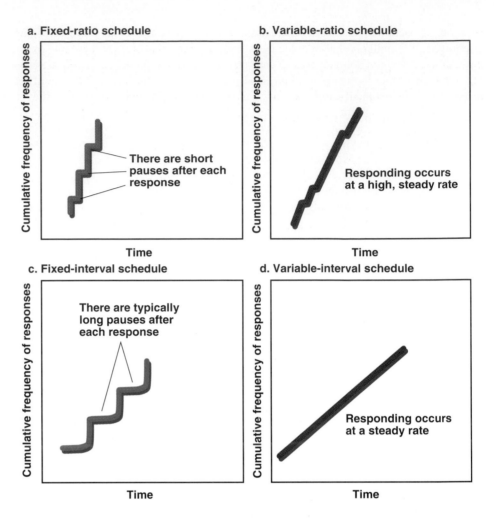

Certain kinds of partial reinforcement schedules produce stronger and lengthier responding before extinction than others. Although many different partial reinforcement schedules have been examined, they can most readily be put into two categories: schedules that consider the *number of responses* made before reinforcement is given, called fixed-ratio and variable-ratio schedules, and those that consider the *amount of time* that elapses before reinforcement is provided, called fixed-interval and variable-interval schedules.

Fixed- and Variable-Ratio Schedules

In a **fixed-ratio schedule,** reinforcement is given only after a certain number of responses. For instance, a pigeon might receive a food pellet every tenth time it pecked a key; here, the ratio would be 1:10. Similarly, garment workers are generally paid on fixed-ratio schedules: They receive several dollars for every blouse they sew. Because a greater rate of production means more reinforcement, people on fixed-ratio schedules are apt to work as quickly as possible (see Figure 5-4).

In a **variable-ratio schedule,** reinforcement occurs after a varying number of responses rather than after a fixed number. Although the specific number of responses necessary to receive reinforcement varies, the number of responses usually hovers around a specific average. A good example of a variable-ratio schedule is a telephone salesperson's job. She might make a sale during the third, eighth, ninth, and twentieth calls without being successful during any call in between. Although the number of responses that must be made before making a sale varies, it averages out to a 20 percent success rate.

fixed-ratio schedule: A schedule whereby reinforcement is given only after a certain number of responses are made

variable-ratio schedule: A schedule whereby reinforcement occurs after a varying number of responses rather than after a fixed number

Under these circumstances, you might expect that the salesperson would try to make as many calls as possible in as short a time as possible. This is the case with all variable-ratio schedules, which lead to a high rate of response and resistance to extinction.

Fixed- and Variable-Interval Schedules: The Passage of Time

In contrast to fixed- and variable-ratio schedules, in which the crucial factor is the number of responses, fixed-*interval* and variable-*interval* schedules focus on the amount of *time* that has elapsed since a person or animal was rewarded. One example of a fixed-interval schedule is a weekly paycheck. For people who receive regular, weekly paychecks, it typically makes relatively little difference exactly how much they produce in a given week.

Because a **fixed-interval schedule** provides reinforcement for a response only if a fixed time period has elapsed, overall rates of response are relatively low. This is especially true in the period just after reinforcement when the time before another reinforcement is relatively great. Students' study habits often exemplify this reality. If the periods between exams are relatively long (meaning that the opportunity for reinforcement for good performance is fairly infrequent), students often study minimally or not at all until the day of the exam draws near. Just before the exam, however, students begin to cram for it, signaling a rapid increase in the rate of their studying response. As you might expect, immediately following the exam there is a rapid decline in the rate of responding, with few people opening a book the day after a test.

One way to decrease the delay in responding that occurs just after reinforcement, and to maintain the desired behavior more consistently throughout an interval, is to use a variable-interval schedule. In a **variable-interval schedule,** the time between reinforcements varies around some average rather than being fixed. For example, a professor who gives surprise quizzes that vary from one every three days to one every three weeks, averaging one every two weeks, is using a variable-interval schedule. Compared to the study habits we observed with a fixed-interval schedule, students' study habits under such a variable-interval schedule would most likely be very different. Students would be apt to study more regularly since they would never know when the next surprise quiz would be coming. Variable-interval schedules, in general, are more likely to produce relatively steady rates of responding than fixed-interval schedules, with responses that take longer to extinguish after reinforcement ends.

Discrimination and Generalization in Operant Conditioning

It does not take a child long to learn that a red light at an intersection means stop and a green light indicates that it is permissible to continue. Just as in classical conditioning, then, operant learning involves the phenomena of discrimination and generalization.

The process by which people learn to discriminate stimuli is known as stimulus control training. In *stimulus control training,* a behavior is reinforced in the presence of a specific stimulus, but not in its absence. For example, one of the most difficult discriminations many people face is determining when someone's friendliness is not mere friendliness, but a signal of romantic interest. People learn to make the discrimination by observing the presence of certain nonverbal cues—such as increased eye contact and touching—that indicate romantic interest. When such cues are absent, people learn that no romantic interest is indicated. In this case, the nonverbal cue acts as a discriminative stimulus, one to which an organism learns to respond during stimulus control training. A *discriminative stimulus* signals the likelihood that reinforcement will follow a response. For example, if you wait until your roommate is in a good mood before you ask to borrow her favorite compact disc, your behavior can be said to be under stimulus control because you can discriminate between her moods.

Just as in classical conditioning, the phenomenon of stimulus generalization, in which an organism learns a response to one stimulus and then applies it to other stimuli, is also found in operant conditioning. If you have learned that being polite produces the

fixed-interval schedule: A schedule that provides reinforcement for a response only if a fixed time period has elapsed, making overall rates of response relatively low

variable-interval schedule: A schedule whereby the time between reinforcements varies around some average rather than being fixed

Nomar Garciaparra, like many baseball players, goes through a ritual of superstitious behaviors before batting. How can his actions be explained in terms of the principles of reinforcement?

reinforcement of getting your way in a certain situation, you are likely to generalize your response to other situations. Sometimes, though, generalization can have unfortunate consequences, such as when people behave negatively toward all members of a racial group because they have had an unpleasant experience with one member of that group.

Superstitious Behavior

When my son, a college senior, takes an exam, he puts on a tie. The reason: Early in his college career, he took an exam wearing a tie (because he had an interview later in the day), and he got an A. From that time on, he wore a tie to every exam.

To learning psychologists, such a ritual is an example of *superstitious behavior.* Superstitious behavior can be explained in terms of learning and reinforcement. As we have seen, behavior that is followed by a reinforcer tends to be strengthened. Occasionally, however, the behavior that occurs prior to the reinforcement is entirely coincidental. Still, an association is made between the behavior and reinforcement.

Imagine, for instance, that a baseball player taps his bat against the ground three times in a row just prior to getting a single. The hit is, of course, coincidental to the batter's tapping the ground, but the player might see it as somehow related. Because the player makes this association, he might tap the ground three times every time he is at bat in the future. And because he will be at least partially reinforced for this behavior— batters usually get a hit 25 percent of the time—his tapping behavior will be maintained, as a superstitious behavior (Van Ginkel, 1990; Matute, 1994, 1995).

Shaping: Reinforcing What Doesn't Come Naturally

Consider the difficulty of using operant conditioning to teach people to repair an automobile transmission. If you had to wait until they chanced to fix a transmission perfectly before you provided them with reinforcement, the Model T might be back in style long before they mastered the repair process.

There are many complex behaviors, ranging from auto repair to zoo management, that we would not expect to occur naturally as part of anyone's spontaneous behavior. For such behaviors, for which there might otherwise be no opportunity to provide reinforcement (because the behavior would never occur in the first place), a procedure known as shaping is used. **Shaping** is the process of teaching a complex behavior by rewarding closer and closer approximations of the desired behavior. In shaping, you start by reinforcing any behavior that is at all similar to the behavior you want the person to learn. Later, you reinforce only responses that are closer to the behavior you ultimately want to teach. Finally, you reinforce only the desired response. Each step in shaping, then, moves only slightly beyond the previously learned behavior, permitting the person to link the new step to the behavior learned earlier.

Shaping allows even lower animals to learn complex responses that would never occur naturally, ranging from lions jumping through hoops to dolphins rescuing divers lost at sea. Shaping also underlies the learning of many complex human skills. For instance, the organization of most textbooks is based on the principles of shaping. Typically, information is presented so that new material builds on previously learned concepts or skills. Thus the concept of shaping could not be presented in this chapter until we had discussed the more basic principles of operant learning. (For a further discussion of the applications of psychological approaches to learning, see the *Psychology at Work* box.)

PsychLink

Psychology of superstition
www.mhhe.com/
feldmaness5–05links

shaping: The process of teaching a complex behavior by rewarding closer and closer approximations to the desired behavior

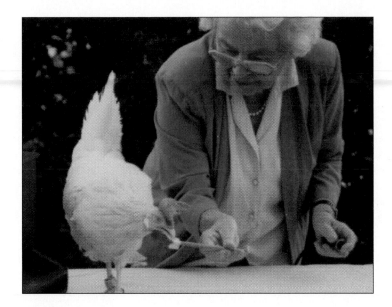

Biological Constraints on Learning: You Can't Teach an Old Dog Just Any Trick

Psychologists Keller and Marian Breland were pleased with their idea: As consultants to a professional animal trainer, they came up with the notion of having a pig place a wooden disk into a piggy bank. With their experience in training animals through operant conditioning, they thought the task would be easy to teach, given that it was certainly well within the range of the pig's physical capabilities. Yet every time they tried out the procedure, it failed. Upon viewing the disk, the pigs were willing to do nothing but root the wooden disk along the ground. Apparently, the pigs were biologically programmed to push stimuli in the shape of disks along the ground.

Their lack of swine success led the Brelands to substitute a raccoon. Although the procedure worked fine with one disk, when two disks were used, the raccoon refused to deposit either of them and instead rubbed the two together, as if it were washing them. Once again, it appeared that the disks evoked biologically innate behaviors that were impossible to replace through even the most exhaustive training (Breland & Breland, 1961).

The Brelands' difficulties illustrate an important point: Not all behaviors can be trained in all species equally well. Instead, there are *biological constraints*, built-in limitations, in the ability of animals to learn particular behaviors. In some cases, an organism will have a special predisposition that will aid in its learning a behavior (such as pecking behaviors in pigeons); in other cases, biological constraints will act to prevent or inhibit an organism from learning a behavior. In either instance, it is clear that animals have specialized learning mechanisms that influence how readily both classical and operant conditioning influence their behavior, and each species is biologically primed to develop particular kinds of associations and to have a difficult time in learning others (Hollis, 1984).

Psychology at Work

Lynne Calero

Dolphin Research Center, Grassy Key, Florida

Education: B.A. in psychology, George Washington University

Home: Big Pine Key, Florida

Lynne Calero

Many people have read about the possible connections between dolphins and humans in terms of both behavior and intellect, but for more than a decade Lynne Calero has seen these similarities firsthand.

An employee of the Dolphin Research Center in Grassy Key, Florida, Calero received her primary exposure to psychology as an undergraduate major at George Washington University in Washington, D.C. "Our facility is a research education facility in which we do training to educate the public, as well as monitoring individual animals' health," she says.

In training dolphins, Calero makes use of the basic principles of learning. "The whole basis of the training done with dolphins and sea lions is operant conditioning and positive reinforcement," she notes.

For instance, one specific type of training aims at getting dolphins to present their tail flukes, thereby permitting medical tests that require blood samples. "All the animals first learn the basics, such as responding to a whistle. The whistle becomes connected with feeding, giving attention, or a back rub.

"From there we gradually get them to position alongside of the dock," she explains, "followed by a series of approximations, as in training with any behavior. With each step we get closer to the tail flukes until the dolphin allows us to hold onto the flukes above the water surface."

Younger dolphins are easier to train, and it takes only a month of training before they will present their flukes. To Calero, this is one example of the unusual intelligence of dolphins. "Certainly their brain anatomy is very complicated. Overall, my impression is that dolphins are incredibly intelligent, as well as being intensely intuitive."

> "Our facility is a research education facility in which we do training to educate the public, as well as monitoring individual animals' health."

> "Overall, my impression is that dolphins are incredibly intelligent, as well as being intensely intuitive and wise."

Evaluate

1. _____ conditioning describes learning that occurs as a result of reinforcement.

2. Match the type of operant learning with its definition:

   1. An unpleasant stimulus is presented to decrease behavior   a. Positive reinforcement

   2. An unpleasant stimulus is removed to increase behavior   b. Negative reinforcement

   3. A pleasant stimulus is presented to increase behavior   c. Positive punishment

   4. A pleasant stimulus is removed to decrease behavior   d. Negative punishment

3. Sandy had had a rough day, and his son's noisemaking was not helping him relax. Not wanting to resort to scolding, Sandy told his son in a serious manner that he was very tired and would like the boy to play quietly for an hour. This approach worked. For Sandy, the change in his son's behavior was

   a. positively reinforcing.

   b. negatively reinforcing.

4. In a _____ reinforcement schedule, behavior is reinforced some of the time, while in a _____ reinforcement schedule, behavior is reinforced all the time.

5. Match the type of reinforcement schedule with its definition.

   1. Reinforcement occurs after a set time period   a. Fixed-ratio

   2. Reinforcement occurs after a set number of responses   b. Variable-interval

   3. Reinforcement occurs after a varying time period   c. Fixed-interval

Rethink

1. How might operant conditioning be used to address serious personal concerns, such as smoking and unhealthy eating?

2. How might you go about "curing" superstitious behavior, such as the rituals people engage in before examinations or athletic competitions? Should we try to extinguish such behavior?

4. Reinforcement occurs after a   d. Variable-ratio
   varying number of responses

6. Fixed reinforcement schedules produce greater resistance to extinction than variable reinforcement schedules. True or false?

Cognitive-Social Approaches to Learning

Prepare

What is the role of cognition and thought in learning?

What are some practical methods for bringing about behavior change, both in ourselves and in others?

Organize

Cognitive-Social Approaches to Learning
  Latent Learning
  Observational Learning
  Violence on Television and in Movies
  The Unresolved Controversy of Cognitive-Social Learning Theory

Consider what happens when people learn to drive a car. They don't just get behind the wheel and stumble around until they randomly put the key into the ignition, and later, after many false starts, accidentally manage to get the car to move forward, thereby receiving positive reinforcement. Instead, they already know the basic elements of driving from prior experience as passengers, when they more than likely noticed how the key was inserted into the ignition, the car was put in drive, and the gas pedal was pressed to make the car go forward.

Clearly, not all learning is due to operant and classical conditioning. In fact, examples like learning to drive a car imply that some kinds of learning must involve higher-order processes in which people's thoughts and memories and the way they process information account for their responses. Such situations argue against regarding learning as the unthinking, mechanical, and automatic acquisition of associations between stimuli and responses, as in classical conditioning, or the presentation of reinforcement, as in operant conditioning.

Instead, some psychologists view learning in terms of the thought processes, or cognitions, that underlie it—an approach known as **cognitive-social learning theory.** Although psychologists using the cognitive-social learning perspective do not deny the importance of classical and operant conditioning, they have developed approaches that focus on the unseen mental processes that occur during learning, rather than concentrating solely on external stimuli, responses, and reinforcements.

In its most basic formulation, cognitive-social learning theory suggests that it is not enough to say that people make responses because there is an assumed link between a stimulus and a response due to a past history of reinforcement for the response. Instead, according to this point of view, people—and even animals—develop an *expectation* that they will receive a reinforcer upon making a response. Support for this point of view comes from several quarters.

cognitive-social learning theory: The study of the thought processes that underlie learning

Latent Learning

Some of the most direct evidence regarding cognitive processes comes from a series of experiments that revealed a type of cognitive-social learning called latent learning. In **latent learning,** a new behavior is learned but not demonstrated until reinforcement is provided for displaying it (Tolman & Honzik, 1930). In the studies, psychologists examined the behavior of rats in a maze such as the one shown in Figure 5-5a. In one representative experiment, a group of rats was allowed to wander around the maze once a day for seventeen days without ever receiving any reward. Understandably, these rats made many errors and spent a relatively long time reaching the end of the maze. A second group, however, was always given food at the end of the maze. Not surprisingly, these rats learned to run quickly and directly to the food box, making few errors.

A third group of rats started out in the same situation as the unrewarded rats, but only for the first ten days. On the eleventh day, a critical experimental manipulation was

latent learning: Learning in which a new behavior is acquired but is not demonstrated until reinforcement is provided

a.   **b.**   **Days**

Figure 5-5 *(a)* In an attempt to demonstrate latent learning, rats were allowed to roam through a maze of this sort once a day for seventeen days. *(b)* Those rats that were never rewarded (the unrewarded control condition) consistently made the most errors, whereas those that received food at the finish every day (the rewarded control condition) consistently made far fewer errors. But the results also showed latent learning: Rats that were initially unrewarded but began to be rewarded only after the tenth day (the experimental group) showed an immediate reduction in errors and soon became similar to the error rate of the rats that had been consistently rewarded. According to cognitive-social learning theorists, the reduction in errors indicates that the rats had developed a cognitive map—a mental representation—of the maze (Tolman & Honzik, 1930). Can you think of other examples of latent learning?

cognitive map: A mental representation of spatial locations and directions

introduced: From that point on, the rats in this group were given food for completing the maze. The results of this manipulation were dramatic, as you can see from the graph in Figure 5-5b. The previously unrewarded rats, who had earlier seemed to wander about aimlessly, showed such reductions in running time and declines in error rates that their performance almost immediately matched that of the group that had received rewards from the start.

To cognitive-social theorists, it seemed clear that the unrewarded rats had learned the layout of the maze early in their explorations; they just never displayed their latent learning until the reinforcement was offered. Instead, the rats seemed to develop a **cognitive map** of the maze—a mental representation of spatial locations and directions.

People, too, develop cognitive maps of their surroundings, based primarily on particular landmarks. When they first encounter a new environment, their maps tend to rely on specific paths—such as the directions we might give someone unfamiliar with an area: "Turn right at the stop sign, make a left at the bridge, and then go up the hill." However, as people become more familiar with an area, they develop an overall conception of it, which has been called an abstract cognitive map. Using such a map, they are eventually able to take shortcuts as they develop a broad understanding of the area (Garling, 1989; Gale et al., 1990; Plumert et al., 1995).

The possibility that we develop our cognitive maps through latent learning presents something of a problem for strict operant conditioning theorists. If we consider the results of Tolman's maze experiment, for instance, it is unclear what the specific reinforcement was that permitted the rats that initially received no reward to learn about the layout of the maze, because there was no obvious reinforcer present. Instead, the results support a cognitive-social view of learning, in which learning might have resulted in changes in unobservable mental processes.

Observational Learning: Learning Through Imitation

Let's return for a moment to the case of a person learning to drive. How can we account for instances in which an individual with no direct experience in carrying out a particular behavior learns the behavior and then performs it? To answer this question, psychologists have proposed another form of cognitive-social learning: observational learning.

According to psychologist Albert Bandura and colleagues, a major part of human learning consists of **observational learning,** which they define as learning through observing the behavior of another person called a *model* (Bandura, 1977). Bandura and his colleagues demonstrated rather dramatically the ability of models to stimulate learning. In what is now considered a classic experiment, young children saw a film of an adult wildly hitting a 5-foot-tall inflatable punching toy called a Bobo doll (Bandura, Ross, & Ross, 1963a, 1963b). Later the children were given the opportunity to play with the Bobo doll themselves and, sure enough, most displayed the same kind of behavior, in some cases mimicking the aggressive behavior almost identically.

Not only negative behaviors are acquired through observational learning. In one experiment, for example, children who were afraid of dogs were exposed to a model—dubbed the Fearless Peer—playing with a dog (Bandura, Grusec, & Menlove, 1967). Following exposure, children who had observed the model were considerably more likely to approach a strange dog than children who had not viewed the Fearless Peer.

According to Bandura, observational learning takes place in four steps: (1) paying attention and perceiving the most critical features of another person's behavior; (2) remembering the behavior; (3) reproducing the action; and (4) being motivated to learn and carry out the behavior. Instead of learning occurring through trial and error, then, with successes being reinforced and failures punished, many important skills are learned through observational processes (Bandura, 1986).

Observational learning is particularly important in acquiring skills for which shaping is inappropriate. Piloting an airplane and performing brain surgery, for example, are behaviors that could hardly be learned using trial-and-error methods without grave cost—literally—to those involved in the learning.

Not all behavior that we witness is learned or carried out, of course. One crucial factor that determines whether we later imitate a model is the consequences of the model's behavior. If we observe a friend being rewarded for putting more time into her studies by receiving higher grades, we are more likely to imitate her behavior than if her behavior only results in her being stressed and tired. Models who are rewarded for behaving in a particular way are more apt to be mimicked than models who receive punishment. Interestingly, though, observing the punishment of a model does not necessarily stop observers from learning the behavior. Observers can still describe the model's behavior—they are just less apt to perform it (Bandura, 1977, 1986, 1994).

Observational learning is central to a number of important issues relating to the extent to which people learn by simply watching the behavior of others. For instance, the degree to which observation of aggression in the media produces subsequent aggression on the part of viewers is a crucial—and controversial—question, as we discuss next.

As this boy watches his father, he is engaging in observational learning. How does observational learning contribute to defining gender roles?

 PsychLink

Social learning theory
www.mhhe.com/
feldmaness5–05links

observational learning: Learning through observing the behavior of another person called a *model*

PsychLink

Violence in the media
www.mhhe.com/
feldmaness5-05links

Albert Bandura examined the principles of observational learning.

Violence on Television and in Movies: Does the Media's Message Matter?

The daughter of a judge from a politically prominent family runs off with her ne'er-do-well boyfriend. They drop LSD and watch, over and over, the ultraviolent Oliver Stone movie "Natural Born Killers," about a young couple who take drugs and kill people for pleasure. One afternoon, out joyriding in rural Mississippi, the boy suggests [according to the girl] "finding an isolated farmhouse and doing a home invasion, robbing a family and killing them, leaving no witnesses . . . as if he was fantasizing from the movie 'Natural Born Killers.'" At a cotton gin on a lonely highway, the boyfriend guns down an innocent citizen, a devoted husband of 40 years, just for the thrill of it. . . . The next day the boy says to the girl, "It's your turn." That night, wearing a hooded poncho, she shoots a convenience-store clerk in cold blood, leaving the mother of three children paralyzed below the neck. (A. G. Miller, 1999, p. 176)

The aftermath of the killers' shooting spree may have a profound effect not just on the individuals directly involved, but on the motion picture industry, because the family of one of the victims sued Oliver Stone, the director of *Natural Born Killers* and Warner Brothers, which released the film, for millions of dollars. Although legal experts suggest that the lawsuit is unlikely to succeed, it raises a critical issue: Does observation of violence and antisocial acts in the media lead viewers to behave in similar ways? Because research on modeling shows that people frequently learn and imitate the aggression that they observe, this question is among the most important being addressed by social psychologists.

Certainly, the amount of violence in the mass media is enormous. Between the ages of 5 and 15, the average American child is exposed to no fewer than 13,000 violent deaths on television; the number of fights and aggressive sequences that children view is still higher. Adult television shows also contain significant violence, with cable television leading the way with such shows as *When Animals Attack* and *World's Scariest Police Shootouts* (Liebert & Sprafkin, 1988; Mifflin, 1998).

Most experts agree that watching high levels of media violence make viewers more susceptible to acting aggressively—for several reasons. For one thing, viewing violence seems to lower inhibitions against the performance of aggression—watching television portrayals of violence makes aggression seem a legitimate response to particular situations. Viewing violence also can distort our understanding of the meaning of others' behavior, predisposing us to view even nonaggressive acts by others as aggressive. Finally, a continual diet of aggression can leave us desensitized to violence, and what

Applying Psychology in the 21st Century

Does Virtual Aggression Lead to Actual Aggression?

Blood flows freely as still-warm corpses lie on the ground. Potential victims beg for mercy, while others moan in pain. Some people catch fire before they are mowed down, falling to the ground, dead.

This is just some of the continual violence that characterizes the computer game Postal. In the game, trigger-happy players act out the role of Postal Dude, who shoots at everything—and everyone—in his path. Like Doom, a favorite game of one of the Columbine High School killers, Postal allows players their choice of a variety of weapons of carnage.

Postal and Doom are just two of many highly realistic, involving, and violent video games now on the market. In fact, one survey found that almost 80 percent of the most popular games involved aggression, with one-fifth of them involving violence against women (Dietz, 1998).

Can playing games like Postal and Doom lead to actual aggression? Increasing research evidence suggests that it might. According to a recent series of studies by psychologists Craig Anderson and Karen Dill (2000), playing violent video games is associated with later aggressive behavior. In one study, for example, they found that college students who frequently played violent video games were more likely to have been involved in delinquent behavior and aggression. Frequent players also had lower academic achievement.

On the other hand, such results do not show that playing violent games causes delinquency, aggression, and lower academic performance; the research only found that the various variables were *associated with* one another. To explore the question of whether violent game play actually caused aggression, Anderson and Dill subsequently conducted a short-term laboratory study. In it, they had participants in an experiment play either a violent video game (Wolfenstein 3D) or one that was nonviolent (Myst). The results were clear: Exposure to the graphically violent video game increased aggressive thoughts and actual aggression.

The finding of a link between playing violent video games and aggressive behavior is consistent with findings from other studies, and it makes sense in light of the research on the consequences of exposure to violence in the media. In fact, the effects of playing video games could be even greater than the effects of merely watching an aggressive television program,

While research has shown that a link exists between playing violent video games and aggressive thoughts and behavior, it has not shown that game playing causes delinquency, real-world aggression, or lower academic achievement. Do you think a definite causal connection will ever be found?

because video games teach something that the mere observation of violence does not: the motor skills involved in aggression. By actually firing virtual weapons at people and objects appearing on the screen, game players presumably hone the skills that would make them more effective in using actual weapons (Cooper & Mackie, 1986; D. Cohen, 1996; Griffiths, 1997).

If a conclusive causal link between playing violent video games and subsequent aggressive acts were established, would you support a ban on such games? Why or why not?

previously would have repelled us now produces little emotional response. Our sense of the pain and suffering brought about by aggression might be diminished (Berkowitz, 1993; Berkowitz & LePage, 1996; Huesmann & Moise, 1996).

Of course, the media are not the only source of aggressive models. For example, many computer and video games involve a significant amount of graphic violence. Does exposure to such violence affect players? For an answer, consider the research findings described in the *Applying Psychology in the 21st Century* box.

EXPLORING DIVERSITY

Does Culture Influence How We Learn?

When a member of the Chilcotin Indian tribe teaches her daughter to prepare salmon, at first she only allows the daughter to observe the entire process. A little later, she permits her child to try out some basic parts of the task. Her response to questions is noteworthy. For example, when the daughter asks about how to do "the backbone part," the mother's response is to repeat the entire process with another fish. The reason? The mother feels that one cannot learn the individual parts of the task apart from the context of preparing the whole fish. (Tharp, 1989)

Looking Back

What is learning?

- Learning, a relatively permanent change in behavior due to experience, is a basic topic of psychology. However, learning must be assessed indirectly by observing performance. (p. 150)

How do we learn to form associations between stimuli and responses?

- One major form of learning is classical conditioning, which occurs when a neutral stimulus—one that brings about no relevant response—is repeatedly paired with a stimulus (called an unconditioned stimulus) that brings about a natural, untrained response. (p. 150)
- Conditioning occurs when the neutral stimulus is repeatedly presented just before the unconditioned stimulus. After repeated pairings, the neutral stimulus brings about the same response as the unconditioned stimulus. When this occurs, the neutral stimulus has become a conditioned stimulus, and the response a conditioned response. (p. 151)
- Learning is not always permanent. Extinction occurs when a previously learned response decreases in frequency and eventually disappears. (p. 153)
- Stimulus generalization occurs when a conditioned response follows a stimulus that is similar to, but not the same as, the original conditioned stimulus. The converse phenomenon, stimulus discrimination, occurs when an organism learns to distinguish between stimuli. (p. 154)

What is the role of reward and punishment in learning?

- A second major form of learning is operant conditioning. According to B. F. Skinner, the major mechanism underlying learning is reinforcement, the process by which a stimulus increases the probability that a preceding behavior will be repeated. (p. 156)
- Primary reinforcers involve rewards that are naturally effective without prior exposure because they satisfy a biological need. Secondary reinforcers begin to act as if they were primary reinforcers through frequent pairings with a primary reinforcer. (p. 158)
- Positive reinforcers are stimuli that are added to the environment and lead to an increase in a preceding response. Negative reinforcers are stimuli that remove something unpleasant from the environment, leading to an increase in the preceding response. (p. 159)
- Punishment decreases the probability that a prior behavior will occur. Positive punishment weakens a response through the application of an unpleasant stimulus, while negative punishment weakens a response by the removal of something positive. In contrast to reinforcement, in which the goal is to increase the incidence of behavior, punishment is meant to decrease or suppress behavior. (p. 160)
- Schedules and patterns of reinforcement affect the strength and duration of learning. Generally, partial reinforcement schedules—in which reinforcers are not delivered on every trial—produce stronger and longer-lasting learning than continuous reinforcement schedules. (p. 161)
- Among the major categories of reinforcement schedules are fixed- and variable-ratio schedules, which are based on the number of responses made, and fixed- and variable-interval schedules, which are based on the time interval that elapses before reinforcement is provided. (p. 162)
- Generalization and discrimination operate in operant conditioning as well as classical conditioning. (p. 163)

- Superstitious behavior results from the mistaken belief that particular ideas, objects, or behavior will cause certain events to occur. (p. 164)
- Shaping is a process for teaching complex behaviors by rewarding closer and closer approximations of the desired final behavior. (p. 164)
- There are biological constraints, or built-in limitations, on the ability of an organism to learn. Because of these constraints, certain behaviors will be relatively easy to learn, whereas other behaviors will be either difficult or impossible to learn. (p. 165)

What is the role of cognition and thought in learning?

- Cognitive-social approaches consider learning in terms of thought processes or cognition. Phenomena such as latent learning—in which a new behavior is learned but not performed until reinforcement is provided for its performance—and the apparent development of cognitive maps support cognitive-social approaches. Learning also occurs through observation of the behavior of models. (p. 167)
- The major factor that determines whether an observed behavior will actually be performed is the nature of reinforcement or punishment a model receives. (p. 169)
- Learning styles are characteristic ways of approaching material, based on a person's cultural background and unique pattern of abilities. One major dimension relates to analytic versus relational approaches to learning. (p. 171)

What are some practical methods for bringing about behavior change, both in ourselves and in others?

- Behavior modification is a method for formally using the principles of learning theory to promote the frequency of desired behaviors and to decrease or eliminate unwanted ones. (p. 174)

Key Terms and Concepts

learning (p. 150)
classical conditioning (p. 151)
neutral stimulus (p. 151)
unconditioned stimulus (UCS) (p. 151)
unconditioned response (UCR) (p. 151)
conditioned stimulus (CS) (p. 151)
conditioned response (CR) (p. 151)
extinction (p. 153)
spontaneous recovery (p. 154)
stimulus generalization (p. 154)
stimulus discrimination (p. 154)
operant conditioning (p. 156)
reinforcement (p. 158)
reinforcer (p. 158)
positive reinforcer (p. 159)

negative reinforcer (p. 159)
punishment (p. 159)
schedules of reinforcement (p. 161)
continuous reinforcement schedule (p. 161)
partial reinforcement schedule (p. 161)
fixed-ratio schedule (p. 162)
variable-ratio schedule (p. 162)
fixed-interval schedule (p. 163)
variable-interval schedule (p. 163)
shaping (p. 164)
cognitive-social learning theory (p. 167)
latent learning (p. 167)
cognitive map (p. 168)
observational learning (p. 169)
behavior modification (p. 174)

Psychology on the Web

1. B. F. Skinner had an impact on society and thought that is only hinted at in this chapter. Find additional information on the Web about Skinner's life and influence. See if you can find out about his ideas for an ideal, utopian society based on the principles of conditioning and behaviorism. Write a summary of what you find.

2. Select a topic discussed in this chapter that is of interest to you (e.g., superstition, teaching complex behaviors by shaping, violence in video games, relational vs. analytic learning styles, behavior modification, etc.). Find at least two sources of information on the Web about your topic and summarize the results of your quest. It may be most helpful to find two different approaches to your topic and compare them.

 Preview

For additional quizzing and a variety of interactive resources, visit the *Essentials of Understanding Psychology* Online Learning Center at

www.mhhe.com/feldmaness5

Epilogue

In this chapter we have discussed several kinds of learning, ranging from classical conditioning, which depends on the existence of natural stimulus-response pairings, to operant conditioning, in which reinforcement is used to increase desired behavior. These approaches to learning focus on outward, behavioral learning processes. We have also been introduced to more cognitive-social approaches to learning, which focus on mental processes and enable learning.

We have also noted that learning is affected by culture and individual differences, with individual learning styles potentially affecting the ways in which people learn most effectively. Finally, we saw some ways in which our learning about learning can be put to practical use, through such means as behavior modification programs designed to decrease negative behaviors and increase positive ones.

Before proceeding to the next chapter—on memory—return to the prologue of this chapter and consider the following questions in relation to Ike, the helpful dog who served Elizabeth Twohy.

1. Is Ike's learning primarily an example of classical conditioning, operant conditioning, or cognitive-social learning? Why?
2. Do you think punishment would be an effective teaching strategy for Ike? Why?
3. In what way would shaping have been used to teach Ike some of his more complex behaviors, such as sorting the recyclables and removing dishes from the dishwasher?

Chapter Six

Memory

Prologue

The Man Who Vanished into His Past

Six days after his disappearance, Terry Dibert was found wandering aimlessly in a wildfire, 800 miles from home, and thinking it was 11 years earlier.

Terry Dibert got up from his desk in the school district headquarters in Bedford, Pennsylvania, and vanished into his past.

That sounds like an opening line to a thriller. But for Mr. Dibert, who left his computer running and his jacket on the back of his chair, it was literally true.

Six days later and 800 miles away, Mr. Dibert, the district's business manager, reappeared near dawn in the midst of a natural disaster. Police officers from Daytona Beach, Florida, found him...wandering on Interstate 95 through the blinding smoke from the wildfires that had shut the highway and forced the evacuation of much of the area.

Mr. Dibert told the police he was a 23-year-old sergeant trying to rejoin his Army unit at Fort Bragg. He was worried about being separated from his wife, who was pregnant with their first child (Sherman, 1999, p. F8).

Looking Ahead

Terry Dibert was accurate—except for one thing: His account was eleven years out of date. When police called Fort Bragg, they found that he had been discharged almost a dozen years earlier, and his wife, whom he thought was pregnant, had delivered the child ten years earlier.

The source of Dibert's strange memory loss proved to be a brain cyst that was pressing against part of the brain that helps store memories. Following surgery to drain the cyst, Dibert's memory returned to normal.

Stories like this illustrate not only the important role memory plays in our lives, but also its fragility. Memory allows us to retrieve a vast amount of information. We are able to remember the name of a friend we haven't talked with for years and to recall details of a picture that hung in our childhood bedroom. At the same time, though, memory failures are common. We forget where we left the keys to the car and fail to answer an exam question about material we studied only a few hours earlier.

In this chapter, we consider the nature of memory. We examine how information is stored and retrieved. We discuss approaches that suggest there are several separate types of memory, and we explain how each type is believed to function in a somewhat different fashion. We examine the problems of retrieving information from memory, the accuracy of memories, and the reasons information is sometimes forgotten. We also consider the biological foundations of memory. Finally, we discuss some practical means of increasing memory capacity.

Prepare

What is memory?
Are there different kinds of memory?

Organize

Encoding, Storage, and Retrieval of Memory
  The Three Systems of Memory
  Contemporary Approaches to Memory

 PsychLink

Reports on memory
www.mhhe.com/
feldmaness5-06links

memory: The process by which we encode, store, and retrieve information

Encoding, Storage, and Retrieval of Memory

You are playing a game of Trivial Pursuit, and winning the game comes down to one question: On what body of water is Bombay located?

As you rack your brain for the answer, several fundamental processes relating to memory come into play. Perhaps you have never been exposed to information regarding Bombay's location, or if you have been exposed to it, perhaps it didn't register in a meaningful way. In other words, your difficulty in answering the question might be traced to the initial encoding stage of memory. *Encoding* refers to the process by which information is initially recorded in a form usable to memory.

On the other hand, even if you had been exposed to the information and originally knew the name of the body of water, you might still be unable to recall it during the game because of a failure in the retention process. Memory specialists speak of *storage,* the maintenance of material saved in the memory system. If the material is not stored adequately, it cannot be recalled later.

Memory also depends on a third process: retrieval. In *retrieval,* material in memory storage is located, brought into awareness, and used. Your failure to recall Bombay's location, then, could rest on your inability to retrieve information that you learned earlier.

In sum, psychologists consider **memory** as the process by which we encode, store, and retrieve information (see Figure 6-1). Each of the three parts of this definition—encoding, storage, and retrieval—represents a different process. You can think of these processes as analogous to the functions of a computer's keyboard (encoding), disk (storage), and screen (retrieval). Only if all three processes have operated will you experience success and be able to recall the body of water on which Bombay is located: the Arabian Sea.

However, before continuing, we should keep in mind the value of memory *failures.* Forgetting is essential to the proper functioning of memory. The ability to forget inconsequential details about experiences, people, and objects helps us to avoid being burdened and distracted by immense stores of meaningless data. Furthermore, forgetting permits us to form general impressions and recollections. For example, the reason our friends consistently look familiar to us is because of our ability to forget their clothing, facial

Figure 6-1 Memory is built on three basic processes—encoding, storage, and retrieval—that are analogous to the functions of a computer's keyboard, disk, and screen. The analogy is not perfect, however, because human memory is less precise than a computer's. How might you modify the analogy to make it more accurate?

blemishes, and other transient features that change from one occasion to the next. Instead, our memories are based on a summary of various critical features—a far more economical use of our memory capabilities. Forgetting unnecessary information, then, is as essential to the proper functioning of memory as is remembering more important material.

The Three Systems of Memory: Memory Storehouses

Although the processes of encoding, storing, and retrieving information are necessary for memory to operate successfully, they do not describe *how* information enters into memory. Many psychologists studying memory suggest that there are different systems or stages through which information must travel if it is to be remembered.

According to one of the most influential and enduring theories, based on the cognitive perspective we first discussed in Chapter 1, there are three kinds of memory storage systems. These storehouses vary in terms of their function and the length of time they retain information (Atkinson & Shiffrin, 1968, 1971).

As shown in Figure 6-2, **sensory memory** refers to the initial, momentary storage of information, lasting only an instant. Information is recorded by the person's sensory system as an exact replica of the stimulus. In a second stage, **short-term memory** holds information for 15 to 25 seconds and stores it according to its meaning rather than as mere sensory stimulation. The third type of storage system is **long-term memory.** Information is stored in long-term memory on a relatively permanent basis, although it might be difficult to retrieve,

sensory memory: The initial, momentary storage of information, lasting only an instant

short-term memory: Memory that holds information for 15 to 25 seconds

long-term memory: Memory that stores information on a relatively permanent basis, although it might be difficult to retrieve

Figure 6-2 In this three-stage model of memory, information initially recorded by the person's sensory system enters sensory memory, which momentarily holds the information. It then moves to short-term memory, which stores the information for 15 to 25 seconds. Finally, the information can move into long-term memory, which is relatively permanent. Whether the information moves from short-term to long-term memory depends on the kind and amount of rehearsal of the material that is carried out (After Atkinson & Shifrin, 1968).

PsychLink

Theory of sensory memory

www.mhhe.com/

feldmaness5-06links

Although we'll be discussing the three types of memory as separate memory stores, keep in mind that these are not mini-warehouses located in particular portions of the brain. Instead, they represent three different types of memory systems with different characteristics. Furthermore, although the three-part model of memory dominated the field of memory research for several decades, recent studies have suggested several newer models, as we'll discuss later. Still, considering memory in terms of three major kinds of stores provides us with a useful framework for understanding how information is both recalled and forgotten.

Sensory Memory

A momentary flash of lightning, the sound of a twig snapping, and the sting of a pinprick all represent stimulation of exceedingly brief duration, but they might nonetheless provide important information that can require some response. Such stimuli are initially—and briefly—stored in sensory memory, the first repository of the information that the world presents to us. Actually, the term *sensory memory* denotes several types of sensory memories, each related to a different source of sensory information. There is **iconic memory,** which reflects information from our visual system; **echoic memory,** which stores auditory information coming from the ears; and corresponding memories for each of the other senses.

iconic memory: Memory of information from our visual system

echoic memory: Memory of auditory information coming from the ears

Regardless of the individual subtypes, sensory memory in general is able to store information for only a very short time. If information does not pass to short-term memory, it is lost for good. For instance, iconic memory seems to last less than a second, although if the initial stimulus is very bright, the image might last a little longer. Echoic memory typically fades within two or three seconds. However, despite the brief duration of sensory memory, its precision is high: Sensory memory can store an almost exact replica of each stimulus to which it is exposed (Darwin, Turvey, & Crowder, 1972; Long & Beaton, 1982; Sams et al., 1993).

If the storage capabilities of sensory memory are so limited and information stored within sensory memory so fleeting, it would seem almost impossible to find evidence for its existence; new information would constantly be replacing older information, even before a person could report its presence. Not until psychologist George Sperling (1960) conducted a series of clever and now-classic studies was sensory memory well understood. Sperling briefly exposed people to a series of twelve letters arranged in the following pattern:

$$\begin{array}{cccc} F & T & Y & C \\ K & D & N & L \\ Y & W & B & M \end{array}$$

When exposed to this pattern of letters for just one-twentieth of a second, most people could accurately recall only four or five of the letters. Although they knew that they had seen more, the memory of these letters had faded by the time they reported the

A momentary flash of lightning leaves a sensory visual memory, a fleeting but exact replica of the stimulus that fades rapidly.

first few letters. It was possible, then, that the information had initially been accurately stored in sensory memory, but during the time it took to verbalize the first four or five letters the memory of the other letters faded.

To test that possibility, Sperling conducted an experiment in which a high, medium, or low tone sounded just after a person had been exposed to the full pattern of letters. People were told to report the letters in the highest line if a high tone were sounded, the middle line if the medium tone occurred, or the lowest line at the sound of the low tone. Because the tone occurred after the exposure, people had to rely on their memory to report the correct row.

The results of the study clearly showed that people had been storing the complete pattern in memory. They were accurate in their recollection of the letters in the line that had been indicated by the tone, regardless of whether it was the top, middle, or bottom line. Obviously, *all* the lines they had seen had been stored in sensory memory. Despite its rapid loss, then, the information in sensory memory was an accurate representation of what people had seen.

By gradually lengthening the time between the presentation of the visual pattern and the tone, Sperling was able to determine with some accuracy the length of time that information was stored in sensory memory. The ability to recall a particular row of the pattern when a tone was sounded declined progressively as the period between visual exposure and tone increased. This decline continued until the period reached about one second in duration, at which point the row could not be recalled accurately at all. Sperling concluded that the entire visual image was stored in sensory memory for less than a second.

In sum, sensory memory operates as a kind of snapshot that stores information—of a visual, auditory, or other sensory nature—for a brief moment in time. But it is as if each snapshot, immediately after being taken, is destroyed and replaced with a new one. Unless the information in the snapshot is transferred to some other type of memory, it is lost.

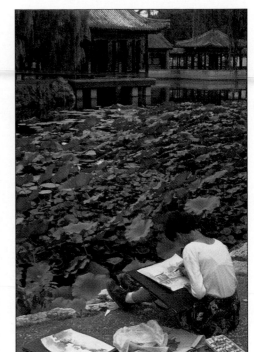

An artist must repeatedly view the subject of a painting in order to capture the image as viewed, using both short-term and long-term memory. Why do you think people tend to close their eyes when recalling a scene or picture?

Short-Term Memory: Giving Memory Meaning

Because the information that is stored briefly in our sensory memory consists of representations of raw sensory stimuli, it is not meaningful to us. For us to make sense of it and to allow for the possibility of long-term retention, the information must be transferred to the next stage of memory, short-term memory. Short-term memory is the memory store in which information first has meaning, although the maximum length of retention there is relatively short.

The specific process by which sensory memories are transformed into short-term memories is not yet clear. Some theorists suggest that the information is first translated into graphical representations or images, and others hypothesize that the transfer occurs when the sensory stimuli are changed to words (Baddeley & Wilson, 1985). What is clear, however, is that unlike sensory memory, which holds a relatively full and detailed—if short-lived—representation of the world, short-term memory has incomplete representational capabilities.

In fact, the specific amount of information that can be held in short-term memory has been identified as seven items, or "chunks," of information, with variations up to plus or minus two chunks. A **chunk** is a meaningful grouping of stimuli that can be stored as a unit in short-term memory. According to George Miller (1956), it could be individual letters or numbers, permitting us to hold a seven-digit phone number (like 226-4610) in short-term memory.

But a chunk might also consist of larger categories, such as words or other meaningful units. For example, consider the following list of twenty-one letters:

P B S F O X C N N A B C C B S M T V N B C

Because the list exceeds seven chunks, it is difficult to recall the letters after one exposure. But suppose they were presented to you as follows:

PBS FOX CNN ABC CBS MTV NBC

 PsychLink

Short-term memory demonstration
www.mhhe.com/
feldmaness5-06links

chunk: A meaningful grouping of stimuli that can be stored as a unit in short-term memory

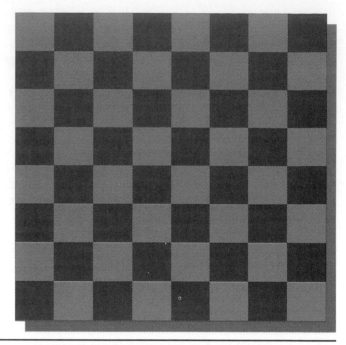

Figure 6-3 Examine the chessboard containing the chess pieces for about five seconds. Then, after covering up the board, try to reproduce the position of the pieces on the blank chessboard. Unless you are an experienced chess player, you are likely to have great difficulty carrying out such a task. Yet chess masters—the kind who win tournaments—do quite well (deGroot, 1966). They are able to reproduce correctly 90 percent of the pieces on the board. In comparison, inexperienced chess players are typically able to reproduce only 40 percent of the board properly. The chess masters do not have superior memories in other respects; they generally test normally on other measures of memory. What they can do better than others is see the board in terms of chunks or meaningful units and reproduce the position of the chess pieces by using these units.

In this case, even though there are still twenty-one letters, you'd be able to store them in short-term memory, because they represent only seven chunks.

Chunks can vary in size from single letters or numbers to categories that are far more complicated. The specific nature of what constitutes a chunk varies according to one's past experience. You can see this for yourself by trying an experiment that was first carried out as a comparison between expert and inexperienced chess players, illustrated in Figure 6-3 (deGroot, 1966; Schneider et al., 1993; Gobet & Simon, 1996).

Although it is possible to remember seven or so relatively complicated sets of information entering short-term memory, the information cannot be held there very long. Just how brief is short-term memory? Anyone who has looked up a telephone number at a pay phone, struggled to find coins, and forgotten the number at the sound of the dial tone knows that information in short-term memory does not remain there very long. Most psychologists believe that information in short-term memory is lost after 15 to 25 seconds—unless it is transferred to long-term memory.

Rehearsal

rehearsal: The repetition of information that has entered short-term memory

The transfer of material from short- to long-term memory proceeds largely on the basis of **rehearsal,** the repetition of information that has entered short-term memory. Rehearsal accomplishes two things. First, as long as the information is repeated, it is maintained in short-term memory. More important, however, rehearsal allows us to transfer the information into long-term memory.

Whether the transfer is made from short- to long-term memory seems to depend largely on the kind of rehearsal that is carried out. If the information is simply repeated over and over again—as we might do with a telephone number while we rush from the phone book to the phone—it is kept current in short-term memory, but it will not necessarily be placed in long-term memory. Instead, as soon as we stop punching in the phone numbers, the number is likely replaced by other information and will be completely forgotten.

On the other hand, if the information in short-term memory is rehearsed using a process called elaborative rehearsal, it is much more likely to be transferred into long-term memory (Craik & Lockhart, 1972). *Elaborative rehearsal* occurs when the information is considered and organized in some fashion. The organization might include expanding the information to make it fit into a logical framework, linking it to another memory, turning it into an image, or transforming it in some other way. For example, a list of vegetables to be purchased at a store could be woven together in memory as items being used to prepare an elaborate salad; they could be linked to the items bought on an earlier shopping trip; or they could be thought of in terms of the image of a farm with rows of each item.

By using organizational strategies such as these—called *mnemonics*—we can vastly improve our retention of information. Mnemonics (pronounced "neh MON ix") are formal techniques for organizing information in a way that makes it more likely to be remembered. For instance, when a beginning musician learns that the spaces on the music staff spell the word *FACE,* or when we learn the rhyme "Thirty days hath September, April, June, and November . . . ," we are using mnemonics (Mastropieri & Scruggs, 1991; Bellezza, Six, & Phillips, 1992; Schoen, 1996; Goldstein et al., 1996; Carney et al., 2000).

Long-Term Memory: The Final Storehouse

Material that makes its way from short-term memory to long-term memory enters a storehouse of almost unlimited capacity. Like a new file we save on our hard drive, the information in long-term memory is filed and coded so that we can retrieve it when we need it.

PsychLink

Long-term memory article
www.mhhe.com/
feldmaness5-06links

Evidence of the existence of long-term memory, as distinct from short-term memory, comes from a number of sources. For example, people with certain kinds of brain damage have no lasting recall of new information following the damage, although information about people and events stored in memory prior to the injury remains intact (Milner, 1966). Because information that was encoded and stored before the injury can be recalled and because short-term memory following the injury appears to be operational— new material can be recalled for a very brief period—we can infer that there are two distinct types of memory, one for short-term and one for long-term storage.

Results from laboratory experiments are also consistent with the notion of separate short- and long-term memories. For example, in one set of studies people were asked to recall a relatively small amount of information (such as a set of three letters). Then, to prevent practice of the initial information, participants were required to recite some extraneous material aloud, such as counting backward by threes (Brown, 1958; Peterson & Peterson, 1959). By varying the amount of time between presentation of the initial material and the need for its recall, investigators found that recall was quite good when the interval was very short but declined rapidly thereafter. After 15 seconds had gone by, recall hovered at around 10 percent of the material initially presented.

Apparently the distraction of counting backward prevented almost all the initial material from reaching long-term memory. Initial recall was good because it was coming from short-term memory, but these memories were lost at a rapid rate. Eventually, all that could be recalled was the small amount of material that had made its way into long-term storage despite the distraction of counting backward.

Contemporary Approaches to Memory: Working Memory, Memory Modules, and Associative Models of Memory

So far, we have relied on the traditional model of memory, which suggests that the processing of information in memory proceeds in three sequential stages: starting with sensory memory, advancing to short-term memory, and potentially ending in long-term memory. However, many contemporary approaches suggest that this traditional model provides an incomplete account of memory. For instance, rather than information being processed sequentially from sensory to short-term to long-term memory stores (a *serial* process), increasing evidence suggests that the brain processes information simultaneously in different memory components (a *parallel* process). These views are exemplified by approaches to short- and long-term memory that we consider next.

Working Memory

working memory: An active "workspace" in which information is retrieved and manipulated, and in which information is held through rehearsal

Rather than seeing short-term memory as an independent way-station through which memories travel, some theorists conceive of short-term memory as an information-processing system known as working memory. **Working memory** is an active "workspace" in which information is retrieved and manipulated, and in which information is held through rehearsal (Baddeley, 1992, 1993, 1995a, 1995b; see Figure 6-4).

In this view, working memory contains a *central executive* processor, which is involved in reasoning and decision making. The central executive coordinates two distinct storage-and-rehearsal systems: the visual store and the verbal store. The *visual store* specializes in visual and spatial information, and the *verbal store* is responsible for holding and manipulating material relating to speech, words, and numbers (Della Sala et al., 1995; Baddeley, 1996; Logie & Gilhooly, 1998).

Working memory permits us to briefly maintain information in an active state so that we can do something with the information. For instance, we use working memory when we're doing a multistep arithmetic problem in our heads, storing the result of one calculation while getting ready to move to the next stage. (I make use of my working memory when I figure a 20 percent tip in a restaurant by first calculating 10 percent of the total bill, then doubling it.)

Some researchers suspect that a breakdown in the central executive might result in the memory losses that are characteristic of Alzheimer's disease, the progressively degenerative disorder that produces loss of memory and confusion (Cherry, Buckwalter, & Henderson, 1996). (We'll discuss Alzheimer's disease and other memory disorders at greater length later in this chapter.)

Figure 6-4 Working memory is an active "workspace" in which information is retrieved and manipulated, and in which information is held through rehearsal (Gathercole & Baddeley, 1993). It consists of a "central executive" that coordinates the visual store (which concentrates on visual and spatial information) and the verbal store (concentrating on speech, words, and numbers).

Long-Term Memory Modules

Just as short-term memory is often viewed in terms of working memory, many contemporary researchers now see long-term memory as made up of several different components, or memory modules. Each of these modules is related to a separate memory system in the brain.

For instance, one major distinction within long-term memory is between declarative and procedural memory. **Declarative memory** is memory for factual information: names, faces, dates, and facts such as a bike has two wheels. In contrast, **procedural memory** (sometimes referred to as "nondeclarative memory") refers to memory for skills and habits, such as how to ride a bike or hit a baseball. Information *about* things is stored in declarative memory; information regarding *how to do* things is stored in procedural memory (Eichenbaum, 1997; Schacter, Wagner, & Buckner, 2000).

The facts in declarative memory can be further subdivided into semantic and episodic memory (Tulving, 1993; Nyberg & Tulving, 1996). **Semantic memory** is memory for general knowledge and facts about the world, as well as memory for the rules of logic that are used to deduce other facts. Because of semantic memory, we remember that $2 \times 2 = 4$, that the ZIP code for Beverly Hills is 90210, and that *memoree* is a misspelling. Thus, semantic memory is somewhat like a mental almanac of facts.

In contrast, **episodic memory** is memory for the biographical details of our individual lives. Memories of what we have done and the kinds of experiences we have had constitute episodic memory. Consequently, our recall of the first time we rode a bike or our first date is based on episodic memories. (To help your long-term memory keep straight the distinctions between the different types of long-term memory, study Figure 6-5.)

Episodic memories can be surprisingly detailed. Consider, for instance, how you'd respond if you were asked to identify what you were doing on a specific day two years ago. Impossible? You might think otherwise as you read the following exchange between a researcher and a participant in a study who was asked, in a memory

The ability to remember specific skills and the order in which they are used is known as procedural memory. If driving involves our procedural memory, is it safe to use a cell phone while driving?

declarative memory: Memory for factual information: names, faces, dates, and the like

procedural memory: Memory for skills and habits, such as riding a bike or hitting a baseball, sometimes referred to as "nondeclarative memory"

semantic memory: Memory for general knowledge and facts about the world, as well as memory for the rules of logic that are used to deduce other facts

episodic memory: Memory for the biographical details of our individual lives

Figure 6-5 Long-term memory can be subdivided into several different types. What type of long-term memory is involved in your recollection of the moment you first arrived on your campus at the start of college?

In addition to procedural memory, driving a car also involves what is known as declarative or explicit memory, which permits us to remember how to get to our destination.

experiment, what he was doing "on Monday afternoon in the third week of September two years ago."

> PARTICIPANT: Come on. How should I know?
> EXPERIMENTER: Just try it anyhow.
> PARTICIPANT: OK. Let's see: Two years ago . . . I would be in high school in Pittsburgh. . . . That would be my senior year. Third week in September—that's just after summer—that would be the fall term. . . . Let me see. I think I had chemistry lab on Mondays. I don't know. I was probably in chemistry lab. Wait a minute—that would be the second week of school. I remember he started off with the atomic table—a big fancy chart. I thought he was crazy trying to make us memorize that thing. You know, I think I can remember sitting . . . (Lindsay & Norman, 1977)

Episodic memory, then, can provide information from events that happened long in the past (Reynolds & Takooshian, 1988). But semantic memory is no less impressive, permitting us to dredge up tens of thousands of facts ranging from the date of our birthday to the knowledge that $1 is less than $5.

Associative Models of Memory

associative models of memory: Models suggesting that memory consists of mental representations of clusters of interconnected information

Our ability to recall detailed information has led some memory researchers to view memory primarily in terms of associations between different pieces of information. **Associative models of memory** suggest that memory consists of mental representations of clusters of interconnected information (e.g., Collins & Quillian, 1969; Collins & Loftus, 1975).

Consider, for example, Figure 6-6, which shows some of the relationships in memory relating to the concept "animal." Associative memory models suggest that thinking about a particular concept leads to recall of related concepts. For example, seeing a bird in the distance could activate our recollections of "robin," which in turn might activate recall of related concepts such as "eats worms" and "has a red breast." Activating one memory triggers the activation of related memories in a process known as *spreading activation.*

priming: A phenomenon in which exposure to a word or concept (called a *prime*) later makes it easier to recall related information, even when one has no conscious memory of the word or concept

Associative memory models help account for **priming,** a phenomenon in which exposure to a word or concept (called a *prime*) later makes it easier to recall related information. Priming effects occur even when people have no conscious memory of the original word or concept (Tulving & Schacter, 1990; Toth & Reingold, 1996; Schacter, 1998).

The typical experiment designed to illustrate priming helps clarify the phenomenon. In priming experiments, participants are rapidly exposed to a stimulus such as a word, an object, or perhaps a drawing of a face. The second phase of the experiment is held after an interval ranging from several seconds to several months. At that point, participants are exposed to incomplete perceptual information that is related to the first stimulus, and they are asked whether they recognize it. For example, the new material might consist of the first letter of a word that had been presented earlier, or a part of a face that had been shown earlier. If participants are able to identify the stimulus more readily than they identify stimuli that have not been presented earlier, priming has taken place.

Priming occurs even when participants report no conscious awareness of having been exposed to a stimulus earlier. For instance, studies have found that people who are anesthetized during surgery can sometimes recall snippets of information that they heard during surgery—even though they have no conscious recollection of the information (Kihlstrom et al., 1990; Sebel, Bonke, & Winogard, 1993).

The discovery that people have memories about which they are unaware has been an important one. It has led to speculation that two forms of memory, explicit and implicit, might exist side-by-side. **Explicit memory** refers to intentional or conscious recollection of information. When we try to remember a name or date that we have

explicit memory: Intentional or conscious recollection of information

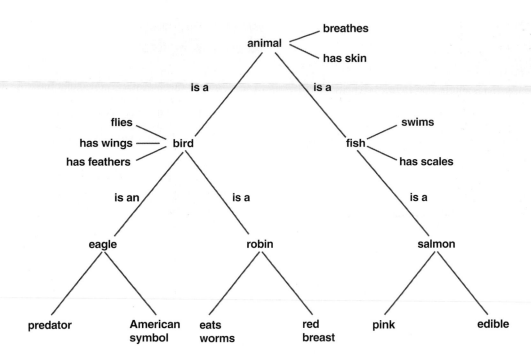

Figure 6-6 Associative models suggest that semantic memory consists of relationships between pieces of information, such as those relating to the concept of "animal," shown in this figure (After Collins & Quillian, 1969).

encountered or learned about previously, we are using explicit memory. In contrast, **implicit memory** refers to memories people are not consciously aware of, but that can affect their subsequent performance and behavior. Skills that operate automatically and without thinking, such as jumping out of the path of an automobile coming toward us as we walk down the side of a road, are stored in implicit memory. Similarly, a feeling of vague dislike for an acquaintance, when we don't know why we have that feeling, could be a reflection of implicit memories. In short, when an event that we are unable to consciously recall affects our behavior, implicit memory is at work (Graf & Masson, 1993; Schacter, Chiu, & Ochsner, 1993; Schacter, 1994, 1995; Underwood, 1996; Tulving, 2000).

implicit memory: Memories people are not consciously aware of, but that can affect their subsequent performance and behavior

The Multiple Models of Memory

We've seen that the way that memory is viewed has been expanded from the three-stage model of memory. Although the traditional view of memory has not been rejected, contemporary views take a broader approach, considering memory in terms of multiple interdependent systems, operating simultaneously, that are responsible for different types of recall. Moreover, greater emphasis has been placed on working memory, in an effort to determine how different types of information can be simultaneously stored and processed.

You might be asking which of these views of memory is most accurate. It's a fair question, but one that is not easily answered at this point. More than most areas of psychology, memory has attracted a great deal of theorizing, and it is probably too early to tell—let alone remember—which of the multiple models proposed by different memory psychologists gives us the most accurate characterization of memory (Collins et al., 1993; Searleman & Herrmann, 1994; Wolters, 1995; Bjork & Bjork, 1996; Conway, 1997).

Implicit memory issues
www.mhhe.com/
feldmaness5-06links

Prepare

What causes difficulties and failures in remembering?

Organize

Recalling Long-Term Memories
   Retrieval Cues
   Levels of Processing
   Flashbulb Memories
   Constructive Processes in Memory
   Memory in the Courtroom
   Autobiographical Memory

Recalling Long-Term Memories

An hour after his job interview, Ricardo was sitting in a coffee shop, telling his friend Laura how well it had gone, when the woman who had interviewed him walked in. "Well, hello, Ricardo. How are you doing?" Trying to make a good impression, Ricardo began to make introductions, but suddenly realized he could not remember the name of the interviewer. Stammering, he desperately searched his memory, but to no avail. "I *know* her name," he thought to himself, "but here I am, looking like a fool. I can kiss this job goodbye."

Have you ever tried to remember someone's name, convinced that you knew it, were unable to recall it no matter how hard you tried? This common occurrence—known as the **tip-of-the-tongue phenomenon**—exemplifies the difficulties that can occur in retrieving information stored in long-term memory (Smith, 1994; Riefer, Keveri, & Kramer, 1995; Schwartz et al., 2000).

Retrieval Cues

One reason recall is not perfect is the sheer quantity of recollections stored in long-term memory. Although the issue is far from settled, many psychologists have suggested that the material that makes its way to long-term memory is relatively permanent (Tulving & Psotka, 1971). If they are correct, this suggests that the capacity of long-term memory is vast, given the broad range of people's experiences and educational backgrounds. For instance, if you are like the average college student, your vocabulary includes some 50,000 words, you know hundreds of mathematical "facts," and you are able to conjure up images—such as the way your childhood home looked—with no trouble at all. In fact, simply cataloging all your memories would probably take years of work.

How do we sort through this vast array of material and retrieve specific information at the appropriate time? One of the major ways is through the use of retrieval cues. A *retrieval cue* is a stimulus that allows us to recall more easily information that is located in long-term memory (Tulving & Thompson, 1973; Ratcliff & McKoon, 1989). It could be a word, an emotion, a

The tip-of-the-tongue phenomenon is especially frustrating in situations in which a person cannot recall the name of someone he or she has just met. Can you think of ways to avoid this common occurrence?

sound; whatever the specific cue, a memory will suddenly come to mind when the retrieval cue is present. For example, the smell of roasting turkey might evoke memories of Thanksgiving or family gatherings (Schab & Crowder, 1995).

Retrieval cues guide people through the information stored in long-term memory in much the same way as the cards in an old-fashioned card catalog guided people through a library, or a search engine like Yahoo! guides people through the World Wide Web. They are particularly important when we are making an effort to *recall* information, as opposed to being asked to *recognize* material stored in memory. In *recall*, a specific piece of information must be retrieved—such as that needed to answer a fill-in-the-blank question or write an essay on a test. In contrast, *recognition* occurs when people are presented with a stimulus and asked whether they have been exposed to it previously, or are asked to identify it from a list of alternatives.

Figure 6-7 Try to recall the names of these characters. Because it is a recall task, it is relatively difficult.

As you might guess, recall is generally a more difficult task than recognition (the task in Figure 6-7 is more difficult than the task in Figure 6-8). Recall is more difficult because it consists of a series of processes: a search through memory, retrieval of potentially relevant information, and then a decision regarding whether or not the information you have found is accurate. If the information appears correct, the search is over, but if it does not, the search must continue. On the other hand, recognition is simpler because it involves fewer steps (Anderson & Bower, 1972; Miserando, 1991).

tip-of-the-tongue phenomenon: The inability to recall information that one realizes one knows—a result of the difficulty of retrieving information from long-term memory

Levels of Processing

One determinant of how well memories are recalled is the way in which material is first perceived, processed, and understood. **Levels-of-processing theory** emphasizes the degree to which new material is mentally analyzed (Craik & Lockhart, 1972; Craik, 1990). Levels-of-processing theory suggests that the amount of information processing that occurs when material is initially encountered is central in determining how much of the information is ultimately remembered. According to this approach, the depth of information processing during exposure to material—meaning the degree to which it is analyzed and considered—is critical; the greater the intensity of its initial processing, the more likely we are to remember it.

levels-of-processing theory: The theory of memory that emphasizes the degree to which new material is mentally analyzed

Because we do not pay close attention to much of the information to which we are exposed, typically only scant mental processing takes place, and we forget new material almost immediately. However, information to which we pay greater attention is processed more thoroughly. Therefore, it enters memory at a deeper level—and is less apt to be forgotten than information processed at shallower levels.

The theory goes on to suggest that there are considerable differences in the ways information is processed at various levels of memory. At shallow levels, information is processed merely in terms of its physical and sensory aspects. For example, we might pay attention only to the shapes that make up the letters in the word *dog*. At an intermediate level of processing, the shapes are translated into meaningful units—in this case, letters of the alphabet. These letters are considered in the context of words, and specific phonetic sounds might be attached to the letters.

At the deepest level of processing, information is analyzed in terms of its meaning. We might see it in a wider context and draw associations between the meaning of the information and broader networks of knowledge. For instance, we might think of

Answer this recognition question:
Which of the following are the names of the seven dwarfs in the Disney movie *Snow White and the Seven Dwarfs*?

Goofy	**Bashful**
Sleepy	**Meanie**
Smarty	**Doc**
Scaredy	**Happy**
Dopey	**Angry**
Grumpy	**Sneezy**
Wheezy	**Crazy**

Figure 6-8 The recognition problem posed above is considerably easier than the recall task in the previous figure.

Five years later the actual criminal was identified, and Jackson was released. For Jackson, though, it was too late. In his words, "They took away part of my life, part of my youth. I spend five years down there, and all they said was 'we're sorry'" (*Time*, 1982).

Unfortunately, Jackson is not the only victim to whom apologies have had to be made; there have been many cases of mistaken identity that have led to unjustified legal actions. Research on eyewitness identification of suspects, as well as on memory for other details of crimes, has shown that witnesses are apt to make substantial errors when they try to recall details of criminal activity (Miller, 2000; Wells et al., 2000).

One reason is the impact of weapons used in crimes. When a criminal perpetrator displays a gun or knife, it acts like a perceptual magnet attracting the eyes of the witnesses. As a consequence, witnesses pay less attention to other details of the crime and are less able to recall what actually occurred (Loftus, Loftus, & Messo, 1987; Steblay, 1992).

Even when weapons are not involved, eyewitnesses are prone to errors relating to memory. For instance, viewers of a twelve-second film of a mugging that was shown on a New York City television news program were later given the opportunity to pick out the assailant from a six-person lineup (Buckhout, 1975). Of some two thousand viewers who called the station after the program, only 15 percent were able to pick out the right person—a percentage similar to random guessing.

One reason eyewitnesses are prone to memory-related errors is that the specific wording of questions posed to them by police or attorneys can affect the way they recall information, as a number of experiments illustrate. For example, in one experiment participants were shown a film of two cars crashing into each other. Some were then asked the question, "About how fast were the cars going when they *smashed* into each other?" On average, they estimated the speed to be 40.8 miles per hour. In contrast, when another group of participants was asked, "About how fast were the cars going when they *contacted* each other?" the average estimated speed was only 31.8 miles per hour (Loftus & Palmer, 1974; see Figure 6-10).

The problem of memory reliability becomes even more acute when children are witnesses, because increasing evidence suggests that children's memories are highly vulnerable to the influence of others (Loftus, 1993; Cassel, Roebers, & Bjorklund, 1996). For instance, in one experiment, 5- to 7-year-old girls who had just had a routine physical examination were shown an anatomically explicit doll. The girls were shown the doll's genital area and asked, "Did the doctor touch you here?" Three of the girls who

Figure 6-10 After viewing an accident involving two cars, subjects were asked to estimate the speed of the collision. Estimates varied substantially, depending on the way the question was worded (Loftus & Palmer, 1974).

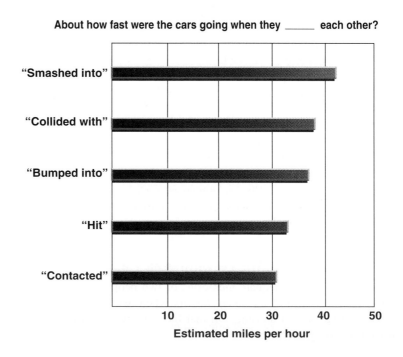

About how fast were the cars going when they _____ each other?

Applying Psychology in the 21st Century

Repressed Memories: Truth or Fiction?

Guilty of murder in the first degree.

That was the jury's verdict in the case of George Franklin, Sr., who was charged with murdering his daughter's playmate. But this case was different from most other murder cases: It was based on memories that had been repressed for twenty years. Franklin's daughter claimed that she had forgotten everything she had once known about her father's crime until two years earlier, when she began to have flashbacks of the event. Gradually, though, the memories became clearer in her mind, until she recalled her father lifting a rock over his head and then seeing her friend lying on the ground, covered with blood. On the basis of her memories, her father was convicted—but then later cleared of the crime following an appeal of the conviction.

Although the prosecutor and jury clearly believed Franklin's daughter, there is good reason to question the validity of *repressed memories*, recollections of events that are initially so shocking that the mind responds by pushing them into the unconscious. Supporters of the notion of repressed memory (who draw on Freud's psychoanalytic theory, first discussed in Chapter 1) suggest that such memories can remain hidden, possibly throughout a person's lifetime, unless they are triggered by some current circumstance, such as the probing that occurs during psychological therapy.

However, memory researcher Elizabeth Loftus (1997, 1998) maintains that so-called repressed memories can well be inaccurate or even wholly false—representing *false memory*. For example, false memories develop when people are unable

As the result of testimony from Eileen Franklin, based on repressed memory, her father was found guilty of murder. The validity of repressed memory, especially in investigating crimes, remains controversial. Can you think of a test to tell whether a recovered memory is accurate or not?

to recall the source of a memory of a particular event about which they have only vague recollections. When the source of the memory becomes unclear or ambiguous, people become confused about whether they actually experienced the event or whether they imagined it. Ultimately, people come to believe that the event actually occurred (Schacter, 1999a; Clancy et al., 2000).

In fact, some therapists have been accused of accidentally encouraging people who come to them with psychological difficulties to recreate false chronicles of childhood sexual experiences. Furthermore, the publicity surrounding well-publicized declarations of supposed repressed memories, such as those of people who claim to be the victims of satanic rituals, makes the possibility of repressed memories seem more legitimate and ultimately might prime people to

recall "memories" of events that never happened (Lynn, 1997).

The controversy regarding the legitimacy of repressed memories is unlikely to be resolved soon. Many psychologists, particularly those who provide therapy, give great weight to the reality of repressed memories. On the other side of the issue are many memory researchers, who maintain that there is no scientific support for the existence of such memories. The challenge for those on both sides of the issue is to distinguish truth from fiction (Brown & Pope, 1996; Pezdek & Banks, 1996; Loftus, 1997; Walcott, 2000).

Can you think of any way to determine which details of a repressed memory are true and which are false? How do you think attorneys and psychologists go about establishing the accuracy or inaccuracy of repressed memories of allegedly criminal actions?

did not have a vaginal or anal exam said that the doctor had in fact touched them in the genital area. And one of those three made up the detail, "The doctor did it with a stick" (Saywitz & Goodman, 1990).

Children's memories are especially susceptible to influence when the situation is highly emotional or stressful. For example, in trials in which there is significant pretrial publicity or where alleged victims are repeatedly questioned, often by untrained interviewers, the memories of alleged victims can be influenced by the type of questions they are asked.

In short, the memories of witnesses are far from reliable, and this is especially true when children are involved (Howe, 1999). The question of the accuracy of memories becomes even more complex, however, when we consider the triggering of memories of events that people at first don't even recall happening. As we discuss in the *Applying Psychology in the 21st Century* box, this issue has raised considerable controversy.

 PsychLink

False memory discussion
www.mhhe.com/
feldmaness5-06links

Figure 6-11 We distort memories for unpleasant events. For example, college students are much more likely to accurately recall their good grades, while inaccurately recalling their poor ones (Bahrick, Hall, & Berger, 1996). Now that you know this, how well do you think you can recall your own high school grades?

autobiographical memories: Our recollections of circumstances and episodes from our own lives

Autobiographical Memory: Where Past Meets Present

Your memory of experiences in your own past might well be a fiction—or at least a distortion of what actually occurred. The same constructive processes that act to make us inaccurately recall the behavior of others also reduce the accuracy of autobiographical memories. **Autobiographical memories** are our recollections of circumstances and episodes from our own lives. Autobiographical memories encompass the episodic memories we hold about ourselves (Stein et al., 1997; Rubin, 1999).

For example, we tend to forget information about our past that is incompatible with how we currently see ourselves. One study found that adults who were well adjusted but who had been treated for emotional problems during the early years of their lives tended to forget important but troubling childhood events, such as being in foster care. College students tend to misremember their bad grades—but remember their good ones (see Figure 6-11; Robbins, 1988; Bahrick, Hall, & Berger, 1996; Stein et al., 1996).

It is not just certain kinds of events that are distorted; particular periods of life are remembered more easily than others. For example, when people reach old age, they remember periods of life in which they experienced major transitions, such as attending college or working at their first job, better than their middle-age years (Rubin, 1985; Newcombe et al., 2000).

EXPLORING DIVERSITY

Are There Cross-Cultural Differences in Memory?

Travelers who have visited areas of the world in which there is no written language often have returned with tales of people with phenomenal memories. For instance, storytellers in some preliterate cultures can recount long chronicles that recall the names and activities of people over many generations. These feats initially led experts to argue that people in preliterate societies develop a different, and perhaps better, type of memory than those in cultures that employ a written language. They suggested that in a society that lacks writing, people are motivated to accurately recall information, particularly information relating to tribal histories and traditions that would be lost if they were not passed down orally from one generation to another (Bartlett, 1932; Cole & Gay, 1972; Rubin, 1995).

However, more recent approaches to cultural differences suggest a different conclusion. For one thing, preliterate peoples don't have an exclusive claim on amazing memory feats. For instance, some Hebrew scholars memorize thousands of pages of text and can recall the locations of particular words on the page. Similarly, poetry singers in Yugoslavia can recall thousands of lines of poetry. Even in cultures in which written language exists, then, astounding feats of memory are possible (Neisser, 1982).

Memory researchers now suggest that there are both similarities and differences in memory across cultures. Basic memory processes such as short-term memory capacity and the structure of long-term memory—the "hardware" of memory—are universal and operate similarly in people of all cultures (Wagner, 1981). In contrast, differences can be seen in how information is acquired and rehearsed—the "software" of memory. Culture determines how people frame information initially, how much they practice learning and recalling it, and the strategies they use to try to recall it.

Storytellers in many cultures can recount hundreds of years of history in vivid detail. Research has found that this amazing ability is due less to basic memory processes than to the ways in which they acquire and retain information.

1. While with a group of friends at a dance, Eva bumps into a man she dated last month. When she tries to introduce him to her friends, she cannot remember his name. What is the term for this?

2. _____ is used when a person is asked to retrieve a specific item from memory.

3. Your mother's friend tells you, "I know exactly where I was and what I was doing when I heard that John Lennon died." What phenomenon explains this type of recollection?

4. The same person could probably also accurately describe in detail what she was wearing when she heard about John Lennon's death, right down to the color of her shoes. True or false?

5. _____ are organized bodies of information stored in memory that bias the way new information is interpreted, stored, and recalled.

6. _____-_____-_____ theory states that the more a person analyzes a statement, the more likely he or she is to remember it later.

1. How do schemas help people process information during encoding, storage, and retrieval? In what ways are they helpful? Can they contribute to inaccurate autobiographical memories?

2. How might courtroom procedure be improved, based on what you've learned about memory errors and biases?

Answers to Evaluate Questions

1. Tip-of-the-tongue phenomenon 2. Recall 3. Flashbulb memory 4. False; small details probably won't be remembered through flashbulb memory. 5. Schemas 6. Levels-of-processing

Forgetting: When Memory Fails

He could remember, quite literally, nothing—nothing, that is, that had happened since the loss of his brain's temporal lobes and hippocampus during experimental surgery to reduce epileptic seizures. Until that time, his memory had been quite normal. But after the operation he was unable to recall anything for more than a few minutes, and then the memory was seemingly lost forever. He did not remember his address, or the name of the person to whom he was talking. He would read the same magazine over and over again. According to his own description, his life was like waking from a dream and being unable to know where he was or how he got there. (Milner, 1966)

As this case illustrates, a person without a normal memory faces severe difficulties. All of us who have experienced even routine instances of forgetting—such as not remembering an acquaintance's name or a fact on a test—understand the very real consequences of memory failure.

The first attempts to study forgetting were made by German psychologist Hermann Ebbinghaus about a hundred years ago. Using himself as the only participant in his study, he memorized lists of three-letter nonsense syllables—meaningless sets of two consonants with a vowel in between, such as *FIW* and *BOZ*. By measuring how easy it was to relearn a given list of words after varying periods of time had passed since initial learning, he found that forgetting occurred systematically, as shown in Figure 6-12. As the figure indicates, the most rapid forgetting occurs in the first nine hours, and particularly in the first hour. After nine hours, the rate of forgetting slows and declines little, even after the passage of many days.

Despite his primitive methods, Ebbinghaus's study had an important influence on subsequent research, and his basic conclusions have been upheld (Wixted & Ebbesen, 1991). There is almost always a strong initial decline in memory, followed by a more gradual drop over time. Furthermore, relearning of previously mastered material is almost always faster than starting from scratch, whether the material is academic information or a motor skill such as serving a tennis ball.

Why do we forget? One reason is that we might not have paid attention to the material in the first place—a failure of *encoding*. For example, if you live in the United States, you have surely been exposed to thousands of pennies during your life. Despite this experience, you probably don't have a clear picture of the details of the coin. (See

Why do we forget information?
What are the biological bases of memory?
What are the major memory impairments?

Forgetting
    Proactive and Retroactive Interference
    The Biological Bases of Memory
    Memory Dysfunctions

Epilogue

In this chapter we have taken a look at memory. We noted that memory comprises the processes of encoding, storage, and retrieval, and we saw that memory can be regarded as having different components. We also encountered several phenomena relating to memory, including the tip-of-the-tongue phenomenon and flashbulb memories. Above all we observed that memory is a constructive process by which interpretations, expectations, and guesses contribute to the nature of our memories.

Before we move on to the next chapter, return briefly to the prologue of this chapter, in which we encountered Terry Dibert and his lost memories of his past. Consider the following questions in light of what you know about memory.

1. Terry Dibert's memory loss is called "retrograde amnesia." What does this mean?
2. What would have been the effects on Dibert's life if his brain cyst had caused anterograde amnesia?
3. Despite his inability to recall recent events, Dibert's memories of older events seemed accurate. Based on what you know about memory, do you believe they were truly accurate? Why or why not?
4. How might investigators use Dibert's case to answer questions about the biological bases of memory? Assuming Dibert gave his consent to PET scans and other means of looking inside his cerebral cortex, what sorts of questions might be explored?

Chapter Seven

Thinking, Language, and Intelligence

Prologue

Many situations require problem-solving skills. The repair of the Hubble space telescope, however, demanded an extraordinary degree of problem-solving effort, which eventually led to a triumphant success.

Housecall in Space

It was a $1.5 billion mistake—a blunder on a grand scale. The finely ground mirror of the Hubble space telescope, designed to provide an unprecedented glimpse into the vast reaches of the universe, was not so finely ground after all.

Despite a variety of quality-control procedures intended to catch any flaws, there was a tiny blemish in the mirror that was not detected until the telescope had been launched into space and started to send back blurry photographs. By then, it seemed too late to fix the mirror.

Or was it? NASA engineers pondered the problem for months, devising and discarding one potential solution after another. Finally, they formulated a daring solution that involved sending a team of astronauts into space. Once there, a space-walking Mr. Goodwrench would install several new mirrors in the telescope, which could refocus the light and compensate for the original flawed mirror.

Although the engineers could not be certain that the $630 million plan would work, it seemed like a good solution, at least on paper. It was not until the first photos were beamed back to earth, though, that NASA knew their solution was A-OK. These photos provided spectacular views of galaxies millions of light years from Earth.

- Information-processing approaches suggest that intelligence should be conceptualized as the way in which people represent and use material cognitively. Rather than focusing on the structure of intelligence, this approach examines the processes underlying intelligent behavior. (p. 235)
- Practical intelligence is intelligence related to overall success in living. Emotional intelligence is the set of skills that underlie the accurate assessment, evaluation, expression, and regulation of emotions. (p. 237)

How can the extremes of intelligence be characterized?

- At the two extremes of intelligence are individuals with mental retardation and the intellectually gifted. The levels of mental retardation include mild, moderate, and severe retardation. (p. 237)
- About one-third of the cases of retardation have a known biological cause; Down syndrome is the most common. Most cases, however, are classified as familial retardation, for which there is no known biological cause. (p. 238)
- There have been a number of advances in educating both people with mental retardation and the intellectually gifted. In mainstreaming, individuals with mental retardation are integrated into regular education classrooms as much as possible. In full inclusion, all students, even those with the most severe educational disabilities, are integrated into regular classes. (p. 239)

Are traditional IQ tests culturally biased?

- Traditional intelligence tests have frequently been criticized for being biased in favor of the white middle-class population. This controversy has led to attempts to devise culture-fair tests, IQ measures that avoid questions that depend on a particular cultural background. (p. 240)
- Issues of race and environmental and genetic influences on intelligence represent major controversies. (p. 241)

To what degree is intelligence influenced by the environment and to what degree is it influenced by heredity?

- Attempting to distinguish environmental from hereditary factors in intelligence is probably futile and certainly misguided. Because individual IQ scores vary far more than group IQ scores, it is more critical to ask what can be done to maximize the intellectual development of each individual. (p. 241)

Key Terms and Concepts

cognitive psychology (p. 212)

thinking (p. 212)

mental images (p. 213)

concepts (p. 214)

prototypes (p. 214)

algorithm (p. 214)

heuristic (p. 214)

means-end analysis (p. 217)

insight (p. 218)

functional fixedness (p. 220)

mental set (p. 220)

creativity (p. 221)

divergent thinking (p. 221)

convergent thinking (p. 221)

language (p. 224)

grammar (p. 224)

phonology (p. 224)

phonemes (p. 224)

syntax (p. 224)

semantics (p. 224)

babble (p. 225)

telegraphic speech (p. 225)

overgeneralization (p. 225)

learning-theory approach (p. 226)

universal grammar (p. 226)

language acquisition device (p. 226)

intelligence (p. 229)

intelligence tests (p. 229)

Psychology on the Web

1. Aside from mental images of sights and sounds, are there mental representations that correspond to the other senses? See if you can answer this question by searching the Web. Summarize your findings in writing.

2. Do animals think? What evidence is there on either side of this question? Find on the Web at least one example of research and/or argument on each side of this question. Summarize your findings and use your knowledge of cognitive psychology to state your position on this question.

3. Many sites on the Web permit you to assess your IQ. Take at least two such tests and compare (a) your results, (b) what mental qualities seemed to be tested on the test, and (c) your impression of the reliability and validity of the tests. Write up your conclusions.

4. Find a way to assess at least one other of your multiple intelligences (i.e., one not tested by the IQ tests you took) on the Web. What sort of intelligence was the test supposed to be testing? What sorts of items were included? How valid and reliable do you think it was, both in and of itself and compared with the IQ tests you took? Summarize your findings in writing.

OLC **Preview**

For additional quizzing and a variety of interactive resources, visit the *Essentials of Understanding Psychology* Online Learning Center at

www.mhhe.com/feldmaness5

Epilogue

The topics in this chapter occupy a central place in the field of psychology. We first examined thinking and problem solving, focusing on the importance of mental images and concepts and identifying the steps commonly involved in solving problems. We discussed language, describing the components of grammar and tracing language development in children. Finally, we considered intelligence. Some of the most heated discussions in all of psychology are focused around this topic, engaging educators, policymakers, politicians, and psychologists alike. The issues include the very meaning of intelligence, its measurement, individual extremes of intelligence, and, finally, the heredity/environment question.

Before we proceed to the next chapter, turn back to the Prologue, where we looked at the ability of NASA scientists to figure out how to restore vision to the damaged Hubble space telescope. Consider the following questions in light of what you have learned about problem solving, creativity, and intelligence.

1. How might the concepts of functional fixedness and mental set have hindered figuring out a solution to the Hubble problem?

2. Do you believe a computer could have created the solution to the Hubble problem, or is there something special about human intelligence that is superior to computer problem solving? Why?

3. Do you think the concept of insight was involved in determining the solution to the repair of the telescope? How?

4. In what ways do you think divergent and convergent thinking are involved in the processes of problem solving?

Chapter Eight

Motivation and Emotion

Prologue

Tour de Lance

Did the same motivation that drove Lance Armstrong to battle cancer help him win the Tour de France?

When Lance Armstrong completed the final leg of the Tour de France before a cheering crowd of a half million people, it meant more than winning the world's most prestigious cycling race. The moment represented a triumph of human motivation and spirit—with a dash of miracle.

Only 33 months earlier, no one would have thought that Armstrong would be the winner of the Tour de France. In fact, the odds were against him ever cycling again. At that time, he learned he had testicular cancer that had spread to his lungs and brain, which contained 12 tumors and two lesions. Doctors gave him a 50–50 chance of surviving.

His treatment was grueling. He suffered through surgery and four rounds of intense chemotherapy, separated by a month each. But he never gave up. Pushing himself, he would ride 20 to 50 miles a day following each of the one-week chemotherapy sessions.

Then the unexpected happened: The cancer disappeared, surprising everyone. And Armstrong picked up where he had left off, training hours each day and entering cycling competitions.

Several years later, Armstrong was crossing the finish line at the Tour de France. It was, he said, a miracle. "Fifteen or 20 years ago, I wouldn't be alive, much less riding a bike or winning the Tour de France. I think it's a miracle" (Abt, 1999, p. D4).

Looking Ahead

What motivation lay behind Armstrong's will to overcome his cancer? Was it the anticipation of the emotional thrill of winning the Tour de France? The potential rewards that would follow if he succeeded? The excitement of participating? The satisfaction of achieving a long-sought goal?

In this chapter, we consider the issues that can help answer such questions, as we address the topic of motivation and the related area of emotion. **Motivation** concerns the factors that direct and energize the behavior of humans and other organisms.

Psychologists who study motivation seek to discover the particular desired goals—the *motives*—that underlie behavior. Motives are exemplified in behavior as basic as drinking to satisfy thirst or as inconsequential as taking a stroll to get exercise. To the psychologist specializing in the study of motivation, underlying motives are assumed to steer one's choice of activities.

The study of motivation, then, consists of identifying why people seek to do the things they do. Psychologists studying motivation ask questions such as these: Why do people choose particular goals for which to strive? What specific motives direct behavior? What individual differences in motivation account for the variability in people's behavior? How can we motivate people to behave in particular ways, such as eating certain foods, quitting smoking, or engaging in safer sexual practices?

Whereas motivation is concerned with the forces that direct future behavior, emotion pertains to the feelings we experience throughout the course of our lives. The study of emotions focuses on our internal experiences at any given moment. Most of us have felt a variety of emotions: happiness at getting an A on a difficult exam, sadness brought about by the death of a loved one, anger at being treated unfairly. Because emotions not only motivate our behavior but can also reflect our underlying motivation, they play an important role in our lives.

We begin this chapter by focusing on the major conceptions of motivation, discussing how the different motives and needs people experience jointly affect behavior. We consider motives that are biologically based and universal in the animal kingdom, such as hunger and sex, as well as motives that are unique to humans, like the needs for achievement, affiliation, and power.

We then turn to the nature of emotional experience. We consider the roles and functions that emotions play in people's lives, discussing a number of theories meant to explain how people understand which emotion they are experiencing at a given moment. Finally, the chapter ends with a look at how emotions are communicated through nonverbal behavior.

motivation: The factors that direct and energize the behavior of humans and other organisms

Prepare

How does motivation direct and energize behavior?

Organize

Explaining Motivation
  Instinct Approaches
  Drive-Reduction Approaches
  Arousal Approaches
  Incentive Approaches
  Cognitive Approaches
  Maslow's Hierarchy
  Applying the Different Approaches
      to Motivation

Explaining Motivation

In just a moment, John Thompson's life changed. That's all it took for him to slip against a piece of farm equipment, which instantly ripped off both his arms.

In the moments following the accident, Thompson demonstrated incredible bravery. Despite his pain and shock, he ran 400 feet to his house. After managing to open the door, he ran inside and dialed for help with a pen gripped in his teeth. When emergency crews arrived 30 minutes later, he told them where to find ice and plastic bags so that his severed arms could be packed for possible surgical reattachment. Thompson's rescuers came none too soon: By the time surgery could start, he had lost half his blood. (Nelson, 1992)

Amazingly, John Thompson's surgery to reattach his arms was a success, and he recovered from his ordeal. But how can we account for his enormous motivation to stay alive?

Like many questions involving motivation, this one has no single answer; biological, cognitive, and social factors combined to fuel his will to survive. The complexity of motivation has led to the development of a variety of conceptual approaches to its understanding. Although they vary in the degree to which they focus on biological, cognitive, and social factors, all seek to explain the energy that guides people's behavior in particular directions.

Instinct Approaches: Born to Be Motivated

When psychologists first sought to explain motivation, they turned to **instincts,** inborn patterns of behavior that are biologically determined rather than learned. According to instinct approaches to motivation, people and animals are born with preprogrammed sets of behaviors essential to their survival. These instincts provide the energy that channels behavior in appropriate directions. Hence, sex might be explained as a response to an instinct for reproduction, and exploratory behavior might be viewed as motivated by an instinct to examine one's territory.

There are several difficulties with such a conception, however. For one thing, there is no agreement on what, or even how many, primary instincts exist. One early psychologist, William McDougall (1908), suggested that there are 18 instincts. Other theorists came up with even more—with one sociologist (Bernard, 1924) claiming that there are exactly 5,759 distinct instincts!

Furthermore, explanations based on the concept of instincts do not go very far in explaining *why* a specific pattern of behavior, and not others, has appeared in a given species. In addition, although it is clear that a significant amount of animal behavior is based on instincts, the variety and complexity of human behavior, much of which is learned, cannot be seen as instinctual.

As a result of these shortcomings, newer explanations have replaced conceptions of motivation based on instincts. However, instinct approaches still play a role in certain theories, particularly those based on the evolutionary approach we discussed in Chapter 1. Furthermore, in later chapters we will discuss Freud's work, which suggests that instinctual drives of sex and aggression motivate behavior.

Drive-Reduction Approaches: Satisfying Our Needs

After rejecting instinct theory, psychologists first proposed simple drive-reduction theories of motivation in its place (Hull, 1943). **Drive-reduction approaches** suggest that when people lack some basic biological requirement such as water, a drive to obtain that requirement (in this case, the thirst drive) is produced.

To understand this approach, we need to begin with the concept of drive. A **drive** is motivational tension, or arousal, that energizes behavior in order to fulfill some need. Many basic kinds of drives, such as hunger, thirst, sleepiness, and sex, are related to biological needs of the body or of the species as a whole. These are called *primary drives.* Primary drives contrast with *secondary drives,* in which no obvious biological need is being fulfilled. The needs involved in secondary drives are created by prior experience and learning. As we will discuss later, some people have strong needs to achieve academically and in their careers. We can say that their achievement need is reflected in a secondary drive that motivates their behavior.

We usually try to satisfy a primary drive by reducing the need underlying it. For example, we become hungry after not eating for a few hours and might raid the refrigerator, especially if our next scheduled meal is not imminent. If the weather turns cold, we put on extra clothing or raise the setting on the thermostat to keep warm. If our body needs liquids in order to function properly, we experience thirst and seek out water.

Homeostasis

The reason for such behavior is homeostasis, a basic motivational phenomenon underlying primary drives. **Homeostasis** is the body's tendency to maintain a steady internal state. Homeostasis operates through feedback loops that bring deviations in body functioning back to a more optimal state, similar to the way a thermostat and furnace work in a home heating system to maintain a steady temperature. Receptor cells throughout the body constantly monitor factors such as temperature and nutrient levels, and when deviations from the ideal state occur, the body adjusts in an effort to return to an optimal state. Many of our fundamental needs, including the need for food, water, stable body temperature, and sleep, operate via homeostasis.

instincts: Inborn patterns of behavior that are biologically determined rather than learned

 PsychLink

Motivation and emotion information
www.mhhe.com/
feldmaness5-08links

drive-reduction approaches to motivation: A theory suggesting that when people lack some basic biological requirement such as water, a drive to obtain that requirement (in this case, the thirst drive) is produced
drive: Motivational tension, or arousal, that energizes behavior in order to fulfill some need

homeostasis: The body's tendency to maintain a steady internal state

Although drive-reduction theories provide a good explanation of how primary drives motivate behavior, they are inadequate when it comes to explaining behaviors in which the goal is not to reduce a drive, but rather to maintain or even to increase a particular level of excitement or arousal. For instance, some behaviors seem to be motivated by nothing more than curiosity, such as rushing to check e-mail messages. Similarly, many people seek thrills through such activities as riding a roller coaster and steering a raft down the rapids of a river. Such behaviors certainly don't suggest that people seek to reduce drives, as drive-reduction approaches would indicate (Mineka & Hendersen, 1985; Loewenstein, 1994).

Both curiosity and thrill-seeking behavior, then, shed doubt on drive-reduction approaches as a complete explanation for motivation. In both cases, rather than seeking to reduce an underlying drive, people and animals appear to be motivated to *increase* their overall level of stimulation and activity. To explain this phenomenon, psychologists have devised an alternative: arousal approaches to motivation.

Arousal Approaches: Beyond Drive Reduction

arousal approaches to motivation: The belief that we try to maintain a certain level of stimulation and activity, increasing or reducing them as necessary

Arousal approaches seek to explain behavior in which the goal is to maintain or increase excitement (Berlyne, 1967; Brehm & Self, 1989). According to **arousal approaches to motivation,** each of us tries to maintain a certain level of stimulation and activity. As with the drive-reduction model, if our stimulation and activity levels become too high, we try to reduce them. But in contrast to the drive-reduction model, the arousal model also suggests that if the levels of stimulation and activity are too low, we will try to *increase* them by seeking stimulation.

People vary widely in the optimal level of arousal that they seek out, with some people seeking out especially high levels of arousal. For example, psychologists have hypothesized that individuals such as comic John Belushi, daredevil Evel Knievel, and bank robbers Bonnie and Clyde exhibited a particularly high need for arousal. You can get a sense of your own preferred level of stimulation by completing the questionnaire in Table 8-1 (Zuckerman, 1991, 1994; Farley, 1986).

Incentive Approaches: Motivation's Pull

incentive approaches to motivation: The theory suggesting that motivation stems from the desire to obtain valued external goals, or incentives

When a luscious dessert is brought to the table after a filling meal, its appeal has little or nothing to do with internal drives or with the maintenance of arousal. Rather, if we choose to eat the dessert, such behavior is motivated by the external stimulus of the dessert itself, which acts as an anticipated reward. This reward, in motivational terms, is an *incentive*.

Incentive approaches to motivation suggest that motivation stems from the desire to obtain valued external goals, or incentives. In this view, the desirable properties of external stimuli—be they grades, money, affection, food, or sex—account for a person's motivation.

Although the theory explains why we might succumb to an incentive (like a mouth-watering dessert) even though internal cues (like hunger) are lacking, it does not provide a complete explanation of motivation, since organisms seek to fulfill needs even when incentives are not apparent. Consequently, many psychologists believe that the internal drives proposed by drive-reduction theory work in tandem with the external incentives of incentive theory to "push" and "pull" behavior, respectively. Thus, at the same time as we seek to satisfy our underlying hunger needs (the push of drive-reduction theory), we are drawn to food that appears particularly appetizing (the pull of incentive theory). Rather than contradicting each other, then, drives and incentives can work together in motivating behavior (Petri, 1996).

Cognitive Approaches: The Thoughts Behind Motivation

cognitive approaches to motivation: The theory suggesting that motivation is a product of people's thoughts and expectations—their cognitions

Cognitive approaches to motivation suggest that motivation is a product of people's thoughts, expectations, and goals—their cognitions. For instance, the degree to which people are motivated to study for a test is based on their expectation of how well studying will pay off in terms of a good grade (Wigfield & Eccles, 2000).

Table 8-1 Do You Seek Out Sensation?

How much stimulation do you crave in your everyday life? You will have an idea after you complete the following questionnaire, which lists some items from a scale designed to assess your sensation-seeking tendencies. Circle either A or B in each pair of statements.

1. A   I would like a job that requires a lot of travelling.
    B   I would prefer a job in one location.

2. A   I am invigorated by a brisk, cold day.
    B   I can't wait to get indoors on a cold day.

3. A   I get bored seeing the same old faces.
    B   I like the comfortable familiarity of everyday friends.

4. A   I would prefer living in an ideal society in which everyone was safe, secure, and happy.
    B   I would have preferred living in the unsettled days of our history.

5. A   I sometimes like to do things that are a little frightening.
    B   A sensible person avoids activities that are dangerous.

6. A   I would not like to be hypnotized.
    B   I would like to have the experience of being hypnotized.

7. A   The most important goal of life is to live it to the fullest and to experience as much as possible.
    B   The most important goal of life is to find peace and happiness.

8. A   I would like to try parachute jumping.
    B   I would never want to try jumping out of a plane, with or without a parachute.

9. A   I enter cold water gradually, giving myself time to get used to it.
    B   I like to dive or jump right into the ocean or a cold pool.

10. A   When I go on a vacation, I prefer the comfort of a good room and bed.
    B   When I go on a vacation, I prefer the change of camping out.

11. A   I prefer people who are emotionally expressive, even if they are a bit unstable.
    B   I prefer people who are calm and even-tempered.

12. A   A good painting should shock or jolt the senses.
    B   A good painting should give one a feeling of peace and security.

13. A   People who ride motorcycles must have some kind of unconscious need to hurt themselves.
    B   I would like to drive or ride a motorcycle.

Scoring   Give yourself one point for each of the following responses: 1A, 2A, 3A, 4B, 5A, 6B, 7A, 8A, 9B, 10B, 11A, 12A, 13B. Find your total score by adding up the number of points and then use the following scoring key:

0–3 very low sensation seeking

4–5 low

6–9 average

10–11 high

12–13 very high

Keep in mind, of course, that this short questionnaire, for which the scoring is based on the results of college students who have taken it, provides only a rough estimate of your sensation-seeking tendencies. Moreover, as people get older, their sensation-seeking scores tend to decrease. Still, the questionnaire will at least give you an indication of how your sensation-seeking tendencies compare with those of others.

(Source: Zuckerman, 1978, 1994)

Cognitive theories of motivation draw a key distinction between intrinsic and extrinsic motivation. *Intrinsic motivation* causes us to participate in an activity for our own enjoyment, rather than for any concrete, tangible reward that it will bring us. In contrast, *extrinsic motivation* causes us to do something for money, a grade, or some other concrete, tangible reward. For example, when a physician works long hours because she loves medicine, intrinsic motivation is prompting her; if she works hard in order to make a lot of money, extrinsic motivation underlies her efforts (Rawsthorne & Elliot, 1999; Ryan & Deci, 2000).

We are more apt to persevere, work harder, and produce work of higher quality when motivation for a task is intrinsic rather than extrinsic. In fact, providing rewards for desirable behavior might cause intrinsic motivation to decline and extrinsic motivation to increase, although this view is controversial (Deci, Koestner, & Ryan, 1999; Eisenberger, Pierce, & Cameron, 1999; Sansone & Harackiewicz, 2000).

In a dramatic demonstration of the differing effects of rewards on motivation, researchers promised a group of nursery school students a reward for drawing with magic markers (an activity for which they had previously shown high motivation). The reward reduced their enthusiasm for the task, for they later showed considerably less zeal for drawing (Lepper & Greene, 1978). It was as if the promise of reward undermined their intrinsic interest in drawing, turning what had been play into work.

Such research suggests the importance of promoting intrinsic motivation and indicates that providing extrinsic rewards (or even just calling attention to them) can undermine the effort and quality of performance. Parents might think twice, then, about offering their children monetary rewards for getting good report cards. Instead, research on intrinsic motivation suggests that better results would come from reminding them of the pleasures that can come from learning and mastering a body of knowledge (Deci, Koestner, & Ryan, 1999: Lepper, Henderlong, & Gingras, 1999).

Maslow's Hierarchy: Ordering Motivational Needs

What do Eleanor Roosevelt, Abraham Lincoln, and Albert Einstein have in common? The common thread, according to a model of motivation devised by psychologist Abraham Maslow, is that each of them fulfilled the highest levels of motivational needs underlying human behavior.

Maslow's model considers different motivational needs to be ordered in a hierarchy, and it suggests that before more sophisticated, higher-order needs can be met, certain primary needs must be satisfied (Maslow, 1970, 1987). The model can be conceptualized as a pyramid (see Figure 8-1) in which the more basic needs are at the bottom and the higher-level needs are at the top. For a particular need to be activated and thereby guide a person's behavior, the more basic needs in the hierarchy must be met first.

The most basic needs are primary drives: needs for water, food, sleep, sex, and the like. To move up the hierarchy, a person must have these basic physiological needs met. Safety needs come next in the hierarchy; Maslow suggests that people need a safe, secure environment in order to function effectively. Physiological and safety needs compose the lower-order needs.

Only when the basic lower-order needs are met can a person consider fulfilling higher-order needs, such as the need for love and a sense of belonging, esteem, and self-actualization. Love and belongingness needs include the need to obtain and give affection and to be a contributing member of some group or society. After these needs are fulfilled, the person strives for esteem. In Maslow's thinking, esteem relates to the need to develop a sense of self-worth by knowing that others are aware of one's competence and value.

Once these four sets of needs are fulfilled—no easy task—the person is able to strive for the highest-level need, self-actualization. **Self-actualization** is a state of self-fulfillment in which people realize their highest potential in their own unique way. Although at first Maslow suggested that self-actualization occurred in only a few, famous individuals, he later expanded the concept to encompass everyday people. For example, a parent with excellent nurturing skills who raises a family, a teacher who year after year creates an environment that maximizes students' opportunities for success, and an artist who realizes her creative potential might all be self-actualized. The important thing is that people feel at ease with themselves and satisfied that they are using their talents to the fullest. In a sense, achieving self-actualization produces a decline in the striving and yearning for greater fulfillment that marks most people's lives and instead provides a sense of satisfaction with the current state of affairs (Jones & Crandall, 1991).

self-actualization: A state of self-fulfillment in which people realize their highest potential in their own unique way

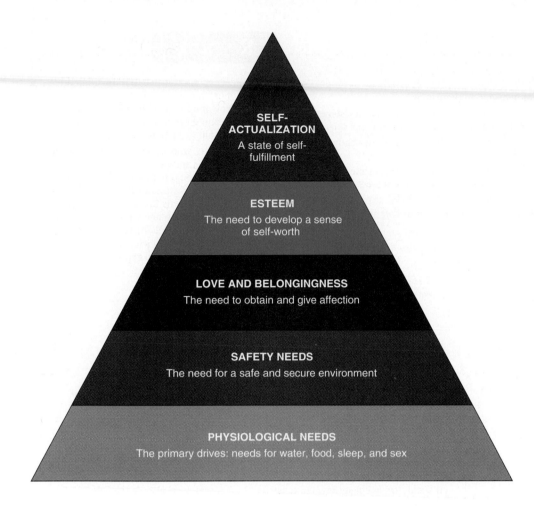

SELF-
ACTUALIZATION
A state of self-
fulfillment

ESTEEM
The need to develop a sense
of self-worth

LOVE AND BELONGINGNESS
The need to obtain and give affection

SAFETY NEEDS
The need for a safe and secure environment

PHYSIOLOGICAL NEEDS
The primary drives: needs for water, food, sleep, and sex

Figure 8–1 Maslow's hierarchy shows how our motivation progresses up the pyramid from a basis in the broadest, most fundamental biological needs to higher-order ones (After Maslow, 1970). Do you agree that lower-order needs must be satisfied before higher-order needs? Do hermits and monks who attempt to achieve spiritual needs while denying basic physical needs contradict Maslow's hierarchy?

From A. Maslow, *Motivation and Personality* 3/e, Copyright © 1970. Reproduced by permission of Pearson Education, Inc., Upper Saddle River, New Jersey.

Although research has been unable to validate the specific ordering of Maslow's stages, and it is difficult to measure self-actualization objectively, Maslow's model is important for two reasons: It highlights the complexity of human needs, and it emphasizes that until more basic biological needs are met, people will be relatively unconcerned with higher-order needs. For example, if people are hungry, their first interest will be in obtaining food; they will not be concerned with such needs as love and self-esteem (Weiss, 1991; Neher, 1991).

 PsychLink
Maslow's self-actualization
www.mhhe.com/
feldmaness5-08links

Applying the Different Approaches to Motivation

The various theories of motivation provide us with several different perspectives on motivation. Which provides the fullest account of motivation? The answer is that many of the approaches are complementary, rather than contradictory. In fact, it often is useful to employ more than one approach in order to understand motivation in a particular instance.

Consider, for example, John Thompson's brave determination after his farm accident (described earlier in the chapter). From the perspective of instinct theory, John could be seen to have an overwhelming instinct to preserve his life at all costs. From the drive-reduction perspective, he was motivated to get medical help in order to end the pain that followed his accident. And from a cognitive perspective, his expectation that surgeons could reattach his arms led him to take action that would maximize the chances of recovery.

In short, applying multiple approaches to motivation to a given situation provides a broader understanding than we might obtain by employing only a single approach. We'll see this fact again as we proceed to consider specific motives—such as the needs for food, achievement, affiliation, and power—where we will draw upon several of the theories to provide us with the fullest account of what motivates our behavior.

Evaluate

1. _____ are forces that guide a person's behavior in a certain direction.
2. Biologically determined, inborn patterns of behavior are known as_____.
3. Your psychology professor tells you, "Explaining behavior is easy! When we lack something we are motivated to get it." Which approach to motivation does your professor subscribe to?
4. By drinking water after running a marathon, a runner tries to keep his or her body at an optimal level of functioning. This process is called_____.
5. I help an elderly person across the street because doing a good deed makes me feel good. What type of motivation is at work here? What type of motivation would be at work if I were to help an elderly man across the street because he paid me $20?
6. According to Maslow, a person with no job, no home, and no friends can become self-actualized. True or false?

Answers to Evaluate Questions

1. Motives 2. instincts 3. Drive reduction 4. homeostasis 5. Intrinsic; Extrinsic 6. False; lower-order needs must be fulfilled before self-actualization can occur.

Rethink

1. Which approaches to motivation are most commonly used in the workplace? How might each approach be used to design employment policies that can sustain or increase motivation?
2. A writer who works all day composing copy for an advertising firm has a hard time keeping her mind on her work and continually watches the clock. After work she turns to a collection of stories she is creating and writes long into the night, completely forgetful of the clock. What ideas from your reading on motivation help to explain this phenomenon?

Prepare

What biological and social factors underlie hunger?

What are the varieties of sexual behavior?

How are needs relating to achievement, affiliation, and power motivation exhibited?

Organize

Human Needs and Motivation
    The Motivation Behind Hunger and Eating
    Sexual Motivation
    The Need for Achievement
    The Need for Affiliation
    The Need for Power

Human Needs and Motivation: Eat, Drink, and Be Daring

As a sophomore at the University of California, Santa Cruz, Lisa Arndt followed a menu of her own making: For breakfast she ate cereal or fruit, with 10 diet pills and 50 chocolate-flavored laxatives. Lunch was a salad or sandwich; dinner: chicken and rice. But it was the feast that followed that Arndt relished most. Almost every night at about 9 P.M., she would retreat to her room and eat an entire small pizza and a whole batch of cookies. Then she'd wait for the day's laxatives to take effect. "It was extremely painful," says Arndt of those days in 1992. "But I was that desperate to make up for my bingeing. I was terrified of fat the way other people are afraid of lions or guns." (Hubbard, O'Neill, & Cheakalos, 1999, p. 59)

Lisa was one of the 5 to 10 million females (and 1 million males) who suffer from an eating disorder. These disorders, which usually appear during adolescence, can bring about extraordinary declines in weight and other physical deterioration. They are extremely dangerous, sometimes resulting in death.

Why are Lisa and others like her subject to such disordered eating, revolving around the motivation to avoid weight gain at all costs? And why do so many other people engage in overeating, leading to obesity?

To answer these questions, we must consider some of the specific kinds of needs that underlie behavior. In this section, we will examine several of the most important human needs. We'll begin with hunger and sex, the primary drives that have received the most attention from researchers, and then turn to secondary drives—those uniquely human strivings, based on learned needs and past experience, that help explain why people strive to achieve, to affiliate with others, and to seek power over others.

The Motivation Behind Hunger and Eating

obesity: The state of being more than 20 percent above the average weight for a person of one's height

More than half the people in the United States are overweight, and more than a fifth are so heavy that they have **obesity,** body weight that is more than 20 percent above the average weight for a person of their height. And the rest of the world is not far behind: the prevalence of obesity around the globe is so great that the World Health Organization has said it has reached epidemic proportions (National Center for Health Statistics, 1994; Taubes, 1998).

Perceptions of ideal weight and body shape vary significantly across different cultures and, within Western cultures, from one time period to another. For instance, many contemporary Western cultures stress the importance of slimness in women—a view that is actually relatively recent. In nineteenth-century Hawaii, women who were considered the most attractive were those who were the most overweight.

Furthermore, for most of the twentieth century—except for a period in the 1920s and the most recent decades—the ideal female figure was relatively full. Even today, weight standards differ among different cultural groups. For instance, African Americans generally judge heavier women more positively than whites do (Silverstein et al., 1986; Hebl & Heatherton, 1998; Rosenthal, 1999).

Regardless of societal standards relating to appearance and weight, there is no question that being overweight is a major health risk. However, controlling weight is complicated, because eating behavior involves a variety of mechanisms. In our discussion of what motivates people to eat, we'll start with the biological aspects of eating.

Biological Factors in the Regulation of Hunger

In contrast to human beings, nonhuman species are unlikely to become obese. Internal mechanisms regulate not only the quantity of their food intake, but also the kind of food they desire. For example, rats that have been deprived of particular foods seek out alternatives that contain the specific nutrients their diet is lacking, and animals given the choice of a wide variety of foods choose a well-balanced diet (Rozin, 1977; Bouchard & Bray, 1996; Woods et al., 2000).

The mechanisms by which organisms know whether they require food or should stop eating are complex. It's not just a matter of an empty stomach causing hunger pangs and a full one alleviating hunger. (Even people whose stomachs have been removed still experience the sensation of hunger.) One important factor is changes in the chemical composition of the blood. In particular, changes in levels of glucose, a kind of sugar, regulate feelings of hunger (Inglefinger, 1944; Rodin, 1985; Campfield et al., 1996).

Glucose levels are monitored by the brain's *hypothalamus,* a tiny brain structure we first discussed in Chapter 2. Increasing evidence suggests that the hypothalamus is the organ primarily responsible for monitoring food intake. Injury to the hypothalamus has radical consequences for eating behavior, depending upon the site of the injury. For example, rats whose *lateral hypothalamus* is damaged might literally starve to death. They refuse food when offered and, unless they are force-fed, eventually die. Rats with an injury to the *ventromedial hypothalamus* display the opposite problem: extreme overeating. Rats with this injury can increase in weight by as much as 400 percent. Similar phenomena occur in humans who have tumors of the hypothalamus (Rolls, 1994; Woods et al., 1998).

Although the hypothalamus clearly plays an important role in regulating food intake, exactly how it operates is still unclear. One hypothesis is that injury to the hypothalamus affects the weight set point by which food intake is regulated. According to this hypothesis, the **weight set point** is the particular level of weight that the body strives to maintain. Acting as a kind of internal weight thermostat, the hypothalamus calls for either greater or less food intake (Nisbett, 1972; Capaldi, 1996; Woods et al., 2000).

weight set point: The particular level of weight that the body strives to maintain

In most cases, the hypothalamus does a good job. People who are not monitoring their weight show only minor weight fluctuations, in spite of substantial day-to-day variations in how much they eat and exercise. However, injury to the hypothalamus drastically raises or lowers the weight set point, and the organism then strives to meet its internal goal by increasing or decreasing its food consumption.

The weight set point is determined at least partly by genetic factors. People seem destined through heredity to have a particular **metabolism,** the rate at which food is converted to energy and expended by the body. People with a high metabolic rate are able to eat virtually as much as they want without gaining weight, whereas people with a low metabolic rate might eat literally half as much and yet gain weight readily (Woods et al., 1998).

metabolism: The rate at which food is converted to energy and expended by the body

- The frequency of marital sex varies widely. However, younger couples tend to have sexual intercourse more frequently than older couples. In addition, most men and women do not engage in extramarital sex. (p. 263)
- Homosexuals are sexually attracted to people of their own sex; bisexuals are sexually attracted to people of the same sex and people of the opposite sex. No explanation of sexual orientation has been confirmed; possibilities include genetic or biological factors, childhood and family influences, and prior learning experiences and conditioning. (p. 263)

How are needs relating to achievement, affiliation, and power motivation exhibited?

- Need for achievement refers to the stable, learned characteristic in which a person strives to attain a level of excellence. Need for achievement is usually measured through the Thematic Apperception Test (TAT), a series of pictures about which a person writes a story. (p. 266)
- The need for affiliation is a concern with establishing and maintaining relationships with others, whereas the need for power is a tendency to seek to exert an impact on others. (p. 266)

What are emotions, and how do we experience them?

- Emotions are broadly defined as feelings that can affect behavior and generally have both a physiological and a cognitive component. There is debate over whether there are separate systems that govern cognitive and emotional responses, and whether one has primacy over the other. (p. 268)

What are the functions of emotions?

- Several theories explain emotions. The James-Lange theory suggests that emotional experience is a reaction to bodily, or visceral, changes that occur as a response to an environmental event and are interpreted as an emotional response. (p. 271)
- In contrast, the Cannon-Bard theory contends that both physiological arousal *and* an emotional experience are produced simultaneously by the same nerve stimulus and that the visceral experience itself does not necessarily differ among differing emotions. (p. 272)
- The Schachter-Singer theory suggests that emotions are determined jointly by a relatively nonspecific physiological arousal and the subsequent labeling of that arousal, using cues from the environment to determine how others are behaving in the same situation. (p. 272)
- The most recent approaches to emotions focus on their biological aspects. For instance, it now seems that specific patterns of biological arousal are associated with individual emotions. Furthermore, new scanning techniques have identified the specific parts of the brain that are activated during the experience of particular emotions. (p. 273)

Key Terms and Concepts

motivation (p. 250)

instincts (p. 251)

drive-reduction approaches to motivation (p. 251)

drive (p. 251)

homeostasis (p. 251)

arousal approaches to motivation (p. 252)

incentive approaches to motivation (p. 252)

cognitive approaches of motivation (p. 252)

self-actualization (p. 254)

obesity (p. 256)

weight set point (p. 257)

metabolism (p. 257)

anorexia nervosa (p. 259)

bulimia (p. 259)

androgens (p. 261)

estrogen (p. 261)

progesterone (p. 261)

ovulation (p. 261)

masturbation (p. 262)

heterosexuality (p. 262)

double standard (p. 262)

extramarital sex (p. 263)

homosexuals (p. 263)

bisexuals (p. 263)

need for achievement (p. 266)

need for affiliation (p. 266)

need for power (p. 267)

emotions (p. 268)

James-Lange theory of emotion (p. 271)

Cannon-Bard theory of emotion (p. 272)

Schachter-Singer theory of emotion (p. 272)

Psychology on the Web

1. Find two different websites that deal with nonverbal behavior. One site should present a fairly "academic" discussion of the topic, and the other should be more informal. (Hint: The terms *nonverbal behavior* and *nonverbal communication* might lead you to more formal discussions of the topic, whereas *body language* might lead you to the less formal discussions.) Compare and contrast your findings from the two sites.
2. Find one or more websites that offer information on losing weight. Evaluate the information on the website(s), using your understanding of obesity discussed in this chapter. Summarize your findings and conclusions in writing.

Epilogue

In this chapter, we discussed motivation and emotions, two interrelated aspects of psychology. The topic of motivation has spawned a great deal of theory and research in its examination of primary and secondary drives. We then turned to a discussion of emotions, beginning with their functions and proceeding to a review of three major theories that seek to explain what emotions are and how they, and their associated physiological symptoms, emerge in the individual.

Before we proceed to Chapter 9, return to the scenario in the prologue to this chapter: how cyclist Lance Armstrong overcame cancer and won the Tour de France. Using your knowledge of motivation and emotion, consider the following questions:

1. Which approach or approaches to motivation—instinctual, drive reduction, arousal, incentive, or cognitive—most effectively explain why an athlete like Armstrong will work exceptionally hard over many years to become a competitive cyclist?

2. How might the need for achievement have contributed to Armstrong's decision to continue competitive cycling after his cancer treatment? Would the need for affiliation have played a role? How?

3. What function might Armstrong's emotions have served in helping him overcome his cancer and continue racing competitively?

4. How can Armstrong's comment about his win in the Tour de France ("I think it's a miracle") be interpreted in terms of your understanding of motivation and emotion?

Preview

For additional quizzing and a variety of interactive resources, visit the *Essentials of Understanding Psychology* Online Learning Center at

www.mhhe.com/feldmaness5

Chapter Nine

Development

Elizabeth Carr

Prologue

The Brave New World of Childhood

A few years ago, when Elizabeth Carr's class was learning how an egg combines with sperm in the mother's body to create a child, she felt compelled to interrupt.

"I piped up to say that not all babies are conceived like that and explained about sperm and eggs and petri dishes," said Elizabeth . . . , the first child in the United States born through in vitro fertilization.

Because her mother's landmark pregnancy was documented in great detail by a film crew, Elizabeth has seen pictures of the egg and sperm that united to become her, the petri dish where she was conceived, the embryonic blob of cells that grew into the bubbly young woman who now plays field hockey and sings in the school chorus. . . .

Elizabeth . . . said that her parents—whose egg and sperm joined in a petri dish at the Jones Institute for Reproductive Medicine in Norfolk, Virginia—have always made it clear that she was created differently from other children. Although she said she had faced taunts of "test tube baby" or "weirdo" a few times at school, she said she had never felt resentful about her conception. "I'm so grateful that they went through all this to have me" (Rosenthal, 1996, A1, B8).

Looking Ahead

Now a bubbly teenager, Elizabeth is just "one of a crowd," as her mother predicted when she was born—a crowd of some 60,000 children in the United States who were born only thanks to the technology of in vitro fertilization (Goldberg, 1999).

Welcome to the brave new world of childhood—or rather, one of the brave new worlds. From new ways of conceiving children to learning how to raise children most sensibly, the issues involved in human development touch each of us.

These issues, along with many others, are addressed by **developmental psychology,** the branch of psychology that studies the patterns of growth and change occurring throughout life. In large part, developmental psychologists study the interaction between the unfolding of biologically predetermined patterns of behavior and a constantly changing, dynamic environment. They ask how our genetic background affects our behavior throughout our lives and whether our potential is limited by heredity. Similarly, they are committed to understanding how the environment works with—or against—our genetic capabilities, how the world we live in affects our development, and how we can be encouraged to reach our full potential.

More than other psychologists, developmental psychologists consider the day-to-day patterns and changes in behavior that occur across the life span. This chapter deals broadly with the entire life cycle, beginning with conception, moving through birth, infancy, and childhood, exploring adolescence and adulthood, and finally proceeding to old age and death.

We begin our discussion of development by examining the approaches used to study the environmental and genetic factors—the nature-nurture issue. Then we consider the very start of development, beginning with conception and the nine months of life prior to birth. We describe both genetic and environmental influences on the unborn individual, and how these can affect behavior throughout the remainder of the life cycle.

Next, we examine the physical and perceptual developments that occur after birth, witnessing the enormous and rapid growth that takes place during the early stages of life. We also focus on the developing child's social world, indicating what draws the child into relationships with others and membership in society. Finally, we discuss cognitive growth during infancy and childhood, tracing changes in the ways children think about the world.

We then examine development from adolescence through young adulthood, middle age, and old age. Our discussion of adolescence focuses on some of the major physical, emotional, and cognitive changes that occur during this transition from childhood to adulthood. Next, we consider early and middle adulthood, stages in which people are at the peak of their physical and intellectual abilities. We discuss the developmental changes people undergo during these periods and their relationship to work, families, and social changes that occur as a consequence of the aging process, and we see that aging can bring about both improvements and declines in various kinds of functioning. We end with a discussion of the ways people prepare themselves for death.

developmental psychology: The branch of psychology that studies the patterns of growth and change occurring throughout life

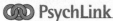
PsychLink
Theories of child development
www.mhhe.com/
feldmaness5-09links

Prepare

How do psychologists study the influences of hereditary and environmental factors in development?

What is the nature of development prior to birth?

What factors affect a child during the mother's pregnancy?

Organize

Nature and Nurture: The Enduring Developmental Issue

How many bald, six-foot-six, 250-pound volunteer fire fighters are there in New Jersey who wear droopy mustaches, aviator-style eyeglasses, and a key ring on the right side of the belt?

The answer is: two. Gerald Levey and Mark Newman are identical twins, separated at birth. Each twin did not even know the other existed until they were reunited—in a fire station—by a fellow fire fighter who knew Newman and was startled to see Levey at a fire fighters' convention.

The lives of the twins, although separate, took remarkably similar paths. Levey went to college, studying forestry; Newman planned to study forestry in college but instead took a job trimming trees. Both had jobs in supermarkets. One has a job installing sprinkler systems; the other installed fire alarms.

Both men are unmarried and find the same kind of woman attractive: "tall, slender, long hair." They share similar hobbies, enjoying hunting, fishing, going to the beach, and watching old John Wayne movies and professional wrestling. Both like Chinese food and drink the same brand of beer. Their mannerisms are also similar—for example, each one throws his head back when he laughs. And, of course, there is one more thing: They share a passion for fighting fires.

Gerald Levey and Mark Newman

The similarities we see in twins Gerald Levey and Mark Newman vividly raise one of the fundamental questions posed by developmental psychologists: How can we distinguish between the causes of behavior that are *environmental* (the influence of parents, siblings, family, friends, schooling, nutrition, and all the other experiences to which a child is exposed) and those causes that are *hereditary* (those based on the genetic makeup of an individual that influence growth and development throughout life)? This question, which we explored when we considered intelligence in Chapter 7, is known as the **nature-nurture issue.** In this context, nature refers to hereditary factors, and nurture to environmental influences.

Although the question was first posed as a nature-*versus*-nurture issue, developmental psychologists today agree that *both* nature and nurture interact to produce specific developmental patterns and outcomes. Consequently, the question has evolved to *how and to what degree* environment and heredity both produce their effects. No one grows up free of environmental influences, nor does anyone develop without being affected by his or her inherited *genetic makeup.* However, the debate over the comparative influence of the two factors remains active, with different approaches and theories of development emphasizing the environment or heredity to a greater or lesser degree (Scarr, 1996; Saudino, 1997; de Waal, 1999).

For example, some developmental theories stress the role of learning in producing changes in behavior in the developing child, relying on the basic principles of learning discussed in Chapter 5. Such theories emphasize the role of environment in accounting for development. In contrast, other approaches emphasize the influence of one's physiological makeup and functioning on development. Such theories stress the role of heredity and *maturation*—the unfolding of biologically predetermined patterns of behavior—in producing developmental change. Maturation can be seen, for instance, in the development of sex characteristics (such as breasts or body hair) that occurs at the start of adolescence. Furthermore, developmental psychologists have been influenced by the work of behavioral geneticists, who study the effects of heredity on behavior, and the theories of evolutionary psychologists, whose goal is to identify behavior patterns that are a result of our genetic inheritance from our ancestors. Both behavioral geneticists and evolutionary psychologists have highlighted the importance of heredity in influencing our behavior (Bjorklund, 1997).

However, developmental psychologists of different theoretical persuasions agree on some points. It seems clear that genetic factors not only provide the potential for particular behaviors or traits to emerge, but also place limitations on the emergence of such behavior or traits. For instance, heredity defines people's general level of intelligence, setting an upper limit which—regardless of the quality of the environment—people cannot exceed. Heredity also provides limits on physical abilities; humans simply cannot run at a speed of 60 miles an hour, nor will they grow to be 10 feet tall, no matter what the quality of their environment (Plomin, 1990; Plomin & McClearn, 1993; Steen, 1996).

Table 9-1 lists some of the characteristics that are most affected by heredity. As you consider these items, keep in mind that these characteristics are not *entirely* determined by heredity, but that environmental factors also play a role.

In fact, in most instances, environmental factors play a critical role in enabling people to develop the capabilities that their genetic background makes possible. Had Albert

PsychLink

Discussion on nature vs. nurture
www.mhhe.com/
feldmaness5-09links

nature–nurture issue: The issue of the degrees to which environment and heredity influence behavior and development

Table 9–1 Characteristics Influenced Significantly by Genetic Factors

Physical Characteristics	Intellectual Characteristics	Emotional Characteristics and Disorders
Height	Memory	Shyness
Weight	Intelligence	Extraversion
Obesity	Age of language acquisition	Emotionality
Tone of voice	Reading disability	Neuroticism
Blood pressure	Mental retardation	Schizophrenia
Tooth decay		Anxiety
Athletic ability		Alcoholism
Firmness of handshake		
Age of death		
Activity level		

Einstein received no intellectual stimulation as a child and not been sent to school, it is unlikely that he would have fulfilled his genetic potential for great intellect. Similarly, it is unlikely that the great athlete and basketball star Michael Jordan would have developed outstanding physical skill if he had not been raised in an environment that nurtured his innate talent and gave him the opportunity to train and perfect his natural abilities.

It is clear that the relationship between heredity and environment is far from simple. As a consequence, developmental psychologists typically take an *interactionist* position on the nature-nurture issue, suggesting that a combination of hereditary and environmental factors influences development. The challenge facing developmental psychologists is to identify the relative strength of each of these influences on the individual, as well as the specific changes that occur over the course of development (Plomin & Neiderhiser, 1992; Wozniak & Fischer, 1993; Saudino & Plomin, 1996).

Determining the Relative Influences of Nature and Nurture

Developmental psychologists use several approaches to determine the relative influence of genetic and environmental factors on behavior. For example, researchers can experimentally control the genetic makeup of laboratory animals by carefully breeding them for specific traits; and by observing animals with identical genetic makeup in varied environments, researchers can ascertain the effects of particular kinds of environmental stimulation. Although generalizing the findings of nonhuman research to a human population must be done only with care, findings from animal research provide important information that, for ethical reasons, could not be obtained by using human participants.

Human twins also are an important source of information about the relative effects of genetic and environmental factors. If **identical twins** (those who are genetically identical) display different patterns of development, such differences have to be attributed to variations in the environment in which the twins were raised. The most useful data come from identical twins (such as Gerald Levey and Mark Newman) who are adopted at birth by different sets of adoptive parents and raised apart in differing environments. Studies of nontwin siblings who are raised in totally different environments also shed some light on the issue. Because they have relatively similar genetic makeups, siblings who show similarities as adults provide strong evidence for the importance of heredity (Lykken et al., 1993; Gottesman, 1997; McClearn et al., 1997).

It is also possible to take the opposite tack. Instead of concentrating on genetically similar people raised in different environments, we could consider people raised in

identical twins: Twins who are genetically identical

similar environments who are genetically dissimilar. If we find, for example, that two adopted children—genetically dissimilar but raised in the same family—develop similarly, we have evidence for the importance of environmental influences on development. Moreover, it is possible to carry out research involving genetically dissimilar animals; by experimentally varying the environment in which they are raised, we can determine the influence of environmental factors (independent of heredity) on development (Segal, 1993; Vernon et al., 1997).

Specific Research Approaches

Because of the unique demands of measuring behavioral change across different ages, developmental researchers have designed several unique methodologies. In the most frequently used, **cross-sectional research,** people of different ages are compared at the same point in time. Cross-sectional studies provide information about differences in development between different age groups.

> **cross-sectional research:** A research method in which people of different ages are compared at the same point in time

Suppose, for instance, we were interested in the development of intellectual ability in adulthood. To carry out a cross-sectional study, we might compare a sample of 25-, 45-, and 65-year-olds on an IQ test. We then can determine whether average IQ test scores differ in each age group.

Cross-sectional research has limitations, however. For instance, we cannot be sure that the IQ score differences we might find in our example are due to age differences alone. Instead, they might reflect cohort differences in educational attainment. A *cohort* is a group of people who grow up at similar times, in similar places, and under similar conditions. In the case of IQ differences, any age differences we find in a cross-sectional study could reflect educational differences among the cohorts studied: People in the older age group might belong to a cohort that was less likely to attend college than those in the younger groups.

One way around the problem is to employ the second major research strategy used by developmental psychologists: a longitudinal study. In **longitudinal research,** the behavior of one or more participants is traced as the participants age. Longitudinal studies assess *change* in intellectual ability over time, unlike cross-sectional studies, which assess *differences* among groups of people.

> **longitudinal research:** A research method that investigates behavior as participants age

For instance, consider how we might investigate intellectual development during adulthood using a longitudinal research strategy. First, we might give IQ tests to a group of 25-year-olds. We'd then come back to the same people twenty years later and retest them at age 45. Finally, we'd return to them once more when they were 65 years old and test them again.

By examining changes over several points in time, we can clearly see how individuals develop. Unfortunately, longitudinal research requires an enormous expenditure of time (as the researcher waits for the participants to get older), and participants who begin a study at an early age might drop out, move away, or even die as the research continues. Moreover, participants who take the same test at several points in time can become "testwise" and perform better each time they take it, having become more familiar with the test.

To make up for the limitations in cross-sectional and longitudinal research, investigators have devised an alternative strategy. Known as **cross-sequential research,** it combines cross-sectional and longitudinal approaches by taking a number of different age groups and examining them over several points in time. For example, investigators might use a group of 3-, 5-, and 7-year-olds, examining them every six months for a period of several years. This technique allows the developmental psychologist to tease out the effects of age changes themselves from other possibly influential factors.

> **cross-sequential research:** A research method that combines cross-sectional and longitudinal research by considering a number of different age groups and examining them over several points in time

Prenatal Development: From Conception to Birth

Our understanding of the biology of *conception*—when a male's sperm cell penetrates a female's egg cell—makes it no less of a miracle. At that single moment, an individual's genetic endowment is established for the rest of her or his life.

(a)   Conception   (b)   23 pairs of chromosomes   (c)   DNA sequence   (d)   Genes

Figure 9-1 Every individual's characteristics are determined by the individual's specific genetic information. At the moment of conception *(a)*, humans receive 23 pairs of chromosomes *(b)*, half from the mother and half from the father. These chromosomes are made up of coils of DNA *(c)*. Each chromosome contains thousands of genes *(d)* that "program" the future development of the body.

The Basics of Genetics

chromosomes: Rod-shaped structures that contain the basic hereditary information

genes: The parts of the chromosomes through which genetic information is transmitted

The one-cell entity that is established at conception contains 23 pairs of **chromosomes,** rod-shaped structures that contain the basic hereditary information. One member of each pair is from the mother and the other is from the father.

Each chromosome contains thousands of **genes**—smaller units through which genetic information is transmitted. Either individually or in combination, genes produce the particular characteristics of each person. Composed of sequences of *DNA (deoxyribonucleic acid)* molecules, genes are the biological equivalent of "software" that programs the future development of all parts of the body's hardware. Humans have some 30,000 different genes (see Figure 9-1).

Some genes are responsible for the development of systems common to all members of the human species—the heart, circulatory system, brain, lungs, and so forth; others control the characteristics that make each human unique, such as facial configuration, height, eye color, and the like. The child's sex is also determined by a particular combination of genes. Specifically, a child inherits an X chromosome from its mother, and either an X or Y chromosome from its father. A child with an XX combination is female; a child with an XY combination is male. Male development is triggered by a single gene on the Y chromosome, and without the presence of that specific gene, the individual will develop as a female.

PsychLink

Publications on genetics
www.mhhe.com/
feldmaness5-09links

As behavioral geneticists are increasingly discovering, genes are also at least partially responsible for a wide variety of personal characteristics, encompassing cognitive abilities, personality traits, and psychological disorders. Of course, few of these characteristics are determined by a single gene. Instead, most traits are the result of a combination of multiple genes, which operate together with environmental influences (Gilger, 1996; Pillard, 1996; Rieder, Kaufmann, & Knowles, 1996; Funder, 1997).

To better understand how genes influence human characteristics and behavior, scientists have mapped the specific location and sequence of every human gene in the massive, multiyear Human Genome Project (first discussed in Chapter 2). As you can see by reading the *Applying Psychology in the 21st Century* box, the Human Genome Project is likely to produce a revolution in health care, as scientists identify the particular genes that are responsible for various disorders.

Development from Zygote to Birth

zygote: The new cell formed by the union of an egg and sperm

When the egg becomes fertilized by the sperm, the result is a one-celled entity called a **zygote** that immediately begins to develop. The zygote starts out as a microscopic speck. Three days after fertilization, though, the zygote increases to around 32 cells,

Applying Psychology in the 21st Century

Cloning, Gene Therapy, and the Coming Medical Revolution

As he chats with the young mother, the doctor flicks a cotton swab into the mouth of her infant son, collecting a small sample of mucus from inside his cheek. In the back room of his office, he inserts the sample into a machine, which extracts DNA from the mucus cells and compares it with the genetic material on a dime-size chip. Minutes later, a computer printer begins to spit out a list of the infant's genes. Fortunately, all but a few of the genes are labeled "normal." It is those few that the doctor discusses as he explains the results to the mother. "Your son's genetic inheritance is generally good," he says, "but he is somewhat predisposed to skin lesions. So starting right away, he should be protected against excessive exposure to the sun." And the doctor warns, "he may well be susceptible to cardiovascular disease later in life. To lessen his risk, after about age two he should begin a lifelong low-fat, high-fiber diet." (Jaroff, 1996, p. 24)

This view of a visit to a pediatrician's office is not so futuristic, for it could become reality within the next few decades. Our increasing understanding of genetics is leading not only to the identification of risk factors in children, but also to the development of new treatments for everything from serious physical illnesses, such as cancer, to psychological disorders like schizophrenia and depression.

This potential medical revolution has been heralded, in part, by an unlikely achievement: the birth of Dolly, a rather ordinary looking sheep with an extraordinary genetic background. Dolly was the first animal to be cloned from the cells of an adult sheep, making her an exact genetic replica of her "parent." Dolly was soon followed by a menagerie of cloned animals, each genetically identical to another member of its species (Pennisi, 1997c; Kolata, 1998).

Dolly, the first adult mammal to be cloned. Is it possible for Dolly to have a different "personality" than her clone?

The ability of scientists to produce clones raises new possibilities of correcting genetic flaws, not only in sheep and other animals, but in humans, and it accelerates the pace of developments in the new field of gene therapy. In *gene therapy,* genes are introduced into existing cells in order to prevent or cure a disorder. For instance, genes targeted to treat a particular disease can be injected into a patient's blood stream. When the genes reach the site of the problem—such as a cancerous tumor—the new genes provide existing cells with a set of new instructions that modify their functioning, thereby potentially curing the disease. It also might be possible to "harvest" defective cells from a child prior to birth. These cells could be treated by gene therapy and reintroduced into the unborn child, thereby repairing the defect (Kmiec, 1999; Levy, 2000; Yan, Kinzler, & Vogelstein, 2000).

Some forms of gene therapy are already in use, and the number of diseases treated by gene therapy is growing. For example, such disorders as AIDS, cystic fibrosis, and rheumatoid arthritis are promising candidates for gene therapy (Weiner, 2000).

Cloning advances are likely to continue to raise significant ethical issues. In one radical possibility, cloning might be employed if both a husband and wife were infertile. In such a case, they might consider cloning one or the other of themselves in order to have at least one child who was genetically similar (in this case, genetically identical) to one of them. The ethical and moral issues of such a procedure, of course, are profound—but the rapid advances in cloning and gene therapy suggest they need to be dealt with now (Angier, 1999; Gordon, 1999; Shiels et al., 1999; Wright, 1999).

Would you choose to be genetically tested so that you could know your susceptibility to future genetic diseases? What if you learned that you had a genetic disorder that was likely to shorten your life?

and within a week it has grown to 100 to 150 cells. These first two weeks are known as the *germinal period.*

Two weeks after conception, the developing individual enters the *embryonic period,* which lasts from week 2 through week 8, and he or she is now called an **embryo.** As the embryo develops through an intricate, preprogrammed process of cell division, it grows 10,000 times larger by 4 weeks of age, attaining a length of about one-fifth of an inch. At this point it has developed a rudimentary beating heart, brain, and intestinal tract, and a number of other rudimentary organs. Although all these organs are at a primitive stage of development, they are clearly recognizable. Moreover, by 8 weeks, the embryo is about an inch long, and has arms, legs, and a face that are discernible.

From 8 weeks and continuing until birth, the developing individual enters the *fetal period* and is now called a **fetus.** At the start of this period, it begins to respond to touch; it bends its fingers when touched on the hand. At 16 to 18 weeks, its movements become

embryo: A developed zygote that has a rudimentary heart, brain, and other organs

fetus: A developing child, from 8 weeks after conception until birth strong enough for the mother to sense the baby's movement. At the same time, hair might begin to grow on the baby's head, and the facial features become similar to those the child will display at birth. The major organs begin functioning, although the fetus could not yet be kept alive outside the mother. In addition, a lifetime's worth of brain neurons are produced—although it is unclear whether the brain is capable of thinking at this early stage.

By 24 weeks, the fetus has many of the characteristics it will display as a newborn. In fact, when an infant is born prematurely at this age, it can open and close its eyes; suck; cry; look up, down, and around; and even grasp objects placed in its hands, although it is still unable to survive for long outside the mother.

age of viability: The point at which the fetus can survive if born prematurely

The fetus continues to develop prior to birth. It begins to grow fatty deposits under the skin and it gains weight. The fetus reaches the **age of viability,** the point at which it can survive if born prematurely, at about 24 weeks, although through advances in medical technology this crucial age is getting earlier. At 28 weeks, the fetus weighs less than 3 pounds and is about 16 inches long. It might be capable of learning: One study found that the infants of mothers who had repeatedly read aloud the Dr. Seuss story *The Cat in the Hat* prior to birth preferred the sound of that particular story over other stories after they were born (Spence & DeCasper, 1982).

As they develop prior to birth, children pass through several *critical periods,* times during development when specific events have their greatest impact. For example, children are particularly sensitive to environmental influences such as drugs during certain certain critical periods before birth. If they are exposed to the drug before or after the critical period, it might have relatively little impact, but if exposure comes during a critical period, its impact will be maximized. Critical periods can also occur after birth; some language specialists suggest, for instance, that there is a period where children are particularly receptive to language (Bornstein & Bruner, 1989; Eisen, Field, & Larson, 1991; Shatz, 1992).

In the final weeks of pregnancy, the fetus continues to gain weight and grow. At the end of the normal 38 weeks of pregnancy, the fetus typically weighs around 7 pounds and is about 20 inches in length.

Genetic Influences on the Fetus

The process of fetal growth that we have just described reflects normal development, which occurs in 95 to 98 percent of all pregnancies. Some people are less fortunate, for in the remaining 2 to 5 percent of cases, children are born with serious birth defects. A major cause of such defects is faulty genes or chromosomes. Here are some of the most common genetic and chromosomal difficulties.

- *Phenylketonuria (PKU).* A child born with the inherited disease phenylketonuria cannot produce an enzyme that is required for normal development. This results in an accumulation of poisons that eventually cause profound mental retardation.

These remarkable photos of live fetuses display the degree of physical development at 4 and 15 weeks.

The disease is treatable, however, if caught early enough. Most infants today are routinely tested for PKU, and children with the disorder can be placed on a special diet that allows them to develop normally.

- *Sickle-cell anemia.* About 10 percent of the African American population has the possibility of passing on sickle-cell anemia, a disease that gets its name from the abnormal shape of the victims' red blood cells. Children with the disease might have poor appetites, swollen stomachs, and yellowish eyes; they frequently die during childhood.
- *Tay-Sachs disease.* Children born with Tay-Sachs disease, a disorder that most often afflicts Jews of eastern European ancestry, usually die by the age of 3 or 4 because of the body's inability to break down fat. If both parents carry the genetic defect producing the fatal illness, their child has a one in four chance of being born with the disease (Navon & Proia, 1989).
- *Down syndrome.* Down syndrome, a cause of mental retardation, occurs when the zygote receives an extra chromosome at the moment of conception, causing retardation. Down syndrome is often related to the mother's age; mothers over 35 and younger than 18, in particular, stand a higher risk than other women of having a child with the syndrome.

Prenatal Environmental Influences

Genetic factors are not the only causes of difficulties in fetal development. Environmental influences—the *nurture* part of the nature-nurture equation—also affect the fetus. Some of the most profound consequences are brought about by **teratogens,** environmental agents such as drugs, chemicals, viruses, or other factors that produce birth defects. Among the major prenatal environmental influences on the fetus:

- *Mother's nutrition and emotional state.* What a mother eats during her pregnancy can have important implications for the health of her baby. Mothers who are seriously undernourished cannot provide adequate nutrition to the growing baby, and they are likely to give birth to underweight babies. Poorly nourished babies are also more susceptible to disease, and a lack of nourishment can adversely affect mental development (Adams & Parker, 1990; Ricciuti, 1993; Sigman, 1995).

  Moreover, the mother's emotional state affects the baby. Mothers who are anxious and tense during the last months of their pregnancies are more apt to have infants who are irritable and who sleep and eat poorly. The reason? One hypothesis is that the autonomic nervous system of the fetus becomes especially sensitive as a result of the chemical changes produced by the mother's emotional state (Kagan, Kearsley, & Zelazo, 1978).
- *Mother's illness.* Several disesases that have a relatively minor effect on the mother's health can have devastating consequences for the developing fetus if contracted during the early part of a woman's pregnancy. For example, rubella (German measles), syphilis, diabetes, and high blood pressure can permanently harm the fetus. The virus that causes AIDS can also be passed from mother to child prior to birth. The virus can also be passed on through breast-feeding after birth (Heyward & Curran, 1988).
- *Mother's use of drugs.* Mothers who take illegal and physically addictive drugs such as cocaine run the risk of giving birth to babies who are similarly addicted. Their newborns suffer painful withdrawal symptoms after birth and sometimes have permanent physical and mental impairment. Even legal drugs taken by pregnant women (who might not know that they have become pregnant) can have a tragic effect. For example, drugs such as the acne medicine Acutane can produce fetal abnormalities (Hannigan et al., 1999; Streissguth et al., 1999; Ikonomidou et al., 2000).
- *Alcohol and nicotine use.* Alcohol and nicotine are dangerous to fetal development. For example, *fetal alcohol syndrome,* a condition resulting in mental and growth retardation, has been found in the children of mothers who

PsychLink

Sickle-cell anemia information
www.mhhe.com/
feldmaness5-09links

teratogens: Environmental agents such as drugs, chemicals, viruses, or other factors that produce birth defects consumed heavy or sometimes even moderate amounts of alcohol during pregnancy. Pregnant mothers who smoke also put their children at considerable risk (DiFranza & Lew, 1995; Mills, 1999; Ness et al., 1999).

A number of other environmental factors have an impact upon the child prior to and during birth (see Table 9-2). It is important to keep in mind, however, that although we have been discussing the influences of genetics and environment separately, neither factor works alone. Furthermore, despite the emphasis here on some of the ways development can go wrong, the vast majority of pregnancies develop without difficulty. And in most instances, subsequent child development also proceeds normally, as we discuss next.

Table 9-2 Environmental Factors Affecting Prenatal Development

Factor	Possible Effect
Rubella (German measles)	Blindness, deafness, heart abnormalities, stillbirth
Syphilis	Mental retardation, physical deformities, maternal miscarriage
Addictive drugs	Low birth weight, addiction of infant to drug, with possible death, after birth, from withdrawal
Smoking	Premature birth, low birth weight and length
Alcohol	Mental retardation, lower-than-average birth weight, small head, limb deformities
Radiation from X rays	Physical deformities, mental retardation
Inadequate diet	Reduction in growth of brain, smaller-than-average weight and length at birth
Mother's age—younger than 18 at birth of child	Premature birth, increased incidence of Down syndrome
Mother's age—older than 35 at birth of child	Increased incidence of Down syndrome
DES (diethylstilbestrol)	Reproductive difficulties and increased incidence of genital cancer in children of mothers who were given DES during pregnancy to prevent miscarriage
AIDS	Possible spread of AIDS virus to infant; facial deformities; growth failure

Evaluate

1. Developmental psychologists are interested in the effects of both _____ and _____ on development.
2. Environment and heredity both influence development, with genetic potentials generally establishing limits on environmental influences. True or false?
3. By observing genetically similar animals in differing environments, we can increase our understanding of the influences of hereditary and environmental factors in humans. True or false?
4. _____ research studies the same individuals over a period of time, whereas _____-_____ research studies people of different ages at the same time.
5. Match the following terms with their definition:

   1. Zygote
   2. Gene
   3. Chromosome

   a. Smallest unit through which genetic information is passed
   b. Fertilized egg
   c. Rod-shaped structure containing genetic information

6. Specific kinds of growth must take place during a _____ period if the embryo is to develop normally.

Rethink

1. What sort of policy might you create for notifying persons who have genetically based disorders that can be identified by genetic testing? Would your policy treat potentially fatal disorders differently from less serious ones? Would it make a distinction between treatable and nontreatable disorders?
2. Given the possible effects of the environment on the developing child, do you think expectant mothers should be subject to legal prosecution for their use of alcohol and other drugs that can seriously harm their unborn children? Defend your position.

Answers to Evaluate Questions

1. heredity (or nature); environment (or nurture) 2. True 3. True 4. Longitudinal; cross-sectional 5. 1-b; 2-a; 3-c 6. critical

The Extraordinary Newborn

His head was molded into a long melon shape and came to a point at the back. . . . He was covered with a thick greasy white material known as "vernix," which made him slippery to hold. In addition to a shock of black hair on his head, his body was covered with dark, fine hair known as "lanugo." His ears, his back, his shoulders, and even his cheeks were furry. . . . His skin was wrinkled and quite loose. . . . His ears were pressed to his head in unusual positions—one ear was matted firmly forward on his cheek. His nose was flattened and pushed to one side. (Brazelton, 1969, p. 3)

Although the description hardly fits that of the adorable babies seen in advertisements, we are in fact talking about a normal, completely developed child just after the moment of birth. Called a **neonate,** the newborn presents itself to the world in a form that hardly meets the standards of beauty against which we typically measure babies. Yet ask any parent: No sight is more beautiful or exciting than the first glimpse of their newborn.

The neonate's strange appearance is brought about by a number of factors. The trip through its mother's birth canal might have squeezed the incompletely formed bones of the skull together and squashed the nose into the head. *Vernix,* its white, greasy covering, is secreted to protect its skin prior to birth, and it might have *lanugo,* a soft fuzz, over its entire body for a similar purpose. Its eyelids could be puffy with an accumulation of fluids because of its upside-down position during birth.

All this changes during the first two weeks of life as the neonate takes on a more familiar appearance. Even more impressive are the capabilities the neonate begins to display from the time it is born—capabilities that grow at an astounding rate over the ensuing months.

Reflexes

The neonate is born with a number of **reflexes**—unlearned, involuntary responses that occur automatically in the presence of certain stimuli. Many of these reflexes are critical for survival and unfold naturally as a part of an infant's ongoing maturation. The *rooting reflex,* for instance, causes neonates to turn their heads toward things that touch their cheeks—such as the mother's nipple or a bottle. Similarly, a *sucking reflex* prompts the infant to suck at things that touch its lips. Among its other reflexes are a *gag reflex* (to clear its throat); the *startle reflex* (a series of movements in which the infant flings out its arms, fans its fingers, and arches its back in response to a sudden noise); and the *Babinski reflex* (the baby's toes fan out when the outer edge of the sole of its foot is stroked).

These primitive reflexes are lost after the first few months of life and replaced by more complex and organized behaviors. Although at birth the neonate is capable of only jerky, limited voluntary movements, during the first year of life the ability to move independently grows enormously. The typical baby is able to roll over by the age of 3 months; it can sit without support at 6 months, stand alone at about $11\frac{1}{2}$ months, and walk by the time it is just over a year old. Not only does the ability to make large-scale movements improve during this time, but fine-muscle movements also become increasingly sophisticated (as illustrated in Figure 9-2).

Development of the Senses: Taking in the World

When proud parents pick up their neonate and peer into its eyes, is the child able to return their gaze? Although it was thought for some time that newborns could see only a hazy blur, most current findings indicate that the capabilities of neonates are far more impressive. Although their eyes have limited capacity to focus on objects that are not within 7 or 8 inches of their face, neonates are able to follow objects moving within

Prepare

What are the major competencies of newborns?

What are the milestones of physical and social development during childhood?

Organize

The Extraordinary Newborn
 Reflexes
 Development of the Senses
The Growing Child
 Physical Development
 Development of Social Behavior

neonate: A newborn child

 PsychLink

Birthing process
www.mhhe.com/
feldmaness5-09links

reflexes: Unlearned, involuntary responses that occur automatically in the presence of certain stimuli

| 3.2 months: rolling over | 3.3 months: grasping rattle | 5.9 months: sitting without support | 7.2 months: standing while holding on | 8.2 months: grasping with thumb and finger |
| 11.5 months: standing alone well | 12.3 months: walking well | 14.8 months: building tower of two cubes | 16.6 months: walking up steps | 23.8 months: jumping in place |

Figure 9–2 Although at birth the neonate is capable of only jerky, limited voluntary movements, during the first year of life the ability to move independently grows enormously. The ages indicate the time when 50 percent of children are able to perform each skill. Remember, however, that when each skill appears varies considerably. For example, 25 percent of children are able to walk well at 11 months, and by 15 months, 90 percent of children are walking well (Frankenburg et al., 1992).

their field of vision. They also show the rudiments of depth perception, as they react by raising their hands when an object appears to be moving rapidly toward the face (Gelman & Au, 1996; Maurer et al., 1999).

You might think that it would be hard to figure out just how well neonates are able to see, given that their lack of both language and reading ability clearly prevents them from saying what direction the *E* on a vision chart is facing. However, a number of ingenious methods, relying on the newborn's biological responses and innate reflexes, have been devised to test perceptual skills (Koop, 1994; Atkinson, 1995).

For instance, infants who are shown a novel stimulus typically pay close attention to it, and, as a consequence, their heart rates increase. But if they are repeatedly shown the same stimulus, their attention to it decreases, as indicated by a return to a slower heart rate. This phenomenon is known as **habituation,** the decrease in the response to a stimulus that occurs after repeated presentations of the same stimulus. By studying habituation, developmental psychologists can tell when a stimulus can be detected and discriminated by a child too young to speak (Peterzell, 1993).

Researchers have developed a number of other methods for measuring neonate and infant perception. One technique involves babies sucking on a nipple attached to a computer. Changes in the rate and vigor of sucking are taken to show that babies can perceive variations in stimuli. Other approaches include examining babies' eye movements and observing which way babies move their heads when presented with a visual stimulus (George, 1999).

Using such research techniques, we now know that infants' visual perception is remarkably sophisticated from birth. At birth, babies show preferences for patterns with contours and edges over less distinct patterns, indicating that they are capable of responding to the configuration of stimuli. Furthermore, even newborns are aware of size constancy, apparently sensitive to the phenomenon that objects stay the same size even though the image on the retina changes size as the distance between the object and the retina varies (Slater, Mattock, & Brown, 1990; Slater, 1996).

habituation: The decrease in the response to a stimulus that occurs after repeated presentations of the same stimulus

In fact, neonates have the ability to discriminate facial expressions—and even to imitate them. As you can see in Figure 9-3, newborns exposed to an adult with a happy, sad, or surprised facial expression are able to produce a good imitation of the adult's expression. Even very young infants, then, can respond to the emotions and moods revealed by their caregivers' facial expressions. This capability provides the foundation for social interactional skills in children (Meltzoff, 1996; Mumme, Fernald, & Herrera, 1996).

Other visual abilities grow rapidly after birth. By the end of their first month, babies can distinguish some colors from others, and after 4 months they can readily focus on near or far objects. By 4 or 5 months, they are able to recognize two- and three-dimensional objects, and they can perceive the gestalt organizing principles that we discussed in Chapter 3. Furthermore, there are rapid improvements in perceptual abilities: Sensitivity to visual stimuli, for instance, becomes three to four times greater at 1 year of age than it was at birth (Slater, 1996; Vital-Durand, Atkinson, & Braddick, 1996).

In addition to vision, infants' other sensory capabilities are quite impressive. Newborns can distinguish different sounds to the point of being able to recognize their own mothers' voices at the age of 3 days. They are also capable of making subtle perceptual distinctions that underlie the language abilities described in Chapter 7. For example, at 2 days of age, infants are able to distinguish between their native tongue and foreign languages, and they can discriminate between such closely related sounds as *ba* and *pa* when they are 4 days old. By 6 months of age, they are capable of discriminating virtually any difference in sound that is relevant to the production of language. Moreover, they are capable of discriminating different tastes and smells at a very early age. There even seems to be something of a built-in sweet tooth: Neonates prefer liquids that have been sweetened with sugar over unsweetened liquids (Bornstein & Arterberry, 1999).

The Growing Child: Infancy Through Middle Childhood

It was during the windy days of March that the problem in the day care center first arose. Its source: 10-month-old Russell Ruud. Otherwise a model of decorum, Russell had somehow learned how to unzip the Velcro chin strap to his winter hat. He would remove the hat whenever he got the urge, seemingly oblivious to the potential health problems that might follow.

But that was just the start of the real difficulty. To the chagrin of the teachers in the day care center, not to speak of the children's parents, soon other children were following his lead, removing their own caps at will.

Russell's mother, made aware of the anarchy at the day care center—and the other parents' distress over Russell's behavior—pleaded innocent. "I never showed Russell how to unzip the Velcro," claimed his mother, Judith Ruud, an economist with the Congressional Budget Office in Washington, D.C. "He learned by trial and error, and the other kids saw him do it one day when they were getting dressed for an outing." (Goleman, 1993, C10)

At the age of 10 months, Russell is asserting his personality, illustrating the tremendous growth that occurs in a variety of domains during the first year of life. Throughout the remainder of childhood, as children move from infancy into middle childhood and the start of adolescence around age 11 or 12, children develop physically, socially, and cognitively in extraordinary ways. In the remainder of this chapter, we'll consider this development.

Physical Development

The most obvious sign of development is children's physical growth. During the first year of life, children typically triple their weight, and their height increases by about half. This rapid growth slows down as the child gets older—think how gigantic adults would be if that rate of growth were constant—and the average rate of growth from age 3 to the beginning of adolescence, around age 13, is a gain of about 5 pounds and 3 inches a year.

The physical changes that occur as children develop are not just a matter of increasing growth; the comparative sizes of the various body parts change dramatically as children age. As you can see in Figure 9-4, the head of the newborn is disproportionately large. However, the head soon becomes more proportional in size to the rest of the body as growth occurs mainly in the trunk and legs.

Development of Social Behavior: Taking on the World

As anyone who has seen an infant smiling at the sight of her or his mother can guess, at the same time as infants are growing physically and honing their perceptual abilities, they are also developing socially. The nature of a child's early social development provides the foundation for social relationships that will last a lifetime.

Attachment, the positive emotional bond that develops between a child and a particular individual, is the most important form of social development that occurs during infancy. The earliest studies of attachment were carried out by animal ethologist Konrad Lorenz (1966). Lorenz focused on newborn goslings, who under normal circumstances instinctively follow their mother, the first moving object to which they are exposed after birth. Lorenz found that goslings whose eggs were raised in an incubator and who viewed him immediately after hatching would follow his every movement, as if he were their mother. He labeled this process *imprinting,* behavior that takes place during a critical period and involves attachment to the first moving object that is observed.

Our understanding of attachment made progress when psychologist Harry Harlow, in a classic study, gave infant monkeys the choice of cuddling a wire "mother" that provided milk, or a soft, terry-cloth "mother" that was warm but did not provide milk. Their

attachment: The positive emotional bond that develops between a child and a particular individual

 PsychLink

Attachment theory and research
www.mhhe.com/
feldmaness5-09links

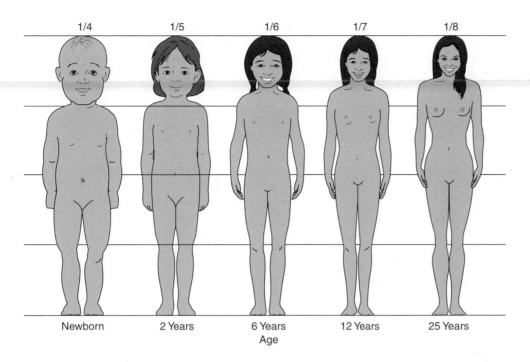

1/4   1/5   1/6   1/7   1/8

Newborn   2 Years   6 Years   12 Years   25 Years
Age

Figure 9-4 As development progresses, the relative size of the head, in relation to the rest of the body, decreases until adulthood is reached. Why do you think the head starts out so large?

choice was clear: They spent most of their time clinging to the warm cloth "monkey," although they made occasional forays to the wire monkey to nurse (Harlow & Zimmerman, 1959). It was obvious that the cloth monkey provided greater comfort to the infants; milk alone was insufficient to create attachment (see Figure 9-5).

Building on this pioneering work with nonhumans, developmental psychologists have suggested that human attachment grows through the responsiveness of infants' caregivers to the signals the babies provide, such as cries, smiles, reaching, and clinging. The greater the responsiveness of the caregiver to the child's signals, the more likely it is that the child will become securely attached. Full attachment eventually develops as a result of a complex series of interactions between caregiver and child (Bell & Ainsworth, 1972). In the course of these interactions, the infant plays as critical and active a role as the caregiver in the formation of the bond. Infants who respond positively to a caregiver produce more positive behavior on the part of the caregiver, which in turn produces an even stronger degree of attachment in the child.

Measuring Attachment

Developmental psychologists have devised a quick and direct way of measuring attachment. Developed by Mary Ainsworth, the *Ainsworth strange situation* consists of a sequence of events involving a child and (typically) his or her mother. Initially, the mother and baby enter an unfamiliar room, and the mother permits the baby to explore while she sits down. An adult stranger then enters the room, after which the mother leaves. The mother then returns, and the stranger leaves. The mother then once again leaves the baby alone, and the stranger returns. Finally, the stranger leaves, and the mother returns (Ainsworth et al., 1978).

Babies' reactions to the experimental situation vary drastically, depending, according to Ainsworth, on their degree of attachment to the mother. One-year-old children who are *securely attached* employ the mother as a kind of home base, exploring independently but returning to her occasionally. When she leaves, they exhibit distress, and they go to her when she returns.

Figure 9-5 Although the wire "mother" dispensed milk to the hungry infant monkey, the soft, terry cloth "mother" was preferred (Harry Harlow Primate Laboratory/University of Wisconsin). Do you think human babies would react the same way? What does this tell us about attachment?

Avoidant children do not cry when the mother leaves, but they seem to avoid her when she returns, as if they were indifferent to her. *Ambivalent* children display anxiety before they are separated and are upset when the mother leaves, but they might show ambivalent reactions to her return, such as seeking close contact but simultaneously hitting and kicking her. A fourth reaction is *disorganized-disoriented;* these children show inconsistent, often contradictory behavior.

The nature of attachment between children and their mothers has far-reaching consequences for later development. For example, children who are securely attached to their mothers tend to be more socially and emotionally competent than their less securely attached peers, and they are viewed as more cooperative, capable, and playful. Furthermore, research has found that children who are securely attached at age 1 show fewer psychological difficulties when they grow older than do avoidant or ambivalent youngsters (Lewis et al., 1984; Ainsworth & Bowlby, 1991; Greenberg, 1997).

On the other hand, children who lack secure attachment do not always have difficulties later in life, and being securely attached at an early age does not guarantee good adjustment later. Furthermore, some cultures foster higher levels of secure attachment than others. In short, attachment style is related to the social environment that children encounter as they are growing up (Hamilton, 2000; Lewis, Feiring, & Rosenthal, 2000; Waters, Hamilton, & Wienfield, 2000).

The Father's Role

Although early developmental research focused largely on the mother-child relation, more recent research has highlighted the father's role in parenting. With good reason: The number of fathers who are primary caregivers for their children has grown significantly, and fathers play an increasing role in their children's lives. For example, in almost 20 percent of families with children, the father is the parent who stays at home caring for preschoolers (U.S. Bureau of the Census, 1997; Parke, 1996).

When fathers interact with their children, their play is often different from that of mothers. Fathers engage in more physical, rough-and-tumble sorts of activities, whereas mothers play more verbally oriented and traditional games such as peekaboo. Despite such behavioral differences, attachment between fathers and children can be similar to attachment between mothers and children. In fact, children are capable of forming multiple attachments simultaneously (Lamb, 1982; Larson, Richards, & Perry-Jenkins, 1994; Genuis & Violato, 2000).

Social Relationships with Peers

By the time they are 2 years old, children start to become less dependent on their parents and more self-reliant, increasingly preferring to play with friends. Initially, play is relatively independent: Even though they might be sitting side by side, 2-year-olds pay more attention to toys than to one another when playing. Later, however, children actively interact, modifying one another's behavior and later exchanging roles during play (Bukowski, Newcomb, & Hartup, 1996).

As children reach school age, their social interactions begin to follow set patterns, and become more frequent. They might engage in elaborate games involving teams and rigid rules. This play serves purposes other than mere enjoyment. It allows children to become increasingly competent in their social interactions with others. Through play they learn to take the perspective of other people and to infer others' thoughts and feelings, even when these are not directly expressed (Asher & Parker, 1991; Cohen, 1993).

In short, social interaction helps children interpret the meaning of others' behavior and develop the capacity to respond appropriately. Furthermore, children learn physical and emotional self-control: They learn to avoid hitting a playmate who wins at a game, to be polite, and to control their emotional displays and facial expressions (e.g., smiling even when receiving a disappointing gift). Situations that provide children with opportunities for social interaction, then, can enhance their social development (Feldman, 1982, 1993; Crick & Dodge, 1994; Fox, 1994).

The Consequences of Day Care

Research on the importance of social interaction is corroborated by work that examines the benefits of day care, which is an important part of an increasing number of children's lives. For instance, almost 30 percent of preschool children whose mothers work outside the home spend their days in day-care centers. More than 80 percent of infants are cared for by people other than their mothers for part of the day during their first year of life. Most of these infants begin day care before the age of 4 months and are enrolled for almost 30 hours per week (NICHD Early Child Care Research Network, 1997; National Research Council, 2000).

Do out-of-the-home child-care arrangements benefit children's development? If they are of high quality, they can. According to the results of a large study supported by the U.S. National Institute of Child Health and Development (NICHD), children who attend high-quality child-care centers might not only do as well as children who stay at home with their parents, but in some respects might do better. Children in child care are generally more considerate and sociable than other children, and they interact more positively with teachers. They can also be more compliant and regulate their own behavior more effectively, and their mothers show increased sensitivity to their children (Lamb, 1996; NICHD Early Child Care Research Network, 1997, 1998, 1999).

In addition, especially for children from poor or disadvantaged homes, child care in specially enriched environments—those with many toys, books, a variety of children, and high-quality care providers—often is more intellectually stimulating than the home environment. Such child care can lead to increased intellectual achievement, demonstrated in higher IQ scores and better language development. In fact, children in child-care centers are sometimes found to score higher on tests of cognitive abilities than children who are cared for by their mothers or by sitters or home day-care providers, and these effects last into adulthood (Wilgoren, 1999; Burchinal et al., 2000).

On the other hand, the outcomes of child care are not universally positive. Children can feel less secure when they are placed in low-quality child care or in multiple child-care arrangements. Furthermore, although the findings are not consistent, some research suggests that infants who are involved in outside care more than twenty hours a week in their first year show less secure attachment to their mothers than those who have not been in day care (Belsky & Rovine, 1988; NICHD Early Child Care Research Network, 1997, 1999).

The key to the success of day care is its quality. High-quality day care produces benefits; low-quality day care provides little or no gain, and can even hinder children's development. In short, significant benefits result from the social interaction and intellectual stimulation provided by high-quality day-care centers—particularly for children from impoverished environments (Harvey, 1999; Burchinal et al., 2000; Campbell, Lamb, & Hwang, 2000).

Parenting Styles and Social Development

Parents' child-rearing practices are critical in shaping their children's social competence. According to classic research by developmental psychologist Diana Baumrind, there are four main parenting styles. **Authoritarian parents** are rigid and punitive and value unquestioning obedience from their children. They have strict standards and discourage expressions of disagreement. **Permissive parents** give their children relaxed or inconsistent direction and, although warm, require little of them. In contrast, **authoritative parents** are firm, setting limits for their children. As the children get older, these parents try to reason with and explain things to them. They also set clear goals and encourage their children's independence. Finally, **uninvolved parents** show little interest in their children. They are emotionally detached, and they view parenting as nothing more than providing food, clothing, and shelter for children. In its most extreme form, uninvolved parents are guilty of neglect, a form of child abuse (Baumrind, 1971, 1980). Table 9-3 summarizes the four parenting styles.

As you might expect, the four parenting styles seem to produce very different kinds of behavior in children (although there are, of course, many exceptions). Children of

"Please, Jason. Don't you want to grow up to be an autonomous person?"

 PsychLink

Comprehensive information on parenting
www.mhhe.com/
feldmaness5-09links

authoritarian parents: Parents who are rigid and punitive and value unquestioning obedience from their children
permissive parents: Parents who give their children lax or inconsistent direction and, although warm, require little of them
authoritative parents: Parents who are firm, set clear limits, reason with their children, and explain things to them
uninvolved parents: Parents who show little interest in their children and are emotionally detached from them

Table 9-3 The Four Main Parenting Styles

Parenting Style	Parent Behavior	Children's Behavior
Authoritarian	Rigid, punitive, strict standards	Unsociable, unfriendly, withdrawn
Permissive	Lax, inconsistent, undemanding	Immature, moody, dependent, low self-control
Authoritative	Firm, sets limits and goals, uses reasoning, encourages independence	Good social skills, likable, self-reliant, independent
Uninvolved	Detached emotionally, sees role as only providing food, clothing, and shelter	Indifferent, rejecting behavior

Source: Baumrind, 1971.

authoritarian parents tend to be unsociable, unfriendly, and relatively withdrawn. Permissive parents' children tends to be immature, moody, and dependent and have low self-control. The children of authoritative parents fare best: Their social skills are high—they are likable, self-reliant, independent, and cooperative. Worst off are children of uninvolved parents; they feel unloved and emotionally detached, and their physical and cognitive development is impeded (Howes, Galinsky, & Kontos, 1998; Saarni, 1999).

Before we rush to congratulate authoritative parents and condemn authoritarian, permissive, and uninvolved ones, it is important to note that many nonauthoritative parents produce children who are perfectly well adjusted. Moreover, as we'll discuss further in Chapter 10, children are born with a particular **temperament**—a basic, innate disposition. Some children are naturally easy-going and cheerful, whereas others are irritable and fussy. The kind of temperament a baby is born with might tend to elicit a particular parenting style (Goldsmith & Harman, 1994; Kendler, 1996; Chess, 1997).

Furthermore, the findings regarding child-rearing styles apply primarily to U.S. society, with its emphasis on children learning to be independent and not relying too heavily on their parents. In contrast, Japanese parents encourage dependence in order to promote the values of cooperation and community life. These differences in cultural values result in very different philosophies of child rearing. For example, Japanese mothers believe it is a punishment to make a young child sleep alone, so many children sleep next to their mothers throughout infancy and toddlerhood (Kagan, Kearsley, & Zelazo, 1978; Miyake, Chen, & Campos, 1985; Kawasaki et al., 1994).

In sum, a child's upbringing is a consequence of the child-rearing philosophy parents hold, the specific practices they use, and the nature of their own and their child's personality. As is the case with other aspects of development, then, behavior is a function of a complex interaction of environmental and genetic factors.

temperament: Basic, innate disposition

Erikson's Theory of Psychosocial Development

In trying to trace the course of social development, some theorists have considered how society and culture present challenges that change as the individual matures. Following this path, psychoanalyst Erik Erikson developed one of the most comprehensive theories of social development. According to Erikson (1963), the developmental changes occurring throughout our lives can be viewed as a series of eight stages of psychosocial development, of which four occur during childhood. **Psychosocial development** involves changes in our interactions and understanding of one another as well as in our knowledge and understanding of ourselves as members of society.

Erikson suggests that passage through each of the stages necessitates resolution of a crisis or conflict. Accordingly, each of Erikson's stages is represented as a pairing of the most positive and most negative aspects of the crisis of the period. Although each

psychosocial development: Development of individuals' interactions and understanding of each other and of their knowledge and understanding of themselves as members of society crisis is never resolved entirely—life becomes increasingly complicated as we grow older—it needs to be resolved sufficiently so that we are equipped to deal with demands made during the following stage of development.

In the first stage of psychosocial development, the **trust-versus-mistrust stage** (birth to $1\frac{1}{2}$ years), infants develop feelings of trust if their physical requirements and psychological needs for attachment are consistently met and their interactions with the world are generally positive. On the other hand, inconsistent care and unpleasant interactions with others can lead to the development of mistrust and leave the infant unable to meet the challenges required in the next stage of development.

In the second stage, the **autonomy-versus-shame-and-doubt stage** ($1\frac{1}{2}$ to 3 years), toddlers develop independence and autonomy if exploration and freedom are encouraged, or they experience shame, self-doubt, and unhappiness if they are overly restricted and protected. According to Erikson, the key to the development of autonomy during this period is for the child's caregivers to provide the appropriate amount of control. If parents provide too much control, children will be unable to assert themselves and develop their own sense of control over their environment; if parents provide too little control, children themselves become overly demanding and controlling.

The next crisis that children face is that of the **initiative-versus-guilt stage** (ages 3 to 6). In this stage, the major conflict is between children's desire to act independently and the guilt that comes from the unintended and unexpected consequences of their behavior. Children in this period come to understand that they are persons in their own right, and they begin to make decisions about their behavior. If parents react positively to their child's attempts at independence, they help their child resolve the initiative-versus-guilt crisis positively.

The fourth and last stage of childhood is the **industry-versus-inferiority stage** (ages 6 to 12). During this period, successful psychosocial development is characterized by increasing competency in all areas, including social interactions and academic skills. In contrast, difficulties in this stage lead to feelings of failure and inadequacy.

Erikson's theory suggests that psychosocial development continues throughout life, and he proposes that there are four more crises to face past childhood (which we discuss later in this chapter). Although his theory has been criticized on several grounds—such as the imprecision of the concepts he employs and his greater emphasis on male development than female development—it remains influential and is one of the few theories that encompass the entire life span.

trust-versus-mistrust stage: According to Erikson, the first stage of psychosocial development, occurring from birth to 18 months of age, during which time infants develop feelings of trust or lack of trust

autonomy-versus-shame-and-doubt stage: The period during which, according to Erikson, toddlers (ages 18 months to 3 years) develop independence and autonomy if exploration and freedom are encouraged, or shame and self-doubt if they are restricted and overprotected

initiative-versus-guilt stage: According to Erikson, the period during which children ages 3 to 6 years experience conflict between independence of action and the sometimes negative results of that action

industry-versus-inferiority stage: According to Erikson, the last stage of childhood, during which children aged 6 to 12 years either develop positive social interactions with others or feel inadequate and become less sociable

Evaluate

1. Researchers studying newborns use _____, or the decrease in the response to a stimulus that occurs after repeated presentations of the same stimulus, as an indicator of a baby's interest.

2. The emotional bond that develops between a child and its caregiver is known as _____.

3. Children develop an attachment to their mothers only; the father's role is important, but children do not become attached to their fathers. True or false?

4. Match the parenting style with its definition:

1. Permissive	a. Rigid; highly punitive; demand obedience
2. Authoritative	b. Give little direction; lax on obedience
3. Authoritarian	c. Firm but fair; try to explain their decisions
4. Uninvolved	d. Emotionally detached and unloving

5. Erikson's theory of _____ development involves a series of eight stages, each of which must be resolved in order for a person to develop optimally.

Rethink

1. In what ways might the infant's major reflexes—the rooting, sucking, gagging, startle, and Babinski reflexes—have had survival value, from an evolutionary perspective? Does the infant's ability to mimic the facial expressions of adults have a similar value?

2. Do you think the growing trend toward greater parental involvement by fathers will have effects on the child-rearing styles to which children are exposed? Will it affect attachment? Psychosocial development? Why or why not?

Answers to Evaluate Questions

1. habituation 2. attachment 3. False; attachment to a father can be as strong as attachment to a mother 4. 1-b; 2-c; 3-a; 4-d 5. psychosocial

Prepare

How does cognitive development proceed during childhood?

Organize

Cognitive Development

Cognitive Development: Children's Thinking About the World

Suppose you had two drinking glasses of different shapes—one short and broad, and one tall and thin. Now imagine that you filled the short, broad one with soda about halfway and then poured the liquid from that glass into the tall one. The soda appears to fill about three-quarters of the second glass. If someone asked you whether there was more soda in the second glass than there had been in the first, what would you say?

You might think that such a simple question hardly deserves an answer; of course there is no difference in the amount of soda in the two glasses. However, most 4-year-olds would be likely to say that there is more soda in the second glass. If you then poured the soda back into the short glass, they would say there is now less soda than there was in the taller glass.

Why are young children confused by this problem? The reason is not immediately obvious. Anyone who has observed preschoolers must be impressed by how far they have progressed from the early stages of development. They speak with ease, know the alphabet, count, play complex games, use tape players, tell stories, and communicate quite ably. Yet, despite this seeming sophistication, there are deep gaps in children's understanding of the world. Some theorists have suggested that children are incapable of understanding certain ideas and concepts until they reach a particular stage of **cognitive development**—the process by which a child's understanding of the world changes as a function of age and experience. In contrast to the theories of physical and social development discussed earlier (such as those of Erikson), theories of cognitive development seek to explain the quantitative and qualitative intellectual advances that occur during development.

cognitive development: The process by which a child's understanding of the world changes as a function of age and experience

Piaget's Theory of Cognitive Development

No theory of cognitive development has had more impact than that of Swiss psychologist Jean Piaget. Piaget (1970) suggested that children throughout the world proceed through a series of four stages in a fixed order. He maintained that these stages differ not only in the *quantity* of information acquired at each stage, but also in the *quality* of knowledge and understanding. Taking an interactionist point of view, he suggested that movement from one stage to the next occurred when the child reached an appropriate level of maturation *and* was exposed to relevant types of experiences. Without such experiences, children were assumed to be incapable of reaching their highest level of cognitive growth.

Piaget's four stages are the sensorimotor, preoperational, concrete operational, and formal operational stages (see Table 9-4). Let's examine each of them and the approximate ages they span.

PsychLink

Theory of cognitive development
www.mhhe.com/
feldmaness5-09links

Table 9–4 Piaget's Stages of Cognitive Development

Stage	Approximate Age Range	Major Characteristics
Sensorimotor	Birth–2 years	Development of object permanence, development of motor skills, little or no capacity for symbolic representation
Preoperational	2–7 years	Development of language and symbolic thinking, egocentric thinking
Concrete operational	7–12 years	Development of conservation, mastery of concept of reversibility
Formal operational	12–adulthood	Development of logical and abstract thinking

Sensorimotor Stage: Birth to 2 Years   During the **sensorimotor stage,** children's understanding of the world is based primarily on touching, sucking, chewing, shaking, and manipulating objects. In the initial part of this stage, children have relatively little competence in representing the environment using images, language, or other kinds of symbols. Consequently, infants have no awareness of objects or people that are not immediately present at a given moment, lacking what Piaget calls **object permanence.** Object permanence is the awareness that objects—and people—continue to exist even if they are out of sight.

How can we know that infants lack object permanence? Although we cannot ask them, we can observe their reactions when a toy that they are playing with is hidden under a blanket. Until the age of about 9 months, children will make no attempt to locate the toy. However, soon after this age they will begin to search actively for the object when it is hidden, indicating that they have developed a mental representation of the toy. Object permanence, then, is a critical development during the sensorimotor stage.

Preoperational Stage: 2 to 7 Years   The most important development during the **preoperational stage** is the use of language, which we described in more detail in Chapter 7. Children develop internal representational systems that allow them to describe people, events, and feelings. They even use symbols in play, pretending, for example, that a book pushed across the floor is a car.

Although children's thinking is more advanced in this stage than in the earlier sensorimotor stage, it is still qualitatively inferior to that of adults. We see this when we observe the preoperational child using **egocentric thought,** a way of thinking in which the child views the world entirely from her or his own perspective. Preoperational children think that everyone shares their own perspective and knowledge. Thus, children's stories and explanations to adults can be maddeningly uninformative, as they are described without any context. For example, a preoperational child might start a story with "He wouldn't let me go," neglecting to mention who "he" is or where the storyteller wanted to go. Egocentric thinking is also seen when children at the preoperational stage play hiding games. For instance, 3-year-olds frequently hide with their faces against a wall, covering their eyes—although they are still in plain view. It seems to them that if *they* cannot see, no one else will be able to see them, because they assume that others share their view.

Another deficiency of preoperational children is demonstrated by their inability to understand the **principle of conservation,** which is the knowledge that quantity can remain the same when shape and other aspects of physical appearance change. Children who have not mastered this concept do not know, for instance, that the amount or volume of a substance (such as a lump of clay) does not change when its shape or configuration is changed. The question about pouring liquid between two glasses—one short and broad, the other tall and thin—with which we began our discussion of cognitive development illustrates this point quite clearly. Children who do not understand the principle of conservation invariably state that the amount of liquid changes as it is poured back and forth. They cannot comprehend that a transformation in appearance does not imply a transformation in amount. Instead, it seems just as reasonable to the child that there is a change in quantity as it does to the adult that there is no change.

There are a number of other ways, some quite startling, in which their failure to understand the principle of conservation affects children's responses. Research demonstrates that principles that are obvious to and unquestioned by adults can be completely misunderstood by children during the preoperational period, and that it is not until the next stage of cognitive development that children grasp the concept of conservation. (Several examples of conservation are illustrated in Figure 9-6.)

Concrete Operational Stage: 7 to 12 Years   The beginning of the **concrete operational stage** is marked by mastery of the principle of conservation. However, there are still some aspects of conservation—such as conservation of weight and volume—that are not fully understood for a number of years.

sensorimotor stage: According to Piaget, the stage from birth to 2 years, during which a child has little competence in representing the environment using images, language, or other symbols

object permanence: The awareness that objects—and people—continue to exist even if they are out of sight

preoperational stage: According to Piaget, the period from 2 to 7 years of age which is characterized by language development

egocentric thought: A way of thinking in which the child views the world entirely from his or her own perspective

principle of conservation: The knowledge that the quantity of a substance remains the same even though its shape or other aspects of its physical appearance might change

concrete operational stage: According to Piaget, the period from 7 to 12 years of age, which is characterized by logical thought and a loss of egocentrism

Children who have not mastered the principle of conservation assume that the volume of a liquid increases when it is poured from a short, wide container to a tall, thin one. What other tasks might a child under 7 have difficulty comprehending?

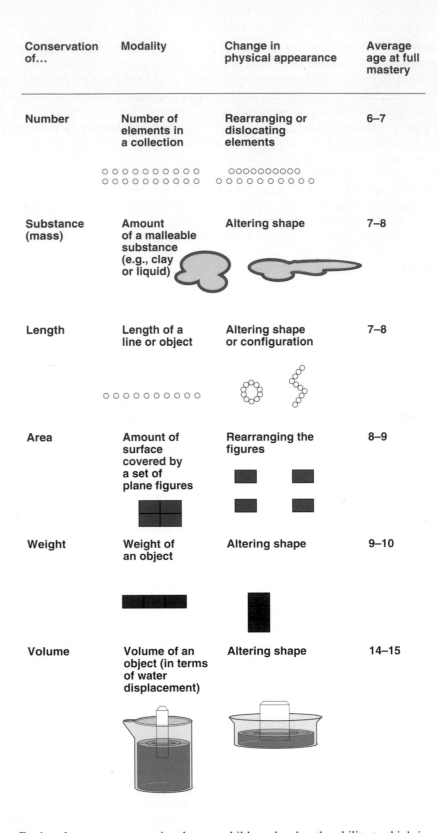

During the concrete operational stage, children develop the ability to think in a more logical manner, and they begin to overcome some of the egocentrism characteristic of the preoperational period. One of the major principles that children grasp during this stage is reversibility, the idea that some changes can be undone by reversing an earlier action. For example, they can understand that when a ball of clay is rolled into a long sausage shape, it is possible to recreate the original ball by reversing the action. They can even conceptualize this principle in their heads, without having to see the action performed before them.

Although children make important advances in their logical capabilities during the concrete operational stage, there is still one major limitation in their thinking: They are largely bound to the concrete, physical reality of the world. For the most part, they have difficulty understanding questions of an abstract or hypothetical nature.

Formal Operational Stage: 12 Years to Adulthood   The **formal operational stage** produces a new kind of thinking that is abstract, formal, and logical. Thinking is no longer tied to events observed in the environment but makes use of logical techniques to solve problems.

The emergence of formal operational thinking is illustrated by how children approach the "pendulum problem," devised by Piaget (Piaget & Inhelder, 1958). The problem solver is asked to figure out what determines how fast a pendulum swings. Is it the length of the string, the weight of the pendulum, or the force with which the pendulum is pushed? (For the record, the answer is the length of the string.)

Children in the concrete operational stage approach the problem haphazardly, without a logical or rational plan of action. For example, they might simultaneously change the length of the string *and* the weight on the string *and* the force with which they push the pendulum. Because they are varying all factors at once, they are unable to tell which factor is the critical one. In contrast, people in the formal operational stage approach the problem systematically. Acting as if they were scientists conducting an experiment, they examine the effects of changes in just one variable at a time. This ability to rule out competing possibilities is characteristic of formal operational thought.

Although formal operational thought emerges during the teenage years, many individuals use this type of thinking infrequently. Moreover, it appears that many people never reach this stage at all; most studies show that only 40 to 60 percent of college students and adults fully reach it, with some estimates running as low as 25 percent in the general population. In addition, in certain cultures—particularly those that are less technologically sophisticated than most Western societies—almost no one reaches the formal operational stage (Chandler, 1976; Keating & Clark, 1980; Super, 1980).

Stages Versus Continuous Development: Was Piaget Right?   No other theorist has given us as comprehensive a theory of cognitive development as Piaget. Still, many contemporary theorists suggest that a better explanation of how children develop cognitively can be provided by theories that do not subscribe to a stage approach. For instance, children are not always consistent in their performance of tasks that—if Piaget's theory were accurate—ought to be performed equally well at a given stage (Siegler, 1994).

Furthermore, some developmental psychologists suggest that cognitive development proceeds in a more continuous fashion than Piaget's stage theory implies. They propose that cognitive development is primarily quantitative in nature, rather than qualitative. They argue that although there are differences in when, how, and to what extent a child is capable of using given cognitive abilities—reflecting quantitative changes—the underlying cognitive processes change relatively little with age (Gelman & Baillargeon, 1983; Case & Okamoto, 1996).

Piaget also underestimated the age at which infants and children are able to understand specific concepts and principles; in fact, they seem to be more sophisticated in their cognitive abilities than Piaget believed. For instance, some evidence suggests that infants as young as 5 months have rudimentary mathematical skills (Wynn, 1995, 2000).

Despite such criticisms, most developmental psychologists agree that, although the processes that underlie changes in cognitive abilities might not unfold in the manner suggested by his theory, Piaget has generally provided us with an accurate account of age-related changes in cognitive development. Moreover, the influence of his theory has been enormous. For example, Piaget suggests that increases in cognitive performance cannot be attained unless both cognitive readiness brought about by maturation *and* appropriate environmental stimulation are present. This view has been influential in determining the nature and structure of educational curricula and how children are taught (see the *Psychology at Work* box on page 304). Piaget's theory

formal operational stage: According to Piaget, the period from age 12 to adulthood, which is characterized by abstract thought

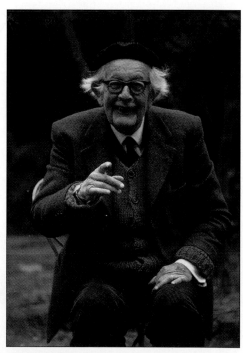

Jean Piaget

Psychology at Work

Michael J. Morrier

Preschool Coordinator

Education: B.A., psychology, University of Massachusetts at Amherst; M.A., special education, University of Georgia

Home: Decatur, Georgia

Michael J. Morrier

Emory University's Walden Early Childhood Program—one of the premier preschools in the United States—not only prepares young children for primary education, but also provides a means for children with developmental disabilities to become successfully integrated into a school setting, according to Michael Morrier, early childhood and research coordinator for the program.

"The program is divided into three sections: the toddler section, which has children from 18 months to 3 years; the preschool, with children aged 3 to 4; and the prekindergarten, with children aged 4 to 5. In each classroom a third of the children are diagnosed with autism, while two-thirds are typically developing children," Morrier explains.

"We use their interests as the topics of our teaching and their learning," he says. "The underlying curriculum is focused on language development, social development, and independence in daily living skills. Everything is individualized for each child."

> "We use their interests as the topics of our teaching and their learning. . . . Everything is individualized for each child."

The Walden program encourages children to interact with one another, according to Morrier. If the children want to go for a snack, they are asked to invite another child to go with them; if they want to play, they ask another child to join in.

"We also are doing research on children's social interests," he notes. "We look at how typical kids develop socially across the age range, and then we look at the group with autism to see what is different.

"Children with autism tend to form three different groups," Morrier explains. "One group avoids interaction entirely; the second group will interact, but only with specific toys, or with toys in general and no people; and the third group appears to want to interact, but the kids in this group don't know what to do, or how to go about it. They want to play, but may end up hitting another child."

When the children leave the program and enter kindergarten they encounter a variety of support systems that differ from the intensive attention they received at Walden. Morrier says, "But all of our students—including the ones with autism—have gone on and have done well."

and methods have also been used to investigate issues surrounding animal cognition, such as whether primates show object permanence (they seem to; Gagnon & Dore, 1994; Funk, 1996).

Information-Processing Approaches: Charting Children's Mental Programs

If cognitive development does not proceed as a series of stages, as Piaget suggested, what *does* underlie the enormous growth in children's cognitive abilities that is apparent to even the most untutored eye? To many developmental psychologists, changes in **information processing**—the ways people take in, use, and store information—account for cognitive development (Siegler, 1998).

According to this approach, quantitative changes occur in children's ability to organize and manipulate information. From this perspective, children become increasingly adept at information processing, much as a computer program might become more sophisticated as a programmer modifies it on the basis of experience. Information-processing approaches consider the kinds of "mental programs" children invoke when approaching problems (Reyna, 1997).

Several significant changes occur in children's information-processing capabilities. For one thing, speed of processing increases with age, as some abilities become more automatic. The speed at which stimuli can be scanned, recognized, and compared with other stimuli increases with age. With increasing age, children can pay attention to stimuli longer and discriminate between different stimuli more readily, and they are less easily distracted (Jensen & Neff, 1993; Mayr, Kliegl, & Krampe, 1996; Miller & Vernon, 1997).

Memory also improves dramatically with age. You may recall from Chapter 6 that adults are able to keep seven, plus or minus two, chunks of information in short-term memory. In contrast, preschoolers can hold only two or three chunks; 5-year-

information processing: The ways people take in, use, and store information

PsychLink

Challenge to Piaget's views
www.mhhe.com/
feldmaness5-09links

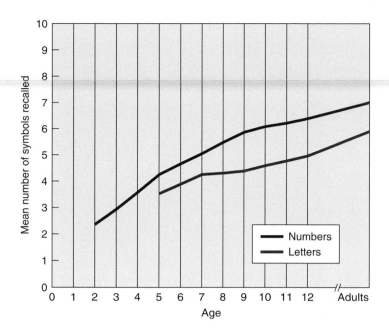

Figure 9-7 Memory span increases with age for both numbers and letters (Dempster, 1981).

olds can hold four; and 7-year-olds can hold five. The size of chunks also grows with age, as does the sophistication and organization of knowledge stored in memory. Still, memory capabilities are impressive at a very early age: Even before they can speak, infants can remember for months events in which they were active participants, according to recent research (Bjorklund, 1985; Rovee-Collier, 1993; Bauer, 1996; see Figure 9-7).

Finally, improvement in information processing is tied to advances in **metacognition,** an awareness and understanding of one's own cognitive processes. Metacognition involves the planning, monitoring, and revising of cognitive strategies. Younger children, who lack an awareness of their own cognitive processes, are often ignorant of their incapabilities. Thus, when they misunderstand others, they might fail to recognize their own errors. It is only later, when metacognitive abilities become more sophisticated, that children are able to know when they *don't* understand. Such increasing sophistication reflects a change in children's *theory of mind,* their knowledge and beliefs about the way the mind operates (Flavell, 1993; Chandler & Lalonde, 1996; Taylor, 1996).

metacognition: An awareness and understanding of one's own cognitive processes

 ## Vygotsky's View of Cognitive Development: Considering Culture

According to Russian developmental psychologist Lev Vygotsky, the culture in which we are raised has an important influence on our cognitive development. In Vygotsky's view, which is increasingly influential, the focus on individual performance of both Piagetian and information-processing approaches is misplaced. Instead, Vygotsky holds, we cannot understand cognitive development without taking into account the social aspects of learning (Vygotsky, 1926/1997; Beilin, 1996; Daniels, 1996).

Vygotsky argues that cognitive development occurs as a consequence of social interactions in which children work with others to jointly solve problems. Through such interactions, children increase their cognitive skills and gain the ability to function intellectually on their own. More specifically, children's cognitive abilities increase when they are exposed to information that falls within their zone of proximal development. The **zone of proximal development,** or **ZPD,** is the level at which a child can almost, but not fully, comprehend or perform a task on his or her own. When children encounter information that falls within the ZPD, they are able to increase their understanding or master a new task. On the other hand, if the information lies outside children's ZPD, they will not be able to master it (Blank & White, 1999; see Figure 9-8).

 PsychLink

Discussion of Vygotsky's theory
www.mhhe.com/
feldmaness5-09links

zone of proximal development (ZPD): According to Vygotsky, the level at which a child can almost, but not fully, comprehend or perform a task on her or his own

Figure 9-8 While the performances of the two children working at a task without aid are similar, Child B benefits more from aid and thus has a larger zone of proximal development (ZPD) than Child A.

Child A

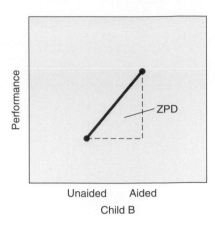

Child B

In short, cognitive development occurs when parents, teachers, or skilled peers assist the child by presenting information that is both new and within the ZPD. This type of assistance is called *scaffolding,* the support for learning and problem solving that encourages independence and growth. Vygotsky claims that scaffolding not only promotes the solution of specific problems, it also aids in the development of overall cognitive abilities (Bruner, 1983; Steward, 1995).

More than other approaches to cognitive development, Vygotsky's theory considers how the specific cultural and social context of society affects intellectual growth. How a child understands the world is seen as an outgrowth of interactions with parents, peers, and other members of the child's culture. Furthermore, as we see next, cultural influences on cognitive development also result in significant differences in scholastic success.

Evaluate

1. _____ suggested four stages of cognitive development, each of which is dependent on maturational and environmental factors.

2. Match the stage of development with the thinking style characteristic of the stage:

   1. Egocentric thought   a. Sensorimotor

   2. Object permanence   b. Formal operational

   3. Abstract reasoning   c. Preoperational

   4. Conservation; reversibility   d. Concrete operational

3. Current research suggests that child development might proceed in a continuous fashion, rather than in stages as suggested by Piaget. True or false?

4. _____-_____ theories of development suggest that how children handle information is critical to their development.

5. According to Vygotsky, information that is within a child's _____ ____ _____ _____ is most likely to result in cognitive development.

Answers to Evaluate Questions

1. Piaget 2. 1-c; 2-a; 3-b; 4-d 3. True 4. Information-processing 5. zone of proximal development

Rethink

1. According to Piaget's theory, children must reach a certain level of maturity before they can learn particular kinds of information. What might be the pros and cons of exposing a child to more complex material at an early age? What might information-processing theory have to say about this?

2. Do you think the widespread use of IQ testing in the United States contributes to parents' views that their children's academic success is largely due to their children's innate intelligence? Why? Would it be possible (or desirable) to change this view?

Adolescence: Becoming an Adult

Prepare

What major physical, social, and cognitive transitions characterize adolescence?

Organize

Adolescence
Physical Development
Moral and Cognitive Development
Social Development

Diana Leary, Age 17: "The school is divided into different groups of kids: the break-dancers, the people who listen to heavy metal, the pretty girls, the ravers and the hip-hop people. But there's no pressure to be in one group or another. If a person is a break-dancer, they can still chill with the ravers. I'm a hip-hopper. We wear baggy jeans and sweatshirts. But if I'm really good friends with a person in the heavy-metal group, I can go chill with them and it's just like, whatever." (Gordon et al., 1999, p. 48)

Trevor Kelson, Age 15: "Keep the Hell Out of My Room!" says a sign on Trevor's bedroom wall, just above an unmade bed, a desk littered with dirty T-shirts and candy wrappers, and a floor covered with clothes. Is there a carpet? "Somewhere," he says with a grin. "I think it's gold." (Fields-Meyer, 1995, p. 53)

Lauren Barry, Age 18: "I went to a National Honor Society induction. The parents were just staring at me. I think they couldn't believe someone with pink hair could be smart. I want to be a high-school teacher, but I'm afraid that, based on my appearance, they won't hire me." (Gordon et al., 1999, p. 47)

Although Diana, Trevor, and Lauren have never met, they share anxieties that are common to adolescence—concerns about friends, parents, appearance, independence, and their futures. **Adolescence,** the developmental stage between childhood and adulthood, is a crucial period. It is a time of profound changes and, occasionally, turmoil. Considerable biological change occurs as adolescents attain sexual and physical maturity. At the same time, these physiological changes are rivaled by important social, emotional, and cognitive changes that occur as adolescents strive for independence and move toward adulthood.

adolescence: The developmental stage between childhood and adulthood

Because many years of schooling precede most people's entry into the workforce in Western societies, the stage of adolescence is a fairly lengthy one, beginning just before the teenage years and ending just after them. No longer children, but considered by society to be not quite adults, adolescents face a period of rapid physical, cognitive, and social change that affects them for the rest of their lives.

Adolescents' development is also being affected by dramatic changes taking place in society. More than half of all children in the United States will spend all or some of their childhood and adolescence in single-parent families. Furthermore, adolescents spend considerably less time with their parents, and more with their peers, than they did several decades ago. Finally, the ethnic and cultural diversity of U.S. adolescents is increasing dramatically. A third of all U.S. adolescents today are of non-European descent, and by the year 2050 the number of adolescents of Hispanic, African American, Native American, or Asian origin will have grown significantly (Carnegie Council on Adolescent Development, 1995; Dreman, 1997).

PsychLink

Adolescent directory
www.mhhe.com/
feldmaness5–09links

Physical Development: The Changing Adolescent

If you think back to the start of your own adolescence, it is likely that the most dramatic changes you remember are of a physical nature. A spurt in height, the growth of breasts in girls, deepening voices in boys, the development of body hair, and intense sexual feelings are a source of curiosity, interest, and sometimes embarrassment for individuals entering adolescence.

The physical changes that occur at the start of adolescence are largely a result of the secretion of various hormones (see Chapter 2), and they affect virtually every aspect of the adolescent's life. Not since infancy has development been so dramatic. Weight and height increase rapidly due to a growth spurt that typically begins

Diana Leary and her mother, Kathryn.

Although puberty begins around age 11 or 12 for girls and 13 or 14 for boys, there are wide variations. What are some advantages and disadvantages of early puberty?

puberty: The period during which maturation of the sexual organs occurs, beginning at about age 11 or 12 for girls and 13 or 14 for boys

around age 10 for girls and age 12 for boys. Adolescents might grow as much as 5 inches in one year.

Puberty, the period when the sexual organs mature, begins at about age 11 or 12 for girls and 13 or 14 for boys. However, there are wide variations. For example, some girls begin to menstruate as early as age 8 or 9 or as late as age 16. In both boys and girls, sexual *attraction* to others begins even before the maturation of the sexual organs, at around the age of 10 (Eveleth & Tanner, 1976; Tanner, 1990; McClintock & Herdt, 1996).

Significant cultural and situational variations occur in the timing of first menstruation. For example, the average Lumi girl in New Guinea does not begin menstruating until she is 18. In Western cultures, the average age at which adolescents reach sexual maturity has been steadily decreasing over the last century, most likely a result of improved nutrition and medical care (Dreyer, 1982).

The age when they enter puberty has important implications for the way adolescents feel about themselves—as well as how others treat them. Early-maturing boys have a distinct advantage over later-maturing boys. They do better in athletics, are generally more popular with peers, and have more positive self-concepts. On the other hand, they are more likely to have difficulties at school, to commit minor acts of delinquency, and to become involved with alcohol abuse. One reason for such behavior seems to be that early-maturing boys are more likely to become friends with older, and therefore more influential, boys, who might lead them into age-inappropriate activities. On balance, though, the consequences of early maturation for boys are basically positive; early maturers, compared to later maturers, are typically somewhat more responsible and cooperative in later life (Duncan et al., 1985; Peterson, 1985; Anderson & Magnusson, 1990).

The picture is different for girls. Although early-maturing girls are more sought after as dates and have better self-esteem than later-maturing girls, some of the consequences of their early physical maturation can be less positive. For example, early breast development can set them apart from their peers and be a source of ridicule (Simmons & Blyth, 1987; Ge, Conger, & Elder, 1996).

Late maturation can produce certain psychological difficulties for both boys and girls. Boys who are smaller and less coordinated than their more mature peers tend to be ridiculed and seen as less attractive, and in time they might come to view themselves in the same way. Similarly, late-maturing girls are at a disadvantage in junior high and early high school. They hold relatively low social status, and they might be overlooked in dating. On the other hand, late-maturing girls report greater satisfaction with their bodies later in high school and college, because late maturers tend to be relatively tall and slim—closer to the current societal ideal of female beauty (Apter et al., 1981; Clarke-Stewart & Friedman, 1987).

Clearly, the rate at which their physical changes occur can affect the way adolescents are viewed by others and how they view themselves. Just as important as physical changes, however, are the psychological and social changes that unfold during adolescence.

Moral and Cognitive Development: Distinguishing Right from Wrong

In a European country, a woman is near death from a special kind of cancer. The one drug that the doctors think might save her is a medicine that a medical researcher has recently discovered. The drug is expensive to make, and the researcher is charging ten times the cost, or $5000, for a small dose. The sick woman's husband, Henry, approaches everyone he knows in hopes of borrowing money, but he can get together only about $2500. He tells the researcher that his wife is dying and asks him to lower the price of the drug or let him pay later. The researcher says, "No, I discovered the drug and I'm going to make money from it." Henry is desperate and considers stealing the drug for his wife.

What would you tell Henry to do?

Table 9-5 Kohlberg's Levels of Moral Reasoning

Level	SAMPLE MORAL REASONING OF SUBJECTS	
	In Favor of Stealing the Drug	Against Stealing the Drug
Level 1 Preconventional morality: At this level, the concrete interests of the individual are considered in terms of rewards and punishments.	"If you let your wife die, you will get in trouble. You'll be blamed for not spending the money to save her, and there'll be an investigation of you and the druggist for your wife's death."	"You shouldn't steal the drug because you'll be caught and sent to jail if you do. If you do get away, your conscience will bother you thinking how the police will catch up with you at any minute."
Level 2 Conventional morality: At this level, people approach moral problems as members of society. They are interested in pleasing others by acting as good members of society.	"If you let your wife die, you'll never be able to look anybody in the face again."	"After you steal the drug, you'll feel bad thinking how you've brought dishonor on your family and yourself; you won't be able to face anyone again."
Level 3 Postconventional morality: At this level, people use moral principles which are seen as broader than those of any particular society.	"If you don't steal the drug, and if you let your wife die, you'll always condemn yourself for it afterward. You won't be blamed and you'll have lived up to the outside rule of the law but you won't have lived up to your own standards of conscience."	"If you steal the drug, you won't be blamed by other people, but you'll condemn yourself because you won't have lived up to your own conscience and standards of honesty."

Kohlberg's Theory of Moral Development

In the view of psychologist Lawrence Kohlberg, the advice you give Henry is a reflection of your level of moral development. According to Kohlberg, people pass through a series of stages in the evolution of their sense of justice and in the kind of reasoning they use to make moral judgments (Kohlberg, 1984). Largely because of the various cognitive limitations that Piaget described, preadolescent children tend to think either in terms of concrete, unvarying rules ("It is always wrong to steal" or "I'll be punished if I steal") or in terms of the rules of society ("Good people don't steal" or "What if everyone stole?").

Adolescents, however, are capable of reasoning on a higher plane, having typically reached Piaget's formal operational stage of cognitive development. Because they are able to comprehend broad moral principles, they can understand that morality is not always black and white and that conflict can exist between two sets of socially accepted standards.

Kohlberg (1984) suggests that the changes occurring in moral reasoning can be understood best as a three-level sequence (see Table 9-5). His theory assumes that people move through the levels in a fixed order, and that they are not capable of reaching the highest level until about the age of 13—primarily because of limitations in cognitive development before then. However, many people never reach the highest level of moral reasoning. In fact, Kohlberg found that only a relatively small percentage of adults rise above the second level of his model (Kohlberg & Ryncarz, 1990).

Although Kohlberg's theory has had a substantial influence on our understanding of moral development, the research support is mixed. One difficulty with the theory is that it pertains to moral *judgments,* not moral *behavior.* Knowing right from wrong does not mean that we will always act in accordance with our judgments. In addition, the theory is primarily applicable to Western society and its moral code; cross-cultural research conducted in cultures with different moral systems suggests that Kohlberg's theory is not necessarily relevant there (Kurtines & Gewirtz, 1995; Coles, 1997; Damon, 1999).

Moral Development in Females

One glaring shortcoming of Kohlberg's research is that he used primarily male participants. Furthermore, psychologist Carol Gilligan (1982, 1987, 1993) argues that because of their distinctive socialization experiences, there is a fundamental difference in how

PsychLink

Kohlberg's theory of moral development
www.mhhe.com/
feldmaness5-09links

PsychLink

Gilligan vs. Kohlberg
www.mhhe.com/
feldmaness5-09links

women and men view moral behavior. According to Gilligan, men view morality primarily in terms of broad principles, such as justice and fairness. In contrast, women see it in terms of responsibility toward individuals and willingness to make sacrifices to help a specific individual within the context of a particular relationship. Compassion for individuals is a more salient factor in moral behavior for women than it is for men (Gilligan, Ward, & Taylor, 1988; Gilligan, Lyons, & Hanmer, 1990).

Because Kohlberg's model conceives of moral behavior largely in terms of abstract principles such as justice, Gilligan finds it inadequate for describing the moral development of females. She suggests that women's morality is centered on individual well-being and social relationships—a morality of *caring*. In her view, the highest levels of morality are represented by compassionate concern for the welfare of others.

Gilligan's conception of morality is very different from that presented by Kohlberg, and it is clear that gender plays an important role in determining what is seen as moral. Furthermore, their differing conceptions of what constitutes moral behavior can lead women and men to regard the morality of a particular behavior in potentially contradictory ways (Handler, Franz, & Guerra, 1992; Wark & Krebs, 1996).

Social Development: Finding Oneself in a Social World

"Who am I?" "How do I fit into the world?" "What is life all about?"

Questions such as these assume particular significance during the teenage years, as adolescents seek to find their place in the broader social world. As we will see, this quest takes adolescents along several routes.

Erikson's Theory of Psychosocial Development: The Search for Identity

Erikson's theory of psychosocial development emphasizes the search for identity during the adolescent years. As noted earlier, psychosocial development encompasses changes in people's understanding of themselves, one another, and the world around them during the course of development (Erikson, 1963).

The fifth stage of Erikson's theory (summarized, with the other stages, in Table 9-6) is labeled the **identity-versus-role-confusion stage** and encompasses adolescence. This stage is a time of major testing, as people try to determine what is unique and special about themselves. They attempt to discover who they are, what their strengths are, and what kinds of roles they are best suited to play for the rest of their lives—in short, their **identity.** Confusion over the most appropriate role to follow in life can lead to lack of a

identity-versus-role-confusion stage: According to Erikson, a time in adolescence of major testing to determine one's unique qualities

identity: The distinguishing character of the individual: who each of us is, what our roles are, and what we are capable of

Table 9-6   A Summary of Erikson's Stages

Stage	Approximate Age	Positive Outcomes	Negative Outcomes
1. Trust-vs.-mistrust	Birth–1½ years	Feelings of trust from environmental support	Fear and concern regarding others
2. Autonomy-vs.-shame-and-doubt	1½–3 years	Self-sufficiency if exploration is encouraged	Doubts about self, lack of independence
3. Initiative-vs.-guilt	3–6 years	Discovery of ways to initiate actions	Guilt from actions and thoughts
4. Industry-vs.-inferiority	6–12 years	Development of sense of competence	Feelings of inferiority, no sense of mastery
5. Identity-vs.-role-confusion	Adolescence	Awareness of uniqueness of self, knowledge of role to be followed	Inability to identify appropriate roles in life
6. Intimacy-vs.-isolation	Early adulthood	Development of loving, sexual relationships and close friendships	Fear of relationships with others
7. Generativity-vs.-stagnation	Middle adulthood	Sense of contribution to continuity of life	Trivialization of one's activities
8. Ego-integrity-vs.-despair	Late adulthood	Sense of unity in life's accomplishments	Regret over lost opportunities of life

stable identity, adoption of a socially unacceptable role such as that of a social deviant, or difficulty in maintaining close personal relationships later in life (Kahn et al., 1985; Archer & Waterman, 1994; Kidwell et al., 1995; Brendgen, Vitaro, & Bukowski, 2000).

During the identity-versus-role-confusion period, pressures to identify what one wants to do with one's life are acutely felt. Because these pressures come at a time of major physical changes as well as important changes in what society expects of them, adolescents can find the period particularly difficult. The identity-versus-role-confusion stage has another important characteristic: a decline in reliance on adults for information, with a shift toward using the peer group as a source of social judgments. The peer group becomes increasingly important, enabling adolescents to form close, adultlike relationships and helping them clarify their personal identities. According to Erikson, the identity-versus-role-confusion stage during adolescence marks a pivotal point in psychosocial development, paving the way for continued growth and the future development of personal relationships.

During the identity-versus-role confusion stage, adolescents seek to determine what is special and unique about themselves, according to Erikson's theory.

During early adulthood, people enter the **intimacy-versus-isolation stage.** Spanning the period of early adulthood (from post-adolescence to the early thirties), the focus is on developing close relationships with others. Difficulties during this stage result in feelings of loneliness and a fear of relationships with others, but successful resolution of the crises of this stage results in the possibility of forming relationships that are intimate on a physical, intellectual, and emotional level.

Development continues during middle adulthood as people enter the **generativity-versus-stagnation stage.** Generativity is the ability to contribute to one's family, community, work, and society, assisting the development of the younger generation. Success in this stage results in positive feelings about the continuity of life; difficulties lead to feelings that one's activities are trivial, a sense of stagnation, or feeling that one has done nothing for upcoming generations. In fact, the person who has not successfully resolved the identity crisis of adolescence might still be floundering in middle adulthood to find an appropriate career.

Finally, the last stage of psychosocial development, the period of **ego-integrity-versus-despair,** comprises later adulthood and continues until death. Success in resolving the difficulties presented by this stage of life is signified by a sense of accomplishment; difficulties result in regret over what might have been achieved but was not.

One of the most noteworthy aspects of Erikson's theory is its suggestion that development does not stop at adolescence but continues throughout adulthood, a view that a substantial amount of research now confirms. For instance, a 22-year study by psychologist Susan Whitbourne found considerable support for the fundamentals of Erikson's theory, determining that psychosocial development continues through adolescence and adulthood. In sum, adolescence is not an endpoint but rather a way-station on the path of psychosocial development (Whitbourne et al., 1992; McAdams et al., 1997).

intimacy-versus-isolation stage: According to Erikson, a period during early adulthood that focuses on developing close relationships

generativity-versus-stagnation stage: According to Erikson, a period in middle adulthood during which we take stock of our contributions to family and society

ego-integrity-versus-despair stage: According to Erikson, a period from late adulthood until death during which we review our life's accomplishments and failures

Stormy Adolescence: Myth or Reality?

Does puberty invariably foreshadow a stormy, rebellious period of adolescence?

At one time most children entering adolescence were thought to be beginning a period fraught with stress and unhappiness. However, psychologists are now finding that this characterization is largely a myth, that most young people pass through adolescence without appreciable turmoil in their lives, and that parents speak easily—and fairly often—with their children about a variety of topics (Steinberg, 1993; Klein, 1998; van Wel, Linssen, & Abma, 2000).

This is not to say that adolescence is completely calm. In most families, there is clearly a rise in the amount of arguing and bickering that goes on. Young teenagers, as part of their search for identity, tend to experience a degree of tension between their attempts to become independent from their parents and their actual dependence on them.

Success in the generativity-versus-stagnation stage results in positive feelings about the continuity of life, while difficulties lead to feelings of triviality regarding one's activities and a sense of stagnation.

PsychLink

Teenage suicide
www.mhhe.com/
feldmaness5-09links

They might experiment with a range of behaviors, flirting with a variety of activities that their parents, and even society as a whole, find objectionable. Happily, though, for the majority of families such tensions tend to stabilize during middle adolescence—around age 15 or 16—and eventually decline around age 18 (Eccles, Lord, & Roeser, 1996; Gullotta, Adams, & Markstrom, 1999).

One reason for the increase in discord during adolescence appears to be the protracted period in which children stay at home with their parents. In prior historical periods—and in some nonwestern cultures today—children leave home immediately after puberty and are considered adults. Today, however, sexually mature adolescents might spend as many as seven or eight years with their parents. Current statistics even hint at an extension of the conflicts of adolescence beyond the teenage years for a significant number of people. Some one-third of all unmarried men and one-fifth of unmarried women between the ages of 25 and 34 continue to reside with their parents (Steinberg, 1989; Gross, 1991).

Another source of strife with parents lies in the way adolescents think. Adolescence fosters *adolescent egocentrism,* a state of self-absorption in which adolescents view the world from their own point of view. Egocentrism leads adolescents to be highly critical of authority figures, unwilling to accept criticism, and quick to fault others. It also makes them believe that they are the center of everyone else's attention, leading to considerable self-consciousness. Furthermore, they develop *personal fables,* the view that what happens to them is unique, exceptional, and shared by no one else. Such personal fables can make adolescents feel invulnerable to the risks that threaten others (Elkind, 1967, 1985; Klacynski, 1997).

Adolescence also introduces a variety of stresses outside the home. Typically, adolescents change schools at least twice (from elementary to middle or junior high, then to senior high school), and relationships with friends and peers are particularly volatile. Many adolescents hold part-time jobs, increasing the demands of school, work, and social activities on their time. Such stressors can lead to tensions at home (Steinberg & Dornbusch, 1991; Cotterell, 1996).

EXPLORING DIVERSITY

Rites of Passage: Coming of Age Around the World

It is not easy for male members of the Awa tribe in New Guinea to make the transition from childhood to adulthood. First come whippings, in which the boys are hit with sticks and prickly branches, both for their own past misdeeds and in honor of those tribesmen who were killed in warfare. In the next phase of the ritual, adults jab sharpened sticks into the boys' nostrils. Then they force a 5-foot length of vine into the boys' throats, until they gag and vomit. Finally, tribesmen cut the boys' genitals, causing severe bleeding.

Although the rites that mark the coming-of-age of boys in the Awa sound horrifying to Westerners, they are comparable to those in other cultures. In some cultures, rites require kneeling on hot coals without displaying pain. In others, girls must toss wads of burning cotton from hand to hand and allow themselves to be bitten by hundreds of ants (Selsky, 1997).

Other cultures have less fearsome, although no less important, ceremonies that mark the passage from childhood to adulthood. For instance, when a girl first menstruates in traditional Apache tribes, the event is marked by dawn-to-dusk chanting. Western religions, too, have several types of celebrations, including bar and bat mitzvahs at age 13 for Jewish boys and girls and confirmation ceremonies for children in many Christian denominations (Myerhoff, 1982; Dunham, Kidwell, & Wilson, 1986; Delaney, 1995; Rakoff, 1995).

In most societies, males, but not females, are the focus of coming-of-age ceremonies. The renowned anthropologist Margaret Mead remarked, only partly in jest, that the preponderance of male ceremonies might reflect that "the worry that boys will not grow up to be men is much more widespread than that girls will not grow up to be women" (Mead,

1949, p. 195). Or it might be that men traditionally have higher status than women, and therefore their transition into adulthood is regarded as more important.

However, there is another explanation for why most cultures place greater emphasis on male rites than female rites. For females, the transition from childhood is marked by a definite, biological event: menstruation. For males, no single event pinpoints entry into adulthood, so they are forced to rely on culturally determined rituals to acknowledge that they have become adults (Chodorow, 1978; Bird & Melville, 1994).

Evaluate

1. _____ is the period during which the sexual organs begin to mature.
2. Delayed maturation typically provides both males and females with a social advantage. True or false?
3. _____ proposed a set of three levels of moral development ranging from reasoning based on rewards and punishments to abstract thinking involving concepts of justice.
4. Erikson believed that, during adolescence, people must search for _____, and that during early adulthood the major task is _____.

Answers to Evaluate Questions

1. Puberty 2. False; both male and female adolescents suffer if they mature late. 3. Kohlberg 4. identity; intimacy

Rethink

1. In what ways do school cultures help or hurt teenage students who are going through adolescence? What school policies might benefit early-maturing girls and late-maturing boys? Would same-sex schools help, as some have argued?
2. Many cultures have "rites of passage" that officially recognize young people as adults. Do you think such rites can be beneficial? Does the United States have any such rites? Would setting up an official designation that one has achieved "adult" status have benefits?

Early and Middle Adulthood: The Middle Years of Life

Prepare

What are the principal kinds of physical, social, and intellectual changes that occur in early and middle adulthood, and what are their causes?

Organize

Early and Middle Adulthood
Physical Development
Social Development
Marriage, Children, and Divorce

Psychologists generally consider early adulthood to begin around age 20 and last until about age 40 to 45, with middle adulthood beginning then and continuing until around age 65. Despite the enormous importance of these periods of life in terms of both the accomplishments that occur within them and their overall length (together they span some 45 years), they have been studied less than any other stage. One reason is that the physical changes that occur during these periods are less apparent and more gradual than changes during other periods of the life span. In addition, the social changes that arise during this period are so diverse that they defy simple categorization. However, developmental psychologists have recently begun to focus on early and middle adulthood, particularly on the social changes in the family and women's careers.

Physical Development: The Peak of Health

For most people, early adulthood marks the peak of physical health. From about 18 to 25 years of age, people's strength is greatest, their reflexes are quickest, and their chances of dying from disease are quite slim. Moreover, reproductive capabilities are at their highest level.

Around age 25, the body starts to become slightly less efficient and more susceptible to disease. Overall, however, ill health remains the exception; most people stay remarkably healthy during early adulthood. (Can you think of any machine other than the body that can operate without pause for so long a period?)

During middle adulthood, people gradually become aware of changes in their bodies. Many people begin to put on weight (although this can be avoided through exercise). Furthermore, the sense organs gradually become less sensitive, and it takes more time to react to stimuli. But generally, the physical declines that do occur during middle adulthood are minor and often unnoticeable (DiGiovanna, 1994).

The major biological change during middle adulthood pertains to reproductive capabilities. During their late forties or early fifties, on average, women begin **menopause,** a process in which they stop menstruating and become infertile. Because menopause is accompanied by a significant reduction in the production of estrogen, a female hormone, menopausal women sometimes experience symptoms such as hot flashes, sudden sensations of heat. However, many symptoms can be treated through *estrogen replacement therapy* (ERT), in which the hormones estrogen and progesterone are taken. However, estrogen replacement therapy poses several dangers, such as an increase in the risk of breast cancer. The uncertainties make the routine use of ERT controversial (LaVecchia, 1996; Swan, 1997).

Menopause was once blamed for a variety of psychological symptoms, including depression and memory loss. However, such difficulties, if they do occur, might be caused by women's expectations about reaching an "old" age in a society that highly values youth.

Furthermore, women's reactions to menopause vary significantly across cultures. According to anthropologist Yewoubdar Beyene, the more a society values old age, the less difficulty its women have during menopause. In a study of women in Mayan villages, she found that women looked forward to menopause, because they then stopped having children. In addition, they didn't even experience some of the classic symptoms of menopause; hot flashes, for example, were unheard of. It is clear that a society's attitudes affect how women experience menopause (Ballinger, 1981; Beyene, 1989; Beck, 1992; Figueiras & Marteau, 1995; Mingo, Herman, & Jasperse, 2000).

For men, the aging process during middle adulthood is somewhat subtler. There are no physiological signals of increasing age equivalent to the end of menstruation in women (there is no male menopause). In fact, men remain fertile and are capable of fathering children until well into old age. On the other hand, some gradual physical declines occur: Sperm production decreases and the frequency of orgasm tends to decline. Once again, though, most psychological difficulties associated with these changes are due not so much to physical deterioration as to societal glorification of youthfulness.

Social Development: Working at Life

Whereas physical changes during adulthood reflect development of a quantitative nature, social developmental transitions are more profound. During this period people typically launch themselves into careers, marriage, and families.

The entry into early adulthood is usually marked by leaving one's childhood home and entering the world of work. People envision the accomplishments they desire in life and make career choices. Their lives often become centered on their careers, which form an important part of their identity (Vaillant & Vaillant, 1990; Levinson, 1990, 1992).

In their early forties, however, people might begin to question their lives as they enter a period called the *midlife transition*. The idea that life will end at some point becomes increasingly influential in their thinking, and they might question their past accomplishments (Gould, 1978). As they face signs of physical aging and feel dissatisfaction with their lives, some individuals experience what has been popularly labeled a *midlife crisis.*

For most people, though, the passage into middle age is relatively calm. Most 40-year-olds view their lives and accomplishments positively enough to proceed relatively smoothly through midlife, and the forties and fifties are often a particularly rewarding period of life. Rather than looking to the future, people concentrate on the present, and their involvement with their families, friends, and other social groups takes on new importance. A major developmental thrust of this period of life is coming to terms with one's circumstances (Whitbourne, 1999).

menopause: The point at which women stop menstruating and are no longer fertile

PsychLink

Medical information on menopause
www.mhhe.com/
feldmaness5-09links

Women's reactions to menopause vary significantly across cultures, and, according to one study, the more a society values old age, the less difficulty its women have during menopause. Why do you think this would be the case?

Finally, during the last stages of adulthood people become more accepting of others and their lives, and less concerned about issues or problems that once bothered them. People come to accept the realization that death is inevitable, and they try to understand their accomplishments in terms of the broader meaning of life. Although people might for the first time begin to label themselves as "old," many also develop a sense of wisdom and feel freer to enjoy life (Gould, 1978; Karp, 1988, 1991).

Marriage, Children, and Divorce: Family Ties

In the typical fairy tale, a dashing young man and a beautiful young woman marry, have children, and live happily ever after. However, such a scenario does not match the realities of love and marriage in the twenty-first century. Today, it is just as likely that the woman and man would first live together, then get married and have children, but ultimately end up getting divorced.

The percentage of unmarried couples in U.S. households has increased dramatically over the last two decades. At the same time, the average age at which marriage takes place is higher than at any time since the turn of the century. These changes have been dramatic, and they suggest that the institution of marriage has changed considerably from earlier historical periods.

When people do marry, the probability of divorce is high, particularly for younger couples. Even though divorce rates appear to be declining since they peaked in 1981, 60 percent of all first marriages still end in divorce. Two-fifths of children will experience the breakup of their parents' marriage before they are 18 years old. Moreover, the rise in divorce is not just a U.S. phenomenon: The divorce rate has accelerated over the last several decades in most industrialized countries except Japan and Italy (Cherlin, 1993; Ahrons, 1995).

Changes in matrimonial and divorce trends have led to a doubling in the number of single-parent households in the United States over the past two decades. More than one-quarter of all family households are now headed by one parent, compared with 13 percent in 1970, and half of all black children and almost one-third of Hispanic children live in homes with only one parent. Furthermore, in most single-parent families, the children reside with the mother, not the father—a phenomenon that is consistent across racial and ethnic groups throughout the industrialized world (Burns & Scott, 1994; U.S. Bureau of the Census, 1997).

PsychLink

Children and divorce
www.mhhe.com/
feldmaness5-09links

What are the consequences for children living in homes with only one parent? Single-parent families are often economically less well off, diminishing children's opportunities. Many single parents are unable to find good child care, and they feel psychological stress and sometimes guilt over the child-care arrangements they must make for economic reasons. Time is always at a premium in single-parent families (Hetherington, 1999; Wallerstein, Lewis, & Blakeslee, 2000). Furthermore, for children of divorce, the parents' separation is often a painful experience that can make it difficult for the children to establish close relationships later in life. Children might blame themselves for the breakup or feel pressure to take sides. Most evidence, however, suggests that children from single-parent families are no less well adjusted than those from two-parent families. In fact, children can be more successful growing up in a harmonious single-parent family than in a two-parent family in which the parents are engaged in continuous conflict with one another (Harold et al., 1997; Kelly, 1999; Clarke-Stewart et al., 2000).

The Changing Roles of Men and Women: The Time of Their Lives

One of the major changes in family life in the last two decades has been the evolution of the roles played by men and women. More women than ever before act simultaneously as wives, mothers, and wage earners—in contrast to women in traditional marriages, in which the husband is the sole wage earner and the wife assumes primary responsibility for care of the home and children.

Close to 75 percent of all married women with school-age children are now employed outside the home, and 56 percent of mothers with children under 6 are working. In the mid 1960s, only 17 percent of mothers of 1-year-olds worked full-time; now, more than half are in the labor force (Darnton, 1990; Carnegie Task Force, 1994).

Most married working women are not free of household responsibilities. Even in marriages in which the spouses hold jobs that have similar status and require similar hours, the distribution of household tasks between husbands and wives has not changed substantially. Working wives are still more likely to view themselves as responsible for traditional homemaking tasks such as cooking and cleaning. In contrast, husbands still view themselves as responsible primarily for such household tasks as repairing broken appliances, putting up screens in the summer, and doing yard work (Perry-Jenkins, 1993; Ganong & Coleman, 1999).

Women's "Second Shift"   The number of hours put in by working mothers can be staggering. One survey found that employed mothers of children under 3 years of age worked an average of ninety hours per week! Sociologist Arlie Hochschild refers to the additional work experienced by women as the "second shift." According to her analysis of national statistics, employed mothers put in an extra month of 24-hour days during the course of a year. Similar patterns are seen in many developing societies throughout the world, with women working at full-time jobs and also having primary responsibilities for child care (Hochschild, 1990; Hochschild, Machung, & Pringle, 1995; Mednick, 1993).

Consequently, rather than women's careers being a substitute for household work, they usually are an addition to the role of homemaker. It is not surprising that some wives feel resentment toward husbands who spend less time on child care and housework than the wives had expected before the birth of their children (Williams & McCullers, 1983; Ruble et al., 1988; Crouter et al., 1999; Stier & Lewin-Epstein, 2000).

Evaluate

1. Emotional and psychological changes that sometimes accompany menopause are probably not due to menopause itself. True or false?
2. Rob recently turned 40 and surveyed his goals and accomplishments to date. Although he has accomplished a lot, he realized that many of his goals will not be met in his lifetime. This stage is called a _____ _____.
3. It is typically in the best interests of children for their parents to remain in a stormy marriage until the children move away from home. True or false?
4. In households where the partners have similar jobs, the usual division of labor is the same as in "traditional" households where the husband works and the wife stays at home. True or false?

Rethink

1. How do you think popular culture contributes to the midlife crisis experienced by some people as they reach their forties? What sorts of cultural changes might ease the midlife crisis or make the phenomenon less prevalent?
2. Given the current divorce rate and the number of households in which both parents work, do you think it is reasonable to still think in terms of a "traditional" household in which the father is the breadwinner and the wife is a homemaker? What problems might such a definition cause for children whose homes do not match this definition?

Answers to Evaluate Questions

1. True 2. midlife transition, 3. False; a stable one-parent home is generally preferable to a two-parent home filled with conflict, 4. True

The Later Years of Life: Growing Old

Prepare

How does the reality of old age differ from the stereotypes about the period?
How can we adjust to death?

Organize

The Later Years of Life
   Physical Changes in Late Adulthood
   Cognitive Changes
   The Social World of Late Adulthood

I've always enjoyed doing things in the mountains—hiking or, more recently, active cliff-climbing. When climbing a route of any difficulty at all, it's absolutely necessary to become entirely absorbed in what you're doing. You look for a crack that you can put your hand in. You have to think about whether the foothold over there will leave you in balance or not. Otherwise you can get trapped in a difficult situation. And if you don't remember where you put your hands or feet a few minutes before, then it's very difficult to climb down.

     The more difficult the climb, the more absorbing it is. The climbs I really remember are the ones I had to work on. Maybe a particular section where it took two or three tries before I found the right combination of moves that got me up easily—and, preferably, elegantly. It's a wonderful exhilaration to get to the top and sit down and perhaps have lunch and look out over the landscape and be so grateful that it's still possible for me to do that sort of thing. (Lyman Spitzer, age 74, quoted in Kotre & Hall, 1990, pp. 358–359)

If you can't quite picture a 74-year-old climbing rocks, some rethinking of your view of old age might well be in order. In spite of the societal stereotype of old age as a time of inactivity and physical and mental decline, *gerontologists*, specialists who study aging, are beginning to paint quite a different portrait of late adulthood.

     By focusing on the period of life that starts at around age 65, gerontologists are making important contributions to clarifying the capabilities of older adults. Their work is demonstrating that significant developmental processes continue even during old age. And as life expectancy increases, the number of people who reach older adulthood will continue to grow substantially. Consequently, developing an understanding of late adulthood has become a critical priority for psychologists (Birren, 1996; Moody, 2000).

PsychLink

Information on aging
www.mhhe.com/
feldmaness5-09links

Physical Changes in Late Adulthood: The Aging Body

Napping, eating, walking, conversing. It probably doesn't surprise you that these relatively nonstrenuous activities represent the typical pastimes of late adulthood. But what is striking about this list is that these activities are identical to the most common leisure activities reported in a survey of college students. Although the students cited more active pursuits—such as sailing and playing basketball—as their favorite activities, in actuality they engaged in such sports relatively infrequently, spending most of their free time napping, eating, walking, and conversing (Harper, 1978).

     Although the leisure activities in which older adults engage might not differ all that much from those of younger people, many physical changes are, of course, brought about by the aging process. The most obvious are those of appearance—hair thinning and turning gray, skin wrinkling and folding, and sometimes a slight loss of height as the thickness of the disks between vertebrae in the spine decreases—but there are also subtler changes in the body's biological functioning (DiGiovanna, 1994).

     For example, sensory capabilities decrease as a result of aging: Vision, hearing, smell, and taste become less sensitive. Reaction time slows, and there are changes in physical stamina. Because oxygen intake and heart-pumping ability decline, the body is unable to replenish lost nutrients as quickly—and therefore the rebound from physical activity is slower. Of course, none of these changes begins suddenly at age 65. Gradual declines in some kinds of functioning start earlier. In

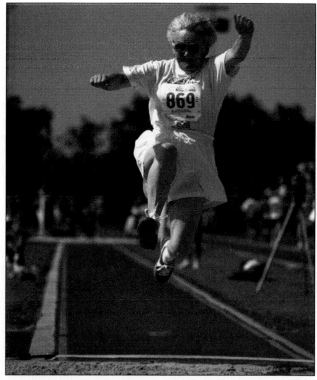

Many people remain active and vigorous during late adulthood, as exemplified by this participant in the Senior Olympics.

Aging process information
www.mhhe.com/
feldmaness5-09links

genetic preprogramming theories of aging: Theories that hold that there is a built-in time limit to the reproduction of human cells, and that after a certain time they are no longer able to divide

wear-and-tear theories of aging: Theories that hold that the mechanical functions of the body simply stop working efficiently when we are old

late adulthood, however, these changes become more apparent (Schneider & Rowe, 1996; Whitbourne, 2000).

What are the reasons for these physical declines? **Genetic preprogramming theories of aging** suggest that there is a built-in time limit to the reproduction of human cells. These theories suggest that after a certain time cells stop dividing or become harmful to the body—as if a kind of automatic self-destruct button has been pushed. In contrast, **wear-and-tear theories of aging** suggest that the mechanical functions of the body simply stop working efficiently as people age. Waste by-products of energy production eventually accumulate, and mistakes are made when cells divide. Eventually the body, in effect, wears out, just like an old automobile (Hayflick, 1994; Ly et al., 2000).

Evidence exists to support both the genetic preprogramming view and the wear-and-tear view, and perhaps both processes contribute to natural aging. It is clear, however, that physical aging is not a disease, but rather a natural biological process. Many physical functions do not decline with age. For example, sex remains pleasurable well into old age (although the frequency of sexual activity decreases), and some people report that the pleasure they derive from sex increases during late adulthood (Olshansky, Carnes, & Cassel, 1990; Gelfand, 2000).

Cognitive Changes: Thinking About—and During—Late Adulthood

At one time, many gerontologists would have agreed with the popular view that older adults are forgetful and confused. Today, however, most research tells us that this is far from an accurate assessment of older people's capabilities.

One reason for the change in view is the availability of more sophisticated research techniques for studying cognitive changes that occur in late adulthood. For example, if we were to give a group of older adults an IQ test, we might find that the average score is lower than the score achieved by a group of younger people. We might conclude that this signifies a decline in intelligence. Yet if we looked a little closer at the specific test, we might find that such a conclusion is unwarranted. For instance, many IQ tests include portions based on physical performance (such as arranging a group of blocks) or on speed. In such cases, poorer performance on the IQ test might be due to decrements in reaction time—a physical decline that accompanies old age and has little or nothing to do with the intellectual capabilities of older adults (Schaie, 1991).

Other difficulties hamper research into cognitive functioning during late adulthood. For example, many older people are less healthy than younger ones; when only *healthy* older adults are compared to healthy younger adults, intellectual differences are far less evident. Furthermore, the average number of years in school is often lower in older adults (for historical reasons) than in the younger ones, and older adults can be less motivated to perform well on intelligence tests than younger people. Finally, traditional IQ tests might be inappropriate measures of intelligence in late adulthood. Older adults sometimes perform better on tests of practical intelligence (of the sort we discussed in Chapter 7) than younger individuals do (Cornelius & Caspi, 1987; Willis & Schaie, 1994; Kausler, 1994).

Still, there are some declines in intellectual functioning during late adulthood, although the pattern of age differences is not uniform for different types of cognitive abilities (see Figure 9-9). In general, skills relating to *fluid intelligence* (which involves reasoning, memory, and information processing) do show declines in old age. On the other hand, skills relating to *crystallized intelligence* (intelligence based on the accumulation of information, skills, and problem-solving strategies) remain steady and in some cases actually improve (Schaie, 1993, 1994; Powell & Whitla, 1994; Salthouse, 1996).

Even when changes in intellectual functioning do occur during late adulthood, people often are able to compensate for any decline. They can still learn what they want to; it might just take more time. Furthermore, when older adults learn strategies for dealing with new problems, this can prevent declines in their performance (Willis & Nesselroade, 1990; Coffey et al., 1999).

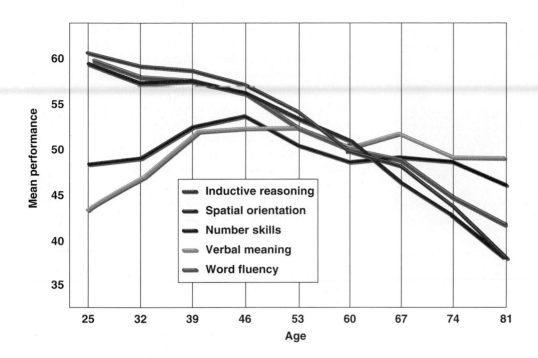

Figure 9-9 Age-related changes in intellectual skills vary according to the specific cognitive ability in question (Schaie, 1994).

Memory Changes in Old Age: Are Older Adults Forgetful?

One of the characteristics most frequently attributed to late adulthood is forgetfulness. How accurate is this assumption?

Most evidence suggests that diminished memory is *not* an inevitable part of the aging process. For instance, research shows that in cultures where older adults are held in high esteem, such as in mainland China, older people are less likely to show memory losses than those living in cultures that expect older people's memory to decline. Similarly, when older people in Western societies are reminded of the advantages of age ("age brings wisdom"), they tend to do better on tests of memory (Levy & Langer, 1994; Levy, 1996).

Even when people do show memory declines during late adulthood, their deficits tend to be limited to particular types of memory. Losses tend to be limited to episodic memories, which relate to specific experiences about our lives. Other types of memories, such as semantic memories (memories of general knowledge and facts) and implicit memories (memories we are not consciously aware of) are largely unaffected by age (Graf, 1990; Russo & Parkin, 1993).

Declines in episodic memories can often be traced to changes in the lives of older adults. For instance, it is not surprising that a retired person who no longer faces the intellectual challenges encountered on the job might well be less practiced in using memory or even be less motivated to remember things, leading to an apparent decline in memory. Even if their long-term memory declines, older adults can usually profit from compensatory efforts. When older adults learn to use the kinds of mnemonic strategies described in Chapter 6, they can not only prevent their long-term memory from deteriorating, but can actually improve it (Kotler-Cope & Camp, 1990; Verhaeghen, Marcoen, & Goossens, 1992; West, 1995).

In the past, older adults with severe cases of memory decline, accompanied by other cognitive difficulties, were viewed as suffering from senility. *Senility* is a broad, imprecise term typically applied to older adults who experience progressive deterioration of mental abilities, including memory loss, disorientation to time and place, and general confusion. Though senility was once thought to be an inevitable state that accompanies aging, the label senile is now viewed by gerontologists as having outlived its usefulness. Rather than senility being the cause of certain symptoms, the symptoms are deemed to be caused by some other factor.

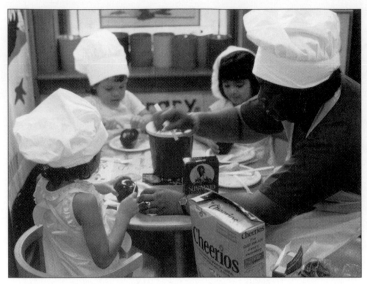

During late adulthood, people can find fulfillment through their contributions to their community and society by working with others.

Some cases of memory loss, however, are produced by actual disease. For instance, *Alzheimer's disease* is a progressive brain disorder, discussed in Chapter 7, that leads to a gradual and irreversible decline in cognitive abilities. In other cases, the declines are caused by temporary anxiety and depression, which can be successfully treated, or might even be due to overmedication. The danger is that people suffering such symptoms will be labeled "senile" and left untreated, thereby continuing their decline—even though treatment would have been beneficial (Selkoe, 1997).

In sum, most declines in cognitive functioning in old age are not inevitable. The key to maintaining cognitive skills might lie in intellectual stimulation. Like the rest of us, older adults need a stimulating environment in order to hone and maintain their skills.

The Social World of Late Adulthood: Old but Not Alone

Just as the view that mental declines are an inevitable outcome of old age has proved to be wrong, so has the view that old age inevitably brings loneliness. Most people in late adulthood see themselves as functioning members of society; only a small minority report that loneliness is a serious problem (Binstock & George, 1996).

disengagement theory of aging: A theory that holds that aging is a gradual withdrawal from the world on physical, psychological, and social levels

There is no single way to age successfully. According to the **disengagement theory of aging,** aging produces a gradual withdrawal from the world on physical, psychological, and social levels (Cummings & Henry, 1961). But such disengagement serves an important purpose, providing the opportunity for increased reflectiveness and decreased emotional investment in others at a time of life when social relationships will inevitably be ended by death.

activity theory of aging: A theory that holds that the elderly who age most successfully are those who maintain the interests and activities they had during middle age

An alternative view of aging is presented by the **activity theory of aging,** which suggests that the people who age most successfully are those who maintain the interests, activities, and level of social interaction they experienced during middle adulthood (Blau, 1973). According to activity theory, late adulthood should reflect a continuation, as much as possible, of the activities in which people participated during the earlier part of their lives.

Both disengagement and activity can lead to successful aging. Not all people in late adulthood need a life filled with activities and social interaction to be happy; as in every stage of life, there are those who are just as satisfied leading a relatively inactive, solitary existence. There are vast individual differences in how people cope with the aging process.

life review: The process in which people in late adulthood examine and evaluate their lives

Regardless of whether people become disengaged or maintain their activities from earlier stages of life, most engage in a process of **life review,** in which they examine and evaluate their lives. Remembering and reconsidering what has occurred in the past, many people in late adulthood come to a better understanding of themselves, sometimes resolving lingering problems and conflicts, and face their lives with greater wisdom and serenity.

Clearly, people in late adulthood are not just marking time until death. Rather, old age is a time of continued growth and development, as important as any other period of life (Butler et al., 1990; Harlow & Cantor, 1996).

BECOMING AN INFORMED CONSUMER OF PSYCHOLOGY

Adjusting to Death

At some time in our lives, we all face death—certainly our own, as well as the deaths of friends, loved ones, and even strangers. Although there is nothing more inevitable in life, death remains a frightening, emotion-laden topic. Certainly, little is more stressful than the death of a loved one or the contemplation of our own imminent death, and preparing for death is one of our most crucial developmental tasks (Aiken, 2001).

Not too long ago, talk of death was taboo. The topic was never mentioned to dying people, and gerontologists had little to say about it. That changed, however, with the pioneering work of Elisabeth Kübler-Ross (1969), who brought the subject of death into the open with her observation that those facing impending death tend to move through five broad stages:

- *Denial.* In this first stage, people resist the idea that they are dying. Even if told that their chances for survival are small, they refuse to admit that they are facing death.
- *Anger.* After moving beyond the denial stage, dying people become angry—angry at people around them who are in good health, angry at medical professionals for being ineffective, angry at God.
- *Bargaining.* Anger leads to bargaining, in which the dying try to think of ways to postpone death. They might decide to dedicate their lives to religion if God saves them; they might say, "If only I can live to see my son married, I will accept death then."
- *Depression.* When dying people come to feel that bargaining is of no use, they move to the next stage: depression. They realize that their lives really are coming to an end, leading to what Kübler-Ross calls "preparatory grief" for their own death.
- *Acceptance.* In this last stage, people accept impending death. Usually they are unemotional and uncommunicative; it is as if they have made peace with themselves and are expecting death with no bitterness.

PsychLink

Death and dying in America
www.mhhe.com/
feldmaness5–09links

It is important to keep in mind that not everyone experiences each of these stages in the same way. In fact, Kübler-Ross's stages pertain only to people who are fully aware that they are dying and have the time to evaluate their impending death. Furthermore, there are vast differences in how specific individuals react to impending death. The specific cause and duration of dying, as well as the person's sex, age, and personality and the type of support received from family and friends, all have an impact on how people respond to death (Zautra, Reich, & Guarnaccia, 1990; Stroebe, Stroebe, & Hansson, 1993).

Few of us enjoy contemplating death. Yet awareness of its psychological aspects and consequences can make its inevitable arrival less anxiety-producing and perhaps more understandable.

Evaluate

1. _____ _____ theories suggest that there is a maximum time limit in which cells are able to reproduce. This time limit explains the eventual breakdown of the body during old age.
2. In contrast to the above theories, _____ - _____ - _____ theories state that the body simply becomes less efficient as time passes.
3. Lower IQ test scores during late adulthood do not necessarily mean a decrease in intelligence. True or false?
4. During old age, a person's _____ intelligence continues to increase, through _____ intelligence might decline.
5. Lavinia feels that, in her old age, she has gradually decreased her social contacts and has become more self-oriented. A proponent of _____ theory interprets the situation as a result of Lavinia's not maintaining her past interests. A supporter of _____ theory views her behavior in a more positive light, suggesting that it is a natural process accompanied by enhanced reflectiveness and declining emotional investment.
6. In Kübler-Ross's _____ stage, people resist the idea of death. In the _____ stage, they attempt to make deals to avoid death, and in the _____ stage, they passively await death.

Rethink

1. Is the possibility that life might be extended for several decades a mixed blessing? What societal consequences might an extended life span bring about?
2. It has been found that people in late adulthood require intellectual stimulation. Does this have implications for the societies in which older people live? In what way might stereotypes about older individuals contribute to their isolation and lack of intellectual stimulation?

Answers to Evaluate Questions

1. Genetic preprogramming 2. wear-and-tear 3. True 4. crystallized; fluid 5. activity; disengagement 6. denial; bargaining; acceptance

Looking**Back**

How do psychologists study the influences of hereditary and environmental factors in development?

- Developmental psychology is the branch of psychology that studies growth and change throughout life. One fundamental question is how much developmental change is due to heredity and how much is due to environment—the nature-nurture issue. Heredity seems to define the upper limits of our growth and change, whereas the environment affects the degree to which the upper limits are reached. (p. 282)
- Cross-sectional research compares people of different ages with one another at the same point in time. Longitudinal research traces the behavior of one or more participants as the participants become older. Finally, cross-sequential research combines the two methods by taking several different age groups and examining them over several points in time. (p. 285)

What is the nature of development prior to birth?

- At the moment of conception, a male's sperm cell and a female's egg cell unite, with each contributing to the new individual's genetic makeup. The union of sperm and egg produces a zygote, which contains 23 pairs of chromosomes—with one member of each pair coming from the father and the other from the mother. Each chromosome contains genes, through which genetic information is transmitted. Genes, which are composed of DNA sequences, are the "software" that programs the future development of the body's hardware. (p. 286)
- After 2 weeks the zygote becomes an embryo. By 8 weeks, the embryo has become a fetus and is responsive to touch and other stimulation. At about 24 weeks it reaches the age of viability, which means it might survive if born prematurely. A fetus is normally born after 38 weeks of pregnancy, weighing around 7 pounds and measuring about 20 inches. (p. 287)
- Genes affect not only physical attributes but also a wide array of personal characteristics, such as cognitive abilities, personality traits, and psychological disorders. (p. 287)

What factors affect a child during the mother's pregnancy?

- Genetic abnormalities produce birth defects such as phenylketonuria (PKU), sickle-cell anemia, Tay-Sachs disease, and Down syndrome. Among the prenatal environmental influences on fetal growth are the mother's nutrition, illnesses, drug intake, and birth complications. (p. 288)

What are the major competencies of newborns?

- Newborns, or neonates, have rooting, sucking, gag, startle, and Babinski reflexes. (p. 291)
- Sensory abilities also increase rapidly; infants can distinguish color, depth, sound, tastes, and smells relatively soon after birth. (p. 291)

What are the milestones of physical and social development during childhood?

- After birth, physical development is rapid; children typically triple their weight in their first year. (p. 294)
- Social development in infancy is marked by the phenomenon of attachment—the positive emotional bond between a child and a particular individual. Attachment is measured in the laboratory using the Ainsworth strange situation and is related to later social and emotional adjustment. (p. 294)

- As children become older, the nature of their social interactions with peers changes. Initially children play relatively independently, but their play becomes increasingly cooperative. (p. 296)
- The different child-rearing styles include authoritarian, permissive, authoritative, and uninvolved. (p. 297)
- According to Erikson, eight stages of psychosocial development involve people's changing interactions and understanding of themselves and others. During childhood, the four stages are trust versus mistrust (birth to 18 months), autonomy versus shame and doubt (18 months to 3 years), initiative versus guilt (3 to 6 years), and industry versus inferiority (6 to 12 years). (p. 298)

How does cognitive development proceed during childhood?

- Piaget's theory suggests that cognitive development proceeds through four stages in which qualitative changes occur in thinking: the sensorimotor stage (birth to 2 years), the preoperational stage (2 to 7 years), the concrete operational stage (7 to 12 years), and the formal operational period (12 years to adulthood). (p. 300)
- Although Piaget's theory has had an enormous influence, some theorists suggest that development is more continuous and that the changes occurring within and between stages are reflective of quantitative advances in cognitive development rather than qualitative changes in thinking. (p. 303)
- Information-processing approaches suggest that quantitative changes occur in children's ability to organize and manipulate information about the world, such as significant increases in speed of processing, attention span, and memory. In addition, there are advances in metacognition, the awareness and understanding of one's own cognitive processes. (p. 304)
- Vygotsky argued that children's cognitive development occurs as a consequence of social interactions in which children and others work together to solve problems. (p. 305)

What major physical, social, and cognitive transitions characterize adolescence?

- Adolescence, the developmental stage between childhood and adulthood, is marked by the onset of puberty, or sexual maturation. The age at which they enter puberty affects how people view themselves and how they are seen by others. (p. 307)
- Moral judgments during adolescence increase in sophistication, according to Kohlberg's three-level model. Although Kohlberg's levels are an adequate description of males' moral judgments, Gilligan suggests that women view morality in terms of caring for individuals rather than in terms of broad, general principles of justice. (p. 308)
- According to Erikson's model of psychosocial development, adolescence can be accompanied by an identity crisis. Adolescence is followed by three stages of psychosocial development that cover the remainder of the life span. (p. 310)

What are the principal kinds of physical, social, and intellectual changes that occur in early and middle adulthood, and what are their causes?

- Early adulthood marks the peak of physical health. Physical changes occur relatively gradually in men and women during early and middle adulthood. (p. 313)
- One major physical change occurs at the end of middle adulthood for women: They begin menopause, after which they are no longer fertile. (p. 314)
- During middle adulthood, people typically experience a midlife transition in which the notion that life is not unending becomes more important. In some

cases this can lead to a midlife crisis, although the passage into middle age is typically relatively calm. (p. 314)

- As aging continues during middle adulthood, people realize in their fifties that their lives and accomplishments are fairly well set, and they try to come to terms with them. (p. 314)
- The most important developmental milestones of adulthood include marriage, family changes, and divorce. Another important determinant of adult development is work. (p. 315)

How does the reality of old age differ from the stereotypes about the period?

- Old age can bring marked physical declines, caused by genetic preprogramming or physical wear and tear. Although the activities of people in late adulthood are not all that different from those of younger people, older adults do experience declines in reaction time, sensory abilities, and physical stamina. (p. 317)
- Intellectual declines are not an inevitable part of aging. Fluid intelligence does decline with age, and long-term memory abilities are sometimes impaired. In contrast, crystallized intelligence shows slight increases with age, and short-term memory remains at about the same level. (p. 318)
- Disengagement theory sees successful aging as a process accompanied by gradual withdrawal from the physical, psychological, and social worlds. In contrast, activity theory suggests that the maintenance of interests and activities from earlier years leads to successful aging. (p. 320)

How can we adjust to death?

- According to Kübler-Ross, dying people move through five stages as they face death: denial, anger, bargaining, depression, and acceptance. (p. 320)

Key Terms and Concepts

developmental psychology (p. 282)
nature-nurture issue (p. 283)
identical twins (p. 284)
cross-sectional research (p. 285)
longitudinal research (p. 285)
cross-sequential research (p. 285)
chromosomes (p. 286)
genes (p. 286)
zygote (p. 286)
embryo (p. 287)
fetus (p. 287)
age of viability (p. 288)
teratogens (p. 289)
neonate (p. 291)
reflexes (p. 291)
habituation (p. 292)
attachment (p. 294)
authoritarian parents (p. 297)
permissive parents (p. 297)
authoritative parents (p. 297)
uninvolved parents (p. 297)
temperament (p. 298)
psychosocial development (p. 298)

trust-versus-mistrust stage (p. 299)
autonomy-versus-shame-and-doubt stage (p. 299)
initiative-versus-guilt stage (p. 299)
industry-versus-inferiority stage (p. 299)
cognitive development (p. 300)
sensorimotor stage (p. 301)
object permanence (p. 301)
preoperational stage (p. 301)
egocentric thought (p. 301)
principle of conservation (p. 301)
concrete operational stage (p. 301)
formal operational stage (p. 303)
information processing (p. 304)
metacognition (p. 305)
zone of proximal development (ZPD) (p. 305)
adolescence (p. 307)
puberty (p. 308)
identity-versus-role-confusion stage (p. 310)
identity (p. 310)
intimacy-versus-isolation stage (p. 311)
generativity-versus-stagnation stage (p. 311)
ego-integrity-versus-despair stage (p. 311)

Psychology on the Web

1. On the Web, check out the current status of the Human Genome Project. Find a picture of part of the genetic map the project is creating, download it, and print it out. Summarize the current status of the project.
2. Find different answers to the question "Why do people die?" Search the Web for scientific, philosophical, and spiritual/religious answers. Write a summary in which you compare the different approaches to this question. Does the thinking in any one realm influence the thinking in the others? How?

Preview

For additional quizzing and a variety of interactive resources, visit the *Essentials of Understanding Psychology* Online Learning Center at

www.mhhe.com/feldmaness5

Epilogue

We have traced major events in human development across the life span, including changes in physical, social, and cognitive abilities. It is clear that children advance rapidly after birth in all these areas, developing abilities upon which they build further in adolescence and later life. We also observed that development continues throughout the life span, even into old age.

As we explored each area of development, we encountered anew the nature-nurture issue, concluding in every significant instance that both nature and nurture contribute to a person's development of skills, personality, and interactions. Specifically, our genetic inheritance—nature—lays down general boundaries within which we can advance and grow, and our environment helps determine the extent to which we take advantage of our potential.

Our consideration of development included a look at the major theories of development, especially Erik Erikson's theory of psychosocial development, Jean Piaget's theory of cognitive development, and Lev Vygotsky's theory of cognitive development, Kohlberg's theory of moral development, and Gilligan's corresponding theory for women.

Before proceeding to the next chapter, turn once again to the prologue that introduced this one, on Elizabeth Carr, who was conceived using in vitro fertilization. Using your knowledge of human development, consider the following questions.

1. Do you think there is any way Elizabeth Carr's birth, infancy, and development differ from those of her classmates who were not conceived through in vitro fertilization? Why or why not?
2. How would you design a longitudinal study of the development of individuals who were conceived through in vitro fertilization? What sorts of questions would this type of study help you answer?
3. What sorts of questions could you examine through a cross-sectional study? A cross-sequential study?
4. If a future Elizabeth Carr were *cloned* from one of her parents, do you think she would turn out to be exactly like that parent, or different in some ways? Why?

Chapter Ten

Personality

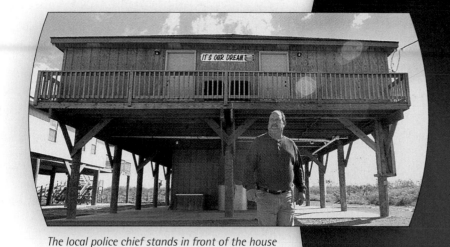

The local police chief stands in front of the house inhabited—and later abandoned—by the man called Tom, who was either a soft-hearted do-gooder or a violent mobster, depending on whom you talked to.

Prologue

Good Guy or Good Fella?

The 60-something man called himself "Tom" and his girlfriend "Helen." He said they were from New York, and they would spend months at a time visiting the Louisiana resort town of Grand Isle.

During his visits, Tom would drive around Grand Isle, offering biscuits to stray dogs. He wept when a dying puppy had to be shot to end its suffering. When he went fishing, he would toss back the small fish. He told a family he befriended how bad it was to permit children to watch violence on television. He bought eyeglasses for a child whose vision needed correction, and bought a family a refrigerator and stove.

"He was a very nice man," said one person who got to know him, and whose children called him "Uncle Tom." "He treated us like family. He was kind. He really had a nice personality. How could you not love him?" (Murphy, 1998, p. A8).

But to criminal investigators at the FBI, he was not so lovable. They said he was a mobster who had run a crime empire that included drug sales and gambling. He was a reputed murderer and bank robber, a man who had held a knife to a banker's throat while extorting $50,000. To the FBI, his pleasant personality was just a front, motivated only by self-interest.

Looking Ahead

Was "Tom" a soft-hearted do-gooder, or, as the FBI contends, a ruthless, greedy mobster, willing to do anything to get ahead?

Many people, like "Tom," have different sides to their personalities, appearing one way to some people and quite differently to others. At the same time, you probably know people whose behavior is so consistent that you can easily predict how they are going to behave, no matter what the situation.

Psychologists who specialize in personality seek to understand the characteristic ways in which people behave. **Personality** is the pattern of enduring characteristics that differentiates a person—those patterns of behaviors that make each of us unique. It is also personality that leads us to act consistently and predictably in different situations and over extended periods of time.

In this chapter we consider a number of approaches to personality. We begin with the broadest and most comprehensive theory: Freud's psychoanalytic theory. Next, we turn to more recent theories of personality. We consider approaches that concentrate on identifying the most fundamental personality traits; on theories that view personality as a set of learned behaviors; on biological and evolutionary perspectives on personality; and on approaches, known as humanistic theories, that highlight the uniquely human aspects of personality. We end our discussion by focusing on how personality is measured and how personality tests can be used.

personality: The pattern of enduring characteristics that differentiates a person—the patterns of behaviors that make each individual unique

Prepare

How do psychologists define and use the concept of personality?

What do the theories of Freud and his successors tell us about the structure and development of personality?

Organize

Psychoanalytic Approaches to Personality

Freud's Psychoanalytic Theory

The Neo-Freudian Psychoanalysts

Psychoanalytic Approaches to Personality

The college student was intent on making a good first impression on an attractive woman he had spotted across a crowded room at a party. As he walked toward her, he mulled over a line he had heard in an old movie the night before: "I don't believe we've been properly introduced yet." To his horror, what came out was a bit different. After threading his way through the crowded room, he finally reached the woman and blurted out, "I don't believe we've been properly seduced yet."

Although this student's error might seem to be merely an embarrassing slip of the tongue, according to one group of personality theorists—*psychoanalysts*—such a mistake is not an error at all (Motley, 1987). Instead, it illustrates one way our behavior is triggered by forces within personality of which we are not aware. These hidden drives, shaped by childhood experiences, play an important role in energizing and directing our everyday behavior.

Freud's Psychoanalytic Theory

psychoanalytic theory: Freud's theory that unconscious forces act as determinants of personality

unconscious: A part of the personality of which a person is not aware, and which is a potential determinant of behavior

Sigmund Freud, an Austrian physician, originated **psychoanalytic theory** in the early 1900s. Freud believed that conscious experience was just the tip of our psychological makeup and experience. In fact, he thought that much of our behavior is motivated by the **unconscious,** a part of the personality of which a person is not aware.

Like the unseen mass of a floating iceberg, the material in the unconscious far surpasses in quantity the information we are aware of. Freud argued that to understand personality, it is necessary to expose what is in the unconscious. But because the unconscious disguises the meaning of the material it holds, the content of the unconscious cannot be observed directly. It is therefore necessary to interpret clues to the unconscious—slips of the tongue, fantasies, and dreams—in order to understand the unconscious processes that direct behavior. A slip of the tongue such as the one quoted earlier (sometimes termed a *Freudian slip*) might be interpreted as revealing the speaker's unconscious sexual desires.

To Freud, much of our personality is determined by our unconscious. Some of the unconscious is made up of the *preconscious,* which contains material that is not threatening and is easily brought to mind, such as the knowledge that $2 + 2 = 4$. But deeper in the unconscious are instinctual drives, the wishes, desires, demands, and needs that are hidden from conscious awareness because of the conflicts and pain they would cause us if they were part of our everyday lives. The unconscious provides a "safe haven" for our recollections of threatening events.

Structuring Personality: Id, Ego, and Superego

To describe the structure of personality, Freud developed a comprehensive theory, which held that personality consists of three separate but interacting components: the id, the ego, and the superego. Freud suggested that the three structures can be diagrammed to show how they are related to the conscious and the unconscious (see Figure 10-1).

Although it might appear that Freud is describing the three components of personality as actual physical structures in the nervous system, they are not. Instead, they represent abstract conceptions of a general *model* of personality that describes the interaction of forces that motivate behavior.

If personality consisted only of primitive, instinctual cravings and longings, it would have just one component: the id. The **id** is the raw, unorganized, inborn part of personality. From the time of birth, the id attempts to reduce tension created by primitive drives related to hunger, sex, aggression, and irrational impulses. These drives are fueled by "psychic energy," or *libido* as Freud called it.

The id operates according to the *pleasure principle,* in which the goal is the immediate reduction of tension and the maximization of satisfaction. However, reality prevents the fulfillment of the demands of the pleasure principle in most cases: We cannot always eat when we are hungry, and we can discharge our sexual drives only when time, place—and partner—are willing. To account for this fact of life, Freud suggested a second component of personality, which he called the ego.

The **ego** strives to balance the desires of the id and the realities of the objective, outside world. In contrast to the pleasure-seeking nature of the id, the ego operates according to the *reality principle,* in which instinctual energy is restrained in order to maintain the safety of the individual and help integrate the person into society. In a sense, then, the ego is the "executive" of personality: It makes decisions, controls actions, and allows thinking and problem solving of a higher order than the id's capabilities permit.

The **superego,** the final personality structure to develop, represents social right and wrong as taught and modeled by a person's parents, teachers, and other significant individuals. The superego has two components, the *conscience* and the *ego-ideal.* The conscience prevents us from behaving in a morally improper way by making us feel guilty if we do wrong, and the ego-ideal, which represents the "perfect person" that we wish we were, motivates us to do what is morally right. The superego helps us control impulses coming from the id, making our behavior less selfish and more virtuous.

The superego and id share an important feature: Both are unrealistic, in that they do not consider the practical realities imposed by society. The superego, if left to operate without restraint, would create perfectionists, unable to make the compromises that life requires. Similarly, an unrestrained id would create a primitive, pleasure-seeking, thoughtless individual, seeking to fulfill every desire without delay. As a result, the ego must compromise between the demands of the superego and the demands of the id.

Developing Personality: A Stage Approach

Freud also provided us with a view of how personality develops in childhood through a series of stages. The sequence he proposed is noteworthy because it explains how experiences and difficulties during a particular childhood stage might predict specific characteristics in adult personality. The theory is also unique in focusing each stage on the major biological function that Freud assumed to be the focus of pleasure in that stage (see Table 10-1).

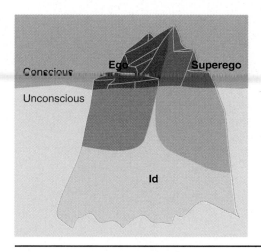

Figure 10-1 In Freud's model of personality, there are three major components: the id, the ego, and the superego. As the iceberg analogy shows, only a small portion of personality is conscious. Why do you think that only the ego and superego have conscious components?

id: The raw, unorganized, inborn part of personality, whose sole purpose is to reduce tension created by primitive drives related to hunger, sex, aggression, and irrational impulses

ego: The part of the personality that provides a buffer between the id and the outside world

superego: According to Freud, the final personality structure to develop; it represents society's standards of right and wrong as handed down by a person's parents, teachers, and other important figures

PsychLink
Freud's works
www.mhhe.com/
feldmaness5-10links

Table 10-1 Freud's Stages of Personality Development

Stage	Age	Major Characteristics
Oral	Birth to 12–18 months	Interest in oral gratification from sucking, eating, mouthing, biting
Anal	12–18 months to 3 years	Gratification from expelling and withholding feces; coming to terms with society's controls relating to toilet training
Phallic	3 to 5–6 years	Interest in the genitals; coming to terms with Oedipal conflict, leading to identification with same-sex parent
Latency	5–6 years to adolescence	Sexual concerns largely unimportant
Genital	Adolescence to adulthood	Reemergence of sexual interests and establishment of mature sexual relationships

oral stage: According to Freud, a stage from birth to 12 to 18 months, in which an infant's center of pleasure is the mouth

fixation: Conflicts or concerns that persist beyond the developmental period in which they first occur

anal stage: According to Freud, a stage from 12 to 18 months to 3 years of age, in which a child's pleasure is centered on the anus

phallic stage: According to Freud, a period beginning around age 3 during which a child's interest focuses on the genitals

Oedipus conflict: A child's sexual interest in his or her opposite-sex parent, typically resolved through identification with the same-sex parent

identification: The process of trying to be like another person as much as possible, imitating that person's behavior and adopting similar beliefs and values

In the first stage of development, called the **oral stage,** the baby's mouth is the focal point of pleasure. During the first 12 to 18 months of life, children suck, mouth, and bite anything that will fit into their mouths. To Freud, this behavior suggested that the mouth is the primary site of a kind of sexual pleasure. Infants who are either overly indulged (perhaps by being fed every time they cried) or frustrated in their search for oral gratification might become fixated at this stage. **Fixation** refers to conflicts or concerns that persist beyond the developmental period in which they first occur. Such conflicts can be due to one's needs being either ignored or overly indulged during the earlier period. For example, fixation might occur if an infant's oral needs were constantly immediately gratified at the first sign of hunger. Fixation at the oral stage might produce an adult who is unusually interested in oral activities—eating, talking, smoking—or who shows symbolic sorts of oral interests: being either "bitingly" sarcastic or very gullible ("swallowing" anything).

From around 12 to 18 months until 3 years of age—where the emphasis in Western cultures is on toilet training—the child enters the **anal stage.** At this point, the major source of pleasure changes from the mouth to the anal region, and children obtain considerable pleasure from both retention and expulsion of feces. If toilet training is particularly demanding, the result may be fixation. Freud suggested that adults who are fixated in the anal stage might show unusual rigidity, orderliness, punctuality—or extreme disorderliness or sloppiness.

At about age 3, the **phallic stage** begins, at which point there is another major shift in the primary source of pleasure for the child. This time, interest focuses on the genitals and the pleasures derived from fondling them. This is also the stage of one of the most important points of personality development, according to Freudian theory: the **Oedipus conflict.** As children focus their attention on their genitals, the differences between female and male anatomy become more salient. Furthermore, at this time, according to Freud, the male unconsciously begins to develop sexual interests in his mother, starts to see his father as a rival, and harbors a wish to kill his father—as Oedipus did in the ancient Greek tragedy. But because he views his father as too powerful, he develops a fear of retaliation in the form of "castration anxiety." Ultimately, this fear becomes so powerful that the child represses his desires for his mother and instead identifies with his father. **Identification** is the process of trying to be like another person as much as possible, imitating that person's behavior and adopting similar beliefs and values. By identifying with his father, a son seeks to obtain a woman like his unattainable mother.

For girls, the process is different. Freud reasoned that girls begin to experience sexual arousal toward their fathers and—in a suggestion that was later to bring serious accusations that he viewed women as inferior to men—that they begin to experience *penis envy:* they wish, said Freud, that they had an anatomical part that, at least to Freud, seems "missing" in girls. Blaming their mothers for their lack of a penis, girls come to believe that their mothers are responsible for their "castration." As with males, though, they find that in order to resolve such unacceptable feelings, they must identify with the same-sex parent by behaving like her and adopting her attitudes and values. In this way, a girl's identification with her mother is completed.

At this point, the Oedipus conflict is said to be resolved, and Freudian theory assumes that both males and females move on to the next stage of development. If difficulties arise during this period, however, all sorts of problems are thought to occur, including improper sex-role behavior and the failure to develop a conscience.

Imitating a person's behavior and adopting similar beliefs and values is part of Freud's concept of identification. How can this concept be applied to the definition of gender roles? Is identification similar in all cultures?

Following the resolution of the Oedipus conflict, typically at around age 5 or 6, children move into the **latency period,** which lasts until puberty. During this period, sexual interests become dormant, even in the unconscious. Then, during adolescence, sexual feelings reemerge, marking the start of the final period, the **genital stage,** which extends until death. The focus during the genital stage is on mature, adult sexuality, which Freud defined as sexual intercourse.

latency period: According to Freud, the period between the phallic stage and puberty during which children temporarily put aside their sexual interests

genital stage: According to Freud, the period from puberty until death, marked by mature sexual behavior (i.e., sexual intercourse)

Defense Mechanisms

Freud's efforts to describe and theorize about the underlying dynamics of personality and its development were motivated by very practical problems that his patients faced in dealing with *anxiety,* an intense, negative emotional experience. According to Freud, anxiety is a danger signal to the ego. Although anxiety can arise from realistic fears—such as seeing a poisonous snake about to strike—it can also occur in the form of *neurotic anxiety,* in which irrational impulses emanating from the id threaten to burst through and become uncontrollable.

Because anxiety, obviously, is unpleasant, Freud believed that people develop a range of defense mechanisms to deal with it. **Defense mechanisms** are unconscious strategies people use to reduce anxiety by concealing its source from themselves and others.

defense mechanisms: Unconscious strategies people use to reduce anxiety by concealing the source of the anxiety from themselves and others

The primary defense mechanism is *repression,* in which unacceptable or unpleasant id impulses are pushed back into the unconscious. Repression is the most direct method of dealing with anxiety; instead of handling an anxiety-producing impulse on a conscious level, one simply ignores it. For example, a college student who feels hatred for her mother might repress these personally and socially unacceptable feelings. The feelings remain lodged within the unconscious, because acknowledging them would provoke anxiety. Similarly, memories of childhood abuse can be repressed (discussed in Chapter 6). Although such memories might not be consciously recalled, they can affect later behavior, and they can be revealed through dreams, slips of the tongue, or symbolically in some other fashion.

If repression is ineffective in keeping anxiety at bay, other defense mechanisms might be used. Freud, and later his daughter Anna Freud (who became a well-known psychoanalyst herself), formulated an extensive list of potential defense mechanisms; the major ones are summarized in Table 10-2 (Cooper, 1989; Conte & Plutchik, 1995; Basch, 1996).

All of us employ defense mechanisms to some degree, according to Freudian theory, and they can serve a useful purpose by protecting us from unpleasant information. Yet some people use them to such an extent that they must constantly direct a large amount of psychic energy toward hiding and rechanneling unacceptable impulses. This makes everyday living difficult. The result is a mental disorder produced by

Table 10-2 Freud's Defense Mechanisms

Defense Mechanism	Explanation	Example
Repression	Unacceptable or unpleasant impulses are pushed back into the unconscious.	A woman is unable to recall that she was raped.
Regression	People behave as if they were at an earlier stage of development.	A boss has a temper tantrum when an employee makes a mistake.
Displacement	The expression of an unwanted feeling or thought is redirected from a more threatening, powerful person to a weaker one.	A brother yells at his younger sister after a teacher gives him a bad grade.
Rationalization	People distort reality in order to justify something that has happened.	A person who is passed over for an award says she didn't really want it in the first place.
Denial	People refuse to accept or acknowledge an anxiety-producing piece of information.	A student refuses to believe that he has flunked a course.
Projection	People attribute unwanted impulses and feelings to someone else.	A man who is angry at his father acts lovingly to his father but complains that his father is angry with him.
Sublimation	People divert unwanted impulses into socially approved thoughts, feelings, or behaviors.	A person with strong feelings of aggression becomes a soldier.
Reaction formation	Unconscious impulses are expressed as their opposite in consciousness.	A mother who unconsciously resents her child acts in an overly loving way to the child.

anxiety—what Freud called "neurosis" (a term rarely used by psychologists today, although it endures in everyday conversation).

Evaluating Freud's Legacy

PsychLink

Questioning Freud's theories
www.mhhe.com/
feldmaness5-10links

Freud's theory has had a significant impact on the field of psychology—and even more broadly on Western philosophy and literature. The ideas of the unconscious, defense mechanisms, and childhood roots of adult psychological difficulties have become accepted by many. Furthermore, Freud's emphasis on the unconscious has been partially supported by current research on dreams (Chapter 4) and implicit memory (Chapter 6), and it has generated an important method of treating psychological disturbances, as we will discuss in Chapter 13 (Westen, 1998; Westen & Gabbard, 1999; Kihlstrom, 1999).

On the other hand, personality psychologists have leveled significant criticisms against the theory. Among the most compelling is the lack of scientific data to support the theory. Although individual case studies *seem* supportive, we lack conclusive evidence showing that the personality is structured and operates along the lines Freud laid out. This is partly due to the fact that Freud's conception of personality is built on unobservable abstract concepts. Moreover, it is difficult to predict how certain developmental difficulties will be displayed in the adult. For instance, a person who is fixated at the anal stage might, according to Freud, be unusually messy—or unusually neat. Freud's theory offers us no way to predict which way the difficulty will be exhibited (Macmillan, 1991; Crews, 1996).

Finally, Freud made his observations—admittedly insightful ones—and derived his theory from a limited population. His theory was based almost entirely on upper-class

Othei
Perso
Huma

"Tell me ;
"OI
his way tc
tempered,
only thing
He seems
"He
Johnetta. "
wonder wt

Friendly. .
The inter(
being discussed
others' behavioi
sistent across di
is outgoing and
tions (Gilbert et
A number
turn now to a di
vides an alternai
mining behavior

Trait Approact

If someone were
two people in th
individual's persc
qualities are mos
Personality
they have develo
dimensions of pei
assume that some
ple possess certai
that can be quanti
For instance, you
We both have a "f
than mine. The m
tify the specific p
ent theorists have

Allport's Trait Th

When personality
dictionary, he can
personality. Althoi
eliminating words
crucial to all trait
Allport answ
of traits: cardinal,
single characterist

Austrian women living in the strict, puritanical era of the early 1900s. How far one can generalize beyond this population is a matter of considerable debate. For instance, in some Pacific Island societies, the role of disciplinarian is played by a mother's oldest brother, not the father. In such a culture, it is unreasonable to argue that the Oedipus conflict would progress in the same way as in Freud's Austrian society, where the father typically was the major disciplinarian. In short, a cross-cultural perspective raises questions about the universality of Freud's view of personality development (Doi, 1990; Brislin, 1993; Altman, 1996).

The Neo-Freudian Psychoanalysts

One important outgrowth of Freud's theorizing was the work done by a series of successors who were trained in traditional Freudian theory but who later rejected some of its major points. These theorists are known as **neo-Freudian psychoanalysts.**

The neo-Freudians placed greater emphasis than Freud on the functions of the ego, suggesting that it had more control than the id over day-to-day activities, and less emphasis on sex as a driving force in people's lives. They also paid greater attention to social factors and the effects of society and culture on personality development.

Jung's Collective Unconscious

One of the most influential neo-Freudians, Carl Jung (pronounced "Yoong"), rejected the notion of the primary importance of unconscious sexual urges. Instead he looked at the primitive urges of the unconscious more positively, suggesting that people had a **collective unconscious,** a set of influences we inherit from our own relatives, the whole human race, and even nonhuman animal ancestors from the distant past. According to Jung, this collective unconscious is shared by everyone and is displayed in behavior that is common across diverse cultures—such as love of mother, belief in a supreme being, and even behavior as specific as fear of snakes.

Jung went on to propose that the collective unconscious contains *archetypes,* universal symbolic representations of a particular person, object, or experience (Jung, 1961). For instance, a mother archetype, which contains reflections of our ancestors' relationships with mother figures, is suggested by the prevalence of mothers in art, religion, literature, and mythology. (Think of the Virgin Mary, Earth Mother, wicked stepmothers of fairy tales, Mother's Day, and so forth!) Jung also suggested that men possess an unconscious feminine archetype affecting how they behave, and that women have a male archetype that colors their behavior.

To Jung, archetypes play an important role in determining our day-to-day reactions, attitudes, and values. For instance, Jung might argue that the popularity of the *Star Wars* movies is due to their use of broad archetypes of good (such as Luke Skywalker) and evil (such as Darth Vader).

Adler and the Other Neo-Freudians

Alfred Adler, another important neo-Freudian psychoanalyst, also considered Freudian theory's emphasis on sexual needs to be misplaced. Adler proposed instead that the primary human motivation is a striving for superiority, not in terms of superiority over others, but as a quest to achieve self-improvement and perfection.

According to Adler, when adults have not been able to overcome the feelings of inferiority that they developed as children, when they were small and limited in their knowledge about the world, they develop an **inferiority complex.** Early social relationships with parents have an important effect on how well

---

neo-Freudian psychoanalysts: Psychoanalysts who were trained in traditional Freudian theory but who later rejected some of its major points
collective unconscious: A set of influences we inherit from our own particular ancestors, the whole human race, and even animal ancestors from the distant evolutionary past
inferiority complex: According to Adler, a complex developed by adults who have not been able to overcome the feelings of inferiority they developed as children, when they were small and limited in their knowledge about the world

PsychLink
Jung's theory
www.mhhe.com/
feldmaness5-10links

In Jungian terms, Darth Vader and Luke Skywalker are archetypes, or universally recognizable symbols of good and evil.

Looking Back

Evaluate

1. Psychoa
forces.

2. Match each s
   1. Ego   b

   2. Id   C

   3. Superego

3. Within the su

4. Which of the
   Freud?
   a. Oral, phallic
   b. Anal, oral, p
   c. Oral, anal, p
   d. Latency, pha

5. In the resoluti
   repress their d
   6. Defense Me
   reduce anxiety

Answers to Evaluate Ques

How do psychologists define and use the concept of personality?

- Personality is the pattern of enduring characteristics that differentiates a person—those patterns of behaviors that makes each person unique. (p. 328)

What do the theories of Freud and his successors tell us about the structure and development of personality?

- According to psychoanalysts, much behavior is caused by unconscious parts of personality that we are unaware of. (p. 328)
- According to Freud's theory, personality is composed of the id, the ego, and the superego. The id is the unorganized, inborn part of personality whose purpose is to immediately reduce tensions relating to hunger, sex, aggression, and other primitive impulses. The ego restrains instinctual energy in order to maintain the safety of the individual and to help the person to be a member of society. The superego represents social right and wrong and consists of the conscience and the ego-ideal. (p. 329)
- Freud's psychoanalytic theory says that personality develops through a series of stages, each of which is associated with a primary biological function. (p. 330)
- Defense mechanisms are unconscious strategies to reduce anxiety for dealing with anxiety related to impulses from the id. (p. 331)
- Freud's psychoanalytic theory has provoked a number of criticisms, especially focusing on its lack of supportive scientific data, the theory's inadequacy in making predictions, and its reliance on a highly restricted population. (p. 332)
- Neo-Freudian psychoanalytic theorists built on Freud's work, although they placed greater emphasis on the role of the ego and paid greater attention to social factors in determining behavior. (p. 333)

What are the major aspects of trait, learning, biological and evolutionary, and humanistic approaches to personality?

- Trait approaches have tried to identify the most basic and relatively enduring dimensions along which people differ from one another—dimensions known as traits. (p. 335)
- Learning approaches to personality concentrate on observable behavior. To the strict learning theorist, personality is the sum of learned responses to the external environment. (p. 338)
- Social cognitive approaches concentrate on the role of cognitions in determining personality and pay particular attention to how self-efficacy determines behavior. (p. 338)
- Biological and evolutionary approaches to personality focus on the inheritance of personality characteristics. (p. 340)
- Humanistic approaches assume that people are basically good. They consider the core of personality in terms of a person's ability to change and improve. (p. 342)
- The major personality approaches differ substantially from one another, which could reflect both their focus on different aspects of personality and the overall complexity of personality. (p. 344)

How can we most accurately assess personality?

- Psychological tests such as the MMPI are standard assessment tools that are intended to objectively measure behavior. They must be reliable, measuring what they are trying to measure consistently, and valid, measuring what they are supposed to measure. (p. 345)

What are the major types of personality measures?

- Self-report measures ask people about a sample range of their behaviors. These reports are used to infer the presence of particular personality characteristics. (p. 347)
- Projective personality tests (such as the Rorschach and Thematic Apperception Test) present an ambiguous stimulus; the observer's responses are then used to infer information about the observer. (p. 348)
- Behavioral assessment is based on the principles of learning theory. It employs direct measurement of an individual's behavior to determine characteristics related to personality. (p. 349)

Key Terms and Concepts

personality (p. 328)
psychoanalytic theory (p. 328)
unconscious (p. 328)
id (p. 329)
ego (p. 329)
superego (p. 329)
oral stage (p. 330)
fixation (p. 330)
anal stage (p. 330)
phallic stage (p. 330)
Oedipus conflict (p. 330)
identification (p. 330)
latency period (p. 331)
genital stage (p. 331)
defense mechanisms (p. 331)
neo-Freudian psychoanalysts (p. 333)
collective unconscious (p. 333)
inferiority complex (p. 333)
trait theory (p. 335)

traits (p. 335)
social cognitive approaches to personality (p. 338)
biological and evolutionary approaches to personality (p. 340)
temperament (p. 340)
humanistic approaches to personality (p. 343)
unconditional positive regard (p. 343)
self-actualization (p. 343)
psychological tests (p. 346)
self-report measures (p. 347)
Minnesota Multiphasic Personality Inventory-2 (MMPI-2) (p. 347)
test standardization (p. 347)
projective personality test (p. 348)
Rorschach test (p. 348)
Thematic Apperception Test (TAT) (p. 348)
behavioral assessment (p. 349)

Psychology on the Web

1. Sigmund Freud is one of the towering figures of psychology, with an influence far beyond his psychoanalytic work. Find further information on the Web about Freud. Pick one aspect of his work or influence (e.g., on therapy, medicine, literature, film, culture and society, etc.) and summarize in writing what you have found, including your attitude toward your findings.
2. Find a website that links to personality tests and take one or two tests—remembering to take them with skepticism. For each test, summarize in writing the aspects of personality that were tested, the theoretical approach that the test appeared to be based on, and your assessment of the trustworthiness of the information you received.

Epilogue

In this chapter, we have discussed the different ways in which psychologists have interpreted the development and structure of personality. The perspectives we've examined range from Freud's analysis of personality, based primarily on internal, unconscious factors, to the externally based view of personality as a learned set of traits and actions that is championed by the learning theorists. We have also noted that there are many ways to interpret personality, and that there is no consensus on what are the key traits central to personality.

Before proceeding to the topic of health psychology in the next chapter, return to the prologue of this chapter and consider the case of "Tom," who was—depending on your perspective—either awfully nice or just awful. Use your understanding of personality to consider the following questions.

1. How might a psychoanalytic approach to personality, using the concepts of id, ego, and superego, apply to the apparent two sides to "Tom"?
2. What sort of profile do you think Tom would have displayed if he had been tested in terms of Cattell's sixteen source traits? Where would he fall on Eysenck's major personality dimensions?
3. Would a personality profile of Tom administered during the time he was involved in mob activities have been different from one administered when he was visiting in Grand Isle? Why?
4. How would an advocate of a social cognitive approach to personality interpret and explain Tom's seemingly contradictory behavior? How might the concepts of observational learning and self-efficacy apply to a case like Tom's?

Chapter Eleven

Health Psychology:

Stress, Coping, and Well-Being

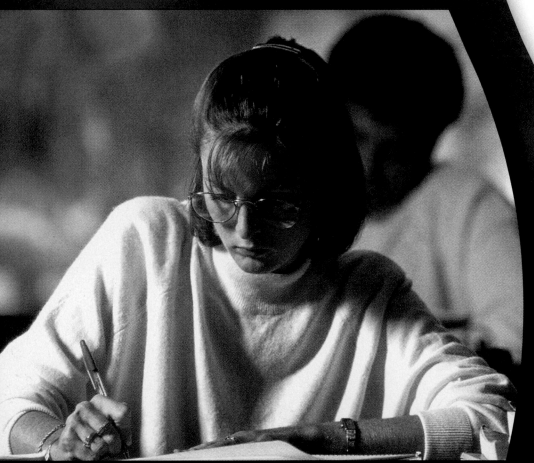

Prologue

So Much to Do, So Little Time to Do It

Feeling pressured by time and the responsibility of completing a large number of tasks can take both a physical and a psychological toll on one's well-being.

Susan Reiche, a public policy manager at AT&T in Basking Ridge, N.J., can handle what work throws at her from 9 to 5. It's what life throws at her between 5 and 9 that pushes her to the limit.

After she flips off her office computer, she hurries to a day care center to pick up her 4-year-old son and then rushes across town to fetch her 7-year-old daughter from an after-school program. She makes a quick trip to the store to buy food for dinner, then zips home, where she lets the dog out, makes dinner, referees a fight or two between the children, feeds the dog, says hello to her husband, gives her son a bath, helps her daughter with her spelling words, tosses a load of laundry into the washing machine, plays with her children, reads with them and puts them to bed.

Finally, about 9 P.M., she has a minute to sit down. Whew. (Kelly, 1999, p. 18)

Looking Ahead

It's not hard to guess what Susan Reiche was experiencing in the four hours from 5:00 P.M. to 9:00 P.M.: stress. For people like her—and that probably includes most of us—the intensity of juggling multiple roles leads to feelings of never having sufficient time, and, in some cases, takes a toll on both physical and psychological well-being.

Stress, and ways of coping with it, have long been central topics of interest to psychologists. However, in recent years the focus has broadened as psychology has come to view stress in the broader context of a new subfield known as health psychology. **Health psychology** investigates the psychological factors related to wellness and illness, including the prevention, diagnosis, and treatment of medical problems. Health psychologists investigate how illness is influenced by psychological factors such as stress. They examine the psychological principles underlying treatments for disease and illness. They are also concerned with issues of prevention: how health problems such as heart disease and stress can be avoided by more healthful behavior.

Health psychologists take a decisive stand on the enduring mind/body issue that philosophers have debated since the time of the ancient Greeks (a debate that psychologists later joined in on and that we first considered in Chapter 1). In their view, the mind and body are clearly linked, and are not two distinct systems (Sternberg, 2000).

Health psychologists recognize that good health and the ability to cope with illness are affected by psychological factors such as thoughts, emotions, and the ability to manage stress. They have paid particular attention to the *immune system,* the complex of organs, glands, and cells that constitute our body's natural line of defense in fighting disease.

In fact, health psychologists are among the primary investigators in a growing field called (somewhat awkwardly) psychoneuroimmunology. **Psychoneuroimmunology (PNI)** is the study of the relationships among psychological factors, the immune system, and the brain. PNI has led to discoveries such as the existence of an association between one's emotional state and the success of the immune system in fighting disease (Baum, Revenson, & Singer, 2000).

In sum, health psychologists view the mind and the body as two parts of a whole human being that cannot be considered independently. This more recent view marks a sharp departure from earlier thinking. Previously, disease was seen as a purely biological phenomenon, and psychological factors were of little interest to most health care workers. In the early twentieth century, the primary causes of death were short-term infections, from which one either rapidly recovered or died. Now, however, the major causes of death, such as heart disease, cancer, and diabetes, are chronic illnesses that often cannot be cured and that can linger for years, posing significant psychological issues (Delahanty & Baum, 2000).

In this chapter we discuss how psychological factors affect health. We first focus on the causes and consequences of stress and ways of coping with it. Next, we explore the psychological aspects of several major health problems, including heart disease, cancer, and ailments resulting from smoking. Finally, we examine the ways in which patient-physician interactions influence our health, and offer suggestions for increasing people's compliance with behavior that will improve their well-being.

health psychology: The branch of psychology that investigates the psychological factors related to wellness and illness, including the prevention, diagnosis, and treatment of medical problems

psychoneuroimmunology (PNI): The study of the relationships among psychological factors, the immune system, and the brain

Prepare

How is health psychology a union between medicine and psychology?

What is stress, how does it affect us, and how can we best cope with it?

Organize

Stress and Coping
   Stress
   Coping with Stress

Stress and Coping

Tara Knox's day began badly: She slept through her alarm and had to skip breakfast in order to catch the bus to campus. Then, when she went to the library to catch up on the reading she had to do before taking a test the next day, the article she needed was missing. The librarian told her that replacing it would take 24 hours. Feeling exasperated, she walked to the computer lab to print out the paper she had completed the night before. However, she couldn't get the computer to read her disk. Although she searched for someone to help her, she was unable to find anyone who seemed to know any more than she did.

It was only 9:42 A.M., and all Tara could think about was how much stress she felt.

Stress: Reacting to Threat and Challenge

Most of us need little introduction to the phenomenon of **stress,** the response to events that threaten or challenge a person. Whether it be a paper or exam deadline, a family problem, or even a cumulative series of events such as those faced by Tara Knox, life is full of circumstances and events, known as *stressors,* that produce threats to our well-being. Even pleasant events—such as planning a party or beginning a sought-after job—can produce stress, although negative events result in greater detrimental consequences than positive ones.

All of us face stress in our lives. Some health psychologists believe that daily life actually involves a series of repeated sequences of perceiving a threat, considering ways to cope with it, and ultimately adapting to the threat, with greater or lesser success. Although adaptation is often minor and occurs without our awareness, adaptation requires major effort when stress is more severe or longer lasting. Ultimately, our attempts to overcome stress can produce biological and psychological responses that result in health problems.

The High Cost of Stress

Stress can take its toll in many ways, producing both biological and psychological consequences. Often the most immediate reaction to stress is biological. Exposure to stressors generates a rise in certain hormones secreted by the adrenal glands, an increase in heart rate and blood pressure, and changes in how well the skin conducts electrical impulses. On a short-term basis, these responses can be adaptive because they produce an "emergency reaction" in which the body prepares to defend itself through activation of the sympathetic nervous system (see Chapter 2). These responses can allow more effective coping with the stressful situation (Akil & Morano, 1996; McEwen, 1998).

However, continued exposure to stress results in a decline in the body's overall level of biological functioning due to the constant secretion of stress-related hormones. Over time, stressful reactions can promote deterioration of bodily tissues such as blood vessels and the heart. Ultimately, we become more susceptible to disease as our ability to fight off infection is lowered (Sapolsky, 1996; Shapiro, 1996; McCabe et al., 2000).

In fact, an entire class of physical problems, known as **psychophysiological disorders,** may result from stress. Once referred to as *psychosomatic disorders* (a term dropped because it implied that the disorders were somehow unreal), psychophysiological disorders are actual medical problems influenced by an interaction of psychological, emotional, and physical difficulties. Among the common psychophysiological disorders are headaches, backaches, indigestion, skin problems, and high blood pressure. Stress has even been linked to the common cold (S. Cohen, 1996; Rice, 2000).

On a psychological level, high levels of stress prevent people from adequately coping with life. Their view of the environment can become clouded (e.g., a minor criticism made by a friend is blown out of proportion). Moreover, at the greatest levels of stress, emotional responses can be so extreme that people are unable to act at all. People under a lot of stress also become less able to deal with new stressors. The ability to contend with future stress, then, declines as a result of past stress.

In short, stress affects us in multiple ways. It can increase the risk that we will become ill; it can directly produce illness; it can make us less able to recover from a disease; and it can reduce our ability to cope with future stress. (For a measure of stress in your life, complete the questionnaire in Table 11-1.)

The General Adaptation Syndrome Model: The Course of Stress

The effects of stress are illustrated in a model devised by Hans Selye (pronounced "SELL-yay"), a pioneering stress theorist (Selye, 1976, 1993). This model, the **general adaptation syndrome (GAS),** suggests that the same set of physiological reactions to stress occurs regardless of the particular cause of stress.

PsychLink

Stress management
www.mhhe.com/
feldmaness5-11links

stress: The response to events that are threatening or challenging

psychophysiological disorders: Medical problems influenced by an interaction of psychological, emotional, and physical difficulties

general adaptation syndrome (GAS): A theory developed by Selye that suggests that a person's response to stress consists of three stages: alarm and mobilization, resistance, and exhaustion

Table 11-1 How Stressful Is Your Life?

Test your level of stress by answering these questions, and adding the score from each box. Questions apply to the last month only. A key below will help you determine the extent of your stress.

1 How often have you been upset because of something that happened unexpectedly?

[ ] 0=never, 1=almost never, 2=sometimes, 3=fairly often, 4=very often

2 How often have you felt that you were unable to control the important things in your life?

[ ] 0=never, 1=almost never, 2=sometimes, 3=fairly often, 4=very often

3 How often have you felt nervous and "stressed"?

[ ] 0=never, 1=almost never, 2=sometimes, 3=fairly often, 4=very often

4 How often have you felt confident about your ability to handle your personal problems?

[ ] 4=never, 3=almost never, 2=sometimes, 1=fairly often, 0=very often

5 How often have you felt that things were going your way?

[ ] 4=never, 3=almost never, 2=sometimes, 1=fairly often, 0=very often

6 How often have you been able to control irritations in your life?

[ ] 4=never, 3=almost never, 2=sometimes, 1=fairly often, 0=very often

7 How often have you found that you could not cope with all the things that you had to do?

[ ] 0=never, 1=almost never, 2=sometimes, 3=fairly often, 4=very often

8 How often have you felt that you were on top of things?

[ ] 4=never, 3=almost never, 2=sometimes, 1=fairly often, 0=very often

9 How often have you been angered because of things that were outside your control?

[ ] 0=never, 1=almost never, 2=sometimes, 3=fairly often, 4=very often

10 How often have you felt difficulties were piling up so high that you could not overcome them?

[ ] 0=never, 1=almost never, 2=sometimes, 3=fairly often, 4=very often

How You Measure Up:

Stress levels vary among individuals—compare your total score to the averages below:

AGE		GENDER	
18-29	14.2	Men	12.1
30-44	13.0	Women	13.7
45-54	12.6		
55-64	11.9		
65 & over	12.0		

MARITAL STATUS	
Widowed	12.6
Married or living with	12.4
Single or never wed	14.1
Divorced	14.7
Separated	16.6

Source: Cohen, 1999.

 PsychLink

General adaptation syndrome
www.mhhe.com/
feldmaness5-11links

The model has three phases. The first stage, the *alarm and mobilization stage,* occurs when people become aware of the presence of a stressor. On a biological level, the sympathetic nervous system (Chapter 2) becomes energized, helping to cope initially with the stressor.

However, if the stressor persists, people move into the next stage of the model. In the *resistance stage,* people prepare themselves to fight the stressor. During resistance, people use a variety of means to cope with the stressor—sometimes successfully—but at a cost of some degree of physical or psychological general well-being.

If resistance is inadequate, people enter the last stage of the model, the *exhaustion stage.* During the exhaustion stage, a person's ability to adapt to the stressor declines to the point where negative consequences of stress appear: physical illness, psychological symptoms in the form of an inability to concentrate, heightened irritability, or, in severe instances, disorientation and a loss of touch with reality. In a sense, people wear out, and their physical reserves are taxed to the limit.

How do people move out of the third stage after they have entered it? Exhaustion sometimes enables people to avoid the stressor. For example, people who become ill from overwork might be excused from their duties for a time, giving them a temporary respite from their responsibilities. At least for a time, then, the immediate stress is reduced.

The GAS model has had a substantial impact on our understanding of stress. By suggesting that the exhaustion of resources in the third stage of the model produces biological damage, it has provided a specific explanation of how stress can lead to illness. Furthermore, the model can be applied to both people and nonhuman species.

Contemporary health psychologists specializing in PNI (psychoneuroimmunology— the study of the relationships among psychological factors, the immune system, and the brain) have taken a broader approach than the GAS. Focusing on the outcomes of stress, they have identified three main consequences (see Figure 11-1). First, stress has direct physiological results, including an increase in blood pressure, increased hormonal activity, and an overall decline in the functioning of the immune system. Second, stress leads people to engage in behavior that is harmful to their health, including increased use of nicotine, drugs, and alcohol, poor eating habits, and decreased sleep. Finally, stress produces indirect consequences that result in declines in health: a reduction in the likelihood of obtaining health care and decreased compliance with medical advice when it is sought (Baum, 1994; McCabe et al., 2000).

The Nature of Stressors: My Stress Is Your Pleasure

As noted above, the general adaptation syndrome model is useful in explaining how people respond to stress, but it is not specific about what constitutes a stressor for a given person. Although certain kinds of events, such as the death of a loved one or participation in combat during a war, are universally stressful, other situations might or might not be stressful to a particular person (Fleming, Baum, & Singer, 1984; Pledge, 1992; Affleck et al., 1994; Krohne, 1996).

Consider, for instance, bungee jumping. Some of us would find jumping off a bridge attached to a slender rubber tether extremely stressful. However, there are those who see such an activity as challenging and fun-filled. Whether or not bungee jumping is stressful depends in part, then, on individual perceptions of the activity.

For people to consider an event to be stressful, they must perceive it as threatening and must lack the resources to deal with it effectively (Folkman et al., 1986). Consequently, the same event might at times be stressful and at other times provoke no stressful reaction at all. For instance, a young man might experience stress when he is turned down for a date—if he attributes the refusal to his unattractiveness or unworthiness. But if he attributes it to some factor unrelated to his self-esteem, such as a previous commitment by the person he asked, the experience of being refused might create no stress at all. Hence, our interpretation of events plays an important role in the determination of what is stressful.

The severity of stress is greatest when important goals are threatened, the threat is immediate, or the anticipation of a threatening event extends over a long period. For example, members of minority groups who feel they are potentially the targets of racist behavior experience significant stress (Clark et al., 1999).

PsychLink
Posttraumatic stress disorder
www.mhhe.com/
feldmaness5-11links

Figure 11-1 Three major types of consequences result from stress: direct physiological effects, harmful behaviors, and indirect health-related behaviors.

Source: Adapted from Baum, 1994.

Hurricane Andrew, which devastated southern Florida in 1992, was a cataclysmic event that caused severe, though in most cases short-term, stress in thousands of people. Why is this type of stress generally less dangerous than many others?

cataclysmic events: Strong stressors that occur suddenly, affecting many people at once (e.g., natural disasters)

posttraumatic stress disorder (PTSD): A phenomenon in which victims of major catastrophes reexperience the original stress event and associated feelings in vivid flashbacks or dreams

personal stressors: Major life events, such as the death of a family member, that have immediate negative consequences that usually fade with time

background stressors: Everyday annoyances, such as being stuck in traffic, that cause minor irritations that can have long-term ill effects if they continue or are compounded by other stressful events

Categorizing Stressors

What kinds of events tend to be seen as stressful? There are three general classes of such events: cataclysmic events, personal stressors, and background stressors.

Cataclysmic events are strong stressors that occur suddenly and typically affect many people simultaneously. Disasters such as tornadoes and plane crashes are examples of cataclysmic events that can affect hundreds or thousands of people simultaneously.

Although it might seem that cataclysmic events would produce potent, lingering stress, this is not always true. In fact, cataclysmic events sometimes produce less stress in the long run than events that initially are not as devastating. One reason is that cataclysmic events have a clear resolution. Once they are over and done with, people can look to the future knowing that the worst is behind them. Moreover, the stress induced by cataclysmic events is shared by others who have also experienced the disaster. This permits people to offer one another social support and a firsthand understanding of the difficulties they are all going through (Kaniasty & Norris, 1995; Hobfoll et al., 1996).

On the other hand, some victims of major catastrophes experience **posttraumatic stress disorder** or **PTSD,** in which the original events and the feelings associated with them are reexperienced in vivid flashbacks or dreams. Depending upon what statistics one accepts, between 5 and 60 percent of the veterans of the Vietnam War suffer from PTSD. Even the Persian Gulf War, which ended quickly, produced some cases of PTSD. People who have suffered child abuse or rape, rescue workers facing overwhelming situations, and victims of any sudden natural disaster or accident that produces feelings of helplessness and terror might suffer from the same disorder (Saigh, 1996; Friedman & Marsella, 1996; Ward, 1997; Davidson, 2000; Woods, 2000).

Symptoms of posttraumatic stress disorder include reexperiencing the event, emotional numbing, sleep difficulties, problems relating to others, alcohol and drug abuse, and—in some cases—suicide. For instance, the suicide rate for Vietnam veterans is as much as 25 percent higher than for the general population (Peterson, Prout, & Schwarz, 1991; Wilson & Keane, 1996; Mazza, 2000). (See the *Psychology at Work* box.)

The second major category of stressor is the personal stressor. **Personal stressors** include major life events such as the death of a parent or spouse, the loss of one's job, a major personal failure, or a diagnosis of a life-threatening illness. Typically, personal stressors produce an immediate major reaction that soon tapers off. For example, stress arising from the death of a loved one tends to be greatest just after the time of death, but people begin to feel less stress and are better able to cope with the loss after the passage of time.

In some cases, though, the effects of stress are lingering. Victims of rape sometimes suffer consequences long after the event, facing major difficulties in adjustment. Similarly, the malfunction of the Three Mile Island nuclear plant in Pennsylvania in the early 1980s, which exposed people to the stressor of a potential nuclear meltdown, produced emotional, behavioral, and physiological consequences that lasted more than a year and a half (Baum, Cohen, & Hall, 1993; Valentiner et al., 1996).

Standing in a long line at a bank and getting stuck in a traffic jam are examples of the third major category of stressor: **background stressors** or, more informally, *daily hassles.* These are the minor irritations of life that we all face time and time again: delays, noisy cars and trucks, broken appliances, other people's irritating behavior, and so on. Another type of background stressor is a long-term, chronic problem, such as experiencing dissatisfaction with school or job, being in an unhappy relationship, or living in crowded quarters without privacy (Lazarus & Cohen, 1977; van Eck, Nicolson, & Berkhof, 1998).

By themselves, daily hassles do not require much coping or even a response on the part of the individual, although they certainly do produce unpleasant emotions and moods.

Yet daily hassles add up—and ultimately they can produce as great a toll as a single, more stressful incident. In fact, the number of daily hassles that people face is associated with psychological symptoms and health problems such as flu, sore throat, and backaches (Chamberlain & Zika, 1990; Roberts, 1995).

The flip side of hassles are **uplifts,** those minor positive events that make one feel good—even if only temporarily. Uplifts range from relating well to a companion to finding one's surroundings pleasing. What is especially intriguing about uplifts is that they are associated with people's psychological health in just the opposite way that hassles are: The greater the number of uplifts experienced, the fewer the psychological symptoms people later report.

Everyone confronts daily hassles, or background stressors, at some point. At what point do daily hassles become more than mere irritants?

Learned Helplessness

Have you ever faced an intolerable situation that you just couldn't resolve, where you finally just gave up and accepted things the way they were? This example illustrates one of the possible consequences of being in an environment in which control over a situation is not possible—a state that produces learned helplessness. According to psychologist Martin Seligman, **learned helplessness** occurs when people conclude that unpleasant or aversive stimuli cannot be controlled—a view of the world that becomes so ingrained that they cease trying to remedy the aversive circumstances, even if they actually can exert some influence (Seligman, 1975; Peterson, Maier, & Seligman, 1993). Victims of the phenomenon of learned helplessness have decided that there is no link between the responses they make and the outcomes that occur.

Take, for example, what often happens to elderly persons when they are placed in nursing homes or hospitals. One of the most striking features of their new environment is that they are no longer independent: They do not have control over the most basic activities in their lives. They are told what and when to eat, and told when they may watch TV or participate in recreational activities. In addition, their sleeping schedules are arranged by someone else. It is not hard to see how this loss of control can have negative effects upon people suddenly placed, often reluctantly, in such a situation.

The results of this loss of control and the ensuing stress are frequently poorer health and even a likelihood of earlier death. These outcomes were confirmed in a classic experiment conducted in a nursing home where elderly residents in one group were encouraged to make more choices and take greater control of their day-to-day activities (Langer & Janis, 1979). As a result, members of the group were more active and happier than a comparison group of residents who were encouraged to let the nursing home staff take care of them. Moreover, an analysis of the residents' medical records revealed that six months after the experiment, the group encouraged to be self-sufficient showed significantly greater health improvement than the comparison group. Even more startling was an examination of the death rate: Eighteen months after the experiment began, only 15 percent of the "independent" group had died—compared with 30 percent of the comparison group.

Other research confirms that learned helplessness has negative consequences, and not just for elderly people. People of all ages report more physical symptoms and depression when they perceive that they have little or no control than when they feel a sense of control over a situation (Rodin, 1986; Joiner & Wagner, 1995; Shnek et al., 1995).

Coping with Stress

Stress is a normal part of life—and not necessarily a completely bad part. For example, without stress, we might not be sufficiently motivated to complete the activities we need to accomplish. However, it is also clear that too much stress can take its toll on both physical and psychological health. How do people deal with stress? Is there a way to reduce its negative effects?

uplifts: Minor positive events that make one feel good

learned helplessness: A state in which people conclude that unpleasant or aversive stimuli cannot be controlled—a view of the world that becomes so ingrained that they cease trying to remedy their aversive circumstances, even if they actually could exert some influence on them

Psychology at Work

Alan Benner

Police Psychologist

Education: B.A., psychology, San Francisco State University; M.A., organizational psychology, San Francisco State University; Ph.D., psychology, Saybrook Institute, San Francisco, California.

Home: Pacifica, California

Alan Benner

By its very nature, the job of a police officer involves high stress. But because of an innovative program developed by psychologist Alan Benner of the San Francisco Police Department, police officers in that city are better able to cope with stress and other psychological problems.

"In order to be a competent law enforcement officer, you often have to repress normal feelings, such as anger, fear, empathy, and revulsion. After a while the ability to do that becomes habitual and unconscious," says Benner, who has been a police officer for more than 34 years. "The problem is, though, that police officers begin to carry these repressed feelings into their personal lives, and that has negative consequences."

Benner's efforts to help police officers cope with the stress of the job begins with their initial training.

"The first thing we do is provide training at the police academy, where the focus is on getting people to understand their normal reactions to abnormal situations. You try to inoculate them against the traumas they encounter," Benner notes. "You also develop peer support teams and get officers used to talking to other officers."

> "In order to be a competent law enforcement officer, you often have to repress normal feelings, such as anger, fear, empathy, and revulsion."

This training is supported by a program, developed by Benner, called CIRT, or Critical Incident Response Team.

"CIRT is composed of four officers who can be reached by pager 24 hours a day. The officers are trained in post-trauma support, which is designed to help officers who may be involved in a traumatic incident such as a shooting or serious accident," Benner explains. "Psychologists and psychiatrists are used as additional resources."

According to Benner, the rationale for CIRT is that police officers are more likely to talk to a fellow officer than to someone outside of their ranks. The program has proven to be quite successful.

"Since 1993 Critical Incident Response Teams have conducted more than 200 separate debriefings involving more than 1,500 officers," says Benner. "Over time CIRT has changed the organizational climate of the job, making people more aware of the impact of their emotions on other aspects of their lives and better able to deal with them."

> "You also develop peer support teams and get officers used to talking to other officers."

---

coping: Efforts to control, reduce, or learn to tolerate the threats that lead to stress

defense mechanisms: Unconscious strategies people use to reduce anxiety by concealing its source from themselves and others

PsychLink

Coping with stress
www.mhhe.com/
feldmaness5-11links

The efforts to control, reduce, or learn to tolerate the threats that lead to stress are known as **coping.** We habitually use certain coping responses to help ourselves deal with stress. Most of the time, we're not aware of these responses—just as we might be unaware of the minor stressors of life until they build up to sufficiently aversive levels (Snyder, 1999).

One means of dealing with stress that occurs on an unconscious level is the use of defense mechanisms. As we discussed in Chapter 10, **defense mechanisms** are reactions that maintain a person's sense of control and self-worth by distorting or denying the actual nature of the situation. For example, one study examined California students who lived in dormitories close to a geological fault. Those who lived in dorms that were rated as being unlikely to withstand an earthquake were significantly more likely to doubt experts' predictions of an impending earthquake than were those who lived in safer structures (Lehman & Taylor, 1988).

Another defense mechanism used to cope with stress is *emotional insulation,* in which a person stops experiencing any emotions at all, thereby remaining unaffected and unmoved by both positive and negative experiences. The problem with defense mechanisms, of course, is that they do not deal with reality but merely hide the problem.

People also use other, more direct and potentially more positive means for coping with stress. Specifically, coping strategies fall into two categories: emotion-focused coping and problem-focused coping. In *emotion-focused coping,* people try to manage their emotions in the face of stress, seeking to change the way they feel about or perceive a problem. Examples of emotion-focused coping include such strategies as accepting sympathy from others or looking at the bright side of a situation. In contrast, *problem-focused coping* attempts to modify the stressful problem or source of the stress.

Problem-focused strategies lead to changes in behavior or to the development of a plan of action to deal with stress. Starting a study group to improve poor classroom performance is an example of problem-focused coping.

In most stressful incidents, people employ *both* emotion-focused and problem-focused strategies. However, they use emotion-focused strategies more frequently when they perceive circumstances as being unchangeable, and problem-focused approaches more often in situations they see as relatively modifiable (Lazarus, 1999; Stanton & Frantz, 1999; Folkman & Moskowitz, 2000).

Coping Style: The Hardy Personality

Most of us cope with stress in a characteristic manner, employing a *coping style* that represents our general tendency to deal with stress in a specific way. For example, you may know people who habitually react to even the smallest amount of stress with hysteria, and others who calmly confront even the greatest stress in an unflappable manner. These kinds of people clearly have quite different coping styles (Taylor, 1991; Taylor & Aspinwall, 1996).

Among those who cope with stress most successfully are people with the coping style of **hardiness**, a personality characteristic associated with a lower rate of stress-related illness. It consists of three components (Kobasa, 1979; Gentry & Kobasa, 1984):

hardiness: A personality characteristic associated with a lower rate of stress-related illness, consisting of three components: commitment, challenge, and control

- *Commitment.* Commitment is a tendency to throw ourselves into whatever we are doing with a sense that our activities are important and meaningful.
- *Challenge.* Hardy people believe that change, rather than stability, is the standard condition of life. To them, the anticipation of change is an incentive rather than a threat to their security.
- *Control.* Hardy people feel a sense of control—they believe that they can influence the events in their lives.

Hardy individuals approach stress optimistically and take direct action to learn about and deal with stressors, thereby changing stressful events into less threatening ones. As a consequence, hardiness acts as a defense against stress-related illness (Wiebe, 1991; Solcova & Tomanek, 1994; Kobasa et al., 1994).

Social Support: Turning to Others

Our relationships with others also help us cope with stress. Researchers have found that **social support,** the knowledge that we are part of a mutual network of caring, interested others, enables us to lower our levels of stress and to cope better with the stress we do undergo (Uchino, Uno, & Holt-Lunstad, 1999; McCabe et al., 2000).

social support: A mutual network of caring, interested others

The social and emotional support that people provide each other helps in dealing with stress in several ways. For instance, such support demonstrates that the person is an important and valued member of a social network, and other people can provide information and advice about appropriate ways of dealing with stress (Hobfoll et al., 1996; Lepore, Ragan, & Jones, 2000). People who are part of a social support network can also provide actual goods and services to help others in stressful situations: by supplying a person whose house has burned down with temporary living quarters, helping a student who is experiencing stress due to poor academic performance study for a test, and so on (Croyle & Hunt, 1991; Peirce et al., 1996).

Surprisingly, the benefits of social support are not limited to the comfort provided by other humans. One study found that owners of pets were less likely than those without pets to require medical care following exposure to stressors. Dogs, in particular, helped diminish the effects of stress (Siegel, 1990, 1993).

"Today, we examined our life style, we evaluated our diet and our exercise program, and we also assessed our behavioral patterns. Then we felt we needed a drink."

Effective Coping Strategies

What are the most effective ways to deal with stress? Researchers have made a number of recommendations for dealing with the problem. There is no universal solution, of course, because effective coping depends on the nature of the stressor and the degree to which it is possible to control it. Still, researchers have developed some general guidelines (Holahan & Moos, 1990; McCain & Smith, 1994; Zeidner & Endler, 1996; Aspinwall & Taylor, 1997):

- *Turn threat into challenge.* When a stressful situation might be controllable, the best coping strategy is to treat the situation as a challenge, focusing on ways to control it. For instance, if you experience stress because your car is always breaking down, you might take an evening course in auto mechanics and learn to deal directly with the car's problems.

- *Make a threatening situation less threatening.* When a stressful situation seems to be uncontrollable, a different approach must be taken. It is possible to change your appraisal of the situation, to view it in a different light, and to modify your attitudes toward it. The old truism "Look for the silver lining in every cloud" is supported by research (Silver & Wortman, 1980; Taylor & Aspinwall, 1996; Salovey et al., 2000).

- *Change your goals.* When faced with an uncontrollable situation, a reasonable strategy is to adopt new goals that are practical in view of the particular situation. For example, a dancer who has been in an automobile accident and has lost full use of her legs might abandon her aspiration to a career in dance, replacing it with the goal of becoming a dance instructor.

- *Take physical action.* Changing your physiological reaction to stress can help you cope. For example, biofeedback, discussed in Chapter 2, can alter your basic physiological processes, allowing you to reduce your blood pressure, heart rate, and other consequences of heightened stress. Exercise can also be effective in reducing stress. Regular exercise improves your overall health and can even reduce your risk for certain diseases, such as breast cancer. Finally, exercise can give you a sense of control over your body and a feeling of accomplishment (Thune et al., 1997; Barinaga, 1997; Langreth, 2000).

- *Prepare for stress before it happens.* A final strategy for coping with stress is *proactive coping:* anticipating and preparing for stress *before* you encounter it. Through proactive coping, you can ready yourself for upcoming stressful events and thereby reduce their negative consequences (Aspinwall & Taylor, 1997).

Evaluate

1. _____ is defined as a response to challenging or threatening events.
2. Match each portion of the GAS with its definition
   1. Alarm
   2. Exhaustion
   3. Resistance

   a. The ability to adapt to stress diminishes; symptoms appear
   b. Activation of the sympathetic nervous system
   c. Various strategies are used to cope with a stressor
3. Stressors that affect a single person and produce an immediate major reaction are known as
   a. Personal stressors
   b. Psychic stressors
   c. Cataclysmic stressors
   d. Daily stressors
4. People with the personality characteristic of _____ seem to be more able to successfully combat stressors.

Rethink

1. Why are cataclysmic stressors less stressful in the long run than other types of stressors? Does the reason relate to the coping phenomenon known as social support? How?

2. Given what you know about coping strategies, how would you train people to avoid stress in their everyday lives? How would you use this information with a group of Gulf War veterans suffering from posttraumatic stress disorder?

Answers to Evaluate Questions

1. Stress 2. 1-b; 2-a; 3-c 3. a 4. hardiness

Psychological Aspects of Illness and Well-Being

Once a week they meet to talk, to cry, sometimes to laugh together. "Is the pain still worse in the mornings?" Margaret asks Kate today.

A petite, graceful woman in her late forties, Kate shakes her head no. "It's getting bad all the time," she says in a voice raw with worry and fatigue. A few weeks ago she learned that the cancer that began in her breast had spread into her bones. Since then she's hardly slept. She knows, as do the other women in the group, that her prognosis isn't good. "Sometimes I'm afraid I'm not going to do that well because it all came on so fast," she tells them. "It's like being in the ocean and the waves are just coming too fast, and you can't get your breath."

They nod in tacit understanding, eight women sitting in a loose circle of chairs here in a small, sparely furnished room at Stanford University Medical Center. They know. All of them have been diagnosed with recurrent breast cancer. . . .

They gather here each Wednesday afternoon to talk with each other and to listen. It's a chance to discuss their fears and find some small comfort, a time to feel they're not alone. And in some way that no one has been able to explain, it may be keeping them alive. (Jaret, 1992, p. 87)

As recently as two decades ago, most psychologists and health-care providers would have scoffed at the notion that a discussion group could improve a cancer patient's chances of survival. Today, however, such methods have gained increasing respectability.

Growing evidence suggests that psychological factors have a substantial impact, both on major health problems that were once seen in purely physiological terms and on our everyday sense of health, well-being, and happiness. We'll consider the psychological components of three major health problems—heart disease, cancer, and smoking—and then consider the nature of people's well-being and happiness.

The A's and B's of Coronary Heart Disease

Have you ever seethed impatiently at being caught behind a slow-moving vehicle, felt anger and frustration at not finding material you needed at the library, or experienced a sense of competitiveness with almost all your classmates?

Many of us experience these sorts of feelings at one time or another, but for some people they represent a pervasive, characteristic set of personality traits (of the type discussed in Chapter 10) known as the **Type A behavior pattern.** Type A individuals are competitive, show a continual sense of urgency about time, are aggressive, exhibit a driven quality regarding their work, and are hostile, both verbally and nonverbally—especially when interrupted while trying to complete a task. On the other hand, people who show the **Type B behavior pattern** are more cooperative, far less competitive, not especially time-oriented, and not usually aggressive, driven, or hostile. Although people are typically not "pure" Type A's or Type B's, showing instead a combination of both behavior types, they generally do fall into one category or the other (Rosenman, 1990; Strube, 1990; see Table 11-2).

Type A people lead fast-paced, driven lives. They put in longer hours at work than Type B's and are impatient with other people's performance, which they typically perceive as too slow. They also engage in "multitasking," concentrating on several activities simultaneously, such as running on a treadmill while watching television and reading a magazine all at the same time.

The Type A behavior pattern is linked to coronary heart disease. Studies have found that men who display the Type A pattern develop coronary heart disease twice as often and suffer significantly more fatal heart attacks compared with those classified as having the Type B pattern. Moreover, the Type A pattern predicts who is going to develop heart disease at least as well as—and independently of—any other single factor, including age,

Prepare

How do psychological factors affect such health-related problems as coronary heart disease, cancer, and smoking?

Organize

Psychological Aspects of Illness and Well-Being
The A's and B's of Coronary Heart Disease
Psychological Aspects of Cancer
Smoking
Well-Being and Happiness

Type A behavior pattern: A pattern of behavior characterized by competitiveness, impatience, tendency toward frustration, and hostility

Type B behavior pattern: A pattern of behavior characterized by cooperation, patience, noncompetitiveness, and nonaggression

 PsychLink

Type A personality
www.mhhe.com/
feldmaness5-11links

Table 11-2 Type Yourself

To get an idea of whether you have the characteristics of a Type A or Type B personality, answer the following questions:

1. When you listen to someone talking and this person takes too long to come to the point, how often do you feel like hurrying the person along?
   _____ Frequently
   _____ Occasionally
   _____ Never

2. Do you ever set deadlines or quotas for yourself at work or at home?
   _____ No
   _____ Yes, but only occasionally
   _____ Yes, once a week or more

3. Would people you know well agree that you tend to get irritated easily?
   _____ Definitely yes
   _____ Probably yes
   _____ Probably no
   _____ Definitely no

4. Would people who know you well agree that you tend to do most things in a hurry?
   _____ Definitely yes
   _____ Probably yes
   _____ Probably no
   _____ Definitely no

Scoring: The more frequently your answers reflect affirmative responses, the more Type A characteristics you hold.

From Jenkins, Zyzsndki & Rosenman, "Coronary-Prone Behavior: One Pattern or Several?" *Psychosomatic Medicine*, 40, pp. 25–43, 1979. Reprinted with permission of Lippincott, Williams and Wilkins Publishers.

PsychLink

Effects of anger on the heart
www.mhhe.com/
feldmaness5-11links

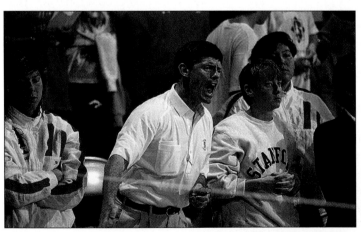

Most people can be classified as primarily either Type A or Type B. Type A's tend to be competitive, time-oriented, aggressive, driven, and hostile— and to be more vulnerable to coronary heart disease than Type B's. Are there types of careers where Type A personalities are more successful than Type B's? Why?

blood pressure, smoking habits, and cholesterol levels in the body (Rosenman et al., 1976; Rosenman et al., 1994; Wielgosz & Nolan, 2000).

Current research suggests that not every component of the Type A behavior pattern is linked to coronary heart disease. Hostility and anger seem to be the key factors, though other negative emotions, such as depression and low self-esteem, are now also thought to be related to heart attacks (Mittleman et al., 1995; McCabe et al., 2000; Williams, Paton, et al., 2000).

Why is Type A behavior, and hostility and anger in particular, linked to coronary heart disease? The most convincing theory is that the Type A behavior pattern produces excessive physiological arousal in stressful situations. This arousal, in turn, results in increased production of the hormones epinephrine and norepinephrine, as well as increased heart rate and blood pressure. Such exaggerated physiological responsivity ultimately produces an increased incidence of coronary heart disease (Blascovich & Katkin, 1993; Sundin et al., 1995).

It's important to keep in mind that not everyone who displays Type A behaviors is destined to have coronary heart disease. For one thing, a firm association between Type A behaviors and coronary heart disease has not been established for women; most studies have been done on males, not females. Furthermore, the evidence relating Type A behavior and coronary heart disease is correlational. Consequently, as we first discussed in Chapter 1, we cannot say for sure whether Type A behavior *causes* heart disease or whether, instead, some other factor causes both heart disease and Type A behavior. In fact, rather than focusing on Type

A behavior as the cause of heart disease, it might make more sense to ask whether Type B behavior *prevents* heart disease (Powell, Shaker, & Jones, 1993; Orth-Gomér, Chesney, & Wenger, 1996).

Psychological Aspects of Cancer

Hardly any disease is more feared than cancer. Most people think of cancer in terms of lingering pain, and being diagnosed with the disease is typically viewed as receiving a death sentence.

Although a diagnosis of cancer is not as grim as you might at first suspect—several kinds of cancer have a high cure rate if detected early enough—cancer remains the second leading cause of death after coronary heart disease. The precise trigger for the disease is not well understood, but the process by which cancer spreads is straightforward. Certain cells in the body become altered and multiply rapidly and in an uncontrolled fashion. As these cells grow, they form tumors, which, if left unchecked, suck nutrients from healthy cells and bodily tissue, ultimately destroying the body's ability to function properly.

Although the processes involved in the spread of cancer are basically physiological, accumulating evidence suggests that the emotional responses of cancer patients to their disease can have a critical effect on its course. For example, one experiment found that people who adopt a fighting spirit are more likely to recover than those who pessimistically suffer and resign themselves to death (Pettingale et al., 1985). The study analyzed the survival rates of women who had undergone the removal of a breast because of cancer.

The results suggested that the survival rates were related to the psychological response of the women three months after surgery (see Figure 11-2). Women who stoically accepted their fate, trying not to complain, and those who felt the situation was hopeless and that nothing could be done, showed the lowest survival rates; most of these women were dead after ten years. On the other hand, the survival rates of women who showed a fighting spirit (predicting that they would overcome the disease and planning to take steps to prevent its recurrence) and the survival rates of women who (erroneously) denied that they had ever had cancer (saying that the breast removal was merely a preventive step) were significantly higher. In sum, according to this study, cancer patients with a positive attitude were more likely to survive than those with a more negative one.

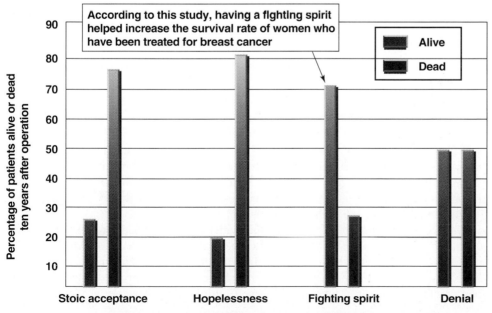

Figure 11-2 The relationship between women's psychological response to breast cancer three months after surgery and their survival ten years after the operation (Pettingale et al., 1985). What implications do these findings have for the treatment of people with cancer?

The ability to fight off disease is related to psychological factors. Here a cell from the body's immune system engulfs and destroys disease-producing bacteria.

 PsychLink

Stress and cancer
www.mhhe.com/
feldmaness5-11links

On the other hand, other research contradicts the notion that the course of cancer is affected by patients' attitudes and emotions. For example, some findings show that although a "fighting spirit" leads to better coping, the long-term survival rate is no better than for patients with a less positive attitude (Watson et al., 1999).

Despite the contradictory evidence, health psychologists believe that patients' emotions might at least partially determine the course of their disease. For example, psychologists specializing in psychoneuroimmunology (PNI) suggest that a patient's emotional state affects the immune system, the body's natural defenses that fight disease. Our bodies produce *lymphocytes,* specialized white blood cells that fight disease, at an extraordinary rate—some 10 million every few seconds—and it is possible that emotions affect this production. In the case of cancer, for instance, it is possible that positive emotional responses might help generate specialized "killer" cells that help control the size and spread of cancerous tumors. Conversely, negative emotions might suppress the ability of the same kinds of cells to fight tumors (Andersen, Kiecolt-Glaser, & Glaser, 1994; Seligman, 1995; Schedlowski & Tewes, 1999).

Other research suggests that "joy"—referring to mental resilience and vigor—is related to the likelihood of survival of patients with recurrent breast cancer. Similarly, cancer patients who are characteristically optimistic report less distress throughout the course of their treatment (Levy et al., 1988; Carver et al., 2000).

Is a particular personality type linked to cancer? Some findings suggest that cancer patients are less emotionally reactive, suppress anger, and lack outlets for emotional release. However, the data are still too tentative and inconsistent to suggest firm conclusions about a link between personality characteristics and cancer. Certainly there is no conclusive evidence that people who develop cancer would not have done so if they had had a different personality or more positive attitudes (Smith, 1988; Zevon & Corn, 1990; Holland, 1996).

What is increasingly clear, however, is that certain types of psychological therapy have the potential to extend the lives of cancer patients. One study found that women with breast cancer who received psychological treatment lived at least a year and a half longer, and experienced less anxiety and pain, than women who did not participate in therapy. Research on patients with other health problems, such as heart disease, also finds that therapy can be beneficial, both psychologically and medically (Spiegel, 1993, 1996a; Galavotti et al., 1997; Frasure-Smith, Lesperance, & Talajic, 2000).

Smoking

Would you stroll into a convenience store and buy an item with a label warning you that its use could kill you? Although most of us would probably answer no, millions make such a purchase every day: a pack of cigarettes. Furthermore, they do this despite clear, well-publicized evidence that smoking is linked to cancer, heart attacks, strokes, bronchitis, emphysema, and a host of other serious illnesses. Smoking is the greatest preventable cause of death in the United States. Worldwide, 3 million people die prematurely each year due to the effects of smoking (Heishman, Kozlowki, & Henningfield, 1997; Kawachi et al., 1997; Noble, 1999).

Why do people smoke, despite all the evidence that it is bad for their health? It is not that they are unaware of the link between smoking and disease; surveys show that most *smokers* agree with the statement "Cigarette smoking frequently causes disease and death." And almost three-quarters of the 48 million smokers in the United States say they would like to quit (Centers for Disease Control, 1994; Wetter et al., 1998).

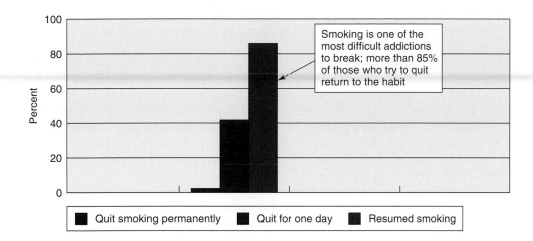

Figure 11-3 The difficulty of quitting smoking is evident in this graph. More than 85 percent of those who tried to quit returned to smoking.

Morbidity and Mortality Weekly Report, July 9, 1993, Center for Disease Control.

Heredity seems to partly determine whether people will become smokers, how much they will smoke, and how easily they can quit. Genetics also influences how susceptible people are to the harmful effects of smoking. For instance, there is an almost 50 percent higher rate of lung cancer in African American smokers than in white smokers. This difference could be due to genetically produced variations in the efficiency with which enzymes are able to reduce the effects of the cancer-causing chemicals in tobacco smoke (Pomerlau, 1995; Heath & Madden, 1995; Richie, 1994).

On the other hand, although genetics plays a role in smoking, most research suggests that environmental factors are the primary cause of the habit. Smokers might at first see smoking as "cool" or sophisticated, as a rebellious act, or as helping them perform calmly under stressful situations. In addition, smoking a cigarette is sometimes viewed as a "rite of passage" for adolescents, undertaken at the urging of friends and viewed as a sign of growing up (Grube, Rokeach, & Getzlaf, 1990; Koval et al., 2000; Wagner & Atkins, 2000).

But ultimately smoking becomes a habit. People begin to label themselves smokers, and smoking becomes part of their self-concept. Moreover, they become dependent on the physiological effects of smoking, because nicotine, a primary ingredient of tobacco, is highly addictive. Ultimately, a complex relationship develops among smoking, nicotine levels, and the smoker's emotional state, in which a certain nicotine level becomes associated with a positive emotional state. As a result, people smoke in an effort to regulate *both* emotional states and nicotine levels in the blood (Leventhal & Cleary, 1980; Gilbert, 1995).

Quitting Smoking

Because smoking has both psychological and biological components, few habits are as difficult to break. Long-term successful treatment typically occurs in just 15 percent of those trying to stop smoking, and once smoking becomes a habit, it is as hard to stop as an addiction to cocaine or heroin. In fact, some of the biochemical reactions to nicotine are similar to reactions to cocaine, amphetamines, and morphine. Many people try to quit and fail, as you can see in Figure 11-3 (Glassman & Koob, 1996; Piasecki et al., 1997; National Council on Aging, 2000).

Among the most effective tools for ending the smoking habit are drugs that replace the nicotine found in cigarettes. Whether in the form of gum, patches, nasal sprays, or inhalers, these products provide a dose of nicotine that reduces dependence

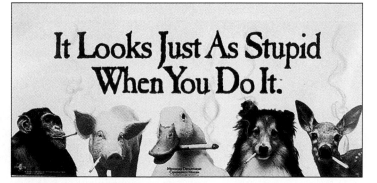

Changes in society's attitudes, and strong anti-smoking campaigns, can go a long way toward reducing tobacco use.

on cigarettes. Another approach is exemplified by the drug Zyban, which, rather than replacing nicotine, raises dopamine levels in the brain, thereby reducing the desire to smoke (Rock, 1999).

Behavioral strategies that view smoking as a learned habit and concentrate on changing the smoking response can also be effective. Initial "cure" rates of 60 percent have been reported, and one year after treatment more than half of those who quit have not resumed smoking. Counseling, either individually or in groups, also increases the rate of success in breaking the habit. The best treatment seems to be a combination of nicotine replacement *and* counseling. What doesn't work? Going it alone: Only 5 percent of smokers who quit cold-turkey on their own are successful (Wetter et al., 1998; Rock, 1999; Noble, 1999).

In the long term, the most effective way to reduce smoking could be changes in societal norms and attitudes toward the habit. Many cities and towns have made smoking in public places illegal, and legislation banning smoking in such places as college classrooms and buildings—based on strong popular sentiment—is being passed with increasing frequency (Gibson, 1997; Jacobson, Wasserman, & Anderson, 1997).

EXPLORING DIVERSITY

Hucksters of Death: Promoting Smoking Throughout the World

In Dresden, Germany, three women in miniskirts offer passers-by a pack of Lucky Strikes and a leaflet that reads: "You just got hold of a nice piece of America." Says a local doctor, "Adolescents time and again receive cigarettes at such promotions."

A Jeep decorated with the Camel logo pulls up to a high school in Buenos Aires. A woman begins handing out free cigarettes to 15- and 16-year-olds during their lunch recess.

At a video arcade in Taipei, free American cigarettes are strewn atop each game. At a disco filled with high school students, free packs of Salems are on each table. (Ecenbarger, 1993, p. 50)

As the number of smokers has declined in the United States, cigarette manufacturers have turned to new markets in an effort to increase the number of people who smoke. In the process, they have employed some dubious marketing techniques.

For instance, in the early 1990s the tobacco company RJ Reynolds developed a new cigarette brand it named "Uptown." The advertising that announced the debut of the cigarette targeted African Americans (Quinn, 1990; Jhally et al., 1995; Ringold, 1996). Given the questionable ethics of targeting a potentially life-threatening product to a minority population, the product introduction caused considerable controversy. Ultimately, the secretary of the U.S. Department of Health and Human Services condemned the tactic, and the manufacturer stopped distributing the brand soon thereafter.

More recently, cigarette manufacturers have turned their sights to other parts of the world, where they see a fertile market of nonsmokers (Sesser, 1993). Although they must often sell cigarettes more cheaply abroad than in the United States, the number of potential smokers still makes it financially worthwhile for the tobacco companies. For instance, in 1995, China opened its market of 298 million smokers—more than the entire U.S. population—to American brands (Hass, 1994). As can be seen in Figure 11-4, overseas sales have surged since the mid 1980s, as sales in the United States have declined (Bartecchi, MacKenzie, & Schrier, 1995).

Clearly, the push into worldwide markets has been successful. In some Latin American cities, as many as 50 percent of teenagers smoke. Children as young as 7 smoke in Hong Kong. The World Health Organization predicts that smoking will prematurely kill some 200 million of the world's children, and that ultimately 10 percent of the world's population will die due to smoking (Ecenbarger, 1993). Clearly, smoking is one of the world's greatest health problems.

PsychLink

Smoking and health
www.mhhe.com/
feldmaness5-11links

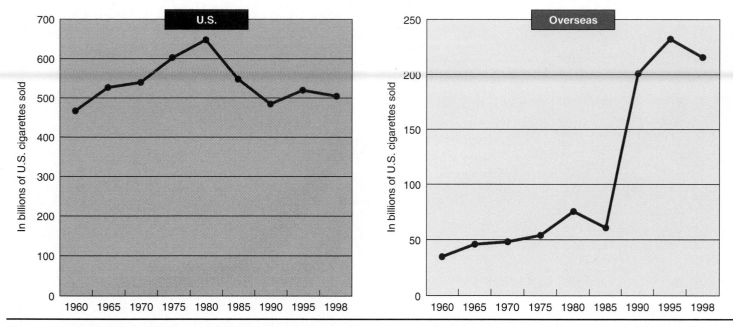

Figure 11-4 Despite the plummeting in sales of cigarettes in the United States, the number sold overseas has dramatically increased.
Source: U.S. Department of Agriculture, 1998.

Well-Being and Happiness

What makes for a good life?

Philosophers and theologians have pondered this question for centuries, and now health psychologists are turning their spotlight on it. They are doing so by investigating **subjective well-being,** people's evaluations of their lives in terms of both their thoughts and emotions. Considered another way, subjective well-being is the measure of how happy people are (Diener, 2000).

Research on subjective well-being shows that happy people share several characteristics (Myers & Diener, 1996; Myers, 2000):

- *Happy people have high self-esteem.* Particularly in Western cultures, which emphasize the importance of individuality, people who are happy like themselves. They see themselves as more intelligent and better able to get along with others than the average person.
- *Happy people have a firm sense of control.* They feel more in control of events in their lives, unlike people who feel they are the pawns of others and who experience learned helplessness.
- *Happy individuals are optimistic.* Their optimism permits them to persevere at tasks and ultimately to achieve more. Their health is also better (Peterson, 2000).
- *Happy people like to be around other people.* They tend to be extroverted and have a supportive network of close relationships.

Perhaps most important, most people are at least moderately happy most of the time. In both national and international surveys, people living in a wide variety of circumstances report being happy. Furthermore—as we consider in the *Applying Psychology in the 21ˢᵗ Century* box—winning the lottery probably won't make you happy. According to a variety of findings, happiness can't be bought.

subjective well-being: People's evaluations of their lives in terms of both their thoughts and their emotions; how happy people are

Applying Psychology in the 21st Century

If You Won the Lottery, Would You Be Happier?

Probably not.

At least that's the implication of an increasing body of research on subjective well-being. This research shows that although winning the lottery brings an initial surge in happiness, a year later winners' level of happiness seems to return to what it was before. The converse phenomenon occurs for people who have suffered serious injuries in accidents: Despite an initial decline in happiness, most victims return to their prior levels of happiness over time (Diener et al., 1999).

Why is the level of subjective well-being so stable? One explanation is that people have a general "set point" for happiness, a marker that establishes the tone for one's life. Although a particular event (a surprise promotion or a job loss, for example) might temporarily elevate or depress one's mood, ultimately people return to their usual general level of happiness.

Although it is not certain how people's happiness set points are initially established, some evidence suggests that genetic factors play a role. Specifically, identical twins who grow up in widely different circumstances turn out to have quite similar levels of happiness (Diener & Diener, 1996; Lykken & Tellegen, 1996; Kahneman, Diener, & Schwarz, 1998).

Most people's well-being set point is relatively high. For example, some 30 percent

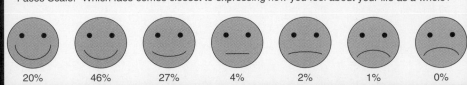

Faces Scale: "Which face comes closest to expressing how you feel about your life as a whole?"

20%   46%   27%   4%   2%   1%   0%

Figure 11–5 Most people in the U.S. rate themselves very happy; only a small percentage indicate that they are not happy (Myers, 2000).

of people in the United States rate themselves as "very happy," and only one in ten rate themselves as "not too happy." Most people declare themselves to be "pretty happy." Such feelings are graphically confirmed by people asked to place themselves on the measure of happiness illustrated in Figure 11-5. The scale clearly illustrates that most people view their lives quite positively.

Similar results are found when people are asked to compare themselves to others. For example, when asked "Who of the following people do you think is the happiest?" survey respondents answered "Oprah Winfrey" (23 percent), "Bill Gates" (7 percent), "the Pope" (12 percent), "Chelsea Clinton" (3 percent), and "yourself" (49 percent), with 6 percent saying they didn't know (Black & McCafferty, 1998).

Demographic groups don't differ much from each other on this measure. Men and women report being equally happy, and African

Americans are only slightly less likely than white Americans to rate themselves as "very happy." Furthermore, happiness is hardly unique to U.S. culture. Even countries that are far from economically prosperous have, on the whole, happy residents (Myers & Diener, 1996; Mroczek & Kolarz, 1998; Schkade & Kahneman, 1998; Staudinger, Fleeson, & Baltes, 1999; Diener, 2000).

The bottom line: Money does *not* seem to buy happiness. Despite the ups and downs of life, most people tend to be reasonably happy, and they adapt to the trials and tribulations—and joys and delights—of life by returning to a steady-state level of happiness.

Why do you think people consistently rate themselves happier than they rate wealthy and powerful people like Oprah Winfrey and Bill Gates? Do you think Winfrey and Gates would agree?

Evaluate

1. Type_____ behavior is characterized by cooperativeness and by being easy-going, whereas Type_____ behavior is characterized by aggression and competitiveness.

2. Type A behavior is known to directly cause heart attacks. True or false?

3. A cancer patient's attitude and emotions might affect that person's_____ system, helping or hindering their fight against the disease.

4. Smokers use smoking to regulate both their nicotine levels and their emotional states. True or false?

Rethink

1. Do you think Type A or Type B behavior is more widely encouraged in the United States? Why?

2. If money doesn't buy happiness, what can you do to make yourself happier? As you answer, consider the research findings on stress and coping, as well as our discussion of emotions in Chapter 8.

Answers to Evaluate Questions

1. B; A. 2. False; Type A behavior is related to a higher incidence of coronary heart disease, but does not necessarily directly cause it. 3. immune 4. True

Psychological Factors Related to Physical Illness: Going to the Doctor

Prepare

How do our interactions with physicians affect our health and compliance with medical treatment?

Organize

Psychological Factors Related to Physical Illness
   Physician–Patient Communication
   Complying with Physicians' Recommendations

When Stuart Grinspoon first noticed the small lump in his arm, he assumed it was just a bruise from the football game he had played the previous week. But as he thought about it more, he considered more serious possibilities and decided that he better get it checked out at the university health service. The visit was less than satisfactory. A shy person, Stuart felt embarrassed talking about his medical condition. Even worse, after answering a string of questions, he couldn't even understand the physician's diagnosis, and was too embarrassed to ask for clarification.

Stuart Grinspoon's attitudes toward health care are shared by many of us. Good medical care does not depend just on physical exams and prescribing a treatment. Several psychological factors are involved in determining the success of a health care provider's effectiveness in diagnosing and treating medical problems.

Physician–Patient Communication

You might be surprised to hear that many patients are reluctant to describe their symptoms to their physicians. But this is a common problem. Many people believe that a skilled physician will easily be able to identify a patient's problems through a thorough physical examination, the way a good mechanic diagnoses car problems. But diagnosing a medical problem is less a science than an art—one in which physicians are not always successful (Leigh & Reiser, 1980; Mentzer & Snyder, 1982; Konrad, 1994).

One source of physician–patient communication difficulties is that physicians have relatively high social prestige and power, which can intimidate patients. Patients might also be reluctant to volunteer information that could cast them in a bad light, and physicians might not be skilled at encouraging their patients to provide information. Physicians often dominate the interview with questions of a technical nature, whereas patients tend to attempt to communicate a personal sense of their illness and the impact it is having on their lives. Add to these communication problems the embarrassment many people feel in discussing personal matters (Beckman & Frankel, 1984; Goleman, 1988).

Patients' reluctance to reveal medical information fully to health care providers and the problems that providers encounter in eliciting information effectively produce major communication difficulties. These factors can prevent providers from understanding the extent of the difficulties that led the patients to seek medical care in the first place (Parrott, Duncan, & Duggan, 2000; see Table 11-3).

The view held by many patients that physicians are "all-knowing" can also result in serious communication problems. For instance, many patients do not understand their treatment, yet fail to ask their physicians for a clearer explanation of a prescribed course of action. About half of all patients are unable to accurately report how long they are to continue taking a medication prescribed for them, and about a quarter do not even know the purpose of the drug. In fact, some patients are not even sure, as they are about to be rolled into the operating room, why they are having surgery (Svarstad, 1976; Atkinson, 1997)!

Another reason for patient–physician communication difficulties is that the information that must be communicated can be too technical for patients who lack fundamental knowledge about the human body and basic medical practices. In response to this problem, some health care providers routinely use baby talk (calling patients "honey" or telling them

PsychLink

Physician communication
www.mhhe.com/
feldmaness5-11links

LookingBack

How is health psychology a union between medicine and psychology?

- The field of health psychology considers how psychology can be applied to the prevention, diagnosis, and treatment of medical problems. (p. 358)

What is stress, how does it affect us, and how can we best cope with it?

- Stress is a response to threatening or challenging environmental conditions. People encounter both positive and negative stressors—circumstances that produce stress. (p. 359)
- Stress produces immediate physiological reactions. In the short term, these reactions can be adaptive, but in the long term they can have negative consequences, including the development of psychophysiological disorders. (p. 359)
- The consequences of stress can be explained in part by Selye's general adaptation syndrome (GAS), which suggests that there are three stages in stress responses: alarm and mobilization, resistance, and exhaustion. (p. 359)
- The way a person interprets an environmental circumstance affects whether that person will consider it to be stressful. Still, there are general classes of events that provoke stress: cataclysmic events, personal stressors, and background stressors or daily hassles. (p. 361)
- Stress can be reduced by developing a sense of control over one's circumstances. Some people, though, develop a state of learned helplessness. (p. 363)
- Coping with stress can take a number of forms, including the unconscious use of defense mechanisms and the use of emotion-focused or problem-focused coping strategies. (p. 363)

How do psychological factors affect such health-related problems as coronary heart disease, cancer, and smoking?

- Coronary heart disease is linked to a specific type of behavior pattern known as Type A. Type A individuals tend to be competitive, show a sense of time urgency and hurriedness, be hostile and aggressive, and be driven. (p. 367)
- There is increasing evidence that a patient's attitudes and emotional responses can affect the course of that patient's disease through links to the immune system. (p. 369)
- Smoking, the leading preventable cause of health problems, has proved to be difficult to control, even though most smokers are aware of the dangerous consequences of smoking. (p. 370)
- Subjective well-being, the measure of how happy people are, is highest in people with high self-esteem, a sense of control, optimism, and a supportive network of close relationships. (p. 373)

How do our interactions with physicians affect our health and compliance with medical treatment?

- Although patients often expect physicians to make a diagnosis from only a physical examination, communicating one's problem to the physician is equally critical. (p. 375)
- Many patients find it difficult to communicate openly with their physicians because of the high social prestige of physicians and the technical nature of medical information. (p. 376)

Key Terms and Concepts

health psychology (p. 358)

psychoneuroimmunology (PNI) (p. 358)

stress (p. 359)

psychophysiological disorders (p. 359)

general adaptation syndrome (GAS) (p. 359)

cataclysmic events (p. 362)

posttraumatic stress disorder (PTSD) (p. 362)

personal stressors (p. 362)

background stressors (p. 362)

uplifts (p. 363)

learned helplessness (p. 363)

coping (p. 364)

defense mechanisms (p. 364)

hardiness (p. 365)

social support (p. 365)

Type A behavior pattern (p. 367)

Type B behavior pattern (p. 367)

subjective well-being (p. 373)

reactance (p. 376)

Preview

For additional quizzing and a variety of interactive resources, visit the *Essentials of Understanding Psychology* Online Learning Center at

www.mhhe.com/feldmaness5

Psychology on the Web

1. Find three or more websites that deal with stress reduction. Gather at least five techniques for reducing stress and summarize them. Write a critique and evaluation of these techniques, using the information you learned about stress in this chapter. Which ones seem to have a sound basis in psychological theory and/or research?

2. Are you a Type A personality or a Type B? Find two websites offering tests that claim to provide the answer. Summarize in writing the nature of each test and compare the results you received from each one.

Epilogue

In this chapter we have explored an important area in which psychology and physiology intersect. We've seen how the emotional and psychological experience of stress can lead to physical symptoms of illness, how personality factors can be related to major health problems, and how psychological factors can interfere with effective communications between physician and patient. We've also looked at the other side of the coin, noting that some relatively simple strategies can help us control stress, affect our illness, and improve our interactions with our physicians.

Turn back to the prologue of this chapter, about Susan Reiche and her hectic after-work schedule, and use your understanding of health psychology and stress to consider these questions.

1. Based on the description of Susan Reiche's day, which of her stressors are personal and which are background stressors? What might happen to "elevate" the stress level of a background stressor to a more serious level? Are there likely to be any uplifts in Reiche's day?

2. How does the general adaptation syndrome (GAS) apply to Reiche's situation? How might events in her life move her along the three stages of the model?

3. What steps would you advise Reiche to take to keep her level of stress under control? How might others in her life be involved in such an effort?

4. Does Reiche appear more likely to have a Type A or a Type B personality? Why?

Chapter Twelve

Psychological Disorders

Lori Schiller, who suffered from schizophrenia, is now a peer counselor at a mental health center and a member of the Board of Directors of the National Alliance for the Mentally Ill.

Prologue

Lori Schiller

Lori Schiller thinks it all began one night at summer camp when she was 15.

Suddenly, she was hearing voices. "You must die! Die! Die!" they screamed. The voices drove her from her bunk, out into the dark, where she thought she could escape. Camp officials found her jumping frantically on a trampoline, screaming. "I thought I was possessed," says Ms. Schiller, now 33. Terrified, she told no one about the voices when she first heard them. The camp sent her home sick. Says Nancy Schiller, her mother: "We thought she had the flu...."

Voices had begun sliding down the telephone wire; they were assaulting her from the TV screen. "The people on TV were telling me it was my responsibility to save the world, and if I didn't I would be killed," she says....

Her behavior became erratic, wilder. On a whim one day, she hopped into her car, drove four hours home to Scarsdale, changed her mind and drove back. She went sky diving. She got stopped by police for speeding. She had fits of hysterical laughter....

As time went on, Lori had more and more trouble concentrating, and more difficulty in controlling her impulses, one of which was to commit suicide. "I used to sit in the library, up all these stairs, and think about jumping," she recalls. Finally, in her senior year, she told her parents she "had problems" and asked to see a counselor. (Bennett, 1992, pp. A1, A10)

Looking Ahead

Although she initially managed to hide her disorder from everyone, Lori Schiller was losing her grip on reality. Less than a year after she graduated from college, her parents convinced her to get treatment. She would spend the next decade in and out of institutions, suffering from schizophrenia, one of the most severe psychological disorders.

Happily, today Schiller is a leader in the mental health field. But her case raises several questions. What caused her disorder? Were genetic factors involved, or were stressors in her life primarily responsible? Were there signs that others should have noticed earlier? Could her schizophrenia have been prevented? What were the specific symptoms of her psychological disorder? And, more generally, how do we distinguish normal from abnormal behavior, and how can Lori's behavior be categorized and classified to pinpoint the specific nature of her problem?

We address some of the issues raised by Lori Schiller's case in this and the following chapter. We begin by discussing the subtle distinctions between normal and abnormal behavior. We examine the various approaches that have been used to explain psychological disorders, ranging from explanations based on superstition to those based on more scientific approaches.

The heart of the chapter consists of a description of the various types of psychological disorders. Using a classification system employed by mental health practitioners, we examine the most significant kinds of disorders. The chapter also includes a discussion of how you can evaluate your own behavior to determine whether it is advisable for you to seek help from a mental health professional.

Prepare

How can we distinguish normal from abnormal behavior?

What are the major perspectives on psychological disorders used by mental health professionals?

What classification system is used to categorize psychological disorders?

Organize

Normal Versus Abnormal
  Defining Abnormality
  Perspectives on Abnormality
  Classifying Abnormal Behavior

 PsychLink

Information on disorders
www.mhhe.com/
feldmaness5-12links

Normal Versus Abnormal: Making the Distinction

Universally that person's acumen is esteemed very little perceptive concerning whatsoever matters are being held as most profitable by mortals with sapience endowed to be studied who is ignorant of that which the most in doctrine erudite and certainly by reason of that in them high mind's ornament deserving of veneration constantly maintain when by general consent they affirm that other circumstances being equal by no exterior splendour is the prosperity of a nation. . . .

It would be easy to conclude that these words were the musings of a madman. The passage does not seem to make any sense at all. But literary scholars would disagree. This passage is from James Joyce's classic *Ulysses* (Joyce, 1934, p. 377), which has beeen hailed as one of the major works of twentieth-century literature.

As this example illustrates, a casual examination of a person's writing is insufficient to determine the degree to which he or she is "normal." But even when we consider more extensive samples of a person's behavior, we find that there might be only a fine line between behavior that is considered normal and that which is considered abnormal.

Defining Abnormality

Because of the difficulty in distinguishing normal from abnormal behavior, psychologists have struggled to devise a precise, scientific definition of "abnormal behavior." For instance, consider the following definitions, each of which has its advantages and disadvantages:

- *Abnormality as deviation from the average.* To employ this statistics-based approach, we simply observe what behaviors are rare or infrequent in a given society or culture and label these deviations from the norm "abnormal."

  The difficulty with such a definition is that some behaviors that are statistically rare clearly do not lend themselves to classification as abnormal. If most people prefer to have cornflakes for breakfast, but you prefer raisin bran, this hardly makes your behavior abnormal. Similarly, based on such a concept of abnormality a person who has an unusually high IQ would be categorized as abnormal simply because a high IQ is statistically rare. A definition of abnormality that rests on deviation from the average, then, is insufficient.

- *Abnormality as deviation from the ideal.* An alternative approach considers abnormality in relation to the standard toward which most people are striving—the ideal. This sort of definition considers behavior abnormal if it deviates enough from some kind of ideal or cultural standard. However, because society has so few standards on which people agree, and the standards that do arise tend to change over time and vary across cultures, the deviation-from-the-ideal approach is inadequate.

- *Abnormality as a sense of personal discomfort.* A more useful definition concentrates on the psychological consequences of the behavior for the individual. In this approach, behavior is considered abnormal if it produces a sense of personal distress, anxiety, or guilt in an individual—or if it is harmful to others in some way.

  Even a definition that relies on personal discomfort has its drawbacks, though. For instance, people with some particularly severe forms of mental disturbance report feeling wonderful, even though their behavior seems bizarre to others. Most of us would consider their behavior abnormal even though they feel a personal state of well-being.

- *Abnormality as the inability to function effectively.* Most people are able to feed themselves, hold a job, get along with others, and in general live as productive members of society. Yet there are those who are unable to adjust to the demands of society or function effectively.

  According to this view of abnormality, people who are unable to function effectively and adapt to the demands of society are abnormal. For example, an unemployed, homeless woman living on the street might be considered unable to function effectively, so her behavior would be viewed as abnormal even if she had chosen to live this way. Her inability to adapt to the requirements of society is what makes her "abnormal," according to this approach.

- *Abnormality as a legal concept.* According to the jury that heard his case, mass murderer Jeffery Dahmer was perfectly sane when he killed his victims. Although you might question this view, it is a reflection of how the law defines abnormal behavior. To the judicial system, the distinction between normal and abnormal behavior rests on the definition of *insanity,* which is a legal, but not a psychological, term. The definition of insanity varies from one jurisdiction to another. In some states, insanity simply means that a defendant could not understand the difference between right and wrong at the time when he or she committed a criminal act. Other states consider whether defendants are substantially incapable of understanding the criminality of their behavior or unable to control themselves. And some jurisdictions do not allow any pleas of insanity (Steadman et al., 1993; Weiner & Wettstein, 1993).

PsychLink
Insanity defense
www.mhhe.com/
feldmaness5–12links

Identifying Normal and Abnormal Behavior: Drawing the Line on Psychological Disorders

Clearly, none of the previous definitions is broad enough to cover all instances of abnormal behavior. Consequently, the distinction between normal and abnormal behavior often remains ambiguous even to trained professionals. Furthermore, what is viewed as abnormal behavior depends largely on cultural expectations for "normal" behavior in a particular society (Scheff, 1999).

Probably the best way to deal with this imprecision is to view abnormal and normal behavior as marking two ends of a continuum rather than as absolute states. Behavior would then be evaluated in terms of gradations, ranging from completely normal functioning to extremely abnormal behavior. Behavior typically falls somewhere between these two extremes. (To learn about someone who deals with life-and-death issues involving the potential of disordered behavior, see the *Psychology at Work* box.)

A person who is unable to function effectively in day-to-day life may be regarded as psychologically abnormal; yet the courts deemed Jeffrey Dahmer, who confessed to a series of gruesome murders, sane and deserving of legal punishment. Why are psychological and legal definitions of abnormality so different? Should they be?

Psychology at Work

Margaret H. Coggins

Senior Research Psychologist, United States Secret Service

Education: B.A., psychology, Dickinson College; M.A., Ph.D., psychology, Catholic University

Home: Reston, Virginia

Margaret H. Coggins

Protecting the president of the United States is the responsibility of the Secret Service, whose agents must be ready at an instant to aid and defend the U.S. leader. And while many agents are literally at the president's side every moment, others—such as psychologist Margaret Coggins—work for his or her safety in the background.

Coggins works closely with agents in the field and with mental health professionals to ensure the safety of U.S. leaders.

"The nature of my work consists of research, liaison, and training and educational work. All are tied to the Secret Service's protective mission," Coggins explained.

"The research program is designed to help the agency better understand the risk factors for violence that may be directed toward the people we protect, as well as helping to prevent and minimize any risk that is out there," she said.

Agents in the field not only must be vigilant in watching people, but must also be knowledgeable about the state of mind of people wishing to harm U.S. leaders or their families. Coggins works to identify the motivations and behaviors of those who are potentially threatening.

"Many of the individuals who come to the attention of the Secret Service are those who have active symptoms of a psychiatric disorder or are found to have a history of mental disorder," she said. "We conduct research on the cases that come to the attention of the Secret Service so we can get a better grasp on the types of behaviors, threats, and motivations. Some people communicate threats but are not likely to do harm, while a few others do pose serious threats."

Bringing together law enforcement with mental health and behavioral science is a major commitment for Coggins. As a result, her staff works closely with mental health specialists to manage the treatment of clients whose behavior could be threatening to people under Secret Service protection.

"One main area of our research has to do with the general understanding and awareness in the mental health community about our protective mission," she noted. "We share some of the same goals, and we have to make the right decisions."

> "We conduct research on the cases that come to the attention of the Secret Service so we can get a better grasp on the types of behaviors, threats, and motivations."

Perspectives on Abnormality: From Superstition to Science

For much of the past, abnormal behavior was linked to superstition and witchcraft. People displaying abnormal behavior were accused of being possessed by the devil or some sort of demonic god. Authorities felt justified in "treating" abnormal behavior by attempting to drive out the source of the problem. This typically involved whipping, immersion in hot water, starvation, or other forms of torture in which the cure was often worse than the affliction (Howells & Osborn, 1984; Berrios, 1996).

Contemporary approaches take a more enlightened view. Today, there are six major perspectives on psychological disorders. These perspectives suggest not only different causes of abnormal behavior but also, as we shall see in the next chapter, different treatment approaches. Furthermore, some are more applicable to particular disorders than others. Table 12-1 summarizes the perspectives and how each can be applied to the case of Lori Schiller described in the Prologue.

The Medical Perspective

medical perspective: The perspective that the root cause of abnormal behavior will be found in a physical examination of the individual, which might reveal a hormonal imbalance, a chemical deficiency, or a brain injury

When people display the symptoms of tuberculosis, we generally find the tuberculin germ in their body tissue. In the same way, the **medical perspective** suggests that when an individual displays symptoms of abnormal behavior, the fundamental cause will be found in a physical examination of the individual, which might reveal a hormonal imbalance, a chemical deficiency, or a brain injury. Indeed, when we speak of mental "illness," "symptoms" of abnormal behavior, and mental "hospitals," we are using terminology associated with the medical perspective.

Because many abnormal behaviors have been linked to biological causes, the medical perspective is a reasonable approach. Yet serious criticisms have been leveled against

Table 12-1 Perspectives on Psychological Disorder

In considering the case of Lori Schiller, discussed in the prologue to this chapter, we can employ each of the different perspectives on abnormal behavior. Note, however, that given the nature of her psychological disorder, some of the perspectives are more applicable than others.

Perspective	Description	Possible Application of Perspective to Schiller's Case
Medical perspective	Assumes that physiological causes are at the root of psychological disorders	Examine Schiller for medical problems, such as brain tumor, chemical imbalance in the brain, or disease
Psychoanalytic perspective	Argues that psychological disorders stem from childhood conflicts	Seek out information about Schiller's past, considering possible childhood conflicts
Behavioral perspective	Assumes that abnormal behaviors are learned responses	Concentrate on rewards and punishments for Schiller's behavior, and identify environmental stimuli that reinforce her behavior
Cognitive perspective	Assumes that cognitions (people's thoughts and beliefs) are central to psychological disorders	Focus on Schiller's perceptions of herself and her environment
Humanistic perspective	Emphasizes people's responsibility for their own behavior and the need to self-actualize	Consider Schiller's behavior in terms of her choices and efforts to reach her potential
Sociocultural perspective	Assumes that behavior is shaped by family, society, and culture	Focus on how societal demands contributed to Schiller's disorder

it. For one thing, there are many forms of abnormal behavior for which no biological cause has been identified. In addition, some critics have argued that the use of the term *illness* implies that people displaying abnormal behavior are not responsible for their actions (Szasz, 1982, 1994).

Still, recent advances in our understanding of the biological bases of behavior have supported the importance of considering physiological factors in abnormal behavior. For instance, we'll see later in this chapter that some of the most severe forms of psychological disturbance, such as major depression and schizophrenia, are influenced by genetic factors and neurotransmitters (Resnick, 1992; Brunner et al., 1993; Crow, 1995; Petronis & Kennedy, 1995).

The Psychoanalytic Perspective

Whereas the medical perspective suggests that biological causes are at the root of abnormal behavior, the **psychoanalytic perspective** holds that abnormal behavior stems from childhood conflicts over opposing wishes regarding sex and aggression. As we discussed in Chapter 10, Freud believed that children pass through a series of stages in which sexual and aggressive impulses take different forms and produce conflicts that require resolution—and that if these childhood conflicts are not dealt with successfully, they remain unresolved in the unconscious and eventually bring about abnormal behavior during adulthood.

To understand the roots of people's disordered behavior, the psychoanalytic perspective scrutinizes their early life history. However, because there is no conclusive way of linking people's childhood experiences with the abnormal behaviors they display as adults, we can never be sure that the causes suggested by psychoanalytic theory are accurate. Moreover, psychoanalytic theory paints a picture of people as having relatively little control over their behavior, because much of it is taken to be guided by unconscious impulses.

On the other hand, the contributions of psychoanalytic theory have been significant. More than any other approach to abnormal behavior, this perspective highlights the fact that people can have a rich, involved inner life and that prior experiences can have a profound effect on current psychological functioning (Horgan, 1996).

psychoanalytic perspective: The perspective that abnormal behavior stems from childhood conflicts over opposing wishes regarding sex and aggression

The Behavioral Perspective

behavioral perspective: The perspective that looks at the behavior itself as the problem

Both the medical and psychoanalytic perspectives look at abnormal behaviors as *symptoms* of some underlying problem. In contrast, the **behavioral perspective** looks at the behavior itself as the problem. Using the principles of learning theory discussed in Chapter 5, behavioral theorists see both normal and abnormal behaviors as responses to a set of stimuli, responses that have been learned through past experience and that are guided in the present by stimuli in the individual's environment. To explain why abnormal behavior occurs, one must analyze how an abnormal behavior has been learned and observe the circumstances in which it is displayed.

The emphasis on observable behavior is both the greatest strength and the greatest weakness of the behavioral approach to abnormal behavior. The behavioral perspective is the most precise and objective approach for examining behavioral displays of particular disorders, such as attention deficit hyperactivity disorder (ADHD), which we'll consider later in this chapter. At the same time, though, critics charge that the perspective ignores the rich inner world of thoughts, attitudes, and emotions that can contribute to abnormal behavior.

The Cognitive Perspective

The medical, psychoanalytic, and behavioral perspectives view people's behavior as being caused by factors largely beyond their control. To many critics, however, people's thoughts cannot be ignored.

cognitive perspective: The perspective that people's thoughts and beliefs are a central component of abnormal behavior

In response to such concerns, some psychologists employ a **cognitive perspective.** Rather than considering only external behavior, as in traditional behavioral approaches, the cognitive approach assumes that *cognitions* (people's thoughts and beliefs) are central to a person's abnormal behavior. A primary goal of treatment using the cognitive perspective is to explicitly teach new, more adaptive ways of thinking.

For instance, suppose that whenever she takes an exam, a student forms the erroneous cognition "Doing well on this exam is crucial to my entire future." Through therapy, such a person might be taught to hold the more realistic, and less anxiety-producing, thought: "My entire future is not dependent on this one exam." By changing cognitions in this way, psychologists working within a cognitive framework seek to help people free themselves from thoughts and behaviors that are potentially maladaptive.

The Humanistic Perspective

humanistic perspective: The perspective that emphasizes people's responsibility for their own behavior, even when such behavior is abnormal

Psychologists who subscribe to the **humanistic perspective** emphasize the responsibility that people have for their own behavior, even when such behavior is seen as abnormal. The humanistic perspective—growing out of the work of Rogers and Maslow (see Chapter 10)—concentrates on what is uniquely human, viewing people as basically rational, oriented toward a social world, and motivated to seek self-actualization (Rogers, 1980).

Humanistic approaches focus on the relationship between the individual and society, considering how people view themselves in relation to others and see their place in the world. People are viewed as having an awareness of life and of themselves that leads them to search for meaning and self-worth. Rather than assuming that a "cure" is required, the humanistic perspective suggests that individuals can, by and large, set their own limits of what is acceptable behavior. As long as they are not hurting others and do not feel personal distress, people should be free to choose what behaviors to engage in.

Although the humanistic perspective has been criticized for its reliance on unscientific, unverifiable information and its vague, almost philosophical, formulations, it offers a distinctive view of abnormal behavior. The perspective stresses the unique aspects of being human and provides a number of important suggestions for helping those with psychological problems.

The Sociocultural Perspective

The **sociocultural perspective** assumes that people's behavior—both normal and abnormal—is shaped by the kind of family group, society, and culture in which they live. According to this view, one's relationships with others can support abnormal behaviors and even cause them to occur. Consequently, the kinds of stresses and conflicts people experience as part of their daily interactions with others in their environment can promote and maintain abnormal behavior.

Statistical support for the position that sociocultural factors shape abnormal behavior can be found in the fact that some kinds of abnormal behavior are far more prevalent among certain social classes than among others. For instance, there tend to be more diagnoses of schizophrenia among members of lower socioeconomic groups than among members of more affluent groups. Proportionally more African Americans than whites are involuntarily hospitalized for psychological disorders. Furthermore, poor economic times tend to be linked to general declines in psychological functioning, and social problems such as homelessness are associated with psychological disorders (Kiesler, 1999; López & Guarnaccia, 2000).

"First off, you're not a nut. You're a legume."

On the other hand, alternative explanations abound for the association between abnormal behavior and social factors. For example, poorer people might be less likely than wealthier people to seek help, and therefore might be more likely to develop symptoms that are severe and warrant a more serious diagnosis. Furthermore, sociocultural explanations provide relatively little specific guidance for the treatment of individuals showing mental disturbance, because the focus is on broader societal factors (Paniagua, 2000).

sociocultural perspective: The perspective that people's behavior—both normal and abnormal—is shaped by the kind of family group, society, and culture in which they live

Classifying Abnormal Behavior: The ABCs of the *DSM*

Crazy. Whacked. Mental. Loony. Insane. Neurotic. Psycho. Strange. Demented. Odd. Possessed.

Society has long placed labels on people who display abnormal behavior. Unfortunately, most of the time these labels have reflected intolerance and have been used with little thought to what the label signifies.

Providing appropriate and specific names and classifications for abnormal behavior has presented a major challenge to psychologists. It is not too hard to understand why, given the difficulties discussed earlier in simply distinguishing normal from abnormal behavior. Yet classification systems are necessary in order to be able to describe and ultimately to diagnose abnormal behavior.

The DSM-IV: Determining Diagnostic Distinctions

Over the years many different classification systems have been used. Some have been more useful than others, and some have been more accepted than others by mental health workers. Today, however, one standard system, devised by the American Psychiatric Association, has emerged in the United States; it is employed by most professionals to diagnose and classify abnormal behavior. This classification system is presented in the ***Diagnostic and Statistical Manual of Mental Disorders,* Fourth Edition *(DSM-IV)*** (American Psychiatric Association, 1994).

The *DSM-IV* presents comprehensive and relatively precise definitions for more than 200 diagnostic categories. By following the criteria presented in the system, diagnosticians can clearly describe the specific problem an individual is experiencing. (Table 12-2 provides a brief outline of the major diagnostic categories.)

One noteworthy feature of the *DSM-IV* is that it is designed to be primarily descriptive and tries to avoid suggesting an underlying cause for an individual's behavior and

Diagnostic and Statistical Manual of Mental Disorders, **Fourth Edition *(DSM-IV):*** The manual of the American Psychiatric Association that presents the diagnostic system used by most U.S. mental health professionals to diagnose and classify abnormal behavior

Table 12-2 Major *DSM-IV* Diagnostic Categories

The following list of disorders represents the major categories from the *DSM-IV*. This is only a partial list of the over 200 disorders found in the *DSM-IV*.

Disorder	Subcategories
Anxiety (problems in which anxiety impedes daily functioning)	Generalized anxiety disorder, panic disorder, phobic disorder, obsessive-compulsive disorder, post-traumatic stress disorder
Somatoform (psychological difficulties displayed through physical problems)	Hypochondriasis, conversion disorder
Dissociative (the splitting apart of crucial parts of personality that are usually integrated)	Dissociative identity disorder (multiple personality), dissociative amnesia, dissociative fugue
Mood (emotions of depression or euphoria that are so strong they intrude on everyday living)	Major depression, bipolar disorder
Schizophrenia (declines in functioning, thought and language disturbances, perception disorders, emotional disturbances, and withdrawal from others)	Disorganized, paranoid, catatonic, undifferentiated, residual
Personality (problems that create little personal distress but lead to an inability to function as a normal member of society)	Antisocial (sociopathic) personality disorder, narcissistic personality disorder
Sexual (problems related to sexual arousal from unusual objects or problems related to sexual functioning)	Paraphilia, sexual dysfunction
Substance-related (problems related to drug dependence and abuse)	Alcohol, cocaine, hallucinogens, marijuana
Delirium, dementia, amnesia, and other cognitive disorders	

problems. Hence, the term *neurotic*—a label that is commonly used by people in their everyday descriptions of abnormal behavior—is not listed as a *DSM-IV* category. The reason is that the term *neurotic* comes directly from Freud's theory of personality. Because the term refers to problems associated with a specific cause and theoretical approach, neurosis is no longer listed as a category.

The *DSM-IV* has the advantage, then, of providing a descriptive system that does not specify a cause or reason behind the problem. Instead, it paints a picture of the behavior that is being displayed. Why should this be important? For one thing, it allows communication between mental health professionals of diverse backgrounds and approaches. In addition, precise descriptive classification enables researchers to make progress in exploring the causes of a problem. If displays of an abnormal behavior cannot be reliably described, researchers will be hard-pressed to find ways of investigating the disorder. Finally, the *DSM-IV* provides a kind of conceptual shorthand through which professionals can describe the behaviors that tend to occur together in an individual (Frances, First, & Pincus, 1995; Halling & Goldfarb, 1996).

Conning the Classifiers: The Shortcomings of the DSM-IV

When clinical psychologist David Rosenhan and eight colleagues sought admission to separate mental hospitals across the United States in the 1970s, each stated that they were hearing voices—"unclear voices" that said "empty," "hollow," and "thud"—and each was immediately admitted to the hospital (Rosenhan, 1973).

However, the truth was that they were conducting a study, and none of them was actually hearing voices. Aside from these misrepresentations, *everything* else they did

PsychLink

Symptoms of disorders
www.mhhe.com/
feldmaness5-12links

and said was their true behavior, including the responses they gave during extensive admission interviews and answers to the battery of tests they were asked to complete. In fact, as soon as they were admitted, they said they no longer heard any voices. In short, each of the pseudo-patients acted in a "normal" way.

We might assume that Rosenhan and his colleagues would be quickly discovered as the impostors they were, but they were not. Instead, each of them was diagnosed as severely abnormal on the basis of observed behavior. Most were labeled as suffering from schizophrenia, and they were kept in the hospital from 3 to 52 days, with the average stay being 19 days. Even when they were discharged, most of the "patients" left with the label *schizophrenia—in remission,* implying that the abnormal behavior had only temporarily subsided and could recur at any time. Most disturbing of all, none of the pseudo-patients was identified by the staff of the hospitals as an impostor—although some of the real patients figured out the ruse.

The results of Rosenhan's classic study illustrate the fact that labeling individuals powerfully influences how their actions are perceived and interpreted. It also points out that determining who is psychologically disordered is not always a clear-cut, accurate process.

Although the *DSM-IV* was developed to provide more accurate and consistent determinations of psychological disorders, it has not been entirely successful. For instance, critics charge that it relies too much on the medical perspective on psychological disorders. It was drawn up by psychiatrists—who are physicians—and some condemn it for viewing psychological disorders primarily in terms of symptoms of some underlying physiological disorder. Moreover, critics suggest that the *DSM-IV* sorts people into inflexible, all-or-none categories, ignoring the degree to which a person displays psychologically disordered behavior.

Other concerns with the *DSM-IV* are more subtle, but equally important. For instance, some critics argue that labeling an individual "abnormal" attaches a lifetime stigma to that person that is dehumanizing. Furthermore, after an initial diagnosis is made, other diagnostic possibilities might be overlooked by mental health professionals, who concentrate on the initial diagnostic category (Szasz, 1961, 1994; Kirk, 1992).

Still, despite the drawbacks inherent in any labeling system, the *DSM-IV* has had an important influence on how mental health professionals approach psychological disorders. It has increased both the reliability and the validity of diagnostic categorization, and it gives us a logical way to organize our examination of the major types of mental disturbance, to which we turn next.

Evaluate

1. One problem in defining abnormal behavior is that:
   a. statistically rare behavior might not be abnormal.
   b. not all abnormalities are accompanied by feelings of discomfort.
   c. cultural standards are too general to use as a measuring tool.
   d. all of the above.

2. If abnormality is defined as experiencing personal discomfort or causing harm to others, which of the following people is most likely to need treatment?
   a. An executive who is afraid to accept a promotion because it would require moving from his ground-floor office to the top floor of a tall office building.
   b. A woman who decides to quit her job and chooses, with great pleasure, to live on the street in order to live a "simpler life."
   c. A man who believes that friendly spacemen visit his house every Thursday, and is glad for their company.
   d. A photographer who enjoys living with nineteen cats in a small apartment.

3. Virginia's mother thinks that Virginia's behavior is clearly abnormal because, despite being offered admission to medical school, Virginia decides to become a waitress instead. What approach is Virginia's mother using to define abnormal behavior?

Rethink

1. Imagine that an acquaintance of yours was recently arrested for shoplifting a $3 pen. What sorts of questions and issues would be raised by proponents of *each* of these perspectives on abnormality: medical, psychoanalytic, behavioral, cognitive, humanistic, and sociocultural?

2. Do you agree or disagree that the *DSM* should be updated every several years? What makes abnormal behavior so variable? Why can't there be one, unchanging definition of abnormal behavior?

4. Which of the following is a strong argument against the medical perspective?

   a. Physiological abnormalities are almost always impossible to identify.

   b. There is no conclusive way to link past experience and behavior.

   c. The medical perspective rests too heavily on the effects of nutrition.

   d. Assigning behavior to a physical problem takes responsibility away from the individual for changing his or her behavior.

5. Cheryl is painfully shy. According to the behavioral perspective, the best way to deal with her "abnormal" behavior is to

   a. treat the underlying physical problem.

   b. use the principles of learning theory to modify her shy behavior.

   c. express a great deal of caring.

   d. uncover her negative past experiences through hypnosis.

Answers to Evaluate Questions

1. d 2. a 3. Deviation from the ideal 4. d 5. b

Prepare

What are the major psychological disorders?

Organize

Major Disorders
   Anxiety Disorders
   Somatoform Disorders
   Dissociative Disorders

Major Disorders

Sally experienced her first panic attack out of the blue, 3 weeks after completing her senior year in college. She had just finished a job interview and was meeting some friends for dinner. In the restaurant, she began to feel dizzy. Within a few seconds, her heart was pounding, and she was feeling breathless, as though she might pass out. Her friends noticed that she did not look well and offered to drive her home. Sally suggested they stop at the hospital emergency room instead. Although she felt better by the time they arrived at the hospital, and tests indicated nothing wrong, Sally experienced a similar episode a week later while at a movie. . . .

Her attacks became more and more frequent. Before long, she was having several attacks per week. In addition, she constantly worried about having attacks. She began to avoid exercise and other activities that produced physical sensations. She also noticed the attacks were worse when she was alone. She began to avoid driving, shopping in large stores, and eating in all restaurants. Some weeks she avoided leaving the house completely. (Antony, Brown, & Barlow, 1992, p. 79)

Sally suffered from panic disorder, one of the specific psychological disorders we'll be considering in the remainder of this chapter. Keep in mind that although we'll be discussing these disorders in a dispassionate manner, each represents a very human set of difficulties that influence, and in some cases considerably disrupt, people's lives.

Anxiety Disorders

All of us, at one time or another, experience *anxiety,* a feeling of apprehension or tension, in reaction to stressful situations. There is nothing "wrong" with such anxiety. Anxiety is a normal reaction to stress that often helps, rather than hinders, our daily functioning. Without some anxiety, for instance, most of us probably would not be terribly motivated to study hard, undergo physical exams, or spend long hours at our jobs.

But some people experience anxiety for no clear reason. When anxiety occurs without external justification and begins to affect a person's daily functioning, it is considered a psychological problem known as an **anxiety disorder.** We'll discuss four types of anxiety disorders: phobic disorder, panic disorder, generalized anxiety disorder, and obsessive-compulsive disorder.

anxiety disorder: Anxiety with no obvious external cause that impairs daily functioning

Table 12-3 Giving Fear a Proper Name

Phobia	Trigger	Phobia	Trigger
Acrophobia	Heights	Herpetophobia	Reptiles
Aerophobia	Flying	Hydrophobia	Water
Agoraphobia	Public spaces	Mikrophobia	Germs
Ailurophobia	Cats	Murophobia	Mice
Amaxophobia	Vehicles, driving	Mysophobia	Dirt or germs
Anthophobia	Flowers	Numerophobia	Numbers
Anthrophobia	People	Nyctophobia	Darkness
Aquaphobia	Water	Ochlophobia	Crowds
Arachnophobia	Spiders	Ophidiophobia	Snakes
Astraphobia	Lightning	Ornithophobia	Birds
Brontophobia	Thunder	Phonophobia	Speaking out loud
Claustrophobia	Closed spaces	Pyrophobia	Fire
Cynophobia	Dogs	Thanatophobia	Death
Dementophobia	Insanity	Trichophobia	Hair
Gephyrophobia	Bridges	Xenophobia	Strangers

Phobic Disorder

Claustrophobia. Acrophobia. Xenophobia. Although these sound like characters in a Greek tragedy, they are actually members of a class of psychological disorders known as phobias. **Phobias** are intense, irrational fears of specific objects or situations. For example, claustrophobia is a fear of enclosed places, acrophobia is a fear of high places, and xenophobia is a fear of strangers. Although the objective danger posed by an anxiety-producing stimulus (which can be just about anything, as you can see from the list in Table 12-3) is typically small or nonexistent, to the individual suffering from the phobia the danger is great, and a full-blown panic attack can follow exposure to the stimulus. Phobic disorders differ from generalized anxiety disorders and panic disorders in that there is a specific, identifiable stimulus that sets off the anxiety reaction.

Phobias might have only a minor impact if those who suffer from them can avoid the stimuli that trigger the fear. If one is not a professional firefighter or tightrope walker, for example, a fear of heights might have little impact on one's daily life. On the other hand, a fear of strangers presents a more serious problem. In one extreme case, a Washington woman suffering from xenophobia left her home just three times in thirty years—once to visit her family, once for a medical operation, and once to purchase ice cream for a dying companion (Adler, 1984).

Panic Disorder

In another type of anxiety disorder, **panic disorder,** *panic attacks* occur that last from a few seconds to several hours. Unlike phobias, which are brought about by specific objects or situations, panic disorders are not triggered by any identifiable stimulus.

phobias: Intense, irrational fears of specific objects or situations

panic disorder: Anxiety that reveals itself in the form of panic attacks that last from a few seconds to as long as several hours

Agoraphobia, the fear of being in a place from which escape is difficult, is one complication that can result from panic disorder. What sort of behavior modification approaches might be used to deal with agoraphobia?

Instead, during an attack, such as the ones experienced by Sally in the case described earlier, anxiety suddenly—and often without warning—rises to a peak, and the individual feels a sense of impending, unavoidable doom. Although symptoms differ from person to person, they might include heart palpitations, shortness of breath, unusual amounts of sweating, faintness and dizziness, an urge to urinate, gastric sensations, and—in extreme cases—a sense of imminent death. After such an attack, it is no wonder that people tend to feel exhausted (Rachman & deSilva, 1996; Pollack & Marzol, 2000).

Panic attacks seemingly come out of nowhere and are unconnected to any specific stimulus. Because they don't know what triggers their feelings of panic, victims of panic attacks can become fearful of going places. In fact, some people with panic disorder develop a complication called *agoraphobia,* the fear of being in a situation in which escape is difficult, and in which help for a possible panic attack would not be available. People with extreme cases of agoraphobia never leave their homes (Langs et al., 2000).

Generalized Anxiety Disorder

generalized anxiety disorder: Long-term, persistent anxiety and worry

People with **generalized anxiety disorder** experience long-term, persistent anxiety and worry. Sometimes their concerns are directed toward identifiable issues involving such things as family, money, work, and health. In other cases, though, people with the disorder feel that something dreadful is about to happen but can't identify what it is, experiencing "free-floating" anxiety.

Because of their persistent anxiety, they cannot concentrate, cannot set their worry and fears aside, and their lives become centered around their worry. Their anxiety can eventually result in medical problems. Because of heightened muscle tension and arousal, individuals with generalized anxiety disorder can begin to experience headaches, dizziness, heart palpitations, or insomnia.

Obsessive-Compulsive Disorder

obsessive-compulsive disorder: A disorder characterized by obsessions or compulsions
obsession: A persistent, unwanted thought or idea that keeps recurring

People with **obsessive-compulsive disorder** are plagued by unwanted thoughts (obsessions) or feel that they must carry out some actions (compulsions) against their will.

An **obsession** is a persistent, unwanted thought or idea that keeps recurring. For example, a student might be unable to stop thinking that she has neglected to put her name on a test and might think about it constantly for the two weeks it takes to get the paper back. A man might go on vacation and wonder the whole time whether he locked his house. A woman might hear the same tune running through her head over and over again. In each case, the thought or idea is unwanted and difficult to put out of mind. Of course, many of us suffer from mild obsessions from time to time, but usually such thoughts persist only for a short period. For people with serious obsessions, however, the thoughts persist for days or months and can consist of bizarre, troubling images.

compulsion: An irresistible urge to repeatedly carry out some act that seems strange and unreasonable

As part of an obsessive-compulsive disorder, people might also experience **compulsions,** irresistible urges to repeatedly carry out some act that seems strange and unreasonable, even to them. Whatever the compulsive behavior, these people experience extreme anxiety if they cannot carry it out, even if it is something they want to stop. The acts involved could be relatively trivial, such as repeatedly checking the stove to make sure all the burners are turned off, or more unusual, such as continuously washing oneself (Rachman & Hodgson, 1980; Carter, Pauls, & Leckman, 1995). For example, consider this case report of a 27-year-old woman with a cleaning ritual:

> Bess would first remove all of her clothing in a preestablished sequence. She would lay out each article of clothing at specific spots on her bed, and examine each one for any indications of "contamination." She would then thoroughly scrub her body, starting at her feet and working meticulously up to the top of her head, using certain washcloths for certain areas of her body. Any articles of clothing that appeared to have been "contaminated" were thrown into the laundry. Clean clothing was put in

the spots that were vacant. She would then dress herself in the opposite order from which she took the clothes off. (Meyer & Osborne, 1987, p. 156)

Unfortunately for those experiencing an obsessive-compulsive disorder, little or no reduction in anxiety results from carrying out a compulsive ritual. People with severe cases lead lives filled with unrelenting tension (Goodman, Rudorfer, & Maser, 1999).

The Causes of Anxiety Disorders

No one cause fully explains all cases of anxiety disorders, and each of the perspectives on abnormal behavior that we discussed earlier has something to say about their causes. However, the medical, behavioral, and cognitive perspectives have been particularly influential in psychologists' thinking about anxiety disorders.

Biological approaches, derived from the medical perspective, have shown that genetic factors play a role in anxiety disorders. For example, if one identical twin has panic disorder, there is a 30 percent chance that the other twin will have it also. Furthermore, recent research shows that a person's characteristic level of anxiety is related to a specific gene that is involved in the production of the neurotransmitter serotonin. This work is consistent with findings indicating that certain chemical deficiencies in the brain appear to produce some kinds of anxiety disorder (Lesch et al., 1996; Rieder, Kaufmann, & Knowles, 1996).

Psychologists employing the behavioral perspective have taken a different approach, emphasizing environmental factors. They consider anxiety to be a learned response to stress. For instance, suppose a young girl is bitten by a dog. When she next sees a dog, she is frightened and runs away—a behavior that relieves her anxiety and thereby reinforces her avoidance behavior. After repeated encounters with dogs in which she is reinforced for her avoidance behavior, she might develop a full-fledged phobia regarding dogs.

Finally, the cognitive perspective suggests that anxiety disorders are an outgrowth of inappropriate and inaccurate cognitions about circumstances in the person's world. For example, a person with an anxiety disorder might view any friendly puppy as a ferocious and savage pit bull, or might see an air disaster looming whenever she or he is in the vicinity of an airplane. According to the cognitive perspective, people's maladaptive thoughts about the world are at the root of anxiety disorders. (For a potentially new form of anxiety disorder, see the *Applying Psychology in the 21st Century* box on page 395.)

PsychLink
Causes of anxiety disorders
www.mhhe.com/
feldmaness5-12links

Somatoform Disorders

Somatoform disorders are psychological difficulties that take on a physical (somatic) form, but for which there is no medical cause. Even though an individual with a somatoform disorder reports physical symptoms, no biological cause exists, or, if there is a medical problem, the person's reaction is greatly exaggerated.

One type of somatoform disorder is **hypochondriasis,** in which people have a constant fear of illness and a preoccupation with their health, taking everyday aches and pains to be symptoms of some dread disease. The "symptoms" are not faked; instead, hypochondriasis is the misinterpretation of these ordinary sensations as evidence of some dread disease—often in the face of inarguable medical evidence to the contrary (Noyes et al., 1993; Cantor & Fallon, 1996).

Another somatoform disorder is conversion disorder. Unlike hypochondriasis, in which there is no actual physical problem, **conversion disorders** involve an actual physical disturbance—such as the inability to see or hear, or to move an arm or leg—but the *cause* of the physical disturbance is purely psychological. There is no biological reason for the problem. Some of Freud's classic cases involved conversion disorders. For instance, one patient of Freud's was suddenly unable to use her arm, without any apparent physiological cause. Later, just as abruptly, she regained its use.

somatoform disorder: Psychological difficulties that take on a physical (somatic) form, but for which there is no medical cause

hypochondriasis: A disorder involving having a constant fear of illness and a preoccupation with one's health

conversion disorder: A major somatoform disorder that involves an actual physical disturbance, such as the inability to use a sensory organ or the complete or partial inability to move an arm or leg

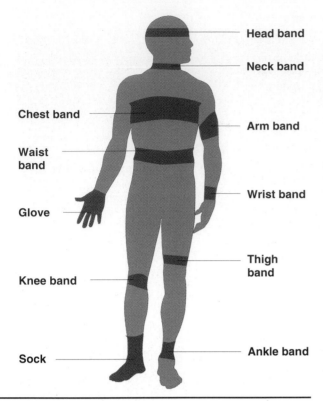

Figure 12-1 Conversion disorders sometimes produce numbness in particular isolated areas of the body (indicated by the shaded areas of the figure). For instance, in glove anesthesia, the area of the body covered by a glove is numb. However, the condition is biologically implausible because of the nerves involved, suggesting that the problem is the result of a psychological disorder rather than actual nerve damage.

 PsychLink

Dissociative disorders
www.mhhe.com/
feldmaness5-12links

dissociative disorder: Psychological dysfunctions characterized by the separation of critical personality facets that are normally integrated; this reduces anxiety by repressing disturbing thoughts or memories

dissociative identity disorder (multiple personality): A disorder in which a person displays characteristics of two or more distinct personalities

dissociative amnesia: A disorder in which the person has significant, selective memory loss

Conversion disorders often have a rapid onset. People wake up one morning blind or deaf, or they experience numbness that is restricted to a certain part of the body. Someone's hand, for example, might become entirely numb, while an area above the wrist, controlled by the same nerves, remains sensitive to touch—something that is biologically implausible. Such a condition is referred to as "glove anesthesia," because the area that is numb is the part of the hand that would be covered by a glove, and not a region related to pathways of the nervous system (see Figure 12-1).

One of the most surprising characteristics of people with conversion disorders is their lack of concern over symptoms that most of us would find very anxiety-producing. Most sighted people would be panic-stricken if they suddenly went blind. For a person in good health to suddenly go blind and react to this with bland dispassion (with *la belle indifférence,* a French phrase meaning "beautiful indifference") hardly seems appropriate.

Dissociative Disorders

The topic of the classic movie *The Three Faces of Eve* and the book *Sybil* (about a girl who allegedly had sixteen personalities) represents a class of disorders that are among the most dramatic: dissociative disorders. **Dissociative disorders** are characterized by the separation (or dissociation) of critical parts of personality that are normally integrated and work together. People who dissociate key parts of their personality are able to prevent disturbing memories or perceptions from reaching their conscious awareness, thereby reducing their anxiety (Ross et al., 1990; Putnam, 1995a; Spiegel, 1996b).

There are several dissociative disorders, and all are rare. A person with **dissociative identity disorder** (or **multiple personality**) displays characteristics of two or more distinct personalities. Each personality has a unique set of likes and dislikes and its own reactions to situations. Some people with multiple personalities even carry several pairs of glasses because their vision changes with each personality. Moreover, each individual personality can be well adjusted when considered on its own (Ross, 1996; Kluft, 1996).

The problem, of course, is that there is only one body available to the various personalities, forcing the personalities to take turns. Because there can be strong variations in personalities, the person's behavior—considered as a whole—can appear very inconsistent. For instance, in the famous case portrayed in *The Three Faces of Eve,* the meek, bland Eve White provided a stunning contrast to the dominant and carefree Eve Black (Sizemore, 1989).

A person with **dissociative amnesia** has significant, selective memory loss. Dissociative amnesia is unlike simple amnesia, which, as we discussed in Chapter 6, involves an actual loss of information from memory, typically due to a physiological cause. In cases of dissociative amnesia, the "forgotten" material is still present in memory—it simply cannot be recalled. The term *repressed memories* is sometimes used to describe the lost memories of dissociative amnesia.

In the most severe forms, individuals cannot recall their names, are unable to recognize parents and other relatives, and do not know their addresses. In other respects, though, they might appear quite normal. Apart from an inability to remember certain facts about themselves, they might be able to recall skills and abilities that they developed earlier. For instance, a chef might not remember where he grew up or received training, but might still be able to prepare gourmet meals.

In some cases of dissociative amnesia, the memory loss is quite profound. For example, a woman—dubbed Jane Doe by her rescuers—was found by a Florida park

Applying Psychology in the 21st Century

Internet Addiction: Real or Virtual?

When Michael Ian Campbell, a would-be actor, was brought before a jury on charges of threatening to "finish what began" at the Columbine High School shootings, his defense was a novel one: Internet addiction. According to his lawyer, who put forward the legal theory, Campbell was so immersed in the world of the Internet that he could not tell fact from fiction. His threat, said his lawyer, was a virtual one, and not made with criminal intent. (Janofsky, 2000)

Whether such "Internet addiction" defenses will be effective in court remains to be seen, but it is clear that the jury is out on whether Internet addiction is an actual, rather than merely "virtual," psychological disorder.

Clearly, some people spend hours each day on the Internet, developing behavior that borders on the compulsive. Some high-use individuals feel anxiety when they are away from a computer, and some try, with little success, to reduce their use of computers and the Internet. These people report that they are unable to stop thinking about computers and the Internet, and some spend increasing amounts of time online, to the neglect of their friends and family. In one court case involving a divorce and custody suit, the husband asserted that his wife spent 10 hours a day on the Internet, neglecting their children. The court supported the husband's claims and awarded him custody of the children. The judge further agreed that the wife's use of the Internet amounted to abnormal behavior (Orzack, 1999).

Who is most vulnerable to compulsive use of the Internet? People who are easily bored, lonely and shy, or depressed appear most vulnerable, along with people who use the Internet as an escape from everyday life and their problems. Ironically, as people use the Internet more, they report becoming less socially engaged with others and more lonely and depressed (Kiesler & Kraut, 1999; Orzack, 1999; Greenfield, 1999).

Although there is evidence that some people use the Internet compulsively, the findings are far from definitive. No specific disorder of Internet addiction or compulsion has been identified by clinical psychologists. In fact, some researchers argue that Internet use itself is not addictive but is instead simply a vehicle that permits people to pursue preexisting obsessions. For example, people using the Internet at very high levels tend to be primarily interested in sex, gambling, trading, and shopping; only a few compulsive users merely surf the Web (Kaiser, 1999; DeAngelis, 2000).

Whether excessive Internet use will eventually be seen as a psychological disorder remains to be seen. Furthermore, it is far from clear whether defendants (such as Michael Ian Campbell) will be able to successfully use an Internet addiction defense in court.

Do you think "Internet addiction" is more than a fascination with new technology? Do you think an "addiction" to television would have been observed when that technology was introduced? How about movies or radio? Are there features of the Internet that make it more addictive than other new technologies? Do you think it is reasonable to argue that such an addiction should excuse antisocial or dangerous behavior?

ranger in the early 1980s. Incoherent, thin, and only partially clothed, Doe was unable to recall her name, her past, and even how to read and write. On the basis of her accent, authorities thought the woman was from Illinois, and interviews conducted while she was given tranquilizing drugs revealed that she had had a Catholic education. However, the childhood memories she revealed were so universal that her background could not be further pinpointed. In a desperate attempt to rediscover her identity, she appeared on the television show *Good Morning America,* and ultimately a couple from Roselle, Illinois, whose daughter had moved to Florida, stepped forward, saying that they were her parents. However, Jane Doe never regained her memory (Carson, Butcher, & Coleman, 1992).

A more unusual form of amnesia is a condition known as **dissociative fugue.** In this state, people take sudden, impulsive trips, sometimes assuming a new identity. After a period of time—days, months, or sometimes even years—they suddenly realize that they are in a strange place and completely forget the period that they had spent wandering. Their last memories are from the time just before they entered the fugue state.

What the dissociative disorders have in common is that they allow people to escape from some anxiety-producing situation. Either the person produces a new personality to deal with stress, or the situation that caused the stress is forgotten or left behind as the individual journeys to some new—and perhaps less anxiety-producing—environment (Spiegel & Cardena, 1991; Putnam, 1995b).

"Jane Doe," who suffered from dissociative amnesia, was found wandering in a Florida park, unable to recall who she was or anything about her past.

dissociative fugue: A form of amnesia in which people take sudden, impulsive trips, sometimes assuming a new identity

Evaluate

1. Kathy is terrified of elevators. She is likely to be suffering from

   a. an obsessive-compulsive disorder

   b. a phobic disorder

   c. a panic disorder

   d. a generalized anxiety disorder

2. Carmen described an incident in which her anxiety suddenly rose to a peak and she felt a sense of impending doom. Carmen had experienced a(n) _____ _____.

3. Troubling thoughts that persist for days or months are known as

   a. obsessions

   b. compulsions

   c. rituals

   d. panic attacks

4. An overpowering urge to carry out a strange ritual is called a(n) _____.

5. In what major way does conversion disorder differ from hypochondriasis?

6. The separation of the personality, providing escape from stressful situations, is the key factor in _____ disorders.

Answers to Evaluate Questions

1. b 2. panic attack 3. a 4. compulsion 5. In conversion disorder, an actual physical disturbance is present. 6. dissociative

Rethink

1. What cultural factors might contribute to the rate of anxiety disorders found in a culture? What perspectives on psychological disorders would best explain cultural contributions to anxiety disorders?

2. Do you think the behavioral perspective would be effective in dealing with dissociative disorders? Why or why not? Which perspective do you think would be most promising for this type of disorder?

Prepare

What are the most severe forms of psychological disorders?

Organize

Mood Disorders
Schizophrenia
Personality Disorders

mood disorder: Disturbances in emotional feelings strong enough to interfere with everyday living

major depression: A severe form of depression that interferes with concentration, decision making, and sociability

 PsychLink

Major depressive disorders
www.mhhe.com/
feldmaness5-12links

Mood Disorders

> I do not care for anything. . . . I do not care to walk, for walking is too strenuous. I do not care to lie down, for I should either have to remain lying, and I do not care to do that, or I should have to get up again, and I do not care to do that either. . . . I do not care at all.

We all experience mood swings. Sometimes we are happy, perhaps even euphoric; at other times we feel upset, saddened, or depressed. Such changes in mood are a normal part of everyday life. In some people, however, moods are so pronounced and lingering—like the feelings described above by philosopher Søren Kierkegaard—that they interfere with the ability to function effectively. In extreme cases a mood can become life-threatening, and in others it can cause the person to lose touch with reality. Situations such as these represent **mood disorders,** disturbances in emotional feelings strong enough to impair everyday living.

Major Depression

President Abraham Lincoln. Queen Victoria. Mark Twain. The common link among these people? Each suffered from periodic attacks of **major depression,** one of the most common mood disorders. Some 15 million people in the United States suffer from major depression, and at any one time, between 6 and 10 percent of the U.S. population is clinically depressed. Almost one in five people in the United States experience major depression at some point in their lives. The cost of depression to society approaches $50 *billion* a year (Cronkite, 1994; Rich, 1997).

Women are twice as likely as men to experience major depression; approximately one-fourth of all females will experience it at some point in their lives. Furthermore, although no one is quite sure why, the rate of depression is going up throughout the world. Results of in-depth interviews conducted in the United States, Puerto Rico, Taiwan, Lebanon, Canada, Italy, Germany, and France indicate that the incidence of depression has increased significantly over previous rates in every area. In fact, in some

Table 12-4 A Test for Depression

This test was distributed by mental health organizations during National Depression Screening Day in the early 1990s, a nationwide event that sought to identify people who suffered from depression severe enough to warrant psychological intervention. On the day of the screening, the organizations received some 30,000 inquiries (Hill, 1992).

To complete the questionnaire, count the number of statements with which you agree:

1. I feel downhearted, blue, and sad.

2. I don't enjoy the things that I used to.

3. I feel that others would be better off if I were dead.

4. I feel that I am not useful or needed.

5. I notice that I am losing weight.

6. I have trouble sleeping through the night.

7. I am restless and can't keep still.

8. My mind isn't as clear as it used to be.

9. I get tired for no reason.

10. I feel hopeless about the future.

Scoring If you agree with at least five of the statements, including either item 1 or 2, and if you have had these symptoms for at least two weeks, help from a professional is strongly recommended. If you answer yes to number 3, you should get help immediately.

---

countries, the likelihood that individuals will suffer major depression at some point in their lives is three times higher than it was for earlier generations. In addition, people are developing major depression at increasingly early ages (Compas, Ey, & Grant, 1993; Weissman & Olfson, 1995; Beckham & Leber, 1997; Culbertson, 1997).

When psychologists speak of major depression, they do not mean the sadness that comes from experiencing one of life's disappointments, something that we have all experienced. Some depression is normal following the breakup of a long-term relationship, the death of a loved one, or the loss of a job. It is even normal following less serious problems, like doing badly on a test or finding that a romantic partner has forgotten one's birthday.

People who suffer from major depression experience similar sorts of feelings, but with much greater severity. They might feel useless, worthless, and lonely and might despair over the future. Moreover, they might experience such feelings for months or even years. They might cry uncontrollably or have sleep disturbances, and they are at risk for suicide. The depth of such behavior and the length of time it lasts are the hallmarks of major depression. (Table 12-4 provides an assessment for depression.)

Mania and Bipolar Disorders

Depression leads to the depths of despair; mania leads to emotional heights. **Mania** is an extended state of intense, wild elation. People experiencing mania feel intense happiness, power, invulnerability, and energy. They might become involved in wild schemes, believing that they will succeed at anything they attempt. Consider, for example, the following description of an individual who experienced a manic episode:

> Mr. O'Reilly took a leave of absence from his civil service job. He purchased a large number of cuckoo clocks and then an expensive car, which he planned to use as a mobile showroom for his wares, anticipating that he would make a great deal of money. He proceeded to "tear around town" buying and selling clocks and other merchandise, and when he was not out, he was continuously on the phone making "deals." He rarely slept and, uncharacteristically, spent every evening in neighborhood bars drinking

mania: An extended state of intense, wild elation

heavily and, according to him, "wheeling and dealing.". . . He was $3000 in debt and had driven his family to exhaustion with his excessive activity and talkativeness. He said, however, that he felt "on top of the world." (Spitzer et al., 1983, p. 115)

A person who sequentially experiences periods of mania and depression has **bipolar disorder** (or, as it used to be known, manic-depressive disorder). The swings between highs and lows might occur as frequently as a few days apart or they might alternate over a period of years. The periods of depression usually are longer than the periods of mania.

Ironically, some of society's most creative individuals have suffered from bipolar disorder. The imagination, drive, excitement, and energy of their manic periods fuel their creativity. For instance, historical analysis of his music shows that composer Robert Schumann was most prolific during his periodic episodes of mania. His output dropped off drastically during his periods of depression (see Figure 12-2). On the other hand, the high output associated with mania does not necessarily lead to higher quality: Schumann created some of his greatest works when he was not manic (Jamison, 1995; Week & James, 1995; Ludwig, 1996).

Despite the creative fires that can be lit by mania, persons who experience this disorder often show a recklessness that produces self-injury—emotionally and sometimes physically. They might alienate others with their talkativeness, inflated self-esteem, and indifference to the needs of others.

Causes of Mood Disorders

Because they are a major mental health problem, mood disorders—and, in particular, depression—have received a good deal of study. Several approaches have been used to explain mood disorders. Psychoanalytic approaches, for example, see depression as the result of feelings of loss (real or potential) or of anger directed at oneself. One psychoanalytic approach sees depression as produced by the loss or threatened loss of a parent early in life; another sees depression as caused by people feeling responsible for the bad things that happen to them and directing their anger inward.

On the other hand, convincing evidence has been found that both bipolar disorder and major depression may have genetic and biochemical roots. Heredity is known to play a role in bipolar disorder: the affliction clearly runs in some families. Furthermore, several neurotransmitters, including serotonin and norepinephrine, appear to play a role in depression (Delgado & Moreno, 2000; Leonard, 2000; Vogel, 2000).

bipolar disorder: A disorder in which a person alternates between periods of euphoric feelings of mania and periods of depression

PsychLink
Bipolar disorder
www.mhhe.com/
feldmaness5–12links

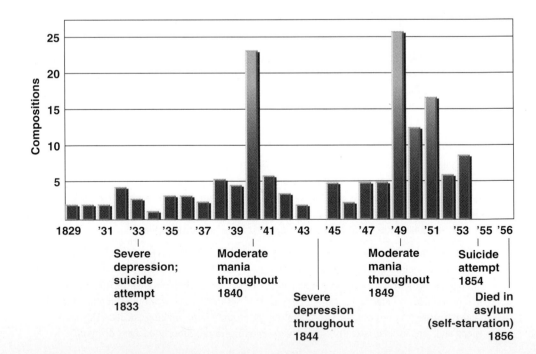

Figure 12–2 The number of pieces written by composer Robert Schumann in a given year is related to his periods of depression and mania (Slater & Meyer, 1959; reprinted in Jamison, 1993). Why do you think mania might be associated with creative productivity in some people?

Some explanations for mood disorders are based on cognitive factors. For example, psychologist Martin Seligman suggests that depression is largely a response to learned helplessness. *Learned helplessness* is a learned expectation that one cannot control the events in one's life and that there is no escape from one's situation. People with these expectations simply give up fighting negative events and submit to them, and develop depression. Other theorists go a step further, suggesting that depression is a result of *hopelessness,* a combination of learned helplessness and an expectation that negative outcomes in one's life are inevitable (Peterson, Maier, & Seligman, 1993; Nunn, 1996; Alloy, Abramson, & Francis, 1999).

Clinical psychologist Aaron Beck has proposed that faulty cognitions underlie people's depressed feelings. Specifically, his cognitive theory of depression suggests that depressed individuals typically view themselves as life's losers, blaming themselves whenever anything goes wrong. By focusing on the negative side of situations, they feel inept and unable to act constructively to change their environment. In sum, their negative cognitions lead to feelings of depression (Sacco & Beck, 1995; Wright & Beck, 1996).

The most recent explanation of depression is drawn from evolutionary psychology. In this view, depression is an adaptive response to pursuing goals that are unattainable. When people fruitlessly pursue an ever-elusive goal, depression kicks in, ending pursuit of the goal. Ultimately, when the depression lifts, people can turn to other, more reasonable goals. In this view, depression serves a positive function, in the long run increasing the chances of survival for particular individuals, who can then pass the behavior to their offspring. Such reasoning, of course, is highly speculative (Nesse, 2000).

The various theories of depression have still not provided a complete answer to an elusive question that has dogged researchers: Why is the incidence of depression twice as high for women as for men? One explanation is that women experience more stress than men at certain points in their lives—such as when a woman must simultaneously earn a living and be the primary caregiver for her children. In addition, women have a higher risk for physical and sexual abuse, typically earn lower wages than men, report greater unhappiness with their marriages, and generally experience chronic negative circumstances (Joiner & Coyne, 1999; Nolen-Hoeksema, Larson, & Grayson, 1999).

But biological factors could also explain some women's depression. For example, 25 to 50 percent of women who take oral contraceptives report symptoms of depression, and depression that occurs following the birth of a child is linked to hormonal changes (Strickland, 1992).

As yet, researchers have discovered no definitive solutions to the puzzle of depression. Many alternative explanations are offered, and most likely mood disorders are caused by a complex interaction of several factors.

The functioning of several areas of the brain is involved in producing the symptoms of depression.

Schizophrenia

I'm a doctor, you know . . . I don't have a diploma, but I'm a doctor. I'm glad to be a mental patient, because it taught me how to be humble. I use Cover Girl creamy natural makeup. Oral Roberts has been here to visit me. . . . This place is where *Mad* magazine is published. The Nixons make Noxon metal polish. When I was a little girl, I used to sit and tell stories to myself. When I was older, I turned off the sound on the TV set and made up dialogue to go with the shows I watched. . . . I'm a week pregnant. I have schizophrenia—cancer of the nerves. My body is overcrowded with nerves. This is going to win me the Nobel Prize for medicine. I don't consider myself schizophrenic anymore. There's no such thing as schizophrenia, there's only mental telepathy. I once had a friend named Camilla Costello. She was Abbot and Costello's

Schizophrenia
www.mhhe.com/
feldmaness5–12links

daughter. . . . I'm in the Pentecostal Church, but I'm thinking of changing my religion. I have a dog at home. I love instant oatmeal. When you have Jesus, you don't need a diet. Mick Jagger wants to marry me. I want to get out of the revolving door. With Jesus Christ, anything is possible. I used to hit my mother. It was the hyperactivity from all the cookies I ate. I'm the personification of Casper the Friendly Ghost. I used to go outside asking the other kids to be my friend when I was little. California's the most beautiful state in the Union. I've been there once, by television. My name is Jack Warden, and I'm an actress. (Sheehan, 1982, pp. 72–73)

This excerpt shows the efforts of a woman with schizophrenia, one of the most severe forms of mental disturbance, to hold a conversation. People with schizophrenia make up by far the largest percentage of people hospitalized for mental disorders. They are also in many respects the least likely to recover from their psychological difficulties.

schizophrenia: A class of disorders involving severe distortions of reality

Schizophrenia refers to a class of disorders involving severe distortions of reality. Thinking, perception, and emotion might deteriorate; there might be a withdrawal from social interaction; and there might be displays of bizarre behavior. Although several types of schizophrenia have been observed (see Table 12-5), the distinctions between them are not always clear-cut (Bentall, 1992; Cannon, 1998). Moreover, the symptoms displayed by persons with schizophrenia can vary considerably over time, and people with schizophrenia can have significantly different symptoms even though they are labeled with the same diagnostic category. Nonetheless, a number of characteristics reliably distinguish schizophrenia from other disorders:

- *Decline from a previous level of functioning.* The individual can no longer carry out activities he or she was once able to do.
- *Disturbances of thought and language.* People with schizophrenia use logic and language in peculiar ways. Their thinking often does not make sense, and their information processing is frequently faulty. They also do not follow conventional linguistic rules (Penn et al., 1997). Consider, for example, the following response to the question "Why do you think people believe in God?"

> Uh, let's, I don't know why, let's see, balloon travel. He holds it up for you, the balloon. He don't let you fall out, your little legs sticking down through the clouds. He's down to the smokestack, looking

Table 12-5 The Major Types of Schizophrenia

Type	Symptoms
Disorganized (hebephrenic) schizophrenia	Inappropriate laughter and giggling, silliness, incoherent speech, infantile behavior, strange and sometimes obscene behavior
Paranoid schizophrenia	Delusions and hallucinations of persecution or of greatness, loss of judgment, erratic and unpredictable behavior
Catatonic schizophrenia	Major disturbances in movement; in some phases, loss of all motion, with patient frozen into a single position, remaining that way for hours and sometimes even days; in other phases, hyperactivity and wild, sometimes violent, movement
Undifferentiated schizophrenia	Variable mixture of major symptoms of schizophrenia; classification used for patients who cannot be typed into any of the more specific categories
Residual schizophrenia	Minor signs of schizophrenia following a more serious episode

through the smoke trying to get the balloon gassed up you know. Way they're flying on top that way, legs sticking out. I don't know, looking down on the ground, heck, that'd make you so dizzy you just stay and sleep you know, hold down and sleep there. I used to be sleep outdoors, you know, sleep outdoors instead of going home. (Chapman & Chapman, 1973, p. 3)

As this selection illustrates, although the basic grammatical structure may be intact, the substance of thinking characteristic of schizophrenia is illogical, garbled, and lacking in meaningful content (see Figure 12-3).

- *Delusions.* People with schizophrenia often have *delusions,* firmly held, unshakable beliefs with no basis in reality. Most commonly, they believe that they are being controlled by someone else, that they are being persecuted by others, or that their thoughts are being broadcast so that others are able to know what they are thinking.

- *Perceptual disorders.* People with schizophrenia do not perceive the world as most other people do. They might see, hear, or smell things differently than others do (see Figure 12-4), and they do not have a normal sense of their bodies. For instance, they could have difficulty determining where their own bodies stop and the rest of the world begins (Ritzler & Rosenbaum, 1974). They might also have *hallucinations,* perceiving things that do not actually exist (McGuire, Shah, & Murray, 1993; Ruppin, Reggia, & Horn, 1996; Reichman & Rabins, 1996).

- *Emotional disturbances.* People with schizophrenia sometimes show a bland lack of emotional response to even the most dramatic events. Or they might display emotion that is inappropriate to a situation. For example, a person with schizophrenia might laugh uproariously at a funeral or might react with anger when being helped by someone.

- *Withdrawal.* People with schizophrenia tend to have little interest in others. They tend not to socialize or hold real conversations with others, although they might talk *at* another person. In the most extreme cases they do not even acknowledge the presence of other people, appearing to be in their own isolated world.

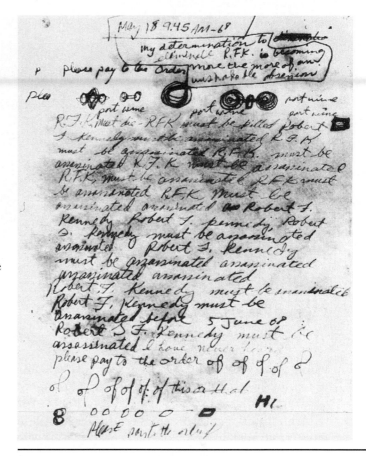

Figure 12–3 This is an excerpt from the diary of the killer of Senator Robert Kennedy who, like his brother President John Kennedy, was assassinated in the 1960s. It shows disturbances of thought and language characteristic of schizophrenia. Kennedy's killer is still in prison, but is seeking parole on the grounds that his schizophrenia is no longer a problem. Would you permit him to go free?
Source: World Wide Photos

The symptoms of schizophrenia follow two primary courses. In *process schizophrenia,* the symptoms develop relatively early in life, slowly and subtly. There could be a gradual withdrawal from the world, excessive daydreaming, and a blunting of emotion, until eventually the disorder reaches the point where others cannot overlook it. In other cases, known as *reactive schizophrenia,* the onset of symptoms is sudden and conspicuous. The treatment outlook for reactive schizophrenia is relatively favorable; process schizophrenia has proved to be much more difficult to treat.

A relatively recent addition to the classifications for schizophrenia distinguishes *positive-symptom schizophrenia* from *negative-symptom schizophrenia* (Fenton & McGlashan, 1994; Tandon, 1995; Hafner & Maurer, 1995). Positive-symptom schizophrenia is indicated by the presence of disordered behavior such as hallucinations, delusions, and extremes of emotionality. In contrast, negative-symptom schizophrenia involves an absence or loss of normal functioning, such as social withdrawal or blunted emotions. The distinction is becoming increasingly important because it suggests that two different underlying processes might explain the roots of schizophrenia—which remains one of the greatest mysteries facing psychologists who deal with disordered behavior (Fenton & McGlashan, 1991; Heinrichs, 1993).

Figure 12–4 These drawings of cats were made by an artist who suffered from schizophrenia.

Solving the Puzzle of Schizophrenia: Biological Causes

Although it is clear that schizophrenic behavior departs radically from normal behavior, its causes are less apparent. It does appear, however, that schizophrenia has both biological and environmental origins.

Let's first consider the evidence pointing to a biological cause of schizophrenia. Because schizophrenia is more common in some families than in others, genetic factors seem to be involved in producing at least a susceptibility to or readiness for developing schizophrenia. For example, research has shown that the closer the genetic link between a person with schizophrenia and another individual, the higher the likelihood that the other person will develop schizophrenia (see Table 12-6; Gottesman & Moldin, 1998; Brzustowicz et al., 2000).

On the other hand, if genetics alone were responsible, the chance that the identical twin of a schizophrenic would have schizophrenia would be 100 percent instead of 48 percent (Table 12-6), because identical twins are genetically identical. Moreover, research that has sought to find a link between schizophrenia and a particular gene has been only partly successful. Apparently schizophrenia is produced by more than genetic factors alone (Franzek & Beckmann, 1996; Lenzenweger & Dworkin, 1998).

Table 12-6 Risk of Developing Schizophrenia, Based on Genetic Relatedness to a Person with Schizophrenia

Relationship	Genetic Relatedness, %	Risk of Developing Schizophrenia, %
Identical twin	100	48
Child of two schizophrenic parents	100	46
Fraternal twin	50	17
Offspring of one schizophrenic parent	50	17
Sibling	50	9
Nephew or niece	25	4
Spouse	0	2
Unrelated person	0	1

Source: Gottesman, 1991.

One of the most intriguing biological hypotheses to explain schizophrenia is that the brains of victims harbor either a biochemical imbalance or a structural abnormality. For example, the *dopamine hypothesis* is that schizophrenia occurs when there is excess activity in the areas of the brain that use dopamine as a neurotransmitter. This hypothesis came to light after the discovery that drugs that block dopamine action in brain pathways can be highly effective in reducing the symptoms of schizophrenia. Other research suggests that dopamine might operate in conjunction with other neurotransmitters such as serotonin (Seeman, 1993; Kapur & Remington, 1996; Abi-Dargham et al., 1997).

Some biological explanations propose that there are structural abnormalities in the brains of people with schizophrenia, perhaps due to exposure to a virus during prenatal development. For example, some research has found abnormal neural circuits in the cortex and limbic system of individuals with schizophrenia. Consistent with such research, different brain functioning has been found in people with schizophrenia compared to those without the disorder (Andreasen et al., 1994; Akbarian et al., 1996; Brown et al., 1996; Lenzenweger & Dworkin, 1998; see Figure 12-5).

Environmental Perspectives on Schizophrenia

Although biological factors provide some pieces of the puzzle of schizophrenia, we still need to consider past and current experiences in the environments of people who develop the disturbance. For instance, psychoanalytic approaches suggest that schizophrenia is a form of regression to earlier experiences and stages of life. Freud believed that people with schizophrenia lack strong enough egos to cope with their unacceptable impulses. They regress to the oral stage—a time in which the id and ego are not yet separated. In this view, individuals suffering from schizophrenia essentially lack an ego and act out impulses without concern for reality.

Although this reasoning is theoretically plausible, there is little evidence to support psychoanalytic explanations. Somewhat more convincing are theories that look to the emotional and communication patterns of families of people with schizophrenia. For instance, some researchers suggest that schizophrenia is a result of high levels of expressed emotion. *Expressed emotion* is an interaction style characterized by criticism, hostility, and emotional intrusiveness by family members. Other researchers suggest that faulty communication patterns lie at the heart of schizophrenia (Weisman et al., 1993; Mueser et al., 1993; Bayer, 1996; Linszen et al., 1997).

Psychologists who take a cognitive perspective on schizophrenia look for cognitive causes for disordered schizophrenic thinking. Some suggest that schizophrenia is the result of *overattention* to stimuli in the environment. Rather than being able to screen out unimportant or inconsequential stimuli and focus on the most important things in the environment, people with schizophrenia might be excessively receptive to virtually everything in their environment. This overloads their information-processing capabilities, which eventually break down. Other cognitivists argue that schizophrenia is the result of *underattention* to certain stimuli: people with schizophrenia fail to focus on important stimuli sufficiently, and pay attention to other, less important information in their surroundings (Braff, 1993).

Although it is plausible that overattention and underattention are related to different forms of schizophrenia, these phenomena do not explain the origins of such information-processing disorders. Consequently, cognitive approaches—like other environmental explanations—are not the full explanation of the disorder.

The Multiple Causes of Schizophrenia

We have seen that several different biological and environmental factors are related to schizophrenia. It is likely, then, that not just one but several causes jointly explain the onset of the disorder. The predominant approach used today, the *predisposition model of schizophrenia,* considers a number of factors simultaneously. This model suggests that individuals might inherit a predisposition or an inborn sensitivity to schizophrenia that makes them particularly vulnerable to stressful factors in the environment. The stressors can vary—social rejection or dysfunctional family communication patterns—but if they

Figure 12-5 Structural changes in the brain have been found in people with schizophrenia. In the first MRI reconstruction of the brain of a patient with schizophrenia, the hippocampus (yellow) is shrunken, and the ventricles (gray) are enlarged and fluid-filled. In contrast, the lower MRI of a brain of a person without the disorder appears structurally different.

Source: N. C. Andreasen, University of Iowa.

are strong enough and are coupled with a genetic predisposition, the result will be the onset of schizophrenia. Similarly, if the genetic predisposition is strong enough, schizophrenia can occur even when the environmental stressors are relatively weak.

In short, schizophrenia is associated with several kinds of biological and environmental factors and is produced by a combination of interrelated variables (Lenzenweger & Dworkin, 1998; McDonald & Murray, 2000; Meltzer, 2000).

Personality Disorders

> I had always wanted lots of things; as a child I can remember wanting a bullet that a friend of mine had brought in to show the class. I took it and put it into my school bag and when my friend noticed it was missing, I was the one who stayed after school with him and searched the room, and I was the one who sat with him and bitched about the other kids and how one of them took his bullet. I even went home with him to help him break the news to his uncle, who had brought it home from the war for him.
>
> But that was petty compared with the stuff I did later. I wanted a Ph.D. very badly, but I didn't want to work very hard—just enough to get by. I never did the experiments I reported; hell, I was smart enough to make up the results. I knew enough about statistics to make anything look plausible. I got my master's degree without even spending one hour in a laboratory. I mean, the professors believed anything. I'd stay out all night drinking and being with my friends, and the next day I'd get in just before them and tell 'em I'd been in the lab all night. They'd actually feel sorry for me. (Duke & Nowicki, 1979, pp. 309–310)

This excerpt provides a graphic first-person account of a person with a personality disorder. **Personality disorders** are different from the other problems we have discussed in this chapter, because people with these psychological maladjustments feel little personal distress. In fact, people with personality disorders frequently lead seemingly normal lives. However, just below the surface lies a set of inflexible, maladaptive personality traits that do not permit them to function appropriately as members of society (Clarkin & Lenzenweger, 1996; Millon & Davis, 1996; Millon & Davis, 1999).

The best-known type of personality disorder is **antisocial personality disorder** (sometimes referred to as sociopathic personality). Individuals with this disturbance show no regard for the moral and ethical rules of society or the rights of others. Although they are intelligent and likable (at least at first), upon closer examination they turn out to be manipulative and deceptive. Moreover, they lack any feelings of guilt or anxiety over their wrongdoings. When people with antisocial personality disorder injure others, they understand intellectually that they have caused the harm but feel no remorse (Lykken, 1995).

People with antisocial personalities are often impulsive, and they are unable to tolerate frustration. They can be extremely manipulative. They also can have excellent social skills, being charming, engaging, and highly persuasive. Some of the best con men have antisocial personalities.

What causes such an unusual constellation of problems? Many factors have been suggested, ranging from a biologically induced inability to appropriately experience emotions to problems in family relationships. For example, many people with antisocial behavior come from a home in which a parent has died or left, or where they have been treated with a lack of affection, a lack of consistency in discipline, or outright rejection. Other explanations concentrate on sociocultural factors, because an unusually high proportion of people with antisocial personalities come from lower socioeconomic groups. Still, no one has been able to pinpoint the specific causes of antisocial personalities, and it is likely that some combination of factors is responsible (Nigg & Goldsmith, 1994; Hare, Hart, & Harpur, 1991; Rosenstein & Horowitz, 1996).

People with **borderline personality disorder** have difficulty developing a secure sense of who they are. As a consequence, they tend to rely on relationships with others to define their identity. The problem with this strategy is that rejections are devastating. People with this disorder are distrustful of others and have difficulty controlling their anger, and their emotional volatility leads them to impulsive and self-destructive behavior.

personality disorder: A mental disorder characterized by a set of inflexible, maladaptive personality traits that keep a person from functioning properly in society

antisocial personality disorder: A disorder in which individuals tend to display no regard for the moral and ethical rules of society or the rights of others

 PsychLink

Antisocial personality
www.mhhe.com/
feldmaness5-12links

borderline personality disorder: A disorder in which individuals have difficulty developing a secure sense of who they are

Individuals with borderline personality disorder often feel empty and alone. They might form intense, sudden, one-sided relationships, demanding the attention of another person and then feeling angered when they don't receive it (Horwitz et al., 1996).

Another example of a personality disturbance is **narcissistic personality disorder,** characterized by an exaggerated sense of self-importance. People with this disorder expect special treatment from others, and at the same time disregard others' feelings. One of the main attributes of the narcissistic personality is an inability to experience empathy for other people.

There are several other categories of personality disorder, ranging in severity from individuals who might simply be regarded by others as eccentric, obnoxious, or difficult, to people who criminally endanger others. Although they are not out of touch with reality in the way that people with schizophrenia are, people with personality disorders live on the fringes of society (Millon et al., 2000).

narcissistic personality disorder: A personality disturbance characterized by an exaggerated sense of self-importance

Attention Deficit Hyperactivity Disorder (ADHD)

You'll find one in almost every elementary school classroom: a student who can't sit still, has trouble concentrating, and is constantly fidgeting. The cause, quite often, is **attention deficit hyperactivity disorder,** or **ADHD,** a disorder marked by inattention, impulsiveness, a low tolerance for frustration, and generally a great deal of inappropriate activity. Although all children show such behavior some of the time, it is so frequent in children diagnosed with ADHD that it interferes with their everyday functioning (Barkley, 1998b; Silver, 1999; Brown, 2000).

ADHD is a surprisingly common disorder; it has been estimated that 3 to 5 percent of the school-age population—or some 3.5 million children under the age of 18—in the United States have ADHD. Children diagnosed with the disorder are often exhausting to parents and teachers, and even their peers find them difficult to deal with.

The cause of ADHD is not known, although most experts feel that it is produced by dysfunctions in the nervous system. For example, one theory suggests that ADHD is caused by unusually low levels of arousal in the central nervous system. To compensate, children with ADHD seek out stimulation in order to increase their arousal. Still, such theories are speculative. Furthermore, because many children occasionally show behaviors characteristic of ADHD, it is often misdiagnosed. It is the frequency and persistence of the symptoms of ADHD that allow for a correct diagnosis, which can only be done by a trained professional (Hinshaw et al., 1997; Barkley, 1998a, 1998b).

attention deficit hyperactivity disorder (ADHD): A learning disability marked by inattention, impulsiveness, a low tolerance for frustration, and a great deal of inappropriate activity

Evaluate

1. States of extreme euphoria and energy paired with severe depression characterize _____ disorder.

2. _____ schizophrenia is characterized by symptoms that are sudden and of easily identifiable onset, whereas _____ schizophrenia develops gradually over a person's lifespan.

3. The _____ _____ states that schizophrenia might be caused by an excess of certain neurotransmitters in the brain.

4. Which of the following theories states that schizophrenia is caused by the combination of a genetic predisposition and environmental stressors?

   a. Learned inattention theory

   b. Predisposition model

   c. Learned helplessness theory

Rethink

1. Do any of the explanations of schizophrenia offer the promise of a treatment or cure of the disorder? Do any of the explanations permit us to predict who will be affected by the disorder? How is explanation different from treatment and prediction?

2. Personality disorders are often not apparent to others, and many people with these problems seem to live basically normal lives without being a threat to others. If these people can function well in society, why should they be considered psychologically disordered?

Answers to Evaluate Questions

1. bipolar 2. Reactive; process 3. dopamine hypothesis 4. b

Prepare

What indicators signal a need for the help of
a mental health practitioner?

Organize

Beyond the Major Disorders
    The Prevalence of Psychological Disorders

Beyond the Major Disorders: Abnormal Behavior in Perspective

The various forms of abnormal behavior described in the *DSM-IV* cover much wider ground than we have been able to discuss in this chapter. Some we have considered in earlier chapters, such as *psychoactive substance-use disorder,* in which problems arise from the abuse of drugs (Chapter 4); and *eating disorders* (Chapter 8). Another important class of disorders that we have previously touched upon is *organic mental disorders.* These are problems that have a purely biological basis. There are other disorders we have not mentioned at all, and each of the classes we have discussed can be divided into several subcategories.

Keep in mind that the specific natures of the disorders included in the *DSM-IV* are reflections of today's Western cultures. The classification system is a snapshot of how its authors viewed mental disorder when the *DSM-IV* was published in 1994. In fact, the development of the latest version of the *DSM* was a source of great debate, in part reflecting social issues.

For example, two disorders were particularly controversial during the revision process. One, the category "self-defeating personality disorder," was ultimately removed from the appendix, where it had appeared in the previous revision. The label *self-defeating personality disorder* was meant to apply to people who neither leave nor take other action regarding relationships in which they receive unpleasant and demeaning treatment. It was typically applied to people who remained in abusive relationships. Although some clinicians argued that it was a valid category, applicable to patients they observed in their clinical practice, it lacked adequate research support. Furthermore, some critics complained that use of the label condemned targets of abuse for their plight—a blame-the-victim phenomenon. For these reasons, the category was removed from the manual.

A second and even more controversial category was "premenstrual dysphoric disorder": severe, incapacitating mood changes or depression related to a woman's menstrual cycle. Some critics argued that the classification simply labeled normal female behavior as a disorder. Former U.S. Surgeon General Antonia Novello suggested that what "in women is called PMS [premenstrual syndrome, a similar classification] in men is called healthy aggression and initiative" (Cotton, 1993, p. 13). Advocates for including the disorder prevailed, however, and "premenstrual dysphoric disorder" appears in the appendix of *DSM-IV* (Hartung & Widiger, 1998).

Such controversies underline the fact that our understanding of abnormal behavior is a reflection of the society and culture in which we live. Future revisions of *DSM* might include a different catalog of disorders. Even now, other cultures might well include a list of disorders that look very different from the list that appears in the current *DSM,* as we discuss next.

⊗⊗ PsychLink

PMS vs. PMDD
www.mhhe.com/
feldmaness5-12links

EXPLORING DIVERSITY

The DSM *and Culture—and the Culture of the* DSM

In most people's estimation, a person who hears voices of the recently deceased is probably a victim of some psychological disturbance. Yet some Plains Indians routinely hear the voices of the dead calling to them from the afterlife.

This is but one example of the role culture plays in the labeling of behavior as "abnormal." In fact, of all the major adult disorders identified in the *DSM,* just four are found across all cultures of the world: schizophrenia, bipolar disorder, major depression, and anxiety disorders. *All* the rest are particular to North America and Western Europe (Kleinman, 1996; López & Guarnaccia, 2000; Cohen, Slomkowski, & Robins, 1999).

Take, for instance, anorexia nervosa, first discussed in Chapter 8. Anorexia nervosa is a disorder in which people, particularly young women, develop inaccurate views of their body appearance, become obsessed with their weight, and refuse to eat, sometimes starving to death. This disorder appears only in cultures holding the societal standard that slender female bodies are most desirable. Most of the world does not have this standard, and likewise does not have anorexia nervosa. Interestingly, there is no anorexia nervosa in all of Asia, with two exceptions: the upper and upper-middle classes of Japan and Hong Kong, where Western influence tends to be great. It is also noteworthy that anorexia nervosa is a fairly recent disorder even in Western cultures. In the 1600s and 1700s it did not occur because the ideal female body in Western cultures at that time was plump.

Similarly, dissociative identity disorder (multiple personality) makes sense as a problem only in societies where a sense of self is fairly concrete. In India, the self is based more on external factors that are relatively independent of the person. There, when an individual displays symptoms of what people in a Western society would call dissociative identity disorder, it is assumed that the person is possessed either by demons (and has a malady) or by gods (and does not need treatment).

Other cultures have disorders that do not appear in the West. For example, in Malaysia, a behavior called "amok" is characterized by a wild outburst in which a person, usually quiet and withdrawn, kills or severely injures another. "Koro" is a condition in Southeast Asian males who develop an intense panic that their penis is about to withdraw into their abdomen. Some West African men develop a disorder when they first attend college they call "brain frag"; it includes feelings of heaviness or heat in the head, as well as depression and anxiety. Finally, *ataque de nervios* is a disorder found most often among Latinos from the Caribbean, characterized by trembling, crying, uncontrollable screams, and incidents of verbal or physical aggression (Stix, 1996; Cohen, Slomkowski, & Robins, 1999; López & Guarnaccia, 2000).

In sum, we should not assume that the *DSM* provides the final word on psychological disorders. The disorders it includes are very much a creation and function of Western cultures at a particular moment in time, and its categories should not be seen as universally applicable.

PsychLink

Dissociative identity disorder
www.mhhe.com/
feldmaness5-12links

The Prevalence of Psychological Disorders: The Mental State of the Union

How common are the kinds of psychological disorders we've been discussing? Here's one answer: Every second person you meet in the United States is likely to suffer, at some point in his or her life, from a psychological disorder.

At least that's the conclusion drawn from a massive study on the prevalence of psychological disorders. In the study, researchers conducted face-to-face interviews with more than 8,000 women and men of ages 15 to 54 years. The sample was designed to be representative of the population of the United States. According to results of the study, 48 percent of those interviewed had experienced a disorder at some point in their lives. In addition, 30 percent had experienced a disorder in any given year (Kessler et al., 1994).

The most common disorder was depression; 17 percent of those surveyed reported having had a major episode at least once in their lifetime (see Figure 12-6). Ten percent of those surveyed had suffered from depression during the current year. The next most frequent disorder was alcohol dependence, which occurred at a lifetime incidence rate of 14 percent. In addition, 7 percent of those interviewed had experienced alcohol dependence during the last year. Other frequently occurring psychological disorders were drug dependence, disorders involving panic (such as an overwhelming fear of talking to strangers or terror of heights), and posttraumatic stress disorder.

The study also found some unexpected gender differences. For example, 12 percent of women experienced posttraumatic stress disorder—a rate twice as high as for men. The researchers concluded that posttraumatic stress disorder, which occurs following a sudden, severe psychological shock, is a major psychological risk for women.

Figure 12-6 The percentage of people in the United States who reported a psychological disorder in the preceding year (Kessler et al., 1994). Are you surprised by the prevalence of psychological disorders?

The results of the study highlight the extent of the need for mental health services. For example, some 14 percent of those interviewed reported having had three or more psychological disorders at some time during their lives. Statistically, the people making up this group, which is the segment of the population most in need of psychological services, tend to be low-income, urban, poorly educated white women in their twenties and thirties.

These findings are supported by survey research conducted over the past 40 years, which shows that the number of people who experienced a "nervous breakdown"—admittedly a crude and imprecise term—had increased from 19 percent in 1957 to 26 percent in the mid 1990s (Swindle et al., 2000).

It is important to keep in mind that the findings are representative only of people living in the United States, and that results in other cultures differ significantly. For instance, cross-cultural surveys show that the incidence of major depression varies significantly from one culture to another. The probability of suffering at least one episode of depression is only 1.5 percent in Taiwan and 2.9 percent in Korea, compared to 11.6 percent in New Zealand and 16.4 percent in France. Such notable differences underscore the importance of considering the cultural context of psychological disorders (Weissman et al., 1996).

The prevalence figures for the United States suggest that psychological disorders are far from rare, and yet significant prejudice and discrimination are directed toward people with psychological disorders. The stigma (a label that leads people to be seen as different and therefore defective) against people who experience a psychological disorder remains real.

BECOMING AN INFORMED CONSUMER OF PSYCHOLOGY

Deciding When You Need Help

After you consider the range and variety of psychological disturbances that can afflict people, it would not be surprising if you began to feel that you are suffering from one (or more) of the problems we have discussed. In fact, there is a name for this perception: *medical student's disease*. Although in the present case it might more aptly be labeled "psychology student's disease," the basic symptoms are the same: feeling that you suffer from the problems you are studying.

Most often, of course, your concerns will be unwarranted. As we have discussed, the differences between normal and abnormal behavior are often so fuzzy that it is easy to jump to the conclusion that one has the symptoms that are involved in serious forms of mental disturbance.

Before coming to such a conclusion, though, it is important to reflect on the fact that over time we all experience a wide range of emotions, and it is not unusual to feel deeply unhappy, to fantasize about bizarre situations, or to feel anxiety about the circumstances of one's life. It is the persistence, depth, and consistency of such behavior that set abnormal reactions apart from normal ones. If you have not previously had serious doubts about the normality of your behavior, reading about others' psychological disorders is probably not a strong reason for you to reevaluate your earlier self-confidence.

On the other hand, many people do have problems that merit concern, and it is important for them to consider the possibility that they might need professional help. Following is a list of symptoms that can arise when the normal problems of everyday living escalate beyond your ability to deal with them yourself (Engler & Goleman, 1992):

- Long-term feelings of distress that interfere with your sense of well-being, competence, and ability to function effectively in daily activities
- Occasions in which you experience overwhelmingly high stress, accompanied by feelings of inability to cope with the situation
- Prolonged depression or feelings of hopelessness, particularly when they do not have any clear cause (such as the death of someone close)

- Withdrawal from other people
- A chronic physical problem for which no physical cause can be determined
- A fear or phobia that prevents you from engaging in everyday activities
- Feelings that other people are out to get you or are talking about and plotting against you
- The inability to interact effectively with others, preventing the development of friendships and loving relationships

This list offers a rough set of guidelines for determining when you might need to seek professional help. In such situations, the least reasonable approach would be to pore over the psychological disorders we have discussed in an attempt to pigeonhole yourself into a specific category. A more reasonable strategy is to consider seeking professional help—a possibility that we discuss in the next chapter.

Evaluate

1. The latest version of the *DSM* is considered to be the conclusive guideline on defining mental disorders. True or False?

2. _____ _____ _____, characterized by severe, incapacitating mood changes or depression related to a woman's menstrual cycle, was eventually added to the appendix of the *DSM-IV* despite controversy surrounding its inclusion.

3. Match the disorder with the culture in which it is most common:

   1. amok   a. India
   2. anorexia nervosa   b. Malaysia
   3. brain frag   c. United States
   4. catatonic schizophrenia   d. West Africa

4. Recent research on the prevalence of psychological disorders has found that _____ is the most common disorder, with 17 percent of those surveyed reporting having had a major episode at least once in their lifetime.

Rethink

1. Why is inclusion in the *DSM-IV* of "borderline" disorders such as self-defeating personality disorder and premenstrual dysphoric disorder so controversial and political? What disadvantages does inclusion bring? Does inclusion bring any benefits?

2. What societal changes would have to occur for psychological disorders to be regarded as the equivalent of appendicitis or another treatable physical disorder? Do you think a person who has been treated for a psychological disorder could become president of the United States? Should such a person become president?

Answers to Evaluate Questions

1. False: the development of the latest version of the was a source of great controversy, in part reflecting issues that divide society. 2. Premenstrual dysphoric disorder 3. 1b, 2c, 3d, 4a 4. depression

Looking Back

How can we distinguish normal from abnormal behavior?

- Definitions of abnormality include deviation from the average, deviation from the ideal, abnormality as a sense of personal discomfort, inability to function effectively, and legal conceptions. (p. 382)
- No single definition is totally adequate, suggesting that abnormal and normal behavior should be considered in terms of a continuum. (p. 382)

What are the major perspectives on psychological disorders used by mental health professionals?

- The medical perspective views abnormality as a symptom of an underlying disease that requires a cure. (p. 384)
- Psychoanalytic perspectives see abnormal behavior as caused by conflicts in the unconscious produced by past experience. (p. 385)
- Behavioral approaches view abnormal behavior not as a symptom of some underlying problem, but as the problem itself. To resolve the problem, one must change the behavior. (p. 386)
- The cognitive approach sees abnormal behavior as the result of faulty cognitions. In this view, abnormal behavior can be remedied through a change in cognitions (thoughts and beliefs). (p. 386)
- Humanistic approaches view people as rational and motivated to get along with others; abnormal behavior is seen as a result of difficulty in fulfilling one's needs. (p. 386)
- Sociocultural approaches view abnormal behavior in terms of difficulties arising from family and other social relationships. (p. 387)

What classification system is used to categorize psychological disorders?

- In the United States, the most widely used system for classifying psychological disorders is the *DSM-IV*—the *Diagnostic and Statistical Manual of Mental Disorders,* Fourth Edition. (p. 387)

What are the major psychological disorders?

- Anxiety disorders are present when a person experiences so much anxiety that it affects daily functioning. Specific types of anxiety disorders include phobic disorder, panic disorder, generalized anxiety disorder, and obsessive-compulsive disorder. (p. 390)
- Somatoform disorders are psychological difficulties that take on a physical (somatic) form, but for which there is no medical cause. Examples are hypochondriasis and conversion disorders. (p. 393)
- Dissociative disorders are marked by the separation, or dissociation, of crucial parts of personality that are usually integrated. The major kinds of dissociative disorders are dissociative identity disorder (multiple personality), dissociative amnesia, and dissociative fugue. (p. 394)

What are the most severe forms of psychological disorders?

- Mood disorders are characterized by emotional states of depression or euphoria so strong that they intrude on everyday living. They include major depression and bipolar disorder. (p. 396)
- Schizophrenia is one of the severest forms of mental illness. Symptoms of schizophrenia include declines in functioning, thought and language disturbances, perceptual disorders, emotional disturbance, and withdrawal from others. (p. 399)

- Strong evidence links schizophrenia to genetic, biochemical, and environmental factors. According to the predisposition model, interactions among these kinds of factors produce the disorder. (p. 402)
- People with personality disorders feel little or no personal distress, but they do suffer from an inability to function as normal members of society. The best-known types of personality disorders are antisocial personality disorder, borderline personality disorder, and narcissistic personality. (p. 404)
- Attention deficit hyperactivity disorder (ADHD), which is marked by inattention, impulsiveness, a low tolerance for frustration, and inappropriate activity, has become a commonly diagnosed (and sometimes misdiagnosed) disorder, particularly among schoolchildren. (p. 405)

What indicators signal a need for the help of a mental health practitioner?

- There are many other categories of disorders, including sexual disorders, psychoactive substance-use disorders, and organic mental disorders. There are significant cultural differences in the nature and prevalence of psychological disorders. (p. 406)
- Students of psychology are susceptible to the same sort of "disease" that afflicts medical students: the perception that they suffer from the problems they are studying. (p. 408)
- The signals that indicate a need for professional help include long-term feelings of psychological distress, feelings of inability to cope with stress, withdrawal from other people, prolonged feelings of hopelessness, chronic physical problems with no apparent causes, phobias and compulsions, paranoia, and an inability to interact with others. (p. 408)

Key Terms and Concepts

medical perspective (p. 384)

psychoanalytic perspective (p. 385)

behavioral perspective (p. 386)

cognitive perspective (p. 386)

humanistic perspective (p. 386)

sociocultural perspective (p. 387)

Diagnostic and Statistical Manual of Mental Disorders, Fourth Edition *(DSM-IV)* (p. 387)

anxiety disorder (p. 390)

phobias (p. 391)

panic disorder (p. 391)

generalized anxiety disorder (p. 392)

obsessive-compulsive disorder (p. 392)

obsession (p. 392)

compulsion (p. 392)

somatoform disorder (p. 393)

hypochondriasis (p. 393)

conversion disorder (p. 393)

dissociative disorder (p. 394)

dissociative identity disorder (multiple personality) (p. 394)

dissociative amnesia (p. 394)

dissociative fugue (p. 395)

mood disorder (p. 396)

major depression (p. 396)

mania (p. 397)

bipolar disorder (p. 398)

schizophrenia (p. 400)

personality disorder (p. 404)

antisocial personality disorder (p. 404)

borderline personality disorder (p. 404)

narcissistic personality disorder (p. 405)

attention deficit hyperactivity disorder (ADHD) (p. 405)

Psychology on the Web

1. On the Web, consulting at least two sources, research the insanity defense as it is used in U.S. courts of law. Summarize your findings, evaluating them against the psychological perspectives you read about in this chapter. Are there differences between legal and psychological interpretations of "sanity"? Do you think such differences are appropriate?

2. Find information on the Web about the controversy surrounding dissociative (or multiple) personality disorder. Summarize both sides of the controversy. Using your knowledge of psychology, state your own opinions on the matter.

Preview

For additional quizzing and a variety of interactive resources, visit the *Essentials of Understanding Psychology* Online Learning Center at

www.mhhe.com/feldmaness5

Epilogue

In this chapter, we discussed a few of the many types of psychological disorders to which people are prone, noting the difficulty that psychologists and physicians have in clearly differentiating normal from abnormal behavior, and looking at some of the approaches that have been taken to explain and treat psychological disorders. We took note of what is currently the most commonly used classification scheme (the *DSM-IV*), and we examined some of the most prevalent forms of psychological disorders. To gain a perspective on the topic of psychological disorders, we discussed the surprisingly broad incidence of psychological disorders in U.S. society and the cultural nature of such disorders.

Before we proceed to focus on treatment of such disorders, turn back to the Prologue, where you read about Lori Schiller. Using the knowledge you gained from this chapter, consider the following questions.

1. Schiller was diagnosed as suffering from schizophrenia. What elements of her behavior seem to fit the description of schizophrenia provided by the *DSM-IV* (and summarized in Table 12-2)?
2. From which type of schizophrenia (disorganized, paranoid, catatonic, undifferentiated, or residual; see Table 12-5) do you think Schiller was probably suffering? Why?
3. Which perspective (medical, psychoanalytic, behavioral, cognitive, humanistic, or sociocultural) do you think provides the best explanation of Schiller's case? Could two or more approaches be used together?
4. Were there signs of psychological disorder in Schiller's actions during adolescence? Why do you think Schiller's family failed to notice that she needed help? Why do you think it took so long for Schiller to tell her parents she had problems?

Chapter Thirteen

Treatment of Psychological Disorders

T

C
Pi
ai

C
Ps
a

Ps
M
th

Ps
Eit
de

Cl
Pri
reç

Eac
Ho
app
tou
a p
thc
me
dec
in c
app

and i
confli
them

impul
by bri
Freud
and th

patien
evolve
consid
explic
hidder
will th

Psych

Classic
and ex
four to
develo
comes
attemp
patient

Correspondent Mike Wallace is one of many people who are benefiting from new drugs that help people cope with depression.

Prologue

Breaking the Silence

In his living room on Martha's Vineyard, . . . CBS newsman Mike Wallace sat and listened to his friend, the author William Styron, talk about how depressed he was. He was so low, remembers Wallace, "I was worried about him taking his life." But Wallace, who had landed in a New York hospital for depression just months before, didn't say a word about his private agonies. "I was still in the closet," he says, "even with my friends" (Solomon, 1996, p. 20).

Ten years later, Wallace was in Washington, D.C., testifying about his mental illness. No longer hiding the fact of his depression, he was there acclaiming the benefits of the drug that ended his depression and changed his life. "I will take Zoloft every day for the rest of my life. And I'm quite content to do it" (Solomon, 1996, p. 20; Buchman, 2000).

Looking Back

What are the goals of psychologically and biologically based treatment approaches?

- Psychotherapy (psychologically based therapy) and biomedical therapy (biologically based therapy) share the goal of resolving psychological problems by modifying people's thoughts, feelings, expectations, evaluations, and ultimately their behavior. (p. 416)

What are the basic kinds of psychotherapies?

- Psychoanalytic treatment, based on Freud's psychodynamic theory, seeks to bring unresolved past conflicts and unacceptable impulses from the unconscious into the conscious, where the problems can be dealt with more effectively. This involves using techniques such as free association and dream interpretation. (p. 417)
- Behavioral approaches to treatment view abnormal behavior itself as the problem, rather than viewing the behavior as a symptom of some underlying cause. To bring about a "cure," according to this view, the outward behavior must be changed. To do this, behavioral approaches use aversive conditioning, systematic desensitization, observational learning, token systems, and contingency contracting. (p. 419)
- Cognitive approaches to treatment see the goal of therapy as a restructuring of a person's belief system into a more realistic, rational, and logical view of the world. (p. 422)

What are humanistic approaches to treatment?

- Humanistic therapy is based on the premise that people have control over their behavior, that they can make choices about their lives, and that it is up to them to solve their own problems. Humanistic therapies, which take a nondirective approach, include client-centered therapy and gestalt therapy. (p. 424)

How does group therapy differ from individual types of therapy?

- In group therapy, several people meet with a therapist to discuss some aspect of their psychological functioning, often centering on a common problem. (p. 426)

How effective is therapy, and which kind of therapy works best in a given situation?

- Most research suggests that, in general, therapy is more effective than no therapy, although how much more effective is not known. (p. 427)
- The answer to the more difficult question of which therapy works best is even less clear. However, particular kinds of therapy are more appropriate for some problems than for others. (p. 428)

How are drug, electroconvulsive, and psychosurgical techniques used today in the treatment of psychological disorders?

- Biological treatment approaches focus on the physiological causes of abnormal behavior, rather than considering psychological factors. Drug therapy, the best example of biomedical treatments, has dramatically reduced the symptoms of mental disturbance. (p. 431)
- Antipsychotic drugs such as chlorpromazine are very effective in reducing psychotic symptoms. Antidepressant drugs, such as Prozac, reduce depression so successfully that they are very widely used. The antianxiety drugs, or minor tranquilizers, are among the most frequently prescribed medications. (p. 432)

- In electroconvulsive therapy (ECT), used only in severe cases of depression, an electric current of 70 to 150 volts is briefly administered to a patient. (p. 434)
- Psychosurgery consists of surgically destroying parts of the brain. (p. 435)
- Community psychology was the stimulus for deinstitutionalization, in which previously hospitalized mental patients were released into the community. (p. 436)

Key Terms and Concepts

psychotherapy (p. 416)
biomedical therapy (p. 416)
psychodynamic therapy (p. 416)
psychoanalysis (p. 417)
behavioral treatment approaches (p. 419)
systematic desensitization (p. 420)
cognitive treatment approaches (p. 422)
cognitive-behavioral approach (p. 422)
rational-emotive behavior therapy (p. 422)
humanistic therapy (p. 425)
client-centered therapy (p. 425)
gestalt therapy (p. 426)
group therapy (p. 426)

family therapy (p. 426)
spontaneous remission (p. 427)
eclectic approach to therapy (p. 429)
drug therapy (p. 431)
antipsychotic drugs (p. 432)
antidepressant drugs (p. 433)
lithium (p. 434)
antianxiety drugs (p. 434)
electroconvulsive therapy (ECT) (p. 434)
psychosurgery (p. 435)
community psychology (p. 436)
deinstitutionalization (p. 436)

OLC **Preview**

For additional quizzing and a variety of interactive resources, visit the *Essentials of Understanding Psychology* Online Learning Center at

www.mhhe.com/feldmaness5

Psychology on the Web

1. Find out more about computer-assisted psychotherapy on the Web. Locate (1) a computerized therapy program, such as ELIZA, that offers "therapy" over the Internet, and (2) a report on "cybertherapy," by which therapists use the Web to interact with patients. Compare the two, describing how each one works.
2. Find more information on the Web about deinstitutionalization. Try to find pro and con arguments for it and summarize the arguments, including your judgment of the effectiveness and advisability of deinstitutionalization.

Epilogue

In this chapter we have examined how psychological professionals treat people with psychological disorders. We considered a range of approaches, including both psychologically based and biologically based therapies. It is clear that substantial progress has been made in recent years, both in terms of treating the symptoms of mental disorders and in understanding their underlying causes.

Before we leave the topic of psychological disorders, turn back to the Prologue, which describes Mike Wallace's liberation from his depression, and consider the following questions.

1. Are people who must take drugs for the rest of their lives in order to avoid the symptoms of depression truly cured? Why or why not?
2. How and why has the social climate changed so that people who suffer from depression, like Mike Wallace, no longer feel compelled to hide the fact that they are taking drugs for the disorder?
3. Do you think that the fact that the rates of depression are considerably higher for women than men contributed to Wallace's initial reluctance to admit to his disorder?
4. Do you think that people who recover from depression can easily reenter the world and take up their lives as if nothing had happened to them? What sorts of adjustments might people have to make?

Chapter Fourteen

Social Psychology

Prologue

From Boy to Girl and Back

When police in a small Texas town responded to a report of a dead body, first they found James Byrd's headless torso. Then, following a trail of blood, they found his head a mile away, and then his right arm, and then other parts of his body.

Ross Byrd, left, and Renee Mullins, children of murder victim James Byrd, Jr., mourn his loss.

Byrd—by all accounts a gentle and peaceful soul—had taken a ride through hell, in which he was chained to the back of a pickup truck and dragged for miles by three white supremacists. Pathologists would later report that Byrd had probably been conscious for the start of his journey, until his head was torn from his body.

Byrd's crime, in the eyes of his killers: He was African American.

Looking Ahead

The hatred and violence shown by Byrd's killers are extreme examples of prejudice and discrimination. Yet many people are the targets of verbal and physical aggression, as well as other forms of discrimination, simply because of their race, ethnicity, sexual preference, physical disability, or other characteristics that somehow set them apart from others.

Why do some people develop, and act on, prejudice? What processes shape the development of such attitudes? How can we improve social conditions to help people live together in harmony?

Each of these questions can be answered only by taking into account findings from the field of social psychology, the branch of psychology that focuses on those aspects of human behavior that unite—and separate—us from one another. **Social psychology** is the study of how people's thoughts, feelings, and actions are affected by others. Social psychologists consider the nature and causes of individual behavior in social situations.

The broad scope of social psychology is conveyed by the kinds of questions social psychologists ask, such as these: How can we convince people to change their attitudes or to adopt new ideas and values? How do we come to understand what others are like? How are we influenced by what others do and think? Why do some people display such violence, aggression, and cruelty toward others that people throughout the world live in fear of annihilation at their hands? And why, on the other hand, do some people place their own lives at risk to help others?

In this chapter, we explore social psychological approaches to these and other issues. Not only do we examine the processes that underlie social behavior, we also discuss strategies for confronting and solving a variety of problems and issues that all of us face—ranging from achieving a better understanding of persuasive tactics to forming more accurate impressions of others.

We begin with a look at how our attitudes shape our behavior, and how we form judgments about others. We'll discuss how we are influenced by others, and we will consider prejudice and discrimination, focusing on their roots and how they can be reduced. After examining what social psychologists have learned about the ways people form friendships and relationships, the chapter concludes with a look at the determinants of aggression and helping.

social psychology: The study of how people's thoughts, feelings, and actions are affected by others

attitudes: Learned predispositions to respond in a favorable or unfavorable manner to a particular person, behavior, belief, or thing

Prepare

What are attitudes and how are they formed, maintained, and changed?

How do we form impressions of what others are like and of the causes of their behavior?

What biases influence how we view others' behavior?

Organize

Attitudes and Social Cognition
    Persuasion
    Social Cognition

 PsychLink

Attitudes
www.mhhe.com/
feldmaness5-14links

Attitudes and Social Cognition

What do Tiger Woods, Rosie O'Donnell, and Bill Cosby have in common?

Each appears in television commercials designed to mold or change our attitudes. Such commercials are part of the barrage of messages we receive each day—from sources as varied as politicians, sales staff in stores, and celebrities—all meant to influence us.

Persuasion: Changing Attitudes

Persuasion is the process of changing attitudes, one of the central concepts of social psychology. **Attitudes** are learned predispositions to respond in a favorable or unfavorable manner to a particular person, behavior, belief, or thing (Eagly & Chaiken, 1993, 1995).

The ease with which attitudes can be changed depends on a number of factors, including these:

- *Message source.* The characteristics of a person who delivers a persuasive message, known as the *attitude communicator,* have a major impact on the effectiveness of that message. Communicators who are physically and socially attractive produce greater attitude change than those who are less attractive. Moreover, the expertise and trustworthiness of a communicator are related to the impact of a message—except when the communicator is believed to have an ulterior motive (Hovland, Janis, & Kelly, 1953; Priester & Petty, 1995).

- *Characteristics of the message.* It is not just *who* delivers a message but *what* the message is like that affects attitude and behavior change. One-sided arguments—in which only the communicator's side is presented—are probably best if the communicator's message is initially viewed favorably by the target (recipient) of the message. But if the target receives a message presenting an unpopular viewpoint, two-sided messages—which include both the communicator's position and the one he or she is arguing against—are more effective, probably because they are seen as more precise and thoughtful. In addition, fear-producing messages ("If you don't practice safer sex, you'll get AIDS") are generally effective, although not always. For instance, if the fear aroused is too strong, such messages can arouse people's defense mechanisms and be ignored (Karlins & Abelson, 1979; Perloff, 1993; L. H. Rosenthal, 1997).

- *Characteristics of the target.* Once a message has been communicated, characteristics of the *target* of the message can determine whether the message will be accepted. For example, intelligent people are more resistant to persuasion than those who are less intelligent. There also seem to be gender differences in persuasibility. Women are somewhat more easily persuaded than men, particularly when they have less knowledge of the message topic. However, the magnitude of the difference between men and women is not large (Eagly, 1989; Rhodes & Wood, 1992; Wood & Stagner, 1994).

Companies use sports stars like Tiger Woods to persuade consumers to buy their products. Can celebrities really affect the purchasing habits of consumers? How?

Whether recipients will be receptive to persuasive messages depends on the type of information processing they use. Social psychologists have discovered two primary information-processing routes to persuasion: central-route and peripheral-route processing. **Central-route processing** occurs when the recipient thoughtfully considers the issues and arguments involved in persuasion. **Peripheral-route processing,** in contrast, occurs when people are persuaded on the basis of factors unrelated to the nature or quality of the content of a persuasive message. Instead, they are influenced by factors that are irrelevant or extraneous to the attitude topic or issue, such as who is providing the message or how long the arguments are (Petty & Cacioppo, 1986; Petty et al., 1994).

In general, central-route processing occurs when targets are highly involved and motivated to comprehend the message. However, if central-route processing is not employed because the target is uninvolved, unmotivated, bored, or distracted, then the nature of the message becomes less important, and peripheral factors more critical (see Figure 14-1). Although both central-route and peripheral-route processing lead to attitude change, central-route processing generally leads to stronger, more lasting attitude change.

central-route processing: Message interpretation characterized by thoughtful consideration of the issues and arguments used to persuade

peripheral-route processing: Message interpretation characterized by consideration of the source and related general information rather than of the message itself

 PsychLink

Dual process persuasion
www.mhhe.com/
feldmaness5-14links

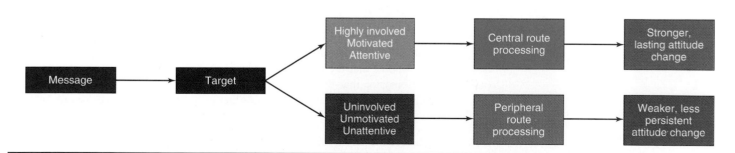

Figure 14–1 Routes to persuasion. Targets who are highly involved, motivated, and attentive use central-route processing when considering a persuasive message, and central-route processing leads to more lasting attitude change. In contrast, uninvolved, unmotivated, and inattentive targets are more likely to use peripheral-route processing, and attitude change is likely to be less enduring. Can you think of particular advertisements that try to produce central-route processing?

The Link Between Attitudes and Behavior

Not surprisingly, attitudes influence behavior. The strength of the link between particular attitudes and behavior varies, of course, but generally people strive for consistency between their attitudes and their behavior. Furthermore, people are fairly consistent in their attitudes. You would probably not hold the attitude that eating meat is immoral and still have a positive attitude toward hamburgers (Kraus, 1995).

Interestingly, not only do our attitudes influence our behavior, but sometimes our behavior shapes our attitudes. Consider, for instance, the following situation:

> You've just spent what you feel is the most boring hour of your life, turning pegs for a psychology experiment. Just as you're finally finished and about to leave, the experimenter asks you to do him a favor. He tells you that he needs a helper for future experimental sessions to introduce subsequent participants to the peg-turning task. Your specific job would be to tell them that turning the pegs is an interesting, fascinating experience. Each time you tell this tale to another participant, you'll be paid $1.

If you agree to help out the experimenter, you could be setting yourself up for a state of psychological tension that is known as cognitive dissonance. According to a major social psychologist, Leon Festinger (1957), **cognitive dissonance** occurs when a person holds two attitudes or thoughts (referred to as *cognitions*) that contradict each other.

A participant in the situation just described is left with two contradictory thoughts: (1) I believe the task is boring; and (2) I said it was interesting with little justification ($1). This should arouse dissonance. How can such dissonance be reduced? One cannot deny having said that the task was interesting without breaking with reality. Relatively speaking, it is easier to change one's attitude toward the task—and thus the theory predicts that participants will reduce dissonance by adopting more positive attitudes toward the task (Johnson, Kelly, & LeBlanc, 1995).

This prediction was confirmed in a classic experiment (Festinger & Carlsmith, 1959). The experiment followed essentially the same procedure outlined earlier. A participant was offered $1 to describe a boring task as interesting. In addition, as a control, other participants were offered $20 to say that the task was interesting. The reasoning behind this condition was that $20 was so much money that participants in this condition had a good reason to be conveying incorrect information; dissonance would *not* be aroused, and *less* attitude change would be expected. The results supported this notion. Participants who were paid $1 changed their attitudes more (becoming more positive toward the peg-turning task) than participants who were paid $20.

We now know that dissonance explains a number of everyday occurrences involving attitudes and behavior. For example, a smoker who knows that smoking leads to lung cancer holds contradictory cognitions: (1) I smoke; and (2) Smoking leads to lung cancer. The theory predicts that these two thoughts will lead to a state of cognitive dissonance. More important, it predicts that the individual will be motivated to reduce such dissonance by one of the following methods: (1) modifying one or both of the cognitions; (2) changing the perceived importance of one cognition; (3) adding cognitions; or (4) denying that the two cognitions are related to each other. Hence the smoker might decide that he really doesn't smoke all that much (modifying the cognition), that the evidence linking smoking to cancer is weak (changing the importance of a cognition), that the amount of exercise he gets compensates for the smoking (adding cognitions), or that there is no evidence linking smoking and cancer (denial). Whatever technique is used, the result is a reduction in dissonance (see Figure 14-2).

Social Cognition: Understanding Others

Regardless of his personal transgressions and his impeachment trial, many Americans genuinely *liked* President Bill Clinton, and his popularity remained high through the end of his second term. Cases like this illustrate the power of our impressions and attest to the importance of determining how people develop an understanding of others. One of the dominant areas of study in social psychology during the last few years has focused

cognitive dissonance: The conflict that occurs when a person holds two attitudes or thoughts (referred to as *cognitions*) that contradict each other

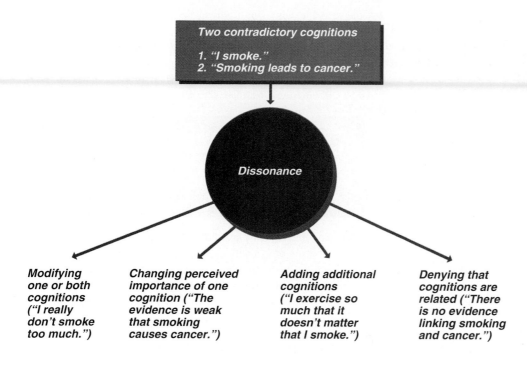

Figure 14-2 The simultaneous presence of two contradictory cognitions ("I smoke" and "Smoking leads to cancer") produces cognitive dissonance, which can be reduced through several methods. What are additional ways that dissonance can be reduced?

on learning how we come to understand what others are like and how we explain the reasons underlying others' behavior (Fiske & Taylor, 1991; Kunda, 1999).

Understanding What Others Are Like

Consider for a moment the enormous amount of information about other people to which we are exposed. How are we able to decide what is important and what is not, and to make judgments about the characteristics of others? Social psychologists interested in this question study **social cognition**—the processes that underlie our understanding of the social world. They have learned that individuals have highly developed **schemas,** sets of cognitions about people and social experiences (see Chapter 6). These schemas organize information stored in memory, represent in our minds the way the social world operates, and give us a framework to categorize, store, remember, and interpret information relating to social stimuli (Fiske & Taylor, 1991; Fiske, 1992a, 1992b).

We typically hold schemas for particular types of people. Our schema for "teacher," for instance, generally consists of a number of characteristics: knowledge of the subject matter he or she is teaching, a desire to impart that knowledge, and an awareness of the student's need to understand what is being said. Our schema for "mother" might include the characteristics of warmth, nurturance, and caring. Regardless of their accuracy, schemas are important because they organize the way in which we recall, recognize, and categorize information about others. Moreover, they allow us to predict what others are like on the basis of relatively little information, because we tend to fit people into schemas even if we don't have much concrete evidence to go on (Bargh et al., 1995).

social cognition: The processes that underlie our understanding of the social world

schemas: Sets of cognitions about people and social experiences

Impression Formation

How do we decide that Sayreeta is a flirt, Jacob is obnoxious, or Hector is a really nice guy? The earliest work on social cognition was designed to examine *impression formation,* the process by which an individual organizes information about another person to form an overall impression of that person. In one classic study, for instance, students were told that they were about to hear a guest lecturer (Kelley, 1950). One group of students was told that the lecturer was "a rather warm person, industrious, critical, practical, and determined"; a second group was told that he was "a rather cold person, industrious, critical, practical, and determined."

 PsychLink

Impression formation
www.mhhe.com/
feldmaness5-14links

Psychology at Work

Ann Altman

Advertising Executive

Education: B.A., psychology/philosophy, University of Florida at Gainesville; M.A., clinical psychology, University of Florida at Gainesville; further work toward an M.B.A., Florida State University

Home: Palm Harbor, Florida

Ann Altman

It is not surprising that over the years the field of advertising has looked to psychology as an important source of ideas for fine-tuning its promotion of products and services and for communicating with potential customers. Nor is it surprising to find people with psychology backgrounds becoming interested in and pursuing careers in advertising. Such is the case with Ann Altman.

Initially Altman pursued a doctorate, spending time in Holland researching the development of language in children with epilepsy. Eventually her interest in communication led her to the international business world of advertis-

> "Interestingly enough, my psychology background has given me the ability to step back and analyze what the client is truly saying, and to understand what the client needs."

ing, where her academic background and strengths in research have proved highly useful in the 15 years she has spent as an advertising executive.

"I apply psychology to everything I do," says Altman, who is the founder and president of the Altman Meder Lawrence Hill Advertising firm. "Advertising is a field of communication that mediates an essential interaction between a company and the audience it is trying to reach. Interestingly enough, my psychology background has given me the ability to step back and analyze what the client is truly saying, and to understand what the client needs."

Altman cites as an example a West German

---

central traits: The major traits considered in forming impressions of others

The simple substitution of "cold" for "warm" was responsible for drastic differences in the way the students in each group perceived the lecturer, even though he gave the same talk in the same style in each condition. Students who had been told he was "warm" rated him considerably more positively than students who had been told he was "cold."

The findings from this experiment led to additional research on impression formation that focused on how people pay particular attention to certain unusually important traits—known as **central traits**—to help them form overall impressions of others. According to this work, the presence of a central trait alters the meaning of other traits. Hence the description of the lecturer as "industrious" presumably meant something different according to which central trait it was associated with—"warm" or "cold" (Asch, 1946; Widmeyer & Loy, 1988).

Other work on impression formation has used information-processing approaches (see Chapter 7) to develop mathematically oriented models of how individual personality traits are combined to create an overall impression. Generally, the results of this research suggest that in forming an overall judgment of a person, we use a psychological "average" of the individual traits we see, in a manner that is analogous to finding the mathematical average of several numbers (Kaplan, 1975; Anderson, 1996).

Of course, as we gain more experience with people and observe them in a variety of situations, our impressions of them become more complex. But, because there usually are gaps in our knowledge of others, we still tend to fit them into personality schemas that represent particular "types" of people. For instance, we might have a schema of "gregarious person" that includes the traits of friendliness, aggressiveness, and openness. The presence of just one or two of the associated traits might be sufficient to make us assign a person to a particular schema (Anderson & Klatzky, 1987; Sherman & Klein, 1994).

However, our schemas are susceptible to error. For example, our mood affects how we perceive others. People who are happy form more favorable impressions and make more positive judgments than people who are in a bad mood (Kenny, 1994; Bernieri et al., 1994).

Even when schemas are not entirely accurate, they serve an important function: They allow us to develop expectations about how others will behave. These expectations permit us to plan our interactions with others more easily, and they simplify a complex social world. (To see how work on social cognition is used in applied settings, see the Psychology at Work box.)

pharmaceutical company that approached her firm needing help in promoting a natural toothpaste in the United States. The company had tried and failed several times to bring the product to the U.S. market, according to Altman.

"We began by establishing focus groups around the product, involving dental professionals, general users, and other groups we thought would be our target audience. We began to see certain patterns," she notes. "We found that the audience of greatest interest was female, aged 35 to 40, and of a certain educational level. Based on that finding, we set up targeted television, newspaper, and direct mail promotions.

"In the first research we did, 9 out of 10 people who tried the product said they would never touch it again because it wasn't foamy or sweet, but we were able to turn that around by finding out more about our participants' expectations and reactions," says Altman. "We have to be accountable to our clients in establishing effective communications between them and their potential customers. Research—practical and targeted, but psychological research nonetheless—plays a big role. It is important that we know what our typical buyers are thinking and expecting. Then we have to prepare them for what we are delivering."

> "Research—practical and targeted, but psychological research nonetheless—plays a big role. It is important that we know what our typical buyers are thinking and expecting."

Attribution Processes: Understanding the Causes of Behavior

Consider the following case:

> When Barbara Washington, a new employee at the Ablex Computer Company, completed a major staffing project two weeks early, her boss, Yolanda, was delighted. At the next staff meeting, she announced how pleased she was with Barbara and explained that *this* was an example of the kind of performance she was looking for in her staff. The other staff members looked on resentfully, trying to figure out why Barbara had worked night and day to finish the project not just on time, but two weeks early. She must be an awfully compulsive person, they decided.

Most of us, at one time or another, have puzzled over another person's behavior. Perhaps it was in a situation similar to the one above, or it may have been under more formal circumstances, such as serving as a judge on a student judiciary board in a cheating case. In contrast to work on social cognition, which describes how people develop an overall impression about others' personality traits, **attribution theory** seeks to explain how we decide, on the basis of samples of an individual's behavior, what the specific causes of that person's behavior are (Weiner, 1985a, 1985b; Jones, 1990; White, 1992).

The general process we use to determine the causes of behavior and other social occurrences proceeds in several steps, illustrated in Figure 14-3. After first noticing that a behavioral event has occurred, we must interpret the meaning of the event. This leads to the formulation of an initial explanation. Depending on the time available, the cognitive resources on hand (such as the attention we can give to the matter), and our motivation (determined in part by how important the event is to us), we might choose to accept our initial explanation or seek to modify it. If we have the time, cognitive resources, and motivation, the event becomes the trigger for deliberate problem solving as we seek a fuller explanation. During the problem formulation and resolution stage, we might try out several possibilities before determining that we have reached a solution (Krull & Anderson, 1997).

In seeking an explanation for behavior, one central question we must answer is whether the cause is situational or dispositional (Heider, 1958). **Situational causes** are elements of the environment. For instance, someone who knocks over a quart of milk and then cleans it up is probably doing so not because he or she is necessarily a terribly neat

attribution theory: The theory of personality that seeks to explain how we decide, on the basis of samples of an individual's behavior, what the specific causes of that person's behavior are

situational causes (of behavior): A perceived cause of behavior that is based on environmental factors

Figure 14–3 The general process we use to determine the causes of others' behavior and social occurrences proceeds in several steps. The kind of explanation we come up with depends on the time available to us, our cognitive resources, and our degree of motivation to come up with an accurate explanation. If time, cognitive resources, and motivation are limited, we'll make use of our first impression, which can be inaccurate.

Is this youngster shy or is he just taking a break from a vigorous game of basketball? In the fundamental attribution error, people over-attribute behavior to dispositional causes, and minimize the importance of situational causes. Do you think something similar can occur between nations?

person, but because the *situation* requires it. In contrast, a person who spends hours shining the kitchen floor is probably doing so because he or she *is* a neat person—hence, the behavior has a **dispositional cause,** prompted by the person's disposition (her or his internal traits or personality characteristics).

In our example involving Barbara, her fellow employees attributed her behavior to her disposition rather than to the situation. But from a logical standpoint, it is equally plausible that there was something about the situation that caused the behavior. If asked, Barbara might attribute her accomplishment to situational factors, explaining that she had so much other work to do that she just had to get the project out of the way, or that the project was not all that difficult and so it was easy to complete ahead of schedule. To her, then, the reason for her behavior might not be dispositional at all; it could be situational.

Biases in Attribution: To Err Is Human

If we always processed information in the rational manner that attribution theory suggests, the world might run a lot more smoothly. Unfortunately, although attribution theory generally makes accurate predictions, people do not always process information about others in such a logical fashion. In fact, research reveals consistent biases in the ways people make attributions. Among the most typical are these:

- *The fundamental attribution error.* One of the most common biases in people's attributions is the tendency to over-attribute others' behavior to dispositional causes, and the corresponding failure to recognize the importance of situational causes. Known as the **fundamental attribution error,** this tendency is quite prevalent in Western cultures. We tend to exaggerate the importance of personality characteristics (dispositional causes) in producing others' behavior, minimizing the influence of the environment (situational factors). For example, we are more likely to jump to the conclusion that someone who is often late to work is too lazy to take an earlier bus (a dispositional cause) than to assume that the cause is due to situational factors, such as the bus always running late. (Ross, 1977; Ross & Nisbett, 1991; Gilbert & Malone, 1995).
- *The halo effect.* Harry is intelligent, kind, and loving. Is he also conscientious? If you were to guess, your response probably would be yes. Your guess reflects the **halo effect,** a phenomenon in which an initial understanding that a person has positive traits is used to infer other uniformly positive characteristics. The opposite would also hold true. Learning that Harry is unsociable and argumentative would probably lead you to assume he is lazy as well. However, few people have uniformly positive or uniformly negative traits, so the halo effect leads to misperceptions of others (Petzold, 1992; Larose & Standing, 1998).
- *Assumed-similarity bias.* How similar to you—in terms of attitudes, opinions, and likes and dislikes—are your friends and acquaintances? Most people believe that their friends and acquaintances are fairly similar to themselves. But this feeling goes beyond just people we know; there is a general

tendency—known as the **assumed-similarity bias**—to think of people as being similar to oneself, even when meeting them for the first time. Given the range of people in the world, this means we're often wrong (Ross, Greene, & House, 1977; Hoch, 1987; Marks & Miller, 1987).

EXPLORING DIVERSITY

Attributions in a Cultural Context: How Fundamental Is the Fundamental Attribution Error?

Not everyone is susceptible to attribution biases in the same way. The kind of culture in which we are raised clearly plays a role in the attributions we make about others' behavior.

Take, for example, the fundamental attribution error, the tendency to overestimate the importance of personal, dispositional factors and underattribute situational causes when determining the causes of others' behavior. The error is pervasive in Western cultures but not in Asian societies.

Many students in Asian societies perform exceptionally well in school, in part because the culture emphasizes academic success and perseverance.

Specifically, social psychologist Joan Miller (1984) found that adult experimental participants in India were more likely to use situational attributions than dispositional ones in explaining events. These findings are the opposite of those based on experimental participants in the United States, and they contradict the fundamental attribution error.

Miller suggested that we can discover the reason for these results by examining the norms and values of Indian society, which emphasize social responsibility and societal obligations to a greater extent than these traits are emphasized in Western societies. She also suggested that the particular language spoken in a culture can lead to different sorts of attributions. For instance, a tardy person using English might say "I am late," suggesting a personal, dispositional cause ("I am a tardy person"). In contrast, users of Spanish who are late say, "The clock caused me to be late." Clearly, the statement in Spanish implies that the cause is a situational one (Zebrowitz-McArthur, 1988).

Cultural differences in attributions can have profound implications. As we first discussed in Chapter 9, for example, parents in Asia tend to attribute good academic performance to effort and hard work (situational factors). In contrast, parents in Western cultures tend to deemphasize the role of effort and to attribute school success to innate ability (a dispositional factor). As a result, Asian students tend to strive harder to achieve and ultimately outperform U.S. students in school (Stevenson, Chen, & Lee, 1993; Lee, Hallahan, & Herzog, 1996).

dispositional causes (of behavior): A perceived cause of behavior that is based on internal traits or personality factors

fundamental attribution error: A tendency to attribute others' behavior to dispositional causes and the tendency to minimize the importance of situational causes

halo effect: A phenomenon in which an initial perception of a person as having positive traits produces the expectation that the person has other uniformly positive characteristics

assumed-similarity bias: The tendency to think of people as being similar to oneself, even when meeting them for the first time

Evaluate

1. A learned predisposition to respond in a favorable or an unfavorable manner to a particular object is called a(n) _____.
2. One brand of peanut butter advertises its product by describing its taste and nutritional value. It is hoping to persuade customers through _____-route processing. In ads for a competing brand, a popular actor happily eats the product—but does not describe it. This approach hopes to persuade customers through _____-route processing.
3. Cognitive dissonance theory suggests that we commonly change our behavior to keep it consistent with our attitudes. True or false?
4. Sopan was happy to lend his textbook to a fellow student who seemed bright and friendly. He was surprised when his classmate did not return it. His assumption that the bright and friendly student would also be responsible reflects the _____ effect.

Rethink

1. Suppose you were assigned to develop a full advertising campaign for a product, including television, radio, and print ads. How might the theories in this chapter guide your strategy to suit the different media?
2. Joan sees Annette, a new coworker, act in a way that seems abrupt and curt. Joan concludes that Annette is unkind and unsociable. The next day Joan sees Annette acting kindly to another worker. Is Joan likely to change her impression of Annette? Why or why not? Finally, Joan sees several friends of hers laughing and joking with Annette, treating her in a very friendly fashion. Is Joan likely to change her impression of Annette? Why or why not?

Answers to Evaluate Questions

1. attitude 2. central; peripheral 3. False; we typically change our attitudes, not our behavior, to reduce cognitive dissonance. 4. halo

Prepare

What are the major sources and tactics of social influence?

Organize

Social Influence
  Conformity
  Compliance
  Obedience

social influence: The process by which the actions of an individual or group affect the behavior of others

conformity: A change in behavior or attitudes brought about by a desire to follow the beliefs or standards of other people

status: Social rank within a group

Social Influence

You have just transferred to a new college and are attending your first class. When the professor enters, your fellow classmates instantly rise, bow to the professor, and then stand quietly, with their hands behind their backs. You've never encountered such behavior, and it makes no sense to you. Is it more likely that you will (1) jump up to join the rest of the class or (2) remain seated?

Based on what research has told us about **social influence,** the process by which the actions of an individual or group affect the behavior of others, the answer to the question would almost always be the first option. As you undoubtedly know from your own experience, pressures to conform can be painfully strong, and they can bring about changes in behavior that, when considered in perspective, otherwise never would have occurred.

Conformity: Following What Others Do

Conformity is a change in behavior or attitudes brought about by a desire to follow the beliefs or standards of other people. The classic demonstration of pressure to conform comes from a series of studies carried out in the 1950s by Solomon Asch (Asch, 1951). In the experiments, participants thought they were participating in a test of perceptual skills with a group of six other participants. The participants were shown one card with three lines of varying length and a second card that had a fourth line that matched one of the first three (see Figure 14-4). The task was seemingly straightforward: The participants had to announce aloud which of the first three lines was identical in length to a "standard" line. Because the correct answer was always obvious, the task seemed easy to the participants.

Indeed, since the participants all agreed on the first few trials, the procedure appeared to be quite simple. But then something odd began to happen. From the perspective of the participant in the group who got to answer last, all of the first six participants' answers seemed to be wrong—in fact, unanimously wrong. And this pattern persisted. Over and over again, the first six participants provided answers that contradicted what the last participant believed to be correct. The dilemma that this situation posed for the last participant was whether to follow his or her own perceptions or to follow the group and repeat the answer that everyone else was giving.

As you might have guessed, this experiment was more contrived than it first appeared. The first six participants were actually confederates (paid employees of the experimenter) and had been instructed to give unanimously erroneous answers in many of the trials. And the study had nothing to do with perceptual skills. Instead, the issue under investigation was conformity.

What Asch found was that in about one-third of the trials, participants conformed to the unanimous but erroneous group answer, with about 75 percent of all participants conforming at least once. However, there were strong individual differences. Some participants conformed nearly all the time, whereas others never did so.

Since Asch's pioneering work, literally hundreds of studies have examined the factors affecting conformity, and we now know a great deal about the phenomenon (Moscovici, 1985; Tanford & Penrod, 1984; Wood et al., 1994). Among the most important variables producing conformity are the following:

- *The characteristics of the group.* The more attractive a group is to its members, the greater its ability to produce conformity (Hogg & Hardie, 1992). Furthermore, a person's relative **status,** the social rank held within a group, is critical: The lower a person's status in the group, the greater the power of the group over that person's behavior.
- *The situation in which the individual is responding.* Conformity is considerably higher when people must make a response publicly than when they can respond privately, as our founding fathers noted when they authorized secret ballots in voting.

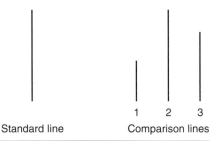

Figure 14-4 Which of the three comparison lines is the same length as the "standard" line? In Asch's conformity experiment, there was always a clear, correct answer, yet participants often conformed to the answers of the other group members. What are some ways that participants in the study could have avoided being influenced by the pressure from the group?

Standard line   Comparison lines
                              1 2 3

- *The kind of task.* People working on tasks and questions that are ambiguous (having no clear answer) are more susceptible to social pressure. Asked to give an opinion, such as on what type of clothing is fashionable, a person is more likely to yield to conformist pressures than if asked a question of fact. In addition, tasks at which an individual is less competent relative to the group create conditions in which conformity is more likely.
- *Unanimity of the group.* Conformity pressures are most pronounced in groups that are unanimous in their support of a position. But what of the case in which people with dissenting views have an ally in the group, known as a **social supporter,** who agrees with them? Having just one person present who shares the unpopular point of view is sufficient to reduce conformity pressures (Allen, 1975; Levine, 1989).

social supporter: A person who shares an unpopular opinion or attitude of another group member, thereby encouraging nonconformity

 PsychLink

Persuasion and control
www.mhhe.com/
feldmaness5-14links

Compliance: Submitting to Direct Social Pressure

Conformity is a phenomenon in which the social pressure is subtle or indirect. But in some situations social pressure is much more obvious, and there is direct, explicit pressure to endorse a particular point of view or to behave in a certain way. Social psychologists call the type of conforming behavior that occurs in response to direct social pressure **compliance.**

compliance: Conforming behavior that occurs in response to direct social pressure

Several specific sales tactics are intended to gain compliance. The following are some of the most common:

- *The foot-in-the-door technique.* A salesperson comes to your door and asks you to accept a small sample. You agree, thinking you have nothing to lose. A little later comes a larger request, which, because you have already agreed to the first one, you have a harder time turning down.

  The salesperson in this case is employing a tried-and-true strategy that social psychologists call the *foot-in-the-door technique:* You first ask a person to agree to a small request and later ask them to comply with a more important one; compliance with the later request increases significantly when the person first agrees to the smaller favor.

  The foot-in-the-door phenomenon was first demonstrated in a study in which a number of experimenters went door-to-door asking residents to sign a petition in favor of safe driving (Freedman & Fraser, 1966). Almost everyone complied with this small, benign request. However, a few weeks later, different experimenters contacted the residents again and made a much larger request: that the residents erect a huge sign reading "Drive Carefully" on their front lawns. The results were clear: 55 percent of those who had signed the petition agreed to the request, whereas only 17 percent of people in a control group who had not been asked to sign the petition agreed.

  Why does the foot-in-the-door technique work? One reason is that involvement with the small request leads to an interest in an issue, and taking an action—any action—makes the individual more committed to the issue, thereby increasing the likelihood of future compliance. Another explanation revolves around people's self-perceptions. By complying with the initial request, individuals might come to see themselves as the kind of person who provides help when asked. Then, when confronted with the larger request, they agree in order to maintain the kind of consistency in attitudes and behavior that we described earlier. Although we don't know which of these two explanations is more accurate, it is clear that the foot-in-the-door strategy is effective (Burger, 1999).

- *The door-in-the-face technique.* A fund raiser asks for a $500 contribution. You laughingly refuse, telling her that the amount is way out of your league. She then asks for a $10 contribution. What do you do? If you are like most people, you'll probably be a lot more compliant than if she hadn't asked for the huge contribution first. The reason lies in

"It's macaroni. We call it pasta as a marketing ploy."

the *door-in-the-face technique,* in which a large request, refusal of which is expected, is followed by a smaller one. This strategy, which is the opposite of the foot-in-the-door approach, has also proved to be effective (Dillard, 1991; Reeves et al., 1991; Abrahams & Bell, 1994).

One example of its success was shown in a field experiment in which college students were stopped on the street and asked to agree to a substantial favor—acting as unpaid counselors for juvenile delinquents two hours a week for two years (Cialdini et al., 1975). Not surprisingly, no one agreed to make such an enormous commitment. But when they were later asked the considerably smaller favor of taking a group of delinquents on a two-hour trip to the zoo, half the people complied. In comparison, only 17 percent of a control group of participants who had not first received the larger request agreed.

The use of this technique is widespread. You may have used it at some point yourself, perhaps by asking your parents for a very large increase in your allowance and later settling for less. Similarly, television writers sometimes sprinkle their scripts with obscenities that they know will be cut by network censors, hoping to keep other key phrases intact (Cialdini, 1988).

- *The that's-not-all technique.* In this technique, you're offered a deal at an inflated price. But immediately following the initial offer, the salesperson offers an incentive, discount, or bonus to clinch the deal.

  Although it sounds transparent, such a practice can be quite effective. In one study, the experimenters set up a booth and sold cupcakes for 75 cents each. In one condition, customers were told directly that the price was 75 cents. But in another condition, they were told the price was $1, but had been reduced to 75 cents. As the that's-not-all technique would predict, more cupcakes were sold at the "reduced" price—even though it was identical to the price in the other experimental condition (Burger, 1986).

- *The not-so-free sample.* If you're ever given a free sample, keep in mind that it comes with a psychological cost. Salespeople provide samples to potential customers in order to instigate the norm of reciprocity. The *norm of reciprocity* is the well-accepted societal standard dictating that we should treat other people as they treat us. Receiving a not-so-free sample, then, suggests the need for reciprocation—in the form of a purchase, of course (Cialdini, 1988).

The techniques devised by social psychologists for promoting compliance are often used by companies seeking to sell their products to consumers, but they are also used by employers to bring about compliance and raise productivity of employees in the workplace. In fact, a branch of psychology, **industrial-organizational (I/O) psychology,** considers such issues as worker motivation, satisfaction, safety, and productivity. I/O psychologists also focus on the operation and design of organizations, asking such questions as how can decision making be improved in large organizations, and how can the fit between workers and their jobs be maximized. Furthermore, as we discuss in the *Applying Psychology in the 21ˢᵗ Century* box, one of the newest frontiers for industrial-organizational psychologists is tracking and targeting consumers virtually.

industrial-organizational (I/O) psychology: The branch of psychology that focuses on work and job-related issues, including productivity, job satisfaction, decision making, and consumer behavior

Obedience: Obeying Direct Orders

Compliance techniques try to gently lead people toward agreement with a request. In some cases, however, requests are geared toward producing **obedience,** a change in behavior in response to the commands of others. Although obedience is considerably less common than conformity and compliance, it does occur in several specific kinds of relationships. For example, we might show obedience to our boss, teacher, or parent, merely because of the power they hold to reward or punish us.

obedience: Conforming behavior in reaction to the commands of others

To acquire an understanding of obedience, consider for a moment how you might respond if a stranger said to you:

Applying Psychology in the 21st Century

Reading Your Mind, Reaching Your Wallet: Using Computer Technology to Increase Compliance

Jennifer Zweben has a weakness: she loves to buy CDs. Her studio apartment in San Jose, California, is littered with new purchases, everything from hip-hop to alternative, classical to techno. She's also a frequent online shopper, usually ringing up an order for CDs or books at least once a month. Indeed, just the other day, Zweben dropped by www.cdnow.com, an online music store, to check the price for her latest must-have.... While reading about the album, she noticed that the Web site had generated a list of other CDs for her to consider. One stood out: "Mermaid Avenue" by Billy Bragg and Wilco. Zweben, Webmaster at IBM Research, had heard a few songs from the album on the radio and liked them. "I'm always scouting for new music," she says, "but I wouldn't have remembered to look for this title on my own." She ... plunked "Mermaid Avenue" into her virtual shopping cart (Lach, 1998, p. 39).

Welcome to the world of virtual persuasion, where compliance pressures are carefully addressed to the specific attitudes and prior behavior of individuals like Jennifer Zweben. Such targeting of website visitors represents the newest use by industrial-organization psychologists of psychographics, a technique that divides people into lifestyle profiles related to purchasing patterns. Psychographics considers such characteristics as a target's age, race, ethnicity, religion, income, marital status, and buying patterns. The technique also examines leisure activities of consumers of particular products. For instance, auto manufacturers know that buyers of minivans are more likely to participate in conversations with friends, go to family gatherings, read, and attend church functions than owners of sport utility vehicles. On the other hand, sport utility vehicle owners are more likely to go to sporting events, work out, hunt, and go out to clubs than minivan owners (Bradsher, 2000; Binkley, 2000).

Web-based persuasion techniques employ past purchasing history and previously stated preferences to build profiles of individuals, permitting sellers to target offers that are most likely to be of interest to given individuals. For example, if someone expresses an interest online

in a new 'N Sync CD, a Web supplier might search its database to see what other CDs were purchased by those who bought 'N Sync CDs. Once it has found this information, it will create a screen on the computer, offering a list of CDs of potential interest—a process called *collaborative filtering*.

Such technology might well move beyond the Web and spawn other persuasion techniques. Consider this scenario: you load up your shopping cart at the supermarket with a week's worth of groceries. After scanning your purchases into the cash register, the clerk reads a message that pops up on a computer screen and says to you, "Do you need dog food today?" You nod and rush back for the dog food, knowing that your buying habits—and the fact that you buy dog food every month or so—lie in the database of the supermarket's computers (Lach, 1998).

Do you think psychographics and collaborative filtering are basically helpful tools for consumers, or are they invasions of privacy? Is there any downside to being led to make purchases that are entirely consistent with what you and others with similar purchasing habits have bought in the past?

I've devised a new way of improving memory. All I need is for you to teach people a list of words and then give them a test. The test procedure requires only that you give learners a shock each time they make a mistake on the test. To administer the shocks you will use a "shock generator" that gives shocks ranging from 30 to 450 volts. You can see that the switches are labeled from "slight shock" through "danger: severe shock" at the top level, where there are three red X's. But don't worry; although the shocks may be painful, they will cause no permanent damage.

Presented with this situation, you would be likely to think that neither you nor anyone else would go along with the stranger's unusual request. Clearly, it lies outside the bounds of what we consider good sense.

Or does it? Suppose the stranger asking for your help were a psychologist conducting an experiment. Or suppose it were your teacher, your employer, or your military commander—all people in authority with some seemingly legitimate reason for their request.

If you still believe it unlikely that you would comply—think again. For the situation presented above describes a now-classic experiment conducted by social psychologist Stanley Milgram in the 1960s (Milgram, 1974). In the study, participants were placed in a situation in which they were told by an experimenter to give increasingly stronger shocks to another person as part of a study on learning (see Figure 14-5). In reality, the experiment had nothing to do with learning; the real issue under consideration was the degree to which participants would comply with the experimenter's requests. In fact, the "learner" supposedly receiving the shocks was actually a confederate who never really received any shocks.

Figure 14–5 This impressive-looking "shock generator" was used to lead participants to believe they were administering electric shocks to another person, who was connected to the generator by electrodes that were attached to the skin.

PsychLink
Perils of obedience
www.mhhe.com/
feldmaness5-14links

Most people who hear a description of the experiment feel that it is unlikely that *any* participant would give the maximum level of shock—or, for that matter, any shock at all. Even a group of psychiatrists to whom the situation was described predicted that fewer than 2 percent of the participants would fully comply and administer the strongest shocks.

However, the actual results contradicted both experts' and nonexperts' predictions. Some 65 percent of the participants eventually used the highest setting on the shock generator, 450 volts, to shock the learner. This obedience occurred even though the learner, who had mentioned at the start of the experiment that he had a heart condition, demanded to be released, screaming "Let me out of here! Let me out of here! My heart's bothering me. Let me out of here!" Still, despite the learner's pleas, most participants continued to administer the shocks.

Why did so many individuals comply with the experimenter's demands? Extensive interviews were carried out with participants following the experiment. They showed that participants were obedient primarily because they believed that the experimenter would be responsible for any potential ill effects that befell the learner. The experimenter's orders were accepted, then, because the participants thought that they personally could not be held accountable for their actions—they could always blame the experimenter (Darley, 1995; Blass, 1996).

The Milgram experiment has been criticized for creating an extremely trying set of circumstances for the participants, thereby raising serious ethical concerns. (Undoubtedly, the experiment could not be conducted today because of ethical considerations.) Other critics have suggested that the conditions in Milgram's experiment did not mirror real-world obedience (Miller, Collins, & Brief, 1995; Blass, 2000).

Despite these concerns, Milgram's research remains one of the strongest laboratory demonstrations of obedience. We need only consider actual instances of obedience to authority to witness some frightening real-life parallels. For instance, a major defense offered after World War II by Nazi officers to excuse their participation in atrocities during the war was that they were "only following orders." Milgram's experiment, which was motivated in part by his desire to explain the behavior of everyday Germans during World War II, forces each of us to ask ourselves this question: Would we be able to withstand the intense power of authority?

Evaluate

1. A _____ _____, or person who agrees with the dissenting viewpoint, is likely to reduce conformity.
2. Who pioneered the study of conformity?
   a. Skinner
   b. Asch
   c. Milgram
   d. Fiala
3. Which of the following techniques asks a person to comply with a small initial request to enhance the likelihood that the person will later comply with a larger request?
   a. Door-in-the-face
   b. Foot-in-the-door
   c. That's-not-all
   d. Not-so-free sample
4. The _____-_____-_____-_____ technique begins with an outrageous request which then makes a smaller request seem reasonable.
5. _____ is a change in behavior that is due to another person's orders.

Answers to Evaluate Questions

1. social supporter 2. b 3. b 4. door-in-the-face 5. Obedience

Rethink

1. Given that persuasive techniques like those described in this section are so powerful, should there be laws against the use of such techniques? Should people be taught defenses against such techniques? Is the use of such techniques ethically and morally defensible?
2. Why do you think the Milgram experiment is so controversial? What sorts of effects might the experiment have had on participants? Do you think the experiment would have had similar results if it had been conducted not in a laboratory setting, but among members of a social group (such as a fraternity or sorority) with strong pressures to conform?

Prejudice and Discrimination

What do you think of when someone says, "He's African American" or "She's Chinese" or "woman driver"?

Most people automatically jump to some sort of impression of what that individual is like. Such views represent **stereotypes,** generalized beliefs and expectations about social groups and their members. Stereotypes, which can be negative or positive, are the outgrowth of our tendency to categorize and organize the vast amount of information we encounter in our everyday lives. All stereotypes oversimplify the world: We view individuals not in terms of their individual characteristics, but in terms of their membership in a particular group (Jussim et al., 1996; Macrae, Stangor, & Hewstone, 1996).

Stereotypes can lead to **prejudice,** the negative (or positive) evaluations of groups and their members. For instance, racial prejudice occurs when a member of a racial group is evaluated in terms of race and not because of her or his own characteristics or abilities.

The most common stereotypes and forms of prejudice have to do with racial, religious, and ethnic categorizations. Over the years, various groups have been called "lazy" or "shrewd" or "cruel" with varying degrees of regularity by members of other groups. Stereotypes remain, even today, despite major progress toward the reduction of legally sanctioned manifestations of prejudice such as school segregation (Katz & Braly, 1933; Johnston, 1996).

Although usually backed by little or no evidence, stereotypes often have harmful consequences. When people act on negative stereotypes, the result is **discrimination**—negative behavior toward members of a particular group. Discrimination can lead to exclusion from jobs, neighborhoods, or educational opportunities, and can result in members of particular groups receiving lower salaries and benefits.

Stereotyping not only leads to overt discrimination; it can actually *cause* members of stereotyped groups to behave in ways that reflect the stereotype, through a phenomenon known as the *self-fulfilling prophecy.* Self-fulfilling prophecies are expectations

Prepare

What are stereotypes, prejudice, and discrimination?
How can we reduce prejudice and discrimination?

Organize

Prejudice and Discrimination
   The Foundations of Prejudice
   Working to End Prejudice
      and Discrimination

stereotypes: Generalized beliefs and expectations about social groups and their members
prejudice: The negative (or positive) evaluations of groups and their members

discrimination: Negative behavior toward members of a particular group about the occurrence of a future event or behavior that act to increase the likelihood that the event or behavior *will* occur. For example, if people think that members of a particular group lack ambition, they might treat them in a way that diminishes their ambition (Harris-Kern & Perkins, 1995; Madon, Jussim, & Eccles, 1997).

⊙⊙ PsychLink
Testing hidden prejudice
www.mhhe.com/
feldmaness5–14links

The Foundations of Prejudice

No one has ever been born disliking a particular racial, religious, or ethnic group. People learn to hate, in much the same way that they learn the alphabet.

According to *social learning approaches* to stereotyping and prejudice, people's feelings about members of various groups are shaped by the behavior of parents, other adults, and peers. For instance, bigoted parents might commend their children for expressing prejudices. Likewise, young children learn prejudice by imitating the behavior of adult models. Such learning starts at an early age; children as young as 3 years of age begin to show preferences for members of their own race (Katz, 1976; Yenerall, 1995).

The mass media also provide a major source of information about stereotypes, not just for children, but for adults as well. Even today, some television shows and movies portray Italians as Mafia-like mobsters, Jews as greedy bankers, and African Americans as promiscuous or lazy. When such inaccurate portrayals are the primary source of information about minority groups, they can lead to the development and maintenance of unfavorable stereotypes (Herrett-Skjellum & Allen, 1996; Coltraine & Messineo, 2000).

Other explanations of prejudice and discrimination focus on how being a member of a particular group can magnify our self-esteem. According to *social identity theory,* we use group membership as a source of pride and self-worth. Slogans such as "Gay pride" and "Black is beautiful" exemplify the argument that group membership gives us self-respect (Tajfel, 1982; Rowley et al., 1998).

However, there is an unfortunate outcome of the use of group membership to provide social respect. In an effort to maximize our sense of self-esteem, we might come to think that our own group is *better* than others. Consequently, we inflate the positive aspects of our own group—and, devalue groups to which we do not belong. Ultimately, we come to view members of other groups as inferior to members of our own (Turner et al., 1992). The end result is prejudice toward members of groups of which we are not a part.

Neither social learning nor social identity approaches provide the full story of stereotyping and prejudice. For instance, some psychologists argue that prejudice results when there is perceived competition for scarce societal resources. Thus, when they must compete for jobs or housing, members of majority groups might perceive (however unjustly or inaccurately) minority group members as hindering their efforts to attain their goals, which can lead to prejudice (Simpson & Yinger, 1985). Other explanations for prejudice emphasize human cognitive limitations that lead us to categorize people on the basis of visually conspicuous physical features such as race, sex, and ethnic group. Such categorization can lead to stereotypes and, ultimately, to discriminatory behavior (Fiske & Morling, 1996; Fiske, 1998).

Like father, like son: Social learning approaches to stereotyping and prejudice suggest that attitudes and behaviors toward members of minority groups are learned through the observation of parents and other individuals. How can this cycle be broken?

Working to End Prejudice and Discrimination

How can we diminish the effects of prejudice and discrimination? Psychologists have developed several strategies that have proven effective, including these:

- *Increasing contact between the target of stereotyping and the holder of the stereotype.* Research has shown that increasing the amount of interaction between people from different groups can reduce negative stereotyping. But only certain kinds of contact are likely to foster a reduction in prejudice and discrimination. Situations where there is relatively intimate contact, where the individuals are of equal status, or where participants must cooperate with one another or are dependent on one another are most likely to reduce stereotyping (Gaertner et al., 1996; Pettigrew, 1997; Oskamp, 2000).

- *Making positive values and norms against prejudice more conspicuous.* It is not always necessary to rely on contact to reduce prejudice and discrimination. Another approach is to demonstrate to people the inconsistencies between values they hold regarding equality and fair treatment of others, and negative stereotyping. For instance, people who are made to understand that their values regarding equality and fairness are inconsistent with their negative perceptions of minority group members are more likely to work actively against prejudice in the future. Similarly, people who hear others vehemently condemn racism are subsequently more likely to strongly condemn racism (Rokeach, 1971; Blanchard, Lilly, & Vaughn, 1991).

- *Providing information about the objects of stereotyping.* Probably the most direct way to change stereotypical and discriminatory attitudes is through education: teaching people to be more aware of the positive characteristics of targets of stereotyping. For instance, when the meaning of puzzling behavior is explained to people holding stereotypes, they might come to appreciate its true significance—even though it might still appear foreign and perhaps even threatening. Furthermore, training in statistical reasoning, which illustrates various logical fallacies, can inhibit the formation of certain stereotypes (Langer, Bashner, & Chanowitz, 1985; Landis et al., 1976; Schaller et al., 1996).

- *Reducing stereotype vulnerability.* Social psychologist Claude Steele suggests that many African Americans suffer from *stereotype vulnerability,* obstacles to performance that stem from awareness of society's stereotypes regarding minority group members. He argues that African American students who receive instruction from teachers who doubt their abilities and who set up special remedial programs to assist them can come to accept society's stereotypes and believe that they are prone to fail (Steele, 1992, 1997).

    Such beliefs can have devastating effects. When confronted with an academic task, African American students might fear that their performance will simply confirm society's negative stereotypes. The immediate consequence of this fear is anxiety that hampers performance. But the long-term consequences can be even worse: Faced with doubts about their ability to perform successfully in academic environments, African Americans might decide that the risks of failure are so great that it is not worth the effort even to attempt to do well. Ultimately, they might "disidentify" with academic success by minimizing the importance of academic endeavors (Steele & Aronson, 1995; Steele, 1997; Stone et al., 1999).

    However, Steele's analysis suggests that it might be possible to overcome the predicament in which African Americans may find themselves. Specifically, intervention programs can train minority group members about their vulnerability to stereotypes and illustrate that the stereotypes are inaccurate. If they can be convinced that they have the potential to be academically successful, members of minority groups might well become immune to the potentially treacherous consequences of negative stereotypes.

 PsychLink

Teaching tolerance project
www.mhhe.com/
feldmaness5-14links

Evaluate

1. Any expectation—positive or negative—about an individual based solely on that person's membership in a group can be a stereotype. True or false?
2. A negative (or positive) evaluation of a group and its members is called:
   a. stereotyping
   b. prejudice
   c. self-fulfilling prophecy
   d. discrimination
3. Paul is a store manager who does not expect women to succeed in business. He therefore offers important, high-profile responsibilities only to men. If the female employees fail to move up in the company, this could be an example of a _____-_____ prophecy.

Answers to Evaluate Questions

1. True 2. b 3. self-fulfilling

Rethink

1. How are stereotypes, prejudice, and discrimination related? In a society committed to equality, which of the three should be changed first? Why?
2. Do you think women can be victims of stereotype vulnerability? In what topical areas might this occur? Can men be victims of stereotype vulnerability?

Prepare

Why are we attracted to certain people, and what progression do social relationships generally follow?
What factors underlie aggression and prosocial behavior?

Organize

Positive and Negative Social Behavior
   Liking and Loving
   Aggression and Prosocial Behavior

Positive and Negative Social Behavior

Are people basically good or bad?

Like philosophers and theologians, social psychologists have pondered the basic nature of humanity. Is it represented by the violence and cruelty we see throughout the world, or is there something special about human nature that permits loving, considerate, unselfish, and even noble behavior?

We turn to two routes that social psychologists have followed in seeking answers to these questions. We first consider what they have learned about the sources of our attraction to others, and we end this chapter with a look at two sides of the coin of human behavior: aggression and helping.

Liking and Loving: Interpersonal Attraction and the Development of Relationships

There is nothing more central in most people's lives than their feelings for others, and consequently it is not surprising that liking and loving have become a major focus of interest for social psychologists. Known more formally as the study of **interpersonal attraction** or **close relationships,** this area addresses the factors that lead to positive feelings for others.

interpersonal attraction (or close relationships): Positive feelings for others; liking and loving

How Do I Like Thee? Let Me Count the Ways

By far the greatest amount of research has focused on liking, probably because it is easier for investigators conducting short-term experiments to produce states of liking for strangers one has just met than to instigate and observe loving relationships over long periods of time. Hence traditional studies have given us a good deal of knowledge about the factors that initially attract two people to each other (Berscheid, 1985; Simpson & Harris, 1994). Among the most important factors considered by social psychologists are the following:

- *Proximity.* If you live in a dormitory or an apartment, consider the friends you made when you first moved in. Chances are you became friendliest with those who lived geographically closest to you. In fact, this is one of the most firmly established findings in the interpersonal attraction literature: *Proximity* leads to liking (Festinger, Schachter, & Back, 1950; Nahome & Lawton, 1975).

- *Mere exposure.* Repeated exposure to a person is often sufficient to produce attraction. Interestingly, repeated exposure to *any* stimulus—a person, picture, compact disc, or virtually anything—usually makes us like the stimulus more. Becoming familiar with a stimulus can evoke positive feelings; the positive feelings stemming from familiarity are then transferred to the stimulus itself. There are exceptions, though. When the initial interactions are strongly negative, repeated exposure is unlikely to cause us to like another person more. Instead, the more we are exposed to him or her, the more we might dislike the individual (Bornstein & D'Agostino, 1994; Kruglanski, Freund, & Bar Tal, 1996).

- *Similarity.* Folk wisdom tells us that birds of a feather flock together. Unfortunately, it also maintains that opposites attract. Social psychologists have come up with a clear verdict regarding which of the two statements is correct: We tend to like those who are similar to us. Discovering that others are similar to us in terms of attitudes, values, or traits promotes our liking them. Furthermore, the more similar others are, the more we like them (Byrne, 1969; Glaman, Jones, & Rozelle, 1996).

    One reason similarity increases the likelihood of interpersonal attraction is that we assume that people with similar attitudes will evaluate us positively. Because there is a strong **reciprocity-of-liking effect** (a tendency to like those who like us), our knowledge that another person evaluates us positively promotes our attraction to that person. In addition, we assume that when we like someone else, that person likes us in return (Condon & Crano, 1988; Metee & Aronson, 1974; Tagiuri, 1958).

- *Physical attractiveness.* For most people, the equation *beautiful = good* is quite true. As a result, people who are physically attractive are more popular than those who are physically unattractive, if all other factors are equal. This finding, which contradicts the values that most people say they hold, is apparent even in childhood—with nursery-school-age children rating popularity on the basis of attractiveness—and continues into adulthood. Indeed, physical attractiveness might be the single most important element promoting initial liking in college dating situations, although its influence eventually decreases when people get to know each other better (Keller & Young, 1996; Langlois et al., 2000; Sangrador & Yela, 2000).

The factors we have discussed are not, of course, the only constituents of liking. For example, surveys have sought to identify the factors critical in friendships. In a questionnaire answered by some 40,000 respondents, the qualities that were most valued in a friend were the ability to keep confidences, loyalty, and warmth and affection, followed closely by supportiveness, frankness, and a sense of humor (Parlee, 1979). The results are summarized in Figure 14-6.

How Do I Love Thee? Let Me Count the Ways

Whereas our knowledge of what makes people like one another is extensive, our understanding of love is more limited in scope and recently acquired. For some time, many social psychologists believed that love was a phenomenon too difficult to observe and study in a controlled, scientific way. However, love is such a central issue in most people's lives that, in time, social psychologists could not resist its allure and became infatuated with the topic (Aron et al., 1997).

As a first step, researchers tried to identify the characteristics that distinguish between mere liking and full-blown love. They discovered that love is not simply liking of a greater quantity, but a qualitatively different psychological state. For instance, at least in its early stages, love includes relatively intense physiological arousal, an all-encompassing interest in another individual, fantasizing about the other, and relatively rapid swings of emotion.

PsychLink
Study of relationships
www.mhhe.com/
feldmaness5-14links

reciprocity-of-liking effect: A tendency to like those who like us

PsychLink
Definition of love
www.mhhe.com/
feldmaness5-14links

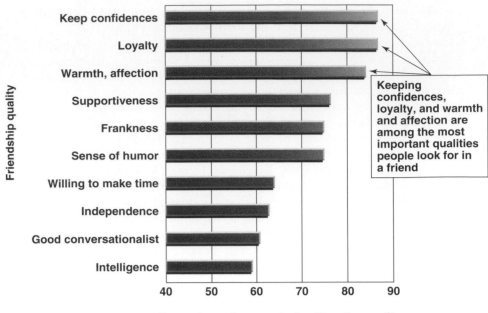

Figure 14-6 These are the key qualities looked for in a friend according to some 40,000 respondents to a questionnaire.

Keeping confidences, loyalty, and warmth and affection are among the most important qualities people look for in a friend

Similarly, love, unlike liking, includes elements of passion, closeness, fascination, exclusiveness, sexual desire, and intense caring. Partners are idealized; we exaggerate their good qualities and minimize their imperfections (Murray & Holmes, 1997).

Other researchers have theorized that there are two main types of love: passionate love and companionate love. **Passionate (or romantic) love** is a state of intense absorption in another person. It includes intense physiological arousal, psychological interest, and caring for the needs of the other. In contrast, **companionate love** is the strong affection we have for those with whom our lives are deeply involved. The love we feel for our parents, other family members, and even some close friends falls into the category of companionate love (Singelis, Choo, & Hatfield, 1995; Baumeister & Bratslavsky, 1999; Regan, 2000).

According to psychologist Robert Sternberg (1986, 1988), an even finer differentiation between types of love is in order. He proposes that love is made up of three components: an *intimacy component,* encompassing feelings of closeness and connectedness; a *passion component,* made up of the motivational drives relating to sex, physical closeness, and romance; and a *decision/commitment component,* encompassing the initial cognition that one loves someone and the longer-term feelings of commitment to maintain love. These three components combine to produce the possible different types of love (see Figure 14-7).

Is love a necessary ingredient of a good marriage? Yes, if you live in United States. On the other hand, it's considerably less important in other cultures. Although mutual attraction and love are the most important characteristics desired in a mate for women and men in the United States, men in China rated good health as most important, and women there rated emotional stability and maturity as most important. In Zulu, South Africa, women rated dependable character first and men rated emotional stability first (Buss et al., 1990; see Table 14-1).

passionate (or romantic) love: A state of intense absorption in someone that includes intense physiological arousal, psychological interest, and caring for the needs of another

companionate love: The strong affection we have for those with whom our lives are deeply involved

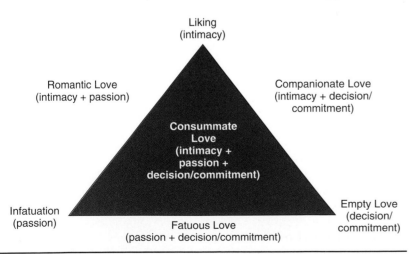

Figure 14-7 According to Sternberg, there are three main components of love: intimacy, passion, and decision/commitment. Different combinations of these components can create other various types of love. Nonlove contains none of the components.

Table 14-1 Rank Ordering of Desired Characteristics in a Mate

	UNITED STATES		CHINA		SOUTH AFRICAN ZULU	
	Females	Males	Females	Males	Females	Males
Mutual attraction—love	1	1	8	4	5	10
Emotional stability and maturity	2	2	1	5	2	1
Dependable character	3	3	7	6	1	3
Pleasing disposition	4	4	16	13	3	4
Education and intelligence	5	5	4	8	6	6
Good health	9	6	3	1	4	5
Good looks	13	7	15	11	16	14
Sociability	8	8	9	12	8	11
Desire for home and children	7	9	2	2	9	9
Refinement, neatness	12	10	10	7	10	7
Ambition and industriousness	6	11	5	10	7	8
Similar education	10	12	12	15	12	12
Good cook and housekeeper	16	13	11	9	15	2
Favorable social status or rating	14	14	13	14	14	17
Similar religious background	15	15	18	18	11	16
Good financial prospect	11	16	14	16	13	18
Chastity (no prior sexual intercourse)	18	17	6	3	18	13
Similar political background	17	18	17	17	17	15

Source: Buss et al., 1990.

Aggression and Prosocial Behavior: Hurting and Helping Others

Drive-by shootings, carjackings, and abductions are just some of the examples of violence that seem all too common today. Yet we also find examples of generous, unselfish, thoughtful behavior that suggest a more optimistic view of humankind. Consider, for instance, people like Mother Teresa, who ministered to the poor in India. Or contemplate the simple kindnesses of life: lending a valued compact disc, stopping to help a child who has fallen off her bicycle, or merely sharing a candy bar with a friend. Such instances of helping are no less characteristic of human behavior than the distasteful examples of aggression. In this last part of the chapter, we explore how social psychologists have sought to explain instances of aggressive behavior and helping behavior (A. G. Miller, 1999).

Hurting Others: Aggression

We need look no farther than our daily paper or the nightly news to be bombarded with examples of aggression, both on a societal level (war, invasion, assassination) and on an individual level (crime, child abuse, and the many petty cruelties that humans are capable of inflicting on one another). Is such aggression an inevitable part of the human condition? Or is aggression primarily a product of particular circumstances that, if changed, could lead to its reduction?

The difficulty of answering such knotty questions becomes quickly apparent as soon as we consider how best to define the term *aggression*. Depending on the definition, examples of inflicted pain or injury might or might not qualify as aggression. It is clear,

PsychLink

Driver aggression/road rage
www.mhhe.com/
feldmaness5-14links

for instance, that a rapist is acting with aggression toward his victim. On the other hand, it is less certain that a physician who causes extreme pain to a patient by carrying out an emergency medical procedure with no available anesthetic should be considered aggressive.

Most social psychologists define aggression in terms of the intent and purpose behind the behavior. **Aggression** involves intentionally inflicting injury or harm on another person (Berkowitz, 1993). Under this definition, it is clear that the rapist in our example is acting aggressively, whereas the physician causing pain during a medical procedure is not.

We turn now to several explanations for aggressive behavior developed by social psychologists (Berkowitz, 1993; Geen & Donnerstein, 1998).

aggression: The intentional infliction of injury or harm on another person

Instinct Approaches: Aggression as a Release

If you have ever punched an adversary in the nose, you might have experienced a certain satisfaction, despite your better judgment. Instinct theories, noting the prevalence of aggression not only in humans but in animals as well, propose that aggression is primarily the outcome of innate—inborn—urges.

Sigmund Freud was one of the first to suggest, as part of his theory of personality, that aggression is a primary instinctual drive (see Chapter 10). Konrad Lorenz, an ethologist (a scientist who studies animal behavior), expanded on Freud's notions by arguing that humans, along with members of other species, have a fighting instinct, which in earlier times ensured protection of food supplies and weeded out the weaker of the species (Lorenz, 1966, 1974). The controversial notion arising from Lorenz's instinct approach is that aggressive energy is constantly being built up within an individual until it is finally discharged in a process called **catharsis.** The longer the energy is built up, says Lorenz, the greater will be the amount of the aggression displayed when it is discharged.

catharsis: The process of discharging built-up aggressive energy

Probably the most controversial idea to come out of instinct theories of aggression is Lorenz's proposal that society ought to provide acceptable means of catharsis through, for instance, participation in sports and games, in order to prevent its discharge in less socially desirable ways. Although the notion makes logical sense, there is no possible way to devise an adequate experiment to test it. Relatively little support exists for instinct theories in general, because of the difficulty in finding evidence for any kind of pent-up reservoir of aggression (Berkowitz, 1993; Geen & Donnerstein, 1983). Most social psychologists suggest that we should look to other approaches to explain aggression.

Frustration–Aggression Approaches: Aggression as a Reaction to Frustration

Suppose you've been working on a paper that is due for a class early the next morning, and your printer runs out of ink just before you can print out the paper. You rush to the store to buy a new ink cartridge, only to find the salesclerk locking the door for the day. Even though the clerk can see you gesturing and literally begging him to open the door, he refuses, shrugging his shoulders and pointing to a sign that indicates when the store will open the next day. At that moment, the feelings you experience toward the salesclerk probably place you on the verge of real aggression, and you are undoubtedly seething inside.

Frustration-aggression theory tries to explain aggression in terms of events like this one. When first put forward, the theory said flatly that frustration *always* leads to aggression of some sort, and that aggression is *always* the result of some frustration, where **frustration** is defined as the thwarting or blocking of some ongoing, goal-directed behavior (Dollard et al., 1939). More recent formulations, however, have modified the original one, suggesting instead that frustration produces anger, leading to a *readiness* to act aggressively. Whether or not actual aggression occurs depends on the presence of *aggressive cues,* stimuli that have been associated in the past with actual aggression or violence and that will trigger aggression again (Berkowitz, 1984). In addition, frustration is assumed to produce aggression only to the extent that the frustration produces negative feelings (Berkowitz, 1989, 1990).

frustration: The thwarting or blocking of some ongoing, goal-directed behavior

What kinds of stimuli act as aggressive cues? They can range from the most overt, such as the presence of weapons, to the subtlest, such as the mere mention of the name of an individual who has behaved violently in the past. For example, in one experiment, angered participants behaved significantly more aggressively when in the presence of a rifle and revolver than in a comparable situation in which no guns were present (Berkowitz & LePage, 1967). Similarly, frustrated participants in an experiment who had viewed a violent movie were more physically aggressive toward a confederate with the same name as the star of the movie than toward a confederate with a different name (Berkowitz & Geen, 1966). It appears, then, that frustration does lead to aggression, at least when aggressive cues are present (Carlson, Marcus-Newhall, & Miller, 1990).

Observational Learning Approaches: Learning to Hurt Others Do we learn to be aggressive? The observational learning (sometimes called social learning) approach to aggression says we do. Taking a view almost the opposite of instinct theories, which focus on innate explanations of aggression, observational learning theory (see Chapter 5) emphasizes that social and environmental conditions can teach individuals to be aggressive. Aggression is seen not as inevitable, but rather as a learned response that can be understood in terms of rewards and punishments.

Observational learning theory pays particular attention not only to direct rewards and punishments that individuals themselves receive, but to the rewards and punishments that models—individuals who provide a guide to appropriate behavior—receive for their aggressive behavior. According to observational learning theory, people observe the behavior of models and the subsequent consequences of the behavior. If the consequences are positive, the behavior is likely to be imitated when observers find themselves in a similar situation.

Suppose, for instance, that a girl hits her younger brother when he damages one of her new toys. Whereas instinct theory would suggest that the aggression had been pent up and was now being discharged, and frustration-aggression theory would examine the girl's frustration at no longer being able to use her new toy, observational learning theory would look to previous situations in which the girl had viewed others being rewarded for their aggression. For example, perhaps she had watched a friend get to play with a toy after he painfully twisted it out of the hand of another child.

Observational learning theory has received wide research support. For example, nursery-school-age children who have watched an adult model behave aggressively and then receive reinforcement for the aggression later display similar behavior themselves, if they have been angered, insulted, or frustrated after exposure (Bandura, 1973, 1983; Anderson & Dill, 2000).

Helping Others: The Brighter Side of Human Nature

Turning away from aggression, we move now to the opposite—and brighter—side of the coin of human nature: helping behavior. Helping behavior, or **prosocial behavior** as it is more formally known, has been considered under many different conditions. However, the question that psychologists have looked at most closely relates to bystander intervention in emergency situations. What are the factors that lead someone to help a person in need?

As we noted in Chapter 1 in the case of Kitty Genovese, one critical factor is the number of others present. When more than one person is witness to an emergency situation, a sense of diffusion of responsibility can arise among bystanders. **Diffusion of responsibility** is the tendency for people to feel that responsibility for acting is shared, or diffused, among those present. The more people present in an emergency, then, the less personally responsible each of them feels—and therefore the less help they provide (Latané & Nida, 1981; Kalafat, Elias, & Gara, 1993; Bickman, 1994; Markey, 2000).

Although the majority of research on helping behavior supports the diffusion-of-responsibility formulation, other factors are clearly involved in helping behavior.

PsychLink

Violence on television
www.mhhe.com/
feldmaness5-14links

prosocial behavior: Helping behavior

diffusion of responsibility: The tendency for people to feel that responsibility for acting is shared, or diffused, among those present

Figure 14-8 The basic steps of helping.

altruism: Helping behavior that is beneficial to others but clearly requires self-sacrifice

Altruism is often the only bright side of a natural disaster. In response to the massive flooding that hit the U.S. Midwest, thousands of volunteers came from other areas of the country to pile sandbags, distribute donated food, and otherwise lend a helping hand.

According to a model developed by Latané and Darley (1970), the process of helping involves four basic steps (see Figure 14-8):

- *Noticing a person, event, or situation that might require help.*
- *Interpreting the event as one that requires help.* Even if an event is noticed, it could be sufficiently ambiguous to be interpreted as a nonemergency situation (Shotland, 1985; Harrison & Wells, 1991). It is here that the presence of others first affects helping behavior. The presence of inactive others could indicate to the observer that a situation does not require help—a judgment the observer might not necessarily make if she or he were the lone observer.
- *Assuming responsibility for taking action.* It is at this point that diffusion of responsibility is likely to occur if others are present. Moreover, a bystander's particular expertise is likely to play a role in determining whether she or he helps. For instance, if people with training in medical aid or lifesaving techniques are present, untrained bystanders are less likely to intervene because they feel they have less expertise. This point was well illustrated in a study by Jane and Irving Piliavin (1972), who conducted a field experiment in which an individual seemed to collapse in a subway car with blood trickling out of the corner of his mouth. The results of the experiment showed that bystanders were less likely to help when a person (actually a confederate) appearing to be an intern was present than when the "intern" was not present.
- *Deciding on and implementing the form of assistance.* After an individual assumes responsibility for helping, he or she must decide how to provide assistance. Helping can range from very indirect forms of intervention, such as calling the police, to more direct forms, such as giving first aid or taking the victim to a hospital. Most social psychologists use a *rewards-costs approach* to predict the nature of assistance a bystander will choose to provide. The general notion is that the rewards of helping, as perceived by the bystander, must outweigh the costs if helping is to occur, and most research tends to support this notion (Bell et al., 1995).

After the nature of assistance is determined, one step remains: the actual implementation of the assistance. A rewards-costs analysis suggests that the least costly form of implementation is the most likely to be used. However, this is not always the case: In some situations, people behave altruistically. **Altruism** is helping behavior that is beneficial to others but clearly requires self-sacrifice. For example, an instance in which a person runs into a burning house to rescue a stranger's child might be considered altruistic, particularly when compared with the alternative of simply calling the fire department (Batson, 1991; Shapiro & Gabbard, 1994).

Some research suggests that people who intervene in emergency situations tend to possess certain personality characteristics that differentiate them from nonhelpers. For example, helpers are more self-assured, sympathetic, and emotionally understanding, and they have greater *empathy* (a personality trait in which someone observing another person experiences the emotions of that person) than nonhelpers (Batson et al., 1995; Sibicky, Schroeder, & Dovidio, 1995).

Still, most social psychologists agree that no single set of attributes differentiates helpers from nonhelpers. For the most part, temporary situational factors (such as the mood we're in) determine whether we will intervene in a situation requiring aid (Eisenberg, 1991; Knight et al., 1994; Bersoff, 1999).

BECOMING AN INFORMED CONSUMER OF PSYCHOLOGY

Dealing with Anger Effectively

At one time or another, almost everyone feels angry. The anger might result from a frustrating situation, or it could be due to the behavior of another individual. How we deal with such anger might determine the difference between a promotion and a lost job or a broken relationship and one that mends itself.

Social psychologists who have studied the topic suggest that there are several good ways to deal with anger, strategies that maximize the potential for positive consequences (Deffenbacher, 1988, 1996; Bass, 1996; Nelson & Finch, 2000). Among the most useful strategies are the following:

- *Look again at the anger-provoking situation from the perspective of others.* By taking others' point of view, you might be able to understand the situation better, and with increased understanding you might become more tolerant of the apparent shortcomings of others.
- *Minimize the importance of the situation.* Does it really matter that someone is driving too slowly and that you'll be late to an appointment as a result? Reinterpret the situation in a way that is less bothersome.
- *Fantasize about getting even—but don't act on it.* Fantasy provides a safety valve. In your fantasies, you can yell at that unfair professor all you want and suffer no consequences at all. However, don't spend too much time brooding: Fantasize, but then move on.
- *Relax.* By teaching yourself the kind of relaxation techniques used in systematic desensitization (see Table 13-2 in the previous chapter), you can help reduce your reactions to anger. In turn, your anger might dissipate.

No matter which of these strategies you try, above all, don't ignore your anger. People who always strive to suppress their anger can experience a variety of unhappy consequences, such as self-condemnation, frustration, and even physical illness (Engebretson & Stoney, 1995; Sharma, Ghosh, & Spielberger, 1995).

Evaluate

1. We tend to like people who are similar to us. True or false?
2. Which of the following sets are the three components of love proposed by Sternberg?
   a. Passion, closeness, sexuality
   b. Attraction, desire, complementarity
   c. Passion, intimacy, decision/commitment
   d. Commitment, caring, sexuality
3. Based on the research evidence, which of the following might be the best way to reduce the amount of fighting a young boy does?
   a. Take him to the gym and let him work out on the boxing equipment.
   b. Take him to see *The Matrix* several times in the hope that it will provide catharsis.
   c. Reward him if he doesn't fight during a certain period.
   d. Ignore it and let it die out naturally.
4. If a person in a crowd does not help in an apparent emergency situation because many other people are present, that person is falling victim to the phenomenon of _____ ___ _____.

Rethink

1. Can love be studied scientifically? Is there an elusive quality to love that makes it at least partially unknowable? How would you define "falling in love"? How would you study it?
2. How would the aggression of a Timothy McVeigh, convicted of blowing up a federal building in Oklahoma City, be interpreted by the three main approaches to the study of aggression: instinct approaches, frustration-aggression approaches, and observational learning approaches? Do you think any of these approaches fits the McVeigh case more closely than the others?

Answers to Evaluate Questions

1. True 2. c 3. c 4. diffusion of responsibility

Looking Back

What are attitudes and how are they formed, maintained, and changed?

- Social psychology is the study of the ways in which people's thoughts, feelings, and actions are affected by others, and the nature and causes of individual behavior in social situations. (p. 442)
- Attitudes are learned predispositions to respond in a favorable or unfavorable manner to a particular object. (p. 442)
- Cognitive dissonance occurs when two cognitions—attitudes or thoughts—contradict each other and are held simultaneously by an individual. To resolve the contradiction, the person might modify the cognition, change its importance, or deny a link, thereby bringing about a reduction in dissonance. (p. 444)

How do we form impressions of what others are like and of the causes of their behavior?

- Social cognition involves the processes that underlie our understanding of the social world. Schemas help us organize information about people and social experiences in memory and allow us to interpret and categorize information about others. (p. 444)
- People form impressions of others in part through the use of central traits, personality characteristics that are given unusually heavy weight when an impression is formed. (p. 446)
- Information-processing approaches have found that we tend to average sets of traits to form an overall impression. (p. 446)
- Attribution theory tries to explain how we understand the causes of behavior, particularly with respect to situational or dispositional factors. (p. 447)

What biases influence how we view others' behavior?

- Even though logical processes are involved, attribution is still prone to error. For instance, the fundamental attribution error is the tendency to over-attribute others' behavior to dispositional causes, and the corresponding failure to recognize the importance of situational causes. (p. 448)
- Other biases include the halo effect and the assumed-similarity bias. (p. 448)

What are the major sources and tactics of social influence?

- Social influence is the area of social psychology concerned with situations in which the actions of an individual or group affect the behavior of others. (p. 450)
- Conformity refers to changes in behavior or attitudes that occur as the result of a desire to follow the beliefs or standards of others. (p. 450)
- Compliance is behavior that occurs as a result of direct social pressure. Tactics for eliciting compliance include the foot-in-the-door, door-in-the-face, that's-not-all, and not-so-free-sample techniques. (p. 451)
- Obedience is a change in behavior in response to the commands of others. (p. 452)

What are stereotypes, prejudice, and discrimination?

- Stereotypes are generalized beliefs and expectations about social groups and their members. (p. 455)
- Prejudice is the negative (or positive) evaluation of groups and their members. (p. 455)
- Stereotyping and prejudice can lead to discrimination, negative behavior toward members of a particular group. (p. 455)

- Self-fulfilling prophecies are expectations about the occurrence of future events or behaviors that increase the likelihood that the events or behaviors will actually occur. (p. 455)
- According to social learning approaches, people learn stereotyping and prejudice by observing the behavior of parents, other adults, and peers. Social identity theory suggests that group membership is used as a source of pride and self-worth, which can lead people to think of their own group as better than others. (p. 456)

How can we reduce prejudice and discrimination?

- Ways to reduce prejudice and discrimination include increasing contact, making positive values against prejudice apparent, and providing information about the target of the attribution or stereotype. (p. 456)
- Stereotype vulnerability relates to the obstacles to performance for minority group members that stem from their awareness of society's stereotypes. (p. 457)

Why are we attracted to certain people, and what progression do social relationships generally follow?

- Among the primary determinants of liking are proximity, mere exposure, similarity, and physical attractiveness. (p. 458)
- Loving is distinguished from liking by the presence of intense physiological arousal, an all-encompassing interest in the other, fantasies about the other, rapid swings of emotion, fascination, sexual desire, exclusiveness, and strong feelings of caring. (p. 459)
- Love can be categorized into two types (passionate and companionate). In addition, the components of love—intimacy, passion, and decision/commitment—combine to form seven different types of love. (p. 460)

What factors underlie aggression and prosocial behavior?

- Aggression is intentional infliction of injury or harm on another person. (p. 461)
- Explanations of aggression include instinct approaches, frustration-aggression theory, and observational learning. (p. 462)
- Helping behavior in emergencies is determined in part by the phenomenon of diffusion of responsibility, which results in a lower likelihood of helping when more people are present. (p. 463)
- Deciding to help is the outcome of a four-stage process consisting of noticing a possible need for help, interpreting the situation as requiring aid, assuming responsibility for taking action, and deciding on and implementing a form of assistance. (p. 464)

Key Terms and Concepts

social psychology (p. 442)
attitudes (p. 442)
central-route processing (p. 443)
peripheral-route processing (p. 443)
cognitive dissonance (p. 444)
social cognition (p. 445)
schemas (p. 445)
central traits (p. 446)
attribution theory (p. 447)
situational causes (of behavior) (p. 447)
dispositional causes (of behavior) (p. 449)

fundamental attribution error (p. 449)
halo effect (p. 449)
assumed-similarity bias (p. 449)
social influence (p. 450)
conformity (p. 450)
status (p. 450)
social supporter (p. 451)
compliance (p. 451)
industrial-organizational (I/O) psychology (p. 452)
obedience (p. 452)

stereotypes (p. 455)

prejudice (p. 455)

discrimination (p. 455)

interpersonal attraction
   (or close relationships) (p. 458)

reciprocity-of-liking effect (p. 459)

passionate (or romantic) love (p. 460)

companionate love (p. 460)

aggression (p. 462)

catharsis (p. 462)

frustration (p. 462)

prosocial behavior (p. 463)

diffusion of responsibility (p. 463)

altruism (p. 464)

Preview

For additional quizzing and a variety of interactive resources, visit the *Essentials of Understanding Psychology* Online Learning Center at

www.mhhe.com/feldmaness5

Psychology on the Web

1. Find examples on the Web of advertisements or other persuasive messages using central-route processing and peripheral-route processing. What type of persuasion appears to be more prevalent on the Web? For what type of persuasion does the Web appear to be most suited? Is there a difference between Web-based advertising and other forms of advertising?

2. Is "hate crimes legislation" a good idea? Use the Web to find at least two discussions of hate crimes legislation—one in favor and one opposed—and summarize in writing the main issues and arguments presented. Using your knowledge of prejudice and aggression, evaluate the arguments for and against hate crimes legislation. State your opinion about whether this type of legislation is advisable.

Epilogue

In this chapter we have touched on some of the major ideas, research topics, and experimental findings of social psychology. We have examined how people form, maintain, and change attitudes; and how they form impressions of others and assign attributions to them. We have also seen how groups, through conformity and tactics of compliance, can influence individuals' actions and attitudes. Finally, we discussed interpersonal relationships, including both liking and loving, and we looked at the two sides of a coin that represent the extremes of social behavior: aggression and prosocial behavior.

Turn back to the prologue of this chapter, which describes the death of James Byrd, who was killed because of his race. Use your understanding of social psychology to consider the following questions.

1. What factors would a social psychologist consider in examining why Byrd's killers initially formed negative attitudes toward African Americans?

2. How would an instinct approach account for the aggression displayed by Byrd's killers? a frustration-aggression approach? an observational learning approach? Which approach appears to you to be most useful in this situation? Why?

3. The public reaction to Byrd's death was horror and outrage. Anger was directed not only at the three killers, but at white supremacists in general. Do you think anger should be directed at the person who harbors prejudice and commits a crime or at the prejudice itself? What difference does that make and why?

Glossary

a

absolute threshold The smallest intensity of a stimulus that must be present for the stimulus to be detected (Ch. 3)

achievement test A test designed to determine a person's level of knowledge in a given subject area (Ch. 7)

action potential An electric nerve impulse that travels through a neuron when it is set off by a "trigger," changing the neuron's charge from negative to positive (Ch. 2)

activation-synthesis theory Hobson's theory that the brain produces random electrical energy during REM sleep that stimulates memories lodged in various portions of the brain (Ch. 4)

activity theory of aging A theory that holds that the elderly who age most successfully are those who maintain the interests and activities they had during middle age (Ch. 9)

adaptation An adjustment in sensory capacity following prolonged exposure to stimuli (Ch. 3)

addictive drugs Drugs that produce a biological or psychological dependence in the user; withdrawal from them leads to a craving for the drug that in some cases can be nearly irresistible (Ch. 4)

adolescence The developmental stage between childhood and adulthood (Ch. 9)

age of viability The point at which the fetus can survive if born prematurely (Ch. 9)

aggression The intentional infliction of injury or harm on another person (Ch. 14)

algorithm A rule that, if applied appropriately, guarantees a solution to a problem (Ch. 7)

all-or-none law The rule that neurons are either on or off (Ch. 2)

altruism Helping behavior that is beneficial to others but clearly requires self-sacrifice (Ch. 14)

anal stage According to Freud, a stage from 12 to 18 months to 3 years of age, in which a child's pleasure is centered on the anus (Ch. 10)

androgens Male sex hormones secreted by the testes (Ch. 8)

anorexia nervosa A severe eating disorder in which people may refuse to eat, while denying that their behavior and appearance—which can become skeletonlike—are unusual (Ch. 8)

antianxiety drugs Drugs that can reduce a person's level of anxiety, essentially by reducing excitability and increasing feelings of well-being (Ch. 13)

antidepressant drugs Medication that improves a depressed patient's mood and feeling of well-being (Ch. 13)

antipsychotic drugs Drugs that temporarily reduce psychotic symptoms such as agitation, overactivity, hallucinations, and delusions (Ch. 13)

antisocial personality disorder A disorder in which individuals tend to display no regard for the moral and ethical rules of society or the rights of others (Ch. 12)

anxiety disorder Anxiety with no obvious external cause that impairs daily functioning (Ch. 12)

aptitude test A test designed to predict a person's ability in a particular area or line of work (Ch. 7)

archival research Research in which existing data, such as census documents, college records, or newspaper clippings, are examined to test a hypothesis (Ch. 1)

arousal approaches to motivation The belief that we try to maintain a certain level of stimulation and activity, increasing or reducing them as necessary (Ch. 8)

association areas One of the major areas of the brain; the site of the higher mental processes such as thought, language, memory, and speech (Ch. 2)

associative models of memory Models of memory as consisting of mental representations of clusters of interconnected information (Ch. 6)

assumed-similarity bias The tendency to think of people as being similar to oneself, even when meeting them for the first time (Ch. 14)

attachment The positive emotional bond that develops between a child and a particular individual (Ch. 9)

attention deficit hyperactivity disorder (ADHD) A learning disability marked by inattention, impulsiveness, a low tolerance for frustration, and a great deal of inappropriate activity (Ch. 12)

attitudes Learned predispositions to respond in a favorable or unfavorable manner to a particular person, behavior, belief, or thing (Ch. 14)

attribution theory The theory of personality that seeks to explain how we decide, on the basis of samples of an individual's behavior, what the specific causes of that person's behavior are (Ch. 14)

authoritarian parents Parents who are rigid and punitive and value unquestioning obedience from their children (Ch. 9)

authoritative parents Parents who are firm, set clear limits, reason with their children, and explain things to them (Ch. 9)

autobiographical memories Our recollections of circumstances and episodes from our own lives (Ch. 6)

autonomic division The part of the nervous system that controls involuntary movement (the actions of the heart, glands, lungs, and other organs) (Ch. 2)

autonomy-versus-shame-and-doubt stage The period during which, according to Erikson, toddlers (ages 18 months to 3 years) develop independence and autonomy if exploration and freedom are encouraged, or shame and self-doubt if they are restricted and overprotected (Ch. 9)

axon The part of the neuron that carries messages destined for other neurons (Ch. 2)

b

babble Speechlike but meaningless sounds made by children from the ages of around 3 months through 1 year (Ch. 7)

background stressors ("daily hassles") Everyday annoyances, such as being stuck in traffic, that cause minor irritations that can have long-term ill effects if they continue or are compounded by other stressful events (Ch. 11)

basilar membrane A vibrating structure that runs through the center of the cochlea, dividing it into an upper and a lower chamber, and containing sense receptors for sound (Ch. 3)

behavior modification A formalized technique for promoting the frequency of desirable behaviors and decreasing the incidence of unwanted ones (Ch. 5)

behavioral assessment Direct measures of an individual's behavior used to describe characteristics indicative of personality (Ch. 10)

behavioral genetics The study of the effects of heredity on behavior (Ch. 2)

behavioral perspective The perspective that looks at the behavior itself as the problem (Ch. 1, 12)

behavioral treatment approaches Treatment approaches that build upon the basic processes of learning, such as reinforcement and extinction (Ch. 13)

biofeedback A procedure in which a person learns to control through conscious thought internal physiological processes such as blood pressure, heart and respiration rate, skin temperature, sweating, and constriction of particular muscles (Ch. 2)

biological and evolutionary approaches to personality The theory that important components of personality are inherited (Ch. 10)

biological perspective The approach that views behavior from the perspective of biological functioning (Ch. 1)

biomedical therapy Therapy that relies on drugs and other medical procedures to improve psychological functioning (Ch. 13)

biopsychologists (or behavioral neuroscientists) Psychologists who specialize in considering the ways in which biological structures and functions of the body affect behavior (Ch. 2)

bipolar disorder   A disorder in which a person alternates between periods of euphoric feelings of mania and periods of depression (Ch. 12)

bisexuals   Persons who are sexually attracted to people of the same sex and people of the opposite sex (Ch. 8)

borderline personality disorder   A disorder in which individuals have difficulty developing a secure sense of who they are (Ch. 12)

bottom-up processing   Perception that consists of recognizing and processing information about the individual components of the stimuli (Ch. 3)

bulimia   A disorder in which a person binges on incredibly large quantities of food, then purges by vomiting or by using laxatives (Ch. 8)

c

Cannon-Bard theory of emotion   The belief that both physiological and emotional arousal are produced simultaneously by the same nerve stimulus (Ch. 8)

case study   An in-depth, intensive investigation of an individual or small group of people (Ch. 1)

cataclysmic events   Strong stressors that occur suddenly, affecting many people at once (e.g., natural disasters) (Ch. 11)

catharsis   The process of discharging built-up aggressive energy (Ch. 14)

central core   The "old brain," which controls such basic functions as eating and sleeping and is common to all vertebrates (Ch. 2)

central nervous system (CNS)   The system that includes the brain and spinal cord (Ch. 2)

central-route processing   Message interpretation characterized by thoughtful consideration of the issues and arguments used to persuade (Ch. 14)

central traits   The major traits considered in forming impressions of others (Ch. 14)

cerebellum (ser uh BELL um)   The part of the brain that controls bodily balance (Ch. 2)

cerebral cortex   The "new brain," responsible for the most sophisticated information processing in the brain; contains the lobes (Ch. 2)

chromosomes   Rod-shaped structures that contain the basic hereditary information (Ch. 9)

chunk   A meaningful grouping of stimuli that can be stored as a unit in short-term memory (Ch. 6)

circadian rhythms   Biological processes that occur repeatedly on approximately a twenty-four-hour cycle (Ch. 4)

classical conditioning   A type of learning in which a neutral stimulus comes to bring about a response after it is paired with a stimulus that naturally brings about that response (Ch. 5)

client-centered therapy   Therapy in which the goal is to reach one's potential for self-actualization (Ch. 13)

cochlea (KOKE lee uh)   A coiled tube in the ear filled with fluid that vibrates in response to sound (Ch. 3)

cognitive approaches of motivation   The theory suggesting that motivation is a product of people's thoughts and expectations—their cognitions (Ch. 8)

cognitive-behavioral approach   An approach used by cognitive therapists that attempts to change the way people think through the use of basic principles of learning (Ch. 13)

cognitive development   The process by which a child's understanding of the world changes as a function of age and experience (Ch. 9)

cognitive dissonance   The conflict that occurs when a person holds two attitudes or thoughts (referred to as cognitions) that contradict each other (Ch. 14)

cognitive map   A mental representation of spatial locations and directions (Ch. 5)

cognitive perspective   The approach that focuses on how people think, understand, and know about the world (Ch. 1)

cognitive perspective   The perspective that people's thoughts and beliefs are a central component of abnormal behavior (Ch. 12)

cognitive psychology   The branch of psychology that focuses on the study of cognition (Ch. 7)

cognitive-social learning theory   The study of the thought processes that underlie learning (Ch. 5)

cognitive treatment approaches   Approaches to treatment that teach people to think in more adaptive ways by changing their dysfunctional cognitions about the world and themselves (Ch. 13)

collective unconscious   A set of influences we inherit from our own particular ancestors, the whole human race, and even animal ancestors from the distant evolutionary past (Ch. 10)

community psychology   A branch of psychology that focuses on the prevention and minimization of psychological disorders in the community (Ch. 13)

companionate love   The strong affection we have for those with whom our lives are deeply involved (Ch. 14)

compliance   Conforming behavior that occurs in response to direct social pressure (Ch. 14)

compulsion   An irresistible urge to repeatedly carry out some act that seems strange and unreasonable (Ch. 12)

concepts   Categorizations of objects, events, or people that share common properties (Ch. 7)

concrete operational stage   According to Piaget, the period from 7 to 12 years of age, which is characterized by logical thought and a loss of egocentrism (Ch. 9)

conditioned response (CR)   A response that, after conditioning, follows a previously neutral stimulus (e.g., salivation at the ringing of a bell) (Ch. 5)

conditioned stimulus (CS)   A once-neutral stimulus that has been paired with an unconditioned stimulus to bring about a response formerly caused only by the unconditioned stimulus (Ch. 5)

cones   Cone-shaped, light-sensitive receptor cells in the retina that are responsible for sharp focus and color perception, particularly in bright light (Ch. 3)

conformity   A change in behavior or attitudes brought about by a desire to follow the beliefs or standards of other people (Ch. 14)

consciousness   The awareness of the sensations, thoughts, and feelings being experienced at a given moment (Ch. 4)

constructive processes   Processes in which memories are influenced by the meaning we give to events (Ch. 6)

continuous reinforcement schedule   Reinforcement of behavior every time it occurs (Ch. 5)

control group   A group that receives no treatment in an experiment (Ch. 1)

convergent thinking   The ability to produce responses that are based primarily on knowledge and logic (Ch. 7)

conversion disorder   A major somatoform disorder that involves an actual physical disturbance, such as the inability to use a sensory organ or the complete or partial inability to move an arm or leg (Ch. 12)

coping   Efforts to control, reduce, or learn to tolerate the threats that lead to stress (Ch. 11)

correlational research   Research that examines the relationship between two sets of variables to determine whether they are associated, or "correlated" (Ch. 1)

creativity   The combining of responses or ideas in novel ways (Ch. 7)

cross-sectional research   A research method in which people of different ages are compared at the same point in time (Ch. 9)

crystallized intelligence   The accumulation of information, skills, and strategies learned through experience and that can be applied in problem-solving situations (Ch. 7)

culture-fair IQ test   A test that does not discriminate against members of any minority group (Ch. 7)

d

daydreams   Fantasies that people construct while awake (Ch. 4)

decay   The loss of information in memory through its nonuse (Ch. 6)

declarative memory   Memory for factual information: names, faces, dates, and the like (Ch. 6)

defense mechanisms   Unconscious strategies people use to reduce anxiety by concealing the source of the anxiety from themselves and others (Ch. 10, 11)

deinstitutionalization   The transfer of former mental patients from institutions into the community (Ch. 13)

dendrites A cluster of fibers at one end of a neuron that receive messages from other neurons (Ch. 2)

dependent variable The variable that is measured and is expected to change as a result of changes caused by the experimenter's manipulation (Ch. 1)

depressants Drugs that slow down the nervous system (Ch. 4)

developmental psychology The branch of psychology that studies the patterns of growth and change occurring throughout life (Ch. 9)

Diagnostic and Statistical Manual of Mental Disorders, Fourth Edition (DSM-IV) The manual of the American Psychiatric Association that presents the diagnostic system used by most U.S. mental health professionals to diagnose and classify abnormal behavior (Ch. 12)

difference threshold The smallest level of stimulation required to sense that a change in stimulation has occurred (Ch. 3)

diffusion of responsibility The tendency for people to feel that responsibility for acting is shared, or diffused, among those present (Ch. 14)

discrimination Negative behavior toward members of a particular group (Ch. 14)

disengagement theory of aging A theory that holds that aging is a gradual withdrawal from the world on physical, psychological, and social levels (Ch. 9)

dispositional causes (of behavior) A perceived cause of behavior that is based on internal traits or personality factors (Ch. 14)

dissociative amnesia A disorder in which the person has significant, selective memory loss (Ch. 12)

dissociative disorder Psychological dysfunctions characterized by the separation of critical personality facets that are normally integrated, allowing stress avoidance by escape (Ch. 12)

dissociative fugue A form of amnesia in which people take sudden, impulsive trips, sometimes assuming a new identity (Ch. 12)

dissociative identity disorder (multiple personality) A disorder in which a person displays characteristics of two or more distinct personalities (Ch. 12)

divergent thinking The ability to generate unusual, yet appropriate, responses to problems or questions (Ch. 7)

double standard The view that premarital sex is permissible for males but not for females (Ch. 8)

dreams-for-survival theory The theory that dreams permit information that is critical for our daily survival to be reconsidered and reprocessed during sleep (Ch. 4)

drive Motivational tension, or arousal, that energizes behavior in order to fulfill some need (Ch. 8)

drive-reduction approaches to motivation A theory suggesting that when people lack some basic biological requirement such as water, a drive to obtain that requirement (in this case, the thirst drive) is produced (Ch. 8)

drug therapy Control of psychological problems through drugs (Ch. 13)

e

eardrum The part of the ear that vibrates when sound waves hit it (Ch. 3)

echoic memory Memory of auditory information coming from the ears (Ch. 6)

eclectic approach to therapy An approach to therapy that uses techniques taken from a variety of treatment methods, rather than just one method (Ch. 13)

ego The part of the personality that provides a buffer between the id and the outside world (Ch. 10)

egocentric thought A way of thinking in which the child views the world entirely from his or her own perspective (Ch. 9)

ego-integrity-versus-despair stage According to Erikson, a period from late adulthood until death during which we review our life's accomplishments and failures (Ch. 9)

electroconvulsive therapy (ECT) A procedure in which an electric current of 70 to 150 volts is briefly administered to a patient's head, causing a loss of consciousness and often seizures (Ch. 13)

embryo A developed zygote that has a rudimentary heart, brain, and other organs (Ch. 9)

emotional intelligence The set of skills that underlie the accurate assessment, evaluation, expression, and regulation of emotions (Ch. 7)

emotions Feelings that generally have both physiological and cognitive elements and that influence behavior (Ch. 8)

endocrine system A chemical communication network that sends messages throughout the nervous system via the bloodstream (Ch. 2)

episodic memory Memory for the biographical details of our individual lives (Ch. 6)

estrogen A female sex hormone (Ch. 8)

evolutionary psychology The branch of psychology that seeks to identify behavior patterns that result from our genetic inheritance from our ancestors (Ch. 2)

excitatory message A chemical message that makes it more likely that a receiving neuron will fire and an action potential will travel down its axons (Ch. 2)

experiment The investigation of the relationship between two (or more) variables by deliberately producing a change in one variable in a situation and observing the effects of that change on other aspects of the situation (Ch. 1)

experimental bias Factors that distort how the independent variable affects the dependent variable in an experiment (Ch. 1)

experimental group Any group receiving a treatment in an experiment (Ch. 1)

experimental manipulation The change that an experimenter deliberately produces in a situation (Ch. 1)

explicit memory Intentional or conscious recollection of information (Ch. 6)

extinction The decrease in frequency, and eventual disappearance, of a previously conditioned response; one of the basic phenomena of learning (Ch. 5)

extramarital sex Sexual activity between a married person and someone who is not his or her spouse (Ch. 8)

f

family therapy An approach that focuses on the family and its dynamics (Ch. 13)

feature analysis A theory of perception according to which we perceive a shape, pattern, object, or scene by reacting first to the individual elements that make it up (Ch. 3)

feature detection The activation of neurons in the cortex by visual stimuli of specific shapes or patterns (Ch. 3)

fetus A developing child, from 8 weeks after conception until birth (Ch. 9)

fixation Conflicts or concerns that persist beyond the developmental period in which they first occur (Ch. 10)

fixed-interval schedule A schedule that provides reinforcement for a response only if a fixed time period has elapsed, making overall rates of response relatively low (Ch. 5)

fixed-ratio schedule A schedule whereby reinforcement is given only after a certain number of responses are made (Ch. 5)

flashbulb memories Memories of a specific, important, or surprising event that are so vivid, they are like a snapshot of the event (Ch. 6)

fluid intelligence Intelligence that reflects information-processing capabilities, reasoning, and memory (Ch. 7)

formal operational stage According to Piaget, the period from age 12 to adulthood, which is characterized by abstract thought (Ch. 9)

frequency theory of hearing The theory that the entire basilar membrane acts like a microphone, vibrating as a whole in response to a sound (Ch. 3)

frustration The thwarting or blocking of some ongoing, goal-directed behavior (Ch. 14)

functional fixedness The tendency to think of an object only in terms of its typical use (Ch. 7)

functionalism An early approach to psychology that concentrated on what the mind does—the functions of mental activity—and the role of behavior in allowing people to adapt to their environments (Ch. 1)

fundamental attribution error   A tendency to attribute others' behavior to dispositional causes and the tendency to minimize the importance of situational causes (Ch. 14)

g

g or g-factor   The single, general factor for mental ability that was assumed to underlie intelligence in some early theories of intelligence (Ch. 7)

gate-control theory of pain   The theory that particular nerve receptors lead to specific areas of the brain related to pain (Ch. 3)

general adaptation syndrome (GAS)   A theory developed by Selye that suggests that a person's response to stress consists of three stages: alarm and mobilization, resistance, and exhaustion (Ch. 11)

generalized anxiety disorder   Long-term, persistent anxiety and worry (Ch. 12)

generativity-versus-stagnation stage According to Erikson, a period in middle adulthood during which we take stock of our contributions to family and society (Ch. 9)

genes   The parts of the chromosomes through which genetic information is transmitted (Ch. 9)

genetic preprogramming theories of aging Theories that hold that there is a built-in time limit to the reproduction of human cells, and that after a certain time they are no longer able to divide (Ch. 9)

genital stage   According to Freud, the period from puberty until death, marked by mature sexual behavior (i.e., sexual intercourse) (Ch. 10)

gestalt laws of organization   A series of principles that describe how we organize bits and pieces of information into meaningful wholes (Ch. 3)

gestalt (geh SHTALLT) psychology   An approach to psychology that focuses on the organization of perception and thinking in a "whole" sense, rather than on the individual elements of perception (Ch. 1)

gestalt therapy   An approach to therapy that attempts to integrate a client's thoughts, feelings, and behavior into a unified whole (Ch. 13)

grammar   The system of rules that determine how our thoughts can be expressed (Ch. 7)

group therapy   Therapy in which people discuss problems in a group (Ch. 13)

h

habituation   The decrease in the response to a stimulus that occurs after repeated presentations of the same stimulus (Ch. 9)

hair cells   Tiny cells covering the basilar membrane that, when bent by vibrations entering the cochlea, transmit neural messages to the brain (Ch. 3)

hallucinogen   A drug that is capable of producing hallucinations, or changes in the perceptual process (Ch. 4)

halo effect   A phenomenon in which an initial perception of a person as having positive traits produces the expectation that the person has other uniformly positive characteristics (Ch. 14)

hardiness   A personality characteristic associated with a lower rate of stress-related illness, consisting of three components: commitment, challenge, and control (Ch. 11)

health psychology   The branch of psychology that investigates the psychological factors related to wellness and illness, including the prevention, diagnosis, and treatment of medical problems (Ch. 11)

hemispheres   The two symmetrical left and right halves of the brain; each controls the side of the body opposite to it (Ch. 2)

heritability   A measure of the degree to which a characteristic is related to genetic, inherited factors (Ch. 7)

heterosexuality   Sexual attraction and behavior directed to the opposite sex (Ch. 8)

homeostasis   The body's tendency to maintain a steady internal state (Ch. 8)

homosexuals   Persons who are sexually attracted to people of their own sex (Ch. 8)

hormones   Chemicals that circulate through the blood and affect the functioning or growth of other parts of the body (Ch. 2)

humanistic approaches to personality   The theory that people are basically good and tend to grow to higher levels of functioning (Ch. 10)

humanistic perspective   The approach that suggests that all individuals naturally strive to grow, develop, and be in control of their lives and behavior (Ch. 1)

humanistic perspective   The perspective that emphasizes people's responsibility for their own behavior, even when such behavior is abnormal (Ch. 12)

humanistic therapy   Therapy in which the underlying assumption is that people have control of their behavior, can make choices about their lives, and are essentially responsible for solving their own problems (Ch. 13)

hypnosis   A trancelike state of heightened susceptibility to the suggestions of others (Ch. 4)

hypochondriasis   A disorder involving having a constant fear of illness and a preoccupation with one's health (Ch. 12)

hypothalamus   A tiny part of the brain, located below the thalamus of the brain, that maintains homeostasis and produces and regulates vital, basic behavior such as eating, drinking, and sexual behavior (Ch. 2)

hypothesis   A prediction, stemming from a theory, stated in a way that allows it to be tested (Ch. 1)

i

iconic memory   Memory of information from our visual system (Ch. 6)

id   The raw, unorganized, inborn part of personality, whose sole purpose is to reduce tension created by primitive drives related to hunger, sex, aggression, and irrational impulses (Ch. 10)

identical twins   Twins who are genetically identical (Ch. 9)

identification   The process of trying to be like another person as much as possible, imitating that person's behavior and adopting similar beliefs and values (Ch. 10)

identity   The distinguishing character of the individual: who each of us is, what our roles are, and what we are capable of (Ch. 9)

identity-versus-role-confusion stage According to Erikson, a time in adolescence of major testing to determine one's unique qualities (Ch. 9)

implicit memory   Memories people are not consciously aware of, but that can affect their subsequent performance and behavior (Ch. 6)

incentive approaches to motivation   The theory suggesting that motivation stems from the desire to obtain valued external goals, or incentives (Ch. 8)

independent variable   The variable that is manipulated by an experimenter (Ch. 1)

industrial-organizational (I/O) psychology The branch of psychology that focuses on work and job-related issues, including productivity, job satisfaction, decision making, and consumer behavior (Ch. 14)

industry-versus-inferiority stage According to Erikson, the last stage of childhood, during which children ages 6 to 12 years either develop positive social interactions with others or feel inadequate and become less sociable (Ch. 9)

inferiority complex   According to Adler, a complex developed by adults who have not been able to overcome the feelings of inferiority they developed as children, when they were small and limited in their knowledge about the world (Ch. 10)

information processing   The way people take in, use, and store information (Ch. 9)

informed consent   A document signed by participants affirming that they have been told the basic outlines of a research study and are aware of what their participation will involve (Ch. 1)

inhibitory message   A chemical message that prevents a receiving neuron from firing (Ch. 2)

initiative-versus-guilt stage   According to Erikson, the period during which children ages 3 to 6 years experience conflict between independence of action and the sometimes negative results of that action (Ch. 9)

insight   A sudden awareness of the relationships among various elements that had previously appeared to be independent of one another (Ch. 7)

instincts   Inborn patterns of behavior that are biologically determined rather than learned (Ch. 8)

intellectually gifted Having an IQ score above 130; about 2 to 4 percent of the population (Ch. 7)

intelligence The capacity to understand the world, think rationally, and use resources effectively when faced with challenges (Ch. 7)

intelligence quotient (IQ) A score that takes into account an individual's mental and chronological ages (Ch. 7)

intelligence tests Tests devised to identify a person's level of intelligence (Ch. 7)

interference The phenomenon by which information in memory displaces or blocks out other information, preventing its recall (Ch. 6)

interneurons Neurons that connect sensory and motor neurons, carrying messages between the two (Ch. 2)

interpersonal attraction (or close relationships) Positive feelings for others; liking and loving (Ch. 14)

intimacy-versus-isolation stage According to Erikson, a period during early adulthood that focuses on developing close relationships (Ch. 9)

introspection A procedure used to study the structure of the mind, in which subjects are asked to describe in detail what they are experiencing when they are exposed to a stimulus (Ch. 1)

j

James-Lange theory of emotion The belief that emotional experience is a reaction to bodily events occurring as a result of an external situation ("I feel sad because I am crying") (Ch. 8)

just noticeable difference The minimum stimulation required to detect the difference between two stimuli (Ch. 3)

l

language The communication of information through symbols arranged according to systematic rules (Ch. 7)

language acquisition device A hypothesized neural system of the brain for understanding language (Ch. 7)

latency period According to Freud, the period between the phallic stage and puberty during which children temporarily put aside their sexual interests (Ch. 10)

latent content of dreams According to Freud, the "disguised" or real meanings of dreams, hidden by more obvious subjects (Ch. 4)

latent learning Learning in which a new behavior is acquired but is not demonstrated until reinforcement is provided (Ch. 5)

lateralization The dominance of one hemisphere of the brain in specific functions (Ch. 2)

learned helplessness A state in which people conclude that unpleasant or aversive stimuli cannot be controlled—a view of the world that becomes so ingrained that they cease trying to remedy their aversive circumstances, even if they actually could exert some influence on them (Ch. 11)

learning A relatively permanent change in behavior brought about by experience (Ch. 5)

learning-theory approach The theory suggesting that language acquisition follows the principles of reinforcement and conditioning (Ch. 7)

levels-of-processing theory The theory of memory that emphasizes the degree to which new material is mentally analyzed (Ch. 6)

life review The process in which people in late adulthood examine and evaluate their lives (Ch. 9)

limbic system The part of the brain located outside the "new brain" that controls eating, aggression, and reproduction (Ch. 2)

lithium A mineral salt used to treat bipolar disorders (Ch. 13)

lobes The four major sections of the cerebral cortex: frontal, parietal, temporal, and occipital (Ch. 2)

long-term memory Memory that stores information on a relatively permanent basis, although it might be difficult to retrieve (Ch. 6)

m

major depression A severe form of depression that interferes with concentration, decision making, and sociability (Ch. 12)

mania An extended state of intense, wild elation (Ch. 12)

manifest content of dreams According to Freud, the overt story line of dreams (Ch. 4)

masturbation Sexual self-stimulation (Ch. 8)

means-end analysis Repeated testing for differences between the desired outcome and what currently exists (Ch. 7)

medical perspective The perspective that the root cause of abnormal behavior will be found in a physical examination of the individual, which might reveal a hormonal imbalance, a chemical deficiency, or a brain injury (Ch. 12)

meditation A learned technique for refocusing attention that brings about an altered state of consciousness (Ch. 4)

memory The process by which we encode, store, and retrieve information (Ch. 6)

memory trace A physical change in the brain that occurs when new material is learned (Ch. 6)

menopause The point at which women stop menstruating and are no longer fertile (Ch. 9)

mental age The average age of individuals who achieve a particular level of performance on a test (Ch. 7)

mental images Representations in the mind that resemble the object or event being represented (Ch. 7)

mental retardation Having significantly below-average intellectual functioning and limitations in at least two areas of adaptive functioning (Ch. 7)

mental set The tendency for old patterns of problem solving to persist (Ch. 7)

metabolism The rate at which food is converted to energy and expended by the body (Ch. 8)

metacognition An awareness and understanding of one's own cognitive processes (Ch. 9)

Minnesota Multiphasic Personality Inventory-2 (MMPI-2) A test used to identify people with psychological difficulties as well as to predict such behavior as job performance (Ch. 10)

mood disorder Disturbances in emotional feelings strong enough to interfere with everyday living (Ch. 12)

motivation The factors that direct and energize the behavior of humans and other organisms (Ch. 8)

motor area The part of the cortex that is largely responsible for the voluntary movement of particular parts of the body (Ch. 2)

motor (efferent) neurons Neurons that communicate information from the nervous system to muscles and glands of the body (Ch. 2)

myelin sheath Specialized cells of fat and protein that wrap themselves around the axon, providing a protective coating (Ch. 2)

n

narcissistic personality disorder A personality disturbance characterized by an exaggerated sense of self-importance (Ch. 12)

narcotics Drugs that increase relaxation and relieve pain and anxiety (Ch. 4)

naturalistic observation Research in which an investigator simply observes some naturally occurring behavior and does not make a change in the situation (Ch. 1)

nature-nurture issue The issue of the degrees to which environment and heredity influence behavior and development (Ch. 9)

need for achievement A stable, learned characteristic in which satisfaction is obtained by striving for and attaining a level of excellence (Ch. 8)

need for affiliation An interest in establishing and maintaining relationships with other people (Ch. 8)

need for power A tendency to seek impact, control, or influence over others, and to be seen as a powerful individual (Ch. 8)

negative reinforcer An unpleasant stimulus whose removal leads to an increase in the probability that a preceding response will occur again in the future (Ch. 5)

neo-Freudian psychoanalysts Psychoanalysts who were trained in traditional Freudian theory but who later rejected some of its major points (Ch. 10)

neonate   A newborn child (Ch. 9)

neurons   Nerve cells, the basic elements of the nervous system (Ch. 2)

neurotransmitters   Chemicals that carry messages across the synapse to the dendrite (and sometimes the cell body) of a receiver neuron (Ch. 2)

neutral stimulus   A stimulus that, before conditioning, does not naturally bring about the response of interest (Ch. 4)

norms   Standards of test performance that permit the comparison of one person's score on the test to the scores of others who have taken the same test (Ch. 7)

O

obedience   Conforming behavior in reaction to the commands of others (Ch. 14)

obesity   The state of being more than 20 percent above the average weight for a person of one's height (Ch. 8)

object permanence   The awareness that objects—and people—continue to exist even if they are out of sight (Ch. 9)

observational learning   Learning through observing the behavior of another person called a model (Ch. 5)

obsession   A persistent, unwanted thought or idea that keeps recurring (Ch. 12)

obsessive-compulsive disorder   A disorder characterized by obsessions or compulsions (Ch. 12)

Oedipus conflict   A child's sexual interest in his or her opposite-sex parent, typically resolved through identification with the same-sex parent (Ch. 10)

operant conditioning   Learning in which a voluntary response is strengthened or weakened, depending on its favorable or unfavorable consequences (Ch. 5)

operationalization   The process of translating a hypothesis into specific, testable procedures that can be measured and observed (Ch. 1)

opponent-process theory of color vision   The theory that receptor cells are linked in pairs, working in opposition to each other (Ch. 3)

optic nerve   A bundle of ganglion axons that carry visual information (Ch. 3)

oral stage   According to Freud, a stage from birth to 12 to 18 months, in which an infant's center of pleasure is the mouth (Ch. 10)

otoliths   Tiny, motion-sensitive crystals within the semicircular canals that sense body acceleration (Ch. 3)

overgeneralization   The phenomenon whereby children apply rules even when their application results in an error (Ch. 7)

ovulation   The point at which an egg is released from the ovaries (Ch. 8)

P

panic disorder   Anxiety that reveals itself in the form of panic attacks that last from a few seconds to as long as several hours (Ch. 12)

parasympathetic division   The part of the autonomic division of the nervous system that acts to calm the body after the emergency situation is resolved (Ch. 2)

partial reinforcement schedule   Reinforcement of behavior some but not all of the time (Ch. 5)

passionate (or romantic) love   A state of intense absorption in someone that includes intense physiological arousal, psychological interest, and caring for the needs of another (Ch. 14)

perception   The sorting out, interpretation, analysis, and integration of stimuli involving our sense organs and brain (Ch. 3)

peripheral nervous system   The part of the nervous system that includes the autonomic and somatic subdivisions; made up of long axons and dendrites, it branches out from the spinal cord and brain and reaches the extremities of the body (Ch. 2)

peripheral-route processing   Message interpretation characterized by consideration of the source and related general information rather than of the message itself (Ch. 14)

permissive parents   Parents who give their children lax or inconsistent direction and, although warm, require little of them (Ch. 9)

personal stressors   Major life events, such as the death of a family member, that have immediate negative consequences that usually fade with time (Ch. 7)

personality   The pattern of enduring characteristics that differentiates a person—the patterns of behaviors that make each individual unique (Ch. 10)

personality disorder   A mental disorder characterized by a set of inflexible, maladaptive personality traits that keep a person from functioning properly in society (Ch. 12)

phallic stage   According to Freud, a period beginning around age 3 during which a child's interest focuses on the genitals (Ch. 10)

phobias   Intense, irrational fears of specific objects or situations (Ch. 12)

phonemes   The smallest basic sound units (Ch. 7)

phonology   The study of the smallest sound units, called phonemes (Ch. 7)

pituitary gland   The "master gland," the major component of the endocrine system, which secretes hormones that control growth (Ch. 2)

place theory of hearing   The theory that different areas of the basilar membrane respond to different frequencies (Ch. 3)

placebo   A false treatment, such as a pill, "drug," or other substance, that has no significant chemical properties or active ingredient (Ch. 1)

positive reinforcer   A stimulus added to the environment that brings about an increase in a preceding response (Ch. 5)

posttraumatic stress disorder (PTSD)   A phenomenon in which victims of major catastrophes reexperience the original stress event and associated feelings in vivid flashbacks or dreams (Ch. 11)

practical intelligence   Intelligence related to overall success in living (Ch. 7)

prejudice   The negative (or positive) evaluations of groups and their members (Ch. 14)

preoperational stage   According to Piaget, the period from 2 to 7 years of age which is characterized by language development (Ch. 9)

priming   A phenomenon in which exposure to a word or concept (called a prime) later makes it easier to recall related information, even when one has no conscious memory of the word or concept (Ch. 6)

principle of conservation   The knowledge that the quantity of a substance remains the same even though its shape or other aspects of its physical appearance might change (Ch. 9)

procedural memory   Memory for skills and habits, such as riding a bike or hitting a baseball, sometimes referred to as "nondeclarative memory" (Ch. 6)

progesterone   A female sex hormone (Ch. 8)

projective personality test   A test in which a person is shown an ambiguous stimulus and asked to describe it or tell a story about it (Ch. 10)

prosocial behavior   Helping behavior (Ch. 14)

prototypes   Typical, highly representative examples of a concept (Ch. 7)

psychoactive drugs   Drugs that influence a person's emotions, perceptions, and behavior (Ch. 4)

psychoanalysis   Psychodynamic therapy that involves frequent sessions and can last for many years (Ch. 13)

psychoanalytic perspective   The perspective that abnormal behavior stems from childhood conflicts over opposing wishes regarding sex and aggression (Ch. 12)

psychoanalytic theory   Freud's theory that unconscious forces act as determinants of personality (Ch. 10)

psychodynamic perspective   The approach based on the belief that behavior is motivated by unconscious inner forces over which the individual has little control (Ch. 1)

psychodynamic therapy   First suggested by Freud, therapy based on the premise that the primary sources of abnormal behavior are unresolved past conflicts and the possibility that unacceptable unconscious impulses will enter consciousness (Ch. 13)

psychological tests   Standard measures devised to assess behavior objectively and used by psychologists to help people make decisions about their lives and understand more about themselves (Ch. 10)

psychology   The scientific study of behavior and mental processes (Ch. 1)

psychoneuroimmunology (PNI)   The study of the relationships among psychological factors, the immune system, and the brain (Ch. 11)

psychophysics   The study of the relationship between the physical aspects of stimuli and our psychological experience of them (Ch. 3)

psychophysiological disorders Medical problems influenced by an interaction of psychological, emotional, and physical difficulties (Ch. 4)

psychosocial development Development of individuals' interactions and understanding of each other and of their knowledge and understanding of themselves as members of society (Ch. 9)

psychosurgery Brain surgery once used to reduce symptoms of mental disorder but rarely used today (Ch. 13)

psychotherapy Treatment in which a trained professional—a therapist—uses psychological techniques to help someone overcome psychological difficulties and disorders, resolve problems in living, or bring about personal growth (Ch. 13)

puberty The period during which maturation of the sexual organs occurs, beginning at about age 11 or 12 for girls and 13 or 14 for boys (Ch. 9)

punishment A stimulus that decreases the probability that a previous behavior will occur again (Ch. 5)

r

random assignment to condition A procedure in which participants are assigned to different experimental groups or "conditions" on the basis of chance and chance alone (Ch. 1)

rapid eye movement (REM) sleep Sleep occupying 20 percent of an adult's sleeping time, characterized by increased heart rate, blood pressure, and breathing rate; erections; eye movements; and the experience of dreaming (Ch. 4)

rational-emotive behavior therapy A form of therapy that attempts to restructure a person's belief system into a more realistic, rational, and logical set of views (Ch. 13)

reactance A negative emotional and cognitive reaction to a restriction of one's freedom that can be associated with medical regimens (Ch. 11)

reciprocity-of-liking effect A tendency to like those who like us (Ch. 14)

reflexes Automatic, involuntary responses to incoming stimuli (Ch. 2)

reflexes Unlearned, involuntary responses that occur automatically in the presence of certain stimuli (Ch. 9)

rehearsal The repetition of information that has entered short-term memory (Ch. 6)

reinforcement The process by which a stimulus increases the probability that a preceding behavior will be repeated (Ch. 5)

reinforcer Any stimulus that increases the probability that a preceding behavior will occur again (Ch. 5)

reliability A test's measuring consistently what it is supposed to measure (Ch. 7)

replication The repetition of research, sometimes using other procedures, settings, and other groups of participants, in order to increase confidence in prior findings (Ch. 1)

resting state The state in which there is a negative electrical charge of about −70 millivolts within the neuron (Ch. 2)

reticular formation The part of the brain from the medulla through the pons made up of groups of nerve cells that can immediately activate other parts of the brain to produce general bodily arousal (Ch. 2)

retina The part of the eye that converts the electromagnetic energy of light into useful information for the brain (Ch. 3)

reuptake The reabsorption of neurotransmitters by a terminal button (Ch. 2)

rods Thin, cylindrical receptor cells in the retina that are highly sensitive to light (Ch. 3)

Rorschach test A test by developed by Swiss psychiatrist Hermann Rorschach that consists of showing a series of symmetrical stimuli to people and then asking them to say what the figures represent to them (Ch. 10)

S

Schachter-Singer theory of emotion The belief that emotions are determined jointly by a nonspecific kind of physiological arousal and its interpretation, based on environmental cues (Ch. 8)

schedules of reinforcement The frequency and timing of reinforcement following desired behavior (Ch. 5)

schemas Organized bodies of information stored in memory that bias the way new information is interpreted, stored, and recalled (Ch. 6)

schemas Sets of cognitions about people and social experiences (Ch. 14)

schizophrenia A class of disorders involving severe distortions of reality (Ch. 12)

self-actualization A state of self-fulfillment in which people realize their highest potential in their own unique way (Ch. 8)

self-actualization According to Rogers, a state of self-fulfillment in which people realize their highest potential (Ch. 10)

self-report measures A method of gathering data about people by asking them questions about a sample of their behavior (Ch. 10)

semantic memory Memory for general knowledge and facts about the world, as well as memory for the rules of logic that are used to deduce other facts (Ch. 6)

semantics The rules governing the meaning of words and sentences (Ch. 7)

semicircular canals Three tubelike structures of the inner ear containing fluid that sloshes through them when the head moves, signaling rotational or angular movement to the brain (Ch. 3)

sensation The processes by which our sense organs receive information from the environment (Ch. 3)

sensorimotor stage According to Piaget, the stage from birth to 2 years, during which a child has little competence in representing the environment using images, language, or other symbols (Ch. 9)

sensory (afferent) neurons Neurons that transmit information from the perimeter of the body to the central nervous system (Ch. 2)

sensory area The site in the brain of the tissue that corresponds to each of the senses, with the degree of sensitivity relating to the amount of tissue (Ch. 2)

sensory memory The initial, momentary storage of information, lasting only an instant (Ch. 6)

shaping The process of teaching a complex behavior by rewarding closer and closer approximations to the desired behavior (Ch. 5)

short-term memory Memory that holds information for 15 to 25 seconds (Ch. 6)

significant outcome Meaningful results that make it possible for researchers to feel confident that they have confirmed their hypotheses (Ch. 1)

situational causes (of behavior) A perceived cause of behavior that is based on environmental factors (Ch. 14)

skin senses The senses that include touch, pressure, temperature and pain (Ch. 3)

social cognition The processes that underlie our understanding of the social world (Ch. 14)

social cognitive approaches to personality The theory that emphasizes the influence of a person's cognitions—thoughts, feelings, expectations, and values—in determining personality (Ch. 10)

social influence The process by which the actions of an individual or group affect the behavior of others (Ch. 14)

social psychology The study of how people's thoughts, feelings, and actions are affected by others (Ch. 14)

social support A mutual network of caring, interested others (Ch. 11)

social supporter A person who shares an unpopular opinion or attitude of another group member, thereby encouraging nonconformity (Ch. 14)

sociocultural perspective The perspective that people's behavior—both normal and abnormal—is shaped by the kind of family group, society, and culture in which they live (Ch. 12)

somatic division The part of the nervous system that specializes in the control of voluntary movements and the communication of information to and from the sense organs (Ch. 2)

somatoform disorder Psychological difficulties that take on a physical (somatic) form, but for which there is no medical cause (Ch. 12)

sound The movement of air molecules brought about by the vibration of an object (Ch. 3)

spinal cord   A bundle of nerves that leaves the brain and runs down the length of the back and is the main means for transmitting messages between the brain and the body (Ch. 2)

split-brain patient   A person who suffers from independent functioning of the two halves of the brain, as a result of which the sides of the body work in disharmony (Ch. 2)

spontaneous recovery   The reemergence of an extinguished conditioned response after a period of rest (Ch. 5)

spontaneous remission   Recovery without treatment (Ch. 13)

stage 1 sleep   The state of transition between wakefulness and sleep, characterized by relatively rapid, low-voltage brain waves (Ch. 4)

stage 2 sleep   A sleep deeper than that of stage 1, characterized by a slower, more regular wave pattern, along with momentary interruptions of "sleep spindles" (Ch. 4)

stage 3 sleep   A sleep characterized by slow brain waves, with greater peaks and valleys in the wave pattern (Ch. 4)

stage 4 sleep   The deepest stage of sleep, during which we are least responsive to outside stimulation (Ch. 4)

status   Social rank within a group (Ch. 14)

stimulants   Drugs that affect the central nervous system by causing a rise in heart rate, blood pressure, and muscular tension (Ch. 4)

stimulus   Energy that produces a response in a sense organ (Ch. 3)

stimulus discrimination   The ability to differentiate between stimuli (Ch. 5)

stimulus generalization   A response to a stimulus that is similar to but different from a conditioned stimulus; the more similar the two stimuli, the more likely generalization is to occur (Ch. 5)

stress   The response to events that are threatening or challenging (Ch. 11)

structuralism   Wundt's approach, which focuses on the basic elements that form the foundation of thinking, consciousness, emotions, and other kinds of mental states and activities (Ch. 1)

subjective well-being   People's evaluations of their lives in terms of both their thoughts and their emotions; how happy people are (Ch. 11)

superego   According to Freud, the final personality structure to develop; it represents society's standards of right and wrong as handed down by a person's parents, teachers, and other important figures (Ch. 10)

survey research   Research in which people chosen to represent some larger population are asked a series of questions about their behavior, thoughts, or attitudes (Ch. 1)

sympathetic division   The part of the autonomic division of the nervous system that acts to prepare the body in stressful emergency situations, engaging all the organism's resources to respond to a threat (Ch. 2)

synapse   The space between two neurons where the axon of a sending neuron communicates with the dendrites of a receiving neuron using chemical messages (Ch. 2)

syntax   The rules that indicate how words and phrases can be combined to form sentences (Ch. 7)

systematic desensitization   A behavioral technique in which gradual exposure to anxiety-producing stimuli is paired with relaxation in order to extinguish the response of anxiety (Ch. 13)

t

telegraphic speech   Sentences that sound as if they were part of a telegram, in which words not critical to the message are left out (Ch. 7)

temperament   A basic, innate disposition that emerges early in life (Ch. 9, 10)

teratogens   Environmental agents such as drugs, chemicals, viruses, or other factors that produce birth defects (Ch. 9)

terminal buttons   Small bulges at the end of axons that send messages to other neurons (Ch. 2)

test standardization   A technique used to validate questions in personality tests by studying the responses of people with known diagnoses (Ch. 10)

thalamus   The part of the brain located in the middle of the central core that acts primarily as a busy relay station, mostly for information concerning the senses (Ch. 2)

Thematic Apperception Test (TAT)   A test consisting of a series of ambiguous pictures about which the person is asked to write a story (Ch. 10)

theories   Broad explanations and predictions concerning phenomena of interest (Ch. 1)

thinking   The manipulation of mental representations of information (Ch. 7)

tip-of-the-tongue phenomenon   The inability to recall information that one realizes one knows—a result of the difficulty of retrieving information from long-term memory (Ch. 6)

top-down processing   Perception that is guided by higher-level knowledge, experience, expectations, and motivations (Ch. 3)

trait theory   A model of personality that seeks to identify the basic traits necessary to describe personality (Ch. 10)

traits   Enduring dimensions of personality characteristics along which people differ (Ch. 10)

treatment   In an experiment, the manipulation implemented by the experimenter (Ch. 1)

trichromatic theory of color vision   The theory that there are three kinds of cones in the retina, each of which responds primarily to a specific range of wavelengths (Ch. 3)

trust-versus-mistrust stage   According to Erikson, the first stage of psychosocial development, occurring from birth to 18 months of age, during which time infants develop feelings of trust or lack of trust (Ch. 9)

Type A behavior pattern   A pattern of behavior characterized by competitiveness, impatience, tendency toward frustration, and hostility (Ch. 11)

Type B behavior pattern   A pattern of behavior characterized by cooperation, patience, noncompetitiveness, and nonaggression (Ch. 11)

u

unconditional positive regard   An attitude of acceptance and respect on the part of an observer, no matter what the other person says or does (Ch. 10)

unconditioned response (UCR)   A response that is natural and needs no training (e.g., salivation at the smell of food) (Ch. 5)

unconditioned stimulus (UCS)   A stimulus that brings about a response without having been learned (Ch. 5)

unconscious wish fulfillment theory   Sigmund Freud's theory that dreams represent unconscious wishes that dreamers desire to fulfill (Ch. 4)

unconscious   A part of the personality of which a person is not aware, and which is a potential determinant of behavior (Ch. 10)

uninvolved parents   Parents who show little interest in their children and are emotionally detached from them (Ch. 9)

universal grammar   Noam Chomsky's theory that all the world's languages share a similar underlying structure (Ch. 7)

uplifts   Minor positive events that make one feel good (Ch. 16)

v

validity   A test's actually measuring what it is supposed to measure (Ch. 7)

variable-interval schedule   A schedule whereby the time between reinforcements varies around some average rather than being fixed (Ch. 5)

variable-ratio schedule   A schedule whereby reinforcement occurs after a varying number of responses rather than after a fixed number (Ch. 5)

variables   Behaviors, events, or other characteristics that can change, or vary, in some way (Ch. 1)

visual illusions   Physical stimuli that consistently produce errors in perception (Ch. 3)

w

wear-and-tear theories of aging   Theories that hold that the mechanical functions of the body simply stop working efficiently when we are old (Ch. 9)

Weber's law   One of the basic laws of psychophysics, that a just noticeable difference is in constant proportion to the intensity of an initial stimulus (Ch. 3)

weight set point   The particular level of weight that the body strives to maintain (Ch. 8)

working memory   An active "workspace" in which information is retrieved and manipulated, and in which information is held through rehearsal (Ch. 6)

Z

zone of proximal development (ZPD) According to Vygotsky, the level at which a child can almost, but not fully, comprehend or perform a task on her or his own (Ch. 9)

zygote   The new cell formed by the union of an egg and sperm (Ch. 9)

References

Abi-Dargham, A., Laruelle, M., Aghajanian, G. K., Charney, D., et al. (1997). The role of serotonin in the pathophysiology and treatment of schizophrenia. *Journal of Neuropsychiatry and Clinical Neurosciences, 9,* 1–17.

Abrahams, M. F., & Bell, R. A. (1994). Encouraging charitable contributions: An examination of three models of door-in-the-face compliance. *Communication Research, 21,* 131–153.

Abt, S. (1999, July 26). Armstrong wins tour and journey. *New York Times,* pp. D1, D4.

Adams, B., & Parker, J. D. (1990). Maternal weight gain in women with good pregnancy outcome. *Obstetrics and Gynecology, 76,* 1–7.

Adler, J. (1984, April 23). The fight to conquer fear. *Newsweek,* pp. 66–72.

Adler, P. A., & Adler, P. (1994). Observational techniques. In N. K. Denzin & Y. S. Lincoln (Eds.), *Handbook of qualitative research.* Thousand Oaks, CA: Sage.

Advances in telepsychology/telehealth. (2000). *Professional Psychology: Research and Practice, 31* (2).

Affleck, G., Tennen, H., Urrows, S., & Higgins, P. (1994). Person and contextual features of daily stress reactivity: Individual differences in relations of undesirable daily events with mood disturbance and chronic pain intensity. *Journal of Personality and Social Psychology, 66,* 329–340.

Aghajanian, G. K. (1994). Serotonin and the action of LSD in the brain. *Psychiatric Annals, 24,* 137–141.

Agras, W. S., & Berkowitz, R. I. (1996). Behavior therapy. In R. E. Hales & S. C. Yudofsky (Eds.), *The American Psychiatric Press synopsis of psychiatry.* Washington, DC: American Psychiatric Press.

Ahissar, M., Ahissar, E., Bergman, H., & Vaadia, E. (1992). Encoding of sound-source location and movement: Activity of single neurons and interactions between adjacent neurons in the monkey auditory cortex. *Journal of Neurophysiology, 67,* 203–215.

Ahrons, C. (1995). *The good divorce: Keeping your family together when your marriage comes apart.* New York: HarperPerennial.

Aiken, L. R. (1996). *Assessment of intellectual functioning* (2nd ed.). New York: Plenum Press.

Aiken, L. R. (1997). *Psychological testing and assessment* (9th ed.). Boston: Allyn & Bacon.

Aiken, L. R. (2001). *Dying, death, and bereavement* (4th ed.). Mahwah, NJ: Erlbaum.

Ainsworth, M. D. S., Blehar, M. C., Waters, E., & Wall, S. (1978). *Patterns of attachment: A psychological study of the strange situation.* Hillsdale, NJ: Erlbaum.

Ainsworth, M. D. S., Bowlby, J. (1991). An ethological approach to personality development. *American Psychologist, 46,* 333–341.

Akbarian, S., Kim, J. J., Potkin, S. G., Hetrick, W. P., et al. (1996). Maldistribution of interstitial neurons in prefrontal white matter of the brains of schizophrenic patients. *Archives of General Psychiatry, 53,* 425–436.

Akil, H., & Morano, M. I. (1996). The biology of stress: From periphery to brain. In S. J. Watson (Ed.), *Biology of schizophrenia and affective disease.* Washington, DC: American Psychiatric Press.

Akmajian, A., Demers, R. A., & Harnish, R. M. (1984). *Linguistics.* Cambridge, MA: MIT Press.

Akutsu, P. D., Sue, S., Zane, N. W. S., & Nakamura, C. Y. (1989). Ethnic differences in alcohol consumption among Asians and Caucasians in the United States: An investigation of cultural and physiological factors. *Journal of Studies on Alcohol, 50,* 261–267.

Alford, B. A., & Beck, A. T. (1997) *The integrative power of cognitive therapy.* New York: Guilford Press.

Allen, M. (1999, September 19). Help wanted: The not-too-high-Q standard. *New York Times,* p. 3.

Allen, V. L. (1975). Social support for nonconformity. In L. Berkowitz (Ed.), *Advances in experimental and social psychology* (Vol. 8). New York: Academic Press.

Alliger, G. M., Lilienfeld, S. O., & Mitchell, K. E. (1996). The susceptibility of overt and covert integrity tests to coaching and faking. *Psychological Science, 7,* 32–39.

Alloy, L. B., Abramson, L. Y., & Francis, E. L. (1999). Do negative cognitive styles confer vulnerability to depression? *Current Directions in Psychological Science, 8,* 128–132.

Allport, G. W. (1961). *Pattern and growth in personality.* New York: Holt, Rinehart & Winston.

Allport, G. W. (1966). Traits revisited. *American Psychologist, 21,* 1–10.

Allport, G. W., & Postman, L. J. (1958). The basic psychology of rumor. In E. D. Maccoby, T. M. Newcomb, & E. L. Hartley (Eds.), *Readings in social psychology* (3rd ed.). New York: Holt, Rinehart & Winston.

Almer, E. (2000, April 22). Online therapy: An arm's length approach. *New York Times,* pp. A1, A11.

Altman, N. (1996). The accommodation of diversity in psychoanalysis. In R. P. Foster, M. Moskowitz, & R. A. Javier (Eds.), *Reaching across boundaries of culture and class: Widening the scope of psychotherapy.* Northvale, NJ: Jason Aronson.

American Academy of Pediatrics. (1999a, July 26). *Circumcision: Information for parents.* Available on the World Wide Web at http://www.aap.org/family/circ.htm.

American Academy of Pediatrics. (1999b). Media education (RE9911). *Pediatrics, 104,* 341–343.

American Association on Mental Retardation (AAMR). (1992). *Mental retardation: Definition, classification, and systems of support.* Washington, DC: Author.

American Psychiatric Association. (1994). *Diagnostic and statistical manual of mental disorders* (4th ed.). Washington, DC: Author.

American Psychiatric Association, Task Force on Electroconvulsive Therapy. (1990). *The practice of electroconvulsive therapy: Recommendations for treatment, training, and privileging.* Washington, DC: American Psychiatric Association.

American Psychological Association (APA). (1988). *Behavioral research with animals.* Washington, DC: Author.

American Psychological Association (APA). (1992). *Ethical principles of psychologists and code of conduct.* Washington, DC: Author.

American Psychological Association (APA). (1993, January/February). Subgroup norming and the Civil Rights Act. *Psychological Science Agenda, 5,* 6.

American Psychological Association (APA). (1999). *Talk to someone who can help.* Washington, DC: American Psychological Association.

Anastasi, A. (1988). *Psychological testing* (6th ed.). New York: Macmillan.

Anastasi, A., & Urbina, S. (1997). *Psychological testing* (7th ed.). Englewood Cliffs, NJ: Prentice Hall.

Andersen, B. L., Kiecolt-Glaser, J.K., & Glaser, R. (1994). A biobehavioral model of cancer stress and disease course. *American Psychologist, 49,* 389–404.

Anderson, C. A., & Dill, K. E. (2000). Video games and aggressive thoughts, feelings, and behavior in the laboratory and in life. *Journal of Personality and Social Psychology, 78,* 772–790.

Anderson, J. (1988). Cognitive styles and multicultural populations. *Journal of Teacher Education, 39,* 2–9.

Anderson, J. A., & Adams, M. (1992). Acknowledging the learning styles of diverse student populations: Implications for instructional design. *New Directions for Teaching and Learning, 49,* 19–33.

Anderson, J. R. (1981). Interference: The relationship between response latency and response accuracy. *Journal of Experimental Psychology: Human Learning and Memory, 7,* 311–325.

Anderson, J. R., & Bower, G. H. (1972). Recognition and retrieval processes in free recall. *Psychological Review, 79,* 97–123.

Anderson, K. B., Cooper, H., & Okamura, L. (1997). Individual differences and attitudes toward rape: A meta-analytic review. *Personality and Social Psychology Bulletin, 23,* 295–315.

Anderson, N. H. (1996). *A functional theory of cognition.* Mahwah, NJ: Erlbaum.

Anderson, S. M., & Klatzky, R. L. (1987). Traits and social stereotypes: Levels of categorization in person perception. *Journal of Personality and Social Psychology, 53,* 235–246.

Anderson, T., & Magnusson, D. (1990). Biological maturation in adolescence and the development of drinking habits and alcohol abuse among young males: A prospective longitudinal study. *Journal of Youth and Adolescence, 19,* 33–42.

Andreasen, N. C., Arndt, S., Swayze II, V., Cizadlo, T., Flaum, M., O'Leary, D., Ehrhardt, J. C., & Yuh, W. T. C. (1994, October 14). Thalamic abnormalities in schizophrenia visualized through magnetic resonance image averaging. *Science, 266,* 294–298.

Angier, N. (1991, January 22). A potent peptide prompts an urge to cuddle. *New York Times,* p. C1.

Angier, N. (1999, May 16). Baby in a box. *New York Times Magazine,* p. 86.

Angoff, W. H. (1988). The nature-nurture debate, aptitudes, and group differences. *American Psychologist, 43,* 713–720.

Ansburg, P. I., & Dominowski, R. L. (2000). Promoting insightful problem solving. *Journal of Creative Behavior, 34,* 30–60.

Antony, M. M., Brown, T. A., & Barlow, D. H. (1992). Current perspectives on panic and panic disorder. *Current Directions in Psychological Science, 1,* 79–82.

Aponte, J. F., & Wohl, J. (2000). *Psychological intervention and cultural diversity.* Needham Heights, MA: Allyn & Bacon.

Apter, A., Galatzer, A., Beth-Halachmi, N., & Laron, Z. (1981). Self-image in adolescents with delayed puberty and growth retardation. *Journal of Youth and Adolescence, 10,* 501–505.

Arafat, I., & Cotton, W. L. (1974). Masturbation practices of males and females. *Journal of Sex Research, 10,* 293–307.

Archambault, D. L. (1992). Adolescence: A physiological, cultural, and psychological no man's land. In G. W. Lawson & A. W. Lawson (Eds.), *Adolescent substance abuse: Etiology, treatment, and prevention.* Gaithersburg, MD: Aspen.

Archer, S. L., & Waterman, A. S. (1994). Adolescent identity development: Contextual perspectives. In C. B. Fisher & R. M. Lerner (Eds.), *Applied developmental psychology.* New York: McGraw-Hill.

Arena, J. M. (1984, April). A look at the opposite sex. *Newsweek on Campus,* p. 21.

Ariel, S. (1999). *Culturally competent family therapy: A general model.* Westport, CT: Greenwood Press.

Aron, A., Melinat, E., Aronon, E. N., Vallone, R. D., & Bator, R. J. (1997). The experimental generation of interpersonal closeness: A procedure and some preliminary findings. *Personality and Social Psychology Bulletin, 23,* 363–377.

Aronow, E., Reznikoff, M., & Moreland, K. (1994). *The Rorschach technique: Perceptual basics, content interpretation, and applications.* Boston: Longwood.

Aronson, E. (1988). *The social animal* (3rd ed.). San Francisco: Freeman.

Asch, S. E. (1946). Forming impressions of personality. *Journal of Abnormal and Social Psychology, 41,* 258–290.

Asch, S. E. (1951). Effects of group pressure upon the modification and distortion of judgments. In H. Guetzkow (Ed.), *Groups, leadership, and men.* Pittsburgh: Carnegie Press.

Asher, S. R., & Parker, J. G. (1991). Significance of peer relationship problems in childhood. In B. H. Schneider, G. Attili, J. Nadel, & R. P. Weissberg (Eds.), *Social competence in developmental perspective.* Amsterdam: Kluwer Academic.

Aspinwall, L. G., & Taylor, S. E. (1997). A stitch in time: Self-regulation and proactive coping. *Psychological Bulletin, 121,* 417–436.

Atkinson, H. (Ed.). (1997, January 21). Understanding your diagnosis. *HealthNews,* p. 3.

Atkinson, J. (1995). Through the eyes of an infant. In R. L. Gregory, J. Harris, P. Heard, & D. Rose (Eds.), *The artful eye.* Oxford: Oxford University Press.

Atkinson, J. W., & Feather, N. T. (1966). *Theory of achievement motivation.* New York: Krieger.

Atkinson, J. W., & Raynor, J. O. (Eds.). (1974). *Motivation and achievement.* Washington, DC: Winston.

Atkinson, J. W., & Shiffrin, R. M. (1971, August). The control of short-term memory. *Scientific American,* pp. 82–90.

Atkinson, R. C., & Shiffrin, R. M. (1968). Human memory: A proposed system and its control processes. In K. W. Spence and J. T. Spence (Eds.), *The psychology of learning and motivation: Advances in research and theory* (Vol. 2, pp. 80–195). New York: Academic Press.

Averill, J. R. (1975). A semantic atlas of emotional concepts. *Catalog of Selected Documents in Psychology, 5,* 330.

Averill, J. R. (1994). Emotions are many splendored things. In P. Ekman & R. J. Davidson (Eds.), *The nature of emotion: Fundamental questions.* New York: Oxford University Press.

Averill, J. R. (1997). The emotions: An integrative approach. In R. Hogan, J. Johnson, & S. Briggs (Eds.), *Handbook of personality psychology.* Orlando: Academic Press.

Aycan, Z. (2000). Cross-cultural industrial and organizational psychology: Contributions, past developments, and future directions. *Journal of Cross-Cultural Psychology, 31,* 110–128.

Baddeley, A. D. (1992, January 31). Working memory. *Science, 255,* 556–559.

Baddeley, A. D. (1993). Working memory and conscious awareness. In A. F. Collins, S. E. Gathercole, M. A. Conway, & P. E. Morris (Eds.), *Theories of memory.* Hillsdale, NJ: Erlbaum.

Baddeley, A. D. (1995a). The psychology of memory. In A. D. Baddeley, B. A. Wilson, & F. N. Watts (Eds.), *Handbook of memory disorders.* Chichester, England: John Wiley.

Baddeley, A. D. (1995b). Working memory. In M. S. Gazzaniga (Ed.), *The cognitive neurosciences.* Cambridge, MA: MIT Press.

Baddeley, A. D. (1996). Exploring the central executive. *Quarterly Journal of Experimental Psychology, Human Experimental Psychology, 49A,* 5–28.

Baddeley, A. D., Gathercole, S., & Papagno, C. (1998). The phonological loop as a language learning device. *Psychological Review, 105,* 158–173.

Baddeley, A. D., & Wilson, B. (1985). Phonological coding and short-term memory in patients without speech. *Journal of Memory and Language, 24,* 490–502.

Baer, J. (1993). *Creativity and divergent thinking: A task-specific approach.* Hillsdale, NJ: Erlbaum.

Baer, L., Rauch, S. L., Callantine, T., Martuza, R., et al. (1995). Cingulotomy for intractable obsessive-compulsive disorder: Prospective long-term follow-up of 18 patients. *Archives of General Psychiatry, 52,* 384–392.

Bahrick, H. P., Hall, L. K., & Berger, S. A. (1996). Accuracy and distortion in memory for high school grades. *Psychological Science, 7,* 265–269.

Bailey, J. M. (1995). Biological perspectives on sexual orientation. In A. R. D'Augelli & C. J. Patteson (Eds.), *Lesbian, gay, and bisexual identities over the lifespan: Psychological perspectives.* New York: Oxford University Press.

Bailey, M., & Pillard, R. C. (1994, January). The innateness of homosexuality. *Harvard Mental Health Letter, 10,* pp. 4–6.

Bailey, J. M., Pillard, R. C., Kitzinger, C., & Wilkinson, S. (1997). Sexual orientation: Is it determined by biology? In M. R. Walsh (Ed.), *Women, men, and gender: Ongoing debates.* New Haven, CT: Yale University Press.

Bailey, J. M., & Zucker, K. J. (1995). Childhood sex-typed behavior and sexual orientation: A conceptual analysis and quantitative review. *Developmental Psychology, 31,* 43–55.

Baird, J. C. (1997). *Sensation and judgment: Complementarity theory of psychophysics.* Mahwah, NJ: Erlbaum.

Baker, R. A. (1998, February). A view of hypnosis. *Harvard Mental Health Letter,* pp. 5–6.

Baker, S. P., Lamb, M. W., Li, G., & Dodd, R. S. (1993). Human factors in crashes of commuter airplanes. *Aviation, Space, and Environmental Medicine, 64,* 63–68.

Ball, E. M., Simon, R. D., Tall, A. A., Banks, M. B., Nino-Murcia, G., & Dement, W. C. (1997, February 24). Diagnosis and treatment of sleep apnea within the community. *Archive of Internal Medicine, 157,* 419–424.

Ballinger, C. B. (1981). The menopause and its syndromes. In J. G. Howells (Ed.), *Modern perspectives in the psychiatry of middle age* (pp. 279–303). New York: Brunner/Mazel.

Bandura, A. (1973). *Aggression: A social learning analysis.* Englewood Cliffs, NJ: Prentice Hall.

Bandura, A. (1977). *Social learning theory.* Englewood Cliffs, NJ: Prentice Hall.

Bandura, A. (1983). Psychological mechanisms of aggression. In R. G. Geen & E. I. Donnerstein (Eds.), *Aggression: Theoretical and empirical reviews, Vol. 1: Theoretical and methodological issues.* New York: Academic Press.

Bandura, A. (1986). *Social foundations of thought and action: A social cognitive theory.* Englewood Cliffs, NJ: Prentice Hall.

Bandura, A. (1988). Self-regulation of motivation and action through goal systems. In V. Hamilton & H. Gordon (Eds.), *Cognitive perspectives on emotion and motivation.* Dordrecht, Netherlands: Kluwer Academic.

Bandura, A. (1994). Social cognitive theory of mass communication. In J. Bryant & D. Zillmann (Eds.), *Media effects: Advances in theory and research.* Hillsdale, NJ: Erlbaum.

Bandura, A. (1997). *Self-efficacy: The exercise of control.* New York: W. H. Freeman.

Bandura, A. (1999). Social cognitive theory of personality. In D. Cervone & Y. Shod (Eds.), *The coherence of personality.* New York: Guilford.

Bandura, A. (2000). Self-efficacy: The foundation of agency. In W. J. Perrig & A. Grob (Eds.), *Control of human behavior, mental processes, and consciousness: Essays in honor of the 60th birthday of August Flammer.* Mahwah, NJ: Erlbaum.

Bandura, A., Grusec, J. E., & Menlove, F. L. (1967). Vicarious extinction of avoidance behavior. *Journal of Personality and Social Psychology, 5,* 16–23.

Bandura, A., Ross, D., & Ross, S. (1963a). Imitation of film-mediated aggressive models. *Journal of Abnormal and Social Psychology, 66,* 3–11.

Bandura, A., Ross, D., & Ross, S. (1963b). Vicarious reinforcement and imitative learning. *Journal of Abnormal and Social Psychology, 67,* 601–607.

Banich, T., & Heller, W. (1998). Evolving perspectives on lateralization of function. *Current Directions in Psychological Science, 7,* 1–2.

Barber, J. (Ed.). (1996). *Hypnosis and suggestion in the treatment of pain: A clinical guide.* New York: W. W. Norton.

Barber, S., & Lane, R. C. (1995). Efficacy research in psychodynamic therapy: A critical review of the literature. *Psychotherapy in Private Practice, 14,* 43–69.

Bargh, J., & Pietromonaco, P. (1982). Automatic information processing and social perception: The influence of trait information presented outside of conscious awareness on impression formation. *Journal of Personality and Social Psychology, 43,* 437–449.

Bargh, J. A., Raymond, P., Pryor, J. B., & Strack, F. (1995). Attractiveness of the underling: An automatic power sex association and its consequences for sexual harassment and aggression. *Journal of Personality and Social Psychology, 68,* 768–781.

Barinaga, M. (1997, May 30). How much pain for cardiac gain? *Science, 276,* 1324–1327.

Barinaga, M. (1999, July 23). Mapping smells in the brain. *Science, 285,* 508.

Barkley, R. A. (1998a, September). Attention-deficit hyperactivity disorder. *Scientific American,* pp. 66–71.

Barkley, R. A. (1998b). *Attention-deficit hyperactivity disorder: A handbook for diagnosis and treatment.* New York: Guilford Press.

Barnard, N. D., & Kaufman, S. R. (1997, February). Animal research is wasteful and misleading. *Scientific American,* pp. 80–82.

Barrett, M. (1999). *The development of language.* Philadelphia: Psychology Press.

Barron, F. (1990). *Creativity and psychological health: Origins of personal vitality and creative freedom.* Buffalo, NY: Creative Education Foundation.

Bartecchi, C. E., MacKenzie, T. D., & Schrier, R. W. (1995, May). The global tobacco epidemic. *Scientific American,* pp. 44–51.

Bartlett, F. (1932). *Remembering: A study in experimental and social psychology.* Cambridge, England: Cambridge University Press.

Bartoshuk, L. (2000, July/August). The bitter with the sweet. *APS Observer,* 11, 33.

Bartoshuk, L., & Beauchamp, G. K. (1994). Chemical senses. *Annual Review of Psychology, 45,* 419–449.

Bartoshuk, L., & Drewnowski, A. (1997, February). Symposium presented at the annual meeting of the American Association for the Advancement of Science, Seattle.

Basch, M. F. (1996). Affect and defense. In D. L. Nathanson (Ed.), *Knowing feeling: Affect, script, and psychotherapy.* New York: W. W. Norton.

Bass, A. (1996, April 21). Is anger good for you? *Boston Globe Magazine,* pp. 20–41.

Batista, A. P., Buneo, C. A., Snyder, L. H., & Anderson, R. A. (1999, July 9). Reach plans in eye-centered coordinates. *Science, 285,* 257–260.

Batson, C. D. (1991). *The altruism question: Toward a social-psychological answer.* Hillsdale, NJ: Erlbaum.

Batson, C. D., Batson, J. G., Todd, R. M., & Brummett, B. H. (1995). Empathy and the collective good: Caring for one of the others in a social dilemma. *Journal of Personality and Social Psychology, 68,* 619–631.

Bauer, P. J. (1996). What do infants recall of their lives? Memory for specific events by one- to two-year-olds. 102nd Annual Convention of the American Psychological Association. (1994, Los Angeles, California, US) *American Psychologist, 51,* 29–41.

Baum, A. (1994). Behavioral, biological, and environmental interactions in disease processes. In S. Blumenthal, K. Matthews, and S. Weiss (Eds.), *New research frontiers in behavioral medicine: Proceedings of the National Conference.* Washington, DC: NIH Publications.

Baum, A., Cohen, L., & Hall, M. (1993). Control and instrusive memories as possible determinants of chronic stress. *Psychosomatic Medicine, 55,* 274–286.

Baum, A. S., Revenson, R. A., & Singer, J. E. (Eds.). (2000). *Handbook of health psychology.* Mahwah, NJ: Erlbaum.

Baumeister, R., & Bratslavsky, E. (1999). Passion, intimacy, and time: Passionate love as a function of change in intimacy. *Personality and Social Psychology Review, 3,* 49–67.

Baumeister, R. F. (1998). The self. In D. T. Gilbert & S. T. Fiske (Eds.), *The handbook of social psychology* (4th ed., Vol. 1). New York: McGraw-Hill.

Baumeister, R. F., Bushman, B. J., & Campbell, W. K. (2000). Self-esteem, narcissism, and aggression: Does violence result from low self-esteem or from threatened egotism? *Current Directions in Psychological Science, 9,* 26–29.

Baumrind, D. (1971). Current patterns of parental authority. *Developmental Psychology Monographs, 4* (1, pt. 2).

Baumrind, D. (1980). New directions in socialization research. *Psychological Bulletin, 35,* 639–652.

Bayer, D. L. (1996). Interaction in families with young adults with a psychiatric diagnosis. *American Journal of Family Therapy, 24,* 21–30.

Baynes, K., Eliassen, J. C., Lutsep, H. L., & Gazzaniga, M. S. (1998, May 8). Modular organization of cognitive systems marked by interhemispheric integration. *Science, 280,* 902–905.

Bazell, B. (1998, August 25). Back pain goes high-tech. *Slate.msn.com,* 1–4.

Bear, M. F., Connors, B. W., & Paradiso, M. A. (2000). *Neuroscience: Exploring the brain.* Philadelphia: Lippincott Williams & Wilkins.

Beatty, J. (2000). *The human brain: Essentials of behavioral neuroscience.* Thousand Oaks, CA: Sage.

Beck, A. T. (1991). Cognitive therapy: A 30-year perspective. *American Psychologist, 46,* 368–375.

Beck, A. T. (1995). Cognitive therapy: Past, present, and future. In M. J. Mahoney (Ed.), *Cognitive and constructive psychotherapies: Theory, research, and practice.* New York: Springer.

Beck, M. (1992, May 25). Menopause. *Newsweek,* pp. 71–79.

Beckham, E. E., & Leber, W. R. (Eds.). (1997). *Handbook of depression* (2nd ed.). New York: Guilford Press.

Beckman, H. B., & Frankel, R. M. (1984). The effect of physician behavior on the collection of data. *Annals of Internal Medicine, 101,* 692–696.

Bedard, W. W., & Persinger, M. A. (1995). Prednisolone blocks extreme intermale social aggression in seizure-induced, brain-damaged rats: Implications for the amygdaloid central nucleus, corticotrophin-releasing factor, and electrical seizures. *Psychological Reports, 77,* 3–9.

Begley, S. (1998b, July 13). You're OK, I'm terrific: "Self-esteem" backfires. *Newsweek,* p. 69.

Begley, S. (2000, April 10). Decoding the human body. *Newsweek,* pp. 50–62.

Beilin, H. (1996). Mind and meaning: Piaget and Vygotsky on causal explanation. *Human Development, 39,* 277–286.

Bell, A., & Weinberg, M. S. (1978). *Homosexuality: A study of diversities among men and women.* New York: Simon & Schuster.

Bell, J., Grekul, J., Lamba, N., & Minas, C. (1995). The impact of cost on student helping behavior. *Journal of Social Psychology, 135,* 49–56.

Bell, S. M., & Ainsworth, M. D. S. (1972). Infant crying and maternal responsiveness. *Child Development, 43,* 1171–1190.

Bellack, A. S., Hersen, M., & Kazdin, A. E. (1990). *International handbook of behavior modification and therapy.* New York: Plenum Press.

Bellezza, F. S., Six, L. S., & Phillips, D. S. (1992). A mnemonic for remembering long strings of digits. *Bulletin of the Psychonomic Society, 30,* 271–274.

Belsky, J., & Rovine, M. (1988). Nonmaternal care in the first year of life and infant-parent attachment security. *Child Development, 59,* 157–167.

Bem, D. J. (1996). Exotic becomes erotic: A developmental theory of sexual orientation. *Psychological Review, 103,* 320–335.

Bem, D. J., & Honorton, C. (1994). Does psi exist? Replicable evidence for an anomalous process of information transfer. *Psychological Bulletin, 115,* 4–18.

Benjamin, J., Li, L., Patterson, C., Greenberg, B. D., Murphy, D. L., & Hamer, D. H. (1996). Population and familial association between the D4 dopamine receptor gene and measures of novelty seeking. *Nature and Genetics, 12,* 81–84.

Benjamin, L. T., Jr. (1997). The psychology of history and the history of psychology: A historiographical introduction. In L. T. Benjamin (Ed.), *A history of psychology: Original sources and contemporary research* (2nd ed.). New York: McGraw-Hill.

Benjamin, L. T., Jr., & Shields, S. A. (1990). Foreword. In H. Hollingworth, *Leta Stetter Hollingworth: A biography.* Bolton: Anker.

Bennett, A. (1992, October 14). Lori Schiller emerges from the torments of schizophrenia. *Wall Street Journal,* pp. A1, A10.

Bennett, M. R. (2000). The concept of transmitter receptors: 100 years on. *Neuropharmacology, 39,* 523–546.

Bennett, W., & Gurin, J. (1982). *The dieter's dilemma: Eating less and weighing more.* New York: Basic Books.

Benson, H. (1993). The relaxation response. In D. Goleman & J. Guerin (Eds.), *Mind-body medicine: How to use your mind for better health.* Yonkers, NY: Consumer Reports.

Benson, H., & Friedman, R. (1985). A rebuttal to the conclusions of Davis S. Holme's article, "Meditation and somatic arousal reduction." *American Psychologist, 40,* 725–726.

Benson, H., Kornhaber, A., Kornhaber, C., LeChanu, M. N., et al. (1994). Increases in positive psychological characteristics with a new relaxation-response curriculum in high school students. *Journal of Research and Development in Education, 27,* 226–231.

Bentall, R. P. (1992). The classification of schizophrenia. In D. J. Kavanagh (Ed.), *Schizophrenia: An overview and practical handbook.* London: Chapman & Hall.

Bergin, A. E., & Garfield, S. L. (1994). (Eds.). *Handbook of psychotherapy and behavior change* (4th ed.). New York: Wiley.

Berkowitz, L. (1984). Aversive conditioning as stimuli to aggression. In R. J. Blanchard & C. Blanchard (Eds.), *Advances in the study of aggression* (Vol. 1). New York: Academic Press.

Berkowitz, L. (1989). Frustration-aggression hypothesis. *Psychological Bulletin, 106,* 59–73.

Berkowitz, L. (1990). On the formation and regulation of anger and aggression: A cognitive-neoassociationistic analysis. *American Psychologist, 45,* 494–503.

Berkowitz, L. (1993). *Aggression: Its causes, consequences, and control.* New York: McGraw-Hill.

Berkowitz, L., & Geen, R. G. (1966). Film violence and the cue properties of available targets. *Journal of Personality and Social Psychology, 3,* 525–530.

Berkowitz, L., & LePage, A. (1967). Weapons as aggression-eliciting stimuli. *Journal of Personality and Social Psychology, 7,* 202–207.

Berlyne, D. (1967). Arousal and reinforcement. In D. Levine (Ed.), *Nebraska symposium on motivation.* Lincoln: University of Nebraska Press.

Berman, R. M., Krystal, J. H., & Charney, D. S. (1996). Mechanism of action of antidepressants: Monoamine hypotheses and beyond. In S. J. Watson (Ed.), *Biology of schizophrenia and affective disease.* Washington, DC: American Psychiatric Press.

Bernard, L. L. (1924). *Instinct: A study in social psychology.* New York: Holt.

Bernieri, F. J., Zuckerman, M., Koestner, R., & Rosenthal, R. (1994). Measuring person perception accuracy: Another look at self-other agreement. *Personality and Social Psychology Bulletin, 20,* 367–378.

Berquier, A., & Ashton, R. (1992). Characteristics of the frequent nightmare sufferer. *Personality and Social Psychology, 101,* 246–250.

Berrettini, W. H. (2000). Genetics of psychiatric disease. *Annual Review of Medicine, 51,* 465–479.

Berrios, G. E. (1996). *The history of mental symptoms: Descriptive psychopathology since the nineteenth century.* Cambridge, England: Cambridge University Press.

Berscheid, E. (1985). Interpersonal attraction. In G. Lindzey & E. Aronson (Eds.), *Handbook of social psychology* (3rd ed.). New York: Random House.

Bersoff, D. N. (1995). *Ethical conflicts in psychology.* Washington, DC: American Psychological Association.

Bersoff, D. N. (1999). Why good people sometimes do bad things: Motivated reasoning and unethical behavior. *Personality and Social Psychology Bulletin, 25,* 28–39.

Betancourt, H., & Lopez, S. R. (1993). The study of culture, ethnicity, and race in American psychology. *American Psychologist, 48,* 1586–1596.

Beutler, L. E., Brown, M. T., Crothers, L., Booker, K., et al. (1996). The dilemma of factitious demographic distinctions in psychological research. *Journal of Consulting and Clinical Psychology, 64,* 892–902.

Beyene, Y. (1989). *From menarche to menopause: Reproductive lives of peasant women in two cultures.* Albany: State University of New York Press.

Bickman, L. (1994). Social influence and diffusion of responsibility in an emergency. In B. Puka (Ed.), *Reaching out: Caring, altruism, and prosocial behavior. Moral development: A compendium, Vol. 7.* New York: Garland.

Bieber, I., et al. (1962). *Homosexuality: A psychoanalytic study.* New York: Basic Books.

Biederman, I. (1981). On the semantics of a glance at a scene. In M. Kubovy and J. R. Pomerangtz (Eds.), *Perceptual organization.* Hillsdale, NJ: Erlbaum.

Biederman, I. (1987). Recognition-by-components: A theory of human image understanding. *Psychological Review, 94,* 115–147.

Biederman, I. (1990). Higher-level vision. In D. N. Osherson, S. Kosslyn, & J. Hollerbach (Eds.), *An invitation to cognitive science: Visual cognition and action.* Cambridge, MA: MIT Press.

Binet, A., & Simon, T. (1916). *The development of intelligence in children (the Binet-Simon scale).* Baltimore: Williams & Wilkins.

Binkley, C. (2000, May 4). Casion chain mines data on its gamblers, and strikes pay dirt. *Wall Street Journal,* pp. A1, A10.

Binstock, R., & George, L. K. (Eds.). (1996). *Handbook of aging and the social sciences* (4th ed.). San Diego: Academic Press.

Birbaumer, N., Ghanayim, N., Hinterberger, T., Iversen, I., Kotchoubey, B., Kubler, A., Perelmouter, J., Taub, E., & Flor, H. (1999, March 25). A spelling device for the paralysed [letter]. *Nature, 398,* 297–298.

Birch, H. G. (1945). The role of motivation factors in insightful problem solving. *Journal of Comparative Psychology, 38,* 295–317.

Bird, G., & Melville, K. (1994). *Families and intimate relationships.* (1994). New York: McGraw-Hill.

Birren, J. E. (Ed.). (1996). *Encyclopedia of gerontology: Age, aging and the aged.* San Diego: Academic Press.

Bjork, D. W. (1993). *B. F. Skinner: A life.* New York: Basic Books.

Bjork, E. L., & Bjork, R. A. (Eds.). (1996). *Memory.* New York: Academic Press.

Bjork, R. A., & Richardson-Klavehn, A. (1989). On the puzzling relationship between environmental context and human memory. In C. Izawa (Ed.), *Current issues in cognitive processes: The Tulane-Floweree symposium on cognition.* Hillsdale, NJ: Erlbaum.

Bjorklund, D. F. (1985). The role of conceptual knowledge in the development of organization in children's memory. In C. J. Brainerd & M. Pressley (Eds.), *Basic process in memory development.* New York: Springer-Verlag.

Bjorklund, D. F. (1997). In search of a metatheory for cognitive development (or, Piaget is dead and I don't feel so good myself). *Child Development, 68,* 144–148.

Blakeslee, S. (1992, August 11). Finding a new messenger for the brain's signals to the body. *New York Times,* p. C3.

Blakeslee, S. (2000, January 4). A decade of discovery yields a shock about the brain. *New York Times,* D1.

Blanchard, F. A., Lilly, R., & Vaughn, L. A. (1991). Reducing the expression of racial prejudice. *Psychological Science, 2,* 101–105.

Blanck, P. D. (Ed.). (1993). *Interpersonal expectations: Theory, research and applications.* Cambridge, England: Cambridge University Press.

Blank, M., & White, S. J. (1999). Activating the zone of proximal development in school: Obstacles and solutions. In P. Lloyd & C. Fernyhough (Eds.), *Lev Vygotsky: Critical assessments: The zone of proximal development, Vol. 3.* New York: Routledge.

Blascovich, J. J., & Katkin, E. S. (Eds.) (1993). *Cardiovascular reactivity to psychological stress and disease.* Washington, DC: American Psychological Association.

Blass, T. (1996). Attribution of responsibility and trust in the Milgram obedience experiment. *Journal of Applied Social Psychology, 26,* 1529–1535.

Blass, T. (Ed.). (2000). *Obedience to authority: Current perspectives on the Milgram paradigm.* Mahwah, NJ: Erlbaum.

Blau, Z. S. (1973). *Old age in a changing society.* New York: New Viewpoints.

Blewett, A. E. (2000). Help cards for patients. *Psychiatric Bulletin, 24,* 276.

Blume, S. B. (1998, March). Alcoholism in women. *Harvard Mental Health Letter,* pp. 5–7.

Boakes, R. A., Popplewell, D. A., & Burton, M. J. (Eds.). (1987). *Eating habits: Food, physiology, and learned behaviour.* New York: Wiley.

Boehm, K. E., Schondel, C. K., Marlowe, A. L., & Rose, J. S. (1995). Adolescents calling a peer-listening phone service: Variations in calls by gender, age, and season of year. *Adolescence, 30,* 863–871.

Bolla, K. I., Cadet, J. L., & London, E. D. (1998). The neuropsychiatry of chronic cocaine abuse. *Journal of Neuropsychiatry and Clinical Neurosciences, 10,* 280–289.

Booth, D. A. (1994). *Psychology of nutrition.* London: Taylor & Francis.

Bornstein, M. H. & Arterberry, M. (1999). Perceptual development. In M. Bornstein & M. Lamb, *Developmental psychology.* Mahwah, NJ: Erlbaum.

Bornstein, M. H., & Bruner, J. S. (Eds.). (1989). *Interaction on human development: Crosscurrents in contemporary psychology services.* Hillsdale, NJ: Erlbaum.

Bornstein, R. F. (1996). Construct validity of the Rorschach Oral Dependency Scale: 1967–1995. *Psychological Assessment, 8,* 200–205.

Bornstein, R. F., & D'Agostino, P. R. (1994). The attribution and discounting of perceptual fluency: Preliminary tests of a perceptual fluency/attributional model of the mere exposure effect. *Social Cognition, 12,* 103–128.

Botting, J. H., & Morrison, A. R. (1997, February). Animal research is vital to medicine. *Scientific American, 276,* 83–86.

Botvin, G. J., & Botvin, E. M. (1992). Adolescent tobacco, alcohol, and drug abuse: Prevention strategies, empirical findings, and assessment issues. *Journal of Developmental and Behavioral Pediatrics, 13,* 290–301.

Botvin, G. J., Schinke, S. P. Epstein, J. A., & Diaz, T. (1994). Effectivenenss of culturally focused and generic skills training approaches to alcohol and drug abuse prevention among minority youths. *Psychology of Addictive Behaviors, 8,* 116–127.

Botvin, G. J., Schinke, S. P., Epstein, J. A., Diaz, T., et al. (1995). Effectiveness of culturally focused and generic skills training approaches to alcohol and drug abuse prevention among minority adolescents: Two-year follow-up results. *Psychology of Addictive Behaviors, 9,* 183–194.

Bouchard, C., & Bray, G. A. (Eds.). (1996). *Regulation of body weight: Biological and behavioral mechanisms.* New York: Wiley.

Bouchard, C., Tremblay, A., Despres, J. P., Nadeau, A., et al. (1990, May 24). The response to long-term overfeeding in identical twins. *New England Journal of Medicine, 322,* 1477–1482.

Bourne, L. E., Dominowski, R. L., Loftus, E. F., & Healy, A. F. (1986). *Cognitive processes* (2nd ed.). Englewood Cliffs, NJ: Prentice Hall.

Bower, G. H., Thompson, S. S., & Tulving, E. (1994). Reducing retroactive interference: An interference analysis. *Journal of Experimental Psychology Learning, Memory, and Cognition, 20,* 51–66.

Bradsher, K. (2000, July 17). Was Freud a minivan or S.U.V. kind of guy? *New York Times,* pp. A1, A16.

Braff, D. L. (1993). Information processing and attention dysfunctions in schizophrenia. *Schizophrenia Bulletin, 19,* 233–259.

Brandimonte, M. A., Hitch, G. J., & Bishop, D. V. (1992). Manipulation of visual mental images in children and adults. *Journal of Experimental Child Psychology, 53,* 300–312.

Braun, A. R., Balkin, T. J., Wesensten, N. J., Gwadry, F., Carson, R. E., Varga, M., Baldwin, P., Belenky, G., & Herscovitch, P. (1998). Dissociated pattern of activity in visual cortices and their projections during human rapid eye movement sleep. *Science, 279,* 91–95.

Brazelton, T. B. (1969). *Infants and mothers: Differences in development.* New York: Dell.

Brehm, J. W., & Self, E. A. (1989). The intensity of motivation. *Annual Review of Psychology, 40,* 109–131.

Brehm, S. S., & Brehm, J. W. (1981). *Psychological reactance.* New York: Academic Press.

Breland, K., & Breland, M. (1961). Misbehavior of organisms. *American Psychologist, 16,* 681–684.

Brendgen, M., Vitaro, F., & Bukowski, W. M. (2000). Deviant friends and early adolescents' emotional and behavioral adjustment. *Journal of Research on Adolescence, 10,* 173–189.

Brewer, J. B., Zhao, Z., Desmond, J. E., Glover, G. H., & Gabrieli, J. D. E. (1998, August 21). Making memories: Brain activity that predicts how well visual experience will be remembered. *Science, 281,* 1185–1187.

Brief psychodynamic therapy, Part I. (1994, March). *Harvard Mental Health Letter,* p. 10.

Brislin, R. (1993). *Understanding culture's influence on behavior.* Fort Worth, TX: Harcourt Brace Jovanovich.

Brody, N. (1990). Behavior therapy versus placebo: Comment on Bowers and Clum's meta-analysis. *Psychological Bulletin, 107,* 106–109.

Bromm, B., & Desmedt, J. E. (Eds.). (1995). *Pain and the brain: From nociception to cognition.* New York: Raven Press.

Brookhiser, R. (1997, January 13). Lost in the weed. *U.S. News and World Report,* p. 9.

Brown, A. S., Susser, E. S., Butler, P. D., Andrews, R. R., et al. (1996). Neurobiological plausibility of prenatal nutritional deprivation as a risk factor for schizophrenia. *Journal of Nervous and Mental Disease, 184,* 71–85.

Brown, D. C. (1994). Subgroup norming: Legitimate testing practice or reverse discrimination? *American Psychologist, 49,* 927–928.

Brown, L. S., & Pope, K. S. (1996). *Recovered memories of abuse: Assessment, therapy, forensics.* Washington, DC: American Psychological Association.

Brown, M. B. (2000). Diagnosis and treatment of children and adolescents with attention-deficit/hyperactivity disorder. *Journal of Counseling and Development, 78,* 195–203.

Brown, R. (1958). How shall a thing be called? *Psychological Review, 65,* 14–21.

Brown, R. (1986). *Social psychology* (2nd ed.). New York: Macmillan.

Brown, S. I., & Walter, M. I. (Eds.). (1993). *Problem posing: Reflections and applications.* Hillsdale, NJ: Erlbaum.

Bruce, B., & Wilfley, D. (1996). Binge eating among the overweight population: A serious and prevalent problem. *Journal of the American Dietetic Association, 96,* 58–61.

Bruce, V., Green, P. R., & Georgeson, M. (1997). *Visual perception: Physiology, psychology and ecology* (3rd ed.). Mahwah, NJ: Erlbaum.

Bruner, J. (1983). *Child's talk: Learning to use language.* Oxford: Oxford University Press.

Brunner, H. G., Nelen, M., Breakefield, X. O., Ropers, H. H., & van Oost, B. A. (1993, October 22). Abnormal behavior associated with a point mutation in the structural gene for monoamine oxidase A. *Science, 262,* 578–580.

Brzustowicz, L. M., Hodgkinson, K. A., Chow, E. W. C., Honer, W. G., & Bassett, A. S. (2000, April 28). Location of major susceptibility locus for familial schizophrenia on chromosome 1q21–q22. *Science, 288,* 678–682.

Buckhout, R. (1975). Eyewitness testimony. *Scientific American,* pp. 23–31.

Buck, L., & Axel, R. (1991, April 5). A novel multigene family may encode odorant receptors: A molecular basis for odor recognition. *Cell, 65,* 167–175.

Bukowski, W. M., Newcomb, A. F., & Hartup, W. W. (Eds.). (1996). *The company they keep: Friendship in childhood and adolescence.* New York: Cambridge University Press.

Burack, J. A., Hodapp, R. M., & Zigler, E. (Eds.). (1998). *Handbook of mental retardation and development.* New York: Cambridge University Press.

Burchinal, M. R., Roberts, J. E., Riggins, R., Jr., Zeisel, S. A., Neebe, E., & Bryant, D. (2000). Relating quality of center-based child care to early cognitive and language development longitudinally. *Child Development, 71,* 338–357.

Burger, J. M. (1986). Increasing compliance by improving the deal: The that's-not-all technique. *Journal of Personality and Social Psychology, 51,* 277–283.

Burger, J. M. (1999). The foot-in-the-door compliance procedure: A multiple-process analysis and review. *Personality and Social Psychology Review, 3,* 303–325.

Burnham, D. K. (1983). Apparent relative size in the judgment of apparent distance. *Perception, 12,* 683–700.

Burns, A., & Scott, C. (1994). *Mother-headed families and why they have increased.* Hillsdale, NJ: Erlbaum.

Bush, P. J., & Osterweis, M. (1978). Pathways to medicine use. *Journal of Health and Social Behavior, 19,* 179–189.

Bushman, B. J. (1993). Human aggression while under the influence of alcohol and other drugs: An integrative research review. *Current Directions in Psychological Science, 2,* 148–152.

Bushman, B. J., & Baumeister, R. F. (1998). Threatened egotism, narcissism, self-esteem, and direct and displaced aggression: Does self-love or self-hate lead to violence? *Journal of Personality and Social Psychology, 75,* 219–229.

Buss, D. M. (1999). Human nature and individual differences: The evolution of human personality. In L. A. Pervin & O. P. John (Eds.), *Handbook of personality: Theory and research* (2nd ed.). New York: Guilford Press.

Buss, D. M., et al. (1990). International preferences in selecting mates: A study of 37 cultures.

Journal of Cross-Cultural Psychology, 21, 5–47.

Butcher, J. N. (1995). Interpretation of the MMPI-2. In L. E. Beutler & M. R. Berren (Eds.), *Integrative assessment of adult personality.* New York: Guilford Press.

Butcher, J. N. (1999). *A beginner's guide to the MMPI-2.* Washington, DC: American Psychological Association.

Butcher, J. N., Graham, J. R., Dahlstrom, W. G., & Bowman, E. (1990). The MMPI-2 with college students. *Journal of Personality Assessment, 54,* 1–15.

Butler, R., Oberlink, M. R., & Schechter, M. (Eds.). (1990). *The promise of productive aging: From biology to social policy.* New York: Springer.

Byne, W. (1996). Biology and homosexuality: Implications of neuroendocrinological and neuroanatomical studies. In R. P. Cabaj & T. S. Stein (Eds.), *Textbook of homosexuality and mental health.* Washington, DC: American Psychiatric Press.

Byrne, D. (1969). Attitudes and attraction. In L. Berkowitz (Ed.), *Advances in experimental social psychology* (Vol. 4, pp. 35–89). New York: Academic Press.

Calmes, J. (1998, March 5). Americans retain puritan attitudes on matters of sex. *Wall Street Journal,* p. A12.

Campbell, J. J., Lamb, M. E., & Hwang, C. P. (2000). Early child-care experiences and children's social competence between 1.5 and 15 years of age. *Applied Developmental Science, 4,* 166–175.

Campfield, L. A., Smith, F. J., Rosenbaum, M., & Hirsch, J. (1996). Human eating: Evidence for a physiological basis using a modified paradigm. [Special Issue: Society for the Study of Ingestive Behavior, Second Independent Meeting.] *Neuroscience and Biobehavioral Reviews, 20,* 133–137.

Cannon, T. D. (1998). Genetic and perinatal influences in the etiology of schizophrenia: A neurodevelopmental model. In M. F. Lenzenweger & R. H. Dworkin (Eds.), *The origins and development of schizophrenia: Advances in experimental psychopathology.* Washington, DC: American Psychological Association.

Cannon, W. B. (1929). Organization for physiological homeostatics. *Physiological Review, 9,* 280–289.

Cantor, C., & Fallon, B. A. (1996). *Phantom illness: Shattering the myth of hypochondria.* Boston: Houghton Mifflin.

Capaldi, E. D. (Ed.) (1996). *Why we eat what we eat: The psychology of eating.* Washington, DC: American Psychological Association.

Carlson, M., Marcus-Newhall, A., & Miller, N. (1990). Effects of situational aggression cues: A quantitative review. *Journal of Personality and Social Psychology, 58,* 622–633.

Carmody, D. (1990, March 7). College drinking: Changes in attitude and habit. *The New York Times,* B12.

Carnegie Council on Adolescent Development. (1995). *Great transitions: Preparing adolescents for a new century.* New York: Carnegie Corporation.

Carnegie Task Force on Meeting the Needs of Young Children. (1994). *Starting points: Meeting the needs of our youngest children.* New York: Carnegie Corporation.

Carney, R. N., & Levin, J. R. (1998). Coming to terms with the keyword method in introductory psychology: A "neuromnemonic" example. *Teaching of Psychology, 25,* 132–135.

Carney, R. N., Levin, J. R., Levin, M. E. & Schoen, L. M. (2000). Improving memory. In M. E. Ware & D. E. Johnson et al. (Eds.), *Handbook of demonstrations and activities in the teaching of psychology: Physiological-comparative, perception, learning, cognitive, and developmental* (2nd ed., Vol. 2). Mahwah, NJ: Erlbaum.

Carroll, J. M., & Russell, J. A. (1997). Facial expressions in Hollywood's portrayal of emotion. *Journal of Personality and Social Psychology, 72,* 164–176.

Carson, R. C., Butcher, J. N., & Coleman, J. C. (1992). *Abnormal psychology and modern life* (9th ed.). New York: HarperCollins.

Carter, A. S., Pauls, D. L., & Leckman, J. F. (1995). The development of obsessionality: Continuities and discontinuities. In D. Cicchetti & D. J. Cohen (Eds.), *Developmental psychopathology: Vol. 2. Risk, disorder, and adaptation.* New York: Wiley.

Carver, C. S., Harris, S. D., Lehman, J. M., Durel, L. A., Antoni, M. H., Spencer, S. M., & Pozo-Kaderman, C. (2000). How important is the perception of personal control? Studies of early stage breast cancer patients. *Personality and Social Psychology Bulletin, 26,* 139–149.

Case, R., & Okamoto, Y. (1996). The role of central conceptual structures in the development of children's thought. *Monographs of the Society for Research in Child Development, 61,* v–265.

Caspi, A., Henry, B., McGee, R. O., Moffitt, T. E., & Silva, P. A. (1995). Temperamental origins of child and adolescent behavior problems: From age three to age fifteen. *Child Development, 66,* 55–68.

Cassel, W. S., Roebers, C. E. M., & Bjorklund, D. F. (1996). Developmental patterns of eyewitness responses to repeated and increasingly suggestive questions. *Journal of Experimental Child Psychology, 61,* 116–133.

Cattell, R. B. (1965). *The scientific analysis of personality.* Chicago: Aldine.

Cattell, R. B. (1967). *The scientific analysis of personality.* Baltimore: Penguin.

Cattell, R. B. (1987). *Intelligence: Its structure, growth, and action.* Amsterdam: North-Holland.

Cattell, R. B., Cattell, A. K., & Catell, H. E. P. (1993). *Sixteen personality factor questionnaire (16PF)* (5th ed.). San Antonio: Harcourt Brace.

Cattell, R. B., Eber & Tatsuoka (1970). *Handbook for the 16PF.* Champaign, IL: Institute for Personality and Ability Testing.

Centers for Disease Control. (1992). *Most students sexually active: Survey of sexual activity.* Atlanta: Author.

Centers for Disease Control and Prevention. (1994). Cigarette smoking among adults—United States, 1993. *Morbidity and Mortality Weekly Report, 43,* 925–930.

Chamberlain, K., & Zika, S. (1990). The minor events approach to stress: Support for the use of daily hassles. *British Journal of Psychology, 81,* 469–481.

Chamberlin, J. (1998, June). Help for students of color. *APA Monitor,* p. 37.

Chandler, M., & Lalonde, C. (1996). Shifting to an interpretive theory of mind: 5- to 7-year-olds' changing conceptions of mental life. In A. J. Sameroff & M. M. Haith (Eds.), *The five to seven year shift: The age of reason and responsibility.* Chicago: University of Chicago Press.

Chandler, M. J. (1976). Social cognition and life-span approaches to the study of child development. In H. W. Reese & L. P. Lipsitt (Eds.), *Advances in child development and behavior* (Vol. 11). New York: Academic Press.

Chapman, L. J., & Chapman, J. P. (1973). *Disordered thought in schizophrenia.* New York: Appleton-Century-Crofts.

Chastain, G., & Landrum, R. E. (Eds.). (1999). *Protecting human subjects: Departmental subject pools and institutional review boards.* Washington, DC: American Psychological Association.

Cheakalos, C., & Heyn, E. (1998, November 2). Mercy mission. *People Weekly,* pp. 149–150.

Chen, J., & Gardner, H. (1997). Alternative assessment from a multiple intelligences theoretical perspective. In D. P. Flanagen, J. L. Genshaft, & P. L. Harrison (Eds.), *Contemporary intellectual assessment: Theories, tests, and issues.* New York: Guilford Press.

Cheney, C. D. (1996). Medical nonadherence: A behavior analysis. In J. R. Cautela & W. Ishaq (Eds.), *Contemporary issues in behavior therapy: Improving the human condition: Applied clinical psychology.* New York: Plenum Press.

Cheng, H., Cao, Y., & Olson, L. (1996, July 26). Spinal cord repair in adult paraplegic rats: Partial restoration of hind limb function. *Science, 273,* 510–513.

Cherlin, A. (1993). *Marriage, divorce, remarriage.* Cambridge, MA: Harvard University Press.

Cherry, B. J., Buckwalter, J. G., & Henderson, V. W. (1996). Memory span procedures in Alzheimer's disease. *Neuropsychology, 10,* 286–293.

Chess, S. (1997, November). Temperament: Theory and clinical practice. *Harvard Mental Health Letter,* pp. 5–7.

Cheston, S. E. (2000). A new paradigm for teaching counseling theory and practice. *Counselor Education and Supervision, 39,* 254–269.

Chi-Ching, Y., & Noi, L. S. (1994). Learning styles and their implications for cross-cultural management in Singapore. *Journal of Social Psychology, 134,* 593–600.

Chin, S. B., & Pisoni, D. B. (1997). *Alcohol and speech.* New York: Academic Press.

Cho, A. (2000, June 16). What's shakin' in the ear? *Science, 288,* 1954–1955.

Chodorow, N. (1978). *The reproduction of mothering.* Berkeley: University of California Press.

Chomsky, N. (1968). *Language and mind.* New York: Harcourt Brace Jovanovich.

Chomsky, N. (1969). *The acquisition of syntax in children from five to ten.* Cambridge, MA: MIT Press.

Chomsky, N. (1978). On the biological basis of language capacities. In G. A. Miller & E. Lennenberg (Eds.), *Psychology and biology of language and thought* (pp. 199–220). New York: Academic Press.

Chomsky, N. (1991). Linguistics and cognitive science: Problems and mysteries. In A. Kasher (Ed.), *The Chomskyan turn.* Cambridge, MA: Blackwell.

Churchland, P. S., & Ramachandran, V. S. (1995). Filling in: Why Dennett is wrong. In B. Dahlbom (Ed.), *Dennett and his critics: Demystifying mind: Philosophers and their critics.* Oxford, England: Basil Blackwell.

Cialdini, R. B. (1988). *Influence: Science and practice* (2nd ed.). Glenview, IL: Scott, Foresman.

Cialdini, R. B. (1997). Professionally responsible communication with the public: Giving psychology a way. *Personality and Social Psychology Bulletin, 31,* 206–215.

Cialdini, R. B., Schaller, M., Houlihan, D., Arps, K., Fultz, J., & Beaman, A. L. (1975). Reciprocal concessions procedure for inducing compliance: The door-in-the-face technique. *Journal of Personality and Social Psychology, 31,* 206–215.

Clancy, S. A., Schacter, D. L., McNally, R. J, & Pitman, R. K. (2000). False recognition in women reporting recovered memories of sexual abuse. *Psychological Science. 11,* 26–31.

Clark, L., & Watson, R. (1999). Temperament. In L. A. Pervin & O. P. John (Eds.), *Handbook of personality: Theory and research* (2nd ed.). New York: Guilford Press.

Clark, R., Anderson, N. B., Clark, V. R., & Williams, D. R. (1999). Racism as a stressor for African Americans: A biopsychosocial model. *American Psychologist, 54,* 805–816.

Clark, R. E., & Squire, L. R. (1998, April 3). Classical conditioning and brain systems: The role of awareness. *Science, 280,* 77–81.

Clarke-Stewart, K. A., & Friedman, S. (1987). *Child development: Infancy through adolescence.* New York: Wiley.

Clarke-Stewart, K. A., Vandell, D. L., McCartney, K., Owen, M. T., & Booth, C. (2000). Effects of parental separation and divorce on very young children. *Journal of Family Psychology, 14,* 304–326.

Clarkin, J. F., & Lenzenweger, M. F. (Ed.). (1996). *Major theories of personality disorder.* New York: Guilford Press.

Clay, R. A. (January, 2000). Psychotherapy *is* cost effective. *Monitor on Psychology,* pp. 39–41.

Clayton, R. R., Leukefeld, C. G., Harrington, N. G., & Cattarello, A. (1996). DARE (Drug Abuse Resistance Education): Very popular but not very effective. In C. B. McCoy & L. R. Metsch (Eds.), *Intervening with drug-involved youth.* Thousand Oaks, CA: Sage.

Cloud, J. (2000, June 5). The lure of ecstasy. *Time,* pp. 60–68.

Coates, T. J., & Collins, C. (1998, July). Preventing HIV infection. *Scientific American,* pp. 96–97.

Coffey, C. E., Saxton, J. A., Ratcliff, G., Bryan, R. N., & Lucke, J. F. (1999). Relation of education to brain size in normal aging: Implications for the reserve hypothesis. *Neurology, 53,* 198–207.

Cohen, D. (1993). *The development of play* (2nd ed.). London: Routledge.

Cohen, D. (1996). Law, social policy, and violence: The impact of regional cultures. *Journal of Personality and Social Psychology, 70,* 961–978.

Cohen, P., Slomkowski, C., & Robins, L. N. (Eds.). (1999). *Historical and geographical influences on psychopathology.* Mahwah, NJ: Erlbaum.

Cohen, S. (1996, June). Psychological stress, immunity, and upper respiratory infections. *Current Directions in Psychological Science, 5,* 86–90.

Cole, M., & Gay, J. (1972). Culture and memory. *American Anthropologist, 74,* 1066–1084.

Coles, R. (1997). *The moral intelligence of children.* New York: Random House.

Collins, A. F., Gathercole, S. E., Conway, M. A. & Morris, P. E. (Eds.). (1993). *Theories of memory.* Hillsdale, NJ: Erlbaum.

Collins, A. M., & Loftus, E. F. (1975). A spreading-activation theory of semantic processing. *Psychological Review, 82,* 407–428.

Collins, A. M., & Quillian, M. R. (1969). Retrieval times from semantic memory. *Journal of Verbal Learning and Verbal Behavior, 8,* 240–247.

Coltraine, S., & Messineo, M. (2000). The perpetuation of subtle prejudice: Race and gender imagery in 1990s television advertising. *Sex Roles, 42*, 363–389.

Compas, B. E., Ey, S., & Grant, K. E. (1993). Taxonomy, assessment, and diagnosis of depression during adolescence. *Psychological Bulletin, 114*, 323–344.

Comuzzie, A. G., & Allison, D. B. (1998, May 29). The search for human obesity genes. *Science, 280*, 1374–1377.

Condon, J. W., & Crano, W. D. (1988). Inferred evaluation and the relation between attitude similarity and interpersonal attraction. *Journal of Personality and Social Psychology, 54*, 789–797.

Conoley, J. C., & Impara, J. C. (Eds.). (1997). *The 12th mental measurements yearbook.* Lincoln, NE: Buros Institute.

Conte, H. R., & Plutchik, R. (Eds.). (1995). *Ego defenses: Theory and measurement.* New York: Wiley.

Conway, M. A. (Ed.). (1997). *Cognitive models of memory.* Cambridge, MA: MIT Press.

Cooklin, A. (2000). Therapy, the family and others. In H. Maxwell (Ed.), *Clinical psychotherapy for health professionals.* London: Whurr.

Cooper, J., & Mackie, D. (1986). Video games and aggression in children. *Journal of Applied Social Psychology, 16*, 726–744.

Cooper, L. A., & Shepard, R. N. (1984, December). Turning something over in the mind. *Scientific American.* pp. 106–114.

Cooper, N. R., Kalaria, R. N., McGeer, P. L., & Rogers, J. (2000). Key issues in Alzheimer's disease inflammation. *Neurobiology of Aging, 21*, 451–453.

Cooper, S. H. (1989). Recent contributions to the theory of defense mechanism: A comparative view. *Journal of the American Psychoanalytic Association, 37*, 865–892.

Corbetta, M., Miezin, F. M., Shulman, G. L., & Petersen, S. E. (1993, March). A PET study of visuospatial attention. *Journal of Neuroscience, 13*, 1202–1226.

Coren, S. (1992). The moon illusion: A different view through the legs. *Perceptual and Motor Skills, 75*, 827–831.

Coren, S., & Aks, D. J. (1990). Moon illusion in pictures: A multimechanism approach. *Journal of Experimental Psychology: Human Perception and Performance, 16*, 365–380.

Coren, S., & Ward, L. M. (1989). *Sensation and perception* (3rd ed.). San Diego: Harcourt Brace Jovanovich.

Cornelius, S. W., & Caspi, A. (1987). Everyday problem solving in adulthood and old age. *Psychology and Aging, 2*, 144–153.

Cornell, T. L., Fromkin, V. A., & Mauner, G. (1993). A linguistic approach to language processing in Broca's aphasia: A paradox resolved. *Current Directions in Psychological Science, 2*, 47–52.

Cotterell, J. (1996). *Social networks and social influences in adolescence.* London: Routledge.

Cotton, P. (1993, July 7). Psychiatrists set to approve DSM-IV. *Journal of the American Medical Association, 270*, 13–15.

Cowley, G. (2000, January 31). Alzheimer's: Unlocking the mystery. *Time*, pp. 46–54.

Craig, I. W., McClay, J., Plomin, R., & Freeman, B. (2000). Chasing behaviour genes into the next millennium. *Trends in Biotechnology, 18*, 22–26.

Craig, R. J. (1999). *Interpreting personality tests: A clinical manual for the MMPI-2, MCMI-III, CPI-R, and 16PF.* New York: Wiley.

Craik, F. I. (1990). Levels of processing. In M. E. Eysenck (Ed.), *The Blackwell dictionary of cognitive psychology,* London: Blackwell.

Craik, F. I., & Lockhart, R. S. (1972). Levels of processing: A framework for memory research. *Journal of Verbal Behavior, 11*, 671–684.

Cramer, J. A. (1995). Optimizing long-term patient compliance. *Neurology, 45*, s25–s28.

Cramer, P. (1996). *Storytelling, narrative, and the Thematic Apperception Test.* New York: Guilford Press.

Crapo, L. (1985). *Hormones, the messengers of life.* New York: Freeman.

Crews, F. (1996). The verdict on Freud. *Psychological Science, 7*, 63–68.

Crick, N. R., & Dodge, K. A. (1994). A review and reformulation of social information-processing mechanisms in children's social adjustment. *Psychological Bulletin, 115*, 74–101.

Crits-Christoph, P. (1992). The efficacy of brief dynamic psychotherapy: A meta-analysis. *American Journal of Psychiatry, 149*, 151–158.

Cronkite, K. (1994). *On the edge of darkness: Conversations about depression.* New York: Doubleday.

Crouter, A. C., Bumpus, M. F., Maguire, M. C., & McHale, S. M. (1999). Linking parents' work pressure and adolescents' well-being: Insights into dynamics in dual-earner families. *Developmental Psychology, 35*, 1453–1461.

Crow, T. J. (1995). A theory of the evolutionary origins of psychosis. *European Neuropsychopharmacology, 5*, 59–63.

Croyle, R. T., & Hunt, J. R. (1991). Coping with health threat: Social influence processes in reactions to medical test results. *Journal of Personality and Social Psychology, 60*, 382–389.

Csikszentmihalyi, M. (1997). *Creativity: Flow and the psychology of discovery and invention.* New York: Basic Books.

Culbertson, F. M. (1997, January). Depression and gender: An international review. *American Psychologist, 52*, 25–31.

Cummings, E., & Henry, W. E. (1961). *Growing old.* New York: Basic Books.

Cwikel, J., Behar, L., & Rabson-Hare, J. (2000). A comparison of a vote count and a meta-analysis review of intervention research with adult cancer patients. *Research on Social Work Practice, 10*, 139–158.

Czeisler, C. A., Duffy, J. F., Shanahan, T. L., Brown, E. N., Mitchell, J. F., Rimmer, D. W., Ronda, J. M., Silva, E. J., Allan, J. S., Emens, J. S., Dijk, D. J., & Kronauer, R. E. (1999, June 25). Stability, precision, and near-24-hour period of the human circadian pacemaker. *Science, 284*, 2177–2181.

Dabbs, J. M., Jr., Hargrove, M. F., & Heusel, C. (1996). Testosterone differences among college fraternities: Well-behaved vs. rambunctious. *Personality and Individual Differences, 20*, 157–161.

Damasio, A. (1999). *The feeling of what happens: Body and emotion in the making of consciousness.* New York: Harcourt Brace.

Damasio, H., Grabowski, T., Frank, R., Galaburda, A. M., & Damasio, A. R. (1994, May 20). The return of Phineas Gage: Clues about the brain from the skull of a famous patient. *Science, 264*, 1102–1105.

Damon, W. (1999, August). The moral development of children. *Scientific American*, pp. 72–78.

Daniels, H. (Ed.). (1996). *An introduction to Vygotsky.* London: Routledge.

Darley, J. M. (1995). Constructive and destructive obedience: A taxonomy of principal-agent relationships. *Journal of Social Issues, 51*, 125–154.

Darnton, N. (1990, June 4). Mommy vs. Mommy. *Newsweek,* pp. 64–67.

Darwin, C. J., Turvey, M. T., & Crowder, R. G. (1972). An auditory analogue of the Sperling partial-report procedure: Evidence for brief auditory storage. *Cognitive Psychology, 3*, 255–267.

Davidson, J. E., Deuser, R., & Sternberg, R. J. (1994). The role of metacognition in problem solving. In J. Metcalfe & A. P. Shimamura (Eds.), *Metacognition: Knowing about knowing.* Cambridge, MA: MIT Press.

Davidson, J. R. T. (2000). Trauma: The impact of post-traumatic stress disorder. *Journal of Psychopharmacology, 14*, S5–S12.

Davidson, R. J. (1994). Complexities in the search for emotion-specific physiology. In P. Ekman & R. J. Davidson (Eds.), *The nature of emotion.* New York: Oxford University Press.

Davidson, R. J., Gray, J. A., LeDoux, J. E., Levenson, R. W., Panksepp, J., & Ekman, P. (1994). Is there emotion-specific physiology? In P. Ekman & R. J. Davidson (Eds.), *The nature of emotion.* New York: Oxford University Press.

Davidson, R. J., Putnam, K. M., & Larson, C. L. (2000, July 28). Dysfunction in the neural circuitry of emotion regulation—a possible prelude to violence. *Science, 289*, 591–594.

DeAngelis, T. (2000, April). Is Internet addiction real? *APA Monitor,* pp. 24–27.

Deary, I. J., & Stough, C. (1996). Intelligence and inspection time: Achievements, prospects, and problems. *American Psychologist, 51*, 599–608.

de Boysson-Bardies, B., & Halle, P. A. (1994). Speech development: Contributions of cross-linguistic studies. In A. Vyt, H. Bloch, & M. H. Bornstein (Eds.), *Early child development in the French tradition: Contributions from current research.* Hillsdale, NJ: Erlbaum.

deCharms, R. C., Blake, D. T., & Merzenich, M. M. (1998, May 29). Optimizing sound features for cortical neurons. *Science, 280*, 1439–1440.

Deci, E. L., Koestner, R., & Ryan, R. M. (1999). A meta-analytic review of experiments examining the effects of extrinsic rewards on intrinsic motivation. *Psychological Bulletin, 125*, 627–668.

Deffenbacher, J. L. (1988). Cognitive relaxation and social skills treatments of anger: A year later. *Journal of Consulting Psychology, 35*, 309–315.

Deffenbacher, J. L. (1996). Cognitive-behavioral approaches to anger reduction. In K. S. Dobson & K. D. Craig (Eds.), *Advances in cognitive-behavioral therapy* (Vol. 2). Thousand Oaks, CA: Sage.

de Gelder, B. (2000, August 18). More to seeing than meets the eye. *Science, 289*, 1148–1149.

deGroot, A. D. (1966). Perception and memory versus thought: Some old ideas and recent findings. In B. Kleinmuntz (Ed.), *Problem solving: Research, method, and theory,* New York: Wiley.

Delahanty, D., & Baum, A. (2000). Stress and breast cancer. In A. S. Baum, R. A. Revenson, & J. E. Singer (Eds.), *Handbook of health psychology.* Mahwah, NJ: Erlbaum.

Delaney, C. H. (1995). Rites of passage in adolescence. *Adolescence, 30*, 891–897.

Delgado, P. L., & Moreno, F. A. (2000). Role of norepinephrine in depression. *Journal of Clinical Psychiatry, 61*, 5–12.

Della Sala, S., Baddeley, A. D., Papagno, C., & Spinnler, H. (1995). Dual-task paradigm: A means to examine the central executive. In J. Grafman, K. J. Holyoak, & F. Boller (Eds.), *Structure and functions of the human prefrontal cortex.* [Annals of the New York Academy of Sciences, Vol. 769.] New York: New York Academy of Sciences.

Delprato, D. J., & Midgley, B. D. (1992). Some fundamentals of B. F. Skinner's behaviorism. *American Psychologist, 47,* 1507–1520.

Dement, W. C. (1976). *Some must watch while some must sleep.* New York: Norton.

Dement, W. C. (1979). Two kinds of sleep. In D. Goleman & R. J. Davidson (Eds.), *Consciousness: Brain, states of awareness, and mysticism* (pp. 72–75). New York: Harper & Row.

Dement, W. C. (1989). Circadian rhythms and sleeping cycles. In D. F. Dinges and R. J. Broughton (Eds.), *Sleep and alertness: Chrono-biological, behavioral and medical aspects of napping.* New York: Lippincott, Williams & Wilkins.

Dement, W. C., & Wolpert, E. A. (1958). The relation of eye movements, body mobility, and external stimuli to dream content. *Journal of Experimental Psychology, 55,* 543–553.

Dempster, F. N. (1981). Memory span: Sources of individual and developmental differences. *Psychological Bulletin, 89,* 63–100.

Denis, M., & Greenbaum, C. (Trans.). (1991). *Image and cognition.* London, England: Harverster Wheatsheaf.

Denmark, G. L., & Fernandez, L. C. (1993). Historical development of the psychology of women. In F. L. Denmark & M. A. Paludi (Eds.), *A handbook of issues and theories.* Westport, CT: Greenwood Press.

Dent, J. (1984, March). *Reader's Digest,* p. 38.

Dentzer, S. (1986, May 5). Can you pass the job test? *Newsweek,* pp. 46–53.

Deregowski, J. B. (1973). Illusion and culture. In R. L. Gregory & G. H. Combrich (Eds.), *Illusion in nature and art* (pp. 161–192). New York: Scribner's.

Desimone, R. (1992, October 9). The physiology of memory: Recordings of things past. *Science, 258,* 245–255.

Detterman, D. K. (Ed.). (1996). *The environment.* Norwood, NJ: Ablex.

Detterman, D. K., Gabriel, L. T., & Ruthsatz, J. M. (2000). Intelligence and mental retardation. In R. J. Sternberg et al. (Eds.), *Handbook of intelligence.* New York: Cambridge University Press.

de Valois, R. L., & de Valois, K. K. (1993). A multi-stage color model. *Vision Research, 33,* 1053–1065.

de Waal, F. B. M. (1999, December). The end of nature versus nurture. *Scientific American,* pp. 94–99.

Diaz-Guerrero, R. (1979). Culture and personality revisited. *Annals of the New York Academy of Sciences, 285,* 119–130.

DiChiara, T. J., & Reinhart, P. H. (1997). Redox modulation of hslo Ca^{2+}-activated K^+ channels. *Journal of Neuroscience, 17,* 4942–4955.

Diener, E. (2000). Subjective well-being: The science of happiness and a proposal for a national index. *American Psychologist, 55,* 34–43.

Diener, E., & Diener, C. (1996). Most people are happy. *Psychological Science, 7,* 181–185.

Diener, E., Suh, E. M., Lucas, R. E., & Smith, H. L. (1999). Subjective well-being: Three decades of progress. *Psychological Bulletin, 125,* 276–302.

Dietz, T. L. (1998). An examination of violence and gender role portrayals in video games: Implications for gender socialization and aggressive behavior. *Sex Roles, 38,* 425–442.

DiFranza, J. R., & Lew, R. A. (1995, April). Effect of maternal cigarette smoking on pregnancy complications and sudden infant death syndrome. *Journal of Family Practice, 40,* 385–394.

DiGiovanna, A. G. (1994). *Human aging: Biological perspectives.* New York: McGraw-Hill.

Dillard, J. P. (1991). The current status of research on sequential-request compliance techniques. [Special issue: Meta-analysis in personality and social psychology.] *Personality and Social Psychology Bulletin, 17,* 283–288.

DiMatteo, M. R. (1997). Health behaviors and care decisions: An overview of professional-patient communications. In D. S. Gochman (Ed.), *Handbook of health behavior research.* New York: Plenum Press.

Dinges, D. F., Pack, F., Williams, K., Gillen, K. A., Powell, J. W., Ott, G. E., Aptowicz, C., & Pack, A. I. (1997). Cumulative sleepiness, mood disturbance, and psychomotor vigilance performance decrements during a week of sleep restricted to 4–5 hours per night. *Sleep, 20,* 267–273.

Dishman, R. K. (1997, January). Brain monoamines, exercise, and behavioral stress: animal models. *Medical Science Exercise, 29,* 63–74.

Dobbins, A. C., Jeo, R. M., Fiser, J., & Allman, J. M. (1998, July 24). Distance modulation of neural activity in the visual cortex. *Science, 281,* 552–555.

Dobelle, W. H. (2000). Artificial vision for the blind by connecting a television camera to the visual cortex. *ASAIO Journal, 46,* 3–9.

Doi, T. (1990). The cultural assumptions of psychoanalysis. In J. W. Stigler, R. A. Shweder, & G. Herdt (Eds.), *Cultural psychology: Essays on comparative human development.* New York: Cambridge University Press.

Dollard, J., Doob, L., Miller, N., Mower, O. H., & Sears, R. R. (1939). *Frustration and aggression.* New Haven, CT: Yale University Press.

Domhoff, G. W. (1996). *Finding meaning in dreams: A quantitative approach.* New York: Plenum Press.

Dorion, A. A., Chantome, M., Hasboun, D., Zouaoui, A., Marsault, C., Capron, C., & Duyme, M. (2000). Hemispheric asymmetry and corpus callosum morphometry: A magnetic resonance imaging study. *Neuroscience Research, 36,* 9–13.

Dortch, S. (1996, October). Our aching heads. *American Demographics,* pp. 4–8.

Doty, R. L., Green, P. A., Ram, C., & Yankell, S. L. (1982). Communication of gender from human breath odors: Relationship to perceived intensity and pleasantness. *Hormones and Behavior, 16,* 13–22.

Dreman, S. (1997). *The family on the threshold of the 21st century.* Mahwah, NJ: Erlbaum.

Dressler, W. W., & Oths, K. S. (1997). Cultural determinants of health behavior. In D. S. Gochman (Ed.), *Handbook of health behavior research.* New York: Plenum Press.

Dreyer, P. H. (1982). Sexuality during adolescence. In B. B. Wolman (Ed.), *Handbook of developmental psychology.* Englewood Cliffs, NJ: Prentice Hall.

Druckman, D., & Bjork, R. A. (1991). *In the mind's eye: Enhancing human performance.* Washington, DC: National Academy Press.

Drummond, D. C., Tiffany, S. T., Glautier, S., & Remington, B. (Eds.). (1995). *Addictive behaviour: Cue exposure theory and practice.* Chichester, England: Wiley.

Dryden, W. (1999). *Rational emotive behavior therapy: A training manual.* New York: Springer.

Dubovsky, S. (1999, February 25). Tuning in to manic depression. *HealthNews, 5,* p. 8.

Dugger, C. W. (1996, December 28). Tug of taboos: African genital rite vs. U.S. law. *New York Times,* pp. 1, 9.

Duke, M., & Nowicki, S., Jr. (1979). *Abnormal psychology: Perspectives on being different.* Monterey, CA: Brooks/Cole.

Duncan, P. D., et al. (1985). The effects of pubertal timing on body image, school behavior, and deviance. [Special Issue: Time of maturation and psychosocial functioning in adolescence: I.] *Journal of Youth and Adolescence, 14,* 227–235.

Duncker, K. (1945). On problem solving. *Psychological Monographs, 58* (5, whole no. 270).

Dunham, R. M., Kidwell, J. S., & Wilson, S. M. (1986). Rites of passage at adolescence: A ritual process paradigm. *Journal of Adolescent Research, 1,* 139–153.

Dupre, D., Miller, N., Gold, M., & Rospenda, K. (1995). Initiation and progression of alcohol, marijuana, and cocaine use among adolescent abusers. *American Journal on Addictions, 4,* 43–48.

Durkin, M. S., & Stein, Z. A. (1996). Classification of mental retardation. In J. W. Jacobson & J. A. Mulick (Eds.), *Manual of diagnosis and professional practice in mental retardation.* Washington, DC: American Psychological Association.

Dusenbury, L., & Botvin, G. J. (1992). Substance abuse prevention: Competence enhancement and the development of positive life options. *Journal of Addictive Diseases, 11,* 29–45.

Dutton, D. G., & Aron, A. P. (1974). Some evidence for heightened sexual attraction under conditions of high anxiety. *Journal of Personality and Social Psychology, 30,* 510–517.

Eagly, A. (1989, May). *Meta-analysis of sex differences.* Paper presented at the annual conference on adversity, University of Massachusetts, Amherst.

Eagly, A. H., & Chaiken, S. (1993). *The psychology of attitudes.* Fort Worth, TX: Harcourt Brace Jovanovich.

Eagly, A. H., & Chaiken, S. (1995). Attitude strength, attitude structure, and resistance to change. In R. E. Petty & J. A. Krosnick (Eds.), *Attitude strength: Antecedents and consequences.* Mahwah, NJ: Erlbaum.

Earley, J. (1999). *Interactive group therapy: Integrating interpersonal, action-oriented and psychodynamic approaches.* New York: Brunner/Mazel.

Eating disorders, Part II. (1997, November). *Harvard Mental Health Letter,* pp. 1–5.

Ebbinghaus, H. (1885/1913). *Memory: A contribution to experimental psychology* (H. A. Roger & C. E. Bussenius, Trans.). New York: Columbia University Press.

Ebomoyi, E. (1987). Prevalence of female circumcision in two Nigerian communities. *Sex Roles, 17,* 13–152.

Eccles, J. S., Lord, S. E., & Roeser, R. W. (1996). Round holes, square pegs, rocky roads, and sore feet: The impact of stage-environment fit on young adolescents' experiences in schools and families. In D. Cicchetti & S. L. Toth (Eds.), *Adolescence: Opportunities and challenges.* Rochester, NY: University of Rochester Press.

Eccleston, C., & Crombez, G. (1999). Pain demands attention: A cognitive-affective model of the interruptive function of pain. *Psychological Bulletin, 125,* 356–366.

Ecenbarger, W. (1993, April 1). America's new merchants of death. *Reader's Digest,* p. 50.

Ecklund, A. (1999, July 12). Now hear this! Deaf since childhood, a TV actress celebrates the gift of hearing. *People Weekly,* pp. 67+.

Edgette, J. H., & Edgette, J. S. (1995). *The handbook of hypnotic phenomena in psychotherapy.* New York: Brunner/Mazel.

Egeth, H. E., & Yantis, S. (1997). Visual attention: Control, representation, and time course. *Annual Review of Psychology, 48,* 269–297.

Eich, E., Macaulay, D., Loewenstein, R. J., & Dihle, P. H. (1997). Memory, amnesia, and dissociative identity disorder. *Psychological Science, 8,* 417–421.

Eichenbaum, H. (1993, August 20). Thinking about brain cell assemblies. *Science, 261,* 993–994.

Eichenbaum, H. (1997). Declarative memory: Insights from cognitive neurobiology. *Annual Review of Psychology, 48,* 547–572.

Eisen, L., Field, T. M., & Larson, S. K. (1991). Environmental effects on the fetus: The examples of alcohol, cocaine, and exercise. In L. Diamant (Ed.), *Mind-body maturity: Psychological approaches to sports, exercise, and fitness.* New York: Hemisphere.

Eisenberg, N. (1991). Meta-analytic contributions to the literature on prosocial behavior. *Personality and Social Psychology Bulletin, 17,* 273–282.

Eisenberger, R., Pierce, W. D., & Cameron, J. (1999). Effects of reward on intrinsic motivation—negative, neutral, and positive: Comment on Deci, Koestner, and Ryan (1999). *Psychological Bulletin, 125,* 677–691.

Ekman, P. (1994a). All emotions are basic. In P. Ekman & R. J. Davidson (Eds.), *The nature of emotion: Fundamental questions.* New York: Oxford University Press.

Ekman, P., & Davidson, R. J. (1994). *The nature of emotion: Fundamental questions.* New York: Oxford University Press.

Elkind, D. (1967). Egocentrism in adolescence. *Child Development, 38,* 1025–1034.

Elkind, D. (1985). Cognitive development and adolescent disabilities. *Journal of Adolescent Health Care, 6,* 84–89.

Elkind, D. (1988). *Miseducation.* New York: Knopf.

Elkins, I. J., McGue, M., & Iacono, W. G. (1997). Genetic and environmental influences on parent-son relationships: Evidence for increasing genetic influence during adolescence. *Developmental Psychology, 33,* 351–363.

Elliot, A. J., & Church, M. A. (1997). A hierarchical model of approach and avoidance achievement motivation. *Journal of Personality and Social Psychology, 72,* 218–232.

Ellis, A. (1974). *Growth through reason.* Hollywood, CA: Wilshire Books.

Ellis, A. (1999). Why rational emotive to rational emotive behavior therapy? *Psychotherapy, 36,* 154–159.

Ellis, A., & Dryden, W. (1997). *The practice of rational emotive behavior therapy* (2nd ed.). New York: Springer.

Embretson, S. E. (1996). Multidimensional latent trait models in measuring fundamental aspects

of intelligence. In I. Dennis & P. Tapsfield (Eds.), *Human abilities: Their nature and measurement.* Mahwah, NJ: Erlbaum.

Engebretson, T. O., & Stoney, C. M. (1995). Anger expression and lipid concentrations. *International Journal of Behavioral Medicine, 2,* 281–298.

Engen, T. (1987, September–October). Remembering odors and their names. *American Scientist, 75,* 497–503.

Engle-Friedman, M., Baker, A., & Bootzin, R. R. (1985). Reports of wakefulness during EEG identified stages of sleep. *Sleep Research, 14,* 152.

Engler, J., & Goleman, D. (1992). *The consumer's guide to psychotherapy.* New York: Simon & Schuster.

Enserink, M. (1999, April 9). Can the placebo be the cure? *Science, 284,* 238–240.

Enserink, M. (2000a, April 21). Are placebo-controlled drug trials ethical? *Science, 288,* 416.

Enserink, M. (2000b, July 28). The violence of the lambs. *Science, 289,* 580–581.

of four repertoires of behavior in a pigeon. *Journal of Comparative Psychology, 101,* 197–201.

Epstein, R. (1996). *Cognition, creativity, and behavior: Selected essays.* Westport, CT: Praeger/Greenwood.

Epstein, R., Kirshnit, C. E., Lanza, R. P., & Rubin, L. C. (1984). Insight in the pigeon: Antecedents and determinants of intelligent performance. *Nature, 308,* 61–62.

Erickson, M. H., Hershman, S., & Secter, I. I. (1990). *The practical application of medical and dental hypnosis.* New York: Brunner/Mazel.

Erikson, E. H. (1963). *Childhood and society* (2nd ed.). New York: W. W. Norton.

Erlandson, D. A., Harris, E. L., Skipper, B. L., & Allen, S. D. (1993). *Doing naturalistic inquiry: A guide to methods.* Newbury Park, CA: Sage.

Estes, W. K. (1991). Cognitive architectures from the standpoint of an experimental psychologist. *Annual Review of Psychology, 42,* 1–28.

Estes, W. K. (1997). Significance testing in psychological research: Some persisting issues. *Psychological Science, 8,* 18–19.

Eveleth, P., & Tanner, J. (1976). *World-wide variation in human growth.* New York: Cambridge University Press.

Eysenck, H. J. (1975). *Eysenck on extroversion.* New York: Wiley.

Eysenck, H. J. (1990). Biological dimensions of personality. In L. A. Pervin (Ed.), *Handbook of personality: Theory and research* (p. 246). New York: Guilford Press.

Eysenck, H. J. (1994a). The Big Five or giant three: Criteria for a paradigm. In C. F. Halverson, Jr., G. A. Kohnstamm, & R. P. Martin (Eds.), *The developing structure of temperament and personality from infancy to adulthood.* Hillsdale, NJ: Erlbaum.

Eysenck, H. J., Barrett, P., Wilson, G., & Jackson, C. (1992). Primary trait measurement of the 21 components of the P-E-N system. *European Journal of Psychological Assessment, 8,* 109–117.

Falk, D., Forese, N., Sade, D. S., & Dudek, B. C. (1999). Sex differences in brain/body relationships of Rhesus monkeys and humans. *Journal of Human Evolution, 36,* 233–238.

Farber, B. A., Brink, D. C., & Raskin, P. M. (Eds.). (1996). *The psychotherapy of Carl Rogers: Cases and commentary.* New York: Guilford Press.

Farley, F. (1986, May). The big T in personality. *Psychology Today,* pp. 44–52.

Fearing, V. G., & Clark, J. (Eds.). (2000). *Individuals in context: A practical guide to client-centered practice.* Chicago: Slack.

Feldman, R. S. (Ed.). (1982). *Development of nonverbal behavior in children.* New York: Springer-Verlag.

Feldman, R. S. (Ed.). (1993). *Applications of nonverbal behavioral theories and research.* Hillsdale, NJ: Erlbaum.

Feldman, R. S., Coats, E. J., & Schwartzberg, S. (1994). *Case studies and critical thinking about psychology.* New York: McGraw-Hill.

Fenton, W. S., & McGlashan, T. H. (1991). Natural history of schizophrenia subtypes: II. Positive and negative symptoms and long-term course. *Archives of General Psychiatry, 48,* 978–986.

Festinger, L. (1957). *A theory of cognitive dissonance.* Stanford, CA: Stanford University Press.

Festinger, L., & Carlsmith, J. M. (1959). Cognitive consequences of forced compliance. *Journal of Abnormal and Social Psychology, 58,* 203–210.

Festinger, L., Schachter, S., & Back, K. W. (1950). *Social pressure in informal groups.* New York: Harper.

Fields-Meyer, T. (1995, September 25). Having their say. *People,* pp. 50–60.

Fields-Meyer, T. (1999, October 25). The whiz kids. *People,* pp. 59–63.

Figueiras, M. J., & Marteau, T. M. (1995). Experiences of the menopause: A comparison between Portugal and the United Kingdom. *Analise Psicologica, 13,* 163–171.

Fine, L. (1994). Personal communication on cultural rituals.

Fink, A. & Kosecoff, J. (1998). *How to conduct surveys: A step-by-step guide.* Thousand Oaks, CA: Sage.

Fink, M. (1999). *Electroshock: Restoring the mind.* New York: Oxford University Press.

Fink, M. (2000). Electroshock revisited. *American Scientist, 88,* 162–167.

Finke, R. A. (1995). Creative insight and preinventive forms. In R. J. Sternberg & J. E. Davidson (Eds.), *The nature of insight.* Cambridge, MA: MIT Press.

Firestein, B. A. (Ed.). (1996). *Bisexuality: The psychology and politics of an invisible minority.* Thousand Oaks, CA: Sage.

Fischer, C. S., Hout, M., Jankowksi, M. S., Lucas, S. R., Swidler, A., & Voss, K. (1996). *Inequality by design: Cracking the bell curve myth.* Princeton, NJ: Princeton University Press.

Fischer, K. W., Shaver, P. R., & Carnochan, P. (1990). How emotions develop and how they organize development. *Cognition and Emotion, 4,* 81–127.

Fisher, C. B., & Fyrberg, D. (1994). Participant partners: College students weigh the costs and benefits of deceptive research. *American Psychologist, 49,* 417–427.

Fisher, K. (1985, March). ECT: New studies on how, why, who. *APA Monitor,* pp. 18–19.

Fiske, S. T. (1992a). Stereotypes work . . . but only sometimes: Comment on how to motivate the "unfinished mind." *Psychological Inquiry, 3,* 161–162.

Fiske, S. T. (1992b). Thinking is for doing: Portraits of social cognition from daguerreotype to laserphoto. *Journal of Personality and Social Psychology, 63,* 877–889.

Fiske, S. T. (1998). Stereotyping, prejudice, and discrimination. In D. T. Gilbert, S. T. Fiske, & G. Lindzey (Eds.), *The handbook of social psychology* (4th ed.). New York: McGraw-Hill.

Fiske, S. T., & Morling, B. (1996). Stereotyping as a function of personal control motives and capacity constraints: The odd couple of power and anxiety. In R. M. Sorrentino & E. T. Higgins (Eds.), *Handbook of motivation and cognition: Vol. 3. The interpersonal context.* New York: Guilford Press.

Fiske, S. T., & Taylor, S. E. (1991). *Social cognition* (2nd ed.). New York: McGraw-Hill.

Flam, F. (1991, June 14). Queasy riders. *Science, 252,* 1488.

Flavell, J. H. (1993). Young children's understanding of thinking and consciousness. *Current Directions in Psychological Science, 2,* 40–43.

Fleming, R., Baum, A., & Singer, J. E. (1984). Toward an integrative approach to the study of stress. *Journal of Personality and Social Psychology, 46,* 939–949.

Folkman, S., Lazarus, R. S., Dunkel-Schetter, C., DeLongis, A., & Green, R. J. (1986). Dynamics of a stressful encounter: Cognitive appraisal, coping, and encounter outcome. *Journal of Personality and Social Psychology, 50,* 992–1003.

Folkman, S., & Moskowitz, J. T. (2000). Stress, positive emotion, and coping. *Current Directions in Psychological Science, 9,* 115–118.

Ford, J. G. (1991). Rogers's theory of personality: Review and perspectives. *Journal of Social Behavior and Personality, 6,* 19–44.

Forer, B. (1949). The fallacy of personal validation: A classroom demonstration of gullibility. *Journal of Abnormal and Social Psychology, 44,* 118–123.

Foreyt, J. P., & Goodrick, G. K. (1994). *Living without dieting.* New York: Warner.

Forrester, M. A. (1996). *Psychology of language: A critical introduction.* Thousand Oaks, CA: Sage.

Fox, R. E. (1994). Training professional psychologists for the twenty-first century. *American Psychologist, 49,* 200–206.

Fox, S., & Spector, P. E. (2000). Relations of emotional intelligence, practical intelligence, general intelligence, and trait affectivity with interview outcomes. It's not all just 'G'. *Journal of Organizational Behavior, 21,* 203–220.

Frances, A., First, M. B., & Pincus, H. A. (1995). *DSM-IV guidebook.* Washington, DC: American Psychiatric Press.

Franks, D. D., & Smith, T. S. (Eds.). (1999). *Mind, brain, and society: Toward a neurosociology of emotion* (Vol. 5). Stamford, CT: Jai Press.

Franzek, E., & Beckmann, H. (1996). Gene-environment interaction in schizophrenia: Season-of-birth effect reveals etiologically different subgroups. *Psychopathology, 29,* 14–26.

Frasure-Smith, N., Lesperance, F., & Talajic, M. (2000). The prognostic importance of depression, anxiety, anger, and social support following myocardial infarction: Opportunities for improving survival. In P. M. McCabe, N. Schneiderman, T. M. Field, & A. R. Wellens (Eds.), *Stress, coping, and cardiovascular disease.* Mahwah, NJ: Erlbaum.

Free, M. L. (2000). *Cognitive therapy in groups: Guidelines and resources for practice.* New York: Wiley.

Freedman, D. S. (1995). The importance of body fat distribution in early life. *American Journal of the Medical Sciences, 310,* S72–S76.

Freedman, J. L., & Fraser, S. C. (1966). Compliance without pressure: The foot-in-the-door technique. *Journal of Personality and Social Psychology, 4,* 195–202.

French, H. W. (1997, February 2). Africa's culture war: Old customs, new values. *New York Times,* pp. 1E, 4E.

Freud, S. (1922/1959). *Group psychology and the analysis of the ego.* London: Hogarth Press.

Friedman, A. F., Lewak, R., Nichols, D. S., & Webb, J. T. (2000). *Psychological assessment with the MMPI-2.* Mahwah, NJ: Erlbaum.

Friedman, M. J., & Marsella, A. J. (1996). Posttraumatic stress disorder: An overview of the concept. In A. J. Marsella, M. J. Friedman, E. T. Gerrity, & R. M. Scurfield (Eds.), *Ethnocultural aspects of posttraumatic stress disorder: Issues, research, and clinical applications.* Washington, DC: American Psychological Association.

Fritsch, J. (1999, October 5). Scientists unmask diet myth: Willpower. *New York Times,* pp. D1, D9.

Fromkin, V. A. (2000). On the uniqueness of language. In K. Emmorey & H. Lane, et al. (Eds.), *The signs of language revisited: An anthology to honor Ursula Bellugi and Edward Klima.* Mahwah, NJ: Erlbaum.

Fromm, E., & Nash, M. (Eds.). (1992). *Contemporary hypnosis research.* New York: Guilford Press.

Funder, D. C. (1991). Global traits: A neo-Allportian approach to personality. *Psychological Science, 2,* 31–39.

Funder, D. C. (1997). *The personality puzzle.* New York: W. W. Norton.

Funk, M. S. (1996). Development of object permanence in the New Zealand parakeet *(Cyanoramphus auriceps). Animal Learning and Behavior, 24,* 375–383.

Furnham, A. (1995). The relationship of personality and intelligence to cognitive learning style and achievement. In D. H. Saklofske & M. Zeidner (Eds.), *International handbook of personality and intelligence: Perspectives on individual differences.* New York: Plenum Press.

Furst, P. T. (1977). "High states" in culture-historical perspective. In N. E. Zinberg (Ed.), *Alternate states of consciousness.* New York: Free Press.

Gaertner, S. L., Rust, M. C., Dovidio, J. F., Bachman, B. A., et al. (1996). The contact hypothesis: The role of a common ingroup identity on reducing intergroup bias among majority and minority group members. In J. L. Nye & A. M. Brower (Eds.), *What's social about social cognition? Research on socially shared cognition in small groups.* Thousand Oaks, CA: Sage.

Gagnon, S., & Dore, F. X. (1994). Cross-sectional study of object permanence in domestic puppies *(Canis familiaris). Journal of Comparative Psychology, 108,* 220–232.

Galanter, E. (1962). Contemporary psychophysics. In R. Brown, E. Galanter, E. Hess, & G. Maroler (Eds.), *New directions in psychology* (pp. 87–157). New York: Holt.

Galanter, M. (Ed.). (1995). *Recent developments in alcoholism: Vol. 12. Alcoholism and women.* New York: Plenum Press.

Galanter, M., & Kleber, H. D. (Eds.). (1999). *The American Psychiatric Press textbook of substance abuse: Abuse treatment* (2nd ed.). Washington, DC: American Psychiatric Press.

Galatzer-Levy, R. M., & Cohler, B. J. (1997). *Essential psychoanalysis: A contemporary introduction.* New York: Basic Books.

Galavotti, C., Saltzman, L. E., Sauter, S. L., & Sumartojo, E. (1997, February). Behavioral science activities at the Center for Disease Control and Prevention: A selected overview of exemplary programs. *American Psychologist, 52,* 154–166.

Gale, N., Golledge, R. G., Pellegrino, J. W., & Doherty, S. (1990). The acquisition and integration of route knowledge in an unfamiliar neighborhood. *Journal of Environmental Psychology, 10,* 3–25.

Gallagher, M., & Rapp, R. R. (1997). The use of animal models to study the effects of aging on cognition. *Annual Review of Psychology, 48,* 339–370.

Gannon, P. J., Holloway, R. L., Broadfield, D. C., & Braun, A. R. (1998, January 9). Asymmetry of chimpanzee planum temporale: Humanlike pattern of Wernicke's brain language area homolog. *Science, 279,* 220–222.

Ganong, L. H. & Coleman, M. (1999). *Changing families, changing responsibilities: Family obligations following divorce and remarriage.* Mahwah, NJ: Erlbaum.

Gao, J., Parsons, L. M., Bower, J. M., Xiong, J., Li, J., & Fox, P. T. (1996, April 26). Cerebellum implicated in sensory acquisition and discrimination rather than motor control. *Science, 272,* 545–547.

Garcia, J. (1990). Learning without memory. *Journal of Cognitive Neuroscience, 2,* 287–305.

Garcia, J., Hankins, W. G., & Rusiniak, K. W. (1974). Behavioral regulation of the milieu intern in man and rat. *Science, 185,* 824–831.

Garcia-Andrade, C., Wall, T. L., & Ehlers, C. L. (1997). The firewater myth and response to alcohol in Mission Indians. *Journal of Psychiatry, 154,* 983–988.

Gardner, H. (1975). *The shattered mind: The person after brain damage.* New York: Knopf.

Gardner, H. (1997). *Extraordinary minds.* New York: Basic Books.

Gardner, H. (1999). *Intelligence reframed: Multiple intelligences for the 21st century.* New York: Basic Books.

Gardner, R. A., & Gardner, B. T. (1969). Teaching sign language to a chimpanzee. *Science, 165,* 664–672.

Garling, T. (1989). The role of cognitive maps in spatial decisions. *Journal of Environmental Psychology, 9,* 269–278.

Garrison, D. W., & Foreman, R. D. (1994). Decreased activity of spontaneous and noxiously evoked dorsal horn cells during transcutaneous electrical nerve stimulation (TENS). *Pain, 58,* 309–315.

Gass, C. S., Luis, C. A., Meyers, T. L., & Kuljis, R. O. (2000). Familial Creutzfeldt-Jakob disease: A neuropsychological case study. *Archives of Clinical Neuropsychology, 15,* 165–175.

Gatchel, R. J., & Turk, D. C. (Eds.). (1996). *Psychological Approaches to Pain Management: A Practitioner's Handbook.* New York: Guilford Press.

Gatchel, R. J., & Weisberg, J. N. (Eds.). (2000). *Personality characteristics of patients with pain.* Washington, DC: American Psychological Association.

Gathercole, S. E., & Baddeley, A. D. (1993). *Working memory and language processing.* Hillsdale, NJ: Erlbaum.

Gazzaniga, M. S. (1998, July). The split brain revisited. *Scientific American,* pp. 50–55.

Ge, X., Conger, R. D., & Elder, G. H., Jr. (1996). Coming of age too early: Pubertal influences on busyness hypothesis. *Social Cognition, 13*, 163–182.

Harris Poll. (2000 February 2). *The power of tobacco addiction*. New York: Harris Interactive.

Harrison, J. A., & Wells, R. B. (1991). Bystander effects on male helping behavior: Social comparison and diffusion of responsibility. *Representative Research in Social Psychology, 19*, 53–63.

Harrison, P. J., Everall, I. P., & Catalan, J. (1994). Is homosexual behaviour hard-wired? Sexual orientation and brain structure. *Psychological Medicine, 24*, 811–816.

Hart, B., & Risley, T. R. (1997). *Use of language by three-year-old children*. Courtesy of Drs. Betty Hart, University of Kansas, Lawrence, and Todd Risley, University of Alaska, Anchorage.

Hartung, C. M., & Widiger, T. A. (1998). Gender differences in the diagnosis of mental disorders: Conclusions and controversies of the *DSM-IV*. *Psychological Bulletin, 123*, 260–278.

Harvey, E. (1999). Short-term and long-term effects of early parental employment on children of the National Longitudinal Survey of Youth. *Developmental Psychology, 35*, 445–459.

Haseltine, W. A. (1997, March). Discovering genes for new medicines. *Scientific American*, pp. 92–97.

Hass, N. (1994, March 21). Fighting and switching. *Newsweek*, pp. 52–53.

Hauri, P. J. (Ed.). (1991). *Case studies in insomnia*. New York: Plenum Press.

Haviland-Jones, J., & Chen, D. (1999, April 17). *Human olfactory perception*. Paper presented at the Association for Chemoreception Sciences, Sarasota, Florida.

Hayflick, L. (1994). *How and why we age*. New York: Ballantine.

Heath, A. C., & Madden, P. A. F. (1995). Genetic influences on smoking behavior. In J. R. Turner, L. R. Cardon, & J. K. Hewitt (Eds.), *Behavior genetic approaches in behavioral medicine: Perspectives on individual differences*. New York: Plenum Press.

Heatherton, T. F., Herman, C. P., & Polivy, J. (1992). Effects of distress on eating: The importance of ego-involvement. *Journal of Personality and Social Psychology, 62*, 801–803.

Hebl, M. R. & Hetherton, T. F. (1998). The stigma of obesity in women: The difference is black and white. *Personality and Social Psychology Bulletin, 24*, 417–426.

Heckhausen, H., Schmalt, H. D., & Schneider, K. (1985). *Achievement motivation in perspective* (M. Woodruff & R. Wicklund, Trans.). Orlando, FL: Academic Press.

Heider, F. (1958). *The psychology of interpersonal relations*. New York: Wiley.

Heinrichs, R. W. (1993). Schizophrenia and the brain: Conditions for neuropsychology of madness. *American Psychologist, 48*, 221–233.

Heishman, S. J., Kozlowski, L. T., & Henningfield, J. E. (1997). Nicotine addiction: Implications for public health policy. *Journal of Social Issues, 53*, 13–33.

Helmuth, L. (2000, August 25). Synapses shout to overcome distance. *Science, 289*, 1273.

Herek, G. M. (1993). Sexual orientation and military service: A social science perspective. *American Psychologist, 48*, 538–549.

Herholz, K. (1995). FDG PET and differential diagnosis of dementia. *Alzheimer Disease & Associated Disorders, 9*, 6–16.

Hermann, C., Kim, M., & Blanchard, E. B. (1995). Behavioral and prophylactic pharmacological

intervention studies of pediatric migraine: An exploratory meta-analysis. *Pain, 60*, 239–255.

Herrett-Skjellum, J., & Allen, M. (1996). Television programming and sex stereotyping: A meta-analysis. In B. R. Burleson (Ed.), *Communication yearbook* (Vol. 19). Thousand Oaks, CA: Sage.

Hermann, D., McEvoy, C., Hertzog, C., Hertel, P., & Johnson, M. (Eds.). (1996). *Basic and applied research. Volume 1: Theory and context. Volume 2: Practical applications*. Mahwah, NJ: Erlbaum.

Herrnstein, R. J., & Murray, C. (1994). *The bell curve: Intelligence and class structure in American life*. New York: Free Press.

Hetherington, E. M. (Ed.). (1999). *Coping with divorce, single parenting, and remarriage: A risk and resiliency perspective*. Mahwah, NJ: Erlbaum.

Heyward, W. L., & Curran, J. W. (1988, October). The epidemiology of AIDS in the U.S. *Scientific American*, pp. 72–81.

Hilgard, E. R. (1975). Hypnosis. *Annual Review of Psychology, 26*, 19–44.

Hill, J. O., & Peters, J. C. (1998). Environmental contributions to the obesity epidemic. *Science, 280*, 1371–1374.

Hinshaw, S. P., Zupan, B. A., Simmel, C., Nigg, J. T., & Melnick, S. (1997). Peer status in boys with and without attention-deficit hyperactivity disorder: Predictions from overt and covert antisocial behavior, social isolation, and authoritative parenting beliefs. *Child Development, 68*, 880–896.

Hipkiss, R. A. (1995). *Semantics: Defining the discipline*. Mahwah, NJ: Erlbaum.

Hirsh, I. J., & Watson, C. S. (1996). Auditory psychophysics and perception. *Annual Review of Psychology, 47*, 461–484.

Hobfoll, S. E., Freedy, J. R., Green B. L., & Solomon, S. D. (1996). Coping in reaction to extreme stress: The roles of resource loss and resource availability. In M. Zeidner & N. S. Endler (Eds.), *Handbook of coping: Theory, research, applications*. New York: Wiley.

Hobson, J. A. (1996, February). How the brain goes out of its mind. *Harvard Mental Health Letter*, pp. 3–5.

Hobson, J. A., & Silverstri, L. (1999, February). Parasomnias. *Harvard Mental Health Letter*, pp. 3–5.

Hoch, S. J. (1987). Perceived consensus and predictive accuracy: The pros and cons of projection. *Journal of Personality and Social Psychology, 53*, 221–234.

Hochschild, A. R. (1990). The second shift: Employed women and putting in another day of work at home. *Utne Reader, 38*, 66–73.

Hochschild, A. R., Machung, A., & Pringle, R. (1995). The architecture of gender: Women, men, and inequality. In D. M. Newman (Ed.), *Sociology: Exploring the architecture of everyday life: Readings*. Thousand Oaks, CA: Sage.

Hocutt, A. M. (1996). Effectiveness of special education: Is placement the critical factor? *Future of Children, 6*, 77–102.

Hoeller, K. (Ed.). (1990). *Readings in existential psychology and psychiatry*. Seattle: Review of Existential Psychology and Psychiatry.

Hogan, R., Hogan, J., & Roberts, B. W. (1996). Personality measurement and employment decisions: Questions and answers. *American Psychologist, 51*, 469–477.

Hogg, M. A., & Hardie, E. A. (1992). Prototypicality, conformity and depersonalized attraction: A self-

categorization analysis of group cohesiveness. *British Journal of Social Psychology, 31*, 41–56.

Holahan, C. J., & Moos, R. H. (1990). Life stressors, resistance factors, and improved psychological functioning: An extension of the stress resistance paradigm. *Journal of Personality and Social Psychology, 58*, 909–917.

Holden, R. R. (2000). Are there promising MMPI substitutes for assessing psychopathology and personality? Review and prospect. In R. H. Dana (Ed.), *Handbook of cross-cultural and multicultural personality assessment*. Mahwah, NJ: Erlbaum.

Holland, J. C. (1996, September). Cancer's psychological challenges. *Scientific American*, pp. 158–161.

Hollingworth, H. L. (1943/1990). *Leta Stetter Hollingworth: A biography*. Boston: Anker.

Hollis, K. L. (1984). The biological function of Pavlovian conditioning: The best defense is a good offense. *Journal of Experimental Psychology: Animal Behavior Processes, 10*, 413–425.

Hollis, K. L. (1997, September). Contemporary research on Pavlovian conditioning: A "new" functional analysis. *American Psychologist, 52*, 956–965.

Holmes, D. S. (1985). To meditate or rest? The answer is rest. *American Psychologist, 40*, 728–731.

Holroyd, J. (1996). Hypnosis treatment of clinical pain: Understanding why hypnosis is useful. *International Journal of Clinical and Experimental Hypnosis, 44*, 33–51.

Holy, T. E., Dulac, C., & Meister, M. (2000, September 1). Responses of vomeronasal neurons to natural stimuli. *Science, 289*, 1569–1572.

Hong, E., Milgram, R. M., & Gorsky, H. (1995). Original thinking as a predictor of creative performance in young children. *Roeper Review, 18*, 147–149.

Honts, C. R., & Kircher, J. C. (1994). Mental and physical countermeasures reduce the accuracy of polygraph tests. *Journal of Applied Psychology, 79*, 252–259.

Honts, C. R., Raskin, D. C., & Kircher, J. C. (1987). Effects of physical countermeasure and their electromyographic detection during polygraphy tests for deception. *Journal of Psychophysiology, 1*, 241–247.

Hoon, P. W., Bruce, K., & Kinchloe, B. (1982). Does the menstrual cycle play a role in sexual arousal? *Psychophysiology, 19*, 21–26.

Horesh, N., Apter, A., Ishai, J., Danziger, Y., et al. (1996). Abnormal psychosocial situations and eating disorders in adolescence. *Journal of the American Academy of Child and Adolescent Psychiatry, 35*, 921–927.

Horgan, J. (1993, December). Fractured functions: Does the brain have a supreme integrator? *Scientific American*, pp. 36–37.

Horgan, J. (1995, November). Get smart, take a test. *Scientific American*, pp. 12–14.

Horgan, J. (1996, December). Why Freud isn't dead. *Scientific American*, pp. 106–111.

Horney, K. (1937). *Neurotic personality of our times*. New York: Norton.

Horwitz, L., Gabbard, G. O., Allen, J. G., Frieswyk, S. H., Colson, D. B., Newsom, G. E., & Coyne, L. (1996). *Borderline personality disorder: Tailoring the psychotherapy to the patient*. Washington, DC: American Psychiatric Press.

Houston, L. N. (1981). Romanticism and eroticism among black and white college students. *Adolescence, 16*, 263–272.

Hovland, C., Janis, I., & Kelly, H. H. (1953). *Communication and persuasion*. New Haven, CT: Yale University Press.

How to lose weight and keep it off. (1990, February). *Consumer Reports Health Letter, 2*, 9–11.

Howard, A., Pion, G. M., Gottfredson, G. D., Flattau, P. E., Oskamp, S., Pfafflin, S. M., Bray, D. W., & Burstein, A. D. (1986). The changing face of American psychology: A report from the committee on employment and human resources. *American Psychologist, 41*, 1311–1327.

Howe, M. L. (1999). *The fate of early memories: Developmental science and the retention of childhood experiences*. Washington, DC: American Psychological Association.

Howells, J. G., & Osborn, M. L. (1984). *A reference companion to the history of abnormal psychology*. Westport, CT: Greenwood Press.

Howes, C., Galinsky, E., & Kontos, S. (1998). Child care caregiver sensitivity and attachment. *Social Development, 7*, 25–36.

Hubbard, K., O'Neill, A., & Cheakalos, C. (1999, April 12). Out of control. *People*, pp. 52–72.

Hubble, M. A., Duncan, B. L., & Miller, S. D. (Eds.). (1999). *The heart and soul of change: What works in therapy*. Washington, DC: American Psychological Association.

Hubel, D. H., & Wiesel, T. N. (1979). Brain mechanisms of vision. *Scientific American*, pp. 150–162.

Hudson, W. (1960). Pictorial depth perception in subcultural groups in Africa. *Journal of Social Psychology, 52*, 183–208.

Huesmann, L. R., & Moise, J. (1996, June). Media violence: A demonstrated public health threat to children. *Harvard Mental Health Letter*, pp. 5–7.

Hull, C. L. (1943). *Principles of behavior*. New York: Appleton-Century-Crofts.

Human Genome Project. (2000, January 19). *http://www.ornl.gov/hgmis/* or *http://www.ornl.gov/hgmis/project/about.html*.

Humphreys, G. W., & Müller, H. (2000). A search asymmetry reversed by figure-ground assignment. *Psychological Science, 11*, 196–200.

Humphreys, L. G. (1992). Commentary: What both critics and users of ability tests need to know. *Psychological Science, 3*, 271–274.

Hunt, E. (1983). On the nature of intelligence. *Science, 219*, 141–146.

Hunt, E. (1994). Problem solving. In R. J. Sternberg (Ed.), *Thinking and problem solving: Handbook of perception and cognition* (2nd ed.). San Diego: Academic Press.

Hunt, M. (1974). *Sexual behaviors in the 1970s*. New York: Dell.

Hunt, M. (1999). *How science takes stock: The story of meta-analysis*. New York: Russell Sage Foundation.

Hyman, R. (1994). Anomaly or artifact? Comments on Bem and Honorton. *Psychological Bulletin, 115*, 19–24.

Iacono, W. G. (1991). Can we determine the accuracy of polygraph tests? In P. K. Ackles, J. R. Jennings, & M. G. H. Coles (Eds.), *Advances in psychophysiology* (Vol. 4). Greenwich, CT: JAI Press.

Iacono, W. G., & Lykken, D. T. (1997). The validity of the lie detector: Two surveys of scientific opinion. *Journal of Applied Psychology, 82*, 426–433.

Ikonomidou, C., Bittigau, P., Ishimaru, M. J., Wozniak, D. F., et al. (2000, February 11). Ethanol-induced apoptotic neurodegeneration and fetal alcohol syndrome. *Science, 287*, 1056–1060.

Inglefinger, F. J. (1944). The late effects of total and subtotal gastrectomy. *New England Journal of Medicine, 231*, 321–377.

Isay, R. A. (1990). *Being homosexual: Gay men and their development*. New York: Avon.

Issac, A. R., & Marks, D. F. (1994). Individual differences in mental imagery experience: Developmental changes and specialization. *British Journal of Psychology, 85*, 479–500.

Iversen, L. L. (2000). *The science of marijuana*. Oxford, England: Oxford University Press.

Izard, C. E. (1990). Facial expressions and the regulation of emotions. *Journal of Personality and Social Psychology, 58*, 487–498.

Izard, C. E. (1991). *The psychology of emotions*. New York: Plenum Press.

Jacobson, P. D., Wasserman, J., & Anderson, J. R. (1997). Historical overview of tobacco legislation and regulation. *Journal of Social Issues, 53*, 75–95.

James, J. E. (1997). *Understanding caffeine: A biobehavioral analysis*. Newbury Park, CA: Sage.

James, W. (1890). *The principles of psychology*. New York: Holt.

Jamison, K. R. (1993). *Touched with fire: Manic depressive illness and the artistic temperament*. New York: Free Press.

Jamison, K. R. (1995, February). Manic-depressive illness and creativity. *Scientific American*, pp. 62–67.

Janofsky, M. (2000, January 13). Defense cites an addiction to the Internet in threat case. *New York Times*, p. A18.

Jaret, P. (1992, November/December). Mind over malady. *Health*, pp. 87–94.

Jaroff, L. (1996, Fall). Keys to the kingdom. *Time* [Special issue: The frontiers of medicine], pp. 24–29.

Jenike, M. A. (1998). Neurosurgical treatment of obsessive-compulsive disorder. *British Journal of Psychiatry, 173*, 79–90.

Jenkins, C. D., Zyzanski, S. J., & Rosenman, R. H. (1978). Coronary-prone behavior: One pattern or several? *Psychosomatic Medicine, 40*, 25–43.

Jenkins, L. S., & Gortner, S. R. (1998). Correlates of self-efficacy expectation and prediction of walking behavior in cardiac surgery elders. *Annals of Behavioral Medicine, 20*, 99–103.

Jenkins, S. R. (1994). Need for power and women's careers over 14 years: Structural power, job satisfaction, and motive change. *Journal of Personality and Social Psychology, 66*, 155–165.

Jensen, A. R. (1998). *The g factor: The science of mental ability*. Wesport, CT: Praeger.

Jensen, J. K., & Neff, D. L. (1993). Development of basic auditory discrimination in preschool children. *Psychological Science, 4*, 104–107.

Jerome, L., DeLeon, P., James, L., & Gedney, J. (2000). The coming of age of telecommunications in psychological research practice. *American Psychologist, 55*, 128–133.

Jevning, R., Anand, R., Biedebach, M., & Fernando, G. (1996). Effects on regional cerebral blood flow of transcendental meditation. *Physiological Behavior, 59*, 399–402.

Jhally, S., Goldman, R., Cassidy, M., Katula, R., et al. (1995). Advertising. In G. Dines & J. M. Humez (Eds.), *Gender, race, and class in media: A text-reader*. Thousand Oaks, CA: Sage.

John, O. P., & Srivastava, R. S. (1999). The big five trait taxonomy: History, measurement, and theoretical perspectives. In L. A. Pervin & O. P. John (Eds.), *Handbook of personality: Theory and research* (2nd ed.). New York: Guilford.

Johnson, D. M., Parrott, G. R., & Stratton, R. P. (1968). Production and judgment of solutions to five problems. *Journal of Educational Psychology Monograph Supplement, 59* (6, pt. 2).

Johnson, G. B., & Emmel, T. (2000). *The living world*, 2nd Edition. New York: McGraw-Hill.

Johnson, J. T., Cain, L. M., Falke, T. L., Hayman, J., & Perillo, E. (1985). The "Barnum Effect" revisited: Cognitive and motivational factors in the acceptance of personality descriptions. *Journal of Personality and Social Psychology, 49*, 1378–1391.

Johnson, R. W., Kelly, R. J., & LeBlanc, B. A. (1995). Motivational basis of dissonance: Aversive consequences of inconsistency. *Personality and Social Psychology Bulletin, 21*, 850–855.

Johnston, D. (1997, October 17). A missing link: LTP and learning. *Science, 278*, 401–402.

Johnston, L. (1996). Resisting change: Information-seeking and stereotype change. *European Journal of Social Psychology, 26*, 799–825.

Johnston, L., Bachman, J., & O'Malley, P. (1999). *Monitoring the future: A continuing study of the lifestyles and values of youth*. Ann Arbor: University of Michigan Institute of Social Research.

Joiner, T. E., & Coyne, J. C. (Eds.). (1999). *The interactional nature of depression: Advances in interpersonal approaches*. Washington, DC: American Psychological Association.

Joiner, T. E., & Wagner, K. D. (1995). Attribution style and depression in children and adolescents: A meta-analytic review. *Clinical Psychology Review, 15*, 777–798.

Jones, A., & Crandall, R. (Eds.). (1991). Handbook of self-actualization. *Journal of Social Behavior and Personality, 6*, 1–362.

Jones, E. E. (1990). *Interpersonal perception*. New York: Freeman.

Jones, J. C., & Barlow, D. H. (1990). Self-reported frequency of sexual urges, fantasies, and masturbatory fantasies in heterosexual males and females. *Archives of Sexual Behavior, 19*, 269–279.

Joseph, R. (1996). *Neuropsychiatry, neuropsychology, and clinical neuroscience: Emotion, evolution, cognition, language, memory, brain damage, and abnormal behavior* (2nd ed.). Baltimore: Williams & Wilkins.

Josephs, R. A., & Steele, C. M. (1990). The two faces of alcohol myopia: Attentional mediation of psychological stress. *Journal of Abnormal Psychology, 99*, 115–126.

Joyce, J. (1934). *Ulysses*. New York: Random House.

Julien, R. M. (1995). *Primer of drug action* (7th ed.). New York: Freeman.

Jung, C. G. (1961). *Freud and psychoanalysis*. New York: Pantheon.

Jussim, L., Fleming, C. J., Coleman, L., & Kohberger, C. (1996). The nature of stereotypes: II. A multiple-process model of evaluations. *Journal of Applied Social Psychology, 26*, 283–312.

Kagan, J., Kearsley, R., & Zelazo, P. R. (1978). *Infancy: Its place in human development*. Cambridge, MA: Harvard University Press.

Kahn, R. S., Davidson, M., & Davis, K. L. (1996). Dopamine and schizophrenia revisited. In S. J. Watson (Ed.), *Biology of schizophrenia and affective disease*. Washington, DC: American Psychiatric Press.

Kahn, S., Zimmerman, G., Csikszentmihalyi, M., & Getzels, J. W. (1985). Relations between identity in young adulthood and intimacy at midlife. *Journal of Personality and Social Psychology, 49,* 1316–1322.

Kahneman, D., Diener, E., & Schwarz, N. (1998). *Well-being: The foundations of hedonic psychology.* New York: Russell Sage Foundation.

Kaiser, J. (1999, September 3). Hold the clicks, they may be addictive. *Science, 285,* 1455.

Kakei, S., Hoffman, D. S., & Strick, P. L. (1999, September 24). Muscle and movement representations in the primary motor cortex. *Science, 285,* 2136–2139.

Kakigi, R., Matsuda, Y., & Kuroda, Y. (1993). Effects of movement-related cortical activities on pain-related somatosensory evoked potentials following CO_2 laser stimulation in normal subjects. *Acta Neurologica Scandinavica, 88,* 376–380.

Kalafat, J., Elias, M., & Gara, M. A. (1993). The relationship of bystander intervention variables to adolescents' responses to suicidal peers. *Journal of Primary Prevention, 13,* 231–244.

Kaniasty, K., & Norris, F. H. (1995, June). Mobilization and deterioration of social support following natural disasters. *Current Directions in Psychological Science, 4,* 94–98.

Kaplan, M. F. (1975). Information integration in social judgment: Interaction of judge and informational components. In M. Kaplan & S. Schwartz (Eds.), *Human development and decision processes.* New York: Academic Press.

Kaplan, R. M., & Saccuzzo, D. P. (1997). *Psychological testing: Principles, applications, and issues* (4th ed.). Pacific Grove, CA: Brooks/Cole.

Kaplan, R. M., Sallis, J. F., Jr., & Patterson, T. L. (1993). *Health and human behavior.* New York: McGraw-Hill.

Kapur, N. (1999). Syndromes of retrograde amnesia: A conceptual and empirical synthesis. *Psychological Bulletin, 125,* 800–825.

Kapur, S., & Remington, G. (1996). Serotonin-dopamine interaction and its relevance to schizophrenia. *American Journal of Psychiatry, 153,* 466–476.

Karlins, M., & Abelson, H. I. (1979). *How opinions and attitudes are changed.* New York: Springer-Verlag.

Karni, A., Tanne, D., Rubenstein, B. S., Askenazy, J. J. M., & Sagi, D. (1992, October). No dreams—no memory: The effect of REM sleep deprivation on learning a new perceptual skill. *Society for Neuroscience Abstracts, 18,* 387.

Karni, A., Tanne, D., Rubenstein, B. S., Askenasy, J. J. M., & Sagi, D. (1994, July 29). Dependence on REM sleep of overnight improvement of a perceptual skill. *Science, 265,* 679–682.

Karp, D. A. (1988). A decade of remembrances: Changing age consciousness between fifty and sixty years old. *Gerontologist, 28,* 727–738.

Karp, D. A. (1991). A decade of reminders: Changing age consciousness between fifty and sixty years old. In B. B. Hess & E. W. Markson (Eds.), *Growing old in America* (4th ed.). New Brunswick, NJ: Transaction.

Katz, A. N. (1989). Autobiographical memory as a reconstructive process: An extension of Ross's hypothesis. *Canadian Journal of Psychology, 43,* 512–517.

Katz, D., & Braly, K. W. (1933). Racial stereotypes of 100 college students. *Journal of Abnormal and Social Psychology, 4,* 280–290.

Katz, P. A. (Ed.). (1976). *Towards the elimination of racism.* New York: Pergamon Press.

Kaufman, A. S., & Lichtenberger, E. O. (1999). *Essentials of WISC-III and WPPSI-R assessment.* New York: Wiley.

Kausler, D. H. (1994). *Learning and memory in normal aging.* San Diego: Academic Press.

Kawachi, I., Colditz, G. A., Speizer, F. E., Manson, J. E., Stampger, M. J., Willett, W. C., & Hennekens, C. H. (1997). A prospective study of passive smoking and coronary heart disease. *Circulation, 95,* 2374–2379.

Kawasaki, C., Nugent, J. K., Miyashita, H., Miyahara, H., et al. (1994). The cultural organization of infants' sleep [Special issue: Environments of birth and infancy]. *Children's Environment, 11,* 135–141.

Kazdin, A. E. (1994). *Behavior modification in applied settings* (5th ed.). Pacific Grove, CA: Brooks/Cole.

Keating, D. P., & Clark, L. V. (1980). Development of physical and social reasoning in adolescence. *Developmental Psychology, 16,* 23–30.

Keefe, F. J., & France, C. R. (1999). Pain: Biopsychosocial mechanisms and management. *Current Directions in Psychological Science, 8,* 137–141.

Keehn, J. D. (1996). *Master builders of modern psychology: From Freud to Skinner.* New York: New York University Press.

Keller, M. C., & Young, R. K. (1996). Mate assortment in dating and married couples. *Personality and Individual Differences, 21,* 217–221.

Kelley, H. (1950). The warm-cold variable in first impressions of persons. *Journal of Personality and Social Psychology, 18,* 431–439.

Kelly, A. L. (1999, June 13). For employed moms, the pinnacle of stress comes after work ends. *New York Times,* p. 18.

Kelly, D. D. (1991). Sexual differentiation of the nervous system. In E. R. Kandel, J. H. Schwartz, & T. M. Jessell (Eds.), *Principles of neural science* (3rd ed.). New York: Elsevier.

Kelly, F. D. (1997). *The assessment of object relations phenomena in adolescents: TAT and Rorschach measures.* Mahwah, NJ: Erlbaum.

Kendler, K. S. (1996). Parenting: A genetic-epidemiologic perspective. *American Journal of Psychiatry, 153,* 11–20.

Kenny, D. A. (1994). *Interpersonal perception.* New York: Guilford Press.

Kessler, R. C., McGonagle, K. A., Zhao, S., Nelson, C. B., Hughes, M., Eshleman, S., Wittchen, H., & Kendler, K. S. (1994). Lifetime and 12-month prevalence of *DSM-III-R* psychiatric disorders in the United States. *Archives of General Psychiatry, 51,* 8–19.

Kidwell, J. S., Dunham, R. M., Bacho, R. A., Pastorino, E., et al. (1995). Adolescent identity exploration: A test of Erikson's theory of transitional crisis. *Adolescence, 30,* 785–793.

Kienker, P. K., Sejnowski, T. J., Hinton, G. E., & Schumacher, L. E. (1986). Separating figure from ground with a parallel network. *Perception, 15,* 197–216.

Kiesler, C. A., & Simpkins, C. G. (1993). *The unnoticed majority in psychiatric inpatient care.* New York: Plenum Press.

Kiesler, D. J. (1999). *Beyond the disease model of mental disorders.* Westport, CT: Praeger.

Kiesler, S., & Kraut, R. (1999, September). Internet use and ties that bind. *American Psychologist, 15,* 783–784.

Kihlstrom, J. F. (1999). Unconscious. In L. A. Pervin & O. P. John (Eds.), *Handbook of personality: Theory and research* (2nd ed.). New York: Guilford Press.

Kihlstrom, J. F., Schacter, D. L., Cork, R. C., Hurt, C. A., & Behr, S. E. (1990). Implicit and explicit memory following surgical anesthesia. *Psychological Science, 1,* 303–306.

Kilborn, P. T. (1991, May 15). "Race norming" tests become a fiery issue. *New York Times,* B1.

Kimble, G. A. (1989). Psychology from the standpoint of a generalist. *American Psychologist, 44,* 491–499.

Kimmel, A. J. (1996). *Ethical issues in behavioral research: A survey.* Oxford, England: Blackwell.

Kimura, D. (1992, September). Sex differences in the brain. *Scientific American,* pp. 119–125.

King, S. H. (1993). The limited presence of African-American teachers. *Review of Educational Research, 63,* 114–149.

Kirk, S. A. (1992). *The selling of DSM: The rhetoric of science in psychiatry.* Hawthorne, New York: Aldine de Gruyter.

Kirsch, I. (Ed.). (1999). *How expectancies shape experience.* Washington, DC: American Psychological Association.

Kirsch, I., & Lynn, S. J. (1995). The altered state of hypnosis: Changes in the theoretical landscape. *American Psychologist, 50,* 846–858.

Kirsch, I., & Lynn, S. J. (1998). Dissociating the wheat from the chaff in theories of hypnosis: Reply to Kihlstrom (1998) and Woody and Sadler (1998). *Psychological Bulletin, 123,* 198–202.

Kirshner, H. S. (1995). Alexias. In H. S. Kirshner (Ed.), *Handbook of neurological speech and language disorders: Neurological disease and therapy* (Vol. 33). New York: Marcel Dekker.

Kitterle, F. L. (Ed.). (1991). *Cerebral laterality: Theory and research.* Hillsdale, NJ: Erlbaum.

Klein, M. (1998, February). Family chats. *American Demographics,* p. 37.

Kleinman, A. (1996). How is culture important for *DSM-IV?* In J. E. Mezzich, A. Kleinman, H. Fabrega, Jr., & D. L. Parron (Eds.), *Culture and psychiatric diagnosis: A DSM-IV perspective.* Washington, DC: American Psychiatric Press.

Kleinman, A., & Cohen, A. (1997, March). Psychiatry's global challenge. *Scientific American,* pp. 86–89.

Klinke, R., Kral, A., Heid, S., Tillein, J., & Hartmann, R. (1999, September 10). Recruitment of the auditory cortex in congenitally deaf cats by long-term cochlear electrostimulation. *Science, 285,* 1729–1733.

Klinkenborg, V. (1997, January 5). Awakening to sleep. *New York Times,* pp. 26–31, 41, 51, 55.

Kluft, R. P. (1996). Dissociative identity disorder. In L. K. Michelson & W. J. Ray (Eds.), *Handbook of dissociation: Theoretical, empirical, and clinical perspectives.* New York: Plenum Press.

Kmiec, E. B. (1999). Gene therapy. *American Scientist, 87,* 240–247.

Knight, G. P., Johnson, L. G., Carlo, G., & Eisenberg, N. (1994). A multiplicative model of the dispositional antecedents of prosocial behavior: Predicting more of the people more of the time. *Journal of Personality and Social Psychology, 66,* 178–183.

Kobasa, S. C. (1979). Stressful life events, personality, and health: An inquiry into hardiness. *Journal of Personality and Social Psychology, 37,* 1–11.

Kobasa, S. C. O., Maddi, S. R., Puccetti, M. C., & Zola, M. A. (1994). Effectiveness of hardiness, exercise and social support as resources against illness. In A. Steptoe & J. Wardle (Eds.), *Psychosocial processes and health: A reader.* Cambridge, England: Cambridge University Press.

Kohlberg, L. (1984). *The psychology of moral development: Essays on moral development* (Vol. 2). San Francisco: Harper & Row.

Kohlberg, L., & Ryncarz, R. A. (1990). Beyond justice reasoning: Moral development and consideration of a seventh stage. In C. N. Alexander & E. J. Langer (Eds.), *Higher stages of human development: Perspectives on adult growth.* New York: Oxford University Press.

Köhler, W. (1927). *The mentality of apes.* London: Routledge & Kegan Paul.

Kolata, G. (1998). *Clone: The road to Dolly and the path ahead.* New York: William Morrow.

Konishi, M. (1993, April). Listening with two ears. *Scientific American,* pp. 66–73.

Konrad, W. (1994, April). Ten things your doctor won't tell you. *Smart Money,* p. 76.

Koocher, G. P., & Keith-Spiegel, P. (1998). *Ethics in psychology: Professional standards and cases* (2nd ed.). New York: Oxford University Press.

Koop, C. B. (1994). Infant assessment. In C. B. Fisher & R. M. Lerner (Eds.), *Applied developmental psychology.* New York: McGraw-Hill.

Koss, M. P. (1993). Rape: Scope, impact, interventions, and public policy responses. *American Psychologist, 48,* 1062–1069.

Kosslyn, S. M. (1981). The medium and the message in mental imagery. *Psychological Review, 88,* 46–66.

Kosslyn, S. M., Seger, C., Pani, J. R., & Hillger, L. A. (1990). When is imagery used in everyday life? A diary study. *Journal of Mental Imagery, 14,* 131–152.

Kosslyn, S. M., & Shin, L. M. (1994). Visual mental images in the brain: Current issues. In M. J. Farah & G. Ratcliff (Eds.), *The neuropsychology of high-level vision: Collected tutorial essays.* Hillsdale, NJ: Erlbaum.

Kotler-Cope, S., & Camp, C. J. (1990). Memory interventions in aging populations. In E. A. Lovelace (Ed.), *Aging and cognition: Mental processes, self-awareness, and interventions.* Amsterdam, Netherlands: North-Holland.

Kotre, J., & Hall, E. (1990). *Seasons of life.* Boston: Little, Brown.

Koval, J. J., Pederson, L. L., Mills, C. A., McGrady, G. A., & Carvajal, S. C. (2000). Models of the relationship of stress, depression, and other psychosocial factors to smoking behavior: A comparison of a cohort of students in Grades 6 and 8. *Preventive Medicine, 30,* 463–477.

Koveces, Z. (1987). *The container metaphor of emotion.* Paper presented at the University of Massachusetts, Amherst.

Kramer, P. (1993). *Listening to Prozac.* New York: Viking.

Kraus, S. J. (1995, January). Attitudes and the prediction of behavior: A meta-analysis of the empirical literature. *Personality and Social Psychology Bulletin, 21,* 58–75.

Kravitz, E. A. (1988). Hormonal control of behavior: Amines and the biasing of behavioral output in lobsters. *Science, 241,* 1775–1782.

Kremer, J. M. D., & Scully, D. M. (1994). *Psychology in sport.* London, England: Taylor & Francis.

Kreuger, L. E. (1989). *The world of touch.* Hillsdale, NJ: Erlbaum.

Kriz, J. (1995). Naturwissenschaftliche Konzepte in der gegenwartigen Diskussion zum Problem der Ordnung (The contribution of natural science concepts to the current discussion of order). *Gestalt Theory, 17,* 153–163.

Krohne, H. W. (1996). Individual differences in coping. In M. Zeidner & N. S. Endler (Eds.), *Handbook of coping: Theory, research, applications.* New York: Wiley.

Kruglanski, A. W., Freund, T., & Bar Tal, D. (1996). Motivational effects in the mere-exposure paradigm. *European Journal of Social Psychology, 26,* 479–499.

Krull, D. S., & Anderson, C. A. (1997). The process of explanation. *Current Directions in Psychological Science, 6,* 1–5.

Kübler-Ross, E. (1969). *On death and dying.* New York: Macmillan.

Kuhl, P. K., Williams, K. A., Lacerda, F., Stevens, K. N., & Lindblom, B. (1992, January 31). Linguistic experience alters phonetic perception in infants by 6 months of age. *Science, 255,* 606–608.

Kulynych, J. J., Vladar, K., Jones, D. W., & Weinberger, D. R. (1994). Gender differences in the normal lateralization of the supratemporal cortex: MRI surface-rendering morphometry of Heschl's gyrus and the planum temporale. *Cerebral Cortex, 4,* 107–118.

Kunda, Z. (1999). *Social cognition: Making sense of people.* Cambridge, MA: MIT Press.

Kupfer, D. J., Reynolds, C. F., III. (1997, January 30). Management of insomnia. *New England Journal of Medicine, 336,* 341–346.

Kurtines, W., & Gewirtz, J. (1995). *Moral development: An introduction.* Boston: Allyn & Bacon.

Kvale, S. (1996). *Interviews: An introduction to qualitative research interviewing.* Newbury Park, CA: Sage.

Kwan, V. S. Y., Bond, M. H., & Singelis, T. M. (1997). Pancultural explanations for life satisfaction: Adding relationship harmony to self-esteem. *Journal of Personality and Social Psychology, 73,* 1038–1051.

Lach, J. (1998, November). Reading your mind, reaching your wallet. *American Demographics,* pp. 39–42.

Laird, J. D., & Bressler, C. (1990). William James and the mechanisms of emotional experience. *Personality and Social Psychology Bulletin, 16,* 636–651.

Lamb, M. (1982). The bonding phenomenon: Misinterpretations and their implications. *Journal of Pediatrics, 101,* 555–557.

Lamb, M. E. (1996). Effects of nonparental child care on child development: An update. *Canadian Journal of Psychiatry, 41,* 330–342.

Lambert, M. J., Shapiro, D. A., & Bergin, A. E. (1986). The effectiveness of psychotherapy. In S. L. Garfield & A. E. Bergin (Eds.), *Handbook of psychotherapy and behavior change* (3rd ed.). New York: Wiley.

Landis, D., Day, H. R., McGrew, P. L., Thomas, J. A., & Miller, A. B. (1976). Can a black "culture assimilator" increase racial understanding? *Journal of Social Issues, 32,* 169–183.

Landry, D. W. (1997, February). Immunotherapy for cocaine addiction. *Scientific American,* pp. 41–45.

Langer, E., Bashner, R. S., & Chanowitz, B. (1985). Decreasing prejudice by increasing discrimination. *Journal of Personality and Social Psychology, 49,* 113–120.

Langer, E., & Janis, I. (1979). *The psychology of control.* Beverly Hills, CA: Sage.

Langlois, J. H., Kalakanis, L., Rubenstein, A. J., Larson, A., Hallam, M., & Smoot, M. (2000). Maxims or myths of beauty? A meta-analytic and theoretical review. *Psychological Bulletin, 126,* 390–423.

Langreth, R. (1996, August 20). Science yields powerful new therapies for pain. *Wall Street Journal,* pp. B1, B4.

Langreth, R. (2000, May 1). Every little bit helps: How even moderate exercise can have a big impact on your health. *Wall Street Journal,* p. R5.

Langs, G., Quehenberger, F., Fabisch, K., Klug, G., Fabisch, H., & Zapotoczky, H. G. (2000). The development of agoraphobia in panic disorder: A predictable process? *Journal of Affective Disorders, 58,* 43–50.

Larose, H., & Standing, L. (1998). Does the halo effect occur in the elderly? *Social Behavior and Personality, 26,* 147–150.

Larson, R. K. (1990). Semantics. In D. N. Osherson & H. Lasnik (Eds.). *Language.* Cambridge, MA: MIT Press.

Larson, R. W., Richards, M. H., & Perry-Jenkins, M. (1994). Divergent worlds: The daily emotional experience of mothers and fathers in the domestic and public spheres. *Journal of Personality and Social Psychology, 67,* 1034–1046.

Lask, B., & Bryant-Waugh, R. (Eds.). (1999). *Anorexia nervosa and related eating disorders in childhood and adolescence.* New York: Brunner/Mazel.

Lasnik, H. (1990). Syntax. In D. N. Osherson & H. Lasnik (Eds.), *Language,* Cambridge, MA: MIT Press.

Latané, B., & Darley, J. M. (1970). *The unresponsive bystander: Why doesn't he help?* New York: Appleton-Century-Crofts.

Latané, B., & Nida, S. (1981). Ten years of research on group size and helping. *Psychological Bulletin, 89,* 308–324.

Lazarus, A. A. (1997). *Brief but comprehensive psychotherapy: The multimodal way.* New York: Springer.

Lazarus, R. S. (1991a). Cognition and motivation in emotion. *American Psychologist, 46,* 352–367.

Lazarus, R. S. (1991b). *Emotion and adaptation.* New York: Oxford University Press.

Lazarus, R. S. (1994). Appraisal: The long and short of it. In P. Ekman & R. J. Davidson (Eds.), *The nature of emotion: Fundamental questions.* New York: Oxford University Press.

Lazarus, R. S. (1995). Emotions express a social relationship, but it is an individual mind that creates them. *Psychological Inquiry, 6,* 253–265.

Lazarus, R. S. (1999). *Stress and emotion: A new synthesis.* New York: Springer.

Lazarus, R. S., & Cohen, J. B. (1977). Environmental stress. In I. Altman & J. F. Wohlwill (Eds.), *Human behavior and the environment: Current theory and research* (Vol. 2). New York: Plenum Press.

Lee, F., Hallahan, M., & Herzog, T. (1996). Explaining real-life events: How culture and domain shape attributions. *Personality and Social Psychology Bulletin, 22,* 732–741.

Lehman, D. R., Lempert, R. O., & Nisbett, R. E. (1988). The effects of graduate training on reasoning: Formal discipline and thinking about everyday-life events. *American Psychologist, 43,* 431–442.

Lehman, D. R., & Taylor, S. E. (1988). Date with an earthquake: Coping with a probable, unpredictable disaster. *Personality and Social Psychology Bulletin, 13,* 546–555.

Lehrer, P. M. (1996). Recent research findings on stress management techniques. In Editorial Board of Hatherleigh Press, *The Hatherleigh guides series.* Vol. 4: *The Hatherleigh guide to issues in modern therapy.* New York: Hatherleigh Press.

Leibel, R. L., Rosenbaum, M., & Hirsch, J. (1995, March 9). Changes in energy expenditure resulting from altered body. *New England Journal of Medicine, 332,* 621–628.

Leibovic, K. N. (Ed.). (1990). *Science of vision.* New York: Springer-Verlag.

Leigh, H., & Reiser, M. F. (1980). *The patient.* New York: Plenum Press.

Leland, J. (2000, May 29). The science of women and sex. *Newsweek,* pp. 48–54.

Lenzenweger, M. F. & Dworkin, R. H. (Eds.). (1998). *The origins and development of schizophrenia: Advances in experimental psychopathology.* Washington, DC: American Psychological Association.

Leonard, B. E. (2000). Evidence for a biochemical lesion in depression. *Journal of Clinical Psychiatry, 61,* 12–17.

Leong, F. L, & Blustein, D. L. (2000). Toward a global vision of counseling psychology. *Counseling Psychologist, 28,* 5–9.

Lepore, S. J., Ragan, J. D., & Jones, S. (2000). Talking facilitates cognitive-emotional processes of adaptation to an acute stressor. *Journal of Personality and Social Psychology, 78,* 499–508.

Lepper, M. R., & Greene, D. (Eds.). (1978). *The hidden costs of reward.* Hillsdale, NJ: Erlbaum.

Lepper, M. R., Henderlong, J., & Gingras, I. (1999). Understanding the effects of extrinsic rewards on intrinsic motivation—Uses and abuses of meta-analysis: Comment on Deci, Koestner, and Ryan (1999). *Psychological Bulletin, 125,* 669–676.

Lerner, R. M., Fisher, C. B., & Weinberg, R. A. (2000). Toward a science for and of the people: Promoting civil society through the application of developmental science. *Child Development, 71,* 11–20.

Lesch, K.-P., Bengel, D., Heils, A., Sabol, S. Z., Greenberg, B. D., Petri, S., Benjamin, J., Muller, C. R., Hamer, D. H., & Murphy, D. L. (1996, November 29). Association of anxiety-related traits with a polymorphism in the serotonin transporter gene regulatory region. *Science, 274,* 1527–1531.

LeVay, S. (1991) A difference in hypothalamic structure between heterosexual and homosexual men. *Science, 253,* 1034–1037.

LeVay, S. (1993). *The sexual brain.* Cambridge, MA: MIT Press.

Levenson, R. W. (1992). Autonomic nervous system differences among emotions. *Psychological Science, 3,* 23–27.

Levenson, R. W. (1994). The search for autonomic specificity. In P. Ekman & R. J. Davidson (Eds.), *The nature of emotion: Fundamental questions.* New York: Oxford University Press.

Levenson, R. W., Ekman, P., Heider, K., & Friesen, W. V. (1992). Emotion and autonomic nervous system activity in the Minangkabau of West Sumatra. *Journal of Personality and Social Psychology, 62,* 972–988.

Leventhal, H., & Cleary, P. D. (1980). The smoking problem: A review of the research and theory in behavioral risk modification. *Psychological Bulletin, 88,* 370–405.

Leventhal, H., & Tomarken, A. J. (1986). Emotion: Today's problems. *Annual Review of Psychology, 37,* 565–610.

Levine, J. M. (1989). Reaction to opinion deviance in small groups. In P. B. Paulus (Ed.), *Psychology of group influence* (2nd ed.). Hillsdale, NJ: Erlbaum.

Levinson, D. J. (1990). A theory of life structure development in adulthood. In C. N. Alexander & E. J. Langer (Eds.), *Higher stages of human development: Perspectives on adult growth.* New York: Oxford University Press.

Levy, B. (1996). Improving memory in old age through implicit self-stereotyping. *Journal of Personality and Social Psychology, 71,* 1092–1107.

Levy, B. L., & Langer, E. (1994). Aging free from negative stereotypes: Successful memory in China and among the American deaf. *Journal of Personality and Social Psychology, 66,* 989–997.

Levy, D. H. (2000, August 20). Are you ready for the genome miracle? *Parade,* pp. 8–10.

Levy, S. (1997, May 19). Big Blue's hand of God. *Newsweek,* p. 72.

Levy, S. M., Lee, J., Bagley, C., & Lippman, M. (1988). Survival hazards analysis in first recurrent breast cancer patients: Seven-year follow-up. *Psychosomatic Medicine, 50,* 520–528.

Lewis, M., Feiring, C., McGuffog, C., & Jaskir, J. (1984). Predicting psychopathology in six-year-olds from early social relations. *Child Development, 55,* 123–136.

Lewis, M., Feiring, C., & Rosenthal, S. (2000). Attachment over time. *Child Development, 71,* 707–720.

Lewis, M., & Haviland-Jones, J. M. (2000). *Handbook of emotions* (2nd ed.). New York: Guilford Press.

LeWitt, P. A. (2000). The challenge of managing mild Parkinson's disease. *Pharmacotherapy, 20,* 2S–7S.

Li, S. (1995). (A comparative study of personality in supernormal children and normal children.) *Psychological Science—China, 18,* 184–186.

Li, Y., Xu, J., Shi, X., & Yan, Y. (1999). Intelligence, memory, and event-related potential in patients with motor neuron disease. *Chinese Mental Health Journal, 13,* 180–181.

Liebert, R. M., & Sprafkin, J. (1988). *The early window: Effects of television on children and youth* (3rd ed.). New York: Pergamon Press.

Lindsay, P. H., & Norman, D. A. (1977). *Human information processing* (2nd ed.). New York: Academic Press.

Linscheid, T. R., Iwata, B. A., Ricketts, R. W., Williams, D. E., & Griffin, J. C. (1990). Clinical evaluation of the self-injurious behavior inhibiting system (SIBIS). *Journal of Applied Behavior Analysis, 23,* 53–78.

Linszen, D. H., Dingemans, P. M., Nugter, M. A., Van der Does, A. J. W., et al. (1997). Patient attributes and expressed emotion as risk factors for psychotic relapse. *Schizophrenia Bulletin, 23,* 119–130.

Lipsey, M. W., & Wilson, D. B. (1993). The efficacy of psychological, educational, and behavioral treatment: Confirmation from meta-analysis. *American Psychologist, 48,* 1181–1209.

Lloyd, J. W., Kameenui, E. J., & Chard, D. (Eds.). (1997). *Issues in educating students with disabilities.* Mahwah, NJ: Erlbaum.

Loewenstein, G. (1994). The psychology of curiosity: A review and reinterpretation. *Psychological Bulletin, 116,* 75–98.

Loftus, E. F. (1993). Psychologists in the eyewitness world. *American Psychologist, 48,* 550–552.

Loftus, E. F. (1997). Memory for a past that never was. *Current Directions in Psychological Science, 6,* 60–65.

Loftus, E. F. (1998, November). The memory police. *APA Observer,* pp. 3, 14.

Loftus, E. F., Loftus, G. R., & Messo, J. (1987). Some facts about "weapon focus." *Law and Human Behavior, 11,* 55–62.

Loftus, E. F., & Palmer, J. C. (1974). Reconstruction of automobile destruction: An example of the interface between language and memory. *Journal of Verbal Learning and Verbal Behavior, 13,* 585–589.

Logie, R. H., & Gilhooly, K. J. (1998). *Working memory and thinking.* Philadelphia: Psychology Press.

Long, A. (1987, December). What is this thing called sleep? *National Geographic, 172,* 786–821.

Long, G. M., & Beaton, R. J. (1982). The case for peripheral persistence: Effects of target and background luminance on a partial-report task. *Journal of Experimental Psychology: Human Perception and Performance, 8,* 383–391.

Loomis, J. M., Golledge, R. G., & Klatzky, R. L. (in press). Navigation system for the blind: Auditory display modes and guidance. In *Presence: Teleoperators and Virtual Environments.*

Loomis, J. M., Klatzky, R. L., Golledge, R. G., Cicinelli, J. G., Pellegrino, J. W., & Fry, P. A. (1993). Nonvisual navigation by blind and sighted: Assessment of path integration ability. *Journal of Experimental Psychology: General, 122,* 73–91.

Looy, H. (1995). Born gay? A critical review of biological research on homosexuality. *Journal of Psychology and Christianity, 14,* 197–214.

López, S. R., & Guarnaccia, P. J. J. (2000). Cultural psychopathology: Uncovering the social world of mental illness. *Annual Review of Psychology, 51,* 571–598.

Lorenz, K. (1966). *On aggression.* New York: Harcourt Brace Jovanovich.

Lorenz, K. (1974). *Civilized man's eight deadly sins.* New York: Harcourt Brace Jovanovich.

Lovaas, O. I., & Koegel, R. (1973). Behavior therapy with autistic children. In C. Thoreson (Ed.), *Behavior modification and education.* Chicago: University of Chicago Press.

Lowe, M. R. (1993). The effects of dieting on eating behavior: A three-factor model. *Psychological Bulletin, 114,* 100–121.

Lown, B. (1999). *The lost art of healing.* New York: Ballantine.

Luborsky, L. (1988). *Who will benefit from psychotherapy?* New York: Basic Books.

Luce, R. D. (1993). *Sound and hearing.* Hillsdale, NJ: Erlbaum.

Luchins, A. S. (1946). Classroom experiments on mental set. *American Journal of Psychology, 59,* 295–298.

Lucy, J. A. (1992). *Language diversity and thought: A reformulation of the linguistic relativity hypothesis.* Cambridge, England: Cambridge University Press.

Lucy, J. A. (1996). The scope of linguistic relativity: An analysis and review of empirical research. In J. J. Gumperz & S. C. Levinson (Eds.), *Rethinking linguistic relativity. Studies in the* social and cultural foundations of language, No. 17. Cambridge, England: Cambridge University Press.

Ludwig, A. M. (1996, March). Mental disturbances and creative achievement. Harvard Mental Health Letter, pp. 4–6.

Luria, A. R. (1968). The mind of a mnemonist. Cambridge, MA: Basic Books.

Ly, D. H., Lockhart, D. J., Lerner, R. A., & Schultz, P. G. (2000, March 31). Mitotic misregulation and human aging. Science, 287, 2486–2492.

Lykken, D. T. (1995). The antisocial personalities. Mahwah, NJ: Erlbaum.

Lykken, D. T., McGue, M., Tellegen, A., & Bouchard, T. J., Jr. (1993). Emergenesis: Genetic traits that may not run in families. American Psychologist, 47, 1565–1577.

Lykken, D. T., & Tellegen, A. (1996). Happiness is a stochastic phenomenon. Psychological Science, 7, 181–185.

Lyman, D. R., Milich, R., Zimmerman, R., Novak, S. P., Logan, T. K., Martin, C., Leukefeld, M. C., & Clayton, R. (1999). Project DARE: No effects at 10-year follow-up. Journal of Consulting and Clinical Psychology, 67, 590–593.

Lynn, S. J., Lock, T. G., Myers, B., & Payne, D. G. (1997). Recalling the unrecallable: Should hypnosis be used to recover memories in psychotherapy? Current Directions in Psychological Science, 6, 79–83.

Lynn, S. J., Neufeld, V., Green, J. P., Sandberg, D., et al. (1996). Daydreaming, fantasy, and psychopathology. In R. G. Kunzendorf, N. P. Spanos, & B. Wallace (Eds.), Hypnosis and imagination. Amityville, NY: Baywood.

Lynn, S. J., & Rhue, J. W. (1988). Fantasy-proneness: Hypnosis, developmental antecedents, and psychopathology. American Psychologist, 43, 35–44.

Macaluso, E., Frith, C. D., & Driver, J. (2000, August 18). Modulation of human visual cortex by crossmodal spatial attention. Science, 289, 1206–1208.

MacKenzie, B. (1984). Explaining race differences in IQ: The logic, the methodology, and the evidence. American Psychologist, 39, 1214–1233.

Mackintosh, N. J. (1998). IQ and human intelligence. Cambridge, England: Oxford University Press.

Macmillan, M. (1991). Freud evaluated: The competed arc. Amsterdam: North-Holland.

Macrae, C. N., Stangor, C., & Hewstone, M. (1996). Stereotypes and stereotyping. New York: Guilford Press.

Mader, S. (2000). Human biology, 6th Edition. New York: McGraw-Hill.

Madon, S., Jussim, L., & Eccles, J. (1997). In search of the powerful self-fulfilling prophecy. Journal of Personality and Social Psychology, 72, 791–809.

Maidment, I. (2000). The use of St John's Wort in the treatment of depression. Psychiatric Bulletin, 24, 232–234.

Mairs, D. A. E. (1995). Hypnosis and pain in childbirth. Contemporary Hypnosis, 12, 111–118.

Malott, R. W., Whaley, D. L., & Malott, M. E. (1993). Elementary principles of behavior (2nd ed.). Englewood Cliffs, NJ: Prentice Hall.

Mann, D. (1997). Psychotherapy: An erotic relationship. New York: Routledge.

Manstead, A. S. R. (1991). Expressiveness as an individual difference. In R. S. Feldman &

B. Rime (Eds.), Fundamentals of nonverbal behavior. Cambridge, England: Cambridge University Press.

Mapes, G. (1990, April 10). Beating the clock: Was it an accident Chernobyl exploded at 1:23 in the morning? Wall Street Journal, pp. A1, A16.

Marcus, G. F. (1996). Why do children say "breaked"? Current Directions in Psychological Science, 5, 81–85.

Margolis, E., & Laurence, S. (Eds.). (1999). Concepts: Core readings. Cambridge, MA: MIT Press.

Marijuana as medicine: How strong is the science? (May, 1997). Consumer Reports, pp. 62–63.

Markey, P. M. (2000). Bystander intervention in computer-mediated communication. Computers in Human Behavior, 16, 183–188.

Marks, G., & Miller, N. (1987). Ten years of research on the false-consensus effect: An empirical and theoretical review. Psychological Bulletin, 102, 72–90.

Martin, A., Haxby, J. V., Lalonde, F. M., Wiggs, C. L., & Ungerleider, L. G. (1995, October 6). Discrete cortical regions associated with knowledge of color and knowledge of action. Science, 270, 102–105.

Martin, L., & Pullum, G. K. (1991). The great Eskimo vocabulary hoax. Chicago: University of Chicago Press.

Maslow, A. H. (1970). Motivation and personality (2nd ed.). New York: Harper & Row.

Maslow, A. H. (1987). Motivation and personality (3rd ed.). New York: Harper & Row.

Masters, W. H., & Johnson, V. E. (1979). Homosexuality in perspective. Boston: Little, Brown.

Mastropieri, M. A., & Scruggs, T. E. (1991). Teaching students ways to remember: Strategies for learning mnemonically. Cambridge, MA: Brookline Books.

Matarazzo, J. D. (1992). Psychological testing and assessment in the 21st century. American Psychologist, 47, 1007–1018.

Matthews, D. B., Best, P. J., White, A. M., Vandergriff, J. L., & Simson, P. E. (1996). Ethanol impairs spatial cognitive processing: New behavioral and electrophysiological findings. Current Directions in Psychological Science, 5, 111–115.

Matute, H. (1994). Learned helplessness and superstitious behavior as opposite effects of uncontrollable reinforcement in humans. Learning and Motivation, 25, 216–232.

Matute, H. (1995). Human reactions to uncontrollable outcomes: Further evidence for superstitions rather than helplessness. Quarterly Journal of Experimental Psychology Comparative and Physiological Psychology, 48, 142–157.

Maurer, D., Lewis, T. L., Brent, H. P., & Levin, A. V. (1999, October 1). Rapid improvement in the acuity of infants after visual input. Science, 286, 108–110.

May, R. (1989). Love and will. New York: Norton.

Mayer, J. D., & Salovey, P. (1997). What is emotional intelligence? In P. Salovey & D. J. Sluyter (Eds.), Emotional development and emotional intelligence. New York: Basic Books.

Mayr, U., Kliegl, R., & Krampe, R. T. (1996). Sequential and coordinative processing dynamics in figural transformations across the life span. Cognition, 59, 61–90.

Mays, V. M., Rubin, J., Sabourin, M., & Walker, L. (1996). Moving toward a global psychology: Changing theories and practice to meet the needs of a changing world. American Psychologist, 51, 485–487.

Mazza, J. J. (2000). The relationship between posttraumatic stress symptomatology and suicidal behavior in school-based adolescents. Suicide and Life-Threatening Behavior, 30, 91–103.

McAdams, D. P., Diamond, A., de St. Aubin, E., & Mansfield, E. (1997). Stories of commitment: The psychosocial construction of generative lives. Journal of Personality and Social Psychology, 72, 678–694.

McCabe, P. M., Schneiderman, N., Field, T., & Wellens, A. R. (Eds.). (2000). Stress, coping, and cardiovascular disease. Mahwah, NJ: Erlbaum.

McCain, N. L., & Smith, J. (1994). Stress and coping in the context of psychoneuroimmunology: A holistic framework for nursing practice and research. Archives of Psychiatric Nursing, 8, 221–227.

McCann, U. D., Mertl, M., Eligulashvili, V., & Ricaurte, G. A. (1999). Cognitive performance in (±) 3,4-methylenedioxymethamphetamine (MDMA, "Ecstasy") users: A controlled study. Psychopharmacology, 143, 417–425.

McCauley, C., & Swann, C. P. (1980). Sex differences in the frequency and functions of fantasies during sexual activity. Journal of Research in Personality, 14, 400–411.

McClearn, G. E., Johansson, B., Berg, S., Pedersen, N. L., Ahern, F., Petrill, S. A., & Plomin, R. (1997, June 6). Substantial genetic influence on cognitive abilities in twins 80 or more years old. Science, 276, 1560–1583.

McClelland, D. C. (1985). How motives, skills, and values determine what people do. American Psychologist, 40, 812–825.

McClelland, D. C. (1993). Intelligence is not the best predictor of job performance. Current Directions in Psychological Research, 2, 5–8.

McClelland, D. C., Atkinson, J. W., Clark, R. A., & Lowell, E. L. (1953). The achievement motive. New York: Appleton-Century-Crofts.

McClintock, M. K., & Herdt, G. (1996). Rethinking puberty: The development of sexual attraction. Current Directions in Psychological Science, 5, 178–183.

McCrae, R. R., & Costa, P. T., Jr. (1999). A five-factor theory of personality. In L. A. Pervin & O. P. John (Eds.), Handbook of personality: Theory and research (2nd ed.). New York: Guilford Press.

McCullough, J. P., Jr. (1999). Treatment for chronic depression: Cognitive behavioral analysis system of psychology (CBASP). New York: Guilford Press.

McDonald, C., & Murray, R. M. (2000). Early and late environmental risk factors for schizophrenia. Brain Research Reviews, 31, 130–137.

McDonald, H. E., & Hirt, E. R. (1997). When expectancy meets desire: Motivational effects in reconstructive memory. Journal of Personality and Social Psychology, 72, 5–23.

McDonald, J. L. (1997). Language acquisition: The acquisition of linguistic structure in normal and special populations. Annual Review of Psychology, 48, 215–241.

McDonald, J. W. (1999, September). Repairing the damaged spinal cord. Scientific American, pp. 65–73.

McDougall, W. (1908). Introduction to social psychology. London: Methuen.

McDowell, D. M., & Spitz, H. I. (1999). Substance abuse. New York: Brunner/Mazel.

McEwen, B. S. (1998, January 15). Protective and damaging effects of stress mediators [Review article]. New England Journal of Medicine, 338, 171–179.

McFadyen, R. G. (1996). Gender, status and "powerless" speech: Interactions of students and lectures. *British Journal of Social Psychology, 35,* 353–367.

McGaugh, J. L. (2000, January 14). Memory— A century of consolidation. *Science, 287,* 248–251.

McGaugh, J. L., Weinberger, N. M., & Lynch, G. (Eds.). (1990). *Brain organization and memory: Cells, systems, and circuits.* New York: Oxford University Press.

McGue, M. (1999). The behavioral genetics of alcoholism. *Current Directions in Psychological Science, 8,* 109–115.

McGuire, P. K., Shah, G. M. S., & Murray, R. M. (1993, September 18). Increased blood flow in Broca's area during auditory hallucinations in schizophrenia. *Lancet, 342,* 703–706.

McGuire, W. J. (1997). Creative hypothesis generating in psychology: Some useful heuristics. *Annual Review of Psychology, 48,* 1–30.

McLaughlin, S., & Margolskee, R. F. (1994). The sense of taste: The internal molecular workings of the taste bud help it distinguish the bitter from the sweet. *American Scientist, 82,* 538–454.

McManus, F., & Waller, G. (1995). A functional analysis of binge-eating. *Clinical Psychology Review, 15,* 845–863.

McMullin, R. E. (2000). *The new handbook of cognitive therapy techniques.* New York: Norton.

McWhirter, D. P., Sanders, S., & Reinisch, J. M. (1990). *Homosexuality, heterosexuality: Concepts of sexual orientation.* New York: Oxford University Press.

Mead, M. (1949). *Male and female.* New York: Morrow.

Mednick, A. (1993). World's women familiar with a day's double shift. *APA Monitor,* p. 32.

Meier, R. P., & Willerman, R. (1995). Prelinguistic gesture in deaf and hearing infants. In K. Emmorey & J. S. Reilly (Eds.), *Language, gesture, and space.* Hillsdale, NJ: Erlbaum.

Mel'nikov, K. S. (1993, October–December). (On some aspects of the mechanistic approach to the study of processes of forgetting.) *Vestnik Moskovskogo Universiteta Seriya 14 Psikhologiya,* 64–67.

Melton, G. B., & Garrison, E. G. (1987). Fear, prejudice, and neglect: Discrimination against mentally disabled persons. *American Psychologist, 42,* 1007–1026.

Meltzer, H. Y. (2000). Genetics and etiology of schizophrenia and bipolar disorder. *Biological Psychiatry, 47,* 171–173.

Meltzoff, A. N. (1996). The human infant as imitative generalist: A 20-year progress report on infant imitation with implications for comparative psychology. In C. M. Heyes & B. G. Galef, Jr. (Eds.), *Social learning in animals: The roots of culture.* San Diego: Academic Press.

Mendez, F. J., & Garcia, M. J. (1996). Emotive performances: A treatment package for children's phobias. *Child and Family Behavior Therapy, 18,* 19–34.

Mental health: Does therapy help? (1995, November). *Consumer Reports,* pp. 734–739.

Mentzer, S. J., & Snyder, M. L. (1982). The doctor and the patient: A psychological perspective. In G. S. Sanders and J. Suls (Eds.), *Social psychology of health and illness* (pp. 161–181). Hillsdale, NJ: Erlbaum.

Merlin, D. (1993). Origins of the modern mind: Three stages in the evolution of culture and cognition. *Behavioral and Brain Sciences, 16,* 737–791.

Mesquita, B., & Frijda, N. H. (1992). Cultural variations in emotions: A review. *Psychological Bulletin, 112,* 179–204.

Metcalfe, J. (1986). Premonitions of insight predict impending error. *Journal of Experimental Psychology: Learning, Memory, and Cognition, 12,* 623–634.

Metee, D. R., & Aronson, E. (1974). Affective reactions to appraisal from others. In T. L. Huston (Ed.), *Foundations of interpersonal attraction* (pp. 235–283). New York: Academic Press.

Meyer, G. J. (2000). Incremental validity of the Rorschach Prognostic Rating scale over the MMPI Ego Strength Scale and IQ. *Journal of Personality Assessment, 74,* 356–370.

Meyer, R. G., & Osborne, Y. V. H. (1987). *Case studies in abnormal behavior* (2nd ed.). Boston: Allyn & Bacon.

Michael, R. T., Gagnon, J. H., Laumann, E. O., & Kolata, G. (1994). *Sex in America: A definitive survey.* Boston: Little, Brown.

Middlebrooks, J. C., Clock, A. E., Xu, L., & Green, D. M. (1994, May 6). A panoramic code for sound location by cortical neurons. *Science, 264,* 842–844.

Middlebrooks, J. C., & Green, D. M. (1991). Sound localization by human listeners. *Annual Review of Psychology, 42,* 135–159.

Mifflin, L. (1998, January 14). Study finds a decline in TV network violence. *New York Times,* p. A14.

Mikamo, K., Takao, Y., Wakutani, Y., & Nishikawa, S. (1994). Effects of mecobalamin injection at acupoints on intractable headaches. *Current Therapeutic Research, 55,* 1477–1485.

Miles, R. (2000, January 14). Diversity in inhibition. *Science, 287,* 244–246.

Milgram, R. M., Dunn, R. S., & Price, G. E. (Eds.). (1993). *Teaching and counseling gifted and talented adolescents: An international learning style perspective.* Westport, CT: Praeger/Greenwood.

Milgram, S. (1974). *Obedience to authority.* New York: Harper & Row.

Miller, A. G. (1999). Harming other people: Perspectives on evil and violence. *Personality and Social Psychology Review, 3,* 176–178.

Miller, A. G., Collins, B. E., & Brief, D. E. (1995). Perspectives on obedience to authority: The legacy of the Milgram experiments. *Journal of Social Issues, 51,* 1–19.

Miller, D. W. (2000, February 25). Looking askance at eyewitness testimony. *Chronicle of Higher Education,* pp. A19–A20.

Miller, G. A. (1956). The magical number seven, plus or minus two: Some limits on our capacity for processing information. *Psychology Review, 63,* 81–97.

Miller, J. G. (1984). Culture and the development of everyday social explanation. *Journal of Personality and Social Psychology, 46,* 961–978.

Miller, J. G. (1999). Cultural psychology: Implications for basic psychological theory. *Psychological Science, 10,* 85–91.

Miller, K. J., & Mizes, J. S. (Eds.). (2000). *Comparative treatments for eating disorders.* New York: Springer.

Miller, L. T., & Vernon, P. A. (1997). Developmental changes in speed of information processing in young children. *Developmental Psychology, 33,* 549–554.

Miller, N. E. (1985, February). Rx: Biofeedback. *Psychology Today,* pp. 54–59.

Miller, N. E., & Magruder, K. M. (Eds.). (1999). *Cost-effectiveness of psychotherapy: A guide for practitioners, researchers, and policymakers.* New York: Oxford University Press.

Miller-Jones, D. (1989). Culture and testing. *American Psychologist, 44,* 360–366.

Millon, T., & Davis, R. (1996). *Disorders of personality: DSM-IV and beyond* (2nd ed.). New York: Wiley.

Millon, T., & Davis, R. (1999). *Personality disorders in modern life.* New York: Wiley.

Millon, T., Davis, R., Millon, C., Escovar, L., & Meagher, S. (2000). *Personality disorders in modern life.* New York: Wiley.

Mills, J. L. (1999). Cocaine, smoking, and spontaneous abortion. *New England Journal of Medicine, 340,* 380–381.

Milner, B. (1966). *Amnesia following operation on temporal lobes.* In C. W. M. Whitty & P. Zangwill (Eds.), *Amnesia.* London: Butterworth.

Milton, J., & Wiseman, R. (1999). Does psi exist? Lack of replication of an anomalous process of information transfer. *Psychological Bulletin, 125,* 387–391.

Mind over matter. (1999). *Discover, 20,* p. 2.

Mineka, S., & Henderson, R. W. (1985). Controllability and predictability in acquired motivation. *Annual Review of Psychology, 36,* 495–529.

Mingo, C., Herman, C. J., & Jasperse, M. (2000). Women's stories: Ethnic variations in women's attitudes and experiences of menopause, hysterectomy, and hormone replacement therapy. *Journal of Women's Health and Gender-Based Medicine, 9* (Suppl. 2), S27–S38.

Minuchin, S., & Nichols, M. P. (1992). *Family healing.* New York: Free Press.

Miserando, M. (1991). Memory and the seven dwarfs. *Teaching of Psychology, 18,* 169–171.

Mittleman, M. A., Maclure, M., Sherwood, J. B., Mulry, R. P., Tofler, G. H., Jacobs, S. C., Friedman, R., Benson, H., & Muller, J. E. (1995, October 1). Triggering of acute myocardial infarction onset by episodes of anger. *Circulation, 92,* 1720–1725.

Miyake, K., Chen, S., & Campos, J. J. (1985). Infant temperament, mother's mode of interaction, and attachment in Japan: An interim report. *Monographs of the Society for Research in Child Development, 50,* 276–297.

Miyashita, Y. (1995, June 23). How the brain creates imagery: Projection to primary visual cortex. *Science, 268,* 1719–1720.

Moghaddam, B., & Adams, B. W. (1998, August 28). Reversal of phencyclidine effects by a group II metabotropic glutamate receptor agonist in rats. *Science, 281,* 1349–1352.

Molfese, V. J. & Molfese, D. L. (2000). *Temperament and personality development across the life span.* Mahwah, NJ: Erlbaum.

Moody, H.R. (2000). *Aging.* Thousands Oaks, CA: Sage Publications.

Moore-Ede, M. (1993). *The twenty-four hour society.* Boston: Addison-Wesley.

Moretti, M. M., & Higgins, E. T. (1990). The development of self-system vulnerabilities: Social and cognitive factors in developmental psychopathology. In R. J. Sternberg & J. Kolligian, Jr. (Eds.), *Competence considered.* New Haven, CT: Yale University Press.

Morrow, J., & Wolff, R. (1991, May). Wired for a miracle. *Health,* pp. 64–84.

Moscovici, S. (1985). Social influence and conformity. In G. Lindzey & E. Aronson (Eds.), *Handbook of social psychology* (3rd ed.). New York: Random House.

Motley, M. T. (1987, February). What I meant to say. *Psychology Today,* pp. 25–28.

Moutoussis, K., & Zeki, S. (1997). A direct demonstration of perceptual asynchrony in vision. *Proceedings of the Royal Society of London, B., Biological Sciences, 264,* 393–399.

Movshon, J. A., & Newsome, W. T. (1992). Neural foundations of visual motion perception. *Current Directions in Psychological Science, 1,* 35–39.

Mroczek, D. K., & Kolarz, C. M. (1998). The effect of age on positive and negative affect: A developmental perspective on happiness. *Journal of Personality and Social Psychology, 75,* 1333–1349.

Mrzljak, L., Bergson, C., Pappy, M., Huff, R., et al. (1996). Localization of dopamine D4 receptors in GABAergic neurons of the primate brain. *Nature, 381,* 245–248.

Mueser, K. T., Bellack, A. S., Wade, J. H., Sayers, S. L., Tierney, A., & Haag, G. (1993). Expressed emotion, social skill, and response to negative affect in schizophrenia. *Journal of Abnormal Psychology, 102,* 339–351.

Mufson, M. J. (1999, September). What is the role of psychiatry in the management of chronic pain? *Harvard Mental Health Letter,* pp. 8–10.

Mukerjee, M. (1997, February). Trends in animal research. *Scientific American,* pp. 86–93.

Mumme, D. L., Fernald, A., & Herrera, C. (1996). Infants' responses to facial and vocal emotional signals in a social referencing paradigm. *Child Development, 67,* 3219–3237.

Murphy, S. (1998, January 4). Whitey Bulger's life on the run. *Boston Globe,* pp. A1, A8–A9.

Murphy, S. T., & Zajonc, R. B. (1993). Affect, cognition, and awareness: Affective priming with optimal and suboptimal stimulus exposures. *Journal of Personality and Social Psychology, 64,* 723–739.

Murray, J. B. (1990). Nicotine as a psychoactive drug. *Journal of Psychology, 125,* 5–25.

Murray, J. B. (1995). Evidence for acupuncture's analgesic effectiveness and proposals for the physiological mechanisms involved. *Journal of Psychology, 129,* 43–461.

Murray, S. L., & Holmes, J. G. (1997). A leap of faith? Positive illusions in romantic relationships. *Personality and Social Psychology Bulletin, 23,* 586–604.

Myerhoff, B. (1982). Rites of passage: Process and paradox. In V. Turner (Ed.), *Celebration: Studies in festivity and ritual.* Washington, DC: Smithsonian Institution Press.

Myers, D. G. (2000). The funds, friends, and faith of happy people. *American Psychologist, 55,* 56–67.

Myers, D. G., & Diener, E. (1996, May). The pursuit of happiness: New research uncovers some anti-intuitive insights into how many people are happy—And why. *Scientific American,* pp. 70–72.

Myerson, J., Rank, M. R., Raines, F. Q., & Schnitzler, M. A. (1998). Race and general cognitive ability: The myth of diminishing returns to education. *Psychological Science, 9,* 139–142.

Nahome, L., & Lawton, M. P. (1975). Similarity and propinquity in friendship formation. *Journal of Personality and Social Psychology, 32,* 205–213.

Nathan, P. E., & Gorman, J. M. (Eds.). (1997). *A guide to treatments that work.* New York: Oxford University Press.

Nathans, J., Davenport, C. M., Maumenee, I. H., Lewis, R. A., et al. (1989, August 25). Molecular genetics of human blue cone monochromacy. *Science, 245,* 831–838.

National Center for Health Statistics (1994). *Report on obesity in the United States.* Washington, DC: Author.

National Center on Addiction and Substance Abuse. (1996, June). *Substance abuse and the American woman.* New York: Author.

National Institute on Drug Abuse. (2000). *Principles of Drug Addiction Treatment: A research-based guide.* Washington, DC: National Institute on Drug Abuse.

National Institutes of Health. (1996). Integration of behavioral and relaxation approaches into the treatment of chronic pain and insomnia. NIH Technology Assessment Panel on Integration of Behavioral and Relaxation Approaches into the Treatment of Chronic Pain and Insomnia. *Journal of the American Medical Association, 276,* 313–318.

National Research Council. (2000). *From neurons to neighborhoods: The science of early childhood development.* Washington, DC: National Academy Press.

Navon, R., & Proia, R. L. (1989, March 17). The mutations in Ashkenazi Jews with adult G(M2) Gangliosidosis, the adult form of Tay-Sachs disease. *Science, 243,* 1471–1474.

Negrin, G., & Capute, A. J. (1996). Mental retardation. In R. H. A. Haslam & P. J. Valletutti (Eds.). *Medical problems in the classroom: The teacher's role in diagnosis and management* (3rd ed.). Austin, TX: PRO-ED.

Neher, A. (1991). Maslow's theory of motivation: A critique. *Journal of Humanistic Psychology, 31,* 89–112.

Neisser, U. (1982). *Memory observed.* San Francisco: Freeman.

Neisser, U. (1996, April). *Intelligence on the rise: Secular changes in IQ and related measures.* Paper presented at a conference at Emory University, Atlanta.

Neisser, U., Boodoo, G., Bouchard, T. J., Jr., Boykin, A. W., et al. (1996). Intelligence: Knowns and unknowns. *American Psychologist, 51,* 77–101.

Neitz, J., Neitz, M., & Kainz, P. M. (1996, November 1). Visual pigment gene structure and the severity of color vision defects. *Science, 274,* 801–804.

Nelson, M. (1992, February 3). Too tough to die. *People Weekly,* pp. 30–33.

Nelson, W. M., III, & Finch, A. J., Jr. (2000). Managing anger in youth: A cognitive-behavioral intervention approach. In P. C. Kendall (Ed.), *Child and adolescent therapy: Cognitive-behavioral procedures* (2nd ed.). New York: Guilford Press.

Ness, R. B., Grisso, J. A., Hirschinger, N., Markovic, N., Shaw, L. M., Day, N. L., & Kline, J. (1999). Cocaine and tobacco use and the risk of spontaneous abortion. *New England Journal of Medicine, 340,* 333–339.

Nesse, R. M. (2000). Is depression an adaptation? *Archives of General Psychiatry, 57,* 14–20.

A new approach to test-taking. (1994, November 15). *New York Times,* p. B9.

Newcombe, N. S., Drummey, A. B., Fox, N. A., Lie, E., & Ottinger-Alberts, W. (2000). Remembering early childhood: How much, how, and why (or why not). *Current Directions in Psychological Science, 9,* 55–58.

Newell, A., & Simon, H. (1972). *Human problem solving.* Englewood Cliffs, NJ: Prentice Hall.

NICHD Early Child Care Research Network. (1997). The effects of infant care on infant-mother attachment security: Results of the NICHD study of early child care. *Child Development, 68,* 860–879.

NICHD Early Child Care Research Network. (1999). Child care and mother-child interaction in the first 3 years of life. *Developmental Psychology, 35,* 1399–1413.

Nickerson, R. S., & Adams, M. J. (1979). Long-term memory for a common object. *Cognitive Psychology, 11,* 287–307.

Nierenberg, A. (1998a, February 17). The physician's perspective. *HealthNews,* pp. 3–4.

Nierenberg, A. (1998b, April 20). Should you take St. John's Wort? *HealthNews,* p. 4.

Nigg, J. T., & Goldsmith, H. H. (1994). Genetics of personality disorders: Perspectives from personality and psychopathology research. *Psychological Bulletin, 115,* 346–380.

Nikles, C. D., II, Brecht, D. L., Klinger, E., & Bursell, A. L. (1998). The effects of current concern- and nonconcern-related waking suggestions on nocturnal dream content. *Journal of Personality and Social Psychology, 75,* 242–255.

Nisbett, R. E. (1968). Taste, deprivation, and weight determinants of eating behavior. *Journal of Personality and Social Psychology, 10,* 107–116.

Nisbett, R. E. (1972). Hunger, obesity and the ventromedial hypothalamus. *Psychological Review, 79,* 433–453.

Nisbett, R. E. (1994, October 31). Blue genes. *New Republic, 211,* 15.

Nisbett, R. E., Krantz, D. H., Jepson, D., & Kunda, Z. (1993). The use of statistical heuristics in everyday reasoning. In R. E. Nisbett (Ed.), *Rules for reasoning.* Hillsdale, NJ: Erlbaum.

Noble, H. B. (1999, March 12). New from the smoking wars: Success. *New York Times,* pp. D1–D2.

Nolen-Hoeksema, S., Larson, J., & Grayson, C. (1999). Explaining the gender differences in depressive symptoms. *Journal of Personality and Social Psychology, 77,* 1061–1072.

Novak, M. A., & Petto, A. J. (1991). *Through the looking glass: Issues of psychological well-being in captive nonhuman primates.* Washington, DC: American Psychological Association.

Noyes, R., Kathol, R. G., Fisher, M. M., Phillips, B. M., et al. (1993). The validity of *DSM-III-R* hypochondriasis. *Archives of General Psychiatry, 50,* 961–970.

Nunn, K. P. (1996). Personal hopefulness: A conceptual review of the relevance of the perceived future to psychiatry. *British Journal of Medical Psychology, 69,* 227–245.

Nyberg, L., & Tulving, E. (1996). Classifying human long-term memory: Evidence from converging dissociations. *European Journal of Cognitive Psychology, 8,* 163–183.

Oatley, K. (1992). *Best laid schemes: The psychology of emotions.* Cambridge, MA: Cambridge University Press.

Oatley, K., & Jenkins, J. M. (1996). *Understanding emotions.* Oxford, England: Blackwell.

O'Brien, C. P., Childress, A. R., McLellan, A. T., & Ehrman, R. (1992). Classical conditioning in drug-dependent humans. In P. W. Kalivas & H. H. Samson (Eds.). *The neurobiology of drug and alcohol addiction. Annals of the New York Academy of Sciences, Vol. 654.* New York: New York Academy of Sciences.

O'Connor, S. C., & Rosenblood, L. K. (1996). Affiliation motivation in everyday experience: A theoretical comparison. *Journal of Personality and Social Psychology, 70,* 513–522.

Ogilvie, R., & Harsh, J. (Eds.). (1994). *Sleep onset: Normal and abnormal processes.* Washington, DC: American Psychological Association.

O'Grady, W. D., & Dobrovolsky, M. (Eds.). (1996). *Contemporary linguistic analysis: An introduction* (3rd ed.). Toronto: Copp Clark Pitman.

O'Hare, D., & Roscoe, S. (1990). *Flightdeck performance: The human factor.* Ames: Iowa State University Press.

Okun, B. F. (1996). *Understanding diverse families: What practitioners need to know.* New York: Guilford Press.

Olds, J., & Milner, P. (1954). Positive reinforcement produced by electrical stimulation of septal area and other regions of rat brain. *Journal of Comparative and Physiological Psychology, 47,* 411–427.

Oliver, M. B., & Hyde, J. S. (1993). Gender differences in sexuality: A meta-analysis. *Psychological Bulletin, 114,* 29–51.

Olshansky, S. J., Carnes, B. A., & Cassel, C. (1990, November 2). In search of Methuselah: Estimating the upper limits to human longevity. *Science, 250,* 634–639.

O'Neil, J. (1999, July 27). For the disabled, special dogs assume special duties. *New York Times,* p. D6.

Oren, D. A., & Terman, M. (1998, January 16). Tweaking the human circadian clock with light. *Science, 279,* 333–334.

Ornstein, R. (1998). *The right mind: Making sense of the hemispheres.* New York: Harcourt Brace.

Orth-Gomer, K., Chesney, M. A., & Wenger, N. K. (Eds.). (1996). *Women, stress and heart disease.* Mahwah, NJ: Erlbaum.

Orth-Gomer, K., & Schneiderman, N. (Eds.). (1995). *Behavioral medicine approaches to cardiovascular disease prevention.* Mahwah, NJ: Erlbaum.

Ortony, A., & Turner, T. J. (1990). What's basic about basic emotions? *Psychological Review, 97,* 315–331.

Orwin, R. G., & Condray, D. S. (1984). Smith and Glass' psychotherapy conclusions need further probing: On Landman and Dawes' re-analysis. *American Psychologist, 39,* 71–72.

Orzack, M. S. (1999). Computer addiction: Is it real or virtual? *Harvard Mental Health Letter,* p. 8.

Oskamp, S. (Ed.) (2000). *Reducing prejudice and discrimination.* Mahwah, NJ: Erlbaum.

Oster, M. I. (1994). Psychological preparation for labor and delivery using hypnosis. *American Journal of Clinical Hypnosis, 37,* 12–21.

Owens, R. E., Jr. (2001). *Language development: An introduction* (5th ed.). Boston: Allyn & Bacon.

Paivio, A. (1971). *Imagery and verbal processes.* New York: Holt, Rinehart & Winston.

Paivio, A. (1975). Perceptual comparison through the mind's eye. *Memory and Cognition, 3,* 635–647.

Paniagua, F. A. (2000). *Diagnosis in a multicultural context: A casebook for mental health professionals.* Thousand Oaks, CA: Sage.

Parke, R. D. (1996). *Fatherhood.* Cambridge, MA: Harvard University Press.

Parlee, M. B. (1979, October). The friendship bond. *Psychology Today,* pp. 43–45.

Parrott, R., Duncan, V., & Duggan, A. (2000). Promoting patients' full and honest disclosure during conversations with health caregivers. In S. Petronio (Ed.), *Balancing the secrets of private disclosures.* Mahwah, NJ: Erlbaum.

Patzwahl, D. R., Zanker, J. M., & Altenmuller, E. O. (1994). Cortical potentials reflecting motion processing in humans. *Visual Neuroscience, 11,* 1135–1147.

Pavlides, C., & Winson, J. (1989). Influences of hippocampal place cell firing in the awake state on the activity of these cells during subsequent sleep episodes. *Journal of Neuroscience, 9,* 2907–2918.

Pavlov, I. P. (1927). *Conditioned reflexes.* London: Oxford University Press.

Pawlik, K., & d'Ydewalle, G. (1996). Psychology and the global commons: Perspectives of international psychology. *American Psychologist, 51,* 488–495.

Payne, D. G. (1986). Hyperamnesia for pictures and words: Testing the recall level hypothesis. *Journal of Experimental Psychology: Learning, Memory, and Cognition, 12,* 16–29.

Peirce, R. S., Frone, M. R., Russell, M., & Cooper, M. L. (1996). Financial stress, social support, and alcohol involvement: A longitudinal test of the buffering hypothesis in a general population survey. *Health Psychology, 15,* 38–47.

Peled, E., Jaffe, P. G., Edleson, J. L. (Eds.). (1995). *Ending the cycle of violence: Community responses to children of battered women.* Thousand Oaks, CA: Sage Publications.

Penn, D. L., Corrigan, P. W., Bentall, R. P., Racenstein, J. M., & Newman, L. (1997). Social cognition in schizophrenia. *Psychological Bulletin, 121,* 114–132.

Penney, J. B., Jr. (2000). Synopsis of neuropsychiatry. In B. S. Fogel, R. B. Schiffer, et al. (Eds.). *Neurochemistry.* Philadelphia: Lippincott-Raven.

Pennisi, E. (1997a, October 24). Enzyme linked to alcohol sensitivity in mice. *Science, 278,* 573.

Pennisi, E. (1997b, August 15). Schizophrenia clues from monkeys. *Science, 277,* 900.

Pennisi, E. (1997c, August 1). Transgenic lambs from cloning lab. *Science, 277,* 631.

Pennisi, E. (2000, May 19). And the gene number is . . . ? *Science, 288,* 1146–1147.

Perez, R. M., DeBord, K. A., & Bieschke, K. J. (Eds.). (2000). *Handbook of counseling and psychotherapy with lesbian, gay, and bisexual clients.* Washington, DC: American Psychological Association.

Perloff, R. M. (1993). *The dynamics of persuasion.* Hillsdale, NJ: Erlbaum.

Perls, F. S. (1970). *Gestalt therapy now: Therapy, techniques, applications.* Palo Alto, CA: Science & Behavior Books.

Perls, F. S., Hefferline, R., & Goodman, P. (1994). *Gestalt therapy: Excitement and growth in the human personality* (2nd ed.). New York: New York Journal Press.

Perry-Jenkins, M. (1993). Family roles and responsibilities: What has changed and what has remained the same? In J. Frankel (Ed.), *The employed mother and the family context.* New York: Springer.

Pervin, L. A. & John, O. P. (Eds.) (1999). *Handbook of personality: Theory and research* (2nd ed.). New York: Guilford Press.

Petersen, S. E., & Fiez, J. A. (1993). The processing of single words studied with positron emission tomography. *Annual Review of Neuroscience, 16,* 509–530.

Peterson, A. (1985). Pubertal development as a cause of disturbance: Myths, realities, and unanswered questions. *Genetic, Social and General Psychology Monographs, 111,* 205–232.

Peterson, C. (2000). The future of optimism. *American Psychologist, 55,* 44–55.

Peterson, C., Maier, S. F., & Seligman, M. E. P. (1993). *Learned helplessness: A theory for the age of personal control.* New York: Oxford University Press.

Peterson, K. C., Prout, M. F., & Schwarz, R. A. (1991). *Post-traumatic stress disorder: A clinician's guide.* New York: Plenum Press.

Peterson, L. R., & Peterson, M. J. (1959). Short-term retention of individual items. *Journal of Experimental Psychology, 58,* 193–198.

Peterzell, D. H. (1993). Individual differences in the visual attention of human infants: Further evidence for separate sensitization and habituation processes. *Developmental Psychobiology, 26,* 207–218.

Petri, H. L. (1996). *Motivation: Theory, research, and applications* (4th ed.). Pacific Grove, CA: Brooks/Cole.

Petronis, A., & Kenedy, J. L. (1995). Unstable genes—unstable mind? *American Journal of Psychiatry, 152,* 164–172.

Pettigrew, T. F. (1997, February). Generalized intergroup contact effects on prejudice. *Personality and Social Psychology Bulletin, 23,* 173–185.

Pettingale, K. W., Morris, T., Greer, S., & Haybittle, J. L. (1985). Mental attitudes to cancer: An additional prognostic factor. *Lancet,* p. 750.

Pettito, L. A. (1993). On the ontogenetic requirements for early language acquisition. In B. de Boysson-Bardies, S. de Schonen, P. W. Jusczyk, P. McNeilage, & J. Morton (Eds.), *Developmental neurocognition: Speech and face processing in the first year of life.* Dordrecht, Netherlands: Kluwer Academic.

Pettito, L. A., & Marentette, P. F. (1991, March 22). Babbling in the manual mode: Evidence for the ontogeny of language. *Science, 251,* 1493–1496.

Petty, R. E., & Cacioppo, J. T. (1986). The elaboration likelihood model of persuasion. In L. Berkowitz (Ed.), *Advances in experimental social psychology* (Vol. 10). New York: Academic Press.

Petty, R. E., Cacioppo, J. T., Strathman, A. J., & Priester, J. R. (1994). To think or not to think: Exploring two routes to persuasion. In S. Savitt & T. C. Brock (Eds.), *Persuasion: Psychological insights and perspectives.* Boston: Allyn & Bacon.

Petzold, P. (1992). Context effects in judgments of attributes: An information-integration approach. In H. G. Geissler, S. W. Link, & J. T. Townsend (Eds.), *Cognition, information processing, and psychophysics: Basic issues.* Scientific psychology series. Hillsdale, NJ: Erlbaum.

Pezdek, K., & Banks, W. P. (Eds.). (1996). *The recovered memory/false memory debate.* New York: Academic Press.

Piaget, J. (1970). Piaget's theory. In P. H. Mussen (Ed.), *Carmichael's manual of child psychology* (3rd ed., Vol. 1). New York: Wiley.

Piaget, J., & Inhelder, B. (1958). *The growth of logical thinking from childhood to adolescence* (A. Parsons & S. Seagrin, Trans.). New York: Basic Books.

Piasecki, T. M., Kenford, S. L., Smith, S. S., Fiore, M. C., & Baker, T. B. (1997). Listening to nicotine: Negative affect and the smoking withdrawal conundrum. *Psychological Science, 8,* 184–189.

Pich, E. M., Pagliusi, S. R., Tessari, M., Talabot-Ayer, D., Hooft van Huijsduijnen, R., & Chiamulera, C. (1997, January 3). Common neural substrates for the addictive properties of nicotine and cocaine. *Science, 275,* 83–86.

Pihlgren, E. M., Gidycz, C. A., & Lynn, S. J. (1993). Impact of adulthood and adolescent rape experiences on subsequent sexual fantasies. *Imagination, Cognition and Personality, 12,* 321–339.

Piliavin, J. A., & Piliavin, I. M. (1972). Effect of blood on reactions to a victim. *Journal of Personality and Social Psychology, 23,* 353–362.

Pillard, R. C. (1996). Homosexuality from a familial and genetic perspective. In R. P. Cabaj & T. S. Stein (Eds.), *Textbook of homosexuality and mental health.* Washington, DC: American Psychiatric Press.

Pinker, S. (1990). Language acquisition. In D. N. Osherson & H. Lasnik (Eds.), *Language.* Cambridge, MA: MIT Press.

Pinker, S. (1994). *The language instinct.* New York: William Morrow.

Pion, G. M., Mednick, M. T., Astin, H. S., Hall, C. C. I., Kenkel, M. B., Keita, G. P., Kohout, J. L., & Kelleher, J. C. (1996). The shifting gender composition of psychology: Trends and implications for the discipline. *American Psychologist, 51,* 509–528.

Pledge, D. S. (1992). Marital separation/divorce: A review of individual responses to a major life stressor. *Journal of Divorce and Remarriage, 17,* 151–181.

Plomin, R. (1990, April 13). The role of inheritance in behavior. *Science, 248,* 183–188.

Plomin, R., & Caspi, R. (1999). Behavioral genetics and personality. In L. A. Pervin & O. P. John (Eds.), *Handbook of personality: Theory and research* (2nd ed.). New York: Guilford Press.

Plomin, R., & McClearn, G. E. (Eds.) (1993). *Nature, nurture and psychology.* Washington, DC: American Psychological Association.

Plomin, R., & Neiderhiser, J. M. (1992). Genetics and experience. *Current Directions in Psychological Science, 1,* 160–163.

Plomin, R., & Petrill, S. A. (1997). Genetics and intelligence: What's new? *Intelligence, 24,* 53–77.

Plous, S. (1996a). Attitudes toward the use of animals in psychological research and education: Results from a national survey of psychologists. *American Psychologist, 51,* 1167–1180.

Plous, S. (1996b). Attitudes toward the use of animals in psychological research and education: Results from a national survey of psychology majors. *Psychological Science, 7,* 352–358.

Plumert, J. M., Carswell, C., De Vet, K., & Ihrig, D. (1995). The content and organization of communication about object locations. *Journal of Memory and Language, 34,* 477–498.

Plummer, W., & Pick, G. (1996, October 10). Beating the blitz. *People Weekly,* pp. 129–132.

Plutchik, R. (1980). *Emotion: A psychorevolutionary synthesis.* New York: Harper & Row.

Polivy, J., & Herman, C. P. (1991). Good and bad dieters: Self-perception and reaction to a dietary challenge. *International Journal of Eating Disorders, 10,* 91–99.

Polk, N. (1997, March 30). The trouble with school testing systems. *New York Times,* p. CN3.

Pollack, A. (2000, May 30). Neural cells, grown in labs, raise hopes on brain disease. *New York Times,* pp. D1, D6.

Pollack, M. H., & Marzol, P. C. (2000). Panic: Course, complications and treatment of panic disorder. *Journal of Psychopharmacology, 14,* S25–S30.

Pomerlau, O. F. (1995). Individual differences in sensitivity to nicotine: Implications of genetic research on nicotine dependence [Special Issue: Genetic, environmental, and situational factors mediating the effects of nicotine]. *Behavior Genetics, 25,* 161–177.

Ponterotto, J. G., Casas, J. M., Suzuki, L. A., & Alexander, C. M. (Eds.). (2001). *Handbook of multicultural counseling.* Thousand Oaks, CA: Sage.

Porkka-Heiskanen, T., Strecker, R. E., Thakkar, M., Bjorkum, A. A., Greene, R. W., & McCarley, R. W. (1997, May 23). Adenosine: A mediator of the sleep-inducing effects of prolonged wakefulness. *Science, 276,* 1265–1268.

Porte, H. S., & Hobson, J. A. (1996). Physical motion in dreams: One measure of three theories. *Journal of Abnormal Psychology, 105,* 329–335.

Porter, R. H., Cernich, J. M., & McLaughlin, F. J. (1983). Maternal recognition of neonates through olfactory cues. *Physiology and Behavior, 30,* 151–154.

Potheraju, A., & Soper, B. (1995). A comparison of self-reported dream themes for high school and college students. *College Student Journal, 29,* 417–420.

Pottieger, A. E., Tressell, P. A., Inciardi, J. A., & Rosales, T. A. (1992). Cocaine use patterns and overdose. *Journal of Psychoactive Drugs, 24,* 399–410.

Powell, D. H., & Whitla, D. K. (1994, February). Normal cognitive aging: Toward empirical perspectives. *Current Directions in Psychological Science, 3,* 27–31.

Powell, L. H., Shaker, L. A., & Jones, B. A. (1993). Psychosocial predictors of mortality in 83 women with premature acute myocardial infarction. *Psychosomatic Medicine, 55,* 426–433.

Pratt, S. I., & Moreland, K. L. (1996). Introduction to treatment outcome: Historical perspectives and current issues. In S. I. Pfeiffer (Ed.), *Outcome assessment in residential treatment.* New York: Haworth Press.

Pressley, M. (1987). Are keyword method effects limited to slow presentation rates? An empirically based reply to Hall and Fuson (1986). *Journal of Educational Psychology, 79,* 333–335.

Pressman, M. R., & Orr, W. C. (1997). *Understanding sleep: The evaluation and treatment of sleep disorders.* Washington, DC: American Psychological Association.

Pribram, K. H. (1984). Emotion: A neurobehavioral analysis. In K. R. Scherer & P. Ekman (Eds.), *Approaches to emotion.* Hillsdale, NJ: Erlbaum.

Price, D. D. (2000, June 9). Psychological and neural mechanisms of the affective dimension of pain. *Science, 288,* 1769–1772.

Priester, J. R. & Petty, R. E. (1995). Source attributions and persuasion: Perceived honesty as a determinant of message scrutiny. *Personality and Social Psychology Bulletin, 21,* 637–654.

Prince, R. J., & Guastello, S. J. (1990). The Barnum effect in a computerized Rorschach interpretation system. *Journal of Personality, 124,* 217–222.

Pulvirenti, L., & Koob, G. F. (1994). Lisuride reduces intravenous cocaine self-administration in rats. *Pharmacology, Biochemistry and Behavior, 47,* 819–822.

Purves, D., Augustine, G. J., Fitzpatrick, D., Katz, L. C., LaMantia, A., & McNamara, J. O. (Eds.). (1997). *Neuroscience.* Sunderland, MA: Sinauer.

Putnam, F. W. (1995a). Development of dissociative disorders. In D. Cicchetti & D. J. Cohen (Eds.), *Developmental psychopathology: Vol. 2. Risk, disorder, and adaptation.* New York: Wiley.

Putnam, F. W. (1995b). Traumatic stress and pathological dissociation. In G. P. Chrousos, R. McCarty, et al. (Eds.), *Stress: Basic mechanisms and clinical implications.* New York: New York Academy of Sciences.

Quinn, M. (1990, January 29). Don't aim that pack at us. *Time,* p. 60.

Rachman, S., & deSilva, P. (1996). *Panic disorder.* Oxford, England: Oxford University Press.

Rachman, S., & Hodgson, R. (1980). *Obsessions and compulsions.* Englewood Cliffs, NJ: Prentice Hall.

Rakoff, V. M. (1995). Trauma and adolescent rites of initiation. In R. C. Marohn & S. C. Feinstein (Eds.), *Adolescent psychiatry: Developmental and clinical studies.* Hillsdale, NJ: Analytic Press.

Ramachandran, V. S. (1995). Filling in gaps in logic: Reply to Durgin et al. *Perception, 24,* 841–845.

Raskin, N. J., & Rogers, C. R. (1989). Person-centered therapy. In R. J. Corsini & D. Wedding (Eds.), *Current psychotherapies* (4th ed.). Itasca, IL: F. E. Peacock.

Ratcliff, R., & McKoon, G. (1989). Memory models, text processing, and cue-dependent retrieval. In H. L. Roediger III & F. I. M. Craik (Eds.), *Varieties of memory and consciousness: Essays in honour of Endel Tulving.* Hillsdale, NJ: Erlbaum.

Rau, H., Weitkunat, R., Brody, S., Buhrer, M., et al. (1996). Biofeedback of R-wave to pulse interval produces differential learning of blood pressure control. *Scandinavian Journal of Behaviour Therapy, 25,* 17–25.

Rawsthorne, L. J., & Elliot, A. J. (1999). Achievement goals and intrinsic motivation: A meta-analytic review. *Personality and Social Psychology Review, 3,* 326–344.

Ray, W. J. (2000). *Methods: Toward a science of behavior and experience* (6th ed.). Belmont, CA: Wadsworth.

Redding, G. M., & Hawley, E. (1993). Length illusion in fractional Müller-Lyer stimuli: An object-perception approach. *Perception, 22,* 819–828.

Rees, G., Frith, C. D., & Lavie, N. (1998). Modulating irrelevant motion perception by varying attentional load in an unrelated task. *Science, 278,* 1616–1619.

Reeves, R. A., Baker, G. A., Boyd, J. G., & Cialdini, R. B. (1991). The door-in-the-face technique: Reciprocal concessions vs. self-presentational explanations. *Journal of Social Behavior and Personality, 6,* 545–558.

Regan, P. C. (2000). Love relationships. In L. T. Szuchman & F. Muscarella (Eds.), *Psychological perspectives on human sexuality.* New York: Wiley.

Reichman, W. E., & Rabins, P. V. (1996). Schizophrenia and other psychotic disorders. In W. E. Reichman & P. R. Katz (Eds.),

Psychiatric care in the nursing home. New York: Oxford University Press.

Reisberg, D. (1997). *Cognition: Exploring the science of the mind.* New York: W. W. Norton.

Reisenzein, R. (1983). The Schachter theory of emotion: Two decades later. *Psychological Bulletin, 94,* 239–264.

Rescorla, R. A. (1988). Pavlovian conditioning: It's not what you think it is. *American Psychologist, 43,* 151–160.

Resnick, S. M. (1992). Positron emission tomography in psychiatric illness. *Current Directions in Psychological Science, 1,* 92–98.

Reyna, V. F. (1997). Conceptions of memory development with implications for reasoning and decision making. In R. Vasta (Ed.), *Annals of child development: A research annual* (Vol. 12, pp. 87–118). London: Kingsley.

Reynolds, R. I., & Takooshian, H. (1988, January). Where were you August 8, 1985? *Bulletin of the Psychonomic Society, 26,* 23–25.

Rhodes, N., & Wood, W. (1992). Self-esteem and intelligence affect influenceability: The mediating role of message reception. *Psychological Bulletin, 111,* 156–171.

Rhodewalt, F., & Fairfield, M. (1991). An alternative approach to Type A behavior and health: Psychological reactance and medical noncompliance. In M. J. Strube (Ed.), *Type A behavior.* Newbury Park, CA: Sage.

Rhue, J. W., Lynn, S. J., & Kirsch, I (Eds.). (1993). *Handbook of clinical hypnosis.* Washington, DC: American Psychological Association.

Ricciuti, H. N. (1993). Nutrition and mental development. *Current Directions in Psychological Science, 2,* 43–46.

Rice, G., Anderson, C., Risch, N., & Ebers, G. (1999, April 23). Male homosexuality: Absence of linkage to microsatellite markers at Xq28. *Science, 284,* 665–667.

Rice, M. L. (1989). Children's language acquisition. *American Psychologist, 44,* 149–156.

Rice, V. H. (Ed.). (2000). *Handbook of stress, coping and health.* Thousand Oaks, CA: Sage.

Rich, F. (1997, May 1). Harnisch's perfect pitch. *New York Times,* p. A35.

Richie, J. (1994, April). Paper presented at the annual meeting of the American Association for Cancer Research, San Francisco.

Rieder, R. O., Kaufmann, C. A., & Knowles, J. A. (1996). Genetics. In R. E. Hales & S. C. Yudofsky (Eds.), *The American Psychiatric Press synopsis of psychiatry.* Washington, DC: American Psychiatric Press, Inc.

Riefer, D. M., Keveri, M. K., & Kramer, D. L. F. (1995). Name that tune: Eliciting the tip-of-the-tongue experience using auditory stimuli. *Psychological Reports, 77,* 1379–1390.

Ringold, D. J. (1996). Social criticisms of target marketing: Process or product? In R. P. Hill (Ed.), *Marketing and consumer research in the public interest.* Thousand Oaks, CA: Sage.

Risch, N., & Merikangas, K. (1996, September 13). The future of genetic studies of complex human diseases. *Science, 273,* 1516–1517.

Risley, R. C., & Rescorla, R. A. (1972). Associations in higher order conditioning and sensory pre-conditioning. *Journal of Comparative and Physiological Psychology, 81,* 1–11.

Ritzler, B., & Rosenbaum, G. (1974). Proprioception in schizophrenics and normals: Effects of stimulus intensity and interstimulus interval. *Journal of Abnormal Psychology, 83,* 106–111.

Robbins, T. W. (1988). Arresting memory decline. *Nature, 336,* 207–208.

Roberts, S. M. (1995). Applicability of the goodness-of-fit hypothesis to coping with daily hassles. *Psychological Reports, 77,* 943–954.

Robertson, L. C., & Ivry, R. (2000). Hemispheric asymmetries: Attention to visual and auditory primitives. *Current Directions in Psychological Science, 9,* 59–63.

Robins, R. W., Gosling, S. D., & Craik, K. H. (1999). An empirical analysis of trends in psychology. *American Psychologist, 54,* 117–128.

Rock, A. (1999, January). Quitting time for smokers. *Money,* pp. 139–141.

Rodin, J. (1985). Insulin levels, hunger, and food intake: An example of feedback loops in body-weight regulation. *Health Psychology, 4,* 1–18.

Rodin, J. (1986, September 19). Aging and health: Effects of the sense of control. *Science, 233,* 1271–1276.

Roffwarg, H. P., Muzio, J. N., & Dement, W. C. (1996). Ontogenic development of the human sleep-dream cycle. *Science, 152,* 604–619.

Rogers, C. R. (1951). *Client-centered therapy,* Boston: Houghton-Mifflin.

Rogers, C. R. (1971). A theory of personality. In S. Maddi (Ed.), *Perspectives on personality.* Boston: Little, Brown.

Rogers, C. R. (1980). *A way of being.* Boston: Houghton Mifflin.

Rogers, P., & Eftimiades, M. (1995, July 24). Abner Louima. *People Weekly,* pp. 42–43.

Rogler, L. H. (1999). Methodological sources of cultural insensitivity in mental health research. *American Psychologist, 54,* 424–433.

Rokeach, M. (1971). Long-range experimental modification of values, attitudes, and behavior. *American Psychologist, 26,* 453–459.

Rolland, J. S., & Walsh, F. (1996). Family therapy: Systems approaches to assessment and treatment. In R. E. Hales & S. C. Yudofsky (Eds.), *The American Psychiatric Press synopsis of psychiatry.* Washington, DC: American Psychiatric Press.

Rolls, E. T. (1994). Neural processing related to feeding in primates. In C. R. Legg & D. A. Booth (Eds.). *Appetite: Neural and behavioural bases.* Oxford, England: Oxford University Press.

Root-Bernstein, R., & Root-Bernstein, M. (1999). *Sparks of genius: The thirteen thinking tools of the world's most creative people.* New York: Houghton Mifflin.

Rorschach, H. (1924). *Psychodiagnosis: A diagnostic test based on perception.* New York: Grune & Stratton.

Roseman, I. J., Wiest, C., & Swartz, T. S. (1994). Phenomenology, behaviors, and goals differentiate discrete emotions. *Journal of Personality and Social Psychology, 67,* 206–221.

Rosen, D. (1999, May 10). Dieting disorder: A physician's perspective. *Harvard Mental Health Newsletter,* p. 4.

Rosen, H. (2000). The creative evolution of the theoretical foundations for cognitive therapy. *Journal of Cognitive Psychotherapy, 14,* 123–134.

Rosenberg, D., & Bai, M. (1997, October 13). Drinking and dying. *Newsweek,* p. 69.

Rosenhan, D. L. (1973). On being sane in insane places. *Science, 179,* 250–258.

Rosenheck, R., Cramer, J., Xu, W., Thomas, J., Henderson, W., Frisman, L., Fye, C., &

Charney, D. (1997). A comparison of clozapine and haloperidol in hospitalized patients with refractory schizophrenia. *New England Journal of Medicine, 337,* 809–815.

Rosenman, R. H. (1990). Type A behavior pattern: A personal overview. *Journal of Social Behavior and Personality, 5,* 1–24.

Rosenman, R. H., Brand, R. J., Sholtz, R. I., & Friedman, M. (1976). Multivariate prediction of coronary heart disease during 8.5 year follow-up in the Western collaborative group study. *American Journal of Cardiology, 37,* 903–910.

Rosenstein, D. S., & Horowitz, H. A. (1996). Adolescent attachment and psychopathology. *Journal of Consulting and Clinical Psychology, 64,* 244–253.

Rosenthal, A. M. (1993, July 27). The torture continues. *New York Times,* p. A13.

Rosenthal, E. (1996, January 10). From Lives Begun in a Lab, Brave New Joy. *The New York Times,* A2, B8.

Rosenthal, E. (1999, December 9). China's chic wasitline: Convex to concave. *New York Times,* pp. A1, A4.

Rosenthal, L. H. (1997). *A new perspective on the relation between fear and persuasion: The application of dual-process models.* Unpublished doctoral dissertation, Dept. of Psychology. University of Massachusetts, Amherst.

Rosenthal, R. (1994). Science and ethics in conducting, analyzing, and reporting psychological research. *Psychological Science, 5,* 127–134.

Rosenzweig, M. R. (1999). Continuity and change in the development of psychology around the world. *American Psychologist, 54,* 252–259.

Rosnow, R. L., & Rosenthal, R. (1997). *Turn away influences that undermine scientific experiments.* New York: Freeman.

Rosnow, R. L., Rotheram-Borus, M. J., Ceci, S. J., Blanck, P. D., & Koocher, G. P. (1993). The institutional review board as a mirror of scientific and ethical standards. *American Psychologist, 48,* 821–826.

Ross, C. A. (1996). *Dissociative identity disorder: Diagnosis, clinical features, and treatment of multiple personality.* Somerset, NJ: Wiley.

Ross, C. A., Miller, S. D., Reagor, P., Bjornson, L., Fraser, G. A., & Anderson, G. (1990). Structured interview data on 102 cases of multiple personality disorder from four centers. *American Journal of Psychiatry, 147,* 596–601.

Ross, L. (1977). The intuitive psychologist and his shortcomings: Distortions in the attribution process. In L. Berkowitz (Ed.), *Advances in experimental social psychology* (Vol. 10, pp. 174–221). New York: Academic Press.

Ross, L., Greene, D., & House, P. (1977). The false consensus effect: An egocentric bias in social perception and attribution processes. *Journal of Experimental Social Psychology, 13,* 279–301.

Ross, L., & Nisbett, R. E. (1991). *The person and the situation.* New York: McGraw-Hill.

Ross, M., & Newby, I. R. (1996). Distinguishing memory from fantasy. *Psychological Inquiry, 7,* 173–177.

Roth, A., & Fonagy, P. (1996). *What works for whom? A critical review of psychotherapy research.* New York: Guilford Press.

Rothblum, E. D. (1990). Women and weight: Fad and fiction. *Journal of Psychology, 124,* 5–24.

Roush, W. (1995, September 1). Can "resetting" hormonal rhythms treat illness? *Science, 269,* 1220–1221.

Routtenberg, A., & Lindy, J. (1965). Effects of the availability of rewarding septal and hypothalamic stimulation on bar pressing for food under conditions of deprivation. *Journal of Comparative and Physiological Psychology, 60,* 158–161.

Rovee-Collier, C. (1993). The capacity for long-term memory in infancy. *Current Directions in Psychological Science, 2,* 130–135.

Rowe, J. B., Toni, I., Josephs, O., Frackowiak, R. S. J., & Passingham, R. E. (2000, June 2). The prefrontal cortex: Response selection or maintenance within working memory? *Science, 288,* 1656–1660.

Rowley, S. J., Sellers, R. M., Chavous, T. M., & Smith, M. A. (1998). The relationship between racial identity and self-esteem in African American college and high school students. *Journal of Personality and Social Psychology, 74,* 715–724.

Rozin, P. (1977). The significance of learning mechanisms in food selection: Some biology, psychology and sociology of science. In L. M. Barker, M. R. Best, & M. Donijan (Eds.), *Learning mechanisms in food selection.* Waco, TX: Baylor University Press.

Rozin, P. (1990). The importance of social factors in understanding the acquisition of food habits. In E. D. Capaldi & T. L. Powley (Eds.), *Taste, experience, and feeding.* Washington, DC: American Psychological Association.

Rubenstein, C. (1982, July). Psychology's fruit flies. *Psychology Today,* pp. 83–84.

Rubin, D. C. (1985, September). The subtle deceiver: Recalling our past. *Psychology Today,* pp. 39–46.

Rubin, D. C. (1995). *Memory in oral traditions.* New York: Oxford University Press.

Rubin, D. C. (1999). *Remembering our past: Studies in autobiographical memory.* New York: Cambridge University Press.

Ruble, D. N., Fleming, A. S., Hackel, L. S., & Stangor, C. (1988). Changes in the marital relationship during the transition to first-time motherhood: Effects of violated expectations concerning division of household labor. *Journal of Personality and Social Psychology, 55,* 78–87.

Runco, M. A., & Sakamoto, S. O. (1993). Reaching creatively gifted students through their learning styles. In R. M. Milgram, R. S. Dunn, & G. E. Price (Eds.), *Teaching and counseling gifted and talented adolescents: An international learning style perspective.* Westport, CT: Praeger/Greenwood.

Ruppin, E., Reggia, J. A., & Horn, D. (1996). Pathogenesis of schizophrenic delusions and hallucinations: A neural model. *Schizophrenia Bulletin, 22,* 105–123.

Russell, J. A. (1991). Culture and the categorization of emotion. *Psychological Bulletin, 110,* 426–450.

Russell, J. A., & Sato, K. (1995). Comparing emotion words between languages. *Journal of Cross Cultural Psychology, 26,* 384–391.

Russo, N. (1981). In L. T. Benjamin, Jr., & K. D. Lowman (Eds.), *Activities handbook for the teaching of psychology.* Washington, DC: American Psychological Association.

Russo, R., & Parkin, A. J. (1993). Age differences in implicit memory: More apparent than real. *Memory & Cognition, 21,* 73–80.

Ryan, R. M., & Deci, E. L. (1996). When paradigms clash: Comments on Cameron and Pierce's claim that rewards do not undermine intrinsic motivation. *Review of Educational Research, 66,* 33–38.

Saarni, C. (1999). *The development of emotional competence.* New York: Guilford Press.

Sacco, W. P., & Beck, A. T. (1995). Cognitive theory and therapy. In E. E. Beckham & W. R. Leber (Eds.), *Handbook of depression* (2nd ed.). New York: Guilford Press.

Sack, R. L., Lewy, A. J., White, D. M., Singer, C. M., Fireman, M. J., & Vandiver, R. (1990). Morning vs. evening light treatment for winter depression: Evidence that the therapeutic effects of light are mediated by circadian phase shift. *Archives of General Psychiatry, 47,* 343–351.

Sackheim, H. A., Luber, B., Katzman, G. P., et al. (1996, September). The effects of electroconvulsive therapy on quantitative electroencephalograms. *Archives of General Psychiatry, 53,* 814–824.

Saggino, A. (2000). The Big Three or the Big Five? A replication study. *Personality and Individual Differences, 28,* 879–886.

Saigh, P. A. (1996). Posttraumatic stress disorder among children and adolescents: An introduction. *Journal of School Psychology, 34,* 103–105.

Salovey, P., Rothman, A. J., Detweiler, J. B., & Steward, W. T. (2000). Emotional states and physical health. *American Psychologist, 55,* 110–121.

Salovey, P., & Sluyter, D. J. (Eds.). (1997). *Emotional development and emotional intelligence.* New York: Basic Books.

Salthouse, T. A. (1996, July). The processing-speed theory of adult age differences in cognition. *Psychological Review, 103,* 403–428.

Sams, M., Hari, R., Rif, J., & Knuutila, J. (1993). The human auditory memory trace persists about 10 sec: Neuromagnetic evidence. *Journal of Cognitive Neuroscience, 5,* 363–370.

Samuda, R. J. (1998). *Psychological testing of American minorities: Issues and consequences.* Thousand Oaks, CA: Sage.

Sandoval, J., Frisby, C. L., Geisinger, K. F., Scheuneman, J. D., & Grenier, J. R. (Eds.). (1998). *Test interpretation and diversity: Achieving equity in assessment.* Washington, DC: American Psychological Association.

Sanes, J. N., Donoghue, J. P., Thangaraj, V., Edelman, R. R., & Warach, S. (1995, June 23). Shared neural substrates controlling hand movements in human motor cortex. *Science, 268,* 1775–1777.

Sangrador, J. L., & Yela, C. (2000). "What is beautiful is loved": Physical attractiveness in love relationships in a representative sample. *Social Behavior and Personality, 28,* 207–218.

Sansone, C., & Harackiewicz, J. M. (Eds.). (2000). *Intrinsic and extrinsic motivation.* Orlando, FL: Academic Press.

Sapolsky, R. M. (1996, August 9). Why stress is bad for your brain. *Science, 273,* 749–750.

Saudino, K. J. (1997). Moving beyond the heritability question: New directions in behavioral genetic studies of personality. *Current Directions in Psychological Science, 6,* 86–90.

Saudino, K. J., & Plomin, R. (1996). Personality and behavioral genetics: Where have we been and where are we going? *Journal of Research in Personality, 30,* 335–347.

Savage-Rumbaugh, E. S., Murphy, J., Sevcik, R. A., Williams, S., Brakke, K., & Rumbaugh, D. M. (1993). Language comprehension in ape and child. *Monographs of the Society for Research in Child Development, 58* (3, 4).

Savage-Rumbaugh, S., & Brakke, K. E. (1996). Animal language: Methodological and interpretive issues. In M. Bekoff & D. Jamieson (Eds.), *Readings in animal cognition.* Cambridge, MA: MIT Press.

Saxe, L. (1994). Detection of deception: Polygraphy and integrity tests. *Current Directions in Psychological Science, 3,* 69–73.

Sayette, M. A. (1993). An appraisal disruption model of alcohol's effects on stress responses in social drinkers. *Psychological Bulletin, 114,* 459–476.

Saywitz, K., & Goodman, G. (1990). [Unpublished study reported in D. Goleman (1990, November 6). Doubts rise on children as witnesses. *New York Times,* pp. C1, C6.]

Scarr, S. (1992). Developmental theories for the 1990s: Development and individual differences. *Child Development, 63,* 1–19.

Scarr, S. (1993). Genes, experience, and development. In D. Magnusson, P. Jules, & M. Casaer (Eds.), *Longitudinal research on individual development: Present status and future perspectives.* Cambridge, England: Cambridge University Press.

Scarr, S. (1996). Behavior genetics and socialization theories of intelligence: Truce and reconciliation. In R. J. Sternberg & E. Grigorenko (Eds.), *Intelligence, heredity, and environment.* New York: Cambridge University Press.

Scarr, S., & Weinberg, R. A. (1976). I.Q. test performance of black children adopted by white families. *American Psychologist, 31,* 726–739.

Schab, F. R. (1991). Odor memory: Taking stock. *Psychological Bulletin, 109,* 242–251.

Schab, F. R., & Crowder, R. G. (Eds.). (1995). *Memory for odors.* Mahwah, NJ: Erlbaum.

Schacter, D. L. (1994). Implicit knowledge: New perspectives on unconscious processes. In O. Sporns & G. Tononi (Eds.), *Selectionism and the brain. International review of neurobiology, Vol. 37.* San Diego: Academic Press.

Schacter, D. L. (1995). Implicit memory: A new frontier for cognitive neuroscience. In M. S. Gazzaniga (Ed.), *The cognitive neurosciences.* Cambridge, MA: MIT Press.

Schacter, D. L. (1998, April 3). Memory and awareness. *Science, 280,* 59–60.

Schacter, D. L. (1999a). *The cognitive neuropsychology of false memories.* Philadelphia: Psychology Press.

Schacter, D. L., Chiu, C.-Y. P., & Ochsner, K. N. (1993). Implicit memory: A selective review. *Annual Review of Neuroscience, 16,* 159–182.

Schacter, D. L., Wagner, A. D., & Buckner, R. L. (2000). Memory systems of 1999. In E. Tulving, F. I. Craik, I. M. Fergus, et al. (Eds.). *The Oxford handbook of memory.* New York: Oxford University Press.

Schachter, S. (1971). Some extraordinary facts about obese humans and rats. *American Psychologist, 26,* 129–144.

Schachter, S., & Singer, J. E. (1962). Cognitive, social, and physiological determinants of emotional state. *Psychological Review, 69,* 379–399.

Schaie, K. W. (1991). Developmental designs revisited. In S. H. Cohen & H. W. Reese (Eds.), *Life-span developmental psychology: Methodological innovations.* Hillsdale, NJ: Erlbaum.

Schaie, K. W. (1993). The Seattle longitudinal studies of adult intelligence. *Current Directions in Psychological Science, 2,* 171–175.

Schaie, K. W. (1994). The course of adult intellectual development. *American Psychologist, 49,* 304–313.

Schaller, M., Asp, C. H., Rosell, M. C., & Heim, S. J. (1996). Training in statistical reasoning inhibits the formation of erroneous group stereotypes. *Personality and Social Psychology Bulletin, 22,* 829–844.

Schapira, A. H. V. (1999). Clinical review: Parkinson's disease. *British Medical Journal, 318,* 311–314.

Scharf, M. (1999, October 1). A new option for insomnia. *HealthNews,* p. 4.

Schedlowski, M., & Tewes, U. (Eds.) (1999). *Psychoneuroimmunology: An interdisciplinary introduction.* New York: Plenum Press.

Scheff, T. J. (1999). *Being mentally ill: A sociological theory* (3rd ed.). Hawthrone, NY: Aldine de Gruyter.

Scheier, M. F., & Carver, C. S. (1992). Effects of optimism on psychological and physical well-being: Theoretical overview and empirical update. [Special issue: Cognitive perspectives in health psychology.] *Cognitive Therapy and Research, 16,* 201–228.

Scherer, K. R. (1984). Les motions: Fonctions et composantes. [Emotions: Functions and components.] *Cahiers de psychologie cognitive, 4,* 9–39.

Scherer, K. R. (1994). Emotion serves to decouple stimulus and response. In P. Ekman & R. J. Davidson (Eds.), *The nature of emotion: Fundamental questions.* New York: Oxford University Press.

Schickedanz, J. A., Shickedanz, D. I., & Forsyth, P. D. (1982). *Toward understanding children.* Boston: Little, Brown.

Schkade, D. A., & Kahneman, D. (1998). Does living in California make people happy? A focusing illusion in judgments of life satisfaction. *Psychological Science, 9,* 340–346.

Schmidt, D. (1999). Stretched dream science: The essential contribution of long-term naturalistic studies. *Dreaming, 9,* 43–69.

Schneider, E. L., & Rowe, J. W. (Eds.). (1996). *Handbook of the biology of aging* (4th ed.). San Diego: Academic Press.

Schneider, K. S. (1996, June 3). Mission impossible. *People,* pp. 65–74.

Schneider, K. S., & Gold, T. (1998, December 7). After the tears. *People,* pp. 126–136.

Schoen, L. M. (1996). Mnemopoly: Board games and mnemonics. *Teaching of Psychology, 23,* 30–32.

Schretlen, D., Pearlson, G. D., Anthony, J. C., Aylward, E. H., Augustine, A. M., Davis, A., & Barta, P. (2000). Elucidating the contributions of processing speed, executive ability, and frontal lobe volume to normal age-related differences in fluid intelligence. *Journal of the International Neuropsychological Society, 6,* 52–61.

Schwarz, N., Bless, H., Strack, F., Klumpp, G.,et al. (1991). Ease of retrieval as information: Another look at the availability heuristic. *Journal of Personality and Social Psychology, 61,* 195–202.

Schwartz, B.L., Travis, D. M., Castro, A. M., & Smith, S. M. (2000). The phenomenology of real and illusory tip-of-the-tongue states. *Memory & Cognition, 28,* 18–27.

Searleman, A., & Herrmann, D. (1994). *Memory from a broader perspective.* New York: McGraw-Hill.

Sears, D. O. (1986). College sophomores in the laboratory: Influences of a narrow data base on social psychology's view of human nature. *Journal of Personality and Social Psychology, 51,* 515–530.

Sears, R. R. (1977). Sources of life satisfaction of the Terman gifted men. *American Psychologist, 32,* 119–128.

Sebel, P. S., Bonke, B., & Winograd, E. (Eds.). (1993). *Memory and awareness in anesthesia.* Englewood Cliffs, NJ: Prentice Hall.

Seeley, R., Stephens, T., & Tate, P. *Anatomy & physiology,* 5th Edition. New York: McGraw-Hill.

Seeman, P. (1993). Schizophrenia as a brain disease: The dopamine receptor story. *Archives of Neurology, 50,* 1093–1095.

Segal, N. L. (1993). Twin, sibling, and adoption methods: Tests of evolutionary hypotheses. *American Psychologist, 48,* 943–956.

Segall, M. H., Campbell, D. T., & Herskovits, M. J. (1966). *The influence of culture on visual perception.* New York: Bobbs-Merrill.

Seidenberg, M. S., & Pettito, L. A. (1987). Communication, symbolic communication, and language: Comment on Savage-Rumbaugh, McDonald, Sevcik, Hopkins, & Rupert (1986). *Journal of Experimental Psychology: General, 116,* 279–287.

Seligman, M. E. P. (1975). *Helplessness: On depression, development, and death.* San Francisco: Freeman.

Seligman, M. E. P. (1995, December). The effectiveness of psychotherapy: The *Consumer Reports* study. *American Psychologist, 50,* 965–974.

Seligman, M. E. P. (1996, October). Science as an ally of practice. *American Psychologist, 51,* 1072–1079.

Selikowitz, M. (1997). *Down syndrome: The facts* (2nd ed.). New York: Oxford University Press.

Selkoe, D. J. (1997, January 31). Alzheimer's disease: Genotypes, phenotype, and treatments. *Science, 275,* 630–631.

Sells, R. (1994, August). *Homosexuality study.* Paper presented at the annual meeting of the American Statistical Association, Toronto.

Selsky, A. (1997, February 16). African males face circumcision rite. *Boston Globe,* p. C7.

Seltzer, L. (1986). *Paradoxical strategies in psychotherapy.* New York: Wiley.

Selye, H. (1976). *The stress of life.* New York: McGraw-Hill.

Selye, H. (1993). History of the stress concept. In L. Goldberger & S. Breznitz (Eds.), *Handbook of stress: Theoretical and clinical aspects* (2nd ed.). New York: Free Press.

Seppa, N. (1996, May). A multicultural guide to less spanking and yelling. *APA Monitor,* p. 37.

Seppa, N. (1997, June). Children's TV remains steeped in violence. *APA Monitor,* p. 36.

Serok, S. (2000). *Innovative applications of gestalt therapy.* New York: Krieger.

Sesser, S. (1993, September 13). Opium war redux. *New Yorker,* pp. 78–89.

Seyfarth, R. M., & Cheney, D. L. (1992, December). Meaning and mind in monkeys (vocalizations and intent). *Scientific American, 267,* 122–128.

Seyfarth, R. M., & Cheney, D. L. (1996). Inside the mind of a monkey. In M. Bekoff & D. Jamieson (Eds.), *Readings in animal cognition.* Cambridge, MA: MIT Press.

Shadish, W. R., Cook, T. D., & Campbell, D. T. (2002). *Experimental and quasi-experimental designs for generalized causal inference.* New York: Houghton Mifflin.

Shapiro, A. P. (1996). *Hypertension and stress: A unified concept.* Mahwah, NJ: Erlbaum.

Shapiro, Y., & Gabbard, G. O. (1994). A reconsideration of altruism from an evolutionary and psychodynamic perspective. *Ethics and Behavior, 4,* 23–42.

Sharma, J., Angelucci, A., & Sur, M. (2000). Induction of visual orientation modules in auditory cortex. *Nature, 404,* 841–847.

Sharma, S., Ghosh, S. N., & Spielberger, C. D. (1995). Anxiety, anger expression and chronic gastric ulcer. *Psychological Studies, 40,* 187–191.

Sharps, M. J., Price, J. L., & Williams, J. K. (1994). Spatial cognition and gender: Instructional and stimulus influences on mental image rotation performance. *Psychology of Women Quarterly, 18,* 413–425.

Shatz, C. J. (1992, September). The developing brain. *Scientific American,* pp. 60–67.

Shaughnessy, J. J., Zechmeister, E. B., & Zechmeister, J. S. (2000). *Research methods in psychology* (5th ed.). New York: McGraw-Hill.

Shawver, L. (1995). *And the flag was still there: Straight people, gay people, and sexuality in the U.S. military.* New York: Harrington Park Press/Haworth Press.

Shaywitz, B. A., Shaywitz, S. E., Pugh, K. R., Constable, R. T., et al. (1995). Sex differences in the functional organization of the brain for language. *Nature, 373,* 607–609.

Shear, J. (Ed.). (1997). *Explaining consciousness: The hard problem.* Cambridge, MA: MIT Press.

Sheehan, S. (1982). *Is there no place on earth for me?* Boston: Houghton Mifflin.

Shelton, R. C., Keller, M. B., Gelenberg, A., Dunner, D. L., Hirschfeld, R., Thase, M. E., Russell, J., Lydiard, B., Crits-Cristoph, P., Gallop, R., Todd, L., Hellerstein, D., Goodnick, P., Keitner, G., Stahl, S. M., & Halbreich, U. (2001, April 18). Effectiveness of St. John's Wort in major depression. *Journal of the American Medical Association, 285,* 1978–1986.

Shepard, R., & Metzler, J. (1971). Mental rotation of three dimensional objects. *Science, 171,* 701–703.

Shepard, R. N., Metzler, J., Bisiach, E., Luzzati, C., Kosslyn, S. M., Thompson, W. L., Kim, I., & Alpert, N. M. (2000). Part IV: Imagery. In M. S. Gazzaniga et al. (Eds.), *Cognitive neuroscience: A reader.* Malden, MA: Blackwell.

Sherman, J. W., & Klein, S. B. (1994). Development and representation of personality impressions. *Journal of Personality and Social Psychology, 67,* 972–983.

Sherman, M. (1999, July 13). The man who vanished into his past. *New York Times,* p. F8.

Shiels, P. G., Kind, A. J., Campbell, K. H., Waddington, D., Wilmut, I., Colman, A., & Schnieke, A. E. (1999, May 27). Analysis of telomere lengths in cloned sheep [letter]. *Nature, 399,* 316–317.

Shier, D., Butler, J., & Lewis, R. (2000). *Hole's essentials of human anatomy and physiology* (7th ed.). New York: McGraw-Hill.

Shnek, Z. M., Foley, F. W., LaRocca, N. G., Smith, C. R., et al. (1995). Psychological predictors of depression in multiple sclerosis. *Journal of Neurologic Rehabilitation, 9,* 15–23.

Shotland, R. L. (1985, June). When bystanders just stand by. *Psychology Today,* pp. 50–55.

Shoulder, K. (1992, August). The empire returns. *Sky,* pp. 40–44.

Shrique, C. L., & Annable, L. (1995). Tardive dyskinesia. In C. L. Shriqui & H. A. Nasrallah (Eds.), *Contemporary issues in the treatment of schizophrenia.* Washington, DC: American Psychiatric Press.

Shuchter, S. R., Downs, N., & Zisook, S. (1996). *Biologically informed psychotherapy for depression.* New York: Guilford Press.

Shurkin, J. N. (1992). *Terman's kids: The groundbreaking study of how the gifted grow up.* Boston: Little, Brown.

Shweder, R. A. (1994). "You're not sick, you're just in love": Emotion as an interpretive system. In P. Ekman & R. J. Davidson (Eds.), *The nature of emotion: Fundamental questions.* New York: Oxford University Press.

Sibicky, M. E., Schroeder, D. A., & Dovidio, J. F. (1995). Empathy and helping: Considering the consequences of intervention. *Basic and Applied Social Psychology, 16,* 435–453.

Siegel, B. (1996b). *The world of the autistic child: Understanding and treating autistic spectrum disorders.* New York: Oxford University Press.

Siegel, J. M. (1990). Stressful life events and use of physician services among the elderly: The moderating role of pet ownership. *Journal of Personality and Social Psychology, 58,* 1081–1086.

Siegel, J. M. (1993). Companion animals: In sickness and in health. *Journal of Social Issues, 49,* 157–167.

Siegel, J. M. (2000, January). Narcolepsy. *Scientific American,* pp. 76–81.

Siegel, R. K. (1989). *Life in pursuit of artificial paradise.* New York: Dutton.

Siegler, R. S. (1994). Cognitive variability: A key to understanding cognitive development. *Current Directions in Psychological Science, 3,* 1–5.

Siegler, R. S. (1998). *Children's thinking* (3rd ed.). Upper Saddle River, NJ: Prentice Hall.

Sigman, M. (1995). Nutrition and child development: More food for thought. *Current Directions in Psychological Science, 4,* 52–55.

Silver, L. B. (1999). *Attention-deficit/hyperactivity disorder: A clinical guide to diagnosis and treatment for health and mental health professionals.* Washington, DC: American Psychiatric Press.

Silver, R. L., & Wortman, C. B. (1980). Coping with undesirable life events. In J. Barber & M. E. P. Seligman (Eds.), *Human helplessness: Theory and application.* New York: Academic Press.

Silverman, K., Evans, S. M., Strain, E. C., & Griffiths, R. R. (1992, October 15). Withdrawal syndrome after the double-blind cessation of caffeine consumption. *New England Journal of Medicine, 327,* 1109–1114.

Silverman, K., Mumford, G. K., & Griffiths, R. R. (1994). Enhancing caffeine reinforcement by behavioral requirements following drug ingestion. *Psychopharmacology, 114,* 424–432.

Silverstein, B., Perdue, L., Peterson, B., Vogel, L., et al. (1986). Possible causes of the thin standard of bodily attractiveness for women. *International Journal of Eating Disorders, 5,* 907–916.

Simmons, R., & Blyth, D. (1987). *Moving into adolescence.* New York: Aldine de Gruyter.

Simonoff, E., Bolton, P., & Rutter, M. (1996). Mental retardation: Genetic findings, clinical implications and research agenda. *Journal of Child Psychology and Psychiatry and Allied Disciplines, 37,* 259–280.

Simpson, G. E., & Yinger, J. M. (1985). *Racial and cultural minorities: An analysis of prejudice and discrimination* (5th ed.). New York: Harper & Row.

Simpson, J. A., & Harris, B. A. (1994). Interpersonal attraction. In A. L. Weber & J. H.

Harvey (Eds.), *Perspectives on close relationships.* Boston: Allyn & Bacon.

Sinclair, J. D. (1990). Drugs to decrease alcohol drinking. *Annals of Medicine, 22,* 357–362.

Singelis, T., Choo, P., & Hatfield, E. (1995). Love schemas and romantic love. *Journal of Social Behavior and Personality, 10,* 15–36.

Singer, J. L. (1975). *The inner world of daydreaming.* New York: Harper & Row.

Sizemore, C. C. (1989). *A mind of my own: The woman who was known as Eve tells the story of her triumph over multiple personality disorder.* New York: Morrow.

Skinner, B. F. (1957). *Verbal behavior.* New York: Appleton-Century-Crofts.

Slater, A. (1996). The organization of visual perception in early infancy. In F. Vital-Durand, J. Atkinson, & O. J. Braddick (Eds.), *Infant vision.* Oxford, England: Oxford University Press.

Slater, A., Mattock, A., & Brown, E. (1990). Size constancy at birth: Newborn infants' responses to retinal and real size, *Journal of Experimental Child Psychology, 49,* 314–322.

Sleek, S. (1995, November). Online therapy services raise ethical question. *APA Monitor,* p. 9.

Sleek, S. (1998, June). Psychologists debate merits of the polygraph. *APA Monitor,* p. 30.

Sloan, E. P., Hauri, P., Bootzin, R., Morin, C., et al. (1993). The nuts and bolts of behavioral therapy for insomnia. *Journal of Psychosomatic Research, 37* (Suppl), 19–37.

Slovic, P., Fischoff, B., & Lichenstein, S. (1976). Cognitive processes and societal risk taking. In J. S. Carroll & J. W. Payne (Eds.), *Cognition and social behavior.* Mahwah, NJ: Erlbaum.

Smith, E. (1988, May). Fighting cancerous feelings. *Psychology Today,* pp. 22–23.

Smith, E. E. (2000). Neural bases of human working memory. *Current Directions in Psychological Science, 9,* 45–49.

Smith, E. E., & Jonides, J. (1999, March 12). Storage and executive processes in the frontal lobes. *Science, 283,* 1657–1661.

Smith, K. A., Williams, C., & Cowen, P. J. (2000). Impaired regulation of brain serotonin function during dieting in women recovered from depression. *British Journal of Psychiatry, 176,* 72–75.

Smith, M. L., Glass, G. V., & Miller, T. J. (1980). *The benefits of psychotherapy.* Baltimore: Johns Hopkins.

Smith, M. V. (1996). Linguistic relativity: On hypotheses and confusions. *Communication and Cognition, 29,* 65–90.

Smith, M., & Lin, K. M. (1996). Gender and ethnic differences in the pharmacogenetics of psychotropics. In M. F. Jensvold, U. Halbreich, & J. A. Hamilton, (Eds.), *Psychopharmacology and women: Sex, gender, and hormones.* Washington, DC: American Psychiatric Press.

Smith, S. M. (1994). Frustrated feelings of imminent recall: On the tip of the tongue. In J. Metcalfe & A. P. Shimamura (Eds.), *Metacognition: Knowing about knowing.* Cambridge, MA: MIT Press.

Snyder, C. R. (1999). *Coping: The psychology of what works.* New York: Oxford University Press.

Snyder, F. (1970). The phenomenology of dreaming. In L. Madow & L. H. Snow (Eds.), *The psychodynamic implications of the physiological studies on dreams.* Springfield, IL: Thomas.

Sohn, D. (1996). Publication bias and the evaluation of psychotherapy efficacy in reviews of the

research literature. *Clinical Psychology Review, 16,* 147–156.

Solcova, I., & Tomanek, P. (1994). Daily stress coping strategies: An effect of hardiness. *Studia Psychologica, 36,* 390–392.

Solomon, C. (1993, December 21). Having nightmares? Chances are, they are about your job. *Wall Street Journal,* pp. A1, A4.

Solomon, J. (1996, May 20). Breaking the silence. *Newsweek,* pp. 20–21.

Sommer, B. B., & Sommer, R. (1997). *A practical guide to behavioral research: Tools and techniques* (4th ed.). New York: Oxford University Press.

Sommerhof, G. (2000). *Understanding consciousness: Its function and brain processes.* Thousand Oaks, CA: Sage.

Sorrentino, R. M., Hewitt, E. C., & Raso-Knott, P. A. (1992). Risk-taking in games of chance and skill: Informational and affective influences on choice behavior. *Journal of Personality and Social Psychology, 62,* 522–533.

Spangler, W. D. (1992). Validity of questionnaire and TAT measures of need for achievement: Two meta-analyses. *Psychological Bulletin, 112,* 140–154.

Spanos, N. P., Burgess, C. A., Roncon, V., Wallace-Capretta, S., et al. (1993). Surreptitiously observed hypnotic responding in simulators and in skill-trained and untrained high hypnotizables. *Journal of Personality and Social Psychology, 65,* 391–398.

Spearman, C. (1927). *The abilities of man.* London: Macmillan.

Spence, J. T. (1985, August). *Achievement American style: The rewards and costs of individualism.* Presidential address, 93rd annual convention of the American Psychological Association, Los Angeles.

Spence, M. J., & DeCasper, A. J. (1982, March). *Human fetuses perceive maternal speech.* Paper presented at the meeting of the International Conference on Infant Studies, Austin, TX.

Sperling, G. (1960). The information available in brief visual presentation. *Psychology Monographs, 74* (whole no. 498).

Sperry, R. (1982). Some effects of disconnecting the cerebral hemispheres. *Science, 217,* 1223–1226.

Spiegel, D. (1993). Social support: How friends, family, and groups can help. In D. Goleman & J. Gurin (Eds.), *Mind-body medicine.* Yonkers, NY: Consumer Reports Books.

Spiegel, D. (1996a, July). Cancer and depression. *British Journal of Psychiatry, 168,* 109–116.

Spiegel, D. (1996b). Dissociative disorders. In R. E. Hales & S. C. Yudofsky (Eds.), *The American Psychiatric Press synopsis of psychiatry.* Washington, DC: American Psychiatric Press, Inc.

Spiegel, D. (1996c). Hypnosis. In R. E. Hales & S. C. Yudofsky (Eds.), *The American Psychiatric Press synopsis of psychiatry.* Washington, DC: American Psychiatric Press.

Spiegel, D. (Ed.). (1999). *Efficacy and cost-effectiveness of psychotherapy.* New York: American Psychiatric Press.

Spiegel, D., & Cardena, E. (1991). Disintegrated experience: The dissociative disorders revisited. *Journal of Abnormal Psychology, 100,* 366–378.

Spiegel, D., Frischholz, E. J., Fleiss, J. L., & Spiegel, H. (1993). Predictors of smoking abstinence following a single-session restructuring intervention with self-hypnosis.

and development of language. Mahwah, NJ: Erlbaum.

Velmans, M. (2000). *Understanding consciousness.* New York: Psychology Press.

Verhaeghen, P., Marcoen, A., & Goossens, L. (1992). Improving memory performance in the aged through mnemonic training: A meta-analytic study. *Psychology and Aging, 7,* 242–251.

Vernon, P. A., Jang, K. L., Harris, J. A., & McCarthy, J. M. (1997). Environmental predictors of personality differences: A twin and sibling study. *Journal of Personality and Social Psychology, 72,* 177–183.

Victor, S. B., & Fish, M. C. (1995). Lesbian mothers and the children: A review for school psychologists. *School Psychology Review, 24,* 456–479.

Vihman, M. M. (1996). *Phonological development: The origins of language in the child.* London, England: Blackwell.

Vital-Durand, F., Atkinson, J., & Braddick, O. J. (Eds.). (1996). *Infant vision.* Oxford, England: Oxford University Press.

Vogel, G. (13 October, 2000). New brain cells prompt new theory of depression. *Science, 290,* 258–259.

von Restorff, H. (1933). Über die wirking von bereichsbildungen im Spurenfeld. In W. Kohler & H. von Restorff, *Analyse von vorgangen in Spurenfeld: I. Psychologische forschung, 18,* 299–342.

Vygotsky, L. S. (1926/1997). *Educational psychology.* Delray Beach, FL: St. Lucie Press.

Wachtel, P. L., & Messer, S. B. (Eds.). (1997). *Theories of psychotherapy: Origins and evolution.* Washington, DC: American Psychological Association.

Wagner, D. A. (1981). Culture and memory development. In H. C. Triandis & A. Heron (Eds.), *Handbook of cross-cultural psychology: Vol. 4. Developmental psychology.* Boston: Allyn & Bacon.

Wagner, E. F., & Atkins, J. H. (2000). Smoking among teenage girls. *Journal of Child and Adolescent Substance Abuse, 9,* 93–110.

Wagner, R. K. (1997). Intelligence, training, and employment. *American Psychologist, 52,* 1059–1069.

Wagner, R. K. (2000). Practical intelligence. In R. J. Sternberg (Ed.), *Handbook of intelligence.* New York: Cambridge University Press.

Waid, W. M., & Orne, M. T. (1982). The physiological detection of deception. *American Scientist, 70,* 402–409.

Walcott, D. M. (2000). Repressed memory still lacks scientific reliability. *Journal of the American Academy of Psychiatry and the Law, 28,* 243–244.

Waldrop, M. W. (1989, September 29). NIDA aims to fight drugs with drugs. *Science, 245,* 1443–1444.

Wall, P. D., & Melzack, R. (1989). *Textbook of pain* (2nd ed.). New York: Churchill Livingstone.

Wallace, R. K., & Benson, H. (1972, February). The physiology of meditation. *Scientific American,* pp. 84–90.

Wallerstein, J. S., Lewis, J., Blakeslee, S., & Lewis, J. (2000). *The unexpected legacy of divorce.* New York: Hyperion.

Wallis, C., & Willwerth, J. (1992, July 6). Schizophrenia: A new drug brings patients back to life. *Time,* pp. 52–57.

Walsh, B. T., & Devlin, M. J. (1998, May 29). Eating disorders: Progress and problems. *Science, 280,* 1387–1390.

Walsh, D. M., Liggett, C., Baxter, D., & Allen, J. M. (1995). A double-blind investigation of the hypoalgesic effects of transcutaneous electrical nerve stimulation upon experimentally induced ischaemic pain. *Pain, 61,* 39–45.

Walter, H. J., Vaughan, R. D., & Wynder, E. L. (1994). Primary prevention of cancer among children: Changes in cigarette smoking and diet after six years of intervention. In A. Steptoe & J. Wardle (Eds.), *Psychosocial processes and health: A reader.* Cambridge, England: Cambridge University Press.

Ward, T. (1997, April 15). Resolving Gulf War syndrome. *HealthNews,* p. 4.

Ward, T. B., Smith, S. M., & Vaid, J. (1997). *Creative thought: An investigation of conceptual structures and processes.* Washington, DC: American Psychological Association.

Ward, W. C., Kogan, N., & Pankove, E. (1972). Incentive effects in children's creativity. *Child Development, 43,* 669–677.

Wark, G. R., & Krebs, D. L. (1996). Gender and dilemma differences in real-life moral judgement. *Developmental Psychology, 32,* 220–230.

Wasserman, E. A., & Miller, R. R. (1997). What's elementary about associative learning? *Annual Review of Psychology, 48,* 573–607.

Waters, E., Hamilton, C. E., & Weinfield, N. S. (2000). The stability of attachment security from infancy to adolescence and early adulthood: General introduction. *Child Development, 71,* 678–683.

Waters, M. (2000, July/August). Bringing minorities into the research fold. *Monitor on Psychology,* pp. 44–47.

Watson, J. B. (1924). *Behaviorism.* New York: Norton.

Watson, J. B., & Rayner, R. (1920). Conditioned emotional reactions. *Journal of Experimental Psychology, 3,* 1–14.

Watson, M., Haviland, J. S., Greer, S., Davidson, J., & Bliss, J. M. (1999, October 16). Influence of psychological response on survival in breast cancer: A population-based cohort study. *Lancet, 354,* 1331–1336.

Webb, W. B. (1992). *Sleep: The gentle tyrant* (2nd ed.). Boston: Anker.

Wechsler, D. (1975). Intelligence defined and undefined. *American Psychologist, 30,* 135–139.

Wechsler, H., Davenport, A., Dowdall, G., Moeykens, B., & Castillo, S. (1994). Health and behavioral consequences of binge drinking in college: A national survey of students at 140 campuses. *Journal of the American Medical Association, 272,* 1672–1677.

Wechsler, H., Kelley, K., Weitzman, E. R., San Giovanni, J. P., & Seibring, M. (2000). What colleges are doing about student binge drinking: A national survey of college administrators. *Journal of American College Health, 48,* 219–226.

Week, D., & James, J. (1995). *Eccentrics: A study of sanity and strangeness.* New York: Villard Books.

Weinberg, M. S., Williams, C. J., & Pryor, D. W. (1991, February 27). Personal communication. Indiana University, Bloomington.

Weinberg, R. A., Scarr, S., & Waldman, I. D. (1992). The Minnesota Transracial Adoption Study: A follow-up of IQ test performance at adolescence. *Intelligence, 16,* 117–135.

Weiner, B. (1985a). *Human motivation.* New York: Springer-Verlag.

Weiner, B. (1985b). "Spontaneous" casual thinking. *Psychological Bulletin, 97,* 74–84.

Weiner, B. A., & Wettstein, R. (1993). *Legal issues in mental health care.* New York: Plenum Press.

Weiner, I. B. (1998). *Principles of Rorschach interpretation.* Mahwah, NJ: Erlbaum.

Weiner, J. (2000, February 7). Curing the incurable. *New Yorker,* pp. 64–73.

Weintraub, M. (1976). Intelligent noncompliance and capricious compliance. In L. Lasagna (Ed.), *Patient compliance.* Mt. Kisco, NY: Futura.

Weisberg, H. F., Krosnick, J. A., & Bowen, B. D. (1996). *An introduction to survey research, polling, and data analysis.* Newbury Park, CA: Sage.

Weisman, A., Lopez, S. R., Karno, M., & Jenkins, J. (1993). An attributional analysis of expressed emotion in Mexican-American families with schizophrenia. *Journal of Abnormal Psychology, 102,* 601–606.

Weiss, A. S. (1991). The measurement of self-actualization: The quest for the test may be as challenging as the search for the self. *Journal of Social Behavior and Personality, 6,* 265–290.

Weissman, M. M., Bland, R. C., Canino, G. J., et al. (1996, July 24–31). Cross-national epidemiology of major depression and bipolar disorder. *Journal of the American Medical Association, 276,* 293–299.

Weissman, M. W., & Olfson, M. (1995, August 11). Depression in women: Implications for health care research. *Science, 269,* 799–801.

Weitzenhoffer, A. M. (1999). *The practice of hypnotism* (2nd ed.). New York: Wiley.

Wells, G. L., Malpass, R. S., Lindsay, R. C. L., Fisher, R. P., Turtle, J. W., & Fulero, S. M. (2000). From the lab to the police station: A successful application of eyewitness research. *American Psychologist, 55,* 581–598.

Wertheimer, M. (1923). Untersuchungen zur Lehre von der Gestalt. II. *Psychol. Forsch., 5,* 301–350. In Beardsley and M. Wertheimer (Eds.), *Readings in perception* (New York: Van Nostrand, 1958).

West, R. L. (1995). Compensatory strategies for age-associated memory impairment. In A. D. Baddeley, B. A. Wilson, & F. N. Watts (Eds.), *Handbook of memory disorders.* Chichester, England: Wiley.

Westen, D. (1998). The scientific legacy of Sigmund Freud: Toward a psychodynamically informed psychological science. *Psychological Bulletin, 124,* 333–371.

Westen, D., & Gabbard, G. O. (1999). Psychoanalytic approaches to personality. In L. A. Pervin & O. P. John (Eds.), *Handbook of personality: Theory and research* (2nd ed.). New York: Guilford Press.

Westera, D. A., & Bennett, L. R. (1994). Population-focused research: A broad-based survey of teens' attitudes, beliefs, and behaviours. *International Journal of Nursing Studies, 31,* 521–531.

Wetter, D. W., Fiore, M. C., Gritz, E. R., Lando, H. A., Stitzer, M. L., Hasselblad, V., & Baker, T. B. (1998). The Agency for Health Care Policy and Research. Smoking cessation clinical practice guideline: Findings and implications for psychologists. *American Psychologist, 53,* 657–669.

Whaley, B. B. (Ed.). (2000). *Explaining illness: Research, theory, and strategies.* Mahwah, NJ: Erlbaum.

Whitbourne, S. K. (1999). Physical changes. In J. C. Cavanaugh & S. K. Whitbourne (Eds.). *Gerontology: An interdisciplinary perspective.* New York: Oxford University Press.

Whitbourne, S. K., & Wills, K. (1993). Psychological issues in institutional care of the aged. In S. B. Goldsmith (Ed.), *Long-term care.* Gaithersburg, MD: Aspen Press.

Whitbourne, S. K., Zuschlag, M. K., Elliot, L. B., & Waterman, A. S. (1992). Psychosocial development in adulthood: A 22-year sequential study. *Journal of Personality and Social Psychology, 63,* 260–271.

White, P. A. (1992). The anthropomorphic machine: Causal order in nature and the world view of common sense. *British Journal of Psychology, 83,* 61–96.

Whorf, B. L. (1956). *Language, thought, and reality.* New York: Wiley.

Wickelgren, I. (1998a, September 11). The cerebellum: The brain's engine of agility. *Science, 281,* 1588–1590.

Wickelgren, I. (1998b, June 26). Teaching the brain to take drugs. *Science, 280,* 2045–2047.

Wickens, C. D. (1984). *Engineering psychology and human performance.* Columbus, OH: Merrill.

Widmeyer, W. N., & Loy, J. W. (1988). When you're hot, you're hot! Warm-cold effects in first impressions of persons and teaching effectiveness. *Journal of Educational Psychology, 80,* 118–121.

Wiebe, D. J. (1991). Hardiness and stress moderation: A test of proposed mechanisms. *Journal of Personality and Social Psychology, 60,* 89–99.

Wiehe, V. R., & Richards, A. L. (1995). *Intimate betrayal: Understanding and responding to the trauma of acquaintance rape.* Thousand Oaks, CA: Sage.

Wielgosz, A. T., & Nolan, R. P. (2000). Biobehavioral factors in the context of ischemic cardiovascular diseases. *Journal of Psychosomatic Research, 48,* 339–345.

Wigfield, A., & Eccles, J. S. (2000). Expectancy-value theory of achievement motivation. *Contemporary Educational Psychology, 25,* 68–81.

Wiggins, J. S. (1997). In defense of traits. In R. Hogan, J. Johnson, & S. Briggs, (Eds.), *Handbook of personality psychology.* Orlando, FL: Academic Press.

Wileman, R., & Wileman, B. (1995). Towards balancing power in domestic violence relationships. *Australian and New Zealand Journal of Family Therapy, 16,* 165–176.

Wilgoren, J. (1999, October 22). Quality day care, early, is tied to achievements as an adult. *New York Times,* p. A16.

Williams, J. E., Paton, C. C., Siegler, I. C., Eigenbrodt, M. L., Nieto, F. J., & Tyroler, H. A. (2000). Anger proneness predicts coronary heart disease risk: Prospective analysis from the Atherosclerosis Risk in Communities (ARIC) study. *Circulation, 101,* 2034–2039.

Williams, J. W., Mulrow, C. D., Chiquette, E., Noel, P. H., Aguilar, C., & Cornell, J. (2000). A systematic review of newer pharmacotherapies for depression in adults: Evidence report summary. *Annals of Internal Medicine, 132,* 743–756.

Williams, S. W., & McCullers, J. C. (1983). Personal factors related to typicalness of career and success in active professional women. *Psychology of Women Quarterly, 7,* 343–357.

Willis, S. L., & Nesselroade, C. S. (1990). Long-term effects of fluid ability training in old-old age. *Developmental Psychology, 26,* 905–910.

Willis, S. L., & Schaie, K. W. (1994). In C. B. Fisher & R. M. Lerner (Eds.), *Applied developmental psychology.* New York: McGraw-Hill.

Wilson, G. T., & Agras, W. S. (1992). The future of behavior therapy. *Psychotherapy, 29,* 39–43.

Wilson, J. P., & Keane, T. M. (Eds.). (1996). *Assessing psychological trauma and PTSD.* New York: Guilford Press.

Windholz, G. (1997, September). Ivan P. Pavlov: An overview of his life and psychological work. *American Psychologist, 52,* 941–946.

Winner, E. (1997). *Gifted children: Myths and realities.* New York: Basic Books.

Winner, E. (2000). The origins and ends of giftedness. *American Psychologist, 55,* 159–169.

Winningham, R. G., Hyman, I. E., Jr., & Dinnel, D. L. (2000). Flashbulb memories? The effects of when the initial memory report was obtained. *Memory, 8,* 209–216.

Winson, J. (1990, November). The meaning of dreams. *Scientific American,* pp. 86–96.

Winter, D. G. (1973). *The power motive.* New York: Free Press.

Winter, D. G. (1987). Leader appeal, leader performance, and the motive profile of leaders and followers: A study of American presidents and elections. *Journal of Personality and Social Psychology, 52,* 196–202.

Winter, D. G. (1988). The power motive in women—and men. *Journal of Personality and Social Psychology, 54,* 510–519.

Witelson, S. F. (1995). Neuroanatomical bases of hemispheric functional specialization in the human brain: Possible developmental factors. In F. L. Kitterle (Ed.), *Hemispheric communication: Mechanisms and models.* Hillsdale, NJ: Erlbaum.

Wixted, J. T., & Ebbesen, E. B. (1991). On the form of forgetting. *Psychological Science, 2,* 409–415.

Wolpe, J. (1990). *The practice of behavior therapy.* Boston: Allyn & Bacon.

Wolters, G. (1995). Het geheugen. Functie, structuur en processen (Memory: Its function, structure, and processes). *Psycholoog, 30,* 369–374.

Wonderlic. (2000, March 7). Wonderlic Personnel Test. Available on the World Wide Web at *http://www.wonderlic.com/wpt.html.*

Wong, M. M., & Csikszentmihalyi, M. (1991). Affiliation motivation and daily experience: Some issues on gender differences. *Journal of Personality and Social Psychology, 60,* 154–164.

Wood, J. M., & Bootzin, R. (1990). The prevalence of nightmares and their independence from anxiety. *Journal of Abnormal Psychology, 99,* 64–68.

Wood, W., Lundgren, S., Ouellette, J. A., Busceme, S., & Blackston, T. (1994). Minority influence: A meta-analytic review of social influence processes. *Psychological Bulletin, 115,* 323–345.

Wood, W., & Stagner, B. (1994). Why are some people easier to influence than others? In S. Savitt & T. C. Brock (Eds.), *Persuasion: Psychological insights and perspectives.* Boston: Allyn & Bacon.

Woodruff-Pak, D. S. (1999). New directions for a classical paradigm: Human eyeblink conditioning. *Psychological Science, 10,* 1–7.

Woods, S. C., Schwartz, M. W., Baskin, D. G., & Seeley, R. J. (2000). Food intake and the regulation of body weight. *Annual Review of Psychology, 51,* 255–277.

Woods, S. C., Seeley, R. J., Porte, D., Jr., & Schwartz, M. W. (1998, May 29). Signals that regulate food intake and energy homeostasis. *Science, 280,* 1378–1383.

Woods, S. J. (2000). Prevalence and patterns of posttraumatic stress disorder in abused and postabused women. *Issues in Mental Health Nursing, 21,* 309–324.

Wozniak, R. H., & Fischer, K. W. (Eds.). (1993). *Development in context: Acting and thinking in specific environments.* Hillsdale, NJ: Erlbaum.

Wright, J. H., & Beck, A. T. (1996). Cognitive therapy. In R. E. Hales & S. C. Yudofsky (Eds.), *The American Psychiatric Press synopsis of psychiatry.* Washington, DC: American Psychiatric Press.

Wright, S. J. (1999). Human embryonic stem-cell research: Science and ethics. *American Scientist, 87,* 352–361.

Wynn, K. (1995). Infants possess a system of numerical knowledge. *Current Directions in Psychological Science, 4,* 172–177.

Wynn, K. (2000). Addition and subtraction by human infants. In D. Muir & A. Slater (Eds.), *Infant development: The essential readings.* Malden, MA: Blackwell.

Wyshak, G., & Barsky, A. (1995). Satisfaction with and effectiveness of medical care in relation to anxiety and depression: Patient and physician ratings compared. *General Hospital Psychiatry, 17,* 108–114.

Yalom, I. D. (1997). *The Yalom reader: On writing, living, and practicing psychotherapy.* New York: Basic Books.

Yan, H., Kinzler, K. W., & Vogelstein, B. (2000, September 15). Genetic testing—present and future. *Science, 289,* 1890–1892.

Yee, A. H., Fairchild, H. H., Weizmann, F., & Wyatt, G. E. (1993). Addressing psychology's problem with race. *American Psychologist, 48,* 1132–1140.

Yenerall, J. D. (1995). College socialization and attitudes of college students toward the elderly. *Gerontology and Geriatrics Education, 15,* 37–48.

Yost, W. A. (1992). Auditory perception and sound source determination. *Current Directions in Psychological Science, 1,* 179–184.

Young, M. W. (2000, March). The tick-tock of the biological clock. *Scientific American,* 64–71.

Yuskauskas, A. (1992). Conflict in the developmental disabilities profession: Perspectives on treatment approaches, ethics, and paradigms. *Dissertation Abstracts International, 53,* 1870.

Zajonc, R. B. (1985). Emotion and facial efference: A theory reclaimed. *Science, 228,* 15–21.

Zajonc, R. B., & McIntosh, D. N. (1992). Emotions research: Some promising questions and some questionable promises. *Psychological Science, 3,* 70–74.

Zamarra, J. W., Schneider, R. H., Besseghini, I., Robinson, D. K., & Salerno, J. W. (1996). Usefulness of the transcendental meditation program in the treatment of patients with coronary artery disease. *American Journal of Cardiology, 77,* 867–870.

Zautra, A. J., Reich, J. W., & Guarnaccia, C. A. (1990). Some everyday life consequences of disability and bereavement for older adults. *Journal of Personality and Social Psychology, 59,* 550–561.

Zebrowitz-McArthur, L. (1988). Person perception in cross-cultural perspective. In M. H. Bond (Ed.), *The cross-cultural challenge to social psychology.* Newbury Park, CA: Sage.

Zeidner, M., & Endler, N. S. (Eds.). (1996). *Handbook of coping: Theory, research, applications.* New York: Wiley.

Zevon, M., & Corn, B. (1990). Paper presented at the annual meeting of the American Psychological Association, Boston.

Zhdanova, I. V., Lynch, H. J., & Wurtman, R. J. (1997). Melatonin: A sleep-promoting hormone. *Sleep, 20,* 899–907.

Zito, J. M. (1993). *Psychotherapeutic drug manual* (3rd ed., rev.). New York: Wiley.

Zuckerman, M. (1978). The search for high sensation. *Psychology Today,* pp. 30–46.

Zuckerman, M. (1991). One person's stress is another person's pleasure. In C. D. Spielberger, I. G. Sarason, Z. Kulczar, & G. L. Van Heck (Eds.), *Stress and emotion: Anxiety, anger, and curiosity.* New York: Hemisphere.

Zuckerman, M. (1994). *Behavioral expression and biosocial expression of sensation seeking.* Cambridge, England: Cambridge University Press.

Zuger, A. (1998, June 2). The "other" drug problem: Forgetting to take them. *New York Times,* pp. C1, C5.

Acknowledgments

Chapter 1

Cartoon by Roz Chast, page 21: © The New Yorker Collection 1998 Roz Chast from cartoonbank.com. All Rights Reserved. **Cartoon, page 23:** © The New Yorker Collection 1993 J. B. Handelsman from cartoonbank.com. All Rights Reserved.

Chapter 2

Figure 2-1: From K. Van de Graaff, *Human Anatomy,* 2000. Copyright © 2000 by the McGraw-Hill Companies, Inc. Reproduced with permission of the McGraw-Hill Companies. **Figure 2-4a:** From S. S. Mader, *Biology,* 2000. Copyright © 2000 by the McGraw-Hill Companies, Inc. Reproduced with permission of the McGraw-Hill Companies. **Figure 2-4b:** From G. B. Johnson, *The Living World,* 2000. Copyright © 2000 by the McGraw-Hill Companies, Inc. Reproduced with permission of the McGraw-Hill Companies. **Figure 2-6:** From E. Loftus & C. Wortmann, *Psychology,* 1989. Copyright © 1989 by the McGraw-Hill Companies, Inc. Reproduced with permission of the McGraw-Hill Companies. **Figure 2-9:** From R. Seeley et al., *Anatomy and Physiology.* Copyright © by the McGraw-Hill Companies, Inc. Reproduced with permission of the McGraw-Hill Companies. **Figure 2-10:** From G. B. Johnson, *The Living World,* 2000. Copyright © 2000 by the McGraw-Hill Companies, Inc. Reproduced with permission of the McGraw-Hill Companies. **Figure 2-11a:** From A. Schneider and B. Tarshih, *Elements of Physiological Psychology.* Copyright © by the McGraw-Hill Companies, Inc. Reproduced with permission of the McGraw-Hill Companies. **Figure 2-15:** From S. S. Mader, *Biology,* 2000. Copyright © 2000 by the McGraw-Hill Companies, Inc. Reproduced with permission of the McGraw-Hill Companies. **Table 2-4:** From http://www.ncbi.nlm.hih.gov/genemap99/map.cgi?CHR=5--U.S. Government maintained website.

Chapter 3

Figure 3-1: From R. Seeley et al., *Anatomy and Physiology.* Copyright © by the McGraw-Hill Companies, Inc. Reproduced with permission of the McGraw-Hill Companies. **Figure 3-3:** From D. Shier, et al., *Hole's Human Anatomy and Physiology,* Copyright © 2000 by the McGraw-Hill Companies, Inc. Reproduced with permission of the McGraw-Hill Companies. **Figure 3-5:** From S. S. Mader, *Biology,* 2000. Copyright © 2000 by the McGraw-Hill Companies, Inc. Reproduced with permission of the McGraw-Hill Companies. **Figure 3-8:** From R. Seeley et al., *Anatomy and Physiology.* Copyright © by the McGraw-Hill Companies, Inc. Reproduced with permission of the McGraw-Hill Companies. **Figure 3-9:** From R. Seeley et al., *Anatomy and Physiology.* Copyright © by the McGraw-Hill Companies, Inc. Reproduced with permission of the McGraw-Hill Companies. **Figure 3-11a&c:** From *Mind Sights* by R. C. Shepard, © 1990 by W. H. Freeman. Reprinted by permission of Henry Holt and Company LLC. **Figure 3-14:** Adapted from Figure 7.38, *Sensation and Perception,* by E. Goldstein, 1984, Wadsworth Group. **Figure 3-15:** From I. Biederman, "Higher Level Vision," in D. N. Osherson, S. Kosslyn and J. Hollerbach (eds.). *An Invitation to Cognitive Science: Visual Cognition and Action,* 1990. Copyright © 1990 MIT Press. Reprinted with permission. **Figure 3-17:** From S. Coren and L. Ward, *Sensation and Perception,* 3rd edition. Copyright © 1989 by John Wiley & Sons, Inc. This material is used by permission of John Wiley & Sons, Inc. **Figure 3-18:** From S. Coren and L. Ward, *Sensation and Perception,* 3rd edition. Copyright © 1989 by John Wiley & Sons, Inc. This material is used by permission of John Wiley & Sons, Inc. **Figure 3-21:** From Gregory & Gombich, *Illusions in Nature and Art,* 1973. **Table 3-1:** Copyright © 1998 Better Hearing Institute, Washington, DC. All Rights Reserved. **Cartoon by Ian Falconer, page 100:** © The New Yorker Collection 1996 Ian Falconer from cartoonbank.com. All Rights Reserved.

Chapter 4

Figure 4-1: From *Sleep* by J. Allen Hobson, © 1989, 1995 by Scientific American Library. Reprinted by permission of Henry Holt and Company, LLC. **Figure 4-3:** From *Secrets of Sleep* by Alexander Borbely. English translation copyright © 1986 by Basic Books, Inc. Copyright © 1984 by Deutsche Verlag-Anstalt GmbH, Stuttgart. Reprinted by permission of Basic Books, a member of Perseus Books, L.L.C. **Figure 4-4:** Reprinted with permission from H. P. Roffwarg, J. N. Munzio and W. C. Dement, "Ontogenic Development of the Human Sleep-Dream Cycle," *Science,* 152, 1996, pp. 604–619. Copyright 1996 American Association for the Advancement of Science. **Figure 4-5:** Dr. Allen R. Braun, N.I.D.C.D., N.I.H. **Figure 4-6:** From W. C. Dement, in D. F. Dinges and Broughton (eds.), *Sleep and Alertness: Chronobiological, Behavioral, and Medical Aspects of Napping,* 1989. Reprinted with permission of Lippincott, Williams and Wilkins Publishers. **Figure 4-7:** From *The Relaxation Response* by Herbert Benson, M.D., with Miriam Z. Klipper. Copyright © 1975 by William Morrow & Company, Inc. Reprinted by permission of HarperCollins Publishers, Inc. **Figure 4-8:** Monitoring the Future Study, 1999. University of Michigan. **Figure 4-9:** From S. S. Mader, *Biology,* 2000. Copyright © 2000 by the McGraw-Hill Companies, Inc. Reproduced with permission of the McGraw-Hill Companies. **Figure 4-10:** From Blakeslee, "Levels of Caffeine in Various Foods," *New York Times,* August 7, 1991. **Figure 4-11:** H. Wechsler, et al., 2000, *Student Survey on Binge Drinking,* Harvard University. **Cartoon by Mischa Richter, page 130:** © The New Yorker Collection 1993 Mischa Richter from cartoonbank.com. All Rights Reserved.

Chapter 5

Figure 5-5: E. C. Tolman and C. H. Honzik, 1930, *Introduction and Removal of Reward and Maze Performance in Rats,* University of California Publications in Psychology, 4, 257–275. **Cartoon by Tom Cheney, page 158:** © The New Yorker Collection 1993 Tom Cheney from cartoonbank.com. All Rights Reserved. **Cartoon by Gahan Wilson, page 168:** © The New Yorker Collection 1995 Gahan Wilson from cartoonbank.com. All Rights Reserved.

Chapter 6

Figure 6-2: Figure from "Human Memory: A Proposed System and Its Control Processes," by R. C. Atkinson and R. M. Shiffrin, from *The Psychology of Learning and Motivation: Advances in Research and Theory,* Volume 2, edited by K. W. Spence and J. T. Spence, copyright © 1968 by Academic Press, reproduced by permission of the publisher. **Figure 6-3:** From A. D. deGroot, "Perception and Memory Versus Thought: Some Old Ideas and Recent Findings," in B. Kleinmuntz, (ed.), *Problem Solving: Research, Method and Theory.* Copyright © 1966 John Wiley & Sons, Inc. This material is used by permission of John Wiley & Sons, Inc. **Figure 6-4:** Adapted from S. E. Gathercole and A. D. Baddeley, 1993, *Working Memory and Language Processing,* Taylor and Francis, Inc. **Figure 6-6:** Figure from "Retrieval Times from Semantic Memory," by A. M. Collins and M. R. Quillian in *Journal of Verbal Learning and Verbal Behavior,* Volume 8, 240–247. Copyright © 1969 by Academic Press. Reproduced by permission of the publisher. **Figure 6-9:** From D. C. Rubin, "The Subtle Deceiver Recalling," *Psychology Today,* September 1995. Reprinted with permission from *Psychology Today* Magazine. Copyright © 1995 Sussex Publishers, Inc. **Figure 6-10:** Figure from "Reconstruction of Automobile Destruction, " by E. F. Loftus and J. C. Palmer in *Journal of Verbal Learning and Verbal Behavior,* Volume 13, 585–589. Copyright © 1974 by Academic Press. Reproduced by permission of the publisher. **Figure 6-11:** From H. P. Bahrick, L. K. Hall, and S. A. Berger, "Accuracy and Distortion in Memory for High School Grades, " *Psychological Science,* 7, 1996, 265–269. Reprinted with permission of Blackwell Publishers. **Figure 6-13:** Figure from R. S. Nickerson and M. J. Adams, *Cognitive Psychology,* Volume 11, page 297. Copyright © 1979 by Academic Press. Reproduced by permission of the publisher. **Figure 6-15:** Courtesy of Dr. Steven E. Peterson, Washington University. **Figure 6-16:** From K. Van De Graaff, *Human Anatomy.* Copyright © by the McGraw-Hill Companies, Inc. Reproduced with permission of the McGraw-Hill Companies. **Cartoon by Roz Chast, page 187:** © The New Yorker Collection 1994 Roz Chast from cartoonbank.com. All Rights Reserved. **Cartoon by Mick Stevens, page 201:** © The New Yorker Collection 1998 Mick Stevens from cartoonbank.com. All Rights Reserved.

Chapter 7

Figure 7-1: Reprinted with permission from R. Shepard and J. Metzler, "Mental Rotation of Three Dimensional Objects," *Science,* 171, pp. 701–703, 1971. Copyright © 1971 American Association for the Advancement of Science. **Figure 7-8:** Data from "A Neural Basis for General Intelligence," by Duncan, *Science,* 289, July 21, 2000, p. 399. **Figure 7-9:** Adaptation of sample items from *Wechsler Intelligence Scales for Children (WISC-III).* The Psychological Corporation. **Figure 7-10:** Reprinted with permission of Wonderlic, Inc., Libertyville, Illinois. **Figure 7-11:** From Robert J. Sternberg, and Richard K. Wagner (eds.), *Practical Intelligence:*

Nature and Origins of Competence in the Everyday World, 1986. Reprinted with permission of Cambridge University Press. **Figure 7-12:** Reprinted with permission from R. J. Sternberg, "The Holey Grail of General Intelligence," *Science,* 289, pp. 399–401, 2000. Copyright © 2000 American Association for the Advancement of Science. **Figure 7-13:** Adapted from "Familial Studies of Intelligence: A Review, " by T. J. Bouchard and M. McGue, *Science,* 212, 1981, p. 1055–1059. **Cartoon by James Stevenson, page 227:** © The New Yorker Collection 1989 James Stevenson from cartoonbank.com. All Rights Reserved. **Cartoon by Roz Chast, page 232:** © The New Yorker Collection 1998 Roz Chast from cartoonbank.com. All Rights Reserved. **Cartoon by W. B. Park, page 235:** © The New Yorker Collection 1983 W. B. Park from cartoonbank.com. All Rights Reserved.

Chapter 8

Table 8-1: From M. Zuckerman, "The Search for High Sensation," *Psychology Today,* February 1978. Reprinted with permission from *Psychology Today* Magazine, Copyright © 1978 Sussex Publishers, Inc. **Figure 8-1:** From A. Maslow, *Motivation and Personality, 3/e,* Copyright © 1970. Reproduced by permission of Pearson Education, Inc., Upper Saddle River, New Jersey. **Figure 8-3:** From K. W. Fischer, P. R. Shaver and P. Carnochan, "How Emotions Develop and How They Organize Development," *Cognition and Emotion,* Vol. 4. Copyright © 1990 by Psychology Press Ltd. Reprinted by permission of Psychology Press Ltd., Hove, UK. **Cartoon by Michael Maslin, page 258:** © The New Yorker Collection 1999 Michael Maslin from cartoonbank.com. All Rights Reserved.

Chapter 9

Figure 9-2: Adapted from Frankenburg, et al., 1992, "The Denver II: A Major Revision and Restandardization of the Denver Developmental Screening Test," *Pediatrics,* 89, 91–97. **Figure 9-4:** Adapted from W. J. Robbins, *Growth,* 1929. Yale University Press. **Figure 9-6:** From Judith A. Schickedanz, et al., *Understanding Children and Adolescents, Fourth Edition.* Copyright © 2001 by Allyn & Bacon. Reprinted by permission. **Figure 9-7:** Adapted from F. N. Dempster, "Memory Span: Sources for Individual and Developmental Differences," *Psychological Bulletin,* 89, 63–100. **Table 9-6:** From L. Kohlberg, "State and Sequence: The Cognitive-Developmental Approach to Socialization." In D. Goslin (ed.) *Handbook of Socialization Theory and Research,* 1969. Reprinted with permission of David Goslin. **Figure 9-9:** From K. W. Schaie, "The Course of Adult Intellectual Development," *American Psychologist,* 49, 304–313. Copyright © 1984 by the American Psychological Association. Reprinted with permission. **Cartoon by Lee Lorenz, page 297:** © The New Yorker Collection 1985 Lee Lorenz from cartoonbank.com. All Rights Reserved. **Cartoon by Roz Chast, page 312:** © The New Yorker Collection 1993 Roz Chast from cartoonbank.com. All Rights Reserved. **Cartoon by Roz Chast, page 321:** © The New Yorker Collection 1993 Roz Chast from cartoonbank.com. All Rights Reserved.

Chapter 10

Figure 10-2: From Cattell, Eber & Tatsuoka, *Handbook for the 16PF.* Copyright © 1970 by the Institute for Personality and Ability Testing. Printed with permission. **Figure 10-3:** From H. J. Eysenck, "Bio-

logical Dimensions of Personality," in L. A. Pervin ed., *Handbook of Personality: Theory and Research.* Copyright © Guilford Publications, Inc. Reprinted with permission. **Figure 10-5:** From Tellegen, et al., "Personality Similarity in Twins Reared Apart and Together," *Journal of Personality and Social Psychology,* 54, pp. 1031–1039, 1989. Copyright © 1988 by the American Psychological Association. Reprinted with permission. **Figure 10-7:** Based on R. P. Halgin and S. K. Whitbourne, *Abnormal Psychology,* 1994, Harcourt Brace, and Minnesota *Multiphasic Personality Inventory* 2, University of Minnesota. **Figure 10-8:** From L. B. Alloy, N. S. Jackson and J. Acocella, *Abnormal Psychology* 8th ed., 1999. Copyright © 1999 The McGraw-Hill Companies, Inc. Reprinted with permission of The McGraw-Hill Companies Inc. **Table 10-3:** From L. A. Pervin ed., *Handbook of Personality: Theory & Research.* Copyright © Guilford Publications, Inc. Reprinted with permission. **Cartoon by Sidney Harris, page 329:** Copyright © by Sidney Harris. **Cartoon by Robert Mankoff, page 343:** © The New Yorker Collection 1991 Robert Mankoff from cartoonbank.com. All Rights Reserved.

Chapter 11

Figure 11-1: Adapted from Baum, A., "Behavioral, Biological and Environmental Interactions in Disease Processes," In S. Blumenthal, K. Matthews, and S. Weiss (eds.), *New Research Frontiers in Behavioral Medicine: Proceedings of the National Conference,* NIH Publications, 1994. **Figure 11-2:** Reprinted with permission from Elsevier Science, *The Lancet,* 1985, Vol. 750. **Figure 11-3:** *Morbidity and Mortality Weekly Report,* July 9, 1993. Center for Disease Control. **Figure 11-4:** US Department of Agriculture, 1998. **Figure 11-6:** From F. M. Andrews and S. B. Withey, *Social Indicators of Well-Being: Americans' Perceptions of Life Quality.* Copyright © 1976 Kluwer Academic/Plenum Publishers. Reprinted with permission. **Table 11-1:** From S. Cohen, T. Kamarck and R. Mermelstein, "A Global Measure of Perceived Stress," *Journal of Health and Social Behavior,* 24. Copyright © American Sociological Association. Reprinted with permission. **Table 11-2:** From Jenkins, Zyzsndki & Rosenman, "Coronary-Prone Behavior: One Pattern or Several?" *Psychosomatic Medicine,* 40, 25–43, 1979. Reprinted with permission of Lippincott, Williams & Wilkins. **Quote, page 357:** From A. L. Kelly, "For Employed Moms, the Pennacle of Stress Comes After Work Ends," *New York Times,* June 13, 1999. Copyright © 1999 by the New York Times Co. Reprinted with permission. **Quote, page 367:** From P. Jaret, "Mind Over Malady," *Health,* November/December 1992, p. 87. Reprinted with permission of Peter Jaret. © 1992. **Cartoon by Edward Koren, page 365:** © The New Yorker Collection 1995 Edward Koren from cartoonbank.com. All Rights Reserved.

Chapter 12

Table 12-4: Personal communication with W. Hill, 1992. Public Affairs Network Coordinator for the American Psychiatric Association. **Figure 12-2:** From Jamison, "The Number of Pieces Written by Composer Robert Schumann," *New York Times,* October 10, 1993. Copyright © 1993 by the New York Times Co. Reprinted by permission. **Table 12-6:** From *Schizophrenia Genesis: The Origins of Madness* by I. I. Gottesman. © 1991 by W. H. Freeman. Reprinted by permission of Henry Holt and Company, LLC. **Quote, page 383:** From *Wall Street*

Journal, Eastern Edition by A. Bennett. Copyright © 1992 Dow Jones & Co., Inc. Reproduced by permission of Dow Jones & Co., Inc. via Copyright Clearance Center. **Quote, page 390:** From M. M. Antony, T. A. Brown, and D. H. Barlow, "Current Perspectives on Pain and Panic Disorder," *Current Directions in Psychological Science,* 1, 1992, page 79. Reprinted with permission of Blackwell Publishers. **Quote, pages 399–400:** Excerpt from *Is There No Place on Earth For Me?* By Susan Sheehan. Copyright © 1982 by Susan Sheehan. This material originally appeared in slightly different form in *The New Yorker,* Spring 1981. Reprinted by permission of Houghton Mifflin Company. All rights reserved. **Quote, page 404:** Excerpt from *Abnormal Psychology,* 1st Edition, by M. Duke and S. Nowicki. Wadsworth Group, a division of Thomson Learning, 1979. **Cartoon by Arnie Levin, page 387:** © The New Yorker Collection 2000 Arnie Levin from cartoonbank.com. All Rights Reserved.

Chapter 13

Figure 13-2: Smith, Mary Lee, Gene V. Glass, and Thomas I. Miller, *The Benefits of Psychotherapy,* Copyright 1980 The Johns Hopkins University Press. Reprinted by permission of The Johns Hopkins University Press. **Figure 13-3:** Copyright © 1995 by Consumers Union of U.S., Inc. Yonkers, NY 10703-1057, a nonprofit organization. Reprinted with permission from the November 1995 issue of *Consumer Reports* for educational purposes only. No commercial use or photocopying permitted. To learn more about Consumers Union, log onto www.ConsumerReports.org. **Figure 13-4:** From D. Mischoulon, "Antidepressants: Choices and Controversy," *Health News,* Copyright © 2000 Massachusetts Medical Society. All rights reserved. **Figure 13-5:** From Howard, et al., "The Changing Face of American Psychology: A Report from the Committee on Employment and Human Resources," *American Psychologist,* 41, pp. 1311–1327, 1986. Copyright © 1986 by the American Psychological Association. Reprinted with permission. **Table 13-2:** Reprinted by permission of Dr. Herbert Benson, Beth Israel Deaconess Medical Center, Boston, Massachusetts. **Quotes, p. 418, 430:** From D. Sue, D. Sue and S. Sue, *Understanding Abnormal Behavior,* Third Edition. Copyright © 1990 by Houghton Mifflin Company. Used with permission. **Cartoon by Donald Reilly, page 423:** © The New Yorker Collection 1994 Donald Reilly from cartoonbank.com. All Rights Reserved. **Cartoon by Gahan Wilson, page 436:** © The New Yorker Collection 1994 Gahan Wilson from cartoonbank.com. All Rights Reserved.

Chapter 14

Figure 14-3: Adapted from Anderson, Krull & Weiner, "Explanations: Processes and Consequences," in Higgins & Kruglanski (eds.), *Social Psychology: Handbook of Basic Principles,* 1996, p. 274. **Figure 14-6:** From M. B. Parlee, "The Friendship Bond," *Psychology Today,* October 1979. Reprinted with permission from *Psychology Today* Magazine. Copyright 1979 Sussex Publishers, Inc. **Figure 14-7:** From R. J. Sternberg, "A Triangular Theory of Love," *Psychological Review,* 93, pp, 119–135, 1986. Copyright © 1986 by the American Psychological Association. Reprinted with permission. **Figure 14-8:** Based on B. Latané and J. M. Darley, 1970. *The Unresponsive Bystander: Why Doesn't He Help?* Appleton-Century-Crofts. **Table 14-1:** From D. M. Buss, et al., "International Preferences in Selecting Mates: A Study of 37 Cultures," *Journal* *of Cross-Cultural Psychology,* 21, pp. 5–47. Copyright © 1990 by Sage Publications. Reprinted by permission of Sage Publications, Inc. **Cartoon by Robert Weber, page 451:** © The New Yorker Collection 1989 Robert Weber from cartoonbank.com. All Rights Reserved.

PHOTOS

Table of Contents

p. ix: © Jon Riley/GETTY IMAGES; **p. x top:** © Alexander Tsiaras/Stock Boston; **p. x bottom:** © Martine Mouchy/GETTY IMAGES; **p. xi top:** © Nicholas Devore III/Network Aspen; **p. xi bottom:** © Joanna B. Penneo/Aurora/PictureQuest; **p. xii:** © Steve Raymer/Corbis Images; **p. xiii top:** © Dwayne Newton/Photo Edit; **p. xiii bottom:** © Michael Schwarz/Getty Images; **p. xiv:** © Look GMBH/eStock Photography/PictureQuest; **p. xv top:** © Jill Sabella/GETTY IMAGES; **p. xv bottom:** © Seth Resnick/Stock Boston; **p. xvi top:** © Vanessa Vick/Photo Researchers; **p. xvi bottom:** © Zigy Kaluzny/GETTY IMAGES; **p. xvii:** © AP/Wide World Photos

Chapter 1

OPENER: © Jon Riley/GETTY IMAGES; **p. 3:** © Monika Graff/Image Works; **p. 7 top:** © Laura Dwight/Photo Edit; **p. 7 bottom:** © Ann Chwatsky/Phototake/PictureQuest; **p. 11 top:** © Bettmann/Corbis Images; **p. 11 bottom:** © The Granger Collection. Photographed by Notman; **p. 13:** Bettmann/Corbis Images; **p. 14:** © Culver Pictures; **p. 15:** © TimePix; **p. 18 left:** © Richard T. Nowitz/National Geographic Image Collection; **p. 18 right:** © Frank Herholdt/GETTY IMAGES; **p. 19:** © Reuters NewMedia/Corbis Images; **p. 23:** © Robert I. M. Campbell/National Geographic Image Collection; **p. 25:** © Bill Aron/Photo Edit; **p. 26:** © James Wilson/Woodfin Camp; **p. 27 top:** Courtesy, Bibb Latane; **p. 27 bottom:** Courtesy, John Darley, Princeton University; **p. 30:** Courtesy, Mary Garrett; **p. 32 top:** © Tom Stewart/Corbis Stock Market; **p. 32 bottom:** © Dan McCoy/Rainbow; **p. 33:** © Douglas Faulkner/Photo Researchers

Chapter 2

OPENER: © Alexander Tsiaras/Stock Boston; **p. 41:** © AP/Wide World Photos; **p. 44:** © John D. Cunningham/Visuals Unlimited; **p. 53:** From Deloukas, et al. October 23, 1998. "A physical map of 30,000 human genes." *Science* 282(5389), 744–746. © 1998 American Association for the Advancement of Science. http://www.ncbi.nlm.nih.gov/genemap/; **Fig. 2.8a–b:** © Science Photo Library/Science Source/Photo Researchers; **Fig. 2.8c:** © Mehau Kulyk/Science Photo Library/Photo Researchers; **Fig. 2.8d:** © Dan McCoy/Rainbow; **Fig. 2.8e:** © Roger Ressmeyer/Corbis Images; **p. 55 top:** © Leonard Lessin/Peter Arnold; **p. 55 bottom:** Artificial Intelligence Laboratory, MIT. Image courtesy of Michael Leventon; **p. 57:** © Gavin Smith/FSP/Getty Images; **Fig. 2.13:** Courtesy, Trustees of the British Museum, Natural History; **p. 62:** From: Damasio H., Grabowski T., Frank R., Galaburda A. M., Damasio A. R. 1994. "The return of Phineas Gage: Clues about the brain from the skull of a famous patient." *Science,* 264:1102–1105, 1994. © 1994 American Association for the Advancement of Science. Department of Neurology and Image Analysis Facility, University of Iowa; **Fig. 2.14:** B. A. Shaywitz et al., 1995. NMR/Yale Medical School

Chapter 3

OPENER: © Martine Mouchy/GETTY IMAGES; **p. 75:** © Everett Collection; **p. 77:** © Curtis Myers/Stock Connection/Picturequest; **p. 80 both:** © Biophoto Associates/Photo Researchers; **Fig. 3.6 (all):** © Joe Epstein/Design Conceptions; **p. 87:** © AP/Wide World Photos; **p. 90:** © VideoSurgery/Photo Researchers; **p. 94 top:** © Prof. P. Motta/Dept. of Anatomy/University "La Sapienza," Rome/SPL/Photo Researchers; **p. 94 bottom:** © Omikron/Photo Researchers; **p. 96 top:** Courtesy, Julie Mennella; **p. 96 bottom:** © Lisa M. McGeady/Corbis Images; **Fig. 3.16 both:** Courtesy, Bela Julesz; **p. 103:** © Cary Wolinsky/Stock Boston; **p. 104:** © Jeff Greenberg/Stock Boston; **Fig. 3.18a:** © John G. Ross/Photo Researchers; **Fig. 3.19b–c:** © Innervisions

Chapter 4

OPENER: © Nicholas Devore III/Network Aspen; **p. 115:** © AP/Wide World Photos; **p. 119 (all):** © Ted Spagna/Photo Researchers; **p. 123:** © Stock Portfolio/Stock Connection/PictureQuest; **p. 126:** © Jose Carrillo/Stock Boston; **p. 128:** © AP, Midland Daily News/Wide World Photos; **p. 134:** © Corbis Images; **p. 137:** © Dr. Dennis Kunkel/PhotoTake; **p. 135:** Courtesy, Princeton Health Press; **p. 138 left:** © Bob Daemmrich/Stock Boston; **p. 138 right:** © IT Int'l/eStock Photography/PictureQuest; **p. 140 top:** © Andrew Brookes/Corbis Stock Market; **p. 140 bottom:** © Lawrence Migdale/Stock Boston; **p. 141:** © Kal Muller/Woodfin Camp

Chapter 5

OPENER: © Joanna B. Penneo/Aurora/PictureQuest; **p. 149:** © AP/Wide World Photos; **p. 151:** © Culver Pictures; **p. 154:** © Pictor International/PictureQuest; **p. 155 both:** © Stuart Ellins; **p. 157:** © Nina Leen/TimePix; **p. 163:** © Chris Stanford/Allsport; **p. 165:** Courtesy, Dr. Marian Bailey; **p. 166:** Courtesy, Lynn Calero; **p. 169:** © Spencer Grant/Stock Boston; **p. 170 top:** From Meltzzoff, A. N. (1988), "Imitation of Televised Models by Infants," *Child Development,* 59, 1221–1229. Photo Courtesy of A. N. Meltzoff & M. Hanak; **p. 170 bottom:** Courtesy, Albert Bandura; **p. 171:** © Michael Newman/Photo Edit

Chapter 6

OPENER: © Steve Raymer/Corbis Images; **p. 181:** © Mary Ann McDonald/Corbis Images; **p. 184:** © Bob Wallace/Stock Boston; **p. 185:** © F. Dewey Webster/Sovfoto/Eastfoto/PictureQuest; **p. 189:** © Arthur Tilley/GETTY IMAGES; **p. 190:** © Susan Werner/PictureQuest; **p. 192:** © Tom McCarthy/Index Stock Imagery; **Fig. 6.7:** © Disney Enterprises, Inc; **p. 197:** © Shahn Kermani/Getty Images; **p. 198:** © Joseph Nettis/Photo Researchers; **Fig. 6.15:** © Dr. Steven E. Peterson/Washington University. From *Scientific American,* 12/93; **Fig. 6.17:** © Cecil Fox/Science Source/Photo Researchers

Chapter 7

OPENER: © Dwayne Newton/Photo Edit; **p. 211:** NASA; **p. 219 (all):** © Superstock; **p. 225:** Courtesy, Dr. Laura Ann Petitto © 1991/ photo by Robert LaMarche; **Fig. 7.11(1):** © TimePix; **Fig. 7.11(2-4):** © Bettmann/Corbis Images; **Fig. 7.11(5):** © Corbis/Vol. #80

Chapter 8

OPENER: © Michael Schwarz/Getty Images; **p. 249:** © AP/Wide World Photos; **p. 258:** © Peter Menzel/Stock Boston; **p. 259:** © Tony Freeman/PhotoEdit; **p. 264:** © Bob Daemmrich/Stock Boston; **Fig. 8.2:** Reprinted by permission of the publisher from THEMATIC APPERCEPTION TEST by Henry A. Murray, Cambridge, Mass.: Harvard University Press, Copyright © 1943 by the Presidents and Fellows of Harvard College, © 1971 by Henry A. Murray; **Fig. 8.5:** George, M. S., et al. "Brain activity during transient sadness and happiness in healthy women." *American Journal of Psychiatry,* 152:341–351, 1995. © 1995, The American Psychiatric Association. Reprinted by permission.

Chapter 9

OPENER: © Look GMBH/eStock Photography/PictureQuest; **p. 281:** © Evan Richman/New York Times Pictures; **p. 283:** © Peter Byron; **Fig. 9.1a:** © D. W. Fawcett/Photo Researchers; **Fig. 9.1b:** © L. Willatt, East Anglian Regional Genetics Service/SPL/Photo Researchers; **Fig. 9.1c:** © Kenneth Eward/Photo Researchers; **Fig. 9.1d:** © Biophoto Associates/Science Source/Photo Researchers; **p. 287:** © AP/Wide World Photos; **p. 288 left:** Photo Lennart Nilsson/Albert Bonniers Forlag, A CHILD IS BORN, Dell Publishing Company; **p. 288 right:** © Petit Format/Science Source/Photo Researchers; **Fig. 9.3:** From: A. N. Meltzoff & M. K. Moore. 1977. "Imitation of facial and manual gestures by human neonates." *Science,* 198: 75–78. © 1977 American Association for the Advancement of Science; **Fig. 9.5:** Harlow Primate Laboratory, University of Wisconsin; **p. 301:** © Laura Dwight/Peter Arnold; **p. 303:** © Farrell Grehan/Corbis Images; **p. 304:** Courtesy, Michael Morrier; **p. 307:** © Najlah Feanny/Saba; **p. 308:** © Danny Lehman/Corbis Images; **p. 311 top:** © C/B Productions/Corbis Stock Market; **p. 311 bottom:** © Julie Houck/Stock Boston; **p. 314:** © Stephen Simpson/GETTY IMAGES; **p. 317:** © Bob Daemmrich/Stock Boston; **p. 320:** © Lori Grinker/Contact Press Images/PictureQuest

Chapter 10

OPENER: © Jill Sabella/GETTY IMAGES; **p. 327:** Republished with permission of Globe Newspaper Company, Inc., from the 1/4/98 issue of *The Boston Globe,* © 1998; **p. 331:** © Tony Freeman/Photo Edit; **p. 333 both:** © Kobal Collection/Lucas-Film/20th Century Fox; **p. 339:** © AP/Wide World Photos; **p. 350:** © Laura Dwight/Corbis Images

Chapter 11

OPENER: © Seth Resnick/Stock Boston; **p. 357:** © Jonathon Nourok/GETTY IMAGES; **p. 362:** © Frank Siteman/Index Stock Imagery; **p. 363:** © Corbis/Vol. #62; **p. 364:** Courtesy, Alan Benner; **p. 368:** © Bob Daemmrich/Stock Boston; **p. 370:** © Prof. S. H. E. Kaufmann & Dr. J. R. Golecki/SPL/Photo Researchers; **p. 371:** © 2001 Buttout.com, Photo by Toni Michaels; **p. 376:** © David Toerge/Black Star

Chapter 12

OPENER: © Vanessa Vick/Photo Researchers; **p. 381:** Courtesy, Lori Schiller; **p. 383:** © AP/Wide World Photos; **p. 384:** Courtesy, Margaret Coggins; **p. 391:** © Owen Franken/Corbis Images; **p. 395:** © Susan Greenwood/Getty Images; **p. 399:** © Wellcome Dept. of Cognitive Neurology/SPL/Photo Researchers; **Fig. 12.3:** © AP/Wide World

Photos; **Fig. 12.4 (all):** © Derek Bayes/TimePix; **Fig. 12.5 (both):** Courtesy, Nancy Andreasen, University of Iowa Hospitals & Clinics

Chapter 13

OPENER: © Zigy Kaluzny/GETTY IMAGES; **p. 415:** © AP/Wide World Photos; **p. 418:** © Bruce Ayres/GETTY IMAGES; **p. 419:** © Jonathan Nourok/PhotoEdit; **p. 421:** © Rick Freedman/Black Star; **p. 426:** © Jon Bradley/GETTY IMAGES; **p. 430:** © Paul Chesley/Photographers/Aspen/PictureQuest; **p. 433:** © Custom Medical Stock Photo; **p. 435:** © Will & Deni McIntyre/Photo Researchers; **p. 436:** © Phyllis Picard/Stock South/PictureQuest

Chapter 14

OPENER: © AP/Wide World Photos; **p. 441, p. 443:** © AP/Wide World Photos; **p. 446:** Courtesy, Ann Altman; **p. 448:** © Myrleen Ferguson Cate/PhotoEdit; **p. 449:** © Mark Wexler/Woodfin Camp; **Fig. 14.4:** © William Vandivert/TimePix; **Fig. 14.5 (both):** From the film OBEDIENCE © 1965 by Stanley Milgram and distributed by Penn. State Media Sales. Permission granted by Alexandra Milgram; **p. 456:** © Barbara Burnes/Photo Researchers; **p. 464:** © AP/Wide World Photos

Name Index

Subject Index

Abnormality. *See also*
    Psychological disorders
    behavioral view, 17, 386
    cognitive theory of, 386
    and culture, 406–407
    definitions of, 384–385
    Freudian view, 385
    humanistic perspective, 386
    medical perspective, 384–385
    psychological viewpoints on,
      16–18, 385–387
    sociocultural perspective, 387
Absolute threshold, 77–78
Accommodation, visual, 81
Acetylcholine, functions of, 48
Achievement motivation, 266
Achievement tests, 232
Action potential, 44–45
Activation-synthesis theory, of
    dreams, 123
Activity theory of aging, 320
Acupuncture, and pain reduction, 97
Adaptation, sensory, 78
Adaptive testing, 234
Addiction. *See also* Drug abuse;
    Psychoactive drugs
    biologically based, 133
    and classical conditioning, 154
    psychologically based, 133
Adler's theory, 333–334
    inferiority complex in,
      333–334
Adolescence, 307–313
    cognitive development, 303
    and culture, 312–313
    definition of, 307
    egocentrism in, 312
    identity development, 310–311
    moral development, 308–310
    personal fable in, 312
    physical development,
      307–308
    psychosocial development,
      310–311
    puberty, 308
    social development, 310–311
    as stormy phase, 311–312
Advertising, cigarette ads, global
    view, 372–373
Afferent neurons, 50
Affiliation, need for, 266
African Americans
    IQ issue, 241–242
    sickle-cell anemia, 289
    stereotype vulnerability of, 457
    and test norms, 346–347
Afterimage, 85–86
Age of viability, fetus, 288
Aggression, 461–463
    anger management, 465

definition of, 462
frustration-aggression theory,
    462–463
instinct theory, 462
and limbic system, 58
observational learning of, 15,
    25, 169–171, 463
and self-esteem, 341
and serotonin levels, 49
and television viewing, 15, 25
and Type A behavior
    pattern, 367
and video games, 171
Aging. *See also* Late adulthood
    activity theory, 320
    disengagement theory, 320
    genetic preprogramming
      theory, 318
    wear-and-tear theories, 318
Agoraphobia, 392
AIDS, prenatal transmission
    of, 289
Ainsworth strange situation, 295
Alcohol abuse
    binge drinking, 115–116,
      137–138
    fetal alcohol syndrome,
      289–290
    help lines, 142
    signs of, 142
Alcohol use, 137–139
    amount/effects of alcohol, 139
    average use, 137
    and culture, 138
    gender differences, 138
    genetic factors, 139
Alcoholics, definition of, 138–139
Algorithms, 214
All-or-none law, 44
Altered states of
    consciousness, 116
Altman, Ann, work in
    psychology, 446
Altruism, elements of, 464
Alzheimer's disease
    and acetylcholine levels, 48
    causation theory, 203
    and memory, 203, 320
American Psychological
    Association (APA)
    Help Center telephone
      number, 436
    research-related guidelines, 31
Amitriptyline, 432
Amnesia, 203–204
    dissociative types of, 394–395
    retrograde and anterograde,
      203–204
Amphetamines, 136–137
Amygdala, 58

Anal stage, 330
Analogies, and problem
    solving, 223
Analytical learning style, 172
Androgens, 261
Anger
    and dying, 321
    management of, 465
Animal magnetism, 128
Animals
    animal research, 33–34
    biological constraints to
      learning, 165
    cloning of, 287
    imprinting and attachment,
      294–295
    language learning, 227
    sexual behavior, 261
Anorexia nervosa, 259
Anterograde amnesia, 204
Antianxiety drugs, 434
Antidepressant drugs, 433–434
Antipsychotic drugs, 432
Antisocial personality
    disorders, 404
Anxiety disorders, 390–393
    causes of, 393
    drug treatment, 434
    generalized anxiety
      disorder, 392
    obsessive-compulsive disorder,
      392–393
    panic disorder, 391–392
    phobias, 391
Aphasia, 62
Apraxia, 62
Aptitude tests, 232
Archetypes, 333
Archival research, elements of, 22
Armstrong, Lance, 249
Arousal approach, to
    motivation, 252
Association areas, cerebral
    cortex, 62
Associative models, of memory,
    190–191
Assumed-similarity bias, 449
Attachment, 294–296
    definition of, 294
    degrees of attachment,
      295–296
    and fathers, 296
    measurement of, 295
Attention
    and schizophrenia, 403
    as two-stage process, 101
Attention deficit hyperactivity
    disorder (ADHD), 405
Attitudes, 442–444
    and behavior, 444

cognitive dissonance, 444
definition of, 442
persuasion and change of,
    442–443
Attributions, 447–449
    biases in attribution, 448–449
    and culture, 449
    dispositional causes of
      behavior, 448
    fundamental attribution
      error, 448
    situational causes of behavior,
      447–448
Auditory area, of brain, 61
Auditory processing disorders,
    Wernicke's aphasia, 62
Authoritarian parents, 297–298
Authoritative parents, 297–298
Autism, punishment, therapeutic
    use of, 160
Autobiographical memory, 198
Autonomic nervous system,
    divisions of, 51, 52
Autonomy-versus-shame-and-
    doubt, 299
Aversive conditioning, 419–420
Axon, 43

Babble, language
    development, 225
Babinski reflex, 291
Balance, and ear, 93
Barbiturates, 140
Basilar membrane, 89, 92
Beck's cognitive therapy,
    423–424
Behavior
    and attitudes, 444
    cognitive dissonance, 444
Behavior modification, 173–175
    analysis of behavior for,
      173–174
    steps in, 174–175
Behavior therapy, 419–422
    aversive conditioning,
      419–420
    behavior modification,
      173–175
    contingency contracting,
      421–422
    evaluation of, 422
    observational learning, 424
    shaping, 164
    systematic desensitization,
      153–154, 420–421
    token system, 421
Behavioral assessment, of
    personality, 349–350
Behavioral genetics, focus of,
    52–53